HOSPITALITY TODAY
AN INTRODUCTION

EDUCATIONAL INSTITUTE BOOKS

HOSPITALITY TODAY
AN INTRODUCTION

Ninth Edition

Rocco M. Angelo, MBA
Michael Cheng, Ph.D., CHE

LEGAL NOTICE

Original author: Rocco M. Angelo

ISBN   978-0-86612-773-8 (print version)

Printed in the USA

1 2 3 4 5 6 7 8 9 10 28 27 26 25 24 23

CONTENTS

6   Understanding the World of Hotels 142

7   Hotel Organization and Management 182

PREFACE

It is a pleasure to introduce the ninth edition of *Hospitality Today*. The content has been updated and some chapters have been altered or removed, but the purpose of the book remains the same: to present and describe opportunities in the hospitality industry while preparing students for a hospitality management career.

As this edition was being created, the world was recovering from the COVID-19 pandemic that wreaked havoc on the industries covered in this book. Travel was at a standstill, hotel occupancies plummeted, and restaurants closed or reverted to takeaway or delivery service. Some businesses failed. But once the threat of COVID-19 waned, it did not take too long for leisure travel to rebound. This rebound was called "revenge travel," with the world's population making up for months of isolation. Hotel occupancies and restaurant activity returned to pre-pandemic levels and in some cases beyond. However, it was not business as usual. The hospitality industry had changed.

Some of the practices of contactless service adopted during the pandemic were accepted by customers and became standard. The use of technology grew in importance, replacing some jobs and changing others. Many restaurants would not have survived without online ordering paired with takeaway or delivery service. Travelers wanted accommodations that felt like home, and the industry responded by developing more extended-stay hotels and adding home rentals to portfolios.

Although the pandemic was an unprecedented challenge, we learned that the hospitality industry is resilient. It recovered from past recessions and now from a pandemic. There are still opportunities within the industry for students, but students must be prepared with skills achieved through education and practical experience.

I had a coauthor for the first six editions of *Hospitality Today* and completed the seventh and eighth editions alone. A book of this scope is better served with another point of view and other talents. It is a pleasure and an honor to introduce my coauthor for this ninth edition, Michael Cheng, Ph.D. Michael is a talented educator, academic leader, and hospitality professional. He brings to the book his keen intelligence, knowledge of global hospitality issues, and experience as a leader of a large and renowned hospitality school. Thank you, Michael.

Rocco M. Angelo, MBA
Chaplin School of Hospitality & Tourism Management
Florida International University
Miami, Florida

ACKNOWLEDGMENTS

I remember meeting Rocco Angelo long before I started my employment at the Chaplin School of Hospitality & Tourism Management at Florida International University. It was at one of the receptions for the International Council on Hotel, Restaurant, and Institutional Education (ICHRIE) conferences that I first heard his name and noticed this stately man with the wits of a person half his age walk in. He then did a little jig as his friends cheered him on. What an impression! This impression never left me, and when I had the opportunity to sit next to Rocco on a bus ride at another ICHRIE conference a few years later, I did everything I could to hold back my fanboy excitement. He recounted how the airline had lost his luggage, and he had to get a whole new set of clothes as he waited for his bag to arrive.

Fast forward to 2015, when I joined the Chaplin School full time and met Rocco again. He told me he had just completed revisions to the eighth edition of this textbook, and it had taken a lot of his time. He said, and I paraphrase, *It almost did me in.* I remember looking at him in awe and thinking to myself, here's a gentleman who is almost twice my age, still showing up to work every day, and he just finished revising the eighth edition of his textbook? What? The amazing accomplishments of Rocco Angelo continue to impress me.

At the end of 2017, when I was appointed as interim dean before subsequently confirmed as the fifth dean of the Chaplin School in 2020, I had the opportunity to work with Rocco on a regular basis. From that point on, I gained a deep appreciation of who Rocco is. He is a true gentleman, a consummate professional, and an avid supporter of and believer in our students. Whenever our students needed anything, he was there for them. When an alum came by, he made sure to greet them and chat with them. He knew all of them and had countless stories of their shenanigans.

Most importantly, Rocco knows our hospitality industry like the back of his hand. He remembers clearly what he did in his days working at Laventhol & Horwath; what transpired when he was a student at Cornell University; what has changed from when our founding dean Gerald Lattin started the Chaplin School in 1972; and what we need to do to stay abreast of new developments, advances in technology, and changes in geopolitical forces. He is the walking encyclopedia of our hospitality industry and thus the perfect author of this textbook, *Hospitality Today*.

At some point during the uncertainty caused by the COVID-19 pandemic, and very likely during the days of remote work, Rocco told me that it was time to update his textbook. But he did not think he could go through the revision process by himself again. And so, that's how I got involved. I had the opportunity to work with a legend who's revered by many and commands respect while doing a jig, and I took it. I have not looked back since.

I'd like to thank Rocco Angelo for trusting in me, for supporting me throughout the whole revision process, and for letting me join him on this ride. I also want to thank my colleagues: Dr. Kristin Malek for her input on updating the chapter "An Introduction to the Meetings and Events Industry," Dr. Clay Dickinson for updating

ACKNOWLEDGMENTS

the chapter "Understanding the World of Hotels," Ed Mugnani, '91, and his team for updating information about contract foodservice management in the chapter "Understanding the Restaurant Industry," and numerous other colleagues and friends for sharing their expertise when I reached out with questions. I hope I have made Rocco proud of the work we've put in together on this revision and that we can continue working together for many, many more years.

Michael Cheng, Ph.D., CHE

Professor Emeritus Rocco M. Angelo

Professor Emeritus Rocco M. Angelo joined Florida International University (FIU) and its Chaplin School of Hospitality & Tourism Management in 1974. Previously, he had been a guest lecturer there in 1972 and 1973. Prior to joining the university, Professor Angelo was the manager of Laventhol and Horwath's (L&H) management advisory services division in New York City. While with L&H, he was responsible for supervising and conducting economic feasibility studies. He was also responsible for operation and control analyses for hotels, restaurants, and country clubs; and tourism studies in the United States, Canada, and the Caribbean. He managed a private club/hotel in New York City and worked in various management positions with Aramark and Loews Hotels. He was a hospitality consultant with Pannell Kerr Forster (now CBRE) in their management advisory services division.

He received Bachelor of Science degrees from both Fordham University and the Nolan School of Hotel Administration at Cornell University, and an MBA from the University of Miami. After graduating from Fordham University, he served in the U.S. Army as a second lieutenant and commanding officer of an antiaircraft gun battery. He was reassigned to higher headquarters as the commanding officer of a group headquarters battery and promoted to first lieutenant.

Angelo was a visiting faculty member at the Nolan School of Hotel Administration from 1968 to 1979. While on leave from FIU in the fall of 1980, he taught at the Glion Institute of Higher Education in Switzerland and later served on the school's advisory board.

He was advisor to the Club Management Institute of the Club Managers Association of America and served on the American Hotel & Lodging Association's Market Research and Feasibility Committee. He also served on the Certification Commission of the American Hotel & Lodging Educational Institute and on the Scholarship and Grant Committee of the American Hotel Foundation.

Angelo was a member of the Corporation of the Culinary Institute of America, has been a trustee of the Caribbean Hospitality Training Institute, and served on the advisory board of Miami-Dade County's Academy of Hospitality and Tourism. He was the interim president of the Southeast Federation of the International Council on Hotel, Restaurant, and Institutional Education, the worldwide association of hospitality and tourism educators. He received the Lamp of Knowledge Lifetime Achievement Award from the American Hotel & Lodging Educational Institute.

In 1993, Angelo was awarded the Statler Professorship, and in 1996, he was appointed Interim Vice President of Development at Florida International University while continuing to serve as associate dean of the Chaplin School. He was honored in 1997 with FIU's Distinguished Service Award. The FIU Alumni Association honored him in 2009 with the Outstanding Faculty Torch Award.

In 2011, the International Council on Hotel, Restaurant, and Institutional Education presented Angelo with the Howard B. Meek Award for lifetime achievement. The award was named for Howard B. Meek, Ph.D., the founding dean of the Nolan School of Hotel Administration.

He received the Dade County Academy of Hospitality & Tourism 2013 South Florida Tourism Professional of the Year Award. The South Florida Chapter of Hospitality Sales and Marketing Association International named him the 2019 Hospitality Legend.

In 2008, the Cornell Nolan School's alumni named him the alumni "Hotelie" of the Year, and in 2022, he was named to the Cornell Hotel Society Hotelie Hall of Fame.

Professor Angelo is also the author of *Understanding Feasibility Studies: A Practical Guide*.

Dr. Michael Cheng

Dr. Michael Cheng is dean at the Chaplin School of Hospitality & Tourism Management at Florida International University (FIU), where he is transforming hospitality, starting with the learner experience. He was previously a tenured associate professor and director of the Food and Beverage Program.

Dr. Cheng has subject matter expertise in competency-based learning, hospitality management, Culinology®, food product development, restaurant development, sensory analysis, and food and beverage management. Prior to joining FIU, Dr. Cheng served at Southwest Minnesota State University as founding director and department chair, director of global studies and MBA programs, and professor of Culinology®.

Dr. Cheng received both his Bachelor of Science degree and Master of Science degree in Restaurant/Foodservice Management from the University of Nebraska-Lincoln (UNL), and his Ph.D. in Hospitality Management from Iowa State University. He has 20 years of experience in teaching and learning in hospitality management and established the world's first and only academic discipline that blends culinary arts and food science—Culinology®.

The Vilcek Foundation recognized Dr. Cheng's achievements by placing him as a finalist for the Vilcek Prize for Creative Promise in the Culinary Arts in 2010. He has been honored three times by the Research Chefs Association (RCA) with the President's Award for his continued innovation, dedication, leadership, and extraordinary contributions to the RCA community. Since establishing the first Culinology® degree program at UNL, Dr. Cheng has been involved with establishing other Culinology® programs, including at Southwest Minnesota State University and Taylor's University, Malaysia.

Dr. Cheng has presented at the National Restaurant Association on Culinology®, as well as at various national and international conferences, such as the Molecular Gastronomy Workshop at University College Cork, Ireland; the Research Chefs

Association Culinology Expo; the League for Innovation; and the World Summit for Deans of Independent Schools of Hospitality & Tourism. In 2022, UNL recognized Dr. Cheng for his success and leadership with an Alumni Masters award.

At FIU, he has led and set new benchmarks for partnerships and fundraising, leading toward the establishment of the first Endowed Professor of Diversity, Equity, and Inclusion in any hospitality program and the creation of the world's only Bacardi Center of Excellence. Dr. Cheng was also the editor-in-chief of the *Journal of Culinary Science & Technology* as well as a published author of several peer-reviewed articles on Culinology® competencies; he has been awarded over $1 million in public and privately funded research grants. Dr. Cheng is a native of Malaysia.

NEW TO THE NINTH EDITION

The ninth edition of *Hospitality Today: An Introduction* is a comprehensive textbook designed to provide a thorough overview of the dynamic and ever-evolving field of hospitality. It covers a wide range of topics, including the various segments of the industry, such as hotels, restaurants, event management, and tourism. In this book, you will learn about the key principles and best practices in hospitality management, including management and leadership of hospitality enterprises, customer service, human resources management, marketing, and operations. This edition also explores the impact of technology on the industry, highlighting the importance of social media marketing, artificial intelligence, and guest experience management. Additionally, you will delve into the crucial role of sustainability and ethical practices in the hospitality industry. New to this edition are case studies, industry spotlights, and real-world scenarios—all designed to equip you with the knowledge and skills necessary for a successful career in the exciting and fast-paced world of hospitality.

Each chapter begins with an outline and a list of learning objectives that you will be familiar with by the end of the chapter. Each chapter ends with a case study, an industry spotlight, and a real-world scenario. You will also have key terms and review questions in each chapter. Appendices at the end of the book present more detailed information related to concepts mentioned in chapters.

The book starts with an overview of the hospitality and tourism industry, followed by a discussion of its various segments. It ends with covering management aspects of the industry as well as unique topics such as hotel ownership, franchising, and ethics.

Chapter 1 explores the meaning of hospitality from multiple angles, starting from the tangible to the intangible. We will look at the challenges of managing a hospitality business and how it is practiced in various settings, including hotels, restaurants, and events. We will also discuss the difference between service and hospitality. Chapter 2 will take you into the exciting world of travel and tourism and discuss how the Fourth Industrial Revolution and artificial intelligence is changing what we know about how people travel and how we choose to experience hospitality. We will also discuss the development of sustainable tourism and why it is important to balance environmental, sociocultural, and economic considerations. In Chapter 3, we will explore the wide range of diverse and exciting career opportunities available in the hospitality industry. From hotel management and event planning to culinary arts and tourism, there are roles that suit a variety of interests and skill sets.

In Chapters 4 through 11, you will gain an appreciation of the restaurant and hotel industries, as well as related segments such as private clubs, cruise lines, and casino hotels. Within each chapter, you will delve into the principles of a specific segment of the hospitality industry, including its special characteristics and effective operations. Understanding the various departments within a hotel or restaurant, such as front office, food and beverage, housekeeping, and sales, will be crucial. Additionally, you will explore the management of restaurants, including menu planning, kitchen operations, and food safety. The unique dynamics of private clubs, cruise lines, and casino hotels will be examined, covering topics such as member/guest relations, onboard operations, entertainment, and responsible gaming practices. Marketing and sales strategies, revenue management, and financial analysis specific to these industries will also be discussed.

In Chapters 12 through 15, we discuss the various aspects of management and marketing in the hospitality industry. Chapter 12 highlights the role of a hospitality manager and discusses the five management functions: planning, organizing, commanding, coordinating, and controlling. Leadership strategies mentioned include attention through vision, meaning through communication, trust through positioning, and self-development. The importance of marketing concepts is also discussed, as well as the distinction between selling and marketing. Chapter 13, which focuses on franchising, is unique in its own right, as franchising is seldom discussed in hospitality textbooks. This chapter introduces concepts such as franchise fees, including initial fees and ongoing royalties, and investments in physical facilities and equipment. Chapter 14, which focuses on hotel management companies, also makes this textbook unique. This chapter has been updated with the latest statistics and discusses hotel management companies and their methods of operation. Chapter 15 defines ethics in the hospitality industry. It also highlights the importance of diversity in the industry, which enables organizations to better serve diverse customers, promotes fairness and equality in the workplace, drives innovation and creativity, enhances competitiveness, and aligns with ethical principles of social justice and equal opportunities.

1

THE MEANING OF HOSPITALITY

Chapter Outline

Learning Objectives

1. Define "hospitality" and summarize how hospitality businesses differ from manufacturing businesses. (pp. 5–10)

2. Explain the importance of strategic planning, describe the strategic planning process, and summarize planning challenges in capacity-constrained businesses. (pp. 10–14)

3. Describe the basic components of a strategic service vision for hospitality companies, summarize keys to delivering good service, and describe Disney's Five Keys. (pp. 14–20)

KEY TERMS

capacity-constrained businesses

chased-demand strategy

hospitality

intangible products

level-capacity strategy

moments of truth

service

strategic planning

SWOT

Hospitality has traditionally been considered a mature industry. That is to say, many assumed it had passed the stage of rapid growth and innovation. But much that we assumed about the hospitality industry changed during the COVID-19 pandemic. Where we once thought there were few new inventions that affected the way we ate and slept away from home, the rapid pace of innovation and integration of technology brought on by the pandemic astounded us all.

When there were fewer hotel and restaurant brands, customers were easily able to tell the difference between the brands because each was unique within its own market niche. Holiday Inn, Hyatt, McDonald's, and T.G.I. Friday's stood for something special and different. Within each chain the architecture, décor, amenities, and menus were similar. But there was a clear difference between chains: McDonald's was known for its hamburgers; chicken was more often associated with KFC. All Holiday Inns had swimming pools; Days Inn did not.

Many of these distinctions are no longer true. As lodging and restaurant chains redefined themselves to appeal to broader markets, their uniqueness began to fade. Chicken is now available not only at KFC but also at McDonald's, Burger King, and Wendy's. Dunkin' sells bagels as well as doughnuts; and if you want a burrito, you can find it at Chili's as well as Chipotle. Many economy hotels now have swimming pools, and the distinctions between hotel brands are blurring. Atriums used to be an exclusive feature of Hyatt, for example; now many hotels have them—they have even become common on cruise ships! Because obvious physical and product differences have faded, consumers have looked for other ways to differentiate one brand from another. There are many possibilities to choose from. One difference is availability. Some lodging chains have many units in just about every major city; others have just a few. Another difference is price. A steak at Outback Steakhouse costs much less than one at Morton's The Steakhouse.

However, the most compelling difference in the minds of many consumers is customer service. Why is this so? Much of the answer has to do with today's busy lifestyles, which have shaped our priorities. The large number of two-income families and the growing number of single-parent families have made time a priority in the way we live our lives. Very few consumers today have the luxury of spending a lot of time shopping to find the best value, the highest quality, or the speediest service. The attitude today is that we demand these things; they are a given and when we don't receive what we expect, we become dissatisfied. The value of hospitality lies in the customer service received by the guests. What is going to keep the guests coming back for more? It is about delivering above and beyond what was promised.

There is another factor at work here. Many studies show that life has become much more stressful in the last 50 years. One way to escape is to purchase a service so that we don't have to do something ourselves. When we do this, we not only relieve some of the pressures of daily life but expect to feel pampered, to feel more important. Someone else is cooking and serving dinner, making the beds, and providing the entertainment. Many service touch points were redefined by the pandemic. The need for social distancing, contactless service, facial coverings, and a heightened attention to sanitation meant those touch points had to evolve, even after successful vaccination thresholds were achieved. Where we once were able to smile warmly at our guests to convey hospitality, we had to find other ways to express our hospitality spirit behind face coverings. The integration of technology and rapid adoption of contactless check-ins at hotels means the first service touch point may no longer be at the front desk of the hotel but instead when the guests first enter their guestrooms. What can you do to make a memorable positive impression on your guests as soon as they step foot in your property if the experience is contactless? As we shall see throughout the chapter, the unexpected is what hospitality is all about.

This chapter will discuss the meaning of hospitality; draw a distinction between service and hospitality and how hospitality businesses are different from manufacturing businesses; highlight the challenges of marketing and managing a hospitality business due to its intangibility, customer-centricity, and focus on unique experiences; discuss the importance of strategic planning and how it can guide an organization toward its desired outcomes; and use examples such as Disney's Five Keys to illustrate how guiding principles serve to create memorable and enjoyable moments.

1.1 WHAT IS HOSPITALITY?

Hospitality refers to the act of being welcoming, friendly, and generous toward guests and visitors. It involves making people feel comfortable, providing them with what they need, and creating a positive and enjoyable experience. Hospitality is contextual, meaning how you experience and exhibit hospitality depends on the situation you are in. How hospitality is applied differs from person to person and situation to situation. While **service** is generally defined as the act of providing assistance, help, or support to someone or fulfilling a particular need or request, hospitality generally means being hospitable—creating a sense of warmth for others and making them feel welcome and at home regardless of their background, beliefs, or culture.

The word *hospitality* evolved from Latin *hospitalitas*, which took its roots from *hospes*, the word for host, guest, stranger, or visitor. Hospitality refers to the relationship between guest and host and the act of being hospitable without the expectation of reward.

This definition is, in many ways, similar to the meaning of service, but providing customer service is not the same as being hospitable. If a customer sits down in a restaurant, orders a sirloin steak grilled medium rare, and after waiting 30 minutes receives a baked chicken breast, we can hardly characterize this as "customer service." Yet it fits the definition of "the act of providing assistance, help, or support to someone or fulfilling a particular need or request"!

For a better understanding of what hospitality can mean, let's look at a real hospitality experience from one of the most highly praised hotels in the world. Many travel writers and frequent-traveler surveys heap praise on the Mandarin Oriental, Bangkok. Authors such as James Michener and Noël Coward have written books while staying there. The Oriental's service is what makes it stand out. How does it achieve this?

Guests who preregister at the Oriental are asked what flight they will be arriving on and whether they would like limousine service to the hotel. (Traffic in Bangkok is horrendous, taxis are hard to come by, and the hotel's limo costs are reasonable.) As soon as guests pass through customs at the Bangkok airport, they are greeted by one of the hotel's airport ambassadors, easy to spot in a bright orange jacket! Remember what hospitality is? The act of being hospitable without the expectation of reward. The airport ambassador takes the guests' baggage claim checks and calls the waiting BMW 7 Series limousine. When the limousine leaves the airport with the guests and their baggage, the airport ambassador calls ahead with the guests' names and car number so that when they pull up to the hotel entrance, the door attendant greets them by name and the assistant manager escorts them immediately to their room for a private check-in. The guests are also greeted by their butler, who serves a welcome drink, familiarizes them with their room or suite,

The art of hospitality means engaging guests beyond meeting their basic service needs.

and offers to unpack for them and press any wrinkled garments. Seasonal fruits in the room are changed out at least once a day, while guests staying in suites also receive pre-printed, personalized stationery. All staff members are trained to greet guests by name and to remember their personal preferences. In order to ensure that the hotel can provide exceptional guest service, there is an employee-to-guest ratio of almost 4 to 1—an impossible level to achieve economically in most countries. Moreover, the hotel runs its own Oriental Hotel Apprenticeship program, which was the first and remains one of the best hospitality schools in Thailand. Top graduates are offered a job at the Oriental, while others easily find positions at other hotels and restaurants.

Every step of the way, the Mandarin Oriental endeavors to exceed its guests' expectations of what it will be like to stay there. First-time guests do not expect to be greeted at the airport by an airport ambassador, be greeted by name when they arrive, be escorted to their room by the assistant manager, find personalized stationery waiting for them in their suites, and so on. It is this ability to exceed expectations that has earned the hotel its coveted outstanding international reputation. This is what hospitality means.

Restaurant and hotel guests have certain expectations. Consider the elements that constitute what we would call "good service" at a fine restaurant. The first impression of what kind of hospitality the restaurant offers is made when guests make a reservation, either online or by telephone. How easy is the website to navigate? How gracious and helpful is the person on the other end of the line? The next impression may be the valet parking. Are cars taken quickly? Are guests welcomed or simply handed valet parking tickets? When they walk through the door, who greets them and how? Is the dining room host well-groomed, polite, and concerned with the guests' needs (e.g., for immediate seating)? How soon after guests are seated does a server acknowledge their presence (often, simple eye contact is enough) and place water and bread on the table? How soon is the order taken? Is the food served on time? Do guests receive what they ordered, correctly prepared? Does the server remember who ordered what? These are just some of the standards that are used when guests form opinions about the restaurant. If all of the parts of this process are performed better than expected— that is, *if reality exceeds expectations*—then

guests rate the service received as better than average, or high. If reality matches expectations— the guests get what they expected, no more and no less—then service is satisfactory. But if reality is less than what is expected, then the service is considered poor. Hospitality is about touch points and all the experiences that make the guests wanting to come back for more.

One further note: price may play an important part in how service is evaluated because it influences customer expectations. When customers buy a hamburger at a quick service restaurant, what they expect is very different from when they buy a hamburger in the dining room of a fine hotel. In the latter case, they expect more because they are paying more. However, when customers order food for delivery or take-out, they expect the food to be of the same quality as when they dine in. This is an important factor that will make your service above satisfactory. The packaging containers can increase the perceived level of food quality and, sometimes, make up for the slight loss of food quality due to the added travel time.

It is important to remember that, in all cases, it is the person who is receiving the service (the customer), not the person who is delivering the service, whose expectations count. Too often managers assume that if they think they are providing good service, it must be so. It is difficult for some managers to recognize that their perceptions may differ considerably from those of their customers. A good manager must always view the service experience from the perspective of the customer. In *Setting the Table: The Transforming Power of Hospitality in Business*, restaurateur Danny Meyer writes that it is important to balance service and hospitality to deliver exceptional experiences: "Understanding the distinction between service and hospitality has been at the foundation of our success. Service is the technical delivery of a product. Hospitality is how the delivery of that product makes its recipients feel. It takes both great service and great hospitality to rise to the top."[1]

With this background, we are now in a position to formulate a more precise definition of hospitality. Danny Meyer centers his philosophy of "enlightened hospitality" on hiring great employees. Hospitality is about trust and empowering staff, and the only way your organization can continuously deliver exceptional hospitality is by ensuring that your employees are as excited about coming to work as you are. When you take care of your staff and make them feel appreciated and valued, they will also make sure that their guests feel valued and "at home." To this day, Marriott International's first core value, "We Put People First," continues to emphasize taking care of their associates so that they will take care of the customers. While service is transactional (the task at hand), hospitality is genuine (the human element of ensuring that guests are happy).

In conclusion, we choose to define hospitality as *meeting customers' needs in the way that they want and expect them to be met.* Superior hospitality, obviously, means exceeding customer expectations.

Knowledge Check

1. How did the COVID-19 pandemic change hospitality touch points?

2. How do expectations of the customer influence how they rate service?

1.2 CHALLENGES IN MANAGING AND MARKETING HOSPITALITY BUSINESSES

Traditionally, the management and marketing of hospitality businesses have been described and studied in the same way as businesses that manufacture products. The view has been that management is management and marketing is marketing; once you understand the basic principles, it doesn't matter much whether you're marketing a bowl of soup in a restaurant or a can of soup in a supermarket.

We no longer believe this. Managing and marketing hospitality require a deep understanding of the unique characteristics of the industry, a customer-centric approach, and the ability to create memorable experiences. Hotels and restaurants—which deal in **intangible products**, meaning products that cannot be seen, touched, or stored, such as comfort, security, and positive experiences—have very different management and marketing challenges than do businesses that create such tangible products as

automobiles or boxes of cereal. Christopher H. Lovelock, a pioneer in the field of services marketing, identified differences between the two[2]. For hospitality businesses:

- The nature of the product is different.

- Customers are more involved in the production process.

- People are part of the product.

- It's harder to maintain quality control standards.

- The services provided can't be inventoried.

- The time factor is more important.

- Distribution channels are different.

Let's take a closer look at each of these differences and consider their implications.

The Nature of the Product

Manufactured goods are tangible products. We can pick them up, carry them around, or physically handle them in some other way. A service, on the other hand, is a performance or process. Marketing hospitality, which of course involves the use of physical objects and goods such as beds and food, is quite a different thing from marketing the goods themselves. For example, when guests choose a hotel, they take into account such factors as the convenience of the location, amenities (spas, free Wi-Fi, etc.), and the kind of service they expect. When they make a reservation, the hotel reserves a certain category of guestroom based on price, size, or location, but seldom reserves the exact room itself (except in the case of a room especially equipped for guests with disabilities). The exact room is not assigned until check-in. When guests arrive, they use the physical facilities and eat the food, but that's not all they are buying. They are also purchasing the performance of services by people who work in the hotel—room service, concierge service, valet service—all of which are intangible. The hotel must manage the production of these services as well as the physical products and also persuade potential guests to buy some things (services) that the hotel cannot show them a picture of or even, in some cases, adequately describe.

The Customer's Role in Production

Customers have no involvement in the production of manufactured goods. Soup is produced and packaged by the food manufacturer in a factory and purchased by a consumer at a supermarket or convenience store. The people who make the soup don't see the people who eat it, and the ones who eat it don't go to the factory when they want a serving. The two activities, production and consumption, are completely separate. This is not true in a hospitality business.

A restaurant or a hotel is, in a very real sense, a factory: a factory where service is produced for customers who come inside, see the workers who are putting together the service, and may even participate in producing it—for example, when guests assemble their own salads at a salad bar and thus become part of the food production and service process. Some kinds of services require more employee–customer interaction than others. But in any case, because it is part of the service (product), the interaction between employees and customers must be managed—a task that a manager of manufactured goods never has to face.

People Are Part of the Product

In a hospitality business like a hotel or restaurant, customers come into contact with both employees and other customers. That makes the other customers a part of the product (which we define as a performance) and often defines the quality of the service. Have you ever been to a movie or play where the people around you wouldn't keep quiet and spoiled some of your enjoyment? What about a restaurant where you went for a quiet, romantic evening, and there was a party of 12 loud people at the next table celebrating someone's birthday? A business traveler who pays $300 or more per night for a room in a city hotel can get very annoyed when their check-in is delayed by a busload of tourists who have just arrived, or when a group of conventioneers insists on being served breakfast before anyone else so they can be finished in time for their first meeting. Similarly, when you are dressed up to attend an elegant reception, the dress of the other guests adds to your own enjoyment.

In short, all the people with whom a guest comes in contact, both other guests and employees, are an integral part of the hospitality experience. They often are the main difference in the quality of the experience that one hotel provides over another.

Maintaining Quality Control

When a factory produces a product, that product can be inspected for quality before it goes out the door. As long as proper quality control procedures and inspections are in place, defective

Everyone, whether other guests or staff, that a guest encounters becomes part of their experience—for better or worse.

products are not delivered. But services, like other live performances, take place in real time. That means mistakes are bound to occur. Christopher H. Lovelock cited a former package-goods marketer who became a Holiday Inn executive and observed:

> *We can't control the quality of our product as well as a Procter & Gamble control engineer on a production line can. … When you buy a box of Ivory, you can reasonably be 99 and 44/100ths percent sure that this stuff will work to get your clothes clean. When you buy a Holiday Inn room, you're sure at some lesser percentage that we'll work to give you a good night's sleep without any hassle, or people banging on the walls, and all the bad things that can happen in a hotel.*[3]

No Inventories

Manufacturers can inventory their products in warehouses until they are needed. But because hospitality is intangible, its products cannot be made in advance or stored for future use. That means there are times when the supply can't be produced on time because the demand is too great. Guests must be turned away from hotels that are completely occupied, or restaurant guests may wait an hour or more for a table. For this

reason, hospitality marketing often focuses on controlling demand.

The Importance of Time

Because most hospitality services are delivered (performed) in the "factory," customers have to be present to receive them (except when they order take-out food from a restaurant; even then, delivery—which is a service—is involved and time is a crucial factor). When customers are present, they expect the service to be performed "on time," which in their minds means "when I want it." In a restaurant, guests not only expect that their orders will be taken promptly but that the food will arrive in a reasonable amount of time. Similarly, in today's fast-paced society, guests expect their food to be delivered in less than an hour once they have placed their order online. Obviously, faster is better and guests often do not take into account unforeseen disruptors, like traffic jams on the delivery route or a rush of dine-in customers at the same time that they place their order at that restaurant. Time, then, often plays a more important role in producing services than in producing goods. Customers must wait for a service to be performed, perhaps just briefly, perhaps for a long time; they don't have to wait for a manufactured good—it is already sitting on the shelf. Since customers must wait for a service, hospitality enterprises

One of the most important parts of working in hospitality is making guests feel like they aren't being ignored during wait times.

must devise strategies to keep them from feeling as though they are being ignored or are not important while they are waiting.

Different Distribution Channels

Companies that manufacture goods move their products from the factory by trucks, trains, or airplanes to wholesalers, distributors, or retailers, who then resell them to the consumer. This is not the case with hospitality companies, where customers may contact "the factory" directly through the hotel or restaurant website. Despite the popularity of online travel agencies (OTAs), direct bookings on the brand website account for 49 percent of U.S. hotel online bookings today. In either case, hospitality businesses must be sensitive to customers dealing directly with them. Even when intermediaries (e.g., travel agents or OTAs) are involved, transferring a service to a customer requires more "people skills" than transferring a physical product from factory to warehouse to retail store.

Knowledge Check

1. How is management affected when the customer has a role in production?

2. What are challenges a hospitality organization may face in maintaining quality control of products or services through intermediary distribution channels?

1.3 ACHIEVING SUPERIOR HOSPITALITY IN A LESS-THAN-PERFECT WORLD

The most important operational competency of top-level service managers is the ability to plan for the future. While day-to-day operations can be performed by others, someone must be thinking about next year and beyond. This is the job of top managers—to develop the strategy for survival that any business needs to succeed. It is also the key to providing superior hospitality, which must begin at the very top of the organizational ladder.

Strategic Planning

Broad, long-range business planning is called **strategic planning**. This is the process of setting goals, defining strategies, and making decisions to guide an organization toward its desired future outcomes. It involves systematically analyzing an organization's internal and external environment, assessing its strengths and weaknesses, identifying opportunities and threats, and developing a comprehensive plan of action. Companies must formulate general business objectives for themselves, otherwise there is bound to be confusion about where they are going and how they intend to get there. These general business objectives are most commonly called a company's mission or values and are expressed as a mission statement or a statement of core values. Here is the value statement of Shake Shack, founded in 2004 by Danny Meyer:

- Hospitality—We go out of our way to ensure that every experience is a memorably positive representation of our culture.

- Team—We hire leaders that are excited about and committed to championship performance, remarkable hospitality, and active personal growth.

- Food and drink—We source and accept only the best ingredients possible and ensure that our food is as good as humanly possible as we balance speed of service and excellence of presentation.

- The Shack—We design, build, and maintain the most engaging, thoughtful, safe, and clean environment for our teams to work in and our guests to gather in.

- Communication—We're aligned with each other every day so that mutual understanding leads to progress, and always listening to ensure that all stakeholders feel heard and know that we are on their side.[4]

Note the basic premise of the list. There is a belief that providing the best possible customer experience is achievable when Shake Shack's leadership and staff follow the company's values and pursue the highest ethical standards, are responsible for their actions, engage in honest communication, embrace individual differences and viewpoints, and so on. You will learn to recognize the importance of all these concepts.

The Strategic Planning Process. Once a mission has been clearly established and articulated, there is a series of steps a company must take to make that mission a guiding force.

Perform a SWOT analysis. SWOT stands for Strengths, Weaknesses, Opportunities, and Threats. To do a SWOT analysis, a company examines the internal and external environment in which it is operating. What are the strengths and weaknesses of its operation? What opportunities exist for growth? What threats exist, either from competitors or changing trends? The ultimate goal of this analysis is to determine how well the company is serving current markets.

Formulate strategies. Strategies might include adding more units; appealing to new market segments, such as wellness-conscious people; or developing new products. Marriott pursued the latter strategy when it developed additional types of Marriott hotels—for example, Courtyard by Marriott (to appeal to travelers who like to stay in limited-service hotels), Residence Inns (to appeal to the extended-stay market), and Fairfield Inns (to appeal to "road warriors"— economy-minded business travelers). Marriott has also expanded its portfolio, revenues, and profits through acquisitions of highly profitable brands, such as Ritz-Carlton, Starwood, Bulgari Hotels & Resorts, and Gaylord Hotels. When Omni Hotels & Resorts made the strategic decision to upgrade its guestrooms, it paid attention to complaints from guests in website reviews and included some of the online suggestions in its redesign plan.

Implement strategies. Once strategies have been developed, they must be implemented. If one of a quick service restaurant chain's strategies for attracting health-conscious guests is to add salads to its menu, then the chain must create salads that can be made in a uniform manner in all of its units. The chain must also identify suppliers for the salad ingredients and devise methods of preparation.

Before a company can implement strategies, some fundamental issues must be addressed:

- *Leadership.* Managers must explain their strategies to employees. Continuing with the restaurant chain example, the chain's managers must explain to employees why salads are being introduced and persuade them that, even if this strategy involves more work, it will produce benefits for them as well as the organization.

- *Organizational structure.* Sometimes the organizational structure must be changed in order to implement a strategy. When Taco Bell decided to concentrate on improving customer service, it freed its unit managers from 15 hours of weekly paperwork so they would have time to coach employees and satisfy customers.

- *Corporate culture.* To implement a strategy, you need employees who buy into the corporate culture or way of doing business. They must share the same values and work ethic. Disney spends two days of employee orientation telling new employees about the history of the company. Walt Disney's life story is retold at length. Early Mickey Mouse cartoons are shown. New hires are taught the Disney language—words and concepts unique to the Disney organization. This helps promote a family or "tribal" feeling. In recent years, one of the biggest drivers of change to corporate culture has been corporate responsibility. Gen Z and millennials are far more interested than previous generations in the values held by their employers and understanding what makes the company tick: its mission, its purpose, and what it is doing for society.

Monitor and evaluate results.
After implementing strategies, managers must monitor them to make sure they are working. Hospitality and travel companies use online surveys to learn what their customers think about their experience. Surveys are an efficient way to determine customer satisfaction with the service provided and the physical facilities.

Tim Firnstahl is the founder of SGE Inc., a restaurant management company in Seattle, Washington. Firnstahl set an objective of making sure that guest satisfaction in all of his restaurants would be guaranteed. Then he developed a plan to reach that objective. He came up with a company slogan: "Your Enjoyment Guaranteed. Always." He reduced this to an acronym—YEGA—that all employees could easily remember. After a series of meetings in which Firnstahl explained what he had in mind, all of his 600 employees signed a contract pledging that they would follow through on the YEGA promise. "We created a YEGA logo and put it everywhere," Firnstahl said: "on report forms, on training manuals, on wall signs. We started *YEGA NEWS* and distributed YEGA pins, shirts, name tags, even underwear. We announced that failure to enforce YEGA would be grounds for dismissal." The final step was empowering employees to make the YEGA objective workable. With this in mind, Firnstahl instituted the idea that employees can and should do anything to keep the customer happy. "In the event of an error or delay, any employee right down to the busboy could provide complimentary wine or dessert, or pick up an entire tab if necessary."[5]

Planning Challenges in Capacity-Constrained Businesses

One important difference between hospitality organizations and manufacturing firms, as pointed out previously, is the inability of hospitality businesses to inventory finished products because of their intangibility. In the manufacturing of goods, peaks and valleys of supply and demand are managed, in part, by finishing and storing goods in advance of when they will be needed. Thus, it is seldom if ever necessary to produce anything instantly to satisfy demand.

Since hospitality businesses cannot manufacture and store services, their financial success depends on how efficiently they match their productive capacity—their staff, equipment, and resources such as operating inventories—to consumer demand at any given moment. This is very difficult. When demand is low, production capacity will be wasted because there will be an oversupply of workers to serve the customers; when demand is higher than production capacity, there will be more guests than the workers or the building can serve and business will be lost. In other words, hotels and restaurants are **capacity-constrained businesses** and therefore must constantly manage both supply (production capacity) and demand.

Managing Supply. Let's first look at strategies for managing supply. In the case of hotels and restaurants, the ability to supply the products manufactured in the service "factory" is fixed. A hotel has a fixed number of beds; a restaurant has a fixed number of seats. These cannot be altered to increase capacity whenever demand is greater than capacity; that is, when there are more guests than there are hotel beds or restaurant seats. That means a good part of the time, hotels and restaurants must follow a **level-capacity strategy**, in which the same amount of capacity is offered no matter how high the demand.

However, some hospitality businesses can follow a **chased-demand strategy**, in which capacity can be varied to suit the demand level—in a limited way. For example, there is a measure of flexibility in some parts of a hotel, such as the space set aside for meetings and conventions. Another common tactic in hospitality firms is to have a certain number of part-time employees who work only when the demand is high. Sometimes firms such as caterers can rent extra equipment and thus increase their capacity as needed. Finally, companies can cross-train employees so that they can be shifted temporarily to other jobs as needed. In the long run, of course, a hotel or restaurant can increase its capacity by enlarging its current property or building a new, larger one. During the COVID-19 pandemic, many restaurants were limited to 25 percent to 50 percent indoor seating capacity. Entrepreneurial restaurateurs were able to regain full capacity by adding and incorporating outdoor dining areas on sidewalks and in parking lots. This strategy allowed the restaurants to increase their sales to a more profitable level, as the fixed costs (rent, insurance, etc.) of a restaurant are the same at 100 percent capacity or 50 percent capacity.

Managing Demand. Because hotel and restaurant capacity is limited, it is important to put most of the strategic planning emphasis on managing demand. One of the goals of managers in a hospitality business is to shift demand from periods when it cannot be accommodated (because the operation is filled to capacity) to periods when it can be. One way to do this is to encourage business during slow periods. Some restaurants offer early-bird specials to increase demand early in the day, and lounges have happy hours to increase demand early in the evening.

While supply cannot be inventoried, sometimes demand can. This happens when managers or employees encourage customers to stand in line or sit in the restaurant's lounge until a table in the dining room becomes available. Taking reservations is another example of inventorying demand.

The most common method used to influence demand in the hotel industry is price. Using pricing strategies to control demand is risky unless the strategies are thoroughly understood. Hotels are faced with pricing decisions every day, such as whether to accept meeting and convention reservations at low group rates or hold on to those guestrooms for later sale at higher rates to individual business travelers. One tool that managers use to make such decisions is revenue management, a system that guides management in selling "the right product to the right customer at the right time for the right price."[6]

Sometimes the product itself can be varied to help balance supply and demand. Restaurants routinely change their menus and level of service between lunch and dinner. Cruise ships reposition themselves to call on ports in the Caribbean in the winter and Alaska in the summer. Sometimes different services can be offered at the same time to accommodate the demand levels of different groups, as with first-class, business-class, and economy-class airline seats—all on the same plane—or concierge floors in hotels.

Finally, communication strategies can play a large part in balancing demand levels. A carefully thought-out advertising schedule can enable resorts to influence demand by appealing to new market segments with special rates during the off-season; similarly, they can keep demand levels high during the regular season by targeting those guest groups willing to pay full rates.

One of the hard realities necessitating these tactics is that hotels and restaurants have a high level of fixed expenses because of their physical plant. These fixed expenses cannot be lowered, so strategies and tactics must be found to utilize a hotel or restaurant to its fullest possible extent—such as the restaurants that expanded their seating capacity to outdoors during the pandemic. Even a marginal increase in business can produce a significant increase in profit once the break-even point is reached.

Integrating Technology. Hospitality legend Ian Schrager says it is the product, not the technology, that defines the guest experience. In hospitality, the product is the intangible benefit received by the guests. Using technology to automate the execution of hotel business such as check-in, check-out, and mobile payment allows hospitality professionals to focus on the amenities provided through the services, the visuals of food and beverage, and the entertainment factor. Technology can make travel easier for guests when they are able to order their food and wine through their mobile devices and then find everything ready for them when they come downstairs to the restaurant. Guests don't necessarily need

Many cruise lines attempt to manage demand by changing their ports of call seasonally over the course of a year.

someone to help them read the menu or select a wine—software can be programmed to provide those suggestions within the app itself. Being able to replace those interactions with a frictionless experience that is customizable is how hospitality businesses can integrate with technology.

1.4 THE STRATEGIC SERVICE VISION

James Heskett, professor emeritus of business administration at Harvard Business School, notes in his book *Managing in the Service Economy* that all successful service companies share what he calls a "strategic service vision"—a blueprint for service managers. There are two components to this blueprint: targeting a market segment and focusing on a service strategy. Let's discuss these elements in more detail, drawing from examples and ideas from the work of Heskett and others.

Targeting a Market Segment

There is no such thing as a product or service that appeals to everyone. Some people want hotels that have a good restaurant because they enjoy dining while they are traveling. Others don't care that much about food but value a hotel with a fitness club and spa where they can relax and exercise. Some travelers want a comfortable guestroom with free Wi-Fi and a desk where they can work; others plan to spend little time in their room. Similarly, a restaurant can't appeal to everyone. People have different tastes in food and different ideas of what constitutes a pleasant experience when dining out. They differ in how much they are willing to pay for a meal.

Since hotels and restaurants cannot hope to appeal to everyone, they single out groups or market segments and attempt to provide products and services that, in the eyes of these consumers, are superior to those of competing hotels and restaurants. For example, the primary market for McDonald's has always been families with young children. Wendy's targets adults who want a hamburger cooked to order—historically, it has made little effort to attract children. At the other end of the hamburger-restaurant scale is Shake Shack, a modern-day version of a roadside burger stand serving hamburgers, chicken, hot dogs, shakes, and beer in an atmosphere designed to appeal to adults.

The furnishings, décor, layout, and design of a hospitality product are all determined by the needs and desires of the targeted market segment. Some markets want little more than a comfortable room with few amenities, while others are looking for a vacation experience.

Focusing on a Service Strategy

The various service concepts that hospitality businesses adopt are not simply amorphous marketing ideas. A hotel or restaurant, including its services, is carefully designed to appeal to a limited segment of the market, and the way hospitality is delivered is tailored to match the expectations of the segment that it targets.

Research has shown that most people believe buying an intangible service like a vacation or even a meal in a restaurant is riskier than buying a manufactured product. With a manufactured product, buyers have a better idea of what they're getting for their money; with intangible products, there may be some surprises. It is that element of uncertainty that poses the biggest challenge to hospitality businesses. That is why it is so important for managers and employees to provide consistent services that meet an operation's standards.

Customer Service Standards. Successful hospitality companies focus a good deal of management attention on establishing quality standards for services, communicating these standards to employees through training programs, and measuring performance. For example, one service standard that is frequently established and easy to measure is waiting time.

Burger King and McDonald's have strict standards for how long customers are expected to wait for their food once it has been ordered. Restaurants often manage expectations by telling guests that they will have to wait longer for a table than is actually the case. When they are given their table earlier than expected, guests conclude that they have been given special attention—thus their feeling of receiving good service is reinforced.

Another quality control technique that restaurants use is to set standards for how quickly a food server should approach a customer after they sit at a table. At some operations, the standard is for a server to go to the table immediately and say, "I'll be with you in a minute." Another restaurant may require bread and butter to be served at the same time to further acknowledge the diners' presence.

Providing consistent services is extremely complex where customer contact is involved, especially when some of the lowest-paid employees make the most contacts.

A former Marriott executive described one strategy he used to deal with the problem:

> The Marriott Bellman booklet is designed to convince our uniformed doormen that they represent an all-important first and last impression for many of our guests, that they must stand with dignity and

The way service is delivered must be tailored to match the expectations of the target market. Leaving flower petals on the sheets during turn-down service, as is done at many resorts, would be strangely out of place at a budget hotel.

good posture, and that they must not lean against the wall or put up their feet when sitting. … Bellmen are often looked at subconsciously by guests as being "Mr. Marriott himself" because many times a guest will speak to and deal with a bellman more often during a visit than with any other employee of the hotel. … They are coached to smile often and to do all they can to make the guest feel welcome and special.[7]

Marriott is known for setting exact standards—including customer service standards—for all of its jobs and for communicating them clearly in writing as well as in training sessions. The company continually measures how well standards are being met with frequent inspections, and it encourages its employees—through profit sharing, stock options, and other bonus programs—to provide good service.

Job Restructuring. An effective service strategy must also provide a means of achieving levels of productivity that will satisfy the business's economic goals as well as customer expectations. One way managers do this in hospitality companies is by job restructuring— changing the nature of the work or the way it is done. For example, at Benihana restaurants, the chef prepares the food at a hibachi in front of guests, combining the jobs of food server and chef. James Heskett observes, "Given the nature of a service concept that combines quality food and entertainment at reasonable prices, as well as the exotic format of a Japanese restaurant, customers of Benihana readily accept a highly economic combination of jobs that is carried out in their full view."[8]

Payroll Control. Along with controlling the quality of service goes controlling payroll and other costs involved in providing that service. Any hotel or restaurant could schedule more than enough employees to give good service all the time, but that would not be profitable. Every operation must provide good, if not superior, service within its own economic constraints. Companies that do the best job of controlling service quality also excel at controlling labor and other costs, since they are closely connected. Payroll control can be achieved by employee training and careful

scheduling, a combination that almost always produces higher productivity and better service.

Remember Seattle restaurateur Tim Firnstahl and YEGA? Part of why Firnstahl designed YEGA was to help him identify systems that were not working and control costs that were out of line. Every time an employee gave a guest a free meal because of bad service, this was reported and considered by Firnstahl to be a "system failure cost." Whenever a meal was given away Firnstahl asked "Why is the system failing?" instead of "Why is the employee failing?" Asking the right question proved to be highly productive.

"Our search for the culprit in a string of complaints about slow food service in one restaurant led first to the kitchen and then to one cook," Firnstahl observed. "But pushing the search one step further revealed several unrealistically complex dishes that no one could have prepared swiftly."[9] A service strategy helped identify a production problem.

Knowledge Check
1. How can a hospitality business align customer service standards with its target market?
2. How do job restructuring and payroll control influence a hospitality business' strategic service mission?

1.5 DELIVERING ON THE HOSPITALITY PROMISE

Many theories and ideas about hospitality have been mentioned so far in this chapter. The bottom line, however, is doing it—delivering on the promise that a company makes to its owners, employees, and customers. It is easy enough to write a mission statement that says, "We intend to be a premier and progressive lodging company," or "Our goal is to deliver the best service of any restaurant chain in our class," but how do you do it? What makes it really happen?

Hundreds of suggestions have been made about how to deliver exceptional hospitality. Any good-sized bookstore has at least a half-dozen books full of practical, tested ideas that work. The Harvard Business School has published hundreds of case histories that detail how and why companies succeed and fail. There are many fine training companies that offer seminars on every aspect of service. With all this information available, it is surprising that there is still so much poor service in the hospitality industry.

Keys to Delivering Memorable Hospitality Experiences

Everyone understands that customers want memorable experiences and that exceptional hospitality leads to better profits. Understanding it is one thing; doing it is another. This chapter does not offer a simple recipe for success or a prescription that can turn a one-star restaurant or hotel into a three- or four-star one—it's not that easy. But any organization that cares about good service can do a number of things to improve. Here are five of them:

1. *Don't forget who you are.* A classic story about forgetting who you are concerns People's Express, which in the early 1980s was the darling of the airline industry. People's Express started as an airline that promised really low fares to leisure travelers who were willing to accept limited service in return. The airline's schedules weren't the most convenient; passengers had to buy a ticket on board instead of getting one ahead of time, and passengers carried their own luggage to the plane. If they wanted a meal during the flight, they paid for it. People's Express employees didn't have a simple job description—they did whatever needed doing. Pilots, for example, also helped out on the ground, which allowed People's Express to save on labor costs. With this simple strategy, in five short years the company's value grew to almost $1 billion.

   As People's Express grew, it acquired more customers and planes. It decided to go after business travelers, and the company added a first-class section. Soon the company's sheer size meant that it had to change the way it did things. With a small customer base, it was acceptable not to take reservations, but when thousands started showing up at the airport, the airline needed some means of forecasting who wanted to go where and when. That meant an expensive computerized

reservations system and reservations agents who knew how to use it—just like the big airlines had. It was OK to ask pilots to help out on the ground when the company only had a few planes, but when it had more than 100, it needed the pilots in the air. Its rapid expansion led to operational and management issues, and the airline struggled to maintain its low-cost structure while dealing with increasing competition from other carriers. All of this affected the company's ability to keep its costs down. It forgot that it had succeeded by being a budget airline that targeted leisure travelers. In 1986, People's Express merged with Continental Airlines in a deal worth $125 million. The merger aimed to combine the low-cost model of People's Express with Continental's larger network and resources. However, integrating the two airlines proved challenging, and People's Express ceased to exist as a separate brand by 1987.

   Companies that succeed create a service strategy for each market segment and stick to it. They make certain that everyone who works for them understands what they are selling and who they want to sell it to. They don't confuse or anger consumers by offering something they don't deliver.

2. *Encourage every employee to act like a manager.* Managers understand the need for repeat business; employees may not. Service-oriented companies motivate, train, and empower their employees to act like the company they work for is their own business. That means really caring when anyone has a problem, whether it's another employee or a guest. It also means making sure that they can solve problems they run into, which in turn requires that they be given the authority to make the necessary decisions. In their book, *Total Customer Service: The Ultimate Weapon*, William H. Davidow and Bro Uttal write about how Embassy Suites, a division of Hilton Hotels Corporation, uses an upside-down organization chart to dramatize the idea that the frontline employees, the ones who deal with guests, are the most important people in the organization. It's not easy to find hotel managers who will accept the idea that when it comes to pleasing guests, the front desk employees may be more important than they are. Embassy Suites does this by hiring

managers who have the right attitude and then training them to help the people who work for them.

3. *Handle moments of truth correctly.* Many of the duties performed by front desk agents or food servers are repetitive and sometimes performed in a depersonalized manner. As a result, guests may feel that they are being treated as mere numbers. To combat this guest perception, some companies have identified what they call **moments of truth**. The concept—popularized by Jan Carlzon, CEO of Scandinavian Airlines System (SAS) in the early 1980s—is still viable today. It refers to the critical interactions or touch points between a customer and a company that significantly influence the customer's perception of the brand. In his book, *Moments of Truth*, Carlzon explains that there was a huge difference in the way SAS defined service levels and the way its customers defined them. "Each of our ten million customers came in contact with approximately five SAS employees, and this contact lasted an average of fifteen seconds each time. Thus SAS is 'created' in the minds of our customers fifty million times a year, fifteen seconds at a time. These fifty million 'moments of truth' are the moments that ultimately determine whether

SAS will succeed or fail as a company. They are the moments when we must prove to our customers that SAS is their best alternative,"[10] Carlzon writes.

Hospitality businesses concentrate their efforts on making sure that moments of truth are handled correctly. For hotels, an important moment of truth occurs when guests check in or out and come face-to-face with a hotel employee. Although there are certain check-in/check-out routines that must be followed, guests should be given individual attention so they feel their needs are being addressed in a personal way. One way to do this is to make certain that front desk employees are trained to look up from their computer screens to give guests a warm welcome (by name, if possible), and continue to smile and make eye contact as they perform their duties for guests. Such seemingly small gestures go a long way toward establishing an overall atmosphere of attentive and pleasing guest service.

4. *Hire good people and keep them happy.* Turnover is the worst enemy for any hospitality business. New people don't know what is expected of them and may have inadequate or incorrect training. They are often unprepared to give good customer service. Superior companies make every effort to recruit, hire,

Guests may experience more "moments of truth" with a door attendant than any other employee.

and hold onto people who have the right personalities. (Many companies today hire for attitude rather than skill. Skills that are learned on the job are often more easily upgraded than attitudes that employees bring with them.) Successful hospitality companies regard their employees as being as important as their customers. That means training their employees well, motivating them, and rewarding them. This strategy is inevitably more cost-efficient and more successful than constantly finding and training new employees.

5. *Respond in a timely manner.* Most guests don't like to wait. Waiting, for them, is a hallmark of poor service. At limited-service establishments, even five minutes may seem too long. At family restaurants, most guests expect their food to be on the table in 30 minutes or less. No one likes to be put on hold when making a reservation for an airline ticket, a hotel room, or a rental car. Long check-in and check-out lines spell disaster. None of these is a necessary evil. Excellent companies are constantly monitoring the waiting time of their guests and looking for ways to decrease it, or at least make it less stressful. As mentioned earlier, integrating technology to allow for frictionless experiences such as self check-ins/check-outs allow the hospitality professional to focus more on the moments of truth.

Each organization and each situation is unique. Managers need to develop their own lists of key service criteria and ways to implement them. It's the difference between winning and losing the battle for satisfied customers.

Service, Disney-Style

A careful look at the way the Walt Disney Company delivers exceptional customer service at its theme parks and resorts provides some insight into how superior customer service is delivered consistently. It starts with Disney's Four Keys: *safety, courtesy, show,* and *efficiency.* The order of these service priorities is important—first safety, next courtesy, then show, and, lastly, efficiency—and Disney personnel must think in that order.

Safety is of course a key element, especially in the theme parks, where the potential for accidents is ever-present. If an elderly person with a walker wants to go on the Haunted Mansion ride in the Magic Kingdom, "cast members" (as all employees are called) are empowered to stop the ride while the guest is helped onto the walkway. At the same time, a recorded announcement is played for those on the ride: "Ladies and gentlemen, the ghosts and goblins have taken over for a minute." This is just one example of how cast members are trained to handle potential safety problems.

Courtesy is generated by Disney's attitude toward its employees and reinforced by specific training techniques in handling guests. A popular Disney saying is, "Our front line is our bottom line." Disney also insists that guests are always guests, whether they are right or wrong. That means they are allowed to be wrong with dignity, never reprimanded or put on the defensive. If a guest has found their car door locked, staff members react in a positive manner even though they know that what has happened is not their fault. They attempt to soften the situation by trying to make the guest feel OK. Body language is also considered a part of courtesy. To give directions, cast members are taught to use the "Disney point": it involves the entire palm or two fingers—never a single finger, which is considered rude! Another dimension of courtesy is the way the Disney cast interacts with guests. In the morning, when people are full of energy and ready to start off on a day of adventure, the staff too is upbeat and chatty. But at night, when people are tired and returning to their rooms or going home, unnecessary conversation is kept to a minimum.

The other two service priorities, *show* (entertainment) and *efficiency,* are obvious throughout the Disney operation. As cast members, all employees have a role in the show at Disney. Part of show integrity is to ensure that a cast member in a Frontierland costume does not appear in Tomorrowland, and that a server in Liberty Tree Tavern talks as if it were 1776. Video monitors, character appearances, and live performances are show elements that entertain guests during long waits for attractions. Parades, shows, and fireworks are used to draw crowds to specific areas of the park. Walt Disney World in Florida efficiently solved a recurring and embarrassing problem for guests: remembering where they left their cars in a parking lot that is larger than California's entire Disneyland complex. When guests cannot find their cars, attendants simply ask them what time they arrived.

With that information, it is easy to tell where to look for a car because specific rows are filled at specific times!

Recently, Disney added a Fifth Key, *inclusion*, to ensure that Disney is welcoming and joyful for all. Josh D'Amaro, chair of parks, experiences, and products for Disney, explained in a Disney Parks blog post that "Inclusion is essential to our culture and leads us forward as we continue to realize our rich legacy of engaging storytelling, exceptional service, and Disney magic."[11]

Disney executives estimate that every cast member has 60 moments of truth every day. Clearly, Disney defines quality service as exceeding guest expectations during every one of those encounters. The Disney company helps its staff exceed guest expectations by paying attention to the smallest details. This meticulous approach pays off, bringing customers back for repeat visits and making Disney World the world's largest single tourist attraction.

Knowledge Check

1. How important is time in Disney's Five Keys to good service?

2. Why is it important for employees in any hospitality business to model Disney's service style in moments of truth?

Because many obvious physical and product differences among hospitality companies have faded, consumers have looked for other ways to differentiate one hotel and restaurant brand from another. The most compelling difference in the minds of many consumers is customer service. Good customer service is defined as meeting customer needs in the way that they want and expect them to be met. Superior service results from exceeding guest expectations.

Hospitality operations, which often deal in intangible services, have very different management and marketing challenges than do companies that deal exclusively in tangible products. For hospitality businesses, the nature of the product is different, customers are more involved in the production process, people are part of the product, services can't be inventoried, the time factor is more important, and distribution channels are different. It is also harder to maintain quality control standards in hospitality businesses.

Broad, long-range business planning is called strategic planning. Companies must formulate general business objectives for themselves; otherwise, there will be confusion about where they are going and how they intend to get there. These general business objectives are most commonly called a company's mission or values and are expressed as a mission or core values statement. Once a mission has been clearly established and articulated, there is a series of steps that a company must take: perform a SWOT analysis, formulate strategies, implement strategies, and monitor and evaluate results.

Hotels and restaurants are capacity-constrained businesses and must constantly manage supply and demand. Supply can be managed to a limited extent, but it is more productive for hospitality businesses to focus on managing demand. Demand can be shifted, inventoried, and controlled by varying prices, changing service levels, or using communications strategies (e.g., advertising) to affect demand.

Successful service companies share a "strategic service vision"—a blueprint for service managers. There are two components to this blueprint: targeting a market segment and focusing on a service strategy. In addition, successful hospitality companies focus a good deal of management attention on establishing quality standards for services, communicating them to employees through training programs, and measuring performance. Job restructuring is another effective strategy.

Companies have found many ways to make certain they deliver on their promise of quality service. Each organization and situation is different. The Walt Disney Company provides one example of how a hospitality company can consistently deliver superior service.

KEY TERMS

capacity-constrained businesses—Businesses that produce products or services that cannot be inventoried or stored for future use. Success depends on their ability to efficiently match productive capacity to consumer demand at any given moment.

chased-demand strategy—A management strategy in which capacity can, to a limited extent, be varied to suit the level of demand.

hospitality—The act of being welcoming, friendly, and generous toward guests or visitors. It involves making people feel comfortable, providing them with what they need, and creating a positive and enjoyable experience for them.

intangible products—The primary products of hospitality-oriented organizations. Intangible products, such as comfort, enjoyment, and pleasant experiences, relate to guests' emotional well-being and expectations. They present very different management and marketing challenges than do tangible products, such as automobiles or boxes of cereal.

level-capacity strategy—A management strategy in which the same amount of capacity is offered, no matter how high the consumer demand.

moments of truth—Critical interactions or touch points between a customer and a company that significantly influence the customer's perception of the brand.

service—The act of providing assistance, help, or support to someone or fulfilling a particular need or request.

strategic planning—The process of setting goals, defining strategies, and making decisions to guide an organization toward its desired outcomes. It involves systematically analyzing an organization's internal and external environment, assessing its strengths and weaknesses, identifying opportunities and threats, and developing a comprehensive plan of action.

SWOT—An acronym for Strengths, Weaknesses, Opportunities, and Threats. A SWOT analysis helps companies assess how well they are serving their current markets, which is an important step in the strategic planning process.

1. Which organization requires both hospitality and customer service at all times?
   a. Pharmacy
   b. Car dealership
   c. Island resort
   d. National bank

2. Which statement accurately describes hospitality and service?
   a. Hospitality and service are synonymous and can be used interchangeably.
   b. Hospitality focuses on meeting customer expectations, while service involves providing assistance and fulfilling needs.
   c. Hospitality refers to providing assistance and support, while service emphasizes creating a positive and enjoyable experience.
   d. Hospitality involves intangible products and service involves tangible products.

3. Which is one of Disney's Five Keys?
   a. Security
   b. Punctuality
   c. Courtesy
   d. Accountability

4. A 35-year-old hotel has 100 rooms. The hotel has no plans to renovate. Which strategy must it follow to maintain business success?
   a. Chased-demand strategy
   b. Banked-executive strategy
   c. Level-capacity strategy
   d. Corporate-executive strategy

5. What is the most important operational competency of top-level service managers?
   a. Managing day-to-day operations
   b. Developing strategies for survival
   c. Providing superior hospitality
   d. Performing a SWOT analysis

6. What is the purpose of performing a SWOT analysis in the strategic planning process?
   a. To determine how well the company is serving current markets
   b. To identify suppliers for new products
   c. To create a company slogan
   d. To implement strategies

7. What is the purpose of monitoring and evaluating results in the strategic planning process?
   a. To determine employee satisfaction
   b. To make sure strategies are working
   c. To create new products
   d. To promote a company's values and culture

8. What is key to delivering memorable hospitality experiences?
   a. Mimicking other companies
   b. Relying on technology for transactions
   c. Encouraging every employee to act like a manager
   d. Appealing to as many segments as possible

9. What concept did Jan Carlzon popularize to combat the guest perception of being treated as a mere number?
   a. First-class section
   b. Moments of truth
   c. Reservations system
   d. Ground staff

10. Which is a challenge in a capacity-constrained business?
   a. Inventorying supply
   b. Finishing and storing goods
   c. Constantly managing supply and demand
   d. Supply chain management

11. Which example constitutes superior service in hospitality?
   a. Gifting a couple checking in to a hotel a bottle of champagne
   b. Offering an omelette station during breakfast hour
   c. Printing a guest's boarding pass for their flight
   d. Extending the business center's hours of operation for guests

12. Which is considered an intangible product or service in a hotel?
   a. High-end bath products
   b. Duvet covers
   c. Complimentary high-speed Wi-Fi
   d. Filtered bottled water

SHORT-ANSWER QUESTIONS

1. How has the hospitality industry changed the way it delivers service?

2. What are some ways hospitality businesses can integrate technology while maintaining a high level of service?

LOST IN COMMUNICATION

On a chilly fall Saturday afternoon around 12:30 p.m., a young woman named Diana arrives with two of her friends at a four-star city-center hotel in New York City. The group has a prepaid reservation. Check-in at the hotel doesn't begin until 3 p.m. Diana attempts to check in early, but there are no available rooms. The morning front desk agent offers to store the group's luggage until check-in, which they graciously accept. The agent confirms with Diana and her friends that the first available room will be secured for them, and they'll be able to check in later that day. The agent suggests that they explore the city in the meantime. Diana and her friends leave the hotel to shop, dine, and see a Broadway play.

When the group arrives back at the hotel around 9 p.m., they attempt to complete the check-in process only to discover that an evening front desk agent released their room to another guest. Cold, angry, and confused, Diana begins arguing with the front desk agents about why the room reserved for her group had been given away. The front desk agents try to provide an explanation and apologize for the mistake. After five minutes of talking, however, they don't offer any solutions. About 10 minutes later, the night auditor tries to help by offering Diana and her friends a one-night stay at a nearby hotel with complimentary round-trip transportation to the hotel.

Frustrated and tired, Diana and her friends accept the offer. They sleep at the neighboring property for one night and return to the original hotel the next morning. The front desk agent, aware of Diana's experience from the previous night, checks the group into a larger suite with two queen beds and a skyline view of Manhattan. Diana and her friends resume their weekend stay without further problems.

When Diana and her friends check out of the hotel on Monday, the final invoice reflects a one-night discount and that 1,000 bonus reward points have been added to Diana's account. The agent on duty apologizes to Diana and invites her to stay at the hotel property again. Diana graciously acknowledges the hotel staff's recovery efforts.

DISCUSSION QUESTIONS

1. What was the problem when Diana and her friends returned from their day of exploring New York City?

2. What key mistake was made when the front desk agents changed shifts?

3. When Diana and her friends returned, what should the on-duty agents have done before or during the moment of truth?

4. How would you assess the hotel's guest recovery response? Do you believe Diana will stay at the property again?

Danny Meyer

Danny Meyer is founder of Shake Shack, a popular modern-day burger restaurant that started as a small roadside stand in New York City. Shake Shack grew into a global phenomenon and became a public company in 2015.

He is also the founder and executive chair of Union Square Hospitality Group (USHG), a renowned hospitality organization based in New York City. Meyer is a prominent figure in the restaurant industry and has made significant contributions to the culinary world.

In 1985, at the age of 27, he opened his first restaurant, Union Square Cafe, marking the beginning of his successful career in hospitality. Over the years, USHG has expanded and now includes several highly acclaimed restaurants, among them Gramercy Tavern, The Modern, and Maialino.

Meyer's leadership at USHG is recognized for fostering a distinctive culture of "enlightened hospitality." He prioritizes the well-being of employees and has established innovative practices in areas such as hiring, leadership, and corporate responsibility. In Setting the Table, published in 2006, he outlines his business and life principles, which have resonated with various industries.

Throughout his career, Meyer has received numerous accolades for his achievements and humanitarian efforts. He was awarded the Julia Child Award in 2017, named one of TIME 100's "Most Influential People" in 2015, and in 2012 received the Aspen Institute's Preston Robert Tisch Award in Civic Leadership, among other honors. His restaurants and individuals associated with USHG have won an unprecedented 28 James Beard Awards, including the prestigious Outstanding Restaurateur award in 2005.

Imagine that you are a restaurant owner who has just received a negative review on social media from a customer. The customer complains that although the food was delicious, the service was lacking in hospitality. As you reflect on this feedback, you start to think about the difference between service and hospitality.

Service refers to the technical aspects of providing a product or service, such as the efficiency and accuracy of the service delivery. Hospitality, on the other hand, refers to the emotional and personal connection between the customer and the service provider. It encompasses factors such as warmth, friendliness, and attentiveness to the customer's needs.

As you consider the negative review, you start to question whether your staff is focusing on providing efficient service at the expense of creating a hospitable atmosphere. You realize that while the food may be excellent, the overall dining experience is just as important to your customers.

What would you do to address this?

2
THE TRAVEL AND TOURISM INDUSTRY

Chapter Outline

Learning Objectives

1. List recent world changes that affect the travel and tourism industry, describe in general terms the size of the industry, and explain the importance of the interrelationships within the industry. (pp. 30–35)

2. Summarize reasons people travel and describe types of travel research. (pp. 35–38)

3. Explain the social impact that travel and tourism can have on a destination, discuss sustainable tourism development and ecotourism, and describe a plan for sound tourism development. (pp. 38–41)

KEY TERMS

demographic information

ecotourism

multiplier effect

price and sights group

psychographic research

quality group

sun and surf group

sustainable tourism development

travel and tourism industry

The hospitality industry is only one of several industries that make up the travel and tourism industry. In this chapter, we'll look at the scope and economic impact of travel and tourism, then examine how businesses within the industry are interrelated. We'll conclude the chapter with a discussion of why people travel, travel and tourism's effect on society, sustainable development, and ecotourism.

2.1 THE CHANGING WORLD

Change is a constant. But never has it been as dramatic as in the twentieth century—more specifically, the period following World War II. The United Nations was established in 1945 as an international organization aimed at promoting peace, security, and cooperation among nations. There was a wave of decolonization as European powers gradually relinquished their colonies in Africa, Asia, and the Middle East, leading to the emergence of numerous independent nations. Advancements in transportation and communication technologies, along with the lowering of trade barriers, led to greater global interconnectedness and trade. But perhaps the most significant postwar change was in technological advancements that transformed various aspects of life. The development of computers, the Internet, telecommunications, space exploration, medical breakthroughs, and other scientific innovations revolutionized industries, communication, and everyday life. The pace of change after 1945 was unprecedented, and there are no signs of it slowing down in the twenty-first century.

More than any other factor, technology is responsible for transforming the way we live. Technological advancement drove much of the world from an agrarian to an industrial society and, beginning in the 1950s, into an information society. The technological revolution that we are living in today has fundamentally changed the way we live, work, and relate to each other. Technology has provided us with the means to travel faster and cheaper, manufacture goods more efficiently, and communicate with one another across the globe almost instantaneously. The Internet, email, smartphones, text and voice messages, teleconferencing, and social media enable us to exchange information as fast as

thoughts are conceived. Satellites and fiber-optic cables link North and South America, Europe, Africa, and Asia, carrying voice and electronic communications faster and clearer every day. Even more significantly, new information-transfer technologies can carry a much greater volume of information and calls.

Today, we are in the midst of the Fourth Industrial Revolution. We do not yet know its full scale, scope, and complexity, but we do know that it is unlike anything we have experienced before. The Fourth Industrial Revolution is characterized by a fusion of technologies that is blurring the lines between physical, digital, and biological spheres. Simply put, it is the union of artificial intelligence (AI), robotics, Internet of Things (IoT), 3D printing, nanotechnology, biotechnology, and quantum computing in our physical lives. Do you know how your casual Internet browsing resulted in purchase suggestions on your Amazon account? That is AI at work.

The world's population is growing. There are more than 8 billion people on the planet today; by 2050, it's estimated there will be 9.7 billion.[1] The global population is also aging (see Exhibit 2.1). In many parts of the world, declining birth rates will produce a population with a larger percentage of older people. The 2020 World Population Data Sheet by the Population Reference Bureau predicts that Western and Southern Europe will have the largest shares of people ages 65 and older in the years ahead, while sub-Saharan Africa will have the smallest. An aging global population presents both opportunities and challenges for the travel and tourism industry. For example, older travelers may have more purchasing power but require proximity to medical care or other accommodations.

There are many other trends affecting travel. In a number of countries, the amount of leisure time is increasing. The United States does not require employers to provide vacation days or holidays. While the average American gets 10 legal holidays per year, Germans receive 30 days of vacation and holidays, as do the French and the British. In fact, workers in most European countries have a minimum of 20 days off to pursue leisure activities.[2]

Many households have two income earners. This often means that there are more discretionary funds for travel and a greater need to take a vacation as a relief from stress. But two workers in one family can also mean shorter vacations. People today tend to take several short vacations during the year rather than a single long one.

Exhibit 2.1 Population Ages 65 and Older by Major World Area

	2022	2030	2050
World	9.7	11.7	16.4
Sub-Saharan Africa	3.0	3.3	4.7
Northern Africa and Southern Asia	5.5	7.0	12.5
Central and Southern Asia	6.4	8.1	13.4
Eastern and South-Eastern Asia	12.7	16.3	25.7
Latin America and the Caribbean	9.1	11.5	18.8
Australia/New Zealand	16.6	19.4	23.7
Oceania[a]	3.9	5.1	8.2
Europe and Northern America	18.7	22.0	26.9

Source: United Nations, *World Population Prospects 2022: Summary of Results*, chrome-extension://efaidnbmnnnibp-cajpcglclefindmkaj/https://www.un.org/development/desa/pd/sites/www.un.org.development.desa.pd/files/wpp2022_summary_of_results.pdf.
[a]Excluding Australia and New Zealand.

Seasonality has become less important in travel. Part of this is due to the increased tendency to take vacations when we can, not when we would like to. Also, more and more attractions tend to be "climate controlled." Dubai has an indoor ski resort that is 278 feet (85 meters) high, with five slopes of varying difficulty.

As a result of an increased awareness of the problems caused by pollution and overdevelopment, sustainable tourism is being embraced by governments, the travel industry, and travelers. People all over the world are eager to visit the Amazon rainforest, the glaciers of Alaska, and the barrier reefs of Australia. The increasing affluence of younger travelers has fueled the adventure travel business. Travelers today are highly invested in trips that are environmentally friendly. Trips today are characterized not by *where* we can be, but by *what* we can be while traveling. From interest in carbon offsets to hotels that are green and environmentally friendly, tourists are seeking more meaning in their travels. This has led tour operators to introduce such options as women-only trips, wellness vacations, and even opportunities for travelers to work with scientists to collect data or be part of a nature restoration project.

The COVID-19 pandemic severely impacted travel worldwide in 2020. The United Nations World Tourism Organization (UNWTO) reported that international tourist arrivals declined by 73 percent in 2020. Lockdowns across the world resulted in an estimated $4.5 trillion loss, compared to 2019. By the end of 2022, international tourism was on track to reach 65 percent of pre-pandemic levels.[3]

In short, we are seeing significant economic, social, and political changes throughout the world. Some bode well for tourism; others, such as terrorism, political instability, and armed conflict, do not. Civil unrest or war in a country or region can greatly affect tourism. Concerns about personal safety, travel advisories, and the disruption of essential services can lead to a significant drop in tourist numbers. Government policies, including visa requirements, entry restrictions, or strict immigration procedures, can also impact tourism. Complicated or restrictive travel regulations can discourage potential tourists from visiting a destination.

2.2 THE NATURE OF THE TRAVEL AND TOURISM INDUSTRY

When the U.S. Senate created the National Tourism Policy Act of 1981 to encourage the growth of tourism, it used the following definition of the **travel and tourism industry**:

> An interrelated amalgamation of those businesses and agencies which totally or in part provide the means of transport, goods, services, and other facilities for travel outside of the home community for any purpose not related to day-to-day activity.[4]

Another definition that is somewhat similar but a bit clearer, and therefore the one we will adopt, is provided by Douglas Frechtling, professor of tourism studies at George Washington University. Frechtling defines the travel and tourism industry as "a collection of organizations and establishments that derive all or a significant portion of their income from providing goods and services purchased on a trip to the traveler."[5]

The travel and tourism industry is made up of a variety of businesses and organizations that provide products and services to travelers. Here are some of the businesses that make up the industry:

- *Accommodations*—Hotels, motels, resorts, vacation rentals, bed and breakfasts, hostels, and other lodging establishments.

- *Transportation*—Airlines, cruise lines, car rental companies, bus companies, train companies, and other transportation services.

- *Food and beverage*—Restaurants, cafés, bars, nightclubs, and other food and beverage establishments.

- *Attractions*—Museums, theme parks, zoos, aquariums, casinos, and other entertainment venues.

- *Travel services*—Travel agencies, tour operators, online travel agencies (OTAs), travel websites, and other travel booking services.

- *Retail*—Gift shops, souvenir shops, travel gear stores, and other retail establishments catering to travelers.

- *Events*—Convention centers, meeting facilities, event planners, and other event-related businesses.

- *Recreation*—Outdoor recreation businesses, such as ski resorts, golf courses, and adventure tourism companies.

- *Wellness*—Spas, yoga and fitness studios, health and wellness retreats, and other businesses catering to wellness travelers.

- *Destination management*—Destination marketing organizations, tourism bureaus, and other organizations responsible for promoting and developing tourism in specific destinations.

These are just a few examples of the types of businesses that make up the travel and tourism industry. The industry is vast and constantly evolving, with new businesses and technologies emerging all the time.

One way to define the size of the travel and tourism industry is to add up the amount of money spent on goods and services by travelers. Unfortunately, it's impossible to do this accurately. While just about everyone would agree that airlines and resorts receive almost all of their business from travelers, what about gift shops and gas stations? These businesses on the whole have no way of knowing what percentage of their customers are travelers and what percentage are local residents. Depending on the location, there may be a wide variation in the amount of business they get from each source. Although there is no way of knowing how much of their revenues are from travelers, for statistical purposes the total receipts of these types of businesses are included in projections of the size and scope of the travel and tourism industry.

Statisticians and economists measure the size of the travel and tourism industry by adding together the receipts of the businesses that compose it. But these figures do not tell the whole story. For example, one could argue that the amount of money a hotel takes in is not a true measure of its economic impact on the surrounding community. The real impact is measured by the salaries the hotel pays its employees, which they in turn spend on housing, clothes, and food for their families; by the taxes the hotel pays to local, state, and federal governments; by the amount of profits generated by local companies who sell goods and services to the hotel; and by the number of jobs the hotel creates. (The pyramid in Exhibit 2.2 is a depiction of the travel and tourism industry's impact on other sectors of the economy.)

Industry analysts have a name for these indirect or hidden benefits—the **multiplier effect**. The multiplier effect is measured by adding up all the expenditures of travelers in a given geographic area and multiplying that figure by a factor (known as the multiplier) to arrive at the amount of additional income that is generated by these expenditures. While the multiplier effect is highly variable among cities and countries around the world, many industry analysts use a figure of 1.6 as a reasonable multiplier on a general basis. Although it is difficult to accurately assess the size of the tourism industry, some figures are available that are truly astounding. In 2019, according to the UNWTO, there were over 1.459 billion international tourist arrivals worldwide; spending on international tourism reached $1.487 trillion; and Spain, the United States, China, and Italy had the most tourist arrivals (see Exhibit 2.3).

However, travel and tourism suffered a staggering 73 percent decline in 2020[6] due to the pandemic, with losses of $910 billion to $1.2 trillion in export revenues, putting 100 million to 120 million jobs at risk. The global tourism industry began to recover as countries reopened borders and relaxed travel restrictions. However, it is likely that the tourism industry will look different in the post-COVID world, with a greater emphasis on sustainable and responsible travel practices, health and safety measures, and technological advancements to enhance the travel experience.

Exhibit 2.2   The Economic Impact of the Travel and Tourism Industry

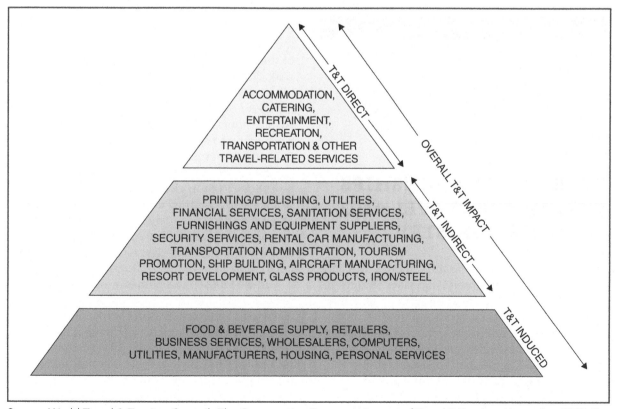

Source: World Travel & Tourism Council, *The Comparative Economic Impact of Travel & Tourism*, November 2012, 2.

Exhibit 2.3   Most Tourist Arrivals 2019

Country	Arrivals (in millions)
France	89
Spain	84
United States	79
China	66
Italy	65
Turkey	51
Mexico	45
Thailand	40
Germany	40
United Kingdom	39

Source: United Nations, *International Tourism Highlights: 2020 Edition*, 2021, https://www.e-unwto.org/doi/pdf/10.18111/9789284422456.

Knowledge Check

1. What is the multiplier effect and how is it measured?

2. What are some ways that the tourism industry will likely change because of the COVID-19 pandemic?

2.3 INTERRELATIONSHIPS WITHIN THE TRAVEL AND TOURISM INDUSTRY

An important and unique feature of the travel and tourism industry is the interrelationship among its various parts. A trip may consist of an airplane flight, a car rental, a stay at a hotel, several restaurant meals, and some gift purchases. Each of these elements must work well in order for travelers to have a pleasant total experience.

For example, suppose the Smiths decide to fly from their home in Minneapolis, Minnesota, to vacation at a theme park in Orlando, Florida.

The sum total of their experiences determines the quality of their vacation and the likelihood of their becoming repeat guests at the theme park. For instance, the Smiths might have a pleasant flight to Florida, but then their rental car could overheat, leaving them stranded for several hours and cutting short the day they were going to spend at the park. Or their hotel could be undergoing refurbishing, so the pool is closed and the usually attractive lobby décor is covered with drop cloths and scaffolding. Even worse—suppose they arrive at the theme park at a particularly busy time and find that the park has closed its parking lot and is not admitting any more visitors that day. Any of these incidents could spoil their entire vacation.

Travel-industry businesses have a symbiotic relationship, a mutual dependency. For any one of them to be entirely successful in pleasing visitors, all of them must do a good job. If the hotel stay was uncomfortable, the Smiths might enjoy the theme park but still feel on the whole that they had a less-than-perfect vacation. If the hotel did its job but the theme park was overcrowded, the net sum of their experience could also be negative. Either way, all of the travel businesses in the area will suffer in the long run if the Smiths do not return or tell their friends in Minneapolis that their trip to the area was a disappointing experience.

Some destinations are so aware of this interrelationship that they go to extreme lengths to control all elements of the travel product. Bermuda, for instance, which is only 21 square miles in size, monitors the standards of all its hotels, restaurants, and attractions because it believes that if a visitor has a bad hotel room or a bad meal, they will go home feeling critical of the whole island. Since more than 40 percent of Bermuda's travel business is repeat, it cannot afford to disappoint its visitors.

Owners and operators of hospitality enterprises often underestimate the importance of the travel and tourism industry's interrelationships when considering how their enterprises are going to attract consumers. Such vacation spots as Hawaii depend on airlines to deliver almost all their visitors. If airline fares are too high, tourism business suffers no matter how strong or how effective marketing efforts are. Atlantic City, New Jersey, is a highly successful destination for motorcoach tours from New York City, but that is entirely a function of the gaming industry that has grown in Atlantic City in the last four decades. Now the casinos depend on the buses, and the buses depend on the casinos. Neither could succeed without the other.

Knowledge Check

1. Why is it important for businesses to recognize interrelationships within the travel and tourism industry?

2. What potential benefits do businesses in the travel and tourism industry have if they strengthen their interrelationships?

2.4 WHY PEOPLE TRAVEL

Over the centuries, travel has developed for business, health, social, and cultural reasons. But at the most basic level, it can be said that the main reason most people travel is to gather information. We want to know how our favorite aunt is doing in Nashville, so we take a trip to visit her. Businesspeople travel to see what is going on in their home office in Chicago or to find out what customers in Madrid, Spain, think of their products. Some of us travel to France to see how the French vintners grow grapes and produce wine. Others go to Beijing to learn more about Chinese culture. Alexis Alford (https://www.lexie limitless.com), the youngest person to travel to all 196 countries before she was 21 (certified by Guinness World Records), chose to travel because she wanted to push the limits of what she thought she could do and see as much of the world as she could in the process. Along the way, she found her purpose: to inspire the people around her, especially young women.

Travel is an important part of our lives. It helps us understand ourselves and others. It is both an effect and a cause of rapid societal change. Technology has played a huge part in all of this. Commercial jet aircraft have brought foreign places closer; communications satellites bring news events from around the world into our living rooms; and the Internet connects us to distant people and places via our personal computers. These technologies have stimulated interest in traveling abroad.

The three most important factors that determine the amount people spend for travel are employment, disposable income, and household wealth. The more money that people who want to travel have, the more likely they are to travel, the more frequently they are likely to travel, and the farther they are likely to travel. Business travel is less susceptible to economic downturns than leisure travel, although not immune. For example, during the Great Recession of 2008–2009, business travel plummeted due to companies tightening their travel budgets. In 2020, at the beginning of the COVID-19 pandemic, business travel came to an abrupt halt due to domestic and global travel restrictions. International and U.S. trade associations and corporate travel agencies predict that as much as 36 percent of business travel has been permanently lost as a result of efficiencies, such as video conferencing, that increased during the pandemic.

It is important to note that not everyone is disposed to travel. Some people by their nature like to stay at home. Others get motion sickness, don't like to fly, or simply won't travel no matter what their economic circumstances. Psychologist Frank Farley has studied the behavior of travelers versus nontravelers. "People who hesitate to travel may do so because of deep-seated fears," says

Farley. "Travelers, though, seem stable enough to expose themselves to uncertainty and adventure. They worry less, feel less inhibited and submissive, and are more self-confident than stay-at-homes."[7] Farley found other differences between people who like to travel and those who would rather stay at home:

Most passionate travelers are risk-takers in many areas of life. They're drawn not only to unknown lands but also to taking chances with their investment portfolios. However, their risk-taking is rational; it's based on a deep sense that they control their destiny. They enjoy life, love to play, and gravitate towards crowds and parties.[8]

The various reasons people travel can be placed into six broad categories:

1. *Recreation*. Recreation includes leisure and activities related to sports, entertainment, and rest. Beach vacations, ski vacations, and adventure travel such as white-water rafting all fall into this category. Destinations such as the Caribbean, Disney World, and national parks benefit largely from recreational travel.

2. *Culture*. People travel for cultural reasons—a desire to learn about things and places that interest them. These interests can be historical, ethnic, educational, or they can relate to the arts or religion. Famous battlegrounds such as the beaches of Normandy, France, or the rolling hills of Gettysburg, Pennsylvania; cathedrals such as St. Peter's Basilica in Vatican City; California's Napa Valley; Kenya's national parks; and the Great Wall of China all have educational, religious, historical, or ethnic significance. Destinations often capitalize on these attributes to stage special events and festivals. The Salzburg Music Festival and Mardi Gras in Rio de Janeiro, Brazil, and New Orleans, Louisiana, are examples of cultural events that are marketed very heavily. Many destination areas and businesses within those areas have their own websites on which they list events, attractions, and other "things to do" for travelers.

3. *Business*. Business travel is a significant portion of all travel. This category includes individual business travelers as well as those attending meetings and conventions.

The trend now is to combine business and recreational travel—thus business meetings and conventions are held at resort hotels, at theme parks, and on cruise ships, and spouses and even children often come along.

4. *Visiting Friends and relatives*. research has shown that much travel involves visiting friends and relatives. This is difficult to measure, however, and has little economic impact compared to recreational, cultural, or business travel.

5. *Wellness*. Many people travel to visit diagnostic centers and receive treatment at clinics, hospitals, or spas, such as the Mayo Clinic in Rochester, Minnesota, or Canyon Ranch in Tucson, Arizona. This type of travel, known as medical tourism, is a growing travel segment with increasing economic impact.

6. *Purpose*. For Generation Z travelers, who are digital natives and largely travel-savvy, travel is all about the experience. They believe that tourism can benefit local communities and have been raised with information about global warming and eco-friendliness. Above all, Gen Z travelers want uniqueness and technological conveniences in their travels. They are willing to partake in budget-friendly travel by contributing to a cause at the destination, whether it's building a watershed in the forest, capturing data for research, or assisting a nonprofit organization.

Psychographic Research

Another kind of research that is helpful in understanding travelers and changing travel patterns is psychographic. **Psychographic research** attempts to classify people's behavior not in terms of their age, education, or gender, but rather in terms of their lifestyle and values. Sometimes this information is more useful than statistical data such as age and income, also called **demographic information**, in deciding what kind of amenities to offer in a resort or how to advertise a particular destination. For instance, the government of Bermuda conducted psychographic research in the United States to determine who would be most interested in going to Bermuda on vacation. In a sample of people who were potential vacationers, three groups emerged:

- The **price and sights group**. These people were interested in seeing the most things for the least amount of money. They wanted tours that covered 10 countries in nine days at a bargain price. For them, the best cruises were the cheapest ones that visited the most ports, and a good hotel was one that offered budget-priced accommodations within walking distance of everything they might want to see.

- The **sun and surf group**. These people sought a vacation where they could lie on a beach and get a golden tan. Value was important, but even more important was finding a destination where there was good weather, guaranteed sunshine, and a beautiful beach where they could soak up the sun and swim in clear waters.

- The **quality group**. The quality of the vacation experience was of paramount importance to this group. Members felt they had worked hard for a vacation and now it was their turn to relax and be taken care of. This group valued destinations and accommodations that were first-class or deluxe. Service was very important—they wanted and expected lots of pampering and were willing to pay a fair price for it. They also wanted gourmet dining and sophisticated entertainment.

In a 2022 study of American travelers, MMGY Travel Intelligence, a travel marketing firm, reported that inflation and the rising cost of travel are leading some Americans to stay home. However, Baby Boomers and higher-income households plan to increase their leisure travel in the coming years. Interest in culinary experiences is driving younger travelers' (Gen Z and millennial travelers) decisions on where they stay.[9] In the coming years, international travel will increase among affluent Americans.

For the most part, today's consumers are technologically savvy. They know how and where to find the help they need to make sound purchasing decisions. For example, travelers shop for the best airline fares and hotel rates on OTA websites such as Expedia and Travelocity. Everyone is wired, and new technologies and tools have erased old limitations. Social media and advertising can greatly influence younger consumers' decision-making, especially appealing videos and pictures posted by a celebrity or influencer.

Travelers today take reliability, comfort, convenience, performance, and more for granted—they expect those things when they travel. Younger travelers prioritize activities and experiences above all but are still influenced by pricing. Of particular note are "bleisure" travelers,

Vacationers in the "sun and surf" group seek a beautiful beach where they can soak up the sun in clear waters.

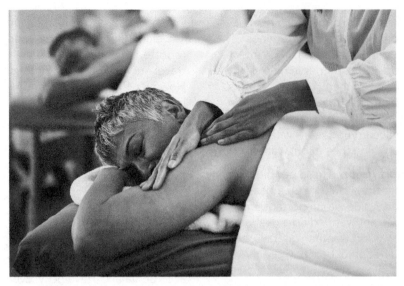

The quality of the vacation experience is of paramount importance for the "quality" group. Members of this group feel they have worked hard for a vacation and now it's their turn to relax and be cared for. They want lots of pampering and are prepared to pay a good price for it.

who are capitalizing on opportunities to extend business trips for leisure.

To attract customers, marketers of hospitality products are learning to offer new points of difference in their product designs and the hospitality experiences they provide. There is no room for an average product anymore. People don't want to sleep in an average hotel or eat average food. Everything has to be special in one way or another. The new consumer mindset is that there is no reason to stick with old travel options when you are good at picking new options.

Knowledge Check

1. What are the six categories that describe why people travel?

2. What is psychographic research and how does it help the travel and tourism industry?

2.5 THE SOCIAL IMPACT OF TRAVEL

Hotels, restaurants, and attractions can shape and change life in a community. For example, Huatulco, Mexico, was a town that hardly rated a dot on the map until Club Med decided to build there. Disney World has changed the character of Orlando and Florida forever.

Travelers to any destination bring money and jobs, but they can also bring problems. Whenever you have increased travel to an area, you must provide additional public services such as police, firefighters, water treatment plants, and solid waste disposal facilities. This may increase the cost of living for residents. Crime may increase. New airports bring with them pollution and noise; new hotels and shopping strips change the character of the local landscape. Residents may have limited or no access to beaches and other property that previously had been public. European cities such as Venice, Italy; Barcelona, Spain; Dubrovnik, Croatia; and Amsterdam, the Netherlands have been victims of overtourism—whereby a destination becomes overwhelmed with an excessive number of tourists, negatively impacting the local environment, infrastructure, economy, and residents' quality of life—and have enacted policies to try and save the soul of their vibrant cosmopolitan destinations. Barcelona has blocked construction of new hotels in its historic center and turned away cruise ships. Amsterdam has increased the tax on hotel rooms and placed restrictions on short-term rentals.

For these and other reasons, many people feel that their communities have been negatively affected by travelers and therefore are not in favor of development that encourages more tourism. Some areas are ambivalent about the benefits of the travel and tourism industry and have not gone out of their way to attract tourists or develop facilities for them. Other communities, like Monroe County, Florida (where Key West is located), feel that they may have let development get out of hand and are now trying to put a cap on it.

There are other problems in developing countries. One is the enormous wealth gap between the travelers who stay in luxurious resorts and the employees who witness for the first time new lifestyles and behaviors that can change their own expectations and values. Local residents often try to emulate the dress styles and consumption patterns of visitors, sometimes eroding an area's culture and traditional values. Racial tensions are not uncommon as a result of these conditions. The seasonality of tourism poses another major problem. When the season is over, often there are large numbers of dislocated, jobless workers who have few other opportunities to earn a comparable living.

Today's hospitality managers are paying more attention to the social costs of travel and tourism. Modern planning methods make more use of impact studies that consider the social and environmental changes to an area that can be brought about by increased travel. Many countries have mounted impressive marketing campaigns in the off-season to attract visitors and keep employment levels high. Countries like Turkey have developed arts and crafts industries so that workers can make products for tourists during the off-season.

Pierre L. van den Berghe, a sociology professor at the University of Washington in Seattle, has studied the cultural impact of tourism in depth. He believes that, on the whole, the impact of tourism is positive:

In complex and unpredictable ways, tourism changes not only the behavior of hosts—their presentation of self— but their very definition of self. Far from destroying local cultures, tourism more commonly transforms and revives them. Of all forms of outside contact and modernization that affect isolated local cultures, tourism is probably the least destructive, precisely because it imparts a marketable value to cultural

diversity. If the quest for authenticity sometimes initially seems to undermine and corrupt local culture, it can revive and reinvigorate traditions that were languishing under the assault of other modernizing forces such as industrialization, urbanization, Christianization, or Western-style schooling. ... Locals often have the vitality to recapture their own heritage, the creativity to invent a new, redefined authenticity, and the resilience to resist the encroachments of the global village. To paraphrase Mark Twain, news of the death of Third and Fourth World cultures is greatly exaggerated. And, where cultures die, tourism is seldom to blame.[10]

Sustainable Tourism Development

One answer to solving some of the problems that tourism brings with it is **sustainable tourism development**, a middle road between unbridled tourism development and public intervention to control tourism expansion. The World Tourism Organization states that "Sustainability principles refer to the environmental, economic, and socio-cultural aspects of tourism development, and a suitable balance must be established between these three dimensions to guarantee its long-term sustainability."[11] Tourism that has a low impact on a locale's environment and culture and conserves the ecosystem while generating income and employment is considered sustainable tourism. Controlling the number of visitors to parks to minimize damage to the flora and fauna and limiting vehicular traffic at cultural sites to reduce air pollution and overcrowding are examples of responsible measures to limit damage to the environment. There is a growing realization that if tourism is to prosper at any location, there must be a balance between the needs of the visitors, the tourism industry, the community visited, and the environment. A sustainable tourism development program protects and enhances a locale's natural resources, conserves the local culture, contributes to cultural understanding, and benefits the economy of the community and its residents.

In 2019, Expedia Group partnered with the United Nations Educational, Scientific and Cultural Organization (UNESCO) and the Tourism Authority of Thailand to launch the first chapter of the UNESCO Sustainable Travel Pledge. Since then, the UNESCO Pledge has expanded to include major chains such as Accor and Iberostar Group, bringing together businesses, academics, startups, small and medium-sized enterprises (SMEs), nongovernmental organizations (NGOs), and members of the public sector looking to create a travel ecosystem that supports sustainable tourism. The UNESCO Pledge now has 4,200 hotels committed to concrete, transparent, and achievable action.

Ecotourism

An example of responsible tourism is **ecotourism**. Ecotourism is described as "responsible travel to natural areas that conserves the environment, sustains the well-being of the local people, and involves interpretation and education."[12] The rainforests in Costa Rica, the animal preserves in Kenya, and the Galapagos Islands are examples of sites that attract travelers who are ecologically and socially conscious. Since many of these sites are fragile and protected, visitation is on a small scale and therefore has a low impact. Simply visiting an ecologically sensitive location is not ecotourism: the visit must have a benefit such as building environmental awareness or providing funds for conservation.

There are a number of private operators of travel and tourism businesses who are invested in ecotourism. Some operators take pains to develop resorts that blend in with their cultural and physical surroundings. Others hire and train local guides and support scientific environmental research. Operators involved in ecotourism are careful that their operations will have minimal impact on the environment or the culture. These kinds of steps are the hallmark of real ecotourism.

Initially, travel to ecologically sensitive sites required forsaking comforts. Not anymore. One example of the many luxury resorts near ecologically sensitive areas is the Arenas Del Mar Hotel in Costa Rica. Located not far from a national park, the hotel uses solar power to heat water, advanced wastewater treatment, and nontoxic biodegradable cleaning products, among other environmentally protective measures. Room rates as high as $2,200 per night are charged during the peak season.[13]

The bottom line is that travel and tourism is an industry that has its benefits and its costs. Societies and governments must recognize both sides of the coin and plan for the proper balance for their own situations.

Planning for Tourism Development

One logical planning sequence for responsible tourism development consists of five steps:

1. *Define the scope of the project.* What is going to be built? Can it be done in a manner that is socially, environmentally, and economically sound?

With a sea lion for company, a photographer captures images on a beach in the Galapagos Islands.

2. *Analyze the market.* What need will this project fulfill? Will the existing infrastructure support it? What about seasonality? What is the demand potential? Who is the competition? Is there an available labor force?

3. *Create a master plan.* How is the land going to be used? What goes where? Is there a need for new roads, airports, or marine facilities?

4. *Determine who is going to develop it.* Some projects are built by governments, others by private developers. In the most successful projects, both are involved. Take Cancun, Mexico, where the development of the area as a resort destination was the result of a government initiative coupled with the desire of international hotel operators to expand into Mexico.

5. *Establish a timetable.* Is this a long-term plan or a short-term one? Is everything going to be done simultaneously or in incremental stages?

Knowledge Check

1. How could an increase in tourism negatively impact a beautiful tropical destination with historically low tourism?

2. Why is sustainable tourism development important?

CHAPTER SUMMARY

Technology has provided us with the means to travel faster and cheaper, produce more food with fewer farmers, manufacture goods more efficiently, and communicate with each other around the globe almost instantaneously. The world's population is changing. There are more of us than ever before, and the population continues to grow—and grow older. Significant technological, economic, social, and political changes occurred throughout the world in the latter part of the twentieth century, and the pace of change shows no sign of slowing down in the twenty-first century. The exponential pace of change brought by the Fourth Industrial Revolution will drastically alter how individuals, governments, and corporations operate, and data literacy will be a necessary skill set for all.

There are many trends that affect travel. These include increased leisure time, greater discretionary funds for travel, less seasonality in travel, growing ecotourism, adventure, and conscious travel. Many of today's trends bode well for tourism; others, such as the persistence of terrorism, do not.

Travel and tourism is now the world's largest industry. We cannot measure its size in receipts alone; adding expenditures such as salaries and food purchases gives a truer measure.

Moreover, the multiplier effect must be added to get the complete picture.

There are many components to the travel and tourism industry, including airlines, hotels, restaurants, and attractions. They are all interrelated, and the success or failure of one component can affect all of them.

Many of today's consumers want to be in charge of the decision-making process while buying hotel rooms and meals and making travel arrangements. They do their own research, using the Internet and other resources, then decide for themselves what they want to see and do, rather than take guided tours. They budget but don't economize; they are willing to spend money on travel and other goods and services so long as they get value. They are motivated by three critical value constructs: self-invention, personal authenticity, and "advantage intangibles."

There is cause for concern about the cultural impact of tourism. Some believe that the effects of tourism can be detrimental. Others maintain that tourism can stimulate economic growth and preserve rather than destroy native cultures. Businesses are recognizing the importance of sustainable tourism development and have joined forces, signing the UNESCO Pledge.

demographic information—Statistical information (such as age and income) about a population, used especially to identify markets.

ecotourism—Responsible travel to natural areas that conserves the environment and improves the well-being of local people.

multiplier effect—The hidden or indirect benefits of travel and tourism to a community, measured by adding up all the expenditures of travelers in the community and then multiplying that figure by a factor (known as the multiplier) to arrive at the amount of income that stays in the community and is generated by these expenditures.

price and sights group—The group of travelers interested in doing the most things for the least amount of money while on vacation.

psychographic research—Research that attempts to classify people's behavior in terms of their lifestyles and values.

quality group—The group of travelers for whom the quality of their vacation is of paramount importance. They want, and are willing to pay for, first-class accommodations and service.

sun and surf group—The group of travelers seeking a vacation spot where there is good weather, guaranteed sunshine, and a beautiful beach.

sustainable tourism development—Tourism that has a low impact on a locale's environment and culture and conserves the ecosystem while generating income and employment.

travel and tourism industry—A collection of organizations and establishments that derives all or a significant portion of its income from providing goods and services to travelers.

1. What travel trend has resulted from an increase in two-income households?
   a. Longer vacations
   b. Shorter vacations
   c. Seasonally influenced vacations
   d. Environmentally friendly vacations

2. Which business would be considered a major component of the travel and tourism industry?
   a. Harvard University
   b. Miami International Airport
   c. Cedars Sinai Medical Center
   d. The Federal Bureau of Investigation

3. Ideally, what is the best way to define the size of the travel and tourism industry?
   a. Reporting the amount of international passengers serviced by a major airport
   b. Surveying the hotel room inventory of a major metropolitan area
   c. Adding up the amount of money spent on goods and services by tourists
   d. Measuring the salaries that hotels pay their employees

4. What is the best example of the multiplier effect?
   a. Completed renovations of a Bay Area bridge
   b. Sargassum collecting along Florida's Atlantic Coast
   c. Increased passenger arrivals in New York City for winter holidays
   d. Increased sales of red snapper fish in restaurants in the Bahamas

5. Which category of travel would a person seeking treatment at a hospital fall into?
   a. Visiting friends and relatives
   b. Wellness
   c. Recreation
   d. Business

6. Which statement describes the relationship among the parts of the travel and tourism industry?
   a. The parts are mostly unrelated.
   b. Effective tourism marketing can overcome issues with any parts.
   c. Destinations should not try to control the relationship between the parts.
   d. The parts are mutually dependent for travelers to enjoy their total experience.

7. A couple that travels to Bali, Indonesia, to stay in a luxury jungle resort is an example of which travel group?
   a. The price and sights group
   b. The quality group
   c. The sun and surf group
   d. The business group

8. Which is the best example of the travel and tourism industry negatively affecting a local community?
   a. Building a new subway system to reduce city traffic
   b. Introducing a study abroad program
   c. Making a once-public beach private
   d. Relocating a technology hub to a new major city

9. What is one step in developing responsible tourism?
   a. Establish a business LLC.
   b. Create a master plan.
   c. Apply for a bank loan.
   d. Obtain a construction permit.

10. What is an example of a destination management organization?
    a. University alumni association
    b. Convention center
    c. Local convention and visitors bureau
    d. Casino

11. Which kind of travel is less susceptible to economic downturns?
    a. Culture
    b. Purpose
    c. Business
    d. Recreation

12. What is the primary responsibility of a sustainable tourism development program?
    a. Break ground for a megahotel resort.
    b. Increase tourism dollars.
    c. Protect and enhance local natural resources.
    d. Commercialize businesses.

SHORT-ANSWER QUESTIONS

1. How are travel and tourism businesses adjusting to rapid shifts in consumer influence?

2. As rapid societal changes occur, what are the positive cultural impacts of tourism?

TRAVELING TO RIO

It's the beginning of 2016. The Summer Olympic Games in Rio De Janeiro, Brazil, are only a few months away. Kali Mendez is a travel agent based in Miami, Florida. She has been one of the top travel agents in South Florida for the past three years, meeting clients' expectations in booking travel arrangements and exceeding expectations with vacation experiences.

Kali's efforts have been so superb that she's been contacted by local government and tourism agencies in Rio De Janeiro to help increase travel between Miami and Rio for the Summer Olympic Games. The local agencies have presented a substantial financial offer to Kali if she can guarantee 50 group bookings to Brazil for the Games. They have also offered Kali an all-expense-paid trip to Rio De Janeiro before March 31, 2016.

Kali is thrilled at the opportunity but has significant concerns regarding tourism in Rio De Janeiro. The city has been experiencing a Zika virus epidemic, economic and political crises, and an increase in pollution and crime. Kali has visited Rio De Janeiro twice, but these concerns were not as great when she visited.

Kali is a trusted agent and never intends to put her clients in harm's way. There is risk here, but nevertheless Kali agrees to take the offer and begins working on her marketing strategy to secure the 50 group bookings.

DISCUSSION QUESTIONS

1. What concerns should Kali address with the government and tourism agencies before agreeing to the offer?

2. What advantages does Kali have that may have led to her agreeing to the offer?

3. How can Kali help ensure that her clients will be safe during their visit?

Hitesh Mehta

Hitesh Mehta is a distinguished professional in the fields of tourism destination physical planning, landscape architecture, architecture, and interior architecture. With over 35 years of experience, he is a highly acclaimed planner and designer, recognized globally for his expertise in sustainable tourism and ecotourism physical planning. Mehta has received numerous international awards in landscape architecture, planning, architecture, urban design, creative writing, and interior design, establishing himself as one of the foremost authorities in his field.

Throughout his career, Mehta has worked and consulted in 67 countries across six continents, contributing his knowledge and skills to various projects. He has played a crucial role in developing sustainable tourism plans for destinations such as Timor-Leste, northwest Bali, Ethiopia, the Maldives, western Uganda, Mayaguana Island in the Bahamas, West Caicos, western Kenya, North and South Madagascar, Nepal, the Virunga Massif in Rwanda, the Democratic Republic of the Congo, Red Center in Australia, Nankun Mountain in China, and many others. Currently, his firm, HM Design, is involved in environmentally and socially friendly sustainable tourism projects in Costa Rica, India, the United States, the Maldives, Kenya, and Liberia.

As one of the founding members of the Global Ecotourism Network, Mehta has made significant contributions to promoting sustainable tourism practices worldwide. He is an accomplished author with three books to his name, including the widely acclaimed *Authentic Ecolodges* published by Harper Design. Mehta was also the longest-serving board member of the International Ecotourism Society and currently holds a position on the board of the International School of Sustainable Tourism in Cavite, Philippines. He is an adjunct professor at the Chaplin School of Hospitality & Tourism Management at Florida International University.

In recognition of his pioneering work in sustainable tourism, Mehta was honored by *National Geographic Adventure* magazine in July 2006 as one of five sustainable tourism pioneers in the world. His ecotourism master planning initiatives have not only contributed to the preservation of endangered habitats but have also made a positive impact in alleviating human poverty. He continues to inspire and influence the field of sustainable tourism through his exceptional contributions and dedication to creating a better future for destinations and communities worldwide.

You are a travel blogger who has been invited to visit a luxury resort in a tropical destination. As you arrive, you notice that the resort is set amid beautiful natural surroundings, but also notice that there are a lot of single-use plastic items being used by the resort, such as straws, cups, and cutlery. You are concerned about the impact of this waste on the local environment and feel conflicted about promoting the resort on your blog without addressing this issue. What would you do?

3

EXPLORING HOSPITALITY CAREERS

Chapter Outline

Learning Objectives

1. Describe in general terms the makeup and size of the lodging and foodservice industries, identify advantages and disadvantages of a career in hospitality, and list the personal characteristics that correspond to each of the three personal skills areas: data, people, and things. (pp. 52–56)

2. Summarize career options in the lodging industry, list the advantages of working in a chain hotel and an independent hotel, and describe typical management positions in lodging operations. (pp. 56–59)

3. Briefly describe segments of the foodservice industry and the career opportunities available within them, outline career options in the club and cruise line industries, and summarize entrepreneurship opportunities within the industry and other career opportunities. (pp. 60–66)

4. Describe career ladders in the hospitality industry; summarize the purpose and contents of a résumé; and explain how to prepare for a job interview, sell yourself during the interview, and effectively follow up after the interview. (pp. 66–70)

KEY TERMS

banquet or catering manager

career path/career ladder

career portfolio

controller

Escoffier, Georges Auguste

food and beverage manager

front office manager

general manager

hospitality industry

hotel manager

housekeeping manager

human resources (HR) manager

information technology (IT) manager

marketing manager

restaurant manager

résumé

revenue manager

sales manager

This chapter focuses on careers in the hospitality industry. The chapter opens with a short discussion of the industry's size. Next, we look at the reasons people go into the hospitality field and how to go about selecting a segment of the industry that interests you. Each segment, from hotels to institutional foodservice, is described. Finally, there are some ideas and suggestions for getting a job in the industry.

3.1 HOSPITALITY TODAY

What *is* the **hospitality industry**? This is not an easy question, and books on the subject offer many different answers. Some view the hospitality industry as comprising four sectors: lodging, food, entertainment, and travel. However, the hospitality industry is usually viewed as encompassing mainly lodging and foodservice businesses. If we define the industry this way, we can include university residence halls, nursing homes, and other institutions (see Exhibit 3.1).

The global hospitality industry has grown tremendously in recent decades. Some of the reasons for this growth are rising consumer global purchasing power, increased demand in international travel, and disruption and innovations that have significantly changed how the industry works. For example, the founders of Airbnb started by renting air mattresses in their San Francisco, California, apartment before becoming the leader in the home-sharing market; Expedia, the first online travel agency (OTA), redefined how people booked travel; and Uber redefined mobility and launched ridesharing. Services and goods that in the past were only available to the privileged few can now be enjoyed by a much larger percentage of the population. For example, in the past 10 years, the number of people who have flown on an airplane or taken a cruise has increased dramatically.

We can get an idea of the hospitality industry's size by examining some of the statistics for the lodging and foodservice industries.

Lodging

It is unknown exactly how many hotels and hotel rooms there are currently worldwide; however, Smith Travel Research estimates that there are about 187,000 hotels worldwide, with an estimated 17.5 million hotel rooms.[1] The American Hotel & Lodging Association estimates that there are over 5.3 million guestrooms and almost 56,000 properties nationwide.[2] The number of rooms continues to increase as new hotels, resorts, and other lodging facilities open every year. Annually, 1.3 billion guests stay in U.S. hotels each year, spending nearly $550 billion at hotels and local businesses.

The U.S. lodging industry employs about 2.3 million people, both part time and full time, representing 1 out of every 25 jobs nationwide. Hotel managers and assistant managers represent about 200,000 jobs. Self-employed managers—primarily owners of small hotels and motels—hold a significant number of those jobs. Clearly, you don't have to work for someone else to succeed in the lodging business!

Exhibit 3.1   The Hospitality Industry

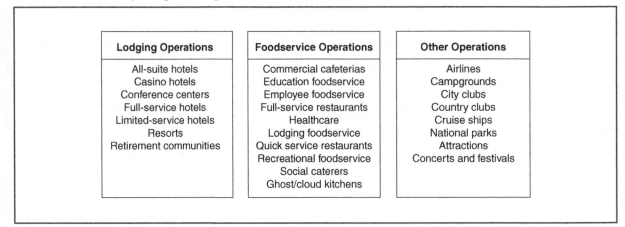

Lodging Operations	Foodservice Operations	Other Operations
All-suite hotels	Commercial cafeterias	Airlines
Casino hotels	Education foodservice	Campgrounds
Conference centers	Employee foodservice	City clubs
Full-service hotels	Full-service restaurants	Country clubs
Limited-service hotels	Healthcare	Cruise ships
Resorts	Lodging foodservice	National parks
Retirement communities	Quick service restaurants	Attractions
	Recreational foodservice	Concerts and festivals
	Social caterers	
	Ghost/cloud kitchens	

Continued expansion of the lodging industry is inevitable. No one knows precisely how many new hotels and other lodging properties will be built in the next decade, or where most of them will be located. All that can be said with certainty is that career opportunities in lodging will continue to grow.

Foodservice

According to the National Restaurant Association, foodservice industry sales were projected to reach $997 billion in 2023, representing about 4 percent of U.S. gross domestic product.[3] For every dollar spent on food overall, 51 cents is spent in a foodservice operation. An estimated 15.4 million people—10 percent of the U.S. workforce—are employed in the industry.[4] The COVID-19 pandemic resulted in a loss of an estimated $235 million in 2020 due to the closures of indoor dining rooms at the onset of the pandemic and reduced seating capacity once restrictions were lifted.

The *State of the Restaurant Industry Report*, published annually by the National Restaurant Association, highlights some interesting facts about the foodservice business:

- The restaurant industry is expected to add 1.6 million jobs over the next decade, with employment reaching 17.2 million by 2030.

- Most eating and drinking places are small businesses. More than 9 out of 10 have fewer than 50 employees.

- Restaurants employ more minority managers and more women managers than any other industry.

- The future is off-premises, and a majority of operators plan to invest in new technology, improving current offerings and adding more payment and service options to satisfy a tech-savvy and younger customer base.

The foodservice industry is broadly classified into two categories: table-service restaurants and limited-service restaurants. Table-service restaurants include family dining, casual dining, and fine dining. Limited-service restaurants include quick service, fast casual, and coffee and snack operations. As can be seen from Exhibit 3.1, other foodservice operations deserve serious consideration as well. For example,

From line cook to award-winning chef, there are plenty of career opportunities in the hospitality industry if cooking is your passion.

contract food companies operate corporate café and dining rooms, snack bars, and catering facilities in office buildings, factories, universities, sports arenas, and retirement homes. Three of the largest companies in these fields are Compass Group, Aramark, and Sodexo. Social caterers such as Crumble Catering and Events in Los Angeles, California, offer opportunities for interesting careers. Many hospitals now have the equivalent of a hotel food and beverage manager in charge of their foodservice. Gourmet meals and wine are available to patients in some hospitals. Hospitals run employee cafeterias, special dining rooms for doctors, and coffee shops for visitors. To maximize kitchen use, some hospitals also market off-premises catering.

Ghost kitchens, or cloud kitchens, a term broadly used to refer to any foodservice operation that prepares food only for off-premises dining with no on-site dining or wait staff, are expected to rise about 25 percent over the next five years as consumers get more accustomed to using food delivery apps. Some of the more notable ghost kitchen operations are Reef Kitchens, which offers a turnkey solution inside shipping containers that can operate up to four to six brands, and Revolving Kitchen and Zuul Kitchens, which offer existing rentable kitchens that include services such as kitchen infrastructure, equipment installation and support, delivery fulfillment, pickup windows, and virtual brand consulting.

Knowledge Check

1. How have the lodging and foodservice industries evolved in recent decades?
2. What impact has the evolution of the hospitality and foodservice industries had on their workforces?

3.2 CAREERS IN THE HOSPITALITY INDUSTRY

Why do people go into the hospitality industry? It is often easy to forget that the hospitality industry is built on service excellence, and people can be a brand's most powerful asset. If you were to ask people who have spent their careers in this business what they like most about it, you would get a wide variety of answers. Some of the most popular are:

■ *The industry offers more career options than most.* No matter what kind of work you enjoy and wherever your aptitudes lie, there is a segment of the industry that can use your talents (take another look at Exhibit 3.1!).

■ *The work is varied.* Because hotels and restaurants are complete production, distribution, and service units, managers are involved in a broad array of activities.

■ *There are many opportunities to be creative.* Hotel and restaurant managers might design new products to meet the needs of their guests; produce training programs for employees; or implement challenging advertising, sales promotion, and marketing plans.

■ *This is a "people" business.* Managers and supervisors spend their workdays satisfying guests, motivating employees, and negotiating with vendors and others.

■ *Hospitality jobs are not nine-to-five jobs.* Hours are highly flexible in many positions. (Some see this as a disadvantage, however.)

■ *There are opportunities for long-term career growth.* If you are ambitious and energetic, you can start with an entry-level job and move up. The industry is full of stories of people who started as bellhops or cooks and rose to high management positions or opened their own successful businesses.

■ *There are perks associated with many hospitality jobs.* If you become the general manager of a resort, you can dine at its restaurants with your family and friends and use its recreational facilities. Airline and cruise employees get free or reduced-fare travel.

Despite these advantages, there are some aspects of the business that many people don't like:

■ *Long hours.* In most hospitality businesses the hours are long. The 40-hour workweek is not the norm, and 50- to 60-hour workweeks are not unusual.

■ *Nontraditional schedules.* Hospitality managers do not work a Monday-through-Friday schedule. In the hospitality field, you will probably often find yourself working when your friends are relaxing. As one manager told his employees, "If you can't come to work

If you are ambitious and energetic, you can start with an entry-level hospitality job and move up quickly. The industry is full of stories of people who started out as bellhops, bartenders, or cooks and rose to high management positions or opened their own successful businesses.

Saturday or Sunday, don't bother to come in on Monday."

- *Pressure.* There are busy periods when managers and employees are under intense pressure to perform.

- *Low beginning salaries.* Entry-level jobs for management trainees tend to be low-paying compared to some other industries.

Selecting an Industry Segment

As we have pointed out, one of the attributes that draws many people to enter the hospitality industry is its breadth of career opportunities. It is difficult to imagine another industry in which there are as many different kinds of work. Before a hotel, restaurant, or club is built, for example, a feasibility study is conducted by a management consulting firm. Research-oriented hospitality graduates often join consulting firms for the opportunity to combine their interest in collecting and analyzing data with their interest in hotels and restaurants. Others work for hotel owners and investors as development officers or asset managers, the guardians of the owner's investment.

Management positions abound in the hospitality industry. Although hotels and restaurants may represent the largest sectors, they are by no means the only ones. Hospitality managers are needed in clubs, hospitals, nursing homes, university and school foodservices, cafeterias, correctional facilities, corporate dining rooms, snack bars, contract management companies, airlines, cruise ships, and many other organizations. Within these organizations, you can go into marketing and sales, rooms management, housekeeping, cooking, engineering, dining-room management, menu planning, security, accounting, food technology, forecasting and planning, computer technology (management information systems), recreation, entertainment, guest relations, and so on. Moreover, you have a wide choice of places to live—you can choose between warm and cold climates; cities, suburbs, and even rural areas; any region of the country or the world. There simply is no other industry that offers more diverse career opportunities.

Skills Inventory. One of the best ways to select a career niche you will be happy with is to start by listing your own skills. What are the tasks

There are plenty of opportunities in the hospitality industry for individuals with people skills.

you do best? Most skills fall into one of three areas: data literacy, human literacy, and technical literacy. In his book *Robot-Proof,* Northeastern University President Joseph Aoun argues that the next generation of college students will need skills to invent, create, and discover—skills that even the most sophisticated artificial intelligence agent cannot do. You will probably find that the majority of your skills will fall into one or two of these areas.

People whose skills fall into data literacy are often good in subjects such as math and science and enjoy working with computers and big data. They tend to like such activities as analyzing information, comparing figures, working with graphs, and solving abstract problems. Such individuals might enjoy doing feasibility studies for a hospitality management consulting firm. They might also be happy in the corporate planning departments of large hotel and restaurant chains, where data is analyzed and demand is forecasted. Most auditors and accountants fall into the data-skills group.

If you like to deal with people, you probably enjoy helping them and taking care of their needs. Human literacy is the ability to engage others, think creatively, and be entrepreneurial. You can take and give advice and instructions. You may also enjoy supervising and motivating other people, and may find that they respond to your leadership. Individuals with people skills are often good at negotiating and selling; they like to bargain and are not afraid to make decisions. In the hospitality industry, general managers and marketing and sales managers of hotels often fall into this category. So do independent restaurant owners, catering managers, and club managers.

The third group involves skills dealing with things. Technological literacy means the nuts and bolts of technical know-how that allow people to navigate in the modern digital world. If you excel in this area, you may also be good at building or fixing things. You like to work with your hands and use tools and gadgets. You enjoy setting things up—when there is a party in your house you like to put up the decorations, for example. As both artificial intelligence and robotics continue to advance, there will be machines built for functions that were once completed by humans. Some of us will find that we are more productive as a result of working with machines. If your skills lie here, you may be attracted to food production jobs. Chefs, bakers, and cooks all like working with things. So do the engineers who manage the hotel's physical plant.

Most of us have skills in more than one area. It is important to identify your skills and rank them according to how much you enjoy using them. More importantly, you should constantly update your skills throughout your career: the half-life of a skill today is 4.5 years and dropping, and many white-collar jobs like accounting will be at risk from automation. The use of robotics with artificial intelligence and speech recognition technology has already begun to replace positions such as butlers and luggage porters in hotels. Chatbots are now widely used by major hotels and travel agencies to provide 24/7 customer service for reservations and inquiries. Fortunately for humans, artificial intelligence agents have a hard time applying knowledge from one context or discipline to another. Aoun writes, "We humans are creative, innovative, entrepreneurial. We are able to interact with other people, work with them, be empathetic. We are able to be culturally agile, work with people with different backgrounds. We are able to be global."[5] By continually strengthening your data, human, and technological literacies, you can help ensure that you won't be replaced by artificial intelligence or a robot one day!

3.3 CAREER OPTIONS

The type of business you choose for your first hospitality job puts you into a definite career slot. While skills and experience are usually transferable within a particular industry segment (e.g., resort hotels), generally you cannot easily jump from one kind of industry segment to another. Managing a Taco Bell is quite different than managing

If you like to work with your hands, you might enjoy working in a food production position, such as hotel chef.

foodservice in a hospital, as is managing a Motel 6 versus a Ritz-Carlton. However, with tenacity and perseverance, you can go from being a hotel manager for Hyatt to being a hotel manager of a large cruise ship, such as the *Queen Mary 2*. Ultimately, it is up to you and the goals that you set for yourself that will help you succeed. Networking is often underrated but is probably the single most important skill that all young professionals should work on. You never know whether someone you spoke to at a conference or business luncheon will open the door for your next big career move. And when the door is opened for you, do not hesitate to make the leap and take a chance! With this in mind, let's take a look at the career options open to you.

Lodging

There are many types of lodging properties to choose from. There are luxury hotels, such as Hotel Drisco in San Francisco and the Four Seasons in London. There are full-service hotels operated by such companies as Marriott International, Hilton Hotels Corporation, IHG Hotels & Resorts, Wyndham Hotels & Resorts, and Hyatt. Resorts are another type of hotel. Some resorts, like the Boca Raton Hotel and Beach Club in Florida and the Arizona Biltmore, are geared to convention groups. Others, such as the Williamsburg Inn in Virginia and the Trapp Family Lodge in Vermont, cater to individuals and small meetings. Finally, there are casino hotels like Resorts World Las Vegas and the Sands Macau. These specialized operations are organized and managed differently from other hotels.

People who choose the lodging industry as a career often do so because they enjoy traveling and living in different places. Hotel management personnel are in great demand, and since most large hotels are operated by chains, managers are often offered opportunities to move into new positions in different geographic locations. Some people enjoy working in large metropolitan areas and in the course of their careers may live in New York, Beijing, and London. Others like warm weather resorts and may start in Miami, then move to a better position in Puerto Rico, then on to Hawaii, and so forth. Managers who like to ski or climb mountains often opt for hotels in the Rocky Mountains, the Cascades, or the Berkshires of New England. Some people enjoy quiet suburban life and move their families to communities where there are independent inns or conference centers. At an independent hotel, you are not as likely to be uprooted from your home and community by a transfer.

Would you rather be part of a large chain or work for an independent operation? There are many opportunities in both areas. The arguments for working for a large chain include:

- *Better training.* Companies such as Ritz-Carlton and Hyatt have very sophisticated operating systems. Being trained in these systems provides valuable additional education and experience.

- *More opportunities for advancement.* Hotel managers of chain properties who wish to advance might be offered opportunities for promotions within their own divisions or, if none are available there, in different divisions. Hotel managers who work for very large hospitality organizations might apply for positions in the timeshare or foodservice divisions of their companies. Since large chains have many units, there are simply more places to climb the ladder of success.

- *Better benefits.* You are more likely to get better life and health insurance benefits, more generous vacation and sick time, use of a company car, moving expenses, stock purchase options, and so forth from a large chain.

A career with an independent operation also offers some advantages, however:

- *More chances to be creative.* You will have a chance to set standards and initiate changes instead of just adhering to company programs and rules.

- *More control.* You are more likely to be in control of your own destiny. In large chains, decisions that involve your salary, advancement, and place of residence are often made by people in corporate headquarters thousands of miles away. In an independent operation, however, you deal on a regular basis with the people who will be deciding your fate. And, as mentioned earlier, with an independent property you are not likely to be transferred.

- *Better learning environments for entrepreneurs.* Independent operations offer better learning environments for entrepreneurs because all of the financial and operating decisions are made on-site. That means you will have a better opportunity to understand how and why things are done the way they are. If you intend to buy your own lodging operation someday, you will learn more at an independent operation than at a chain where data are forwarded to headquarters for analysis.

Executive and Management Positions within Lodging Operations. Whether the lodging property is part of a chain or an independent operation, as a hospitality student you have a wide variety of management positions open to you. Many people enjoy aiming for the top administrative job of general manager, but others prefer to specialize in such areas as:

- Catering
- Food and beverage
- Finance and accounting
- Human resources (HR)
- Marketing and sales
- Hotel management
- Revenue management
- Information technology (IT)

Let's take a look at management positions in these areas.

The **general manager** is the chief operating officer of a hotel or restaurant. They are responsible for attracting guests and making sure they are safe and well-served while visiting. The general manager supervises hotel staff and administers policies established by the owners or chain operators. Chains such as InterContinental Hotels Group and Marriott have very specific service, operating, and decorating standards. The general manager must see that all departments adhere to those standards.

Most general managers hold frequent meetings with their department heads. If a convention is about to arrive, for example, the general manager will want to make sure that the staff is aware of all the details necessary to

make the conventioneers' stays pleasant—details regarding limousine service, check-in procedures, banquets, meeting rooms, audiovisual facilities, entertainment, and so on.

The general manager's main responsibility is the financial performance of the business. The compensation a general manager receives is often tied to the profitability of the business they manage. Hiring and firing when necessary is also part of a general manager's job. The general manager can be involved in union negotiations as well.

Good general managers are skilled at getting along with people. They are able to forge positive relationships with employees, guests, and members of the community. They believe in teamwork and know how to get things done through other people. Effective general managers are also technically proficient. They do not subscribe to "seat of the pants" managing; instead, they study problems and carefully formulate short- and long-term solutions.

Catering managers promote and sell the hotel's banquet facilities. They plan, organize, and manage the hotel's banquets, which can range from formal dinners to picnic buffets. Knowledge of food costs, preparation techniques, and pricing is essential. Good catering managers are also aware of protocol, social customs, and etiquette. Creativity and imagination are useful qualities as well.

Food and beverage managers direct the production and service of food and beverages. They are responsible for training the dining room and kitchen staffs and ensuring quality control. Food and beverage managers at large properties work with their head chefs to plan menus and with their beverage managers to select wines and brands of liquor. At small properties, the food and beverage manager has sole responsibility for these tasks. Menu pricing and cost control are also the province of the food and beverage manager.

Food and beverage managers must have a keen interest in food and wines and an up-to-date knowledge of food trends and guests' tastes. Because food and beverage service is offered from 15 to 24 hours per day, managers in this field must be prepared to work long shifts and endure periods of pressure—dealing with unexpectedly large dinner crowds, serving a banquet, and so on.

The **controller** is in charge of the accounting department and all of its functions, such as the management of credit, payroll, guest accounts, and all cashiering activities. The controller also prepares budgets and daily, weekly, and monthly reports showing revenues, expenses, and other statistics that managers require. Controllers are detail-oriented people and favor an analytical approach to business problems.

Human resources (HR) managers are responsible for overseeing the management and administration of the human resources function within an organization. They play a critical role in attracting, developing, and retaining a qualified workforce while ensuring compliance with employment laws and regulations. They are also in charge of employee relations, which includes counseling employees, developing and administering programs to maintain and improve employee morale, monitoring the work environment, and so on. People who choose human resources as a career usually have a good deal of empathy and are excellent negotiators.

The marketing and sales function at a hotel consists of several different activities. Sometimes a large hotel will have two managers overseeing marketing and sales. In that case, the **marketing manager** develops and implements a marketing plan and budget. The marketing plan lays out how the hotel intends to attract business. It includes sections on meeting and convention sales, local sales, advertising, and promotion plans. The marketing manager is also in charge of corporate accounts and may work with an advertising and public relations agency. The **sales manager** conducts sales programs and makes sales calls on prospects for group and individual business. They usually report to the marketing manager. People who work in marketing and sales tend to be service-oriented and possess good communication skills.

Hotel managers are often the executives in charge of daily hotel operations. Their areas of responsibility include the front office, reservations, and housekeeping, as well as such sources of revenue as gift shops and recreational facilities. Additionally, they may be responsible for the food and beverage department. In small operations, hotel managers are also in charge of security. They report directly to the general manager and share responsibility for compliance with budgets and forecasts. Hotel managers are good leaders and have many of the same qualities that general managers have.

The **revenue manager** recommends room-rate strategies based on demand and market conditions. This function is becoming increasingly important as hotels strive to optimize profitability. Decisions must be made daily about how to sell the right room to the right customer at the right price and through the right channel, whether it be the company website, an OTA, or a travel agent. Strong analytical skills are required, along with an understanding of the interaction of supply, demand, and the market environment.

The **front office manager** is responsible for all front desk operations, including managing front desk employees. This includes budgeting, scheduling, hiring and training, and managing. A hotel's front desk is the first point of contact for all guests and must be staffed at all times. The front desk is responsible for providing a range of customer service, including greeting guests, helping them check in, collecting payments, and answering questions. They may need to deal with complaints and manage guest key cards, and some also provide concierge services, such as recommending restaurants or transportation services.

Housekeeping, one of the most important functions in hotels, is also the most often overlooked position. What can be more important than a clean bathroom and tidy hotel room to a hotel guest? While many college graduates do not aspire to be housekeepers, they must learn how housekeeping functions and its important contribution to the overall positive experience of every guest. A **housekeeping manager** is responsible for coordinating the housekeeping staff and making sure they have all the supplies and equipment needed to do the job. This includes hiring, firing, training, scheduling, and budgeting.

Information technology (IT) managers are the computer experts in a hotel. They are in charge of the computers used for reservations, room assignments, telephones, guestroom status reports, accounting functions, and labor and productivity reports. They often know how to write simple computer programs and easy-to-follow instructions for using computers. They have an aptitude for problem-solving and oral and written communication skills.

The salaries for these hotel management positions vary according to the area of the country and the world, the size of the property, and the work experience of the individual. Appendix A lists hotel management positions, titles, and advancement opportunities.

Foodservice

There is also a wide variety of job opportunities and geographic locations to choose from within the foodservice industry. There are three broad categories within the industry:

- *Commercial restaurant services*—Includes table-service and limited-service restaurants, which can be independently owned or chain (company-owned or franchised).

- *Noncommercial restaurant services*—Includes business, education, government, and institutional organizations that operate their own restaurant services. Disney theme parks use a hybrid model—the company also has third-party operating participants with world-famous chefs in addition to operating their own foodservices.

- *Other*—Includes managed services, lodging, retail-host restaurants (healthcare and personal-care stores, general-merchandise and variety stores, food and grocery stores, airports and gasoline-service stations, miscellaneous retailers); recreation outlets and sports centers (movie theaters, bowling lanes, fitness centers); mobile catering; and vending and non-store retailers (sales of hot food, sandwiches, pastries, coffee and other hot beverages).

Commercial Restaurant Services. Those who are interested in commercial restaurant services often choose between independently owned or chain restaurants. Within the chain restaurant concept, investors can buy a franchise model, such as McDonald's, and independently operate the quick service restaurant following the franchisor's standards. With franchises, individual business owners are responsible for the success or failure of their independent location. With chain restaurants, the parent company owns all of the business locations and handles the management for the entire business from its corporate headquarters. Therefore, the parent company is responsible for the success or failure of each restaurant. Dave & Buster's is an example of a chain owner and operator that does not franchise its business within the United States. However, it does franchise its business model internationally, as each country is governed by a different set of rules regarding ownership, investment, and operations.

Independent restaurants represent a broad cross section of dining options.

Independent Restaurants. Independent restaurants—defined by the Independent Restaurant Coalition as privately owned restaurants that have fewer than 20 establishments and whose primary source of revenue comes from food and beverage—represent a broad cross section of dining options that include fine dining restaurants, neighborhood restaurants, local bars, café, bistros, corner pizza parlors, and mobile food trucks. The menus vary from haute cuisine to comfort food, traditional and ethnic fare, farm-to-table cooking, and trendy or experimental fusion.[6]

At the top of the restaurant spectrum are fine dining restaurants, which are for the most part owned and operated by independent entrepreneurs. Within the trade, these restaurants are sometimes called "white tablecloth" restaurants. Most of their patrons are on expense accounts. Masa in New York City and Restaurant Guy Savoy in Las Vegas are perennial favorites in this class.

Guests at fine dining restaurants usually receive superior service. Some of these establishments, for example, feature French service in which meals are served from a cart or *gueridon* by formally dressed personnel. Tables are waited on by servers, a *chef de rang*, and an apprentice called a *commis de rang*. In the back of the house there is a classic kitchen in the tradition of **Escoffier**, with an executive chef and a brigade of cooks organized into departments, each headed by a *chef de partie*. Escoffier (1847–1935), a French chef, is considered the father of modern cookery. His two main contributions were (1) the simplification of classical cuisine and the classical menu, and (2) the reorganization of the kitchen.

Contrary to popular belief, fine dining restaurants are not necessarily high-profit ventures.

Often, their rent and labor costs are high, and there is intense competition for a limited number of guests. These restaurants are usually open for both lunch and dinner (some only offer dinner). The work starts early in the morning, when much of the food is purchased fresh and delivered for cooking that day, and runs until midnight or even later.

Next, there are neighborhood restaurants, which include family dining and fast-casual restaurants. Examples of family dining restaurants abound and can be found in many local neighborhoods. Often, family dining restaurants are table-service restaurants with a comfortable and laid-back atmosphere and an affordably priced menu. The cuisine ranges from home-style cooking to mainstream ethnic fare, such as Mexican or Korean.

The largest category of independent restaurants is fast-casual restaurants. Examples of fast-casual restaurants are plentiful. These restaurants are characterized by the limited service offered. In most fast-casual restaurants, the customer walks up to the counter to order and pay for their food and beverage. A food runner then delivers the food to their table when it is ready, or, if it is a pre-prepared item or beverage, they receive the item immediately after completing the transaction at the counter. Fast-casual restaurants have lower labor costs because they do not need servers or have a host stand. The menus are often simplified and offer a limited selection of alcoholic beverages, if any.

Many hospitality students aspire to run and eventually own their own restaurant. Depending on the type of restaurant, the investment to open an independent restaurant ranges from $500,000 to over $1 million. The average independently owned and operated restaurant makes between $350,000 and $750,000 in sales per year, depending on its business model. Independently owned restaurants are integral to the economic, social, and cultural workings of local economies and help revitalize neighborhoods, stimulate economic activity in other local businesses, contribute to public programs through generation of large sales taxes, and foster civic pride.

Chain Restaurants. Chain restaurants are typically characterized as casual dining, quick service, or fast-casual restaurants with multiple locations in many cities across the country or globally. They can be table-service restaurants or offer limited service. Chain restaurants can be owned and operated by a parent company such as Darden Restaurants, which has a portfolio of full-service

casual dining restaurant brands that include Olive Garden, LongHorn Steakhouse, Cheddar's Scratch Kitchen, Bahama Breeze, Seasons 52, The Capital Grille, Eddie V's Prime Seafood, and Yard House. Chain restaurants can also be franchised and owned and operated by a private investor. Two such examples are Buffalo Wild Wings and McDonald's. Some chain restaurant companies that used to franchise, such as Chipotle Mexican Grill, have changed their business strategy and no longer offer franchise agreements. As previously mentioned, brands like Dave & Busters that do not offer franchises in the United States but offer them internationally do so for a reason—to maintain the quality of brand standards in the country where they are headquartered and have legal permission to operate. Starbucks is another such example. In an interview with *Entrepreneur* in 2003, then-Starbucks CEO Howard Schultz said,

> *We believed very early on that people's interaction with the Starbucks experience was going to determine the success of the brand. The culture and values of how we related to our customers, which is reflected in how the company relates to our [employees], would determine our success. And we thought the best way to have those kinds of universal values was to build around company-owned stores and then to provide stock options to every employee, to give them a financial and psychological stake in the company.[7]*

Fast-casual restaurant chains are the fastest-growing sector of the restaurant business. Similar to quick service restaurants, their menus rarely change and their strategy calls for delivering a large number of meals at fairly low prices. The primary difference between fast-casual and quick service restaurants is the quality of the food sold. While the free-standing buildings occupied by quick service restaurants are characterized by drive-through lanes and include specially built food-production kitchens filled with specially designed equipment, fast-casual restaurants do not offer drive-through service due to the slightly longer time it takes to prepare the food. They have the same limited-service business concept with counter service and no wait staff. Successful fast-casual and quick service chains depend on a large number of units so that they can engage in regional and national marketing and advertising programs. Expansion is usually accomplished through franchising, although some of the largest quick service chains own as many as 30 percent of their units. Annual sales revenue per unit varies, from $2.6 million at McDonald's to $1.8 million at Chipotle to under $500,000 at Subway.

Chain restaurants recruit the majority of their managers from hospitality schools. Entry-level jobs for graduates with hospitality degrees are often on the assistant manager level, with progression to manager, then district manager responsible for a group of restaurants, and then regional manager. Such well-known companies as Shake Shack, Applebee's, Chili's, Outback Steakhouse, and Olive Garden lead the pack. These companies are popular career choices for hospitality graduates because they offer many opportunities for advancement.

Many hospitality students bypass quick service management opportunities. This is often a mistake. Many of these jobs pay well and offer security and excellent benefit packages. For example, Burger King multiunit managers can earn between $55,000 and $100,000 per year, plus benefits and bonuses. In addition, if you dream of owning your own franchise, the franchise company may help you if you've worked well in one of their units. Domino's Pizza recruits many of its franchisees from its store managers and helps them arrange financing. Burger King and McDonald's have leasing programs that allow successful managers to lease units and pay the rent out of sales until they can afford to buy their unit.

Noncommercial Restaurant Services.
The noncommercial foodservice industry generates approximately $67 billion annually, according to a 2020 economic impact study by the National Restaurant Association. While this may seem like a small share of the $900 billion foodservice industry as a whole, the potential for growth and opportunity within this industry segment may prove to be attractive and advantageous to hospitality job seekers.

Noncommercial foodservices or contracted foodservices operate in a wide variety of industries, venues, and settings, including hospitals, schools and colleges, senior living communities, airports, casinos, and Fortune 500 companies, like Google, Amazon, and Microsoft. To put it plainly, noncommercial foodservice can exist just about anywhere that offers food as an amenity.

Managed foodservice companies, as you will read more about, can supply food for schools and hospitals, but the majority of these institutions tend to handle their own foodservice programs.

Most public schools belong to the National School Lunch Program, established by the federal government in 1946. The purpose of this program is twofold: (1) to create a market for agricultural products produced by U.S. farmers and (2) to serve a nutritious lunch to schoolchildren at a low cost. Public elementary schools tend to offer only those menu items that qualify for government support, but many high schools add items such as hamburgers, french fries, and even diet sodas. High school food managers work hard to come up with creative and innovative menu plans to keep students in school cafeterias. Even the look of school cafeterias has changed as managers have developed new methods of merchandising food.

Colleges and universities have also experienced changes in their foodservice programs. Because more students live off-campus now, there is a trend toward flexible meal plans in which students have a choice of how many meals they wish to purchase from the institution. To compete successfully, many universities have opened special table-service restaurants in addition to their traditional cafeterias. Another move has been to offer a more varied dining menu, featuring salad bars and popular items such as croissant sandwiches, bagels, lox and cream cheese, and even Belgian waffles for breakfast. Some universities have brought branded quick service outlets such as Pizza Hut and Taco Bell on campus. Many have implemented online ordering, with pickup at different locations on campus.

Hospital programs are usually administered by a trained dietitian or a professional foodservice manager working with one. Menus are generally simple and nourishing. In the past, most hospitals had a central kitchen where all foods were prepared and then sent in insulated carts or trays to the patients' rooms. Some hospitals have decentralized their foodservice. With a decentralized system, the hospital purchases frozen entrées and portion-packed salads and keeps them in small pantries in various parts of the hospital. The meals are then plated and heated in microwave ovens as needed. Another trend has been the attempt to turn hospital foodservice from a cost center into a revenue center. Some hospitals sell take-home food to doctors and other employees and even do outside catering.

As you can see, institutions are beginning to compete with commercial foodservice operations for consumers. This means that there are more opportunities than ever before for hospitality students to enter what is clearly a growing field.

Other foodservice categories include managed foodservices, hotel restaurants, retail-host restaurants, recreation and sports venues, mobile catering, vending, and non-store retailers.

Managed Foodservice Companies. Managed foodservice companies are generally hired by organizations whose major business purpose is not foodservice, but they provide it as an amenity for their employees. The biggest users of managed foodservices are large manufacturing and industrial corporations where workers have a short lunch period. The three largest managed services enterprises, which employ hundreds of thousands of people globally and are publicly traded, are Compass Group (U.K.), Aramark (U.S.), and Sodexo (France). Autogrill (Italy), Elior Group (France), and SSP Group (U.K.) are also well-known providers.

Contractors operate in spaces that are owned by another entity, whether that be the government, a business, or a property management company—all of which are often referred to as "clients" by the service operator. The operator will manage everything from product purchasing, menu development, catering, and retail to marketing, ordering technology, and vending. As it relates to airlines, meals are cooked and prepackaged in central commissaries and then delivered to the airplanes for preparation and service as needed.

While sales volume is important, another key metric to the success of an operation is participation, or the number of people who are using the service. The scale of service can vary between hosting and catering large events, like the Academy Awards, to providing daily meals at breakfast and lunchtime.

The service is often subsidized by the contracting company, which may supply the space and utilities and, in some cases, underwrite some or all of the food costs. Schools and colleges, hospitals, sports arenas, airlines, cruise ships, and even correctional facilities use contract food companies.

Working as a contracted foodservice provider has many attractive benefits that may be harder to come by in a typical restaurant and bar setting. In most cases, a job with a contracted foodservice account could consist of traditional hours, working Monday through Friday with holidays. The juxtaposition of consistency and creativity also exists on the job, giving a professional the ability to anticipate what the day-to-day might be, such

as how many meals will be served, while providing the freedom to transform menus and experiences for the guest.

Managed foodservice companies are somewhat unusual because the manager must please two employers—the manager's home office and the client that has contracted for the service. Many managed food programs, such as those at schools and hospitals, have specific nutritional requirements as well. Others, such as airline programs, require a knowledge of advanced food technology.

Opportunities for career growth are expansive. Because many of the dominant contracted foodservice employers operate in several lines of business and industry segments across the world, an employee could have a greater chance at professional progression and longevity within one company.

Additionally, roles in noncommercial foodservice are not limited to positions one might generally think of, like general manager, catering manager, or chef. Contracted foodservice companies are structured like any other business, employing people in finance, human resources, sales, marketing and public relations, technology, wellness and sustainability, and more.

There is no shortage of creativity and innovation available to a working professional in noncommercial foodservice. Gone are the days of the cafeteria—many of the spaces where service is provided are designed to create an experience that defies the drab and monotonous atmosphere the word evokes. Much of the entire foodservice operation is centered on elevating the guest experience through excellence in cooking, wellness, hospitality, and technology.

As millennials and Generation Z increasingly represent the customer base, culinarians in the noncommercial foodservice industry are inspired to satisfy their desire for adventurous menus that include sustainably sourced ingredients and authentic, ethnic flavors. Likewise, wellness offerings, including organic, plant-based, and gluten-free options, are often key client and customer priorities. A popular emerging trend involves the concept of "grazing," allowing a guest to create what goes on their plate by grabbing a small amount of a variety of foods. Convenience and speed of service are also important factors in providing a strong digital guest experience, driving technology solutions like mobile ordering, badge pay, self-pay kiosks, and frictionless transactions.

Full-service hotel restaurants can dramatically enhance the guest experience.

Hotel Restaurants. Many full-service hotels have signature restaurants that can dramatically enhance the overall guest experience by offering excellent food and first-class customer service. These restaurants are usually managed and staffed by the hotel, but the trend is shifting toward arrangements with local restaurant groups to operate on-premises restaurants. The organizational structure of a hotel restaurant is similar to a chain restaurant that is managed by a parent company. Many of the management functions, such as human resources, accounting, training, and development, are handled centrally by the hotel management team.

Retail-Host Restaurants. This industry term, defined by the National Restaurant Association, refers to all the on-site restaurants operating in airports, grocery and convenience stores, drug stores, and even gasoline stations. Depending on its host location, management and operation of retail-host restaurants can range from complicated to fairly standard. In airports, the restaurants are typically franchises of specialty coffee, quick service, casual dining, or local favorite brands.

HMSHost is the largest travel retail company in the United States and partners with some of the most famous and beloved national brands for travelers seeking familiarity while on the road. The operation and management of a retail-host restaurant will vary depending on its concept and location. At Paradies Lagardère, the largest travel retail company in the world, each of the retail-host restaurants has a dedicated general manager. Unlike managed foodservice companies that are operating foodservice for their clients, travel retail companies invest heavily in each of their locations

to ensure their financial success while providing support from headquarters.

Retail-host restaurants within a convenience or grocery store give customers the option of freshly prepared meals that are reasonably priced and the convenience of buying a meal without having to stop at another location.

Recreation and Sports Venues. This category of foodservice includes movie theaters, bowling lanes, and recreation and sport facilities that are largely self-operated and owned. Food concepts range from healthy grab-and-go menu items and snacks such as nachos, hot dogs, and burgers to full-service restaurants and bars with chef-driven menus, as offered by IPIC Theaters.

Mobile Caterers. Mobile catering is another part of the foodservice industry that many hospitality graduates become interested in. Catering is another business that is most often started by independent entrepreneurs, as it requires very little startup capital—facilities can be rented as needed, equipment can usually be leased on a short-term basis from restaurant supply houses, and food servers can be hired as needed. In some cases, caterers provide only food; in others, they are responsible for tables, chairs, utensils, tents, servers, and decorations.

Vending and Non-Store Retailers. The last category of foodservice is vending and non-store retailers. The National Automatic Merchandising Association reports vending machines collect an estimated $20 million to $30 million per year in annual gross sales in the United States. However, picking the right location is crucial to the success of the vending machine, and understanding the needs and wants of your customer base at that location will make or break your business. Most managed foodservice companies also offer vending services.

Management Positions within Foodservice. A restaurant is usually a small business with an average monthly revenue of $111,860.70.[8] That means most of the management opportunities in this field, even with large chains, lie in operations or hands-on management, as opposed to corporate positions in an office. The duties of a foodservice manager are similar across the spectrum of foodservice operations, from an independent restaurant to a cruise ship to a retirement home.

The Dave & Buster's restaurant chain has a general manager who is responsible for the financial performance of the restaurant, as well as its community engagement and marketing strategy. The general manager oversees the unit as a whole, while day-to-day operations and facility and inventory management are the responsibility of the assistant general manager. Next are senior managers, who are responsible for training and development of their employees and supervising area operation managers, such as the amusement manager, kitchen manager, and special events manager. Many commercial foodservice operations have a similar management structure and division of duties.

Smaller restaurants typically only have a **restaurant manager**, someone who oversees operations and ensures the restaurant's efficient functioning and overall success. They are responsible for managing various aspects of the restaurant, including staff supervision, customer service, financial performance, and administrative tasks. Other typical foodservice management positions include chef, maître d', and banquet manager. Appendix B lists foodservice management positions, titles, and advancement opportunities.

Clubs

Clubs are another career option open to you. Clubs are very different from other types of hospitality businesses because the "guests"— the club members—are in many cases also the owners. There are country clubs, city clubs, luncheon clubs, yacht and sailing clubs, military clubs, tennis clubs, even polo clubs—all with clubhouses and other facilities that must be managed. Some, like the Yale Club of New York City, offer complete hotel services. Others are like the Ocean Reef Club in Key Largo, Florida— open to members only and boasting a complete suite of amenities, including a private airport and marina and two championship 18-hole golf courses. Large clubs have many of the same positions found in hotels and restaurants: a general manager, a food and beverage director, a catering director (weddings and parties are an important part of club operations), and a controller.

Today there are more than 14,000 recreational and social clubs in the United States that lease or own their facilities and have them run by professional managers. Most clubs are nonprofit organizations owned by and run for the benefit of the members. Some clubs are built by developers as part of housing developments and are proprietary, for-profit enterprises.

Many hospitality managers enjoy working in clubs. First of all, unlike chain foodservice and hotel operations, there is a chance to exercise imagination and creativity in such matters as menu selection, party planning, and sporting events. Secondly, you interact with the owners (members) in a more direct way. Moreover, clubs with sports facilities often host celebrity tournaments that bring with them media coverage. This can make the job even more stimulating. Since the nature of clubs often requires specialized training and knowledge (in such areas as golf, tennis, and marina operations), club managers often come up through the ranks.

Cruise Lines

There are opportunities both on shore and at sea within the cruise industry. Shoreside positions include marketing, accounting, provisioning, itinerary planning, and hotel operations. At sea, there are the same kinds of jobs any fine resort has. Salaries are competitive. People who are attracted to travel may enjoy operations jobs at sea but should be prepared to spend a minimum of 9 out of every 12 months away from home. Living conditions don't allow for much privacy either, but many like the feeling of extended family that often occurs among staff members on a ship. Most people who aspire to work in the cruise industry usually start at sea and learn all the different positions before landing a position on shore. Crew members who are successful and ambitious can find plentiful promotion opportunities, and many cruise lines report high employee retention.

Entrepreneurship

The Marriott hospitality empire began with J. Willard Marriott, Sr.'s nine-seat root beer stand in Washington, D.C. Conrad Hilton, Sr. opened his first hotel in a small Texas town. Chipotle was started by Steve Ells for the purpose of earning enough money to fund a fine dining restaurant. Wendy's, Starbucks, Motel 6, and many other well-known hospitality brand names also had modest beginnings before developing into global enterprises. Each of these businesses was founded by someone who had a vision for their business and a desire to be an entrepreneur. Entrepreneurship is a challenging but potentially greatly rewarding career option.

There are many hospitality school alumni who are entrepreneurs; some having formed partnerships and companies with classmates who brought complementary talents to the union. But how does one begin? Generally, it starts with an idea for a different or better type of restaurant, hotel, catering business, sports bar, or some other type of hospitality product or service. The U.S. Small Business Administration recommends 10 guiding steps for starting a business. Some are sound business practices and others are legal requirements:[9]

Step 1: Write a Business Plan

Step 2: Get Business Assistance and Training

Step 3: Choose a Business Location

Step 4: Finance Your Business

Step 5: Determine the Legal Structure of Your Business

Step 6: Register a Business Name ("Doing Business As")

Step 7: Get a Tax Identification Number

Step 8: Register for State and Local Taxes

Step 9: Obtain Business Licenses and Permits

Step 10: Understand Employer Responsibilities

It might be necessary to hire a consultant or call on experienced friends to critique the project. If that is the case, all of their comments should be examined carefully. Some entrepreneurs tend to be blinded by their passion for their creation.[10]

Other Career Options

Graduates of hospitality programs are sought after by firms that provide goods and services to hotels and restaurants. There are career opportunities with food distributors, hotel and restaurant equipment suppliers, and technology companies. Consulting firms, hotel developers, and equity investors also value the education and the operational experience of hospitality school graduates. There are positions in marketing, sales, and market research with chambers of commerce and convention and visitors bureaus for graduates of travel and tourism programs. As you can see, hospitality career options are vast and not limited to managing a hospitality enterprise, although that is the career preference for many.

Knowledge Check

1. What are the advantages of working for a large hotel chain? What are the advantages of working for an independent hotel?

2. What are some career options in the foodservice industry outside of commercial and noncommercial foodservice?

3.4 LOOKING FOR A JOB

Many hospitality students have a preconceived idea of the job they want in the industry. They may have had an enjoyable part-time or summer job in a restaurant or hotel, for example. Their parents, a family friend, or someone else they admire may have been in the business and advised them to take a particular position. In the view of career counselors, however, it's better to keep an open mind. If you don't explore other career possibilities, you might overlook opportunities that could be more appealing in the long run. A sound understanding of your goals and lifestyle, and a thorough knowledge of the companies that might be interested in what you offer, is an important foundation for your career search.

Every job you take should move you closer to your final goal. If you look at jobs as stepping stones that you take on the way to your ultimate career goal, also known as a **career path** or **career ladder** (see Exhibit 3.2), there are several questions you should answer before you decide whether a job is right for you:

■ What can I learn from this job that will contribute to my career goals?

Exhibit 3.2 Typical Hospitality Career Paths

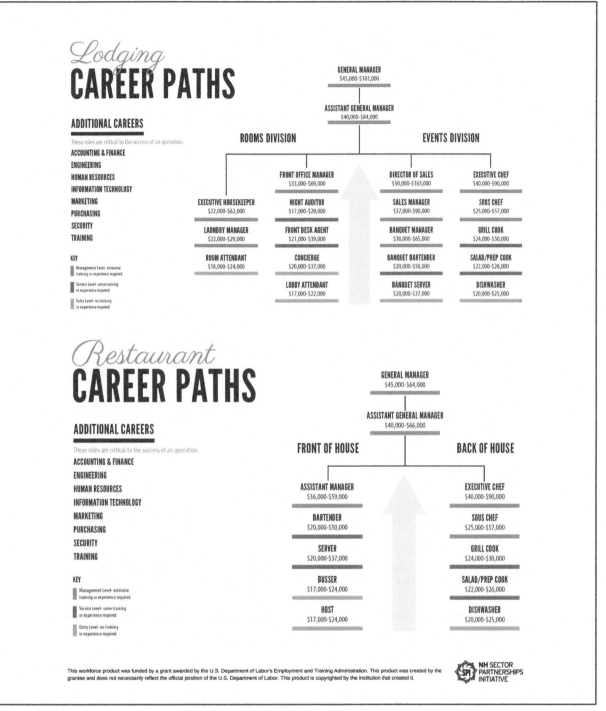

Source: "Hospitality Career Guides," Explore NH Careers, http://explorenhcareers.com/industry/hospitality-career-guides/.

- What are the long-term opportunities for growth in this company?

- What is this company's reputation among the people I know? Is it a good place to work? Does it deliver on its promises to employees?

- How good is the training program? Will the company really make an effort to educate me?

- What is the starting salary? What about other benefits? Do they add up to a competitive package?

- How do I feel about the location? Will I be living in a place where I can be happy? What about proximity to friends and relatives?

Your First Moves

While you are still in school, you probably will want to gain some job experience in the hospitality industry. To do that, you will need some basic knowledge of how to prepare a résumé and handle a job interview. The following sections contain information that may be useful to you.

Your Résumé. Whether you apply for a position online or in person, a basic tool you will need is a well-prepared and attractive **résumé**. A résumé is a concise document that provides a summary of an individual's education, work experience, skills, and qualifications. There are many excellent books in bookstores and libraries on creating résumés; our best advice is to find one and read it!

Purpose of a résumé. A résumé is an *advertisement for yourself*. Its purpose is to convince the person doing the hiring that they should not fill the job without talking to you first. Résumés have other purposes as well. They introduce you to your prospective employer and provide a brief summary of your educational and employment background. However, their main purpose is to presell you to the company, to persuade the interviewer before the interview starts that you may be the best person for the job.

Contents of a résumé. Once you understand the purpose of a résumé, the information that goes into one and in what order becomes clearer.

Start with the length. Unless you have been in the workforce for a number of years, your résumé should typically be one page in length. Remember that your résumé will end up in a file with many others. The interviewer will likely only skim résumés to find the most likely candidates. A sample résumé is provided in Appendix C.

Career Portfolio. Your résumé may be the mainstay document for summarizing your experience, education, skills, and personal qualifications, but it has its limitations. Basically, a résumé is a snapshot that provides the reader with a quick summary view of an applicant's qualifications—which is a valuable feature for the recruiter who is reading many résumés. But this also means that potentially valuable information that might help you land a job is left out. How can you differentiate yourself from the scores of other students who are applying for the same job? One way to do this is to create a **career portfolio**. A career portfolio expands on your résumé by providing additional information that might be of interest to an employer, including information regarding your talents, communications skills, creativity, leadership qualities, social responsibility, critical thinking, and teamwork. Here are some items that might be included in a career portfolio:

- Résumé

- Professional certifications

- Examples of term papers that showcase your ability to write and think critically

- Leadership positions in student organizations

- Professional licenses

Preparing for the Interview. You should know as much as possible about your prospective employer before you walk in the door. You want to be informed because that will make it easier for you to hold a conversation and you will sound more enthusiastic. If you're applying to work at a property within a hotel or restaurant chain, there's a lot of information about most of these chains on the Internet.

Dressing for the Interview. The way you are dressed makes a big difference in the way you are perceived. If you are applying for a management position, you should consider how you would dress if you were on the job, and then dress slightly better. Research shows that reactions to clothing styles, colors, and combinations are fairly predictable. Remember that you want to project a professional, responsible image. The interview is not the time to make a bold or unusual fashion statement.

How to Be Interviewed. An interview is your opportunity to sell yourself, or rather to sell your prospective employer on offering you a job. Once you get the offer, you can decide whether to take it, but the name of the game is to convince the interviewer to hire you.

Going into an interview with this attitude can have several results. First, it gives you a sense of confidence. You are not going to sit back and wait to see what the interviewer asks because they might not ask about the things that make you a superior candidate. You are going to control, to the extent that you can, what is talked about. This is not as hard as it sounds. One good way to start off and gain control of the interview is to ask questions. If you have done your homework about the company, some questions will naturally occur to you. Asking questions shows that you are a person who is very interested in working for the company. The answers to your questions may give you clues that will help you sell the interviewer on hiring you.

The more you know about the company (and the interviewer) before you start answering questions, the better job you can do of answering them. Generally, industry recruiters look for people who not only possess specific skills but also understand the dynamics of our changing business. They want good communicators and leaders who can motivate others, show them what needs to be done, and teach them how to do it. Industry recruiters look for well-rounded individuals who understand financial issues, legislative issues, ethics issues, and, above all, human resources issues.

Often, interviewers have a checklist of topics they want to cover in the interview. Don't be put off; you can still ask your questions in between their questions. Always answer their questions directly and honestly. If you don't know the answer to something, say so. The best thing you can do is sound positive. You want to be remembered after you leave the room as someone who is enthusiastic, confident, energetic, and dependable. Shape every answer to reinforce those images.

Under no circumstances should you say anything bad about a former employer. To do so suggests that you might be disloyal or dishonest.

Finally, encourage the interviewer to make you an offer. Like any good salesperson, ask for the order! Once you have a job offer, you can weigh it along with other possibilities.

You should always write a follow-up thank-you letter after you leave the interview. Thank the interviewer for the time they spent with you and for considering you for the position. If you were impressed with the company, say so! Tell the interviewer that you're certain you can make a contribution and you hope you'll be hearing from them soon.

If you are offered a job, respond within the time requested. You might have additional questions, so contact the person making the offer to clarify details. If you need more time to make your decision, ask for it. When you have decided, be prompt in letting your prospective employer know. If you call to turn down the offer, follow up with a letter in which you thank the person for their interest in you. Remember that you may meet this recruiter again during your career under different circumstances.

Using Social Media to Advance the Job Search. You are probably one of the billions of users of social media. How you use this communication tool can help or hinder your job search—and, indeed, your career. Employers and recruiters use social media to get a clearer picture of candidates beyond what is on the résumés or in their career portfolios. What you post on your Facebook, Instagram, X, TikTok, or Threads account can give a clue to your personality, how you might fit in with a company's culture, and your professionalism. Any photos you post or comments you make should depict you in a proper manner.

There are many online networking platforms that are used for business and career-related purposes, such as LinkedIn, Indeed, Glassdoor, and Xing (Germany). One of the most popular platforms is LinkedIn, where you can find and reach people who have similar professional goals, who can be useful in a job search, or with whom you can share information or advice about your field. Users can connect with colleagues, classmates, industry professionals, and potential employers, expanding their professional network. To get started on any of these networking platforms, you will need to create a profile and add a professional-quality photo. Update your profile as you add to your accomplishments. Make social media work for you to advance your career.

The hospitality industry's growth in recent decades has been due in part to the average individual's higher standard of living, higher level of education, and longer life span. The greater opportunities available in rapidly developing societies have also contributed to industry expansion.

The hospitality industry offers many career options. The work is varied, and there are numerous opportunities for advancement. Some people, however, don't like the occasional pressures and long hours that go along with many hospitality jobs. Management positions in a hotel include general manager, catering manager, food and beverage manager, controller, HR manager, marketing and sales manager, resident manager, and IT manager. Management positions in a restaurant include general manager, restaurant manager, food and beverage manager, and banquet or catering manager.

It's important to select the segment of the industry that will best suit you. To do this, you must know whether you work best with data, people, or things. Once you have considered your strengths and weaknesses, you are in a position to evaluate areas of specialization. Your choices include hotels, restaurants, clubs, catering operations, managed and contract foodservice companies, institutional foodservice, and more.

Three important job-seeking skills are preparing a good résumé and career portfolio, dressing correctly for an interview, and conducting yourself appropriately during an interview. The purpose of your résumé is to gain an interview. It is an advertisement for you; use it to emphasize your special skills and experience. The purpose of your career portfolio is to differentiate you from other applicants. Research the company you will interview with, dress appropriately for your interview, and "sell yourself." Use social media to advance your career.

KEY TERMS

banquet or catering manager—A hotel manager responsible for arranging and planning food and beverage functions for (1) conventions and smaller hotel groups, and (2) local banquets booked by the sales department.

career path/career ladder—A series of positions an individual may take on the way to their ultimate career goal. Some companies lay out sample career paths or ladders for their employees.

career portfolio—A job search tool that expands on a job applicant's résumé by giving additional information about the applicant's talents, communications skills, creativity, leadership qualities, social responsibility, critical thinking, and teamwork.

controller—Manages the accounting department and all of its functions, including management of credit, payroll, guest accounts, and cashiering activities.

Escoffier, Georges Auguste—A French chef (1847–1935) who is considered the father of modern cookery. His two main contributions were (1) the simplification of classical cuisine and the classical menu, and (2) the reorganization of the kitchen.

food and beverage manager—Directs the production and service of food and beverages.

front office manager—Responsible for all hotel front desk operations, including managing front desk employees.

general manager—The chief operating officer of a hotel or restaurant.

hospitality industry—Lodging and foodservice businesses that provide short-term or transitional lodging and/or food.

hotel manager—A person in charge of daily hotel operations. Areas of responsibility include the front office, reservations, and housekeeping, as well as such sources of revenue as gift shops and recreational facilities. May be responsible for the food and beverage department as well.

housekeeping manager—Responsible for coordinating the housekeeping staff and making sure they have all the supplies and equipment needed to do the job. This includes hiring, firing, training, scheduling, and budgeting.

human resources (HR) manager—Responsible for overseeing the management and administration of the HR function within an organization. They play a critical role in attracting, developing, and retaining a qualified workforce while ensuring compliance with employment laws and regulations. They are also in charge of employee relations, which includes counseling employees, developing and administering programs to maintain and improve employee morale, monitoring the work environment, and so on.

information technology (IT) manager—Oversees a hotel's computerized management information systems. May write simple computer programs and instruction manuals for employees.

marketing manager—Develops and implements a marketing plan and budget.

restaurant manager—Oversees the operations of a restaurant, ensuring its efficient functioning and overall success. They are responsible for managing various aspects of the restaurant, including staff supervision, customer service, financial performance, and administrative tasks.

résumé—A concise document that provides a summary of an individual's education, work experience, skills, and qualifications.

revenue manager—Recommends room rate strategies based on demand and market conditions.

sales manager—Conducts sales programs and makes sales calls on prospects for group and individual business. Reports to the marketing manager.

1. Which would be an example of a table-service restaurant?
   a. Hospital cafeteria
   b. Ghost kitchen
   c. Fine dining restaurant
   d. Coffee shop

2. A person with strong skills in data literacy would be well suited to which hospitality area?
   a. Front office reservations
   b. Revenue management
   c. Food production
   d. Sales

3. Which position in a hotel is often overlooked?
   a. IT manager
   b. Revenue manager
   c. Housekeeping manager
   d. Food and beverage manager

4. What is the most important skill a young professional should develop?
   a. Digital communication
   b. Personal budgeting
   c. Management
   d. Networking

5. Which operation offers the most opportunity for sophisticated training?
   a. Large chain hotel
   b. Independent hotel
   c. Independent caterer
   d. Independent restaurant

6. Which foodservice operation requires minimal startup capital?
   a. Fast-casual restaurant
   b. Independent restaurant
   c. Hotel restaurant
   d. Mobile caterer

7. Which is a managed foodservice company?
   a. Aramark
   b. McDonald's
   c. The Ritz-Carlton
   d. Darden Restaurants

8. To get a sense of the work environment in a company, which question is most appropriate to ask during an interview?
   a. What is the worst part of your job?
   b. Which employee is the most problematic?
   c. How many people have been laid off in the past year?
   d. How would you describe the way your team works together?

9. The initial purpose of a résumé is to
   a. provide a complete work history.
   b. convince your supervisor of a salary raise.
   c. advertise or introduce yourself as a professional.
   d. help you remember work highlights during an interview.

10. What is an advantage of having a career portfolio?
    a. It provides a brief snapshot of qualifications.
    b. It guarantees a recruiter's interest.
    c. It replaces the need for a résumé.
    d. It expands on a résumé.

11. What is one way to gain control of an interview?
    a. Try to prevent the interviewer from asking questions that you don't want to answer.
    b. Be on the defensive about questions regarding past employers.
    c. Convince the interviewer that you need the job.
    d. Ask well-researched questions.

12. Which social media platform is most catered to networking?
    a. Instagram
    b. Facebook
    c. LinkedIn
    d. Twitter

SHORT-ANSWER QUESTIONS

1. What are the advantages and disadvantages of a career in hospitality?

2. How can a skills inventory help you decide on a career path?

DECISIONS, DECISIONS, DECISIONS

Chris is a 23-year-old student enrolled in a hospitality management graduate program at a local university. He has worked in hospitality and tourism for seven years, including positions in sports retail, fast food, catering, sporting events, and bartending. Masterful in multiple fields and loved by customers in each of his jobs, he maintains great relationships with former employers and has been asked to return to some of them as an on-call employee.

Chris decides that he needs to gain hotel experience if he wants to climb the career ladder. He lands a job at a local resort as a full-time night auditor while taking nine credits of graduate work each semester. Despite the crazy schedule and long hours of studying, Chris is incredibly determined.

After about 12 months on the job, Chris has gained plenty of experience. His managers are very flexible with his schedule because they know he is a student. However, new opportunities are arising for Chris at school and in his career.

When Chris enters his final year of graduate school, his professor recommends that he apply for a one-month study abroad program in London and Paris to help him earn final elective credits and give him international career experience. The study abroad program will be covered by a scholarship, which will relieve a lot of his financial burden. Simultaneously, Chris has also been offered a paid six-month management internship with a major hotel brand, but the offer is only available while he's enrolled as a student.

Chris has been so busy finishing his final two semesters that he hasn't had a chance to evaluate these opportunities or what will happen after graduation. One thing is for sure—he will need to resign from his current resort job if he wants to pursue these other opportunities. Chris wants to make the right decision. He also doesn't want to keep burning himself out or not finish his degree program. Lastly, he doesn't want to disappoint the resort where he works, since they've been very considerate of his growth as an employee.

DISCUSSION QUESTIONS

1. What are some disadvantages of Chris's chosen career?

2. As an employee, what advantages does Chris have?

3. Which opportunity do you think is most beneficial for Chris's career?

4. If Chris decides to leave the resort, do you think management will respect his decision?

David Grutman

David Grutman is a globally renowned innovator and entrepreneur in the hospitality field. He is known for creating immersive experiential venues with distinct atmospheres, infusing high energy and transportive luxury across a one-of-a-kind portfolio of restaurants, hotels, bars, and nightclubs.

In 2008, Grutman opened the nightclub LIV at Fontainebleau after garnering wide acclaim for his prior work in founding the Miami Marketing Group (which specialized in seamlessly merging the fields of nightlife and entertainment). Immediately, LIV garnered worldwide buzz and a celebrity clientele, which it has continued to sustain over the past decade. LIV is especially beloved for its Sunday night party, which attracts world-famous athletes, musicians, and movie stars. Following the success of LIV, Grutman opened Story, another Miami Beach nightclub, in 2013.

Since then, Grutman—a native Floridian—founded Groot Hospitality in Miami. Since its launch, Groot has developed a sizable and impressive portfolio, with a focus on the South Florida market and a recent expansion to Texas and Nevada. In 2015, Grutman entered the dining space with the launch of Komodo, a 300-seat, ultra-popular restaurant located in Miami's Brickell neighborhood. He solidified his leading position in the hospitality business with what came next: the opening of Swan and Bar Bevy, also in the Design District, for which he partnered with the multihyphenate talent Pharrell Williams. Swan has become a top-tier contender in the region's restaurant scene, mixing luxuriant décor with contemporary food, along with an inimitable bar scene. Swan draws an A-list international crowd, in large part due to Grutman's gregarious and hospitable nature. Put simply, he is the ultimate host.

In the Miami area, Groot also owns the restaurants Gekkō, The Key Club, Papi Steak, and Strawberry Moon. Grutman also spearheaded the conception and execution of The Goodtime Hotel. Komodo Dallas, now open in the Texas city's Epic Development neighborhood, is Groot's first property outside of Florida. Somewhere Else will be Grutman and Groot's first resort, arriving in 2024 on Atlantis Paradise Island in The Bahamas.

These venues are individually influential, yet it's their combined contribution to the region's overall hospitality roster that places them on the leading edge: Miami and Miami Beach have long been known for their extensive food, beverage, and hotel offerings, but Grutman has helped to usher in a new paradigm. He has reestablished the Miami area as a contemporary hotspot by imagining dining, hospitality, and nightlife through a lens of lavish design; in-demand talent; and a frisson of celebrity, social media moments, and, most importantly, escapist fun.

Outside of hospitality, Grutman pursues additional business and personal interests. He is the creative director and co-owner of Prince, the athletics and lifestyle company. Grutman also teaches an annual seminar at Florida International University called The David Grutman Experience, which focuses on what it takes to conceptualize and create a leading hospitality platform. He has guest lectured at the prestigious School of Hotel Administration at Cornell University, the University of Miami, and Harvard Business School.

You are a recent hospitality management graduate who has just landed an entry-level job at a hotel. You are excited to start your career in the industry, but you are also wondering what your long-term career prospects are. You are curious about the different career ladders in the hospitality industry and how you can progress in your career. Identify and explain different career ladders in the industry.

4

UNDERSTANDING THE RESTAURANT INDUSTRY

Chapter Outline

Learning Objectives

1. Describe in general terms the size of the restaurant industry, list restaurant industry segments, and describe eating and drinking places. (pp. 80–88)

2. Describe foodservice outlets in lodging operations; the transportation, recreation and sports, business and industry, education, healthcare, and retail foodservice markets; corrections and military foodservice; and contract foodservice management companies. (pp. 88–93)

3. Summarize some of the pitfalls of starting a new restaurant, cite reasons restaurants may fail, and outline some of the issues involved in starting a new restaurant, such as developing a concept, selecting a site, and having a feasibility study done. (pp. 93–99)

KEY TERMS

areas of dominant influence (ADI)

bars and taverns

capital investment budget

casual dining restaurant

catering

cyclical menu

ethnic restaurant

family dining restaurant

fast-casual restaurant

feasibility study

fine dining restaurant

food hall

full-service restaurant

fusion cuisine

limited-service restaurant

operating budget

quick service restaurant (QSR)

table-service restaurant

This chapter describes the diversity and complexity of the various segments of the restaurant industry. We will take a look at eating and drinking establishments; hotel food and beverage operations; foodservice for airlines, trains, and cruise lines; the recreational, business and industry, education, healthcare, retail, corrections, and military markets; and contract foodservice management companies. Since owning their own restaurant is the dream of many who enter the restaurant industry, there is also a section on how to start a new restaurant. The chapter concludes with a discussion of technology that is being deployed today in restaurants.

4.1 TODAY'S RESTAURANT INDUSTRY

The restaurant industry runs the gamut from gourmet establishments to hot dog stands. It is difficult to quantify exactly how many restaurants exist in the world due to the nature of the restaurant industry. As you have learned, the foodservice industry consists of commercial, noncommercial, and other enterprises, such as managed foodservices and retail-host outlets. In this chapter, we will focus more closely on commercial restaurant enterprises, which include **table-service restaurants** (where customers or guests are seated at tables and served by wait staff) and **limited-service restaurants**, also known as quick service restaurants (QSRs) or fast-casual restaurants, where guests are provided fast and efficient food service with minimal table service. These restaurants can be independently owned or chain (company-owned or franchised).

In the United States, restaurant revenue was worth $937 billion in 2022, and the restaurant industry employed almost 15 million people in about one million establishments. The National Restaurant Association estimates that the restaurant industry will have sales in the United States exceeding $1.2 trillion by 2030 and will employ more than 17 million people. The overall impact of the industry on the U.S. economy is estimated at $1.8 trillion. Restaurant industry sales equal 4 percent of the U.S. gross domestic product. The percentage

of the food dollar spent away from home is 51 percent.[1]

The COVID-19 pandemic resulted in restaurant revenues for 2020 contracting to $678 billion, down $186 billion from 2019. After years of growth and expanded employment in the restaurant industry, the trend was quickly and dramatically reversed by the pandemic, forcing restaurants to close with a few days' notice and decimating millions of jobs within weeks. With the closure of dining rooms and the shift to off-premises sales, monthly revenue at restaurants, bars, and other food and drinking businesses fell by more than 50 percent in the early months of the pandemic, from $66 billion in February 2020 to $30 billion in April 2020.[2] Even with creative pivoting to take-out, delivery, in-restaurant grocery stores, expanded outdoor seating in parking lots, and pop-up concepts within restaurants, the industry continued to struggle. The fine dining and casual dining sectors were hit harder than quick service, whose business model relied less on dine-in customers. An estimated 110,000 restaurant locations were closed temporarily or permanently during the pandemic in 2020.[3] Even so, pent-up demand for restaurant meals remains high, and operators are poised to benefit from the rebounding consumer optimism and growing opportunities in off-premises sales.

The U.S. restaurant industry is truly an equal-opportunity employer. It employs more minority managers than any other industry; 52 percent of restaurant managers are women; 12 percent are Black or African American; and 25 percent are Hispanic. Forty percent are between the ages of 16 and 24. Roughly one in four restaurant job openings in 2019 were filled by people hired for their first regular job.[4] Someone entering the foodservice field might work for a small, independent operator who runs a sandwich shop, an ice cream stand, or even a fine dining restaurant. A **fine dining restaurant** features a luxury setting and an exciting menu (not necessarily French or haute cuisine, however) and employs well-trained, creative chefs and skilled servers.

Working at an independent operation is good training for future entrepreneurs. Eight in 10 restaurant owners started in an entry-level position. Another career track might begin in the management training program of a large corporation like Darden Restaurants, which operates the full-service restaurants Olive Garden, LongHorn Steakhouse, Cheddar's Scratch Kitchen, Seasons 52, The Capital Grille, Bahama Breeze, Eddie V's Prime Seafood, and Yard House. There are many opportunities in the quick service field with McDonald's, Starbucks, and other companies. The Walt Disney Corporation runs a huge number of diverse food operations and actively recruits hospitality graduates to manage its theme park restaurants and snack bars. Airline meals are supplied by in-flight catering operators such as Gategroup and LSG Sky Chefs. Many big banks, insurance companies, and advertising agencies have executive dining rooms run by professional foodservice managers. Managed foodservice companies such as Aramark, Sodexo, the Compass Group, and others place managers in executive or employee dining facilities; in schools, colleges, and universities; and at tourist attractions, such as the Getty Center and J. Paul Getty Museum in Los Angeles. As you can see, there are many career choices in the restaurant industry.

As we look toward 2030, the National Restaurant Association rates the following as the five most likely workforce developments:

- Women will hold a larger proportion of upper-management jobs in the restaurant industry.

- Minorities will hold a larger proportion of upper-management jobs in the restaurant industry.

- The average number of employees per restaurant location will decline.

- The restaurant industry workforce will become more diverse.

- The restaurant industry will remain very labor-intensive despite technological developments.

It is important for us to remember that we have to continually strengthen our data, human, and technological literacies so we don't get left behind by the disruptive changes brought on by the Fourth Industrial Revolution.

Restaurant Industry Segments

The restaurant industry includes many different types of facilities and markets. For reporting and other purposes, the industry can be divided into three broad segments:

- *Commercial restaurant services*—Includes table-service and limited-service restaurants, commercial cafeterias, snack and alcoholic beverage bars, social caterers, and bars and taverns.

- *Noncommercial restaurant services*—Includes business, education, government, and institutional organizations that operate their own restaurant services.

- *Other services*—Includes managed services, lodging, retail-host restaurants, recreation and sports, mobile catering, vending, and non-store retailers.

Commercial Restaurant Services.
The commercial restaurant services sector constitutes the largest segment of the restaurant industry, accounting for 71 percent of total industry sales. This segment includes table-service restaurants, limited-service restaurants, commercial cafeterias, social caterers, snack and alcoholic beverage bars, and bars and taverns. Almost 84 percent of this segment's sales come from table-service and limited-service restaurants, which offer the most opportunities for hospitality students. For this reason, most of this section deals with these industry segments.

Table-service restaurants. There is a wide variety of table-service restaurants. The biggest differentiator between table-service and limited-service restaurants is the level of service provided. Table-service restaurants that offer a comprehensive dining experience are called full-service restaurants. A **full-service restaurant** provides table service; a diverse menu with appetizers, entrées, desserts, and beverages; and a staff of servers to assist customers throughout their meal. Full-service restaurants often have clean table settings, ambience, and such features as reservations, private dining, and catering services. They aim to provide quality food, professional service, and a pleasant atmosphere for leisurely meals, celebrations, or social gatherings. Guests at full-service restaurants are seated at a table when they arrive. A server leaves them with menus, takes their drink orders, and returns to deliver drinks and takes food orders. The server or a food runner brings the food, and the server returns with the check when the guests are finished.

Full-service restaurants consist of fine dining, casual dining, or family dining establishments. Each are characterized by the level of cuisine offered, menu price, and atmosphere. These characteristics are not mutually exclusive. Many full-service restaurants—as well as other restaurant operations—can fit into more than one category. Full-service restaurants usually feature a dozen or more main-course items on the menu that are cooked to order.

Level of cuisine. Restaurants such as steak houses and seafood restaurants are full-service restaurants as defined in terms of menu. However, not all steak houses or seafood restaurants offer the same level of cuisine. For example, both Outback Steakhouse and Morton's The Steakhouse specialize in beef, but their menu offerings and prices are very different. An average check for two at Outback Steakhouse can total less than $75 but could be almost four times that amount at Morton's The Steakhouse. Morton's is considered a fine dining steakhouse while Outback is considered a family dining steakhouse.

Restaurants also provide a unique service that attracts customers; that is, they provide flavor and taste sensations that cannot be easily duplicated in your home kitchen. The popularity of global and ethnic cuisines in the United States has been a driving force behind new **ethnic restaurants**, featuring cuisines such as Chinese, Italian, and Mexican. For example, Cédric Vongerichten, son of French chef Jean-Georges Vongerichten, opened his first solo venture, Wayan, in New York City in 2019. Wayan offers Indonesian cuisine with a modern French flair. The unique and varied menu combines seasonal products and savory Southeast Asian flavors. The service is impeccable and luxurious. Another example of ethnic restaurants that feature a specific cuisine as their distinctive theme is Café China, located in midtown Manhattan. Behind unassuming heavy steel doors in a 2,000-square-foot space is a restaurant known for its authentic Sichuan food. The service is casual, and the menu prices are reasonable, averaging around $10 per dish. Yet, this is a restaurant that was awarded one Michelin star from 2012 to 2019. The owners, Wang Yiming and Zhang Xian, a couple from China who quit their well-paid financial jobs in New York, did not want to emulate the widely available Americanized Chinese food and instead sought to open a true-to-its-roots, signature Sichuan-cuisine restaurant away from the Chinatown district in New York City.

Price. When the focus is on price, restaurants can be categorized as luxury, high-priced, mid-priced, or low-priced. An example of a luxury restaurant is Chef Thomas Keller's Per Se, in New York City, where dinner for two—appetizer, entrée, dessert,

Well-trained, creative chefs staff the kitchens of luxury restaurants.

coffee, and accompanying bottle of wine—would cost over $300 per person. Luxury restaurants are generally small and independently operated. They feature well-trained, creative chefs and employ skilled dining-room servers headed by a maître d'hôtel and a cadre of captains. Some luxury restaurants offer tableside cooking. To provide the necessary—and expected—high level of service, luxury restaurants employ more kitchen and dining-room employees per guest than do other types of restaurants.

Some luxury restaurants are tourist attractions famous the world over, such as the Eiffel Tower Restaurant in Paris. Others, such as Nobu in New York City, cater to "regulars"—members of the jet set, movie stars, corporate executives, and others who lead the lifestyle of the rich and famous. Typically, such establishments are owned or co-owned by a chef who supervises the cooking in the kitchen. While fine dining restaurants have historically featured French cuisine, this is no longer the case. Today's top restaurants often feature regional specialties and **fusion cuisine**, which blends ingredients and flavors from all over the globe, as exemplified by Wayan. The industry is led today by innovative young chefs, many of whom have been trained in the United States at institutions like the Culinary Institute of America in Hyde Park, New York, and Johnson & Wales University in Providence, Rhode Island.

High-priced restaurants are also usually independently owned and operated, but most have larger seating capacities than luxury restaurants. Menus are extensive, and service can range from formal at New York's Per Se to casual at Joe's Stone Crab in Miami Beach. Every year, *Restaurant Business* ranks the top 100 independent full-service restaurants in America in order of total sales. The Top 20 list appears in Exhibit 4.1. As you can see, a higher price does not necessarily mean higher sales. Rather, it is the number of customers served that is important to the profitability of the restaurant.

Atmosphere. Some restaurants are known primarily for their atmosphere—that is, for their unique architecture, décor, and setting. Restaurant design is all about creating the perfect dining experience for the customer, and the experience starts from the first point of contact, whether it is on a website, by phone, or at a curbside. Whether it is the entryway, the waiting area, dining room, private dining space,

or the energy of the bar area, every component of restaurant design is purposeful. Restaurants are designed for social interactions, so if you are opening an Asian-themed restaurant in a downtown commercial building, the guest's first impression begins when they walk into the office building. As an example, Komodo, by Groot Hospitality, is located in an office building that is quite nondescript. But as you head to the host stand, you pass a 20-foot-long glass window behind which hangs a row of perfectly roasted and shiny Peking ducks; a chef can be seen, too, hard at work. Your senses are heightened before you even arrive at the host stand. Upon being greeted by hosts dressed in black, you are walked to your table—passing a busy bar with a view of the open kitchen—and seated in a multilevel dining room with a swanky, clubby feel and floating "bird's nest" seating.

Not all restaurants are designed to evoke a nightclub feel. Crate and Barrel in Chicago opened its first on-site full-service restaurant, where it can showcase its tools and tableware in a real-life setting. Other restaurants, like Elm Street Taproom in Somerville, Massachusetts, feature local artists and their artwork to incorporate area icons. The power of social media and influencers is also another factor to consider. At Cosme in New York City's Flatiron District, whose upscale contemporary Mexican cuisine features local and seasonal ingredients from the Hudson Valley and surrounding region, each table has a spotlight positioned above the table to allow diners to capture that perfect picture to share on social media. Cosme's dining room features a color palette with warm, inviting tones to ensure that diners feel comfortable as they enjoy their meals.

Casual dining restaurants. Full-service restaurants can be categorized in other ways besides level of cuisine, menu, or atmosphere. For example, **casual dining restaurants** are distinguishable by their combination of décor, informal atmosphere, and eclectic menus that draw from ethnic and traditional offerings. Casual dining is one of the largest segments of the full-service restaurant category (see Exhibit 4.2). Almost all casual dining restaurants are chain affiliated—Olive Garden, Outback Steakhouse, and BJ's Restaurant & Brewhouse are casual dining restaurants. Applebee's and Chili's are two of the largest chains in the segment. Part of Applebee's success is the

Exhibit 4.1 Top 20 Independent Full-Service Restaurants

Rank	Restaurant	Sales	Avg. Ck	Meals Served
1.	Komodo Miami, Fla.	$ 41,000,000	$115	285,000
2.	The Boathouse Orlando Orlando, Fla.	39,863,628	44	921,785
3.	Swan Miami, Fla.	31,000,000	85	185,000
4.	Maple & Ash (Chicago) Chicago, Ill.	30,285,684	106	285,714
5.	Mila Miami Beach, Fla.	27,350,000	134	203,990
6.	Alinea Chicago, Ill.	27,072,500*	650*	41,650
7.	Top of the World Las Vegas, Nev.	25,672,308	133	218,586
8.	Shooters Waterfront Fort Lauderdale, Fla.	25,025,370	68	419,972
9.	Prime 112 Miami Beach, Fla.	24,750,000	155	210,000
10.	Paddlefish Orlando, Fla.	23,795,000*	52*	485,000
11.	Capa Orlando, Fla.	23,547,000*	121*	197,000
12.	Maple & Ash (Scottsdale) Scottsdale, Ariz.	23,487,122	95	247,232
13.	Commander's Palace New Orleans, La.	23,184,000*	89*	264,000
14.	Taste of Texas Houston, Texas	23,180,522	64	356,894
15.	Joe's Seafood, Prime Steak & Stone Crab (Washington, D.C.) Washington, D.C.	22,477,000*	94*	255,000
16.	Gibsons Italia Chicago, Ill.	22,342,704	116	209,788
17.	Joe's Seafood, Prime Steak & Stone Crab (Chicago) Chicago, Ill.	22,292,000*	99*	210,000
18.	Papi Steak Miami Beach, Fla.	22,000,000	240	91,667
19.	Marion Miami, Fla.	21,989,000*	85*	255,000
20.	Buddakan (NYC) New York, N.Y.	21,800,593	91	177,000

Source: Restaurant Business, *Top 100 Independents*, https://www.restaurantbusinessonline.com/top-100-independents.
Note: *Restaurant Business estimate.

Exhibit 4.2   Top 20 Full-Service Restaurant Chains, Ranked by Gross Domestic Sales

Rank	Chain	Gross Domestic Sales (2021 sales in millions)
1.	Applebee's Neighborhood Grill + Bar	$4,168
2.	Olive Garden	3,593
3.	Texas Roadhouse	3,439
4.	IHOP	3,017
5.	Chili's	3,006
6.	Denny's	2,462
7.	The Cheesecake Factory	2,293
8.	Cracker Barrel	2,227
9.	Outback Steakhouse	2,176
10.	LongHorn Steakhouse	1,810
11.	Red Robin	1,399
12.	BJ's Restaurant & Brewhouse	1,087
13.	First Watch	751
14.	Carrabba's Italian Grill	653
15.	Bonefish Grill	544
16.	Dave & Buster's	437
17.	Ruth Chris Steak House	418
18.	Chuy's	397
19.	Fleming's Prime Steakhouse & Wine Bar	333
20.	Famous Dave's	304

Source: Nicole Duncan, "Full-Service Restaurant Chains, Ranked by Sales," *FSR* magazine, August 2022, https://www.fsrmagazine.com/2022-fsr-50/rankings.

attention the chain devotes to the location of each restaurant. Although there is uniformity in the chain's concept, 40 percent of Applebee's menu items are tailored to regional food preferences. The Hard Rock Café, which is a chain that started in London and now has restaurants in major cities around the world, is a casual dining restaurant featuring rock-and-roll music memorabilia from Elvis Presley to contemporary stars.

Family dining restaurants. Another mainstay in the full-service restaurant category caters to families, with an emphasis on satisfying the needs of children (see Exhibit 4.3). **Family dining restaurants** serve breakfast, lunch, and dinner, offering traditional menu items. Their pricing falls between casual dinner houses and quick service restaurants. A major source of revenue for some family dining restaurants

(such as Cracker Barrel) is an on-site gift shop. Other examples of chain-affiliated family dining restaurants are IHOP, Denny's, Waffle House, Bob Evans Restaurants, Perkins Restaurant & Bakery, and Village Inn.

But not all family dining restaurants are chain affiliated. Many are located in smaller communities on the outskirts of a city or in rural areas where the population is spread out. These small businesses often become the cornerstone of their community, part of the American Dream for many women, minorities, and immigrants. Almost half of all adults surveyed say their first regular job was in the restaurant industry, and 7 out of 10 millennials and Generation X-ers have worked in the restaurant industry. With relatively low financial investment compared to a casual dining restaurant in a bustling city, these family dining restaurants support the local economy by providing jobs for

Exhibit 4.3   Top 8 Family Dining Restaurant Chains, Ranked by Domestic System Sales

Rank	Chain	Domestic System Sales (2021 sales in millions)
1.	IHOP	$2,997
2.	Denny's	2,462
3.	Cracker Barrel	2,418
4.	Waffle House	1,279*
5.	First Watch	751
6.	Bob Evans	750
7.	Perkins Restaurant & Bakery	496*
8.	Black Bear Diner	350

Source: Technomic's Top 500 Chain Restaurant Report.
Note: *Technomic estimate.

young adults as well as a refuge for senior citizens looking to stay in touch with their friends.

Fast-casual restaurants. Fast-casual restaurants are the fastest-growing sector of the restaurant business. **Fast-casual restaurants** combine elements of quick service and casual dining—they offer higher-quality food and a more upscale dining experience compared to traditional quick service chains, while still maintaining speed and affordability. They have limited menus, similar to quick service restaurants, but utilize higher-quality ingredients in meals that are made to order. Fast-casual restaurants typically follow the limited-service business model, with counter service and no wait staff, except they do not have drive-throughs. During the COVID-19 pandemic, many fast-casual restaurants offered walk-up service, where customers placed an online order in advance and drove up to the curb to pick up their orders.

In addition to take-out options, many fast-casual restaurants offer a sit-down dining room with unique décor where customers can enjoy their meals. The menus are often highly customizable and innovative. Menu prices are lower than at fine dining restaurants but can be comparable to casual dining restaurants. Examples of successful chain-operated fast-casual restaurants are Panera Bread, Shake Shack, Chipotle Mexican Grill, and Au Bon Pain.

In the United States, fast-casual restaurants are poised to grow by $150.1 billion during 2020–2024, according to Technavio.[5] Evolving consumer tastes, demand for more authenticity, and creative restaurant concepts are the biggest drivers behind this growth.

Quick service restaurants. The distinguishing features of **quick service restaurants** are a narrow selection of food, limited service, and focus on speed of preparation and delivery. Quick service restaurants focus on convenience. Burger King, KFC, and Taco Bell fall into this category. Because convenience is such an important element of a quick service restaurant's appeal, many stay open from early morning until very late at night and remain open on major holidays.

Exhibit 4.4 lists the top 20 restaurant chains in the United States. Note that the vast majority are quick service restaurants. One-quarter of quick service restaurants specialize in hamburgers, and the leader of the pack is McDonald's, with more than 39,000 units serving nearly 69 million customers each day in over 100 countries. The largest McDonald's in the world is in Orlando, Florida; it seats more than 400 people on three levels and has a broader selection of items, including hot ham and cheese sandwiches, customizable pasta dishes, pizzas, and Belgian waffles. One of the most distinctive McDonald's locations is in the underground of the Louvre, in Paris.

McDonald's is a leader in innovative marketing approaches. Some McDonald's units offer computers with limited Internet access and computer game kiosks for kids. In Boca Raton, Florida, the customers of one McDonald's can eat amid a small museum that displays motorcycle paraphernalia and a Harley-Davidson. In Hong Kong, there is a McDonald's at the racetrack; a McDonald's in Rovaniemi, Finland, has a drive-through unit designed for snowmobiles.

Exhibit 4.4 Top 20 Restaurant Chains, Ranked by U.S. System-Wide Sales

Rank	Chain	Category	U.S. System-Wide Sales (2021 sales in millions)
1.	McDonald's	Burger	$45,960
2.	Starbucks*	Snack	24,300
3.	Chick-fil-A*	Chicken	16,700
4.	Taco Bell	Global	12,600
5.	Wendy's	Burger	11,111
6.	Dunkin'	Snack	10,416
7.	Burger King	Burger	10,033
8.	Subway*	Sandwich	9,350
9.	Domino's	Pizza	8,641
10.	Chipotle	Global	7,547
11.	Sonic Drive-In	Burger	5,835
12.	Panera Bread*	Sandwich	5,650
13.	Pizza Hut	Pizza	5,500
14.	KFC	Chicken	5,100
15.	Popeyes Louisiana Kitchen	Chicken	4,775
16.	Dairy Queen	Snack	4,494
17.	Arby's	Sandwich	4,462
18.	Panda Express	Global	4,452
19.	Little Caesars*	Pizza	4,185
20.	Jack in the Box	Burger	4,077

Source: QSR, *QSR Magazine*, August 2022.
Note: *Includes figures estimated by QSR.

Starbucks, the second-largest restaurant chain, started as Starbucks Coffee; however, in 2011 "Coffee" was dropped from the title to reflect the chain's increased emphasis on food and its expanded food menu. Chick-fil-A leapfrogged over Taco Bell, Wendy's, and Burger King to become the third-largest chain restaurant by sales—simply by focusing on details. If you want to operate a Chick-fil-A, you can operate only one restaurant, and you must manage hands-on, giving it your full attention.

The type or number of menu items alone does not determine who is successful in the quick service category. A commitment to good service and providing nutritional menu choices has taken center stage. McDonald's guarantees hot food; fast, friendly service; and double-checked drive-through accuracy. A survey of operators, customers, and chefs conducted by the National Restaurant Association found that customers have become more health-conscious and concerned about sustainability and how and where their food was produced. Thirty-eight percent of adults surveyed said they would choose one restaurant over another if it used locally sourced food.[6]

Hospitality school graduates tend to look at careers in quick service restaurants last, preferring to work for major fine dining restaurants. But quick service companies offer graduates a chance to assume positions of great responsibility quickly, and the pay is very good due to liberal bonus and incentive plans.

Social catering. Catering refers to the business of providing food, beverages, and related services for special occasions. It involves preparing, delivering, and serving meals at a specific location chosen by a client, such as a venue, office, or private residence. Many restaurants offer catering as an additional source of revenue, but there are companies that do catering only. Catering can provide for a crowd of 500 or a gathering of a dozen guests at a host's home. The late Michael Roman, founder of Catersource Conference & Tradeshow, wrote, "Catering is the selling, producing, and performing of outstanding foodservice usually in situations that are not ideal for anyone, under pressure circumstances, with a lot of people watching chefs as they work, and a host wishing to pay the least amount of money possible."[7]

The major difference between table-service restaurants and catering is that all catering is pre-sold, meaning you already know how much to prepare and when, and your profits are pre-defined. Then again, catering is likely the only foodservice business where guests will haggle for a lower price. In today's market, catering gives many restaurants more visibility in the marketplace and can help draw new customers to restaurants. Catering companies can also have on-premises or off-premises operations. For instance, Bill Hansen Catering has a facility at Villa Woodbine in Coconut Grove, Florida, and also does off-premises catering. Exquisite Catering by Robert in North Miami handles strictly off-premises catering and has invested in a fleet of delivery trucks for that purpose.

Bars and taverns. Bars and taverns are locations where drinks, especially alcoholic drinks, are served, sometimes with limited food options. They could be local neighborhood bars frequented after work or social meeting places known for imaginative and exciting cocktails. They could also be sports bars with many televisions and many types of snack foods. Another form of bar is a disco bar or nightclub that offers late-evening entertainment and provides music, such as LIV in the Fontainebleau Hotel in Miami Beach. Other types of bars and taverns are lounges, adult entertainment establishments, gay and lesbian bars, piano bars, karaoke bars, wine bars, microbreweries, brew pubs, and English and Irish pubs.

Food halls. The growth of food halls has exploded in recent years and, before the advent of ghost kitchens, was often considered the next stage of restaurant evolution. A **food hall** is a type of marketplace or large indoor space that features a diverse collection of vendors, stalls, and eateries in a communal setting. It is a modern take on traditional markets and offers a wide range of culinary options in a single location. Unlike food courts located in

malls that often consist of QSR chains, food halls are often in landmark buildings like Julia and Henry's in downtown Miami, or on the ground floors of mixed-use buildings like Urban Space Vanderbilt located next to New York City's Grand Central Station. Food halls also tend to focus on local restaurants rather than chain restaurants. The vendors in food halls use either an on-site shared kitchen or the kitchens of the local restaurants. They are run by entrepreneurs, celebrity chefs, and some up-and-coming chefs.

The cuisine in food halls runs from comfort foods to gourmet fare worthy of any white tablecloth restaurant. Perhaps the most recognizable food hall in the United States is Eataly, the multilevel Italian food destination with locations in New York, Chicago, Boston, Dallas, Los Angeles, and Las Vegas. Eataly was founded in Turin, Italy, by Oscar Farinetti. Eataly food halls are known for their extensive selection of Italian food products, ingredients, and culinary experiences. They typically offer fresh produce, meats, seafood, cheeses, bakery items, pasta, and wine. Customers can explore and purchase high-quality products or dine at the various on-site restaurants and food counters.

The Ferry Building Marketplace in San Francisco is home to the Bay Area's most prestigious farmers market and houses over two dozen restaurants, including celebrated spots like The Slanted Door and Boulettes Larder, while supporting local food entrepreneurs from La Cocina, a nonprofit organization that helps food microbusinesses launch, grow, and formalize their operations. A rotating stand at the Ferry Building allows food entrepreneurs an opportunity to showcase their food products as they refine their marketing approach, collect immediate feedback, and build their customer base and brand.

Cruise lines. Cruise lines put a great deal of emphasis on their foodservice. Industry surveys cite the food served shipboard as one of the top reasons for taking a cruise and selecting a specific line. Royal Caribbean International's 168,666-ton *Quantum of the Seas* carries 4,180 passengers and a crew of 1,500; fully 30 percent of the crew works in the kitchen. Royal Caribbean has won numerous international awards for its food. Some of the other cruise lines contract their food and beverage service out to the Apollo Group, an award-winning company cited for its outstanding foodservice by *Onboard Hospitality Magazine*, *Condé Nast Traveler*, and *Porthole Cruise Magazine*.

Noncommercial Restaurant Services.

Noncommercial restaurant services include business, education, government, or institutional organizations that operate their own foodservices, making up almost 7.5 percent ($67 million) of total industry sales. The primary distinguishing factor for this segment is that the food and beverage service provided is not a primary goal of the business entity or institution; rather, it is in addition to other services provided and is typically operated at a break-even level or subsidized. You may wonder why anyone would operate a foodservice if it wasn't to make a profit. The answer is simple: In many manufacturing facilities, employees usually only have 30 minutes for a meal break. If the employer does not provide foodservices on-site, the employees must bring their own meals every day. Productivity could be impacted if the employees cannot concentrate on their work because they are thinking about food. In this case, it is better for the employer to provide food and beverage services or contract with a managed foodservice company to provide it. Other examples include universities and hospitals, where employees and customers (students and patients) would have to leave the premises to buy food and thus waste valuable time traveling.

Education.

The education market includes schools that operate their own dining services and those that contract with foodservice companies. This more than $30.3 billion annual market is made up of foodservice in colleges, universities, and primary and secondary schools. One of the biggest changes in college foodservice programs has been the gradual shift from mandated meal plans to à la carte operations. Due in part to this shift, many college foodservice operators have become revenue producers instead of revenue consumers for their institutions.

Another change in college foodservice is the growing use of brands. Today's students grew up eating at branded restaurants and they expect to see these familiar brands at school. Starbucks, Chick-fil-A, and Subway, among others, are found on campuses across the country.

More than 49.8 million primary and secondary school students eat lunch at school each day. One company, Chartwells School Dining Services (a division of the Compass Group), manages the foodservice at seven public schools in Chester, Pennsylvania, serving 5,000 students each day. The challenge for Chartwells and other contract companies is to provide nutritional meals that are similar to the quick service food that appeals to students.

Some school districts and universities still believe they can outdo contract food companies. For example, the Hillsborough County Public School system in Florida operates its own foodservice. The University of Notre Dame's dining service, once managed by an external foodservice contract company—also known as managed foodservices—is now being run by the university for its more than 13,000 students. Universities that run their dining services divisions as self-supporting enterprises are expected to turn at least a small profit. Notre Dame considers its dining and other auxiliary services a major contributor of revenue to the university's academic mission, which unfortunately also drives the rising cost of higher education.

Healthcare.

The healthcare market consists of three principal segments: hospitals and other medical centers, nursing homes, and retirement communities (including congregate food sites—community-sponsored meal centers for senior citizens). Many experts believe that there is enormous potential for foodservice management companies in the healthcare market. This can be attributed to a combination of factors—rapidly changing lifestyles, an aging population, skyrocketing medical costs, restricted federal funds, and a lack of family support systems. Sodexo, Aramark, and the Compass Group have over 2,000 healthcare accounts in North America and the United Kingdom. Each of these companies provides everything from bedside meals for patients to foodservice in staff and visitor dining rooms and cafeterias, some of which feature mall-style food courts with such well-known brands as Burger King, Wendy's, Starbucks, and Subway.

Many healthcare facilities run their own foodservice departments, and some are quite extensive. One example is the Florida Hospital Medical Center, which serves as a community hospital for Orlando and a major tertiary referral hospital for Central Florida and much of the Southeast United States, the Caribbean, and Latin America. The facility has a nutritional services department that boasts impressive foodservice statistics: it serves seven hospitals; provides meals for 1,785 beds; serves 1.8 million meals each year; and grosses almost $12 million in retail food sales. Many hospitals operate vending machines, visitor coffee shops, employee cafeterias, special dining

The healthcare foodservice market continues to grow.

facilities for doctors, daycare food programs for employees' children, regular patient food programs, and special patient food programs that can include gourmet meals (with accompanying wines) served in patient rooms.

Corrections foodservice. Correctional institutions—state and federal prisons and local jails—constitute another segment of the foodservice industry. Correctional institutions often have a hard time attracting and retaining foodservice staff because they cannot offer much professional career growth. However, the unique challenge they do offer can be attractive to some people. A prison must offer a **cyclical menu**—a menu that changes every day for a certain number of days, then repeats the cycle without being overly repetitive. The menu must have the flexibility to meet special religious and medical dietary needs while still offering a bit of creativity in preparation and presentation. Theft is another problem encountered by prison foodservice systems, so stringent controls must be used. Food costs are a further constraint on operations. Correctional institutions often have limited budgets for foodservice; economies of scale can thus make a substantial difference in the type and variety of food that can be offered to inmates.

Because they enjoy economies of scale, managed foodservice companies are now successfully competing in this area. For example,

Aramark, through its Correctional Services group, operates the foodservice at more than 500 correctional facilities in North America and provides other support, such as laundry management and commissary services. Aramark's IN2WORK vocational training program prepares inmates for their transition to the community by offering skills training and classroom instruction in food production.

Military foodservice. Military foodservice is a very specialized area. Nevertheless, it deserves mention because of its diversity in terms of geography, type of facility, and size. Positions in military foodservice can be both enlisted and officer positions within the armed forces. Examples of these jobs include foodservice specialists who are responsible for the preparation, cooking, and serving of meals in military dining facilities; foodservice managers who oversee the operations of a dining facility or foodservice operation; dietitians and nutritionists who provide expert guidance on nutrition and dietary needs for military personnel; and many others involved in ensuring the safety of food and managing supply and logistics. Both civilian and military personnel are employed by military dining facilities all over the world.

All military foodservice specialists are enlisted service members who must complete basic military training, which includes time spent in a classroom and in the field, as well as achieve competencies in tactical and survival skills, physical training, military life and customs, and weapons training. Job training for foodservice specialists consists of classroom and simulated field instruction, which often includes setting up and dismantling field kitchens for practice in food preparation.

Other segments. Other segments of the restaurant industry include managed services, lodging, retail-host restaurants, recreation and sports, and ghost kitchens. This segment is broad and sometimes combined with the commercial restaurant services segment, as they are both profit oriented.

Managed Services. The managed services segment, also known as business and industry, consists of non-foodservice businesses that offer on-site foodservice to their employees. The difference between managed services and noncommercial foodservices is that managed services are profit oriented. Their clients range from manufacturing plants to banks and technology companies. Because foodservice is not their primary business focus, most businesses that provide employee meals use managed foodservice companies, such as Sodexo, Aramark, and the Compass Group, to provide this amenity (see Exhibit 4.5). These companies manage employee restaurants, corporate cafés, executive dining rooms, coffee bars, catering services, and convenience stores for office-building employees. In many large office buildings, all these types of facilities and services are available. Unlike free-standing, single-concept restaurants, many managed foodservice locations have multiple restaurant concepts. For example, at a corporate headquarters, the foodservice might consist of an upscale corporate café, a quick service outlet, a table-service restaurant, and banquet facilities. Food trucks are now a part of the managed foodservices scene as well. For example, the contract food company Bon Appetit, a division of the Compass Group, introduced a grilled-cheese food truck at the Seattle headquarters of Starbucks in addition to operating three restaurants in the building.

The lines between commercial restaurant services (table-service, limited-service, fast-casual, etc.) and managed foodservice companies are blurring, as some managed foodservice companies are also hired to operate restaurants and other foodservice outlets in convention centers, sports arenas, tourist attractions, colleges and schools, and healthcare facilities. Managed foodservice companies face increasing competition in the business and industry market from quick service and casual dining restaurants

Exhibit 4.5   Top 10 Contract Food Management Companies

Rank	Company	2021 Revenue (in millions of dollars)
1.	Compass Group North America	$15,200
2.	Sodexo Inc.	7,795
3.	Aramark[a]	6,809
4.	Delaware North Companies	2,800
5.	HMSHost[b]	1,541
6.	Elior North America	1,440
7.	Healthcare Services Group Inc.[c]	820.6
8.	AVI Foodsystems Inc.	726
9.	Thompson Hospitality	700
10.	Southwest Foodservice Excellence	483

Source: Mike Buzalka, "Top 50 Contract Companies," *Food Management*, March 31, 2022, https://www.food-managem ent.com/top-50-contract-companies/get-rankings-50-largest-contract-management-companies-2022.
[a]Revenue figure is for U.S. food and support services only.
[b]Revenue figure is for North American operations only.
[c]Revenue figure is for dietary and nutrition services unit only.

and have responded by entering into agreements with some of these companies to operate franchises or by developing competing concepts.

In addition to foodservice, some managed foodservice management companies provide janitorial services, grounds maintenance, laundry, and other support services for their clients. This diversification has enhanced management opportunities in the field. For example, a foodservice manager for a college may be offered a higher salary for also managing janitorial services in the building in which the foodservice outlet is located. Managed foodservice companies offer numerous careers in restaurant management. Many contractors recruit on college campuses.

Lodging. Foodservice outlets in lodging operations range from gourmet restaurants to coffee shops and even quick service outlets. Lodging foodservice sales are tremendous: total hotel food sales are in the tens of billions each year.[8] Hotels and motels are now marketing their foodservice outlets aggressively. According to Jean-Georges Vongerichten, an outstanding chef who operates hotel and free-standing restaurants in the United States, Europe, and Asia, "The expectations for a hotel restaurant are far superior to what they were 10 years ago. This is true for both the United States and Europe."[9] Hotel foodservice can be a powerful marketing tool. The presence of the renowned chef Michael Mina in Miami Beach's Fontainebleau Hotel suggests that the hotel itself is also a world-class facility. Some hotels choose to enter a contract whereby restaurateurs operate the hotel's on-site restaurants. This allows management to focus on the core business of the hotel.

Retail-Host. The retail-host segment refers to the on-site restaurants that are operating in airports, grocery and convenience stores, drugstores, and even gasoline stations. Travelers eat at highway stops; on airplanes, ships, and trains; at airport terminals and train stations; and at other facilities in the transportation market.

In airports, the restaurants typically are franchises of major brands, such as Starbucks, Dunkin', McDonald's, Chili's, Buffalo Wild Wings, or local favorites. As the largest travel retail operator in the United States, HMSHost partners with local and celebrity chefs to operate restaurants in airports. For example,

Rick Bayless operates Tortas Frontera in Chicago's O'Hare International Airport. This partnership allows millions of travelers each day to experience Chef Bayless's unique Mexican flavors without needing to leave the airport or make a reservation at his restaurant.

Depending on the host site, the retail-host operator must decide what the restaurant's purpose will be and how it physically fits in its host-site's real estate, whether it is an airport, train station, gasoline station, convenience store, or grocery store. Retail-host restaurants within a convenience or grocery store give customers the option of freshly prepared meals that are reasonably priced and the convenience of buying them in one stop.

As more and more Americans choose to eat food prepared outside the home, the take-out and delivery segment of the market presents opportunities for expansion in the retail-host segment. Several major department stores, like Macy's and Nordstrom, have added dining areas within their stores. In fact, the Walnut Room at Macy's in Chicago was the first restaurant opened in a department store. It opened in 1890, when Macy's was known as Marshall Field's. The goal was to keep customers in the store for more shopping.

A good part of retail business take-out sales comes at the expense of traditional restaurants and quick service outlets. This is due, among other reasons, to increased marketing by convenience stores and supermarkets of their prepared take-out foods. Supermarkets are increasing the size and scope of their take-out food operations. Some industry observers expect the average supermarket to increase in size from its present 30,000 to 50,000 square feet to 200,000 square feet (2,790–4,650 square meters to 18,600 square meters). Much of that space will be devoted to precooked take-out dishes and sit-down foodservice areas. Many supermarkets already offer take-out salad bars in addition to their traditional deli sections. Using ovens in their bakeries, many of today's supermarkets are preparing a complete line of food products for their small in-store restaurants and cafeterias. Supermarket research shows that supermarket produce is perceived to be fresher than produce sold in most restaurants. Some supermarkets are taking advantage of this perception by selling a wide range of freshly prepared salad and vegetable dishes. Some have hired chefs to work in open kitchens so customers can see that dishes are prepared with fresh—not frozen—ingredients.

Recreation and Sports. The recreation and sports market includes foodservice facilities located at sports arenas, stadiums, racetracks, movie theaters, bowling alleys, amusement parks, municipal convention centers, and other attractions. In many cases, recreational-market foodservice facilities are concessions run by contract food companies such as Sodexo Live! and Delaware North Companies Sportservice, Inc.

The food served at recreational facilities varies greatly. For example, theme parks such as Walt Disney World sell everything from lollipops in kiosks to lobster tails in gourmet restaurants. Yankee Stadium has a location where baseball fans can see butchers from Lobel's, one of New York City's most famous butcher shops, preparing prime steaks to be served in places throughout the stadium. The concessionaire is Legends Hospitality Management, the 13th-largest contract foodservice management company, which was formed by the New York Yankees and the Dallas Cowboys to operate concessions and catering at their home stadiums. Aramark has foodservice contracts for five National Basketball Association teams and six National Hockey League teams.

Ghost Kitchens. The COVID-19 pandemic sent restaurateurs scrambling to figure out how to make up for lost revenue and adapt to off-premises sales. With the closure of indoor dining everywhere at the onset of the pandemic, many restaurants pivoted to delivery and take-out. The pandemic also accelerated the adoption of technology as consumers became adept at ordering food online. To mitigate the losses from indoor dining, restaurants invested heavily in their online presence, thus creating entirely new brands that live online. Many of these concepts use online delivery companies like Uber Eats for online ordering, pickup, and delivery. Capitalizing on this growing market, Uber's founder and former CEO Travis Kalanick started CloudKitchens. CloudKitchens builds and operates kitchen facilities that host multiple concepts under one roof. Delivery-only brands, such as Cosmic Wings by Applebee's and It's Just Wings by Chili's, are another way that restaurants expanded their revenue during the pandemic.

The popularity of ghost kitchens can be attributed to a familiar consumer habit: direct-to-consumer online shopping. Consumers trust brands based on their digital presence alone and willingly order products that are delivered directly to their door. This direct-to-consumer channel is now being used in the restaurant industry and can be very successful, potentially creating a $1 trillion global opportunity by 2030, according to a recent report from Euromonitor.[10] In addition to convenience, ghost kitchens benefit from labor savings, as staff can be used for multiple concepts and cuisines and there is no wait staff.

However, ghost kitchens are not without their challenges—the food needs to be suited for delivery and consumers need to regard you as a delivery brand. With some 1,500 ghost kitchens, the United States lags behind Asia's estimated 7,500-plus ghost kitchens.[11] Looking into the future, ghost kitchens can meet consumers' need for what they want wherever they're at, as the delivery infrastructure continues to strengthen. For restaurants, it also means a single brand can offer an online delivery-only menu that differs from its fast-casual or table-service dine-in-only menus. The possibilities are endless!

> **Knowledge Check**
>
> 1. What characterizes a casual dining restaurant? What characterizes a quick service restaurant?
>
> 2. How did restaurants pivot during the COVID-19 pandemic? What are some challenges restaurants face in implementing these changes?

4.2 STARTING A NEW RESTAURANT

Many students dream of owning their own restaurant. To be sure, huge fortunes have been made in the restaurant business. The Marriott empire grew from a single Hot Shoppe Restaurant, opened in 1927 in Washington, D.C., by J. Willard Marriott, a 27-year-old sheep herder from Salt Lake City, Utah. One of the largest-grossing independent restaurants in the United States, the Tavern on the Green in Manhattan, was the creation of Warner LeRoy, whose father, Mervyn LeRoy, produced the movie *The Wizard of Oz*. Warner LeRoy made his fortune by understanding the meaning of showmanship in the restaurant business—his employees often referred to him as a "food impresario." Norman Brinker, creator of many casual dining restaurants, started out as a buser and went on to create Chili's and other successful restaurant chains.

The restaurant business is one of the easiest businesses to enter. Novices see few barriers—comparatively little capital and virtually no experience is needed. Used commercial ovens, stoves, and other fixtures are readily available. Almost any location will do—they think—and no special skills or technology are required. Most of the labor can be obtained at minimum wage. Anyone can cook, right?

Staying in business is the real challenge. Being a good cook, a popular host, and a creative promoter are not enough when it comes to running a successful restaurant. Because the business is far more complicated than it appears, those who study the industry at colleges or universities have a much better chance of succeeding. Without business knowledge, prospects can be bleak. The National Restaurant Association estimates a 30 percent failure rate in the restaurant industry. That means one in three restaurants won't be open after their first year.[12] Actual figures may be even higher since many restaurants simply close their doors when they have exhausted their capital and become unrecorded failures. Due to the COVID-19 pandemic, an estimated 11 percent of restaurants nationwide have closed permanently.[13]

Why Do Restaurants Fail?

There are several reasons why so many restaurants fail every year:

- *Lack of business knowledge.* The first and most important reason restaurants fail is due to an operator's simple lack of business knowledge. Successful restaurant operators have a working knowledge of marketing, accounting, finance, law, engineering, and human resources. Knowing and loving food is not enough to operate a thriving foodservice operation. Tim and Nina Zagat, the creators of the Zagat guides and surveys that rate restaurants in a number of cities, observed in the *Wall Street Journal* that "a good restaurateur must exhibit unerring real estate instinct, a grasp of financial controls, a flair for interior design, and a sense of popular trends. [They need] to be adept at hospitality, publicity, and procurement."[14]

- *Lack of technical knowledge.* The second reason for failure is an operator's lack of technical knowledge. Attorneys, accountants, movie stars, and sports figures have all tried the restaurant business. In general, those who have succeeded either invested capital or simply lent their names to the enterprise in return for a share of the profits; they left the planning and operating to professional restaurateurs. Successful restaurant operators must understand site selection, menu planning, recipe development, purchasing, production techniques, and sophisticated service procedures that make it possible to deliver a consistent and reliable experience that meets guest expectations.

- *Lack of sufficient working capital.* A third reason for restaurant failure is a lack of sufficient working capital. In the restaurant business, where word-of-mouth recommendations are so important, it takes time to develop a solid guest base. New restaurants usually lose money for a while. Many new operators badly underestimate the amount of capital they will need (to pay for food, labor, and fixed operating expenses) until they reach the break-even point, which can be six months to a year down the road—or never.

Building a Successful Restaurant

Let's assume that you have enough business knowledge, technical knowledge, and capital to start a restaurant and keep it going until you reach the break-even point. What's the first step? How do you decide what kind of restaurant it should be and where it should be located?

Many would-be restaurateurs approach this issue by first deciding what kind of restaurant they would like to have and then picking a location they're comfortable with. You might want to operate an Italian restaurant in the neighborhood where you live, for example. You may then decide to negotiate a lease in a nearby shopping center where some space is available, come up with a name, and hire a contractor to "build out"—do the interior construction needed to add finishing touches to the restaurant, such as Roman columns, trellises with hanging grapes or other details suggesting an Italian setting.

While this approach might succeed, modern management theory suggests that you are putting the proverbial cart before the horse. In the above scenario, you decided on the restaurant's concept and location without any regard for who your guests are likely to be or who your competitors are. The big chain restaurants and franchisors have a different approach. Their focus is more on marketing—they have already identified their customers (e.g., families with children), and their task now becomes one of finding and serving them. Fred Turner, former president of McDonald's, was quoted as saying, "We lead the industry because we follow the customers."[15] Part of what makes McDonald's successful is that its product and service concepts are developed in response to customer and potential customer input. For example, McDonald's started serving breakfast not to keep stores open longer— although that was a consideration—but because it recognized customer demand for earlier hours and breakfast items.

The Concept. Before selecting a concept for your restaurant, you should first ask yourself the following questions:

- Who are the people I hope to attract? Are they families, businesspeople, tourists, or other guest groups?

- What guest needs am I trying to satisfy? Do these people want quick service or a fine dining experience?

- Where do these people live and work? Are they located near my proposed location?

- When do they buy? Do they eat out at lunch and dinner, or only at dinner? What are their peak days and hours for dining out?

- How do they buy? Do they dine in, take out, or want delivery?

- How much competition is there now? How much competition is there likely to be in the near future?

- What are the current competitors' menus, prices, and hours of operation?

Only after you have addressed all these questions are you ready to develop a concept.

Before selecting a concept for your restaurant, you should first ask yourself questions such as, "Who are the people I hope to attract?" and "What guest needs am I trying to satisfy?"

The concept consists of not only the products and services your proposed restaurant will offer but also the manner in which you will present them. The restaurant's name, atmosphere, location, and menu prices are all elements of the concept. In other words, the concept is the physical embodiment of the answers to the questions you have just asked. It is your idea of a restaurant that will attract the customers you have targeted.

How do you arrive at a concept? A new restaurant's concept can come from an existing concept—as when a restaurant chain expands—or from individuals who create fresh concepts, usually after considering the questions posed above. In either case, the foundation of the concept is the menu. Will it be ethnic, regional American, eclectic, traditional, limited? One way to address this question is to study market trends in terms of the popularity of various menu items. Much of this information is available in trade media research (e.g., magazines such as *Restaurant Business* and *Nation's Restaurant News*) as well as from trade associations like the National Restaurant Association. At this point, you will need to decide whether your concept is a table-service restaurant, a fast-casual restaurant, a ghost kitchen, a bar, or any of the models previously discussed.

Once you've decided on the menu, you can put many other aspects of the concept into place—number of seats, type of service, hours of operation, pricing structure, and the investment required.

You may modify the final investment figure several times in the course of creating your restaurant. To begin with, market research is likely to influence some of the elements of the concept; remember that the focus must be on the potential guests' needs and preferences. Resource limitations may pose another constraint. Most restaurateurs do not have unlimited funds. Even large restaurant chains are concerned with how long it will take a new restaurant to break even and make a profit. This means that the amount of capital available for investment may be established early on, and that amount, in turn, may affect many elements of the concept (e.g., some elements may have to be scaled back if investment capital is lacking).

Site Selection. Another important decision you must make about your proposed restaurant is its location. A restaurant site can be an undeveloped lot where a new building must be constructed, or a lot with an existing restaurant (or a building that can be converted). Of course, there is no such thing as a universally ideal restaurant site. Some restaurants should be in areas where there is a substantial amount of foot traffic; others should be near a busy highway intersection. Many quick service restaurants consider their primary, secondary, and tertiary markets to be within a one-, two-, and three-mile radius, respectively. On the other hand, table-service restaurants regard these markets to be within a one-, three-, and five-mile radius. Still others rely on neighborhoods with certain predetermined characteristics, such as a minimum number of households within a certain radius or a minimum average household income. In any case, a restaurant's site has a tremendous influence on its success.

Expanding restaurant chains like Chili's and Olive Garden offer examples of how site selection works. Most chains start by selecting cities or metropolitan areas with a certain-size population that has an average disposable income within a certain range. For instance, one chain's criterion might be "to locate our new restaurants in cities of more than 250,000 people, where the average annual household income is $30,000 or more." If you want to open a Denny's franchise, they require a permanent population of 40,000 people minimum and a median household income of $32,000–$50,000 within their trade area. Often, rather than thinking in terms of cities or metropolitan areas, sites are selected in specific **areas of dominant influence (ADI)**—locations reached by major television station signals as measured by Arbitron, a national TV rating service. By selecting a site in this manner, a chain knows in advance that it will be able to advertise economically using television.

Restaurant sites often fall into one of four areas:

- *Central-city business and shopping districts.* These are near office buildings, downtown department stores, or major commercial hotels.

- *Shopping centers.* Modern shopping centers provide a focus in suburban communities. City government offices, churches, recreational facilities such as movie theaters and fitness centers, and restaurants usually are in or near shopping centers.

- *Planned communities.* Planned communities can be large suburban developments or urban renewal projects.

- *Highway intersections.*

Usually, large restaurant chains carefully analyze market data in new locations to match potential guest profiles with chain standards. Outback Steakhouse used to focus on establishing sites in residential neighborhoods, where it thought its dinner-only concept would find the most patrons. While it hasn't abandoned those areas, Outback has discovered other successful sites for its restaurants. These include expressway interchanges, shopping malls, and hotel districts that are some distance from suburban communities. With prime real estate becoming harder to find, Outback is also building restaurants in secondary locations.[16]

A good site possesses specific characteristics. First, the site must be easily visible. If the proposed location is off a highway, it should be near a clearly marked or well-known exit. It should also be possible to put up a sign that can be seen from the highway far enough in advance from either direction so that a driver can slow down and exit safely. If the restaurant is in a major shopping complex, the site should not be off in a corner where no one will see it. It should be visible from the parking lot, where shoppers entering the mall or movie theater are bound to notice it.

Second, a good site is easily accessible. Some otherwise favorable sites are rejected because they are hard to find or located on side streets or one-way streets that are inconvenient for customers. Moreover, the restaurant must be accessible to the market it intends to serve. Depending on the type of restaurant, "accessible" can range from a few minutes' walk to a one-hour drive. Restaurants that serve upscale markets or have unique themes may have a large geographic range, while limited-menu or quick service restaurants tend to serve markets no more than 5 square miles (13 square kilometers) in size.

The third consideration is parking. There must be sufficient spaces on-site for peak periods unless valet parking off-site is provided to accommodate busy times.

The fourth consideration is availability. Can the property be rented or purchased? When? Are there any zoning restrictions?

A fifth factor to consider is affordability. An undeveloped lot may require extensive and costly site preparation. Are power and other utilities readily available, or must they be brought in? What are the terms of the purchase? If you are buying a building on the lot, is the seller willing to help with the financing? Are the taxes reasonable? Can the building be leased? Will the landlord pay for remodeling costs and other improvements, or must you pay? Since under-capitalization is a major cause of restaurant failure, you must be careful not to commit yourself to higher rent or remodeling costs than you can afford. You should be conservative when deciding what you can afford because business may not go as well as you expect.

The feasibility study. After finding a possible site, restaurateurs usually have a **feasibility study** done to determine the potential success of the proposed restaurant. These studies are commissioned by developers, prepared by consultants, and similar to the feasibility studies that are done for new hotels. The major difference is that the demand for hotel rooms is usually generated by travelers or others coming from outside a hotel's immediate area, while the demand for restaurants is mostly local. Therefore, local market characteristics are more important for restaurants. Feasibility studies help a restaurateur decide whether a particular location is right and whether a restaurant has a good chance of success.

In addition to data on local population characteristics, a good deal more information is available from many sources. The National Restaurant Association publishes a number of studies that provide data for feasibility analysts:

- Restaurant Spending Report

- Table-Service and Quick Service Restaurant Trends

- Restaurant Industry Forecast

- Restaurant Performance Index
- Restaurant Trendmapper
- Employment by State

The Bureau of Labor Statistics publishes an annual Consumer Expenditure Survey based on consumer interviews and purchase diaries. This survey is available from the U.S. Government Printing Office in Washington, D.C.[17] Using this survey and data collected from specific zip codes and other sources, research services can report exactly how often people in those zip codes eat out, which meals they like to eat, and how much they spend. A computer database called PRIZM, available through the Claritas Corporation, provides demographic and lifestyle information for the entire United States by zip code.

As you can see, feasibility studies can draw from many sources to produce qualitative and quantitative analyses of proposed restaurant operations. A feasibility study can identify possible guest markets for a proposed restaurant, evaluate the proposed site, and analyze the financial prospects of the restaurant.

The financial analysis portion of the study also contains a **capital investment budget**, a financial plan that outlines the projected spending on long-term assets or capital projects over a specified period. The purpose of a capital investment budget is to make certain that enough capital will be available for the following items:

- Land and construction costs (or extended lease costs on an existing building)
- Equipment
- Furniture and fixtures
- Working capital
- Pre-opening expenses for inventory
- Pre-opening staff salaries and training expenses
- Pre-opening advertising and promotion

Finally, the study should contain a proposed operating budget for the restaurant's first three years. An **operating budget** outlines the anticipated income and expenses of a business over a specific period, typically a fiscal year. Without this information, it's impossible to tell when the proposed restaurant will make money.

The budget lets investors and managers know how much cash will be required to meet initial expenses until the restaurant makes a profit. The budget may reveal that the restaurant, as conceived, will never make money, and therefore adjustments must be made.

Restaurant Technology

The hospitality industry has traditionally been slow to adopt new technologies, but COVID-19 changed everything. During the height of the pandemic, online ordering, deliveries, and contactless payment became crucial to the survival of a restaurant. Technology and innovation have helped save the industry and transformed it to become more efficient and automated. From online ordering, self check-out, and mobile payment to robotic servers driven by artificial intelligence (AI), there has never been a more exciting time to be in the restaurant industry.

According to the National Restaurant Association's *State of the Restaurant Industry* report, many operators are planning to invest more in service-based technology, such as online or app ordering, reservations, mobile payments, or delivery payments, followed by upgrading their hardware to include tablets, table-service ordering systems, or kiosks. Over 50 percent of consumers would like to see technology used to improve customer service, make ordering and payment easier, and provide more detailed information about food, such as nutrition, allergen information, and sourcing. When it comes to robots and drones, Generation Z and millennials are more excited about trying them than older adults.

Here are some restaurant technologies being deployed today:

- *Cloud-based point-of-sale (POS) systems.* A POS system is a necessity for all restaurants to run efficiently, as it tracks and records customer orders, menu items sold, payments, and inventory. Some systems also include human resources functions, like time-tracking and scheduling. As online ordering continues to soar in popularity, restaurants are forced to work with multiple food-delivery vendors in order to retain market share; but not all food-delivery vendors use the same ordering platform. In this case, a cloud-based POS system that can seamlessly integrate all orders may be the most helpful. Additionally, deployment of touchscreen POS in the restaurant along with self-ordering kiosks designed to streamline the customer experience will require a system capable of "talking" to all the various platforms.

- *Restaurant chatbots.* As more and more of the restaurant experience takes place online prior to guests' arrival, it is important to have a website that is interactive and helpful. Restaurant chatbots are driven by AI and can deliver automated, immediate, text-based responses to customers, making them extremely valuable for customer service because they are available on a 24/7 basis.

- *Augmented-reality menus.* While augmented reality has already been used to improve the customer experience in retail, healthcare, education, and training, it is still being experimented with in the hospitality industry. For example, augmented reality can be used to show 3D images of items on a restaurant menu as well as preparation, nutrition, and allergen information. It can also be connected to the ordering and POS systems, thus streamlining the customer experience.

With technology evolving at breakneck speed, there are plenty of opportunities for restaurateurs to upgrade the overall customer experience and allow personalization on all levels. This also aligns with changing demographics, as millennials are now the dominant consumer and more likely to be adept with technology.

Knowledge Check

1. Why are both a capital investment budget and a three-year operating budget important for a feasibility study?

2. How has the adoption of new technology changed the restaurant industry in recent years?

Foodservice is a huge industry. Career opportunities abound throughout the various industry segments, which include commercial restaurant services, noncommercial restaurants services, managed services, lodging, retail-host, recreation and sports, and ghost kitchens. The commercial restaurant services sector constitutes the largest segment of the restaurant industry, accounting for 71 percent of total industry sales. This segment includes table-service and limited-service restaurants, commercial cafeterias, snack and alcoholic beverage bars, social caterers, and bars and taverns.

Over 88 percent of sales from the commercial restaurant services segment are from full-service and quick service restaurants. Consequently, these restaurants offer the most opportunities for hospitality students. Full-service restaurants are generally categorized in terms of level of cuisine offered, menu, or atmosphere. The distinguishing features of quick service restaurants are that they offer a narrow selection of food, provide limited service, and focus on speed of preparation and delivery.

Compared to other industries, the restaurant industry offers unmatched opportunities for entrepreneurship. Restaurant entrepreneurs have followed various paths to success. Some have created entire restaurant chains; others have nourished a single restaurant to perfection. However, success is far from guaranteed: approximately 70 percent of new restaurants that open in a given year will be out of business within 10 years. Restaurants often fail because their operators lack business and technical knowledge, or because there is insufficient working capital.

Successful restaurateurs start by focusing on the needs and preferences of their potential guests. Then they develop a restaurant concept. Next, they select a site. During the site-selection process, a feasibility study is done to analyze the local market. Such studies typically include a financial analysis and capital investment budget.

Today's restaurant operators and patrons are more technologically savvy than before. The ability to integrate technology seamlessly into the dining experience and create more opportunities for interaction will increase check averages for operators.

areas of dominant influence (ADI)—A term used in the television industry to describe areas covered by the signals of major television stations as measured by Arbitron, a national TV rating service.

bars and taverns—Locations where drinks, especially alcoholic drinks, are served, sometimes with limited food options. It can be a local neighborhood corner bar or a sports bar with many televisions and many types of snack foods.

capital investment budget—A financial plan that outlines the projected spending on long-term assets or capital projects over a specified period. Also known as a capital expenditure budget or capital budget.

casual dining restaurant—A restaurant distinguishable by a combination of décor, informal atmosphere, and eclectic menu that draws from ethnic and traditional offerings.

catering—The business of providing food, beverages, and other related services for special events, gatherings, or occasions. It involves preparing, delivering, and serving meals at a specific location chosen by the client, such as a venue, office, or private residence.

cyclical menu—A menu that changes every day for a certain number of days, then repeats the cycle. A few cycle menus change regularly but without any set pattern. Also known as a cycle menu.

ethnic restaurant—A restaurant featuring a particular cuisine, such as Chinese, Italian, or Mexican.

family dining restaurant—A restaurant that caters to families—with an emphasis on satisfying the needs of children—and serves breakfast, lunch, and dinner, while offering traditional menu items.

fast-casual restaurant—A restaurant that combines elements of quick service and casual dining. These establishments offer higher-quality food and a more upscale dining experience compared to traditional quick service chains, while still maintaining speed and affordability.

feasibility study—A study commissioned by developers and prepared by consultants that seeks to determine the potential success of a proposed business on a proposed site.

fine dining restaurant—A restaurant that features luxury dining and an exciting menu (not necessarily French or haute cuisine, however), and employs well-trained, creative chefs and skilled food servers. Fine dining restaurants are generally small and independently operated, with more employees per guest than other types of restaurants.

food hall—A type of marketplace or large indoor space that features a diverse collection of food vendors, stalls, and eateries in a communal setting. It is a modern take on traditional markets and offers a wide range of culinary options in a single location.

full-service restaurant—A restaurant that provides table service; a diverse menu with appetizers, entrées, desserts, and beverages; and a staff of servers to assist customers throughout their meal. Full-service restaurants often have additional amenities such as reservations, private dining, and catering services.

fusion cuisine—A style of cooking in which chefs take ingredients or techniques from more than one cuisine and create new dishes with the results.

limited-service restaurant—Also known as quick service or fast-casual restaurants, they provide fast and efficient food service with minimal table service. These restaurants are designed to offer quick meals to customers who are looking for convenience, speed, and affordability.

operating budget—A financial plan that outlines the anticipated income and expenses of an organization or business over a specific period, typically a fiscal year.

quick service restaurant (QSR)—A restaurant that offers a narrow selection of food, provides limited service, and focuses on speed of preparation and delivery.

table-service restaurant—A restaurant where customers or guests are seated at tables and served by wait staff.

1. Which restaurant would be considered a fast-casual restaurant?
   a. Morton's The Steakhouse
   b. Joe's Stone Crab
   c. Waffle House
   d. Chipotle

2. Which characteristic determines whether a restaurant is a full-service restaurant?
   a. It offers table service and such amenities as reservations, private dining, and catering.
   b. It operates within a medical center.
   c. It focuses on convenience.
   d. It offers tableside preparation.

3. Which cuisine is likely to be featured in New York City's Chinatown district?
   a. Italian
   b. Brazilian
   c. Mediterranean
   d. Sichuan

4. Which is a unique challenge of foodservice in a correctional institution?
   a. Dealing with construction costs
   b. Offering a cyclical menu
   c. Dismantling kitchens
   d. Choosing a location

5. Which is a common reason for restaurant failure?
   a. Poor menu conceptualization
   b. Lack of business knowledge
   c. Health inspection failure
   d. Lack of theft control

6. Which area has the most potential for a successful casual dining chain restaurant?
   a. An area of a large city that is undergoing massive roadway construction
   b. An area that has recently experienced a natural disaster
   c. A planned community near a mid-sized city
   d. A village near a national park

7. Which should be the first step in building a restaurant?
   a. Developing a concept
   b. Finding a business partner
   c. Applying for a business loan
   d. Obtaining a construction permit

8. Which are good characteristics for site selection?
   a. Efficiency, affordability, visibility, flexibility, and security
   b. Creativity, variety, affordability, safety, and cleanliness
   c. Visibility, accessibility, parking, availability, and affordability
   d. Affordability, parking, variety, efficiency, and security

9. Which organization publishes studies that provide data for feasibility analysts?
   a. National Restaurant Association
   b. Food and Drug Administration
   c. Better Business Bureau
   d. Smith Travel Research

10. A feasibility study should have a proposed operating budget of how many years?
   a. 10 years
   b. 5 years
   c. 3 years
   d. 1 year

11. Which restaurant technology is driven by artificial intelligence?
   a. Online ordering
   b. Restaurant chatbots
   c. Augmented reality menus
   d. Cloud-based point-of-sale system

12. What percentage of restaurants fail within 10 years of opening?
   a. 30 percent
   b. 65 percent
   c. 70 percent
   d. 80 percent

SHORT-ANSWER QUESTIONS

1. In what ways will the restaurant industry change by 2030?

2. How do advancements in restaurant technology align or not align with the desires of different demographics?

SURVIVAL MODE

Twin brothers and real estate investors Tyrone and Kenny open their first table-service restaurant in the spring of 2019. The restaurant features Caribbean soul food and has a live-music stage. Having worked in real estate their entire careers, the brothers are excited to venture into the restaurant industry. The restaurant is near a sports arena where football, tennis, car racing, and other major events take place.

The restaurant has a rocky start—there are staffing issues that result in turnover and issues with food cost and quality control. The restaurant receives negative reviews for several months until the brothers decide to make a change. They contact a consultant with 20 years of hospitality and restaurant industry experience to help solve their operational challenges. The restaurant starts to see satisfactory profit and service improvement by the fall of 2019.

With the restaurant gaining popularity from its nightly music performances and feeder business from the sports arena, it earns a significant profit by the start of 2020. Everything goes well until March of 2020, when the COVID-19 pandemic hits and threatens to shut down the restaurant.

The brothers are stunned and afraid that their business will not survive. Additionally, their consultant, who still has a contract with them until the end of 2020, is forced to quarantine due to COVID-19 exposure.

As many restaurants are forced to develop new revenue-earning strategies, the brothers feel they have no choice but to reevaluate their own strategies, despite their growing success prior to the pandemic. If they don't take action, the brothers could lose everything they worked so hard for.

DISCUSSION QUESTIONS

1. What were some factors in the success of the restaurant before the pandemic?

2. What is the advantage of hiring a consultant with hospitality industry knowledge?

3. What strategies could the brothers implement during the pandemic to maintain revenue streams?

Mashama Bailey

Chef Mashama Bailey is co-founder and partner of The Grey, headquartered in historic downtown Savannah, Georgia. At The Grey, Bailey developed her personal take on port city Southern food, tapping into the experiences of her youth to create layered and soulful dishes. While she was born in the Bronx and raised in Queens, Bailey attended grammar school in Savannah at Charles Ellis and spent many summers at her grandparents' home in Waynesboro, Georgia.

Bailey learned to cook from the women in her family. Her mom, grandmothers, and aunts gave her the best kind of education—a real-world one. She attended the Institute for Culinary Education to round out her home-cooking expertise and studied in France. Prior to launching The Grey in 2014, she spent a dozen years cooking throughout New York City—the last four at Prune, on Manhattan's Lower East Side, under the tutelage of her friend and mentor, Gabrielle Hamilton.

As the chef of The Grey and its related restaurants, Bailey has earned a number of accolades, including the James Beard Foundation Award for Best Chef–Southeast in 2019 and its Outstanding Chef award in 2022. She also chairs the board of the Edna Lewis Foundation, working to preserve and celebrate Lewis's legacy, which she credits as a heavy influence. Bailey surrounds herself with family, friends, and food, and she is a firm believer in the old adage that you learn something new every day.

Samantha has been working as a server at a popular downtown restaurant for the past two years. She enjoys her job and the lively atmosphere of the restaurant, but Samantha feels she has hit a ceiling in terms of her career growth. While she has received positive feedback from customers and her managers, she has not been given any opportunities to take on more responsibility or advance to a higher position.

Samantha is considering her options for career growth within the industry but is unsure of her next steps. She has a degree in hospitality management and has considered applying for management positions at other restaurants, but she is hesitant to leave her current job where she is well-liked and comfortable.

She has also considered starting her own restaurant or catering business, but she is daunted by the financial and logistical challenges that come with entrepreneurship.

As Samantha weighs her options, she is also grappling with the reality of the restaurant industry's notoriously low wages and lack of benefits. She wants to continue working in the industry she loves, but she is also looking for a path that will provide her with financial stability and opportunities for advancement.

What advice would you give Samantha? What steps could she take to advance her career in the restaurant industry, and what are the potential risks and rewards of each path? How can she balance her desire for career growth with the need for financial stability and job security?

5

RESTAURANT ORGANIZATION AND MANAGEMENT

Chapter Outline

Learning Objectives

1. Describe the importance of guest information and restaurant ambience to a restaurant's success, and summarize rules for creating menus. (pp. 110–115)

2. Give examples of guest menu preferences in different parts of the United States and the rest of the world, describe menu categories, and summarize the importance of menu design and menu pricing. (pp. 115–119)

3. Summarize the impact of computers and the Internet on restaurant controls; identify methods of financial and operational control; list the control points of the food cost control cycle; and describe the menu planning, forecasting, purchasing, receiving, storing, and issuing control points of the cycle. (pp. 120–128)

4. Describe the producing, serving, and customer payment control points of the food cost control cycle, outline methods of food cost analysis, and explain how managers can control labor and beverage costs. (pp. 128–132)

KEY TERMS

ambience	dogs	plowhorses
balance sheet	financial controls	prime costs
bar's par	first-in, first-out (FIFO)	primes
blind receiving	fixed menu	purchase specification
budgeting	food cost	puzzles
cash flow statement	food cost percentage	requisition form
contribution margin	gross profit	specialty menu
cost of food sold	income statement	standard recipe
direct purchase	perpetual inventory system	stars

In this chapter we will focus first on organizing a restaurant for success. We will discuss the importance of guests, ambience, and menus. Then we will describe financial and operational controls for restaurants, including accounting systems, budgeting, menu planning, forecasting, purchasing, receiving and storing, issuing, producing, serving, customer payment, food cost analysis procedures, and computerized point-of-sale (POS) systems. We will briefly consider labor costs, then conclude the chapter with a discussion of beverage control.

5.1 ORGANIZING FOR SUCCESS

Restaurant managers must have a broad base of skills to run a restaurant successfully. These include marketing skills (to bring guests in) and quality control and service skills (to satisfy guests so they will want to return). Of course, having guests does not guarantee a profit; restaurants have gone bankrupt even when running at capacity every night. Often, the difference between successful and unsuccessful foodservice operations is that the successful ones are organized. Managers of well-organized restaurants are able to budget and control expenses so they maximize profits. Even the success of managers of nonprofit or subsidized operations, such as school food programs, is measured in financial terms—by their ability to control expenses and operate within their budget limitations.

All types of foodservice operations have the same mission—to prepare and serve food while staying within financial guidelines. Because their mission is the same, they all operate under similar principles of management and control.

Three elements crucial to the success of any restaurant are its guests, ambience, and menu.

Guests

Everything starts with the guest or customer. Finding and holding on to this elusive creature is the most important factor in the success of any business. Once you understand where guests will come from and what needs they will have, you can determine the feasibility and optimal location or structure of any new foodservice operation.

But a thorough knowledge of guests tells us a good deal more than simply where to put the restaurant. Guests' wants and needs guide new restaurateurs in formulating menus, determining ambience, setting the level and style of service, and creating advertising and marketing plans.

The marketing research that goes into a feasibility study for a new restaurant is only the beginning. Guest research must be updated continually because we live in a dynamic society where markets change quickly. Continual research makes it possible not only to measure current guest preferences but also to discover trends— how those preferences are changing and how fast.

Restaurants with long, successful track records and loyal guests have sometimes lost their guests' allegiance virtually overnight. According to management consultants Albrecht and Zemke, guest loyalty "must be based on a continuously satisfying level of service."[1]

The key word is "continuously." It is not hard to find examples of restaurants that lost touch with their guests and either failed or fell under the control of new companies with new concepts. For example, Sambo's, a limited-menu chain popular for many years, derived its name and décor from the children's story "Little Black Sambo." The civil rights movement focused attention on the racial aspects of Sambo's concept, and the chain died a painful death. The Royal Castle hamburger chain started during the Depression, offering 24-hour service and five-cent hamburgers. Over the years, the units became too small, old-fashioned, and limited in their menu choices. Soon the land on which the 175 restaurants rested was worth more than the company, and the company was liquidated. Then there was the Victoria Station restaurant chain. It had an attractive concept— restaurants in the form of a cluster of railroad cars that served extraordinarily good roast beef and generous drinks at reasonable prices. But beef consumption began to decrease, and the restaurant's concept became less popular. The owners tried many new concepts, one after the other, leaving customers guessing about what they might find on their next visit. Eventually, most customers went elsewhere.

Guest attitudes and desires change constantly. At the moment, fast-casual dining restaurants are the most popular segment of commercial restaurants. This segment, a combination of quick service and casual dining, features menus that use quality ingredients, counter service, and a casual dining environment where guests can sit down and enjoy their food. Examples of fast-casual dining restaurants are Panera Bread, Shake Shack, and Chipotle Mexican Grill. Evolving consumer tastes, demand for more authenticity, and creative restaurant concepts are the biggest drivers behind this growth.

Dining out, it seems, has become more routine than occasional. Many people see dining out as an affordable indulgence. The National Restaurant Association reports that 63 percent of adults say restaurants are an essential part of their lifestyle. There are over one million restaurant locations in the United States, and that number is growing.[2]

Smoking in restaurants is a good example of how consumer preferences have changed over the years. In the 1960s, every restaurant offered ashtrays on every table. By the end of the 1980s, surveys showed that more than three-quarters of guests wanted separate smoking and no-smoking restaurants. Today, almost all of the most populated states in the United States have either state or local ordinances banning smoking in restaurants and bars. McDonald's has implemented 100 percent no-smoking policies in all of its company-owned units in the United States and has urged its franchisees to do the same.

Nutrition awareness has dramatically changed the way guests view menus. Freshness has become an important attribute for menu items, partly because it denotes a more nutritious and therefore healthier product. Restaurant analysts have seen an increased demand for locally sourced food. There has also been an increase in the popularity of plant-based proteins in sandwiches, breakfast sandwiches, and burgers.[3]

However, a trend taking hold or losing ground is not a reason in itself to make dramatic changes in methods of operation. Few trends are universal. Different regions of the country and different countries have their own values; what is true in California may be less true or not true at all in Vermont. Therefore, restaurateurs should use national surveys and studies only as guides. Whether they apply to your city and your restaurant can only be determined by asking your guests.

Ambience

In successful foodservice operations, all types of elements play a role. The décor, lighting, furnishings, tableware, menu, methods and personalities of the servers, and even the guests all combine to create a feeling about or an identity for a restaurant—that is, they create the restaurant's atmosphere or mood, its **ambience**. Ambience often leads guests to choose one restaurant over another. For some patrons, a restaurant's ambience may be as important as the food, or even more important. Swan in Miami's Design District, owned and operated by hospitality mogul David Grutman and singer–producer Pharrell Williams, features a palette of soft pinks and grays, jewel-like finishes, and artwork by fashion illustrator David Downton. Inside the main dining room is a horseshoe-shaped bar covered in scalloped tile and backed with pink onyx. The whole restaurant is designed to provide visually appealing spaces and dishes that are highly shareable on social media. These restaurants often focus on creating unique and aesthetically pleasing environments that encourage customers to capture and post their experiences online.

A restaurant's ambience can even enhance how its food tastes to guests. One reason restaurateurs like to locate seafood restaurants next to the water is that there is a suggestion that the fish they serve are fresh. The restaurants in the Fuddruckers hamburger chain feature a glass-enclosed refrigerated room where fresh sides of beef hang; customers can view the beef while they stand in line. This reinforces Fuddruckers' claim that its hamburgers are fresh and made on the premises, and may help convince customers that Fuddruckers' hamburgers taste better than those made from frozen patties.

A legendary industry story about designing a restaurant's ambience to satisfy the clientele comes from the early days of McDonald's. Founder Ray Kroc decided to concentrate on reaching families with young children. Why? Research showed that this was a large and growing market segment. The research also showed that the children often cast the deciding vote on which restaurant a family visited. With this information in mind, Kroc and his associates designed a restaurant that not only served food children would like but also served it in a setting where small children would feel comfortable. Kroc ordered cameras mounted on 3-foot-high tripods to photograph a prototype McDonald's restaurant. Looking at the restaurant through the eyes of a child made the necessity for some changes immediately evident. Counters, for example, were lowered so a child could order without having to strain or stand on tiptoe. Seats and tables were also lowered. The interior was accented with bright yellow and red—the same colors used on many toys at the time.

Décor, lighting, tableware, menu, and other factors combine to create a restaurant's ambience. As you can see, these two restaurants have a very different ambience.

Benihana is another restaurant chain that owes much of its success to ambience. Japanese immigrant Rocky Aoki, the chain's founder, was a stickler for authentic detail. Not only did he train his chefs at a special school in Tokyo before bringing them to the United States, but he also imported wooden beams from Japan at great expense to create the atmosphere of an authentic Japanese inn. Many of Aoki's advisors told him that this was an unnecessary expense, since the same look could be produced with American materials, but Aoki refused to compromise.

Restaurant designers today talk about "fusing the décor with the region." Colonial-style furnishings and fabrics are often used in New England inns. Nautical themes are popular for restaurants located in seaports, and Southwest native décor predominates in cities like Santa Fe, New Mexico. A well-known restaurant designer, Ken Fulk, whose works include ZZ's Sushi Bar, Swan, Goodtime Hotel, and Strawberry Moon, all in Miami, believes spaces should be carefully curated and edited with the utmost restraint. "It's not about throwing everything at the wall to see what sticks, but creating a setting that invites you in, to stay a while, to curl up by a fire—or, you know, to stay and party till the wee hours of the night—in turn, creating more stories, more history."[4]

The ambience of a restaurant's building can dictate the restaurant's concept. For example, some restaurants are housed in landmark buildings (the Space Needle in Seattle, Washington, to name one) or historic railroad stations. In Europe, castles, country houses, and châteaus are favored locales for restaurants because of their distinctive character.

A sense of place is related to ambience. Chef Thomas Keller says it is "the experience … that is going to leave a lasting memory."[5] As an example, when you walk up to The French Laundry in Yountville, California, you immediately see the beautiful culinary gardens across the street. The sun is setting behind the vineyards, and you are surrounded by lush greenery. You start to feel relaxed, in anticipation of the fine dining you will experience shortly. The service is meticulous and nothing is rushed. In fact, an average dinner takes around three hours. After dinner, you can ask for a tour of the kitchen and even meet Keller himself! To most diners, this is the experience that will leave a lasting memory.

Menu

A restaurant's menu is usually the most important element of its success. For that reason, we will discuss menus in some detail. A menu is much more than a list of items for sale. The menu helps define and explain what the restaurant is all about. It should represent what its guests expect and want. There is also a more subtle dimension. The menu should state what the restaurant does best. Unfortunately, what a restaurant does best sometimes changes. This is often the case with independent restaurants that are showcases for famous chefs. Cooking is a creative process; dishes conceived by one chef are not always as deftly executed by assistants and successors. This is one of the main reasons the menus of gourmet independent restaurants should and do change—so the restaurants they represent can put their best foot forward.

Freshness is an important attribute. Here, the chef tends to a rooftop herb and vegetable garden.

Basic Rules. There are some basic rules that good restaurateurs follow when creating menus:

- *Give guests what they want.* Offer your guests what they are looking for at your restaurant. If your restaurant emphasizes convenience and speed of service, then do not include items on your menu that take a long time to prepare. If Italian specialties are what you promise, you must offer more than just spaghetti and lasagna.

- *Use standard recipes.* **Standard recipes** are formulas for producing a food or beverage item that specify ingredients, the required quantity of each ingredient, preparation procedures, portion size and portioning equipment, garnish, and any other information necessary to prepare the item (see Exhibit 5.1). Standard recipes are an essential part of quality control. Guests who come to your restaurant for the Dover sole *à la meunière* expect it to look and taste the same every time they come back for it.

- *Match the menu to the staff's abilities.* Make certain that all of the items on the menu can be correctly prepared and served by your staff. Servers' abilities are especially important when the menu includes items that are prepared tableside.

- *Take equipment into account.* Consider the limitations of your kitchen equipment.

Menu items that call for grilling should not be broiled; grilled items do not taste the same as broiled items. Dishes that should have authentic wood-smoke flavors require a hickory or mesquite grill.

- *Provide variety and balance.* Present a variety of items, colors, and textures in your menu. Much of any restaurant's business is repeat, especially at lunchtime. Daily or weekly specials can ensure that there are varying choices for guests. Strive for balance, so foods complement each other or contrast nicely. Cream soups should not be followed by main courses with cream sauces. Some items should be heavy, others light. Since poultry and meat are white or brown, liven up their presentation with colorful vegetables.

- *Pay attention to the season.* Food costs are higher and quality is lower when you use fresh fruit or vegetables that are out of season. Menu items calling for fresh ingredients that are not readily available should perhaps be dropped from the menu until the ingredients are in season again.

- *Keep nutrition in mind.* Probably a certain number of your guests are committed to eating nutritious meals. Many of today's consumers try to eat a balanced diet. They may also be interested in reducing their intake of salt, fat, or sugar. Don't make that difficult to do in your restaurant.

Exhibit 5.1   Sample Standard Recipe

			Fish Fillet Amandine		
Yield: _____ Size: _____		Yield: 60 Size: 6 oz	IX. MAIN DISHES—FISH 2 Baking Temperature: 450ºF Baking Time: 14–15 min		
Amount	**Ingredients**	**Amount**	**Procedure**		
_____	Fish fillets, fresh or frozen, 6 oz portion	22 ½ lb	1. Defrost fillets if frozen fish is used. 2. ARRANGE defrosted or fresh fillets.		

_____	Almonds, toasted, chopped or slivered	1 lb	3. To toast almonds:
			
			    a. Spread on sheet pans.
			
			    b. Place in 350ºF oven until lightly toasted.
			
			    Approximate time: 15 min		

_____	Margarine or butter, softened	2 lb 8 oz	4. Add almonds, lemon juice, lemon peel, salt, and pepper to softened margarine or butter. 5. Mix thoroughly. 6. Spread margarine mixture on fillets as uniformly as possible. 7. Bake at 450ºF for approx. 15 min or until fish flakes when tested with fork. 8. Sprinkle lightly with chopped parsley or sprigs of parsley when served.		
_____	Lemon juice	½ cup			
_____	Lemon peel, grated	2¾ oz			
_____	Salt	4 tbsp			
_____	Pepper, white	1 tbsp			
_____	Weight: Margarine-almond mixture	4 lb			

■ *Use food wisely.* Strive for a menu that will produce profits. Carefully plan how to use perishable items and make full use of leftovers. Throwing away food is like throwing away money. Smart chefs use meat and vegetable scraps (left over from preparing other menu items) for stews and soups. Day-old bread can be used for stuffings and croutons. Good menu planners automatically think of daily specials that chefs can prepare using leftovers from the previous day's production.

Chefs create and test new dishes as part of developing standard recipes.

Menu Preferences. Successful restaurant chains know that menu preferences vary significantly by region. In the United States, people in New England have significantly different tastes than people in the South or West. Germans from Berlin prefer different dishes than their Bavarian cousins in Munich. The food in central China (Sichuan, Chongqing, and Hunan regions) is much spicier than food in northern China (Beijing, Xi'an, and Inner Mongolia). Darden Restaurants (which operates eight restaurant chains, the largest being Olive Garden) is careful to make sure that although the restaurants in each of its chains look alike and have many of the same basic items, regional preferences are taken into account. Olive Garden, for example, has many different menus for its more than 650 restaurants. By offering seasonal and "test" menu items and conducting tens of thousands of customer interviews nationwide, Olive Garden was able to put together a data bank to help design new menus. This research showed executives that customers in coastal areas preferred more seafood dishes on the menus, while those in the Midwest preferred more meat options. Before entering a new market, Olive Garden executives sample food at potential competitor restaurants to measure local spice preferences.

Global food chains keep their signature items on all menus the world over, but they also add items that appeal to local tastes. McDonald's serves fried yucca sticks in Venezuela and an egg, rice, beans, and chorizo platter for breakfast in Mexico. In the Middle East, regional menu items include a folded tortilla sandwich filled with spiced beef. In China, Pizza Hut, a division of Yum! Brands, Inc., serves French restaurant-style escargot in garlic oil and ostrich-topped pizza. Pizza Huts in Hong Kong offer many more pasta dishes than their counterparts in the United States because the Chinese have never been large consumers of cheese.[6]

Menu Categories. There are two main menu categories based on how the menu is scheduled: fixed menus and cyclical menus. Menus can be further categorized as breakfast, lunch, dinner, or specialty menus. A third menu category that is less prevalent is the chef's table menu. This menu type is often found at fine dining restaurants and features menu items that use the freshest ingredients available that day, selected and expertly prepared by the chef and their team. One example of a restaurant with a chef's table menu is Per Se in New York City, by Chef Thomas Keller. *Omakase*, meaning a meal consisting of dishes selected by the chef, is growing in popularity all across the United States, and many sushi restaurants specializing in omakase have been recognized by the coveted Michelin Guide.

Fixed menus. A **fixed menu**, also known as a static menu, is typically used for several months or longer before it is changed. Daily specials may be offered, but a set list of items forms the basic menu.

Quick service operations are examples of restaurants with fixed menus. They can get away with offering the same menu items every day because the items they serve—typically hamburgers, chicken, pizza, or Mexican foods—appeal to a broad market. Many chain-operated full-service restaurants also feature fixed menus.

One of the principal advantages of a fixed menu is its simplicity. Purchasing, staffing, and inventory control are straightforward and uncomplicated. Even the equipment requirements are minimal and less complex. But there are disadvantages. A fixed menu provides no variety and few options for coping with increased costs other than raising menu prices. One solution to the lack of variety is to expand the fixed menu from time to time by adding new menu items on a temporary or permanent basis. Burger King's Impossible Whopper and Taco Bell's Triplelupa are both examples of temporary items, also called limited time offers (LTOs). LTOs are a way to boost sales before the end of a quarter or experiment with new menu items to gauge customer feedback. At Arby's, gyros became a permanent menu item after they were introduced first as an LTO. Both Burger King and McDonald's added salads and desserts on a permanent basis to provide more variety and achieve a higher average check per customer.

Some restaurants, such as independent family restaurants, offer daily specials to put a little variety in their fixed menus. The specials are usually printed on a separate sheet and inserted into the regular menu. Adding daily specials to an otherwise fixed menu helps keep regular customers who occasionally want to try something different.

Cyclical menus. A cyclical menu is a menu that changes every day for a certain number of days before the cycle is repeated. Desktop publishing makes changing printed cyclical menus easy and inexpensive.

Institutional foodservice operations and commercial operations that are likely to serve guests for an extended period of time use cyclical menus. A cruise ship where guests typically stay for a week needs a seven-day cyclical menu so different menus can be offered each day. Menus can be numbered and may run from #1 to #7 before starting with #1 again. Cruise lines that offer longer cruises or whose clientele often take back-to-back cruises may use a much longer cycle menu; Seabourn Cruise Line has a 14-day-cycle menu. Hospitals, where patients might be confined for prolonged periods, sometimes use long cycles. Nursing homes may use a very long cycle menu.

Specialty menus. Specialty menus differ from typical breakfast, lunch, and dinner menus. They are usually designed for holidays and other special events or for specific guest groups. Most restaurants offer a specialty menu featuring turkey and ham at Thanksgiving and Christmas, for example. Catered events such as birthdays, weddings, bar and bat mitzvahs, and other social occasions may call for specialty menus. In some cases, specialty banquet menus may be created. There are many other kinds of specialty menus used by restaurants, such as children's, early-bird, beverage, senior citizens', dessert, and take-out.

Specialty menus are marketing tools—extra incentives to bring patrons in. Their only limit is the menu planner's imagination.

Menu Design. Like a brochure for a hotel, a menu is a sales tool and motivational device. A menu's design can affect what guests order and how much they spend. The paper, colors, artwork, and copy all can influence guest decisions and help establish a restaurant's ambience and image; therefore, the look and language of the menu should be closely tied to the restaurant's concept. For example, The Fat Duck, a three-Michelin-star restaurant in Bray, United Kingdom, owned by Chef Heston Blumenthal, is famous for its innovative and experimental approach to food, taking diners on a unique gastronomic journey. Its website invokes a sense of imagination and encourages the diner to question everything—especially when it comes to food. The menu (Exhibit 5.2) is called "Sensorium," named after the parts of the brain or the mind concerned with the reception and interpretation of sensory stimuli. The menu is delivered to guests in an unusual format and its items are creatively laid out in different colors to awaken their curiosity.

When guests sit down at a restaurant table, there is no question about whether they are going to buy something; the question is how much they are going to spend. Blackboards, tent cards, QR codes, well-trained food servers, and—most important—a well-designed menu can influence that decision and ultimately affect the restaurant's bottom line. News Cafe, an iconic South Beach restaurant frequented by locals and celebrities such as the late fashion designer Gianni Versace, has a well-designed menu (Exhibit 5.3) that looks like a newspaper with pictures and boxed elements meant to draw guests' attention to the café's specials, thus encouraging them to spend

Exhibit 5.2 Format and Layout of The Fat Duck's "Sensorium" Menu

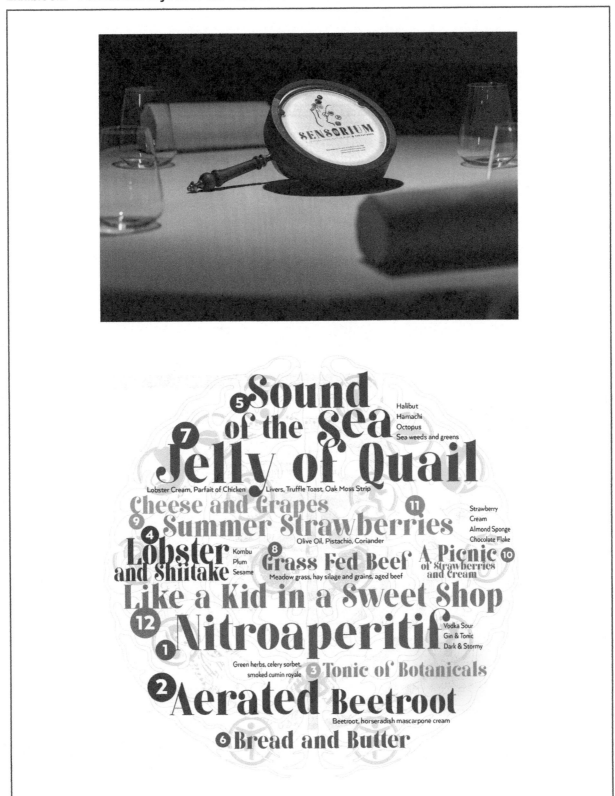

Exhibit 5.3 Sample Menu from News Cafe, Miami Beach

more. In spite of technological advances spurred by the COVID-19 pandemic, 66 percent of adults still prefer paper menus over digital menus if given the choice.[7] However, opportunities exist for augmented reality integration and enhanced guest interaction with digital menus.

Menu Prices. The goal in establishing menu prices is to bring in sufficient revenue to cover operating costs and overhead and to provide a reasonable return on investment. In other words, price is related to costs and investment. Clearly, a restaurant with a low investment and low operating costs should be able to charge less than a restaurant with high costs and a larger investment. Quick service restaurants use computer-designed, standardized facilities and specialized equipment to prepare their menu items. The result is a relatively low investment cost plus low operating costs since the menu and the equipment are designed for use by unskilled labor and with a limited menu in mind. Other operating costs are also kept to a minimum because only absolutely necessary things are added to the system for the smooth functioning of the unit. Therefore, prices in quick service restaurants can be kept low.

On the other hand, restaurants such as Daniel (Chef Daniel Boulud's restaurant in New York City) are designed to offer extraordinary dining. These restaurants have lavish appointments, are located on valuable real estate, and provide luxury service with a menu requiring highly skilled chefs, cooks, dining room captains, and servers. Luxury restaurants charge high prices to cover their high food and operating costs and high overhead. They can do this because their guests are willing to pay for a fine dining experience.

A number of mathematical models and other methods are used to set menu prices. Most of them involve a markup over food and labor costs. Whatever method is used, you should ask some basic questions after pricing menu items:

- Are these prices appropriate for my type of operation? Cafeterias usually charge less than table-service restaurants for the same items, for example.

- Will my guests feel that I am offering a good price/value relationship? In other words, will they feel they're getting a good deal for their money?

- Are my prices competitive? What do similar restaurants in this same locale charge?

- Do these prices deliver a fair profit? Profit, of course, depends on many factors, but people who invest in restaurants generally expect their original investment to be paid back in three to five years.

Remember that, for most menu items, the lowest price you can charge a customer is governed by the need for the restaurant to make a profit, but the highest price you can charge is governed by the customer's perception of the item's quality and value.

The popularity of delivery apps for online ordering has created a unique menu pricing phenomenon. Some delivery apps charge restaurants as much as 30 percent of the overall bill for a commission fee, on top of the delivery fee. Restaurateurs who had to rely solely on take-out and delivery sales as their primary revenue during the pandemic were faced with the dilemma of how to increase sales when their dining rooms were shuttered or at less than 100 percent capacity. Consequently, most restaurateurs adopted a different set of menu prices for online orders placed through delivery apps. New York City is among the municipalities that passed commission limits whereby third-party delivery services cannot charge more than 15 percent per order and no more than 5 percent for other fees, such as credit card processing and better placement on apps. Even though most restaurants use a third-party delivery vendor, 6 out of 10 consumers say they would prefer to order directly from the restaurant.[8]

Knowledge Check

1. How have changes in consumer preference influenced the restaurant industry?

2. What are some basic rules for creating menus?

5.2 RESTAURANT CONTROLS

Control is one of management's fundamental responsibilities. Effective control is a result of establishing standards based on the needs of guests and the goals of the business. This principle holds true for all types of foodservice operations. Whether the establishment is a fine dining restaurant, a quick service outlet, or even an institutional foodservice operation, managers must establish standards for financial performance, operations, and quality control. Without standards, there can be no real management, only organized confusion.

Clearly, running a successful foodservice operation requires attention to details. Each day, managers must keep track of reservations, the number of people in the restaurant, what guests are ordering, and how much guests are spending. They also need to be aware of the restaurant's inventory, operating costs, and profit picture. The answer to keeping track of all these things lies with information technology. Computers, computer networks, and the Internet have revolutionized the restaurant industry.

Look at what is happening right now. Restaurant operators are collecting reservations from all over the world using their own websites and other Internet reservations systems, such as OpenTable, Eat App, Resy, Yelp, and Table Agent. OpenTable lists approximately 60,000 restaurants around the world, displays their addresses and menus, shows a photo of each establishment, and takes and confirms reservations. According to a study published by the National Restaurant Association, 26 percent of restaurant patrons used the Internet to make a reservation, and 43 percent said they were likely to use a smartphone or tablet to make future restaurant reservations.[9]

Computer-based food and beverage systems have revolutionized restaurants by increasing the efficiency of front- and back-of-the-house operations. With a POS system, servers need not roam far from their dining room stations and can still get their food and beverage orders to the kitchen or the bar by using a touchscreen terminal in the dining room or a wireless handheld device that transmits the order to either a printer or a video display. These terminals and handheld devices also allow servers to print and settle guest checks, whether guests pay via contactless or mobile payment, cash, credit card, or—in the case of hotel restaurant customers—charges to their guest folio.

For high-volume table-service restaurants, a table management system can be invaluable in improving service by reducing the guest's wait, allowing staff to utilize tables as soon as they are free, and balancing workload. The system, which can be part of a reservations and wait-list management system, is managed through touchscreen monitors that graphically display the table layout at the host's station as well as stations throughout the restaurant. As a table becomes available, the server indicates its availability by touching the table icon, causing the corresponding icon on the host's screen to be identified.

Back-of-the-house computer operations include labor and scheduling management programs and an inventory/purchasing (I/P) system. Menu items sold are transmitted to the I/P system, where they are broken down into their major ingredients and those ingredients are deducted from inventory. Management reports—covering such topics as sales analysis, server sales, menu mix, complimentary meals and beverages, and labor costs—can be generated at any interval during the meal period or at the close of business.

In the following sections, we will take a look at the financial and operational controls—many enhanced by the use of computers—that restaurant managers use in order to meet guest expectations and achieve their operations' financial goals.

Financial Controls

Financial controls are tools managers use to measure the worth of a restaurant and its level of sales, costs, and profitability. They include such documents as balance sheets, statements of income, and statements of cash flow. Managers use an accounting system to gather the financial information that makes control possible.

Accounting Systems. An accounting system that provides usable and sufficient information for management decisions is the basis for sound financial control. One such accounting system is the *Uniform System of Accounts for Restaurants*. This system is similar to the *Uniform System of Accounts for the Lodging Industry* in that it establishes categories of revenues and expenses, as well as formats for financial statements. The *Uniform System of Accounts for Restaurants* provides a common language for the restaurant industry, so operators can compare the performance of their restaurant with other restaurants in the same chain, with similar establishments in different chains, or with industry performance as a whole.

The following sections discuss three important components of the *Uniform System of Accounts for Restaurants*: the balance sheet, the income statement, and the statement of cash flow.

The balance sheet. A restaurant's **balance sheet** is a financial statement that provides a snapshot of its financial position at a specific point in time. It presents a summary of a restaurant's assets, liabilities, and shareholders' equity and shows the balance between these three components. It is similar in many ways to a hotel's balance sheet (in fact, to any business's balance sheet), but there are differences. For example, although many restaurants accept credit cards as well as cash, they are actually cash businesses since the credit card companies rapidly redeem the charges. Therefore, unlike many other kinds of businesses, restaurants do not have high levels of accounts receivable on their balance sheets—that is, money due to them from customers.

The income statement. A restaurant **income statement**, also known as a profit and loss (P&L) statement, is a financial statement that summarizes the revenues, expenses, and resulting net income or loss of a restaurant over a specific period. It provides a detailed breakdown of a restaurant's financial performance, specifically its ability to generate profits. Whereas a hotel has a number of services for sale, a restaurant basically sells only food and, in some cases, alcoholic beverages. (There are exceptions, of course, such as theme restaurants, which may also sell T-shirts, caps, and other souvenirs; and restaurants with gift shops.) Hence, the income statement generally is uncomplicated and relatively easy to understand.

Exhibit 5.4 shows an income statement for the fictional Key Biscayne Restaurant. Note the division of sales into food and beverage sales. (Food sales include sales of nonalcoholic beverages; beverage sales are sales of alcoholic beverages.) The cost of sales is also divided into food and beverage categories, representing the cost of the food and beverages sold to guests. "Merchandise & Other" includes income derived

from gift shop sales, service charges, cover and minimum charges, and banquet room rentals. Although this other income can be profitable, it is usually not very significant in foodservice operations. The "Labor" expense line relates to the entire operation, divided into "Management," "Staff," and "Employee Benefits" categories.

"Noncontrollable Expenses" relate to the fixed costs of the restaurant, such as rent, real estate taxes, insurance on the building and its contents, and equipment leases. The levels of these expenses do not vary with sales, as labor and other controllable expenses do—with the exception of rent on the land or building(s), which may contain a percentage clause related to sales. (For example, the rent may be $20,000 per year plus 2 percent of gross sales.)

The cash flow statement. A restaurant **cash flow statement** is a financial statement that tracks the inflow and outflow of cash from a restaurant over a specific period. It provides insights into the sources and uses of cash, allowing owners and stakeholders to understand how cash is being generated and utilized within the business. Cash receipts and cash payments are organized into operating, investing, and financing activities. An example of cash flow from operating activities is the inflow of cash from customers and the outflow of cash paid to suppliers. Investing activities include the outflow of cash to purchase new kitchen equipment and the inflow of selling unused equipment. Borrowing funds to finance the operation of the restaurant is a cash inflow financing activity, while the repayment of loans or payment of dividends to investors is a cash outflow.

Operational Controls

Budgeting. Budgeting—the forecasting of revenues, expenses, and profits—is another tool managers must use to track a restaurant's performance and make necessary adjustments. The headquarters of many chain restaurants downloads the sales figures from each restaurant in the chain on a daily basis, using a process called "polling." Managers at headquarters then compare actual sales with forecasted sales and take appropriate action. If sales are down, management can increase advertising, lower prices, add promotional

Exhibit 5.4 Sample Income Statement

Key Biscayne Restaurant

Income Statement

Month Ending January 31, 20XX

	Amounts	Percentage*
Sales:		
Food	$ 577,823	77.9%
Beverages	149,092	20.1
Merchandise & Other	–14,835	2.0
Total Sales	741,750	100.0
Cost of Sales:		
Food	184,900	32.0
Beverages	45,736	30.7
Merchandise & Other	5,934	40.0
Total Cost of Sales	236,570	31.9
Labor:		
Management	74,175	10.0
Staff	133,465	18.0
Employee Benefits	45,900	6.2
Total Labor	253,540	34.2
Prime Cost	490,110	66.1
Other Controllable Expenses:		
Direct Operating Expenses	51,923	7.0
Music & Entertainment	6,676	0.9
Marketing	17,802	2.4
Utilities	18,544	2.5
General & Administrative Expenses	40,055	5.4
Repairs & Maintenance	12,610	1.7
Total Other Controllable Expenses	147,610	19.9
Controllable Income	104,030	14.0
Noncontrollable Expenses:		
Occupancy Costs	44,505	6.0
Equipment Leases	3,704	0.5
Depreciation & Amortization	11,126	1.5
Total Noncontrollable Expenses	59,335	8.0
Restaurant Operating Income	44,698	6.0
Corporate Overhead	2,225	0.3
Interest Expense	742	0.1
Other (Income)/Expense	1,480	0.2
Income before Income Taxes	40,331	5.4

*All percentages are calculated as a percentage of Total Sales except Food, Beverages, and Merchandise & Other Costs, which are based on their respective sales.

items to the menu, or take other steps. Without standards and budgeting procedures, restaurant managers allow difficult situations to develop past the point where anything can be done, and financial disaster becomes an almost certainty.

Many management experts feel that budgeting for the first year of operation for any foodservice enterprise is as much an art as a science. The reason, of course, is that the venture is new—there are no sales-history records on which to base forecasts of the number of guests to expect and the expenses that are likely to be incurred. If, however, a new restaurant is a franchise restaurant, the franchisor can assist its managers in coming up with a first-year budget based on the franchisor's experience with similar restaurants in the chain. Entrepreneurs starting independent restaurants can make use of information from the annual *State of the Restaurant Industry* report issued by the National Restaurant Association and Deloitte (the audit, consulting, and financial advisory firm). The restaurants in the report are grouped according to whether they offer full service or limited service, and the full-service restaurants are further segmented into average-check-per-person groupings (under $15, $15 to $24.99, and $25 and over). Once a restaurant has been running for a year or more and has a track record, the forecaster's work becomes easier.

Since food is the primary tangible item for sale in a restaurant, the procedures related to menu planning, the acquisition of food products, and the processing of food through storage, production, and service are important elements of a restaurant's control system. Equally important is control over labor costs.

The cost of food sold plus payroll costs and employee benefits (such as paid vacation, sick leave, employee meals, and bonuses) constitute the largest costs of operation. Together they are known as **prime costs**, representing approximately 60 percent of sales. While all expenses must be controlled, prime costs are management's major concern.

In the following sections, we will discuss strategies for controlling food, labor, and beverage costs.

Controlling Food Costs. Food cost is defined as the cost of food used in the production of a menu item. To control food costs, most restaurants use a system of control points that are linked in a cycle similar to the one shown in Exhibit 5.5. A problem anywhere in the food cost control cycle can weaken the operation's control over food costs. Let's take a closer look at each of the cycle's control points.

Menu planning. Once a restaurant is in operation, ongoing market research is needed to update the existing menu or develop a new one. Such research includes periodic analyses of menu items sold. Computerized POS systems make this analysis easier. Sales of menu items can be tracked by meal period or, if necessary, by the hour. This information can help menu planners develop a menu guests will like. (The choice of menu items is not unlimited, however; menu planners must keep in mind their operation's concept, equipment,

Exhibit 5.5   Food Cost Control Cycle

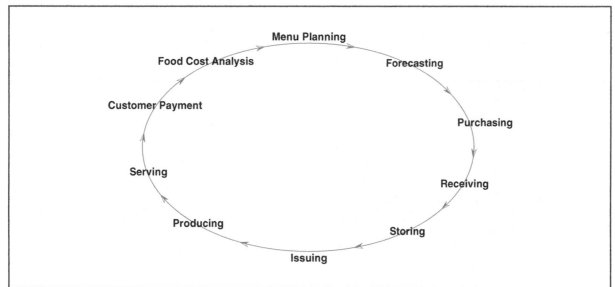

staff, and budget.) With such research in hand, the planner can remove menu items that are not selling and replace them with items that may prove more popular.

To achieve an optimal mix of popular and profitable menu items, restaurant managers perform a menu analysis. The following discussion is not intended to give you a detailed understanding of menu analysis; its purpose is to introduce you to the subject and acquaint you with some of the methods used in the industry.

There are a number of ways to analyze a menu. The earliest was proposed by Jack Miller, who used a "cost percentage" scheme that suggests that the best menu items ("winners") are those that achieve the lowest food cost percentage and the highest popularity.[10] A second method, proposed by Michael Kasavana and Donald Smith of the Boston Consulting Group, places all menu items into a chart consisting of four labeled sections: stars, plowhorses, puzzles, and dogs. Under this system, the best items (**stars**) are those that produce the highest **contribution margin** (the menu item's selling price minus the cost of the food that went into preparing the item) and the largest sales volume.[11] **Plowhorses**, on the other hand, are popular menu items with a low contribution margin. Conversely, **puzzles** are unpopular menu items with a high contribution margin, and **dogs** are unpopular menu items with a low contribution margin (see Exhibit 5.6).

A third method, suggested by David V. Pavesic, states that the best items, the **primes**, are those with a low food cost and a high contribution margin, which is weighted by sales volume.[12] All of these methods rely on averages to separate the winners from the losers.

David K. Hayes and Lynn Huffman suggested a fourth method that creates an individual P&L statement for each menu item. Their system calculates the P&L for each item by allocating all variable and fixed costs incurred in the restaurant among the items on the menu. Variable costs are those that change when business volume changes (e.g., costs for servers or table linens). A fixed cost is an item, such as insurance, that does not vary according to volume. The best menu items, according to Hayes and Huffman, are those that contribute the greatest profit.

Finally, Mohamed E. Bayou, professor of accounting at the University of Michigan-Dearborn, and Lee B. Bennett, an experienced restaurant-chain controller, proposed a method (see Exhibit 5.7) that begins by analyzing the profitability of the restaurant as a whole and then the profitability of each of its meal segments (breakfast, lunch, dinner, and catering). Once this is done, a margin for each menu category, such as appetizers, entrées, and desserts, is calculated. From there, a margin for each item within the category is established. On the surface, this procedure sounds complicated, but when Bayou and Bennett surveyed the managers of 103 table-service restaurants in southeastern Michigan, they found that 55 percent used an approach similar to their "segment-contribution analysis" method.[13]

Professor Stephen Miller suggested that "the proliferation of personal computers and low-cost, easy-to-use software means virtually any organization can quickly and easily perform menu analyses anytime at little or no additional expense."[14] Miller called his system "the Simplified Menu-Cost Spreadsheet." Under Miller's system, a spreadsheet listing all ingredients and their costs is first set up, then the cost of menu items and side dishes is calculated. From there, you can calculate your **gross profit** (selling price minus cost of food) based on your established selling price. The **food cost percentage** is a financial metric used in the restaurant industry to measure the proportion of a restaurant's revenue that is spent on the cost of ingredients and food items used in menu preparation. It is calculated by dividing the total cost of food by selling price. A higher food cost percentage means you will have a lower contribution margin, and vice versa. An example of a menu-cost spreadsheet is shown in Exhibit 5.8.

Exhibit 5.6 Menu Engineering Matrix

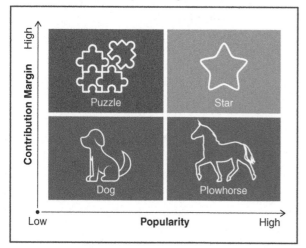

Exhibit 5.7   Levels of Profitability Analysis

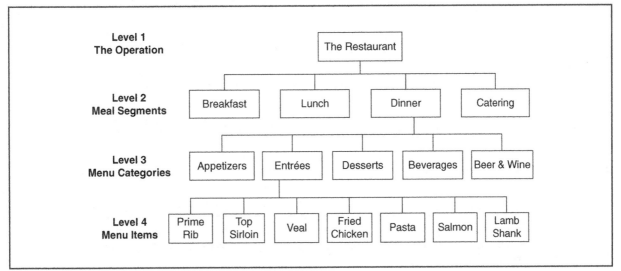

Source: Mohamed E. Bayou and Lee B. Bennett, "Profitability Analysis of Table-Service Restaurants," *Cornell Quarterly*, April 1992, p. 53.

Exhibit 5.8   Sample Menu-Cost Spreadsheet

Menu Item	Cost per Entrée	Cost of Side Dishes	Total Cost	Selling Price	Food Cost %	Gross Profit
Beef Kabob	$ 8.55	$3.10	$11.65	$24.00	48.54%	$12.35
Chicken Kiev	6.62	2.48	9.10	20.00	45.50	10.90
Eggplant Parm	5.07	2.79	7.86	19.00	41.36	11.14
Filet Mignon	15.34	3.02	18.36	46.00	39.91	27.64
Fried Shrimp	7.78	2.41	10.19	22.00	46.31	11.81
Lamb Kabob	10.16	3.10	13.26	28.00	47.35	14.74
London Broil	8.79	2.45	11.24	27.00	41.62	15.76
Perch	7.52	2.78	10.30	26.00	39.62	15.70
Pork Chops	7.48	2.41	9.89	24.00	41.20	14.11
Prime Rib	13.26	2.92	16.18	35.00	46.22	18.82
Salmon	11.57	3.10	14.67	28.00	52.39	13.30
Scallops	12.65	3.10	15.75	32.00	49.21	16.25
Strip Steak	9.14	2.67	11.81	26.00	45.42	14.19
Veg Platter	7.25	1.84	9.09	21.00	43.28	11.91

Forecasting. Once the menu is created and a restaurant has been open long enough for a sales pattern to be established, management should forecast total expected business by meal period and menu item in order to determine purchasing needs and plan production. Accurate forecasting keeps food costs down because food is not purchased to be left sitting in a storeroom, perhaps to spoil before it is needed.

Purchasing. In any foodservice operation, the goal in purchasing is to keep food costs at a planned,

Exhibit 5.9   Sample Purchase Specification Format

_____

(name of food and beverage operation)

1. Product name:

2. Product used for:

> Clearly indicate product use (such as olive garnish for beverage, hamburger patty or grill-fry for sandwich, etc.).

3. Product general description:

> Provide general quality information about desired product. For example, "Iceberg lettuce; heads to be green and firm without spoilage, excessive dirt, or damage. No more than 10 outer leaves. Packed 24 heads per case."

4. Detailed description:

> Purchaser should state other factors that help to clearly identify desired product. Examples of specific factors, which vary by product being described, may include:
>
> | | | |
> |---|---|---|
> | ■ Geographic origin | ■ Grade | ■ Density |
> | ■ Variety | ■ Product size | ■ Specific gravity |
> | ■ Type | ■ Portion size | ■ Container size |
> | ■ Style | ■ Brand name | ■ Edible yield, trim |

5. Product test procedures:

> Test procedures can occur at the time the product is received and/or after product is prepared/used. For example, products that should be at a refrigerated temperature upon delivery can be tested with a thermometer. Portion-cut meat patties can be randomly weighed. Lettuce packed 24 heads per case can be counted.

6. Special instructions and requirements:

> Any additional information needed to clearly indicate quality expectations can be included here. Examples include bidding procedures, if applicable, labeling and/or packaging requirements, and special delivery and service requirements.

budgeted level by obtaining the right product for the best price. To accomplish this, purchase specifications must be developed for all food items used in the restaurant so bids based on those specifications can be obtained from suppliers. A **purchase specification** is a detailed description of a food item for ordering purposes (see Exhibit 5.9). The description might include size by weight ("3 lb. chicken") or by volume ("#2 can"); grade ("Rib of Beef—USDA Prime" or "Peaches—Fancy"); and packaging ("Iceberg Lettuce—24 count" or "Eggs—30 dozen").

According to Lendal H. Kotschevar, author of *Management by Menu* and other foodservice industry texts, most food specifications should include the following:

- Name of the item;

- Grade of the item, brand, or other quality information;

- Packaging method, package size, and special requirements;

- Basis for price—by the pound, case, piece, or dozen; and

- Miscellaneous factors required to get the right item, such as the number of days beef should be aged, the region in which the item is produced, and the requirement that all items be inspected for wholesomeness.[15]

Purchase specifications enable the restaurant's purchaser to communicate to suppliers an exact description of what is needed to meet the restaurant's standards. Veteran operators are able to establish these specifications based on need and personal experience. Beginners and others who would like assistance can turn to sources such as the U.S. Department of Agriculture at https://www.usda.gov.

Once you have developed purchase specifications, the next task is to determine how much of each item to purchase. As explained earlier, the best way to accomplish this is to forecast the number of guests you expect and identify the menu items they are most likely to order. Delivery schedules also play a part in determining how much to order. Delivery schedules depend in part on the restaurant's location in relation to its suppliers—the greater the distance, the costlier the deliveries. Many restaurants order large quantities of the items they can stock up on (such as nonperishable items)

so fewer deliveries are needed. Restaurants typically like to receive fresh fish and produce daily; meats twice weekly; canned and frozen items weekly or biweekly; and nonperishable items, such as napkins or sugar packets, quarterly or even semiannually. The level of inventory already on hand and the available storage space are other obvious factors in determining how much to order. Computers make it easier to track inventory levels closely and make rate-of-consumption information on individual items readily available. Once this is done, supplies can be ordered directly on the Internet.

Receiving. Acceptable receiving procedures mandate that the employees receiving the food items clearly understand the food specifications adopted by the restaurant. Receiving clerks help keep food costs down by verifying that:

- The items delivered are those ordered and correspond to the quantity on the supplier's invoice.

- The quoted price and the invoice price are the same.

- The quality and size of the items delivered match the restaurant's specifications.

In addition, receiving clerks handle the initial processing of invoices and deliver the food to the kitchen or to storage areas. Some operators favor a **blind receiving** system. With this system, suppliers give the receiving clerk a list of items being delivered but not the quantities or weights. This forces the clerk to count or weigh the incoming products and record their findings on the invoice. Later these figures are compared with (1) the supplier's invoice received by the accounting office, and (2) the restaurant's purchase order.

Receiving clerks must check large shipments on a random basis for quality and count. Items that do not meet the restaurant's standards are generally returned and a credit is recorded on the invoice. Those items that are acceptable are placed in storage, ready to be used as needed.

Controlling the receiving process is an important part of keeping food costs down because receiving is an area in which dishonest employees or suppliers can take advantage of employers. For example, suppliers may deliver a lower-grade product than ordered with the hope that it will pass unnoticed or use extra packing material to increase the weight of goods delivered.

Storing. Food storage facilities consist of dry storerooms, refrigerators, and freezers. Ideally, food storage areas should:

■ Have adequate capacity

■ Be close to receiving and food preparation areas

■ Have suitable temperature and humidity levels

■ Be secure from unauthorized personnel

■ Be protected from vermin and insects

In addition, careful consideration should be given to storage shelves and the arrangement of items within the storage facility. Obviously, the items used most frequently should be stored near the entrance. Sometimes goods are stored on shelves by groups (e.g., vegetables might be one group) and then alphabetically within those groups (asparagus, broccoli, cauliflower, corn, etc.).

A standard inventory system of **first-in, first-out (FIFO)** is almost always adopted. With this system, older products (those received first) are stored in front so that they will be used first; newer shipments are stored behind them for later use. Proper storage reduces spoilage and waste.

Issuing. Formal procedures for transferring food from storage to production or service areas are an essential part of any control system. The purpose of such procedures is to keep track of inventory usage and make sure only authorized employees take food from storage.

In some instances, a small amount of food goes directly from the receiving area to the kitchen or dining room, bypassing the issuing system used to requisition food from storage areas. This is known as a **direct purchase**. Most direct purchases consist of items that will be used that day, such as fresh-baked goods and fresh fish. Foodservice operations can calculate their daily food costs by adding together direct purchases and storeroom issues.

The bulk of the inventory received in each shipment goes to various storage areas. Items from storage are issued using a requisition system. A **requisition form** identifies the person who ordered the items and the type, amount, and price of each item. Sometimes the area the items are going to—for example, the pantry or kitchen range area—is identified. Although many operations manually calculate

the cost of requisitioned food, the trend is to use computerized systems to calculate this cost. Some operators track food by categories such as meat, fish, fresh produce, or staples. This enhances control by showing how the restaurant uses specific food categories and, within each category, specific food items.

Modern foodservice operations with relatively uncomplicated menus have been the first to adopt computerized issuing. For computerized issuing to work, standard recipes must be used. When food is requisitioned for a specific menu item, the computer determines the quantity to be issued based on the standard recipe. Computerized issuing systems work best in hospitals, schools, and other institutional foodservice operations that prepare large numbers of the same meal types. Few hotels have adopted the system due to their many different restaurant concepts and menus. But as new software becomes available, this technology is expected to spread.

Producing. Standard recipes are essential in controlling food costs. With a standard recipe, managers can calculate exactly how much it should cost to produce each menu item. As a result, managers have something to compare actual costs with and can take into consideration the cost of producing menu items when setting menu prices. Standard recipes are also important in controlling labor costs since employees using such recipes require less training and supervision.

Standard recipes play a major role in customer satisfaction. By using standard recipes, operators are able to provide consistency in quality and quantity no matter who is in the kitchen. Standard recipes enable restaurants to ensure that every time a repeat customer orders a particular item, the same product and portion will be served.

Serving. If service is not friendly and efficient, all other efforts in the control cycle are in vain because most guests will stop going to a restaurant where they receive poor service. Well-trained food servers who know the menu and have good people skills can help overcome production problems. However, if servers are not attentive to the needs of guests, the best efforts of the chef and others in the kitchen will not be enough to produce a satisfactory experience. It is a mistake to assume that operations that do not offer table service need not be concerned with their level

Servers have a tremendous impact on guests' experience—and the bottom line.

of service. Even the food servers in a cafeteria serving line help set the mood for guests.

Customer payment. Obviously, a restaurant cannot recoup its food costs if customer payments are not collected. There is no one universal payment system—systems vary from operation to operation. Here are some of the ways payment can be settled:

- The guest pays a cashier who tabulates the food order (as in a cafeteria).

- The guest pays an order-taker/cashier who rings up the order on a cash register before the food is delivered (as in quick service operations).

- The server writes the order and prices on a check, or the order is machine-printed and priced on a check. The check is then settled in one of the following ways: (1) the guest pays the cashier; (2) the guest pays the server, who pays the cashier; (3) the guest pays the server, who maintains a bank or carries a mobile payment collection device that is connected wirelessly to the restaurant's POS system; or (4) the guest scans the QR code on the check and uses their own contactless payment system, such as Apple Pay, to pay the bill.

The goal of any cash control system is to ensure that what comes out of the kitchen is in fact served, recorded as a sale, and paid for. In establishments where the server takes the order, the server writes the order on a check. The original is kept for presentation to the guest for payment at the end of the meal and will eventually be placed in the cash register. A duplicate is carried to the kitchen so production personnel know what to prepare. As mentioned earlier, computerized POS systems can help servers perform this process faster and with less legwork. Servers input the order into a handheld or stationary POS terminal in the dining room. The order is electronically transmitted to the kitchen, where it is shown on a video display monitor or printed by a small work-station printer. Whether checks are recorded manually or by computer, control records (i.e., the machine data, the check, and the duplicate check) are created that can be reconciled at the end of the meal.

Food cost analysis. A common statistic used throughout the foodservice industry is the food cost percentage. This number represents the cost of food sold to guests in a given period (e.g., the month of June), divided by food sales for the same period.

To reach the **cost of food sold**, one must deduct meals that are consumed but not sold, such as complimentary meals. The cost of food sold is based on beginning inventories, closing inventories, and food purchases for the period between the two inventories, minus complimentary meals. The following figures illustrate how this works:

Beginning Inventory	$20,000
Add Food Purchases	+ 15,000
Total	$35,000
Deduct Closing Inventory	– 4,000
Cost of Food Consumed	$31,000
Deduct Employee Meals	($1,500)
and Complimentary Meals ($500)	– 2,000
COST OF FOOD SOLD	$29,000

Assume food sales for this period (e.g., the month of June) were $100,000. To compute the food cost percentage, the formula is:

$$\frac{\$29{,}000 \text{ (cost of food sold)}}{\$100{,}000 \text{ (food sales)}} = 0.29 \times 100 = 29\%$$

In this example, 29 percent reflects the actual cost of food sold (expressed as a percentage of food sales) during June. This percentage has little value unless it can be compared to a goal or an acceptable food cost percentage range established by management.

How do managers come up with a food cost goal or an acceptable range within which food costs should fall? They often use a standard cost system based on standard recipes. Since each standard recipe is an exact formula for making X number of menu items, the exact or standard cost of preparing a menu item can be computed. Continuing with our example, the restaurant manager can total the standard costs for all the menu items sold during June, divide this figure by the total menu item sales for June, multiply by 100, and come up with the **standard food cost percentage**, which would match the actual food cost percentage for June if everything worked exactly as it should have. Assuming the manager assessed standard food costs in June at $27,000, the standard food cost percentage would be calculated as follows:

$$\frac{\$27{,}000 \text{ (standard food costs)}}{\$100{,}000 \text{ (food sales)}} = 0.27 \times 100 = 27\%$$

In this case, the standard food cost percentage for June is 27 percent. The actual food cost percentage for June was 29 percent—2 percentage points higher than the standard. Since a standard food cost represents the ideal cost that

management can expect if everything goes exactly as planned, the actual food cost percentage is almost always higher than the standard food cost percentage. Management at each restaurant must determine an acceptable limit for actual food costs. For example, one operation may set a limit of 2 percentage points over standard food costs. This means that if the standard food cost percentage for a period of time is 22 percent, an actual food cost percentage of 24 percent or below for that time period is acceptable.

Each individual menu item has a standard food cost percentage and, of course, some menu items have a higher food cost percentage than others. However, it is unwise to decide to keep an item on the menu or add a new one by looking at the item's food cost percentage alone. The following comparison between two menu items shows why:

	8 oz. Filet Mignon	Smoked Salmon
Menu Price	$24.00	$14.00
Standard Food Cost %	52%	25%
Gross Profit	$11.52	$10.50

The smoked salmon has a lower food cost percentage, which is desirable, but the filet mignon provides a higher gross profit. Obviously, it's preferable to sell the filet mignon, despite the higher costs associated with it, because its gross profit gives the operation $1.02 more ($11.52–$10.50) to cover other costs and add to profits. Another consideration is the cost of labor that goes into preparing the menu item. An 8-ounce filet mignon may have a higher food cost, but the labor associated with preparing it is lower than the labor associated with smoking a whole salmon.

The food cost percentage is a crucial indicator of a restaurant's financial performance and operational efficiency. A lower food cost percentage generally indicates better control over ingredient costs and a higher potential for profitability. It allows restaurant owners and managers to monitor and manage food costs, analyze trends over time, make informed pricing decisions, identify potential cost-saving opportunities, and evaluate the financial impact of menu changes or promotions.

Controlling Labor Costs. The cost of payroll and employee benefits averages about 30 percent of sales for most full-service restaurants. This is a high figure when you consider that restaurants have more entry-level and minimum-wage employees than most other businesses. Foodservice is highly labor-intensive, and quality service on any level demands that employees be well-trained, efficient, and productive. Quick service restaurants and cafeterias have lower payroll costs primarily because of their methods of service and, in the case of quick service restaurants, their limited menu and production-line system of food preparation. Labor shortages in the restaurant industry have also resulted in the adoption of new service styles. Once you may have expected to sit down at a cool new restaurant and be waited on; now it is not unusual to get in a line, place your order, and pay before you find an open table.

Commercial foodservice establishments have a unique problem in controlling payroll. The amount of money an operation must allocate to payroll depends on two factors: (1) the rates of pay for employees, and (2) the time required to do a given job—that is, productivity. While payroll costs escalate every year, productivity does not. Indeed, many full-service restaurants prepare and serve food today with the same type of equipment and in the same way as did restaurateurs many years ago. (Even quick service restaurants with new technology will always need a base staff.) As a result, the industry, for the most part, has responded to higher payroll costs by raising menu prices rather than increasing employee productivity, adhering to the conventional wisdom that you cannot raise productivity when you are dealing with low-paid personnel.

You also can't raise productivity if there aren't enough customers in the restaurant. Even the hardest-working employees can't be productive if there is no one to serve. And even the best managers can only trim payroll costs to a certain point because a minimum number of employees must be on hand when a restaurant opens, even when business is projected to be terrible. Therefore, keeping payroll costs in line depends in part on having a concept and menu that appeal to the target market and having a marketing program strong enough to keep guest demand high.

Controlling Beverage Costs. In recent years, the dangers of excessive alcohol use have gained greater recognition in the United States and elsewhere. Nevertheless, wine, malt beverages (beer, ale, stout), and distilled spirits—the major categories of alcoholic beverages—are still an important part of restaurant revenue. Alcoholic beverages account for 10 to 15 percent of sales in casual dining chains and 20 to 30 percent in upscale restaurants. These sales are extremely profitable because of the high markup on beverages. In fine dining restaurants, a markup of 100 percent for a bottle of wine is not unusual. Most drinks are easy to pour or mix, and the labor and beverage costs combined represent a small part of the sales price.

For restaurant managers, purchasing alcoholic beverages is relatively uncomplicated compared to purchasing food. Purchase specifications are limited to brand (Dewars White Label scotch, Budweiser beer, Robert Mondavi wine); size (liters, quarts, fifths, kegs); and, in the case of wine, vintages. Competitive bidding is usually not necessary. Some states, known as monopoly or control states, set beverage prices and allow beverage purchases to be made only from state-owned stores. Most states, however, are license states. In these, operators can buy from private wholesalers licensed by the state. Even in these states, state laws are typically designed to limit price wars, and prices do not vary a great deal among wholesalers. Most license states publish a monthly master list of wholesalers in the state, the beverages they carry, and the prices they charge.

Receiving is also straightforward. For example, weighing or checking for wholesomeness is not necessary. The receiving clerk simply verifies that what was ordered—brand, size, amount, and vintage—is what was delivered and billed on the invoice.

With beverages, secure storage is of prime importance. Access to beverage storage areas should be limited to authorized personnel. All items should be grouped by brand. Wine bottles should be stored on their side or bottom-up to keep the cork moist. Temperature control during storage is crucial. For example, the ideal storage temperature for red wines is 65°F (18.3°C) and for white wines 45°F to 50°F (7.2°C to 10°C).

Issuing is generally done by requisition. If a restaurant has more than one bar, separate requisitions are written by personnel at each bar. Some operations stamp their liquor bottles with their name or logo to prevent unscrupulous bartenders from bringing in their own bottles, pouring drinks from them, and pocketing the money.

In most operations, a perpetual inventory of beverage items is maintained either manually or by computer. A **perpetual inventory system** is a record that shows what should be on hand in the storeroom at any one time. It is compiled from daily invoices and requisitions by adding each day's purchases and subtracting each day's issues. Of course, inventory levels should be checked by a physical count on a regular basis, usually monthly. The perpetual inventory system is particularly helpful for purchasing managers since it tracks inventory usage on a daily, weekly, and monthly basis.

Control over individual drink sales may take one or more forms. Many operators have employed automated systems with electronic or mechanical devices attached to each bottle that record every drink poured. The advantages are obvious. The manager or owner can easily determine how many drinks have been sold and thus what the receipts should be. The system reduces loss from spillage and overpouring and prevents a bartender from underpouring or offering complimentary drinks to friends. The disadvantage of an automated system is that it impedes those bartenders who make pouring drinks a theatrical presentation.

Managers can control the amount of beverages on hand at a bar by establishing a "par." A **bar's par** is the amount of each type of beverage that managers want available behind the bar. It is based largely on expected consumption. Levels are set high enough so the bar will not run out of an item during a bartender's shift, but not so high that theft is encouraged. At the end of each shift, empty bottles are replaced so the bar's beverage stock is at par for the next shift.

Beverage control is crucial to running any establishment that sells beverages to customers. Product consistency and the threat of theft are the primary areas of concern. Only through proper controls can these concerns be addressed and customer satisfaction and profitability ensured.

Knowledge Check

1. What are the benefits of using online reservations systems and computer-based food systems for patrons and restaurant staff?

2. What control points make up the food cost control cycle?

Foodservice operations that are organized for success focus on their guests. Since guest preferences and tastes constantly change, a restaurant's management team should keep track of local and national trends and conduct ongoing research of its own customers to make sure that the restaurant's concept and menu reflect current preferences.

A restaurant's ambience is also important to its success. Décor, lighting, furnishings, and other features should all be a natural extension of a restaurant's concept.

A third important element of a successful restaurant is its menu. A good menu offers customers what they want, is based on standard recipes that can be prepared and served by the restaurant's staff, takes into account equipment limitations, and lists a variety of items. Menus can be categorized as either fixed or cyclical. Menus can be further categorized as breakfast, lunch, dinner, or specialty menus. A menu is primarily a sales tool that should be constructed and presented with marketing in mind.

Pricing menu items correctly is also a key element of organizing for success. Menu prices are related to costs and investment. Basic considerations when setting menu prices include the type of operation, the customers' perception of the price/value relationship, the competition, and the desired level of profit.

Sound financial management is achieved through efficient budgeting, using a system such as the *Uniform System of Accounts for Restaurants*. Components of this system include a balance sheet and an income statement. A successful operation keeps its costs within budgeted levels. Prime costs are the most important costs for management to control. Prime costs consist of the cost of food and the cost of payroll and related employee benefits.

There are many control points in the food cost control cycle that help restaurant managers keep food costs down. The first is menu planning. A correctly planned menu has few, if any, unpopular menu items. This helps control food costs by reducing or eliminating the need to purchase food for unpopular menu items; such food may spoil and have to be thrown away before it is used. Accurate forecasting also helps reduce food costs because unnecessary food is not ordered. A restaurant's purchaser can minimize food costs by obtaining the right products for the best price. Purchase specifications play an important role in this. If suppliers have a restaurant's purchase specifications in hand as they're formulating a bid, their bids are more likely to be truly comparable since they are all basing their bids on the same criteria.

Receiving procedures can also affect food cost. What is received must be verified and compared with what was ordered.

Storing and issuing also require attention if food cost is to be adequately controlled. Storage facilities must protect the operation's inventory from deterioration and theft. Issuing procedures allow managers to keep track of inventory and calculate a daily food cost figure. Daily food cost is calculated by adding together direct purchases and storeroom issues.

Standard recipes that yield standard portions reduce food waste. Standard recipes also reduce food and labor costs. The cost of preparing menu items can only be calculated accurately when standard recipes are used.

Service and cash control concerns include the manner in which customer payments are handled. This varies by type of establishment, but the goal of all cash control systems is to ensure that what comes out of the kitchen is in fact served, recorded, and paid for. Getting instant reporting from computerized POS systems can make a substantial difference to restaurant operators. Computers connect the dining room to the kitchen and generate customer checks, sales reports, and inventory lists.

Food cost calculation is essential for the operation of a successful and profitable establishment. A restaurant's overall food cost percentage for a given period is calculated by dividing the cost of food sold during the period by total food sales during the same period. Each menu item has its own food cost percentage and contribution margin. Although, as a rule, a low food cost percentage is desirable for a menu item because a high contribution margin results. Some items with high food cost percentages also have high contribution margins. Therefore, operators

CHAPTER SUMMARY

should keep contribution margins as well as food cost percentages in mind when making decisions about whether to drop or add menu items.

Payroll expenses, including employee benefits, represent about 30 percent of sales in the foodservice industry, but payroll costs vary considerably by type of establishment.

Alcoholic beverages account for approximately 29 percent of sales in medium-priced full-service restaurants—sales that have a high profit margin. Purchasing beverages is fairly uncomplicated since purchase specifications are largely limited to brands and sizes, and competitive bidding is not necessary. Receiving is also straightforward. Issuing is usually tracked by a perpetual inventory system that shows what ought to be on hand in the beverage storeroom. These records should be checked by taking a physical inventory on a regular basis, usually monthly. Finally, a bar par, based mostly on expected consumption, is established at each bar.

ambience—The décor, lighting, furnishings, and other factors that create a feeling about or an identity for a restaurant.

balance sheet—A financial statement that provides a snapshot of a restaurant's financial position at a specific point in time. It presents a summary of a restaurant's assets, liabilities, and shareholders' equity and shows the balance between these three components.

bar's par—The amount of each type of beverage established for behind-the-bar storage, based on expected consumption.

blind receiving—A receiving system in which the supplier gives the receiving clerk a list of items being delivered but not the quantities or weights, thereby forcing the clerk to count or weigh the incoming products and record the results. These results are later compared with the supplier's invoice.

budgeting—The forecasting of revenues, expenses, and profits.

cash flow statement—A financial statement that tracks the inflow and outflow of cash from a restaurant over a specific period. It provides insights into the sources and uses of cash, allowing owners and stakeholders to understand how cash is being generated and utilized within the business.

contribution margin—A food or beverage item's selling price minus the cost of the ingredients used to prepare the item.

cost of food sold—The cost of the food sold to a guest. It is calculated based on beginning inventories, closing inventories, and food purchases for the period between the two inventories, minus complimentary meals.

direct purchase—Food sent directly from the receiving area to the kitchen or dining room rather than to a storage area.

dogs—Unpopular menu items with a low contribution margin.

financial controls—Tools that managers use to measure the worth of a restaurant and its level of sales, costs, and profitability.

first-in, first-out (FIFO)—An inventory method used to rotate and issue stored food, so items that have been in storage the longest are used first.

fixed menu—A menu with a set list of items that is used for several months or longer before it is changed. Also known as a static menu.

food cost—The cost of food used in the production of a menu item.

food cost percentage—A financial metric used in the restaurant industry to measure the proportion of a restaurant's revenue that is spent on the cost of ingredients and food items used in menu preparation. It is calculated by dividing the total cost of food by selling price.

gross profit—Selling price minus the cost of food.

income statement—Also known as a profit and loss (P&L) statement, it summarizes the revenues, expenses, and resulting net income or loss of a restaurant over a specific period. It provides a detailed breakdown of a restaurant's financial performance, specifically its ability to generate profits.

perpetual inventory system—A system for tracking inventory by keeping a running balance of inventory quantities—that is, recording all additions to and subtractions from stock.

plowhorses—Popular menu items with a low contribution margin.

prime costs—The cost of food sold plus payroll costs (including employee benefits). These are a restaurant's highest costs.

primes—Menu items with a low food cost and a high contribution margin.

purchase specification—A detailed description—for ordering purposes—of the quality, size, weight, and other characteristics desired for a particular item.

puzzles—Unpopular menu items with a high contribution margin.

requisition form—A written order used by employees that identifies the type, amount, and value of items needed from storage.

KEY TERMS

specialty menu—A menu that differs from the typical breakfast, lunch, or dinner menu. Specialty menus are usually designed for holidays and other special events or for specific guest groups. Examples include children's, beverage, dessert, and banquet menus.

standard recipe—A formula for producing a food or beverage item specifying ingredients, the required quantity of each ingredient, preparation procedures, portion size and portioning equipment, garnish, and any other information necessary to prepare the item.

stars—Popular menu items with high contribution margins.

1. Which is the most important success factor for a restaurant?
   a. Guest satisfaction and loyalty
   b. High check average
   c. Menu organization
   d. Location

2. Why should restaurateurs use national surveys as guides only?
   a. The information becomes quickly outdated.
   b. The information may not apply to their region.
   c. The information focuses on nutrition only.
   d. The information focuses on national chains only.

3. Why is ambience an important success factor for a restaurant?
   a. It establishes a restaurant's identity and enhances the guest experience.
   b. It is the easiest thing to change based on customer preference.
   c. It is the main influence on menu conceptualization.
   d. It is the main determinant of guest satisfaction.

4. Which menu creation rule is essential for quality control?
   a. Match the menu to the staff's abilities.
   b. Give guests what they want.
   c. Keep nutrition in mind.
   d. Use standard recipes.

5. What is the main difference between fixed menus and cyclical menus?
   a. Fixed menus are typically used for several months. Cyclical menus change every day for a certain number of days.
   b. Fixed menus generate a low-check average. Cyclical menus generate a high-check average.
   c. Fixed menus provide variety. Cyclical menus follow strict dietary guidelines.
   d. Fixed menus offer new specials daily. Cyclical menus change seasonally.

6. What does a balance sheet show?
   a. The results of operations for a stated period of time
   b. A restaurant's financial position on any given day
   c. Estimated food costs
   d. Invoice payments

7. What appears on an income statement?
   a. Sales, expenses, and net income
   b. Forecasted sales and costs
   c. Payments and refunds
   d. Profit and loss

8. Which example best describes the FIFO method?
   a. Serving potato salad made on July 6 instead of potato salad made on July 1
   b. Using milk purchased on April 26 first and then using milk purchased on April 28
   c. Storing a fresh package of beef in a refrigerator in front of a six-day-old package of beef
   d. Uncorking a bottle of red wine produced in 2003 rather than a bottle produced in 1999

9. How many control points are in the food cost control cycle?
  a. 7
  b. 8
  c. 9
  d. 10

10. A purchase specification includes what information?
  a. Grade of an item
  b. Shape of an item
  c. Cleaning instructions
  d. Nutritional information

11. What is the formula for calculating standard food cost percentage?
  a. Food sales divided by standard food costs
  b. Standard food costs divided by food sales
  c. Food sales divided by cost of food waste
  d. Cost of food waste divided by food sales

12. What is the best method for controlling beverage stock at a bar?
  a. Train bartenders to use the 1-2-3 count method.
  b. Install cameras that monitor the bar.
  c. Do a nightly inventory.
  d. Establish a bar par.

SHORT-ANSWER QUESTIONS

1. How important is it for restaurants to keep track of local and national trends?

2. How could rising food costs affect a restaurant's menu?

MENUS AND MARKETING

A student-run café operated by the culinary program of a major university has just reopened after being closed during the COVID-19 pandemic in 2020. The members of the program's graduating class are in their final practicum course. As part of their course, the students and their senior instructor operate the café's back of the house Monday through Friday from 8 a.m. to 1 p.m. International student assistants have been hired to operate the café's front of house. The café features a large dining area for guests. Because of its location, the café's patrons include students, college staff and faculty, and outside visitors who walk by or work in neighboring buildings.

The course instructor created a small, fixed menu that consists of made-to-order hot sandwiches, premade cold sandwiches and salads, and warm pastries. The beverage menu includes bottled juices, sport drinks, water, and cans of soda. Made-to-order beverages include various coffee and tea selections. The cyclical menu offers a soup of the day, a hot lunch of the day, and other specialty items, such as vegan and vegetarian options. The cyclical menu rotates every week and features the same items until a new semester starts.

The café had a grand reopening, which featured a robot that provided table service to alleviate the lunch rush. But four months after the reopening, sales have declined by 30 percent. Since the café is a business of the university, it does minimal marketing. One major complaint of guests is that food items on the cyclical menu sell out one hour before the café closes. Additional complaints have included wait times for food, incorrect orders, and product consistency and quality (which has resulted in food waste of cold items). In addition, the robot has become nonoperational and the return on its investment has not been worthy.

Will business continue to decline if the café continues to operate in its current style?

DISCUSSION QUESTIONS

1. What are some success factors of the café?

2. What are key issues with the café's service and food?

3. What modifications could be made to the café's menu or service to improve operations?

Alex Kuk

Alex Kuk is a fourth-generation restaurateur who has dedicated his life to the hospitality industry, mentoring future generations and making a positive impact on the community through food and education. With a rich family legacy in the restaurant business, Kuk's journey began at a young age, working in his grandfather's restaurant, Wan's Mandarin House, then located near Miami's renowned Calle Ocho.

Driven by a passion for the industry, Kuk pursued higher education at the Chaplin School of Hospitality & Tourism Management at Florida International University. There, he earned bachelor's and master's degrees in hospitality management, immersing himself in comprehensive studies and gaining invaluable knowledge. During his time at FIU, Kuk played an integral role on the inaugural committee for the Food Network South Beach Wine and Food Festival, showcasing his commitment to the culinary world. Additionally, he served as an adjunct professor at FIU's Miami and Tianjin, China, campuses, imparting his wisdom and expertise to aspiring hospitality professionals.

Kuk's professional experience encompasses working at various renowned restaurants and hotels in the Miami area, including Houston's, Loews Miami Beach Hotel, and Sushi Maki. The breadth of his industry exposure has provided him with a comprehensive understanding of different culinary concepts and service standards.

In 2014, driven by a desire to create something of their own, Kuk and his business partner, Diego Ng, embarked on a new venture. They opened Temple Street Eatery in Fort Lauderdale, Florida, introducing a fast-casual dining concept that celebrates Asian American comfort food. With its focus on intangible service, seasonal ingredients, and constantly changing customer preferences, the hospitality business presents ongoing challenges. Kuk emphasizes the importance of attention to detail, as even the smallest aspects can significantly impact the overall experience for guests.

Despite his busy schedule, Kuk remains closely connected to his alma mater, serving as a member of the board of directors for the FIU Alumni Association. This role allows him to contribute to the growth and development of the next generation of hospitality professionals, supporting their journey to excellence.

You are the manager of a popular Italian restaurant in a bustling city. Your restaurant has always been known for its authentic Italian cuisine, great service, and lively atmosphere. However, you have recently received some negative feedback from customers regarding your restaurant's environmental practices.

One customer wrote on a review site that she was disappointed to see that your restaurant uses single-use plastic straws and utensils, and that many of the menu items contain ingredients that are not sustainably sourced. Another customer left a comment on social media expressing concern about the amount of food waste he witnessed while dining at your restaurant.

As a manager, you recognize the importance of environmental sustainability and want to address these concerns. However, you also know that making significant changes to your restaurant's practices could be expensive and time-consuming. You need to come up with a plan that will satisfy your customers while also being practical for your business.

What steps would you take to address these concerns? Would you consider making changes to your menu or sourcing practices? How would you communicate any changes to your customers, and would you expect pushback? How would you balance the desire to be environmentally responsible with the need to maintain profitability and keep your restaurant running smoothly?

6

UNDERSTANDING THE WORLD OF HOTELS

Chapter Outline

Learning Objectives

1. Briefly describe the dynamic hotel industry and summarize information about important hotel guest segments. (pp. 144–150)

2. Describe center-city, resort, suburban, highway, and airport hotels, including their services and facilities, and summarize their historical development. (pp. 151–156)

3. Explain various ways hotels can be owned and operated, distinguish chain hotels from independent hotels, and explain how hotels can be categorized by price. (pp. 156–161)

4. Describe the following hotel categories: boutique/lifestyle hotels, all-suite hotels, conference centers, timeshare properties, condominium hotels, seniors housing, and Airbnb. (pp. 161–166)

5. Outline the following steps in developing and planning new hotels: site selection, the feasibility study, and financing. (pp. 167–171)

KEY TERMS

airline-related guests

airport hotels

all-suite hotel

bleisure

boutique hotels

budget hotels

center-city hotels

condominium hotel

conference centers

construction financing loan

convention and association groups

corporate groups

corporate individuals

economy hotels

feasibility study

first-class/luxury hotels

franchise

franchisee

franchisor

government and military travelers

guest mix

hard costs

highway hotels

hotel chain

independent hotel

leisure travelers

lifestyle hotel

long-term stay/relocation guests

management company

mid-price hotels

permanent financing loan

regional getaway guests

resort hotels

segmenting

select-service hotels

seniors housing

soft brands

soft costs

suburban hotels

take-out

timeshare condominiums

tourist courts

This chapter examines the dynamic hotel industry. We will discuss types of hotel guests and the various types of hotels they patronize. You will learn about hotel branding concepts and some of the differences between chain and independent hotels. Major industry players will be identified so you can become familiar with the business philosophies of the most successful hotel companies. The growing trend of independent hotels joining or investing in a major brand's platform while retaining their own names and branding will be discussed. Finally, there is a section on developing and planning new hotels. Included in this section is information on the use and structure of feasibility studies.

6.1 HOTELS: A DYNAMIC INDUSTRY

The hotel industry is undergoing many changes. The demand for hotels is affected as the economic fortunes of countries, regions, and cities rise and fall. Each year, companies and hotels change ownership, and new companies and brands enter the marketplace. Brand names that are popular today may not be around in the next decade. For example, Renaissance Hotels of Hong Kong acquired Stouffer Hotels (formerly a U.S.-based company) from the Nestlé Corporation of Switzerland and converted the Stouffer properties into Renaissance hotels, which were then acquired by Marriott International. The Stouffer hotel name no longer exists.

As you can see, the hotel industry is a global industry. U.S.-based Marriott has hotels in 131 countries; Hilton has hotels in 118 countries; the French company Accor has hotels in 110 countries; and InterContinental Hotels Group (IHG), headquartered in London, operates hotels in 100 countries and territories. Marriott's acquisition of Starwood Hotels & Resorts Worldwide in 2016 added 30 new hotel brands to its portfolio, making it the largest hotel company in the world.

The COVID-19 pandemic resulted in the most devastating year on record for the hotel industry because of low occupancy, massive job losses, and hotel closures across the United States. Travel was brought to an abrupt stop with the closure of international borders and the lockdown in the early stages of the pandemic.

Industry experts like Smith Travel Research (STR) estimated that hotels will be one of the last industries to recover. Regardless, the hotel industry is resilient, and hotels across the world have already implemented countless innovations focused on creating an environment that is safe and welcoming for guests.

Industry Trends

In the 1960s, the development of new locations fueled the expansion of the hotel industry. Prior to that time, hotels were built primarily in city centers and resort areas. As commerce and industry spread from urban centers to rural, suburban, and airport locations, hotel companies like Hilton Hotels Corporation, Sheraton Hotels & Resorts, and Marriott recognized opportunities to develop their brands in these new locations.

In the 1970s, intense competition among established and emerging hotel chains created a need for chains to better differentiate their product. Some did this with architecture and décor—for example, the atrium lobby became the signature for Hyatt Hotel Corporation's Regency brand. Hotel companies adopted distinctive motifs—Ritz-Carlton's décor was traditional, whereas Hyatt's was contemporary.

Pampering the hotel guest was the strategy of the 1980s. Room and bathroom amenities—specialty soaps, sewing kits, mouthwash, shampoo, and a variety of other personal-care items—could be found in most hotels, whatever the rate category. Of course, the higher-rate hotels provided the most elaborate amenity packages. Some first-class and luxury hotels set aside one or more guest floors as "club" areas. For a higher rate, club guests could enjoy a number of special services, including an exclusive club desk for check-in and check-out, and complimentary breakfasts, afternoon teas, evening cocktails, and before-bed snacks served in the club's private lounge. Exercise rooms—even complete spa facilities—were added to many hotels to satisfy travelers' growing interest in physical fitness. Hotels with predominantly business-traveler markets added business centers to provide secretarial and translating services as well as computer and fax capabilities.

In the early 1990s, the concept of quality service as a differentiating factor came to the fore. Hotel companies implemented quality-assurance programs and referred to the quality of their

Hotels added exercise rooms to satisfy travelers' interest in physical fitness.

service in their advertising. For the first time, a hotel company—Ritz-Carlton—won the prestigious Malcolm Baldrige National Quality Award.

As the 1990s progressed, the industry emphasized innovation and new business strategies. Segmentation was one of the most important strategies implemented by many hotel chains to increase their market share. Actually, the concept was not new. Hilton and Sheraton each had established hotel and inn divisions 40 years before; the hotels were in cities, the inns in suburbs, at airports, and off highways. But in the 1990s, segmentation was based on market, not on location. Between 1992 and 1996 there were 25 new brand announcements. Some of these brands were divisions of established chains, such as Marriott's TownePlace Suites.

At the end of the twentieth century and the beginning of the twenty-first, mergers, acquisitions, and joint ventures changed lodging's competitive environment worldwide. Hoteliers started emphasizing technology and sustainability as they focused more closely on the guest experience. This included the implementation of mobile check-in and check-out, keyless entry systems, in-room automation, and mobile concierge services. Many hotels have implemented sustainable practices to reduce their environmental impact, such as energy-efficient building designs, water

conservation measures, recycling programs, the use of eco-friendly materials, and initiatives to support local communities and ecosystems. Hotels understand that prioritizing the guest experience is crucial for guest satisfaction, loyalty, and positive reviews.

Technology

The rapid evolution of technology continues to shape guest experiences, streamline operations, and drive innovation within the hospitality sector. Advances such as digital room keys, contactless check-in and payments, and mobile app capabilities already allow guests to have a seamless experience. New technology will allow hotels to add compelling upsell options during and after the reservations process. Revenue management will leverage artificial intelligence (AI) to determine optimal pricing for hotel guests interested in using their amenities, from spas to curated restaurant experiences.

Guests will be able to bring their own streaming devices when they travel and seamlessly use the hotel room's TV. Robot-assisted room service will be the norm and front desk staff will be equipped with translation apps to help manage the influx of international travelers. Guests will have 24/7 access to concierge services via their smartphones through a QR code rather than an app. Self-service markets will proliferate with self check-out, saving on staffing costs and adding a new source of revenue. Augmented reality and virtual reality advances will allow guests to experience a new hotel and its surrounding area prior to their arrival.

Sustainability

Sustainability is a big trend today within the hotel industry. Individual hotels and even the headquarters buildings of hotel chains are now being built with environmental concerns in mind. For example, Hilton moved its headquarters during the summer of 2009 from Beverly Hills, California, to a new building in Virginia that is LEED Gold certified ("LEED" stands for Leadership in Energy and Environmental Design).

The LEED certification program was introduced in 2000 by the U.S. Green Building Council, a nonprofit organization. The program contains benchmarks for the design, construction, and operation of sustainable buildings that focus on five categories (with prerequisites and points for each):

■ Sustainable site development

■ Water savings

■ Energy efficiency

■ Materials selection

■ Indoor environmental quality[1]

The outcome of the LEED assessment determines which of four levels a hotel or other building will achieve: certified, silver, gold, or platinum. There is a rating system for new buildings (LEED for New Construction and Major Renovations) and existing buildings (LEED for Existing Buildings: Operations and Maintenance). The goal of the program is to encourage a move toward sustainable practices. By the end of 2013, there were 150 new hotels and three existing properties in the United States that were certified, with more than 1,300 registered to go through the certification process. One of the first hotels to receive LEED certification was the Orchard Garden Hotel in San Francisco. Since the Orchard Garden received its certification, the cost of sustainability has been decreasing. Stefan Mühle, the hotel's general manager, says that

some "green" building materials are becoming mainstream and less expensive.[2] A challenge for hoteliers who are seeking LEED certification is that the program was designed for office buildings, not hotels. A hotel-specific certification is being created.

The Green Globe Certification is an official announcement to the public that a hotel is environmentally efficient. But certification isn't necessary to create an eco-sensitive hotel operation. Almost all of the major hotel chains have initiated green policies. For example, Wyndham Worldwide, as part of its Wyndham Green Program has adopted sustainable staff uniforms and green cleaning products. As Marriott hotels use up their inventory of supplies, it is being replaced with greener products. In Europe, Scandic Hotels has replaced bottled water in restaurants and meetings with filtered water from taps. It appears that the "green revolution" is here to stay, and many hotel companies are responding.

Hotel Mergers

The following are just some of the notable acquisitions that have occurred in the hotel industry:

■ The Blackstone Group, in the biggest hotel deal in history, acquired Hilton in 2007 for $26 billion. Six years later, it took Hilton public and raised $2.5 billion in a record initial public offering for a lodging company.

■ Marriott acquired the Gaylord Hotels brand for $210 million and spent $13 billion to merge with Starwood in 2016 to become the world's largest hotel chain.

■ In 2014, Hilton Worldwide sold the landmark Waldorf Astoria hotel in New York City to the Anbang Insurance Group of China for $1.95 billion, but it continues to manage the iconic 1,232-room hotel.

■ IHG acquired Kimpton Hotels & Restaurants for $430 million in 2014.

Acquisitions are not the only vehicle for growth. Hotel companies have expanded through partnerships and alliances. For example, Thayer Lodging Group, owners of Interstate Hotels and formerly the largest independent hotel management company in the United States, formed a 50/50 joint venture with Jin Jiang International (Holdings) Co. LTD, helping each company expand globally. Interstate Hotels & Resorts was acquired by Aimbridge Hospitality in 2019, making it the largest hotel management company, with over 1,500 hotels across the Americas, Europe, and Asia.

New hotel companies have started as well. China's Plateno Hotel Group, the largest hotel chain in Asia with nine brands, started in 2005 with a budget brand, 7 Days Inn. It focuses on budget and mid-scale hotel brands and has been recognized for its innovative use of technology and data analytics to enhance the guest experience. In 2015, Plateno Group was acquired by Jin Jiang, one of the largest hotel companies in China.

Brand proliferation continued in the new century as established chains launched new concepts or acquired existing ones. Between 2005 and 2006, 25 brands were introduced. An additional 43 brands were introduced from 2007 to 2014. One new brand, citizenM, is a Netherlands-based company. Others are brand extensions of existing chains: for example, Aloft by Starwood and Choice Hotel's Cambria Hotels.[3]

Soft Brands. Hotel **soft brands**, also known as soft brand collections or collections of independent hotels, are established when independent hotels join a larger parent brand or group while retaining their individual identity and unique characteristics. Soft brands offer independent hotels the opportunity to benefit from a well-established brand's reservations and revenue management systems, distribution channels, loyalty programs, and marketing power while maintaining their distinct branding, style, and management. In such an arrangement, these soft brand independent hotels gain the advantage of economies of scale that can be achieved in purchasing and negotiating rates with online travel agencies (OTAs), while the chain expands its market presence and gets an additional source of revenue.

Marriott's soft brand is known as the Autograph Collection. Hilton has the Curio Collection, and Choice features the Ascend Hotel Collection. The famous Algonquin Hotel in New York City and the Pier One Sydney Harbour in Australia are two of a growing number of Marriott's Autograph Collection hotels. Hilton has the Jewel Dunn's River Resort and Spa in Ocho Rios, Jamaica, and the Reichshof Hamburg in Germany, among others. Fueled by consumer demand for more individual and unique guest experiences and the popularity of boutique hotels and lifestyle brands, soft brand collections continue to expand, mostly in the upper upscale class.

6.2 HOTEL GUESTS

Hotels are in the business of attracting guests. The most important guest segments that constitute the market for the hotel industry are:

- Corporate individuals
- Leisure travelers
- Corporate groups
- Convention and association groups
- Long-term stay/relocation guests
- Airline-related guests
- Government and military travelers
- Regional getaway guests[4]
- Bleisure travelers

We will take a look at each of these guest segments in the following sections.

Corporate Individuals. Corporate individuals are hotel guests who are traveling for business purposes and are not part of any group. They usually stay one or two nights. The leading factors that determine the hotels they select are:

- Location
- Connectivity, fast Wi-Fi and Internet
- Room rate
- Complimentary breakfast
- Comfortable lobby for working and socializing
- Fitness center

Business travelers' use of the Internet to make hotel reservations is steadily increasing. Their preferences are a hotel chain's website first, followed by OTAs such as Expedia and Travelocity.

As millennials and Generation Z move into the workforce, it is not surprising that more business travelers are using smartphones, tablets, and laptops to plan their travel. At every stage of their travel, they are able to use this technology. They can book a flight or hotel on their smartphone, check in and board a flight with their phones, read emails and draft business plans with in-flight Wi-Fi, and even translate languages or secure ground transportation with their phones.

In a study done by Choice Hotels International, location was the most important factor for business travelers when selecting a hotel. Sixty-one percent of those polled stated that the quality of the room was also a critical factor, with Wi-Fi the next most important amenity. Technology plays a key role in the booking process for business travelers. According to this study, 76 percent of business travelers booked their rooms online and 60 percent used their smartphone or tablet to check into the hotel.[5]

Business travelers care about recognition and special treatment. Frequent-stay programs such as Marriott Bonvoy Rewards, Hilton Honors, and World of Hyatt have proven particularly effective with part of this market segment. Individual corporate travelers are often members of airline frequent-flyer programs, and they may choose to patronize hotels (and rental car companies) tied in with such programs.

Leisure Travelers. Leisure travelers often travel with their families on sightseeing trips or on trips to visit friends or relatives (VFR travel). Except at resorts, they typically spend only one night at the same hotel, and a room may be occupied by a couple as well as one or more children. Because they typically travel during peak season, leisure travelers usually pay high rates unless they are members of such organizations as the American Automobile Association (AAA) or the American Association of Retired Persons (AARP), which have been able to negotiate discounts with many hotels. Leisure travelers are also using Facebook and Instagram to make their travel decisions and rely more on recommendations from friends they know rather than celebrities, influencers, or the properties themselves to get ideas or inspiration for trip activities.

Corporate Groups. Corporate groups travel purely for business purposes. Unlike individual corporate travelers, however, they are usually attending a small conference or meeting at their

A business traveler typically desires a room with a desk, good lighting, and an Internet connection.

Leisure travelers often travel as a family during peak seasons.

hotel or at another facility in the area, and their rooms are booked in blocks by their company or a travel agency. These travelers usually stay from two to four days. While top managers are typically assigned single rooms, middle- and lower-level managers often share rooms.

Corporate groups favor hotels that offer intimate meeting rooms and private dining facilities. Several conference centers with these features have been constructed in suburban locations conveniently located near major cities and airports. The idea is to do away with big-city distractions and give participants a chance to interact not only during meetings but between them as well.

Convention and Association Groups. Generally, what distinguishes **convention and association groups** from other corporate groups is their size. The number of people in a convention or association group can run well into the thousands. For example, the annual meeting of the American Association of Orthodontists typically attracts about 14,000 delegates, and every year the National Restaurant Show in Chicago attracts approximately 45,000 visitors. Modest-size hotels with limited function space often compete for this group business in slow periods by offering extremely competitive rates. Convention delegates usually share rooms and

stay three to four days. Large convention groups choose their venues several years in advance, so a hotel's selling efforts are often prolonged and may involve cooperation from airlines and local convention and visitors bureaus.

Long-Term Stay/Relocation Guests. Long-term stay/relocation guests are primarily individuals or families relocating to an area and requiring lodging until permanent housing can be found. Often, they are corporate, government, or military personnel. Their needs include limited cooking facilities and more living space than is available in a typical hotel room. All-suite and extended-stay hotels such as Hilton's Embassy Suites and Residence Inns by Marriott are examples of products designed specifically for the needs of long-term guests. A Residence Inn unit is about twice the size of an average hotel room and typically contains a living area, a bedroom, extra closet space, and a small kitchen.

Airline-Related Guests. Airlines negotiate rates with hotels for airplane crew members and for passengers who need emergency accommodations because they are stranded by some unforeseen event, such as a winter storm. Rooms for these **airline-related guests** are usually booked in blocks at rock-bottom prices.

Government and Military Travelers. Government and military travelers are reimbursed on fixed per diem allowances, which means they only receive a certain amount for lodging expenses no matter what they have to pay for a room. Therefore, as a general rule, these guests stay only in places that have negotiated acceptable rates with their organizations or offer very low rates.

Regional Getaway Guests. Regional getaway guests are important to hotels that normally cater to commercial and convention groups on weekdays. Such hotels promote special weekend packages designed to entice nearby residents to leave the kids at home, check into a hotel for Friday and Saturday nights, and enjoy a night or two "on the town." Family packages are also available. Rates are discounted substantially and often include some meals and entertainment. During the pandemic, when much of the world was unable to travel, "staycations" became the norm and many hotel properties offered packages for couples and families who wanted a different experience for a short time. Another unintended benefit of the pandemic has been the ability to work remotely, leading to a rise in digital nomads. According to MBO Partners, the number of digital nomads grew by 96 percent in 2020 compared with 2019 figures, from 3.2 million to 6.3 million, according to the analyst's 2020 *State of Independence in America* report.[6] Some countries, such as Finland, Mauritius, and Barbados, offered 90-day digital nomad visas that allowed foreigners to work while traveling.

Bleisure Travelers. Bleisure is a term that combines the words *business* and *leisure*. It is on the rise and is one of the biggest trends in business travel. Popularized by millennials, bleisure travel is when a traveler blends work travel with leisure travel to save on vacation costs and create a better work–life balance. Bleisure travelers are significantly more satisfied with their quality of life and their work–life balance since they take time for themselves while on business trips. They are also more likely to prioritize self-care on the road, including following a healthy diet and regularly exercising. Worldwide, more than a third of business travelers will add a leisure component to their trip, whether it is an excursion, sightseeing, or meeting with family and friends. Many bleisure travelers will extend their trips into the weekend in order to explore a new destination.

Guest Mix. Guest mix refers to the variety or mixture of guests who stay at a hotel. A hotel's guest mix might consist of 60 percent individual business travelers, 20 percent conventioneers, and 20 percent leisure travelers, for example. However, since the pandemic, the ratio of business travelers to leisure travelers has changed. With travel restrictions, quarantine requirements, and reduced travel demand, many hotels saw a significant decrease in international and business travelers. They have seen an increase in leisure travelers, including road-trippers, domestic tourists, and individuals looking for a change of scenery while working remotely.

Guest mix is carefully managed in successful hotels. With few exceptions, hotels—no matter where they are located or what their price structures are—strive to capture multiple market segments. A hotel's guest mix depends on its location, size, facilities, and operating philosophy. To fill up rooms not booked by convention groups, hotels geared to convention sales seek individual business travelers and vacationers willing to pay nondiscounted rates. At any one time, a hotel such as the 2,000-room New York Hilton in Manhattan will lodge several groups: individual business travelers, families on vacation, airline crews, and government employees. By diversifying their guest base, hotels hope to minimize the effect of seasonality, economic recessions, and changing market dynamics.

There are dangers inherent in this strategy, however. Sometimes different kinds of guests do not mix well together. For example, business executives paying top rates for their rooms may be annoyed to find a noisy tour group blocking their way to the coffee shop in the morning. Some luxury hotels control their mix very carefully, only allowing groups on weekends and, even then, setting up special facilities for group registration and dining so the groups will not interfere with regular guests.

Knowledge Check

1. What are some things that define hotel guest segments?

2. How are regional getaway guests important to the hotel industry?

6.3 HOTEL CATEGORIES

It is important to understand the ways in which hotels are categorized. Hotels can be categorized by location, ownership, price, and other factors (e.g., service, guestroom format, or clientele).

Location

Many hospitality publications and consulting firms categorize hotels by location. Some of the most generally recognized hotel-location categories are:

- Center-city
- Resort
- Suburban
- Highway
- Airport

Center-City. After the Great Depression of the 1930s, there was a considerable amount of rebuilding and construction in the United States as part of President Franklin Roosevelt's New Deal. One result of that program was that by 1941, when the country entered World War II, most cities had at least one downtown hotel built to create jobs and stimulate the economy. Major cities like New York, Chicago, and Los Angeles had many downtown hotels, some of them internationally famous. These hotels were usually built near railroad stations because at that time railroad stations were located at or near the center of a city's business district. This followed the pattern that had been established in other major cities of the world as early as the late nineteenth century. London's Savoy Hotel, built in 1889, and Frankfurt's Parkhotel are early examples of this trend. In New York City, the Commodore (the Hyatt Grand Central New York now occupies the site) was built right over Grand Central Station. In St. Louis, the Head House (now the St. Louis Union Station Hotel) was part of Union Station. Other popular downtown locations for hotels were near centers of government, such as city halls and courts, and in financial districts, such as stock exchanges and Chicago's Merchandise Mart.

After World War II the face of the world began to change. In the United States, automobiles and airplanes replaced trains as the favored means of transportation. Autos and good road systems made suburbs possible. Soon those suburbs were attracting office parks, shopping centers, airports, and other businesses. Downtown areas in many parts of the country began to decline. This was not the case in Europe, where trains remained a popular means of transportation. Consequently, the downtown centers of major European capitals continued to flourish.

But most Americans were not ready to let their downtown metropolitan areas die. In the mid-1960s, a trend began (and continues today) to restore and rebuild downtown areas. This included building new hotels and refurbishing many of the old ones. In 1969 the Parker House in Boston was totally renovated and is now operated by Omni Hotels & Resorts. In Seattle, the Four Seasons Hotels & Resorts purchased the historic Olympic Hotel from Westin Hotels & Resorts (which is now a Fairmont Hotel). In 1986 the Willard Hotel—the hotel of choice in Washington, D.C., for foreign dignitaries, several presidents-elect, and other notables in the nineteenth century—was reopened as an IHG hotel after $113 million was invested in its restoration. The 3,000-room Conrad Hilton Hotel in Chicago, built in 1927, was closed in 1984 and reopened in 1988 as the Chicago Hilton and Towers after a $180 million renovation. It is known as the Hilton Chicago today.

Many of the downtown or **center-city hotels** today are properties built within the last 40 years. Along with these hotels, skyscrapers such as the John Hancock Building in Chicago and the Columbia Center in Seattle have sprung up. These buildings kept corporate headquarters in town and attracted new businesses as well. As you would expect, the hotels that surround them attract mostly business travelers during the week and tourists on weekends. In general, center-city hotels achieve the highest average room rate of all the non-resort hotel categories. These hotels cost more to develop and operate than hotels in other categories because of the high cost of real estate, construction, and urban wages.

Most of today's center-city hotels are full-service facilities operated or managed by hotel chains. In addition to rooms, center-city hotels may have a coffee shop as well as other restaurants, at least one bar or cocktail lounge, room service, laundry and valet services, a business center, a newsstand and gift shop, and a health club.

Many older center-city hotels have no parking facilities on the premises and must offer valet services to park guests' automobiles off-site. Consequently, parking fees can be high. Some of these hotels contract at special rates with nearby independent garages, thus lowering their costs somewhat.

Mixed-use development projects have been gaining popularity in downtown areas. One such example is the Miami Worldcenter, which spans approximately 27 downtown acres. The development features a diverse range of components, including luxury condominiums, hotels, retail shops, restaurants, entertainment venues, and office spaces. The project also includes public spaces, green areas, and pedestrian-friendly streets, creating a lively and walkable environment. This area aims to offer a unique shopping experience with a mix of national and international brands, dining options, and entertainment venues.

Resort. Resort hotels are generally found in destinations that are desirable vacation spots because of their climate, scenery, recreational attractions, or historic interest. Mountains and seashores are favorite locales. It is not unusual for resorts to have elaborately landscaped grounds with hiking trails and gardens as well as extensive sports facilities such as golf courses and tennis courts.

The Romans were the first to build hotels for recreational purposes, usually near hot springs. Famous spas dating back to the Roman Empire still exist, though in modern form, in Baden-Baden, Germany; Bath, England; and other countries. In the United States, early resorts were linked to the transportation system—the highways, rivers, and railroads. Reputedly, the first American resort advertisement appeared in 1789 for Gray's Ferry, Pennsylvania. Guests were offered fishing tackle and free weekly concerts. Transportation to and from nearby cities was provided by "a handsome State Waggon mounted on steel springs, with two good horses."[7]

Early American resorts were also built around hot or mineral springs. The Greenbrier in White Sulphur Springs, West Virginia; the nearby Homestead in Hot Springs, Virginia (which owns 15,000 acres of Allegheny Mountain forests); and the many facilities in Saratoga Springs, New York, all survive today as popular vacation destinations.

Major growth in U.S. resorts came in the nineteenth century. The Mountain View House in Whitefield, New Hampshire, opened in 1865. The Hotel del Coronado near San Diego opened its doors in 1888. That was the same year Henry Flagler opened the Ponce de Leon in St. Augustine, Florida, followed by the Royal Poinciana in Palm Beach in 1893 and the Royal Palm Hotel in Miami in 1896. Another great resort, the Grand Hotel on Michigan's Mackinac Island, opened in 1887 and has preserved its original turn-of-the-century atmosphere to this day—helped greatly by the island's ban on all automobiles.

The first American resorts were summer retreats only. In the winter, fashionable people stayed in the cities to work and attend the opera, theater, and other cultural events; they went to the mountains and seashore in the hot summer

Source: National Park Service. The Ahwahnee in Yosemite National Park. The hotel was commissioned in the 1920s to bring more affluent visitors to Yosemite.

months to escape the heat of the city. California resorts were the first to solicit winter vacation business, followed by Florida hoteliers who recognized the potential profit in offering those in northern cities a way to get out of the cold.

European resorts also were first built as summer retreats, only later becoming popular in the winter as well. The Palace, a famous Swiss resort in St. Moritz, was founded in 1856 by Johannes Badrutt. His clientele came only in the summer until, one year, Badrutt made a bet with some of his wealthy British guests. He told them that if they visited him in the winter, he would charge them nothing if they did not agree that wintering in St. Moritz was more pleasant and not as cold as staying home in London. They came, and Badrutt won his bet. Today the Palace dominates St. Moritz and remains one of Europe's most luxurious resorts, attracting royalty and celebrities from all over the globe.

A resort's guest base may vary greatly according to the season. For example, in Palm Springs, California, the winter months are the peak season. That is when movie stars and other celebrities are in town, and rates are at their highest. In the summer, when temperatures often approach 100 degrees in the shade, the same resorts offer bargain prices to tour operators, conventioneers, and individual guests who could never afford to come during the cooler months.

Early resorts did not have extensive entertainment or recreational facilities. The principal activities consisted of dining, walking, climbing, horseback riding, swimming, and lawn games. These resorts all featured large verandas with comfortable chairs for sitting, reading, and enjoying the scenery. Dinner was served early, and many guests retired to their rooms by 10 p.m. On weekends there might be a dinner dance. Contemporary resorts offer much more to their guests. In Las Vegas resorts, for example, there are nightly shows featuring star entertainment, all-night casinos, discos, elaborate health spas, two or even three golf courses, tennis courts, boating, arts and crafts classes, and children's programs. Fine dining is an important part of all resort operations. Guests expect it and are not willing to pay high room prices unless the resort has a superior restaurant.

All-inclusive resorts were first created by Gerard Blitz in 1950 when he founded Club Méditerranée (Club Med), offering accommodation, relaxation, sunshine, beaches, and sports, with the idea that "the aim of life is to be happy, the place to be happy is here, and the time to be happy is now."[8] The concept behind an all-inclusive resort was that you could have a safe, fun vacation at an affordable price with no hidden expenses. This included all the amenities you could find in a hotel, including world-class dining,

Club Med Kani, Maldives, is an all-inclusive resort.

entertainment, and cultural activities. Twenty years later, Jamaica's Issa family opened the Negril Beach Village (now Hedonism II) and included the cost of travel, gratuities, and activities in the price of the stay. Thus, the modern all-inclusive resort was born.

In 1981, the late Gordon "Butch" Stewart built the first Sandals Resort in Montego Bay, Jamaica, and grew that into 20 Sandals and Beaches Resorts on 10 islands across the Caribbean—in Jamaica, Antigua, St. Lucia, Bahamas, Grenada, Barbados, Curaçao, Turks & Caicos, and St. Vincent. Today, Sandals Resorts International remains the world's only 5-Star Luxury Included vacation. While Stewart never laid claim to starting the all-inclusive, couples-only format, he was known as "King of All-Inclusives" with his continuous innovation and commitment to the "we can do it better" principle of pleasing his guests.

Industrywide, the majority of all-inclusive resorts are in the Caribbean and Latin America, where the weather is more stable and warmer. However, the costs of supplies and imports vary greatly, as most goods have to be imported to the islands.

Successful resorts achieve higher occupancy and higher sales per room than other categories of hotels. However, resorts are the most expensive hotels to operate. They average a higher number of employees per room, and thus their payrolls are much higher than for other kinds of hotels.

Resort hotels that offer conference and convention facilities attract business travelers and corporate groups. These facilities are typically equipped with state-of-the-art technology and can accommodate a range of events, from small meetings to large-scale conferences and conventions. Examples include Gaylord, Omni, Grand Hyatt, Marriott, and Westin. These resort hotels typically offer a combination of business and leisure amenities, with conference facilities and meeting spaces complemented by recreational facilities such as spas, golf courses, and other activities. This allows guests to balance work and play while enjoying the amenities and attractions of a resort setting. In smaller resorts, the guest mix may be skewed toward leisure visitors, but groups and meetings nevertheless remain important target markets. Because of the significance of the revenue from business guests, many resorts added or increased amenities that are important to this market segment, such as full-service business centers.

Suburban. With the rebirth of American cities in the two decades after World War II, the U.S. economy expanded rapidly, and construction of major office buildings in downtown areas reached a new peak of activity. Landowners soon realized that new buildings commanded a much higher rent than older ones, and real estate prices in many downtown areas doubled and tripled.

Many corporations that did not want to pay the higher downtown rents moved to the suburbs. Land there was available at a more reasonable price and, with improved highway systems, proliferating suburban housing developments, and gigantic new suburban shopping centers, it made sense to relocate. IBM, for example, moved its world headquarters from Manhattan to Armonk, New York. Many of the other large business tenants in Manhattan moved to Connecticut, New Jersey, and upstate New York.

Inevitably, a strong demand arose for building new hotels near these suburban businesses. Land developers recognized this need and found meeting it particularly attractive. Unlike suburban townhouses and rental apartments, a hotel seemed to be a more profitable investment. After all, when you rented out a new apartment, you were tied into a lease at a set price for a year or more. Inflation could easily erode your profits because you could not raise the rent whenever you wanted to cover increased costs. A hotel was different; you were not locked into fixed rates at all. If your costs went up, you could raise rates in less than 24 hours. While many land developers did not know the first thing about running a hotel, a solution was readily available. Large hotel chains were selling franchises, and management companies were available to completely take over the new hotels from those developers who were not really interested in hotelkeeping.

In addition to the new businesses, there were other reasons for locating hotels in the suburbs. Newer and larger hotels offering parking space and other amenities could be built much more economically in suburban locations than downtown. Moreover, the growth of motels (which were on their way to being called motor hotels), combined with the need for suburban accommodations, further eroded the desirability of building hotels downtown.

Today, it is difficult to distinguish between a **suburban hotel** and any other kind of hotel. It is the location that makes the difference.

Nevertheless, there are some characteristics that suburban hotels have in common:

- As a group, they tend to be somewhat smaller than downtown hotels. Many suburban properties have 250 to 500 rooms and limited banquet facilities.

- They are primarily chain affiliated; just about every major chain operates suburban properties.

- Their major source of revenue is from business-meeting and convention attendees and from individual business travelers.

- They often have the same kinds of facilities that center-city hotels offer. Because they depend heavily on local patronage, restaurants in suburban hotels frequently offer superior dining experiences. Hotel services such as laundry, valet, and room service are on a par with center-city standards.

- Many of these properties have sports and health facilities as well as swimming pools.

- Suburban hotels are often cornerstones of their communities. They frequently host weddings and bar/bat mitzvahs as well as weekly meetings of such major service clubs as Rotary and Kiwanis.

Highway. As soon as America began to develop its highway system in the 1920s and 1930s, small **tourist courts** began to spring up along major roads such as the Boston Post Road (U.S. Highway 1) from Maine to Florida. At first, these tourist courts were a row of simple cabins with direct access to the outside. Many of them did not even have private baths. These early motels averaged 20 cabins or rooms and were usually owned by a couple who lived on the premises and did all the work. No effort was made to provide food or other services. Because rooms were sometimes rented for just a few hours with no questions asked, early highway motels in some communities developed an unsavory reputation.

It was not until after World War II, when the pent-up demand for automobiles and travel was finally released, that the highway motel business really grew. With the new interstate highways came a need for families and businesspeople to have a safe and comfortable place to stay en route to their destination. One of the first to recognize this need was Kemmons Wilson, whose Holiday Inn chain was launched in 1952 in Memphis, Tennessee. One of Wilson's major innovations was to put a restaurant in his motel so that travelers could eat a meal without leaving the property. This upgraded the status of these properties considerably, making them more like hotels. Soon the evolution from tourist court to motel to motor hotel was complete. Today's **highway hotels** offer the same facilities found in downtown and suburban hotels, but with a distinct identity of their own.

Most highway hotels feature a large sign that can be seen from the highway and an entrance where travelers can leave their automobiles while they check in. Parking space is plentiful, and the atmosphere is informal. Beyond that, the distinction blurs—a highway hotel can be just like any other hotel except that it is on the highway.

Most highway hotels are franchised. The nature of highway hotels—often located away from urban centers—presents management and quality-control problems that can best be solved by independent entrepreneurs operating a franchise. Guests spend less time at this kind of hotel than in other kinds of hotels; consequently, total sales per room are generally lower. Like most other types of hotels, highway properties depend mainly on commercial traffic.

Airport. It did not take long for hotel chains to identify another growing need for hotel space—guestrooms near airports. The majority of **airport hotels** today are affiliated with chains. Even though airport hotels tend to have difficulty attracting weekend guests because most airline travel occurs on weekdays, airport hotels enjoy some of the highest occupancy rates in the lodging industry. In fact, demand can be too high at times. A problem that airport hotels face is the need to respond to a high demand almost immediately. A severe snowstorm or an airline strike can fill up an airport hotel instantly and put a severe strain on the rooms division and foodservice facilities.

Airport hotels in the United States and Europe have begun changing from facilities designed just for overnight guests to hotels that can accommodate the needs of business travelers who may plan to stay more than one night and might require meeting space. Why are they changing? Because fewer guests are airline passengers. Busy industrial parks have sprung up in areas surrounding major airports. Hotels near the airports serving London, Brussels, and Frankfurt draw much of their business from executives visiting nearby firms, and many of these executives arrive by auto.

How the Government Categorizes Lodging.

The U.S. government, along with Canada and Mexico, has its own way of categorizing hotels and other lodging properties. The basis of government classification is the North American Industry Classification System (NAICS). Industries in the Accommodation subsector (subsector 721) provide lodging for short-term accommodation to travelers, vacationers, and others. The Traveler Accommodation group of the subsector includes hotels, motels, and bed-and-breakfast inns.

Ownership

There are various ways hotels can be owned and operated. Hotels can be:

1. Independently owned and operated

2. Independently owned but leased to an operator who may or may not have a franchise

3. Owned by a single entity or group that has a franchise and hires a hotel management company to operate the property

4. Owned and operated by a branded chain

5. Owned by a single entity or group and operated by a branded chain

An **independent hotel** is not connected with any established hotel company and is owned by an individual or group of investors. A **management company** contracts with hotel owners to operate their hotels. The management company may or may not have any of its own funds invested. It is usually paid by a combination of fees plus a share of revenues and profits. A **hotel chain** is a group of affiliated hotels.

A **franchise** is the authorization granted by a hotel chain to an individual hotel to use the chain's trademark, operating systems, and reservations system in return for a percentage of the hotel's revenues plus certain other fees, such as advertising fees. A **franchisor** is the party granting the franchise; Holiday Inn Worldwide is

an example of a franchisor. A **franchisee** is the party granted the franchise.

Chain Hotels. Hotel chains account for a large percentage of the world's hotel room inventory. The largest of these chains, Marriott, has a global presence in 110 countries with over 5,700 properties spread across 30 brands. Marriott's merger with Starwood in 2016 created the world's largest hotel empire and completely revamped their loyalty program, Bonvoy, which was announced in 2019. The merger gave Marriott more leverage with corporate travel departments that often look for one giant chain for all their employees. In addition, Marriott will have more influence over Expedia and Priceline, the two giant OTAs that sell rooms on behalf of hotel companies in exchange for a commission.

In the past, the world's most deluxe hotels were independent. There was a perception that a chain could not possibly achieve the level of service of an independent hotel owned and operated by hoteliers who were there every day. This is no longer true. Some travel writers consider the Mandarin Oriental Hotel, Bangkok to be one of the world's best hotels, and it is part of the Mandarin chain of 29 hotels. The Ritz-Carlton Hotel Company, a division of Marriott, manages a chain of hotels in the United States and abroad. It was awarded—twice—the Malcolm Baldrige National Quality Award (in 1992 and 1999), which was created by Congress to recognize quality achievements. It is the only hotel company ever to win this prestigious award. Four Seasons Hotels and Resorts of Toronto, Ontario, Canada, operates first-class hotels all over the world, including London's famous Inn on the Park.

Exhibit 6.1 lists the top 25 hotel chains. It should be noted that the figures in the exhibit can be somewhat misleading without a more complete understanding of these organizations. For example, the "Hotels" column does not indicate how many of the properties are company-owned, franchised, under management contract, or simply independent hotels that have banded together solely to advertise and set up a common reservations system. The largest chains on the list are primarily franchisors or management companies, or both. For example, Jin Jiang International is a Chinese state-owned travel and hotel conglomerate headquartered in Shanghai. It has three core businesses: hotel management and investment, tourist services, and transport

Exhibit 6.1   Top 25 Hotel Chains

Rank 2021	Company/Headquarters	Rooms 2021	Hotels 2021
1.	Marriott International Bethesda, Maryland, USA	1,446,600	7,795
2.	Jin Jiang International Holdings Co. Ltd. Shanghai, China	1,239,274	11,959
3.	Hilton McLean, Virginia, USA	1,065,413	6,777
4.	IHG Hotels & Resorts Atlanta, Georgia, USA	885,706	6,032
5.	Wyndham Hotels & Resorts Parsippany, New Jersey, USA	810,051	8,950
6.	Accor Paris, France	777,714	5,298
7.	Huazhu Group Ltd. Shanghai, China	753,216	7,830
8.	Choice Hotels International Rockville, Maryland, USA	575,735	7,139
9.	BTG Hotels (Group) Co. Ltd. Beijing, China	475,124	5,916
10.	BWH Hotel Group Phoenix, Arizona, USA	348,07	3,963
11.	GreenTree Hospitality Group Ltd Shanghai, China	337,153	4,659
12.	Qingdao Sunmei Group Co. Ltd. Qingdao, China	288,293	5,804
13.	Hyatt Hotels Corp. Chicago, Illinois, USA	284,944	1,162
14.	Dossen International Group Guangzhou, China	254,774	3,025
15.	Aimbridge Hospitality Plano, Texas, USA	226,797	1,517
16.	Delonix Group (New Century H&R) Hangzhou, China	144,468	863

(Continued)

Exhibit 6.1   Top 25 Hotel Chains (*Continued*)

Rank 2021	Company/Headquarters	Rooms 2021	Hotels 2021
17.	G6 Hospitality Carrollton, Texas, USA	116,669	1,409
18.	Westmont Hospitality Group Houston, Texas USA	88,363	795
19.	Meliá Hotels International Palma de Mallorca, Spain	83,772	316
20.	Whitbread Dunstable, England	80,000	820
21.	The Ascott Ltd. Singapore	78,000	750
22.	Minor Hotel Group Bangkok, Thailand	75,621	527
23.	Toyoko Inn Co. Ltd. Tokyo, Japan	72,559	331
24.	Extended Stay America Charlotte, North Carolina, USA	71,500	650
25.	Highgate New York, New York, USA	70,002	409

Source: *Hotels Magazine*, July/August 2022, p. 34.

and logistics. Jin Jiang Hotels partners with hotel groups such as Marriott, Hilton, InterContinental, Fairmont Raffels, and Accor.

OYO Rooms, on the other hand, is a virtual hospitality brand headquartered in India with a global presence. Founded in 2013 by Ritesh Argawal, OYO partners with hotels to create a branded guest experience across cities by licensing its brand, ensuring common standards, and providing distribution in return for a royalty fee, much like franchising. Their portfolio ranges from the OYO Townhouse, which is similar to a mid-scale hotel targeted at millennials, to OYO Vacation Homes, a vacation home brand rental.

All of the hotels under the Wyndham and Choice brands are franchised. Marriott, IHG, and Hilton hotels have both franchised and managed hotels in their portfolios. Companies such as

Marriott develop a hotel and sell it once it has achieved a stable income stream but retain the management. Best Western International does not own, franchise, or manage any of its properties. The only affiliation among Best Western hotels is that all of them are part of a common reservations and marketing system.

Independent Hotels. Most hotels that are classified as independent are independently owned and managed but are allied with a referral or marketing association. Three such associations are Preferred Hotels & Resorts Worldwide, The Leading Hotels of the World, and Relais & Chateaux. Las Brisas Acapulco in Mexico and the Maybourne Beverly Hills in California are Preferred hotels. The Halekulani in Hawaii and the One&Only The Palm, Dubai, are members of The Leading Hotels of the World. Relais & Chateaux properties include Lake Placid Lodge in upstate New York and Las Mañanitas in Cuernavaca, Mexico.

It is sometimes difficult to differentiate hotels that are independent from those that are managed or owned by chains. For example, the Pierre Hotel in New York City, which many consider to be a fine independent hotel, is owned and managed by the Taj Hotels chain.

Price

Another way of categorizing—or **segmenting**— hotels is by the prices they charge. Hotel chains create several different brands or hotel names that offer different benefits and charge different prices. This is a favored strategy for marketing manufactured consumer products. For example, General Motors manufactures an economy automobile line (Chevrolet), a mid-price automobile line (Buick), and a luxury car line (Cadillac). The idea is that different segments of the consumer market are attracted to different brands at different price levels, and if you want to sell a car to everyone, you must have different kinds of cars at different prices. When Henry Ford started his automobile business, his intention was to offer only one kind of car—a basic black Model T that he could sell for the lowest-possible price of $500. It was not until General Motors demonstrated that it could sell more cars by having a range of brands at different price levels that Ford decided to change his strategy of offering only one product at a rock-bottom price.

Similarly, in the lodging industry the major hotel chains started by offering only one kind of brand. Initially, these were mid-price products introduced by Sheraton, Hilton, and Marriott in the 1940s and 1950s. They were priced to appeal to the largest segment of the traveling public— mid-level business executives. Top executives in those days would not dream of staying at a chain hotel—they stayed at independent properties or properties that may have been part of a group but were perceived to be unique or independent, such as the St. Regis Hotel in New York City, one of Starwood's brands.

As the market for mid-price hotels became saturated, some of the leading hotel chains developed new concepts to appeal to a growing economy-minded market. Also, there was increasing demand from families and businesspeople for more spacious, reasonably priced hotel accommodations. The industry responded by developing several full-service and select-service brands at different prices.

Today, most hotel chains have properties in one or more full- or select-service segments. For example, through development and acquisition, Marriott has chosen to enter every price category in an effort to maximize its market share. Marriott adheres to the philosophy that if it is no longer possible to appeal to everyone with one kind of hotel, then it will build or acquire as many kinds of hotels as necessary to ensure that as many people as possible who stay in hotels will stay at a Marriott property (see Exhibit 6.2). On the other hand, Four Seasons identifies its expertise not in the management of hotels in general, but in the management of luxury hotels. To maintain this specialized identity, Four Seasons manages only first-class hotels that appeal to its current guest base.

Three broad categories of hotels distinguished by price are (1) select-service—economy and budget, (2) mid-price—full-service and select-service, and (3) first-class/luxury. We will take a brief look at each of these categories in the following sections.

Select-Service: Economy and Budget. There are many **select-service hotels** in the marketplace today, including Hyatt Place, Hilton Garden Inn, Courtyard by Marriott, and Sheraton Inn Four Points. Select-service hotels do not offer the full range of services customarily associated with hotels, such as restaurants and bars. The first hotel chain to go after a low-price consumer market was Holiday Inn. Holiday Inns were not budget properties, however. Their construction costs were relatively high because they included restaurants and other amenities and services, and their aim was to provide a better product than previously available on the highway.

It was not until the 1960s that the first budget motels were introduced: Motel 6 in California, Days Inn in Georgia, and La Quinta in Texas. Sam Barshop, founder of La Quinta, explained his idea this way: "We have a very simple concept. What we're doing is selling beds. Not operating restaurants, not running conventions—just selling beds." By eliminating the restaurants and the lobby and meeting space that Holiday Inns

Exhibit 6.2   How Marriott Segments the Market

Signature Brand
Marriott Hotels
Luxury Brands
The Ritz-Carlton
St. Regis Hotels
JW Marriott
Premium Brands
Marriott
Sheraton
Delta Hotels Marriott
Select Brands
Courtyard by Marriott
Four Points by Sheraton
SpringHill Suites by Marriott
Protea Hotels Marriott
Fairfield by Marriott
Extended-Stay Brands
Marriott Executive Apartments
Residence Inn by Marriott
TownePlace Suites by Marriott

Source: Marriott (website), https://www.hotel-development.marriott.com/brands.

offered, La Quinta and other budget properties were able to offer Holiday Inn–type rooms at 25 percent less. Some chains, like Motel 6, sold rooms for as low as $6. They were able to offer such low prices by using modular and prefabricated construction materials and choosing less-than-ideal locations where land costs were lower. These chains offered hardly any amenities. In the early days, some had a coin slot in their guestroom television sets for pay-as-you-view TV!

The early budget motel segment has evolved into two price levels, **economy hotels** (the lowest-rate hotels) and **budget hotels** (select-service hotels with slightly higher rates than economy hotels). Both of these hotel segments have a low per-room construction cost. Because they provide limited services and facilities, labor and other operating costs are well below those for full-service hotels. However, pricing varies by market area and is affected by inflation. Generally, rates are offered at 20 to 50 percent below prevailing mid-market rates. Of course, hotel rates are constantly changing. Holiday Inn, once at the low end of the price scale, is now considered a mid-price hotel. However, Holiday Inn developed a concept, called Holiday Inn Express, to compete at the low end of the market. Choice Hotels International, the eighth-largest hotel company worldwide, developed Comfort Inn and Comfort Inn Suites as part of its low-price strategy.

Mid-Price. In the 1960s, Sheraton, Hilton, Ramada, Quality Inns, and Holiday Inn used the term "inn" to designate their mid-price products. At that time the **mid-price hotel** segment was the fastest-growing segment of the industry. Fueled by a growing economy and the growth of automobile and commercial air traffic, a strong need existed for mid-price lodging facilities with restaurants and some other amenities (such as lounges and meeting space) previously found only in higher-priced establishments. Today, however, the term "inn" no longer identifies a specific price category. For example, Days Inn is an economy product.

Mid-price hotels are attractive to many consumers who want to trade up from the economy/budget segment. When the rate difference between first-class and mid-price hotels is not significant, travelers are drawn to the higher-class hotels; but when rates are significantly different, mid-price hotels become more attractive. The challenge for mid-price hotels is to maintain a guest-pleasing, clearly drawn middle position between increasingly upscale hotels in the economy/budget segment and first-class hotels with low (for the segment) room rates.

Four Points by Sheraton is a mid-price concept that is, in some cases, a rebranding of Sheraton Inns. Although the facilities have not necessarily changed, the name has changed because the term "inn" was considered to represent a limited facility. Holiday Inn Select and Hilton Garden Inns are other brands that compete in the mid-price segment.

First-Class/Luxury. At the top of the price scale, there is a range of **first-class/luxury hotels**, from the full-service hotels of Hyatt, Hilton, and Marriott to the luxury properties of Four Seasons, Ritz-Carlton, and IHG. Before these chains offered successful luxury hotels, "luxury chain hotel" was considered a contradiction in terms. By definition, a luxury hotel used to be an independent property in which the owner/manager was present to greet

guests and see that their every need was satisfied. A perfect example of this kind of property was the Ritz Hotel in Paris on the Place Vendôme. Its founder, the legendary César Ritz, set unusually high standards for facilities and services. But Ritz also recognized the marketing advantages that could accrue from having more than one Ritz Hotel and so, with his partner Georges Auguste Escoffier, he acquired an equity interest in the Carlton Hotel in London and then formed the Ritz-Carlton chain. Other luxury chains followed. One highly successful example is the Canada-based Four Seasons hotel company. The company's strategy is to operate only mid-size hotels of exceptional quality and have the finest hotel or resort in each destination where it locates.

STR Hotel Classifications. STR Benchmarking classifies branded hotels into chain scale segments based on average daily rates. The following are the STR chain scale segments, with examples of global chains in each segment:

- *Luxury Chains:* Four Seasons, Mandarin Oriental Hotel Group
- *Upper Upscale Chains:* Marriott, Hilton
- *Upscale Chains:* Crowne Plaza, Radisson
- *Upper Midscale Chains:* Best Western Plus, Drury Inn
- *Midscale Chains:* Ramada, Quality Inn
- *Economy Chains:* Motel 6, Jinjiang Inn

Other Hotel Categories

Other hotel categories include boutique/lifestyle hotels, all-suite hotels, conference centers, timeshare properties, condominium hotels, seniors housing, and Airbnb. We will take a look at each of these categories in the following sections.

Boutique/Lifestyle Hotels. Although the Boutique & Lifestyle Lodging Association (BLLA) makes a distinction between boutique and lifestyle hotels, the terms are sometimes used interchangeably. Throughout the industry, the definition of a **boutique hotel** can vary widely. Initially, it was understood that a boutique hotel was small—typically 100 rooms and under. However, STR now defines the boutique segment as having 150 to 300 rooms, and most boutique hotels do indeed fall within that range. Generally, the features of a boutique hotel are described by using such words as "cultural," "historical," and "authentic." By contrast, a **lifestyle hotel** has contemporary design and décor, provides unique services, and has high-quality technology features in the guestrooms.

"Boutique" was first applied to a hotel in 1984, when Ian Schrager and his partner, Steve Rubell, opened Morgans Hotel in New York City. Later, Schrager opened hotels where he introduced "lobby socializing" by creating lobbies that invited guests and others to meet and socialize within them. His lobby designs were adopted by Starwood when it developed the W hotel. Since then, other chains have followed, including Canopy by Hilton, Marriott's Edition, Andaz by Hyatt, and Hotel Indigo by IHG.

All-Suite Hotels. There are a number of all-suite hotel chains in the industry, including Embassy Suites and Residence Inn by Marriott. Although all-suite chains can be viewed as a different kind of hotel chain, they also provide a way for traditional hotel chains to expand their product.

When **all-suite hotels** were first introduced, the concept was simple—two connected hotel rooms for approximately the price of one, at a price much lower than that of a traditional hotel suite. One room was furnished as a typical hotel guestroom with a bed, the other with a fold-out sofa (or a table and chairs) in place of the bed. The first all-suite hotel was built in 1961—the Lexington Apartments and Motor Inn in Grand Prairie, Texas. It took 11 years for one of the major chains to embrace the idea; Guest Quarters Suite Hotels opened its first property in Atlanta in 1972. Residence Inns developed an all-suite concept in the early 1980s and had more than 100 hotels when it was acquired by Marriott in 1987.

All-suite hotels were originally positioned to attract extended-stay travelers, but they proved popular with other kinds of travelers as well. An all-suite hotel gave guests more private space, but the trade-off was that much of the hotel's public space—the lobby, meeting rooms, health club, and (most importantly) restaurant and kitchen—was eliminated.

All-suites continue to develop and be embellished; today, there are all-suite hotels that are upscale, mid-price, extended-stay, and resort. Some of these hotels still embrace the original concept, but others have restored the lobbies, restaurants, health clubs, and other features.

All-suite hotels appeal to several kinds of travelers. Business travelers are still the primary target and account for two-thirds of the guests. Executives find all-suites attractive because they

Boutique hotels are smaller hotels with unique design identities.

can hold private meetings in their room outside of a bedroom setting. Families also like all-suites. The children can sleep in their own alcove on bunk beds or on the convertible sofa in the living room, leaving the parents with the master bedroom. And the ranges and microwave ovens that are part of many all-suite guestrooms are great for preparing meals or popping popcorn while watching the news or a movie.

Conference Centers. Although all hotels with meeting facilities compete for conferences, there are specialized properties called **conference centers** that almost exclusively book conferences, executive meetings, and training courses. They are either residential venues or day-meeting centers with no accommodations.

According to the International Association of Conference Centers, for a facility to be classified as a conference center, a minimum of 60 percent of its total sales must come from conferences and, of the facility's total meeting space, 60 percent must be devoted exclusively to meetings.[9]

Conference centers almost always have more audiovisual equipment on-site than is available at other hotels. Theaters, videotaping facilities, closed-circuit television, secretarial services, and translation facilities are common amenities. Conference centers are usually accessible to major market areas but are in less busy locations. They range in size from 20 guestrooms (The Council House in Racine, Wisconsin) to 1,042 guestrooms (the Q Center in St. Charles, Illinois). Revenues from conference centers are as much as 15 percent higher than those from full-service hotels.

As with other kinds of hotels and resorts, conference centers can be classified according to usage. There are four general classifications:

■ *Executive conference centers*, which cater to high-level meetings and seminars.

■ *Corporate-owned conference centers*, used primarily for in-house training.

■ *Resort conference centers*, which provide extensive recreation and social facilities in addition to conference facilities.

■ *College and university conference centers*, which tend to be used mostly by academic groups. These facilities range from dormitory accommodations to modern hotels.

Such hotel chains as Hilton and Marriott include conference centers among their hotel brands. Conference centers operated by American Express, General Electric, and American Airlines are used expressly for private meetings and conferences. Private and public universities (e.g., Columbia, Duke, Babson, and the universities of Virginia and Pennsylvania) have entered the conference-center business with great success, attracting overseas visitors and weekend meetings.

One company that specializes in conference-center management is Benchmark Resorts & Hotels of Woodlands, Texas. Its merger with Pyramid Hotel Group in 2021 formed Benchmark Pyramid (subsequently rebranded as Pyramid Global Hospitality), making it one of the most owner-focused, experiential companies in the industry. Pyramid Global manages more than 210 properties in the United States, Europe, and the Caribbean, and is the largest third-party manager of independent and experiential hotels, resorts, and conference centers.

Timeshare Properties. During the 1960s and 1970s, when inflation was a serious problem in many countries, timesharing—which first started in the French Alps in the 1960s—seemed like an idea whose time had come. Many people enjoyed taking their vacation every year at the same time and at the same place. Many Californians, for example, went to Hawaii every winter for a week or two, rented a hotel room at the same property, played the same golf course, and had a group of friends who would go at the same time. The more affluent Californians bought condominiums, but most people didn't think it made sense to buy a $40,000 to $100,000 condominium that they might use for only a few weeks each year.

The **timeshare condominium** concept seemed the perfect answer. Instead of selling people entire condominiums, developers reasoned, why not sell them only one-twelfth of one, which would give them the use of it for 30 days—or even one-fiftieth of one, which would allow buyers to use the condo for one week every year? (Typically, timeshare properties set aside two weeks each year for maintenance, so one year, for sales purposes, consisted of 50 weeks.) Buyers could pick their own month or week and actually own the condo for that period of time. If they could not go on their designated week, they could trade with other owners. By buying a block of time in a timeshare condominium, they would not only be assured of getting the accommodations they wanted when they wanted them, but their rate would stay the same over the years even if hotel-room rates doubled or tripled. Moreover, if they got bored with going to the same place every year, they could join an exchange company such as Interval International or RCI (a division of Wyndham Worldwide) and trade the use of their timeshare unit for another timeshare unit somewhere else in the world. For example, Interval International has 2,800 affiliated resorts in 75 countries, and 1.8 million timeshare owners as members. Disney, Marriott, and Four Seasons timeshare divisions are some of the brands that are clients of the exchange company.

The timeshare concept arrived in the United States in the 1970s. Problems with the first timeshare developments occurred when too many unscrupulous developers tried to unload bankrupt or aging hotels and condominiums by luring purchasers with high-pressure sales tactics. In a number of cases, management of such facilities was left to unsuspecting buyers who lacked the technical expertise needed to operate a timeshare property. Consequently, many properties were poorly maintained, and a number went bankrupt. The federal government and most states enacted consumer protection laws and policies, including a grace period for buyers to reconsider their decision to purchase a timeshare. It was not until the 1980s, when respected companies such as Disney entered the arena, that timesharing became a serious contender for the vacation market. Other well-regarded companies soon followed: Hilton, Marriott, Hyatt, and Four Seasons.

Hotel companies entered the timeshare business for a number of reasons. First, of course, is the potential for profit. The average vacation-ownership package includes a two-bedroom unit and costs about $16,000 for one week. If a unit is sold out for the year (as just mentioned, timeshare properties usually set aside two weeks each year for maintenance, so a sellout would mean that the unit was sold for 50 weeks), the total revenue on that unit is $800,000. After deducting approximately 50 percent for sales and marketing costs, about $400,000 remains to cover general and administrative costs and profit.

The timeshare business has other advantages for hotel companies, especially in mixed-use projects—a project comprising timeshare units and a resort hotel, for example. With this type of mixed-use project, operating expenses such as housekeeping can be shared between the resort and the timeshare units, and timeshare residents can increase the resort's food and beverage revenue.

From a management standpoint, there are significant differences between managing traditional hotels and timeshare facilities. Timeshare properties—where there is deeded interest—are considered harder to manage because owners are always present and concerned about their investment. Managers must deal with numerous owners, all of whom have their own ideas about improvements. Selling must be handled more aggressively and sales costs are considerably higher for timeshare properties than for traditional hotels. After all, when a deeded interest is involved, you are selling a piece of property, not simply an overnight stay. Salespersons with strong closing techniques are required for the initial sellout period.

At first, the majority of timeshare units sold were deeded one-week intervals. While this type is still popular, many timeshare resorts and companies now offer more flexible systems, such as vacation clubs that feature point systems. They do not include a deeded interest but are structured more like a membership. These point systems enable buyers to purchase a minimum number of points, rather than time or property; buyers "spend" these points like currency to select their timeshare location, preferred time of year, number of nights, and type of unit. Buyers can use their points all at once or spread them throughout the year for shorter vacations. Timeshare units may be sold on a floating-week basis as well. This method allows the owner to select a period in which the week purchased will be used. For example, a family may want the option of choosing their one week during the summer season when school is out. The average timeshare owner is 48 years old, is college educated, makes more than $92,000 per year, and owns their primary residence.[10]

Timesharing is big business. There are more than 5,000 timeshare resorts worldwide, with over six million unit owners. The United States currently dominates the industry, with more than 1,500 timeshare resorts. Florida and California have the highest number. The leading timeshare companies (in terms of units) are Wyndham, Marriott, Vacation Resorts International (VRI), and Westgate.

Condominium Hotels. Somewhat similar to timeshare properties are properties known as condominium hotels. (In a timeshare hotel, the owner has a deed for 1/52 of a unit and can use the unit for one week per year; a condominium room or apartment is wholly owned by the purchaser.) Also called condo hotels or even condotels, condominium hotels first surfaced in the 1960s and weathered some difficult early years as a result of dishonest practices by some developers. A **condominium hotel** is a building or complex with individual rooms that are sold to individual owners, who then have the option to use the unit for personal purposes or place it in a rental program managed by a hotel operator. Investors stay in their rooms whenever they wish and inform management of the times during the year when they will not be using their rooms. When an investor does not occupy their hotel room, it is placed in the pool of hotel rooms available for rent to vacationers and other travelers. Investors expect to receive a gain from the increase in value of the condominium hotel over time, as well as ongoing income from the rental of their rooms.

After years of little growth in the condominium hotel segment, the concept has become popular in resort areas such as South Florida, Hawaii, and Las Vegas, and even in some cities like New York and San Francisco. The difficulty in obtaining financing for full-service and resort hotel projects has made mixed-use properties that include a transient hotel and a condominium hotel component attractive to developers. By selling hotel rooms or apartments as condominium units, the developer can transfer much of the development costs to the purchasers of the condominiums.

There are three types of mixed-use condominium hotels:

- One type has a number of condominium units in the hotel that are sold to people who use them as a primary residence. These residences are not placed in a rental pool. The Ritz-Carlton in Boston is an example of this type of development.

- Another type of mixed-use condominium hotel has condominium units located in a separate wing of the hotel, such as the Ritz-Carlton in Key Biscayne, Florida. These units are vacation homes, not primary residences, and are rented to transient guests by the hotel when the owners are away.

- There is a type of mixed-use condominium hotel in which each room is sold as a condominium to one or more investors. In this case, the owners are interested in a return on their investment rather than an additional residence. An example of this type of condominium hotel is the Westin Grand Vancouver in British Columbia, Canada.[11]

In all types of condominium hotels, the permanent residents and the transient guests receive the customary hotel services, such as housekeeping and room service.

Seniors Housing. Seniors housing is hard to define because each state uses unique terms and regulatory controls for this portion of the lodging industry. What follows is a generally accepted classification of the various types of seniors housing:

- *Independent-living units.* Independent-living units are apartments, condominiums, or co-ops for seniors who function independently (i.e., those who have no serious health problems requiring assistance of some kind).

- *Congregate communities.* Congregate communities are made up of rental units with tie-ins to services such as meals, housekeeping, transportation, and social activities.

- *Assisted-living facilities.* Assisted-living facilities are apartments with private bathrooms and kitchenettes for seniors who need assistance with the activities of daily living (bathing, dressing, or eating), but who do not require continuous skilled-nursing care.

- *Continuing-care retirement communities.* Continuing-care retirement communities provide a full range of long-care services, such as home care and independent-living, assisted-living, and skilled-nursing care.

Adding to the confusion about seniors housing is the fact that several of these categories can exist in the same facility. For example, a single seniors-housing development might offer independent, congregate, and assisted-living units to meet the various needs of its clientele.

Seniors housing has gotten the attention of hotel corporations and major real estate developers with hotel interests. The reason for this growing interest is the "graying of America," which so many marketing people have commented on and written about. In the past, many elderly Americans moved in with their children; retired to states like Florida, Arizona, or California; or entered nursing homes. Today's senior citizens are a different breed. For example, the very term "senior" is rejected by some older citizens. They think of themselves as active, mature people with distinct needs. They are, on the whole, more educated and affluent than their parents. And many of them prefer the new varieties of seniors housing to other options.

There is no doubt that these new "life care" centers (as they are sometimes called to distinguish them from "healthcare" facilities like nursing homes) are targeted at the affluent because prices are typically high. Residents can buy apartments or rent them; they typically get small studios or one- or two-bedroom apartments with small kitchens where they can prepare their own meals, although usually at least two meals per day are included in the rent or maintenance plans. Often there are scheduled activities every day, including trips to shopping malls and grocery stores, movies, and fitness centers.

Marriott was one of the first hotel companies to enter this market when it established its Senior Living Services division in 1984. The division has since been sold to Sunrise Senior Living in McLean, Virginia, which is now one of the largest provider of seniors housing in the United States. The largest is Brookdale, based in Brentwood, Tennessee, with a total capacity of 113,000 residents in all of its locations.

Airbnb. Short-term home rentals and apartment exchanges have been available to travelers for many years. However, the concept had never been done on the scale that Airbnb has created in a relativity short time period. Airbnb was founded by two friends when, due to economic circumstances, they had to rent space in their apartment. They recognized the possibilities for a new business concept and, after adding a third partner, they

launched their website in August 2008. The website provided a convenient online platform that allowed hosts to offer their homes, apartments, or rooms to travelers. The company has grown to more than 8 million listings in 220 countries. Airbnb markets its experiences as local and unique. People who book with Airbnb are looking for unique experiences, are willing to experiment more, and want to feel part of a local culture.

Airbnb has revolutionized the lodging industry in more ways than initially expected. First and foremost, it has kept hotel rates in check, especially during peak periods in cities when inventory is low and demand is high, by offering an alternative form of lodging. Airbnb rooms are more plentiful in cities with high demand for accommodations and higher-priced hotels, such as Miami, New York, and San Francisco. The flexibility of hosts to enter the market with their listings during peak demand periods means that more inventory will be available during holiday seasons or when a major event, like Formula 1, comes to the city.

Airbnb and other short-term rental companies are not without detractors. The hotel industry has tried to curb the growth of short-term rentals through lobbying and legislation. Some cities around the world have passed laws outlawing or limiting short-term rentals. There are legal challenges pending in Berlin, Barcelona, and New York. On the other hand, Amsterdam and Paris have passed laws friendly to short-term rentals. As competition from short-term rentals continues to intensify, the lodging industry is looking at new ways to tout more prominently the benefits of staying at their hotels, such as consistency of experience, daily housekeeping, and amenities like spas and fitness centers.

Hotels have also started listing their properties on Airbnb, which plays well into travelers' affinity for brand loyalty because Airbnb gets a very high rating for brand advocacy. For consumers who have never experienced a vacation rental, a survey from Goldman Sachs found out that while 79 percent of guests prefer a hotel over Airbnb, that number drops to 40 percent once they've experienced Airbnb.[12]

Knowledge Check

1. What is an advantage of a hotel chain diversifying its brands?

2. How can hotels be categorized by price?

6.4 DEVELOPING AND PLANNING NEW HOTELS

Before a new hotel is built, (1) a site is selected, (2) a feasibility study is conducted to determine the potential success of the planned hotel, and (3) financing is arranged.

Site Selection

Choosing the site for a hotel is usually first in a series of critical decisions affecting the eventual success of the hotel. The site must be accessible to the market it hopes to attract. If the location is downtown, for example, it should be convenient to the central business district, the financial district, the entertainment district, or a major convention hall. It also should be accessible by public transportation. If it is a highway location, whether the highway is a major route and will continue to be one should be established. Many of the old "ma and pa" tourist courts and motels were put out of business when new freeways and turnpikes bypassed their locations. On the other hand, the site criteria for resort hotels might be quite different. Many resorts are deliberately developed off main routes and might not be easily accessible. One example of a hotel in a somewhat isolated location is Amangiri in Utah, a resort in the middle of the desert that can only be reached by a private road. The luxury resort is known for its stunning architecture and its secluded location, which offers guests the opportunity to enjoy the natural beauty of the surrounding landscape in peace and quiet.

The site must be adaptable to the type and size of the proposed hotel. A 400-room commercial hotel with meeting space cannot be built on a site where zoning laws prohibit a building of that size. Zoning ordinances could also limit the type and size of ancillary facilities that would make the property more attractive and marketable, such as restaurants and lounges. Parking requirements are another consideration. Many cities have ordinances that dictate the number of parking spaces that must be available to employees and guests. That requirement must be satisfied before a hotel can be constructed.

The Feasibility Study

After the site is selected, a market study and financial analysis to determine the potential return on investment, called a **feasibility study**, is conducted. This study can help investors decide whether the hotel project they are considering is economically viable. Among other things, a feasibility study determines the size and scope of the potential guest market for the new hotel. It would be unwise to construct a hotel without first making sure that a market for it exists and learning about the market's size and characteristics. The kinds of questions the study should address include: What kind of hotel is most likely to succeed in this location? What types of guests is it likely to attract? How much will these guests be willing to pay? What occupancy rate can be expected? How many competitors are there and where are they located? Are there any other hotels planned for the area, and if so, at what stage of development are they in the planning process?

A feasibility study helps prospective owners in a number of ways. They can use the study to help them obtain financing and negotiate contracts for a franchise, lease, or management contract. A feasibility study can guide planners and architects of the facility. A study also helps the new hotel's management team formulate operating and marketing plans and prepare the initial capital and operating budget.

Feasibility studies are typically conducted at the request of lenders, investors, franchisors, or management companies. Usually, the person or persons conducting the study are independent consultants, although it is not uncommon for developers, management companies, or institutional investors to conduct their own study as well.

The person or consulting firm commissioned to conduct a feasibility study should have expertise and experience in hotel marketing, operations, and finance. There are a number of domestic and international companies that are considered experts in these disciplines, including HVS Global Hospitality Services and PricewaterhouseCoopers. Personnel in these firms are often graduates of hospitality management schools.

Most feasibility studies are performed to determine the suitability of a location for a hotel-chain property. Hotel chains already have brand recognition, tested hotel concepts, and established markets. Consumers have definite expectations of these hotels. Therefore, an important purpose of a feasibility study is to find out whether the proposed site and hotel can meet these expectations.

The Report. The final product of a feasibility study is a written report that typically includes the following sections.

Market area characteristics. This section contains a review of demographic and relevant economic data for the area surrounding the site. The purpose is not to provide an in-depth economic evaluation, but to obtain a sampling of those factors that support or reject the need for the proposed hotel. For example, a profile of the commercial and industrial sectors of the area can indicate the degree of economic stability and strength of the market. Population statistics, along with growth trends and income levels, are valuable for determining the potential demand for hotel restaurants and catering facilities. Employment statistics are helpful as well. Not only are they another indicator of economic strength, but they also may be useful in forecasting potential

employment problems or opportunities in operating the hotel. Highway traffic counts, air arrivals and departures, and tourism statistics often are analyzed in relation to their potential impact on the proposed project.

Site and area evaluation. The father of the modern American hotel, Ellsworth Statler, was reputed to have said that there were three reasons for a hotel's success: location, location, and location. That maxim may be as true today as it ever was. As pointed out earlier, convenience and accessibility are key components to a new hotel's success. There may be a real demand, but if the proposed hotel is not easily accessible to the source of that demand, it cannot succeed. Moreover, the proposed hotel should ideally be *more accessible than existing or proposed competing hotels.*

Accessibility is a relative concept, of course, and varies according to the kind of facility proposed. Club Med has built one of the largest hospitality organizations of its kind by going into areas that are, by definition, inaccessible—except to its own guests. To make sure that guests can get to its hotels, Club Med often charters aircraft and buses, and it has even developed airports in partnership with governments (as was necessary in Mexico).

Accessibility is a relative concept that varies according to the type of facility proposed. Some hotels are built in remote areas.

Resort hotels may not need to be accessible by automobile as long as they are convenient to get to by air, train, bus, or even ferry (e.g., ferries serve Nantucket Island in Massachusetts). On the other hand, highways are the lifelines of motels.

Finally, the reputation of the area may well be an important factor in determining the feasibility of the proposed hotel. Travelers avoid areas with high crime rates, blatant poverty, or political unrest. Unless there is an overriding reason for building a hotel in these areas, they are best avoided.

Competition analysis. A good feasibility study carefully describes all the competition and proposed future competition in the area to reveal the size and nature of the market as it currently exists. Facilities, services, and price levels of competitors are noted. This section of the report is a good place to look for opportunities that may have been overlooked or simply not taken advantage of by competitors. There may not be a fine dining restaurant in the area, for example, or there may be a need for a health club—both of which a hotel could include in its concept.

Demand analysis. The feasibility study must answer a number of questions about potential guests. Who are they and where are they going to come from? How many are there? Is this number likely to grow or decline in the future? Which hotels are they going to now? How are we going to take these guests away from those hotels? (It should be noted that other than the existing demand for hotels within a competitive set, additional demand can be created by a new hotel that is unlike any of the competition.) A detailed approach to demand analysis is a vital part of any sound marketing plan.

On the one hand, if demand is expected to be generated from local industry and commercial activity, then surveys of potential guests in the area are one of the best ways to confirm that demand. On the other hand, if the potential market is anticipated to come from incoming travelers such as conventioneers and sightseers, measured by current occupied room nights and a projection of future room demand by market segment, then the market survey should be extended to cover those groups. The market as a whole must be quantified, measured by current occupied room nights and a projection of future room demand by market segment. Then

the potential for the proposed property to gain a fair share of that market must be appraised.

Proposed facilities and services. After analyzing market-area characteristics, evaluating the site, reviewing the competition, and preparing a demand analysis, the next step in a feasibility study is the proposal of facilities and services. At this stage, the analysts conducting the study are expected to recommend the size and type of facilities the proposed hotel should have, as well as the services that should be provided. Their goal is to establish a market difference that gives the hotel a competitive advantage. Recommendations may cover architectural and design considerations as well as overall concept and ambience.

Financial estimates. The last section of the study contains estimates of revenues and expenses, based on (1) the proposed hotel's type and the services it will offer, and (2) the size of the projected guest demand.

Feasibility studies vary at this point. Some will present estimates of operating results only. Others, at the request of those commissioning the study, provide additional information, such as (1) the fixed charges that can be anticipated—for example, property taxes, the cost of insurance on buildings and contents, and interest on borrowed capital and depreciation; and (2) an analysis of the expected return on investment (ROI). A study that includes ROI is a true feasibility study. (However, in order to calculate the return on investment, an estimate of construction and development costs must be obtained, usually from other experts.) Most studies end at the point of forecasting income before fixed charges—that is, they estimate only operating revenues and expenses. Those studies are known as market studies with estimates of operating revenues and expenses. Exhibit 6.3 lists financial risks and rewards in the hotel industry.

Financing

Investors who are asked to participate in the financing of a new hotel look carefully at several components, known as hard costs:

■ *The land on which the hotel will be built.* How large is the site? What condition is it in?

Exhibit 6.3   Hotel Industry Financial Rewards and Risks

Hotel Industry Financial Rewards/Benefits	
Type of Reward/Benefit	**Explanation**
Favorable Tax Treatment	Personal property within a hotel can be depreciated over a short period of time. As such, hotels generate tax shelter benefits via associated depreciation and amortization write-offs.
Potential for Significant Profits	As soon as the income from a hotel reaches the break-even point, profits tend to increase rapidly. A large portion of hotel expenses are fixed and do not vary significantly with occupancy; therefore profits increase with occupancy.
Potential for Value Appreciation	The financial returns from a hotel investment are derived from the annual cash flow after debt service (equity dividend), mortgage amortization, and the potential value appreciation realized when a property is sold. Mortgage amortization also creates equity.
Inflation Hedge	Hotel rates can be adjusted daily, within the limits of market conditions.
Part of a Global Industry	Travel and tourism is the world's largest employer and industry, with strong growth prospects over the next 10 years.
Intangibles	Trophy-asset and investment-grade hotel properties can strengthen an investor's portfolio, prestige, and standing in the financial community.
Financial Risk in the Hotel Industry	
Type of Risk	**Explanation**
Cyclicity and Operating Leverage	Small movements in occupancy and average daily rate have had profound impacts on net operating income. A hotel's significant operating leverage heightens its sensitivity to economic cycles and necessitates underwriting to a higher debt service coverage ratio than for other property types. Because of the higher operating leverage inherent to the lodging sector, investors can naturally expect higher return potential compared to other types of real estate investments. However, the downside risk in the hotel industry is greater if economic or company-specific issues produce insufficient cash flow to cover the high fixed-cost structure of this asset class.
Interest Rate Risk	The unexpected change in interest rates is a risk. Changes in interest rates impact hotel investments because they are highly leveraged. This means that increased interest rates lower returns or can make a proposed project not feasible.
	Additionally, required investor returns tend to move with interest rates.
	With interest rates rising, the value of the future is discounted. Higher interest rates make it harder to earn those profits. The rise in interest rates will also cause price/earnings ratio multiples to decline.
Supply-Side Risk	A spike in hotel construction gives pause to investors and triggers scrutiny. The critical issue is whether supply is growing faster than demand. Many hotel markets are currently suffering from supply growth that is running ahead of demand. Part of the reason is that the capital suppliers are hotel companies, not traditional real estate financing sources.

Source: Adapted from *PKF Consulting.*

What is its appraised value? What is its market value? What has comparable land sold for in the last year?

- *The building.* What construction costs are involved? How long will it take to construct the hotel?

- *Furniture, fixtures, and equipment (FF&E).* What is needed to decorate rooms and public areas? What types of equipment are necessary? How much will FF&E cost?

In addition to these **hard costs**, there are components known as **soft costs** that should be factored into any financing package:

- *Architectural fees.* These include site elevations, final blueprints from which contractors will work, and models.

- *Pre-opening expenses.* Certain members of the management team will be on board months before opening day. New managers and employees must be trained. Security guards will be needed to protect the property. An advertising campaign should begin several months before opening day. Working capital will also be needed until the hotel is open and generating its own.

- *Financing costs.* Financing costs include interest on loans and brokerage fees paid to lenders.

There are two general types of hotel financing—permanent financing loans and construction financing loans.

Permanent financing loans are long-term mortgage loans—traditionally no longer than 25 years. Long-term mortgage loans are obtained from institutions such as insurance companies, pension funds, and banks. These lending institutions provide financing and charge interest at what the going rate is when the loan is made. In addition, they sometimes take an equity position in the property—that is, they become part-owners of the hotel. Historically, these institutions have put up as much as 65 to 75 percent of the cost of the project. The developer, either alone or with partners, provides the remainder, as lenders do not wish to loan money to projects if the developer is unwilling or unable to risk any of their own funds.

A **construction financing loan** is obtained from a bank or a group of banks. It is a short-term loan for use while the hotel is being built, with repayment to be made in three years or less. In most cases, the construction financing loan is approved only after permanent financing, known as "**take-out**," has already been granted, since once the hotel opens and the permanent financing is in place, part of the permanent financing will be used to pay off the construction financing loan.

Knowledge Check

1. What is a feasibility study and what does it cover?

2. What options exist for financing a hotel?

CHAPTER SUMMARY

The hotel industry is dynamic. Each year, companies and hotels change ownership, and new companies and brands enter the marketplace. The hotel industry is also global. Mergers, acquisitions, and joint ventures have changed the competitive environment in many parts of the world.

There is more awareness about environmental concerns among hotel owners and customers, resulting in more eco-friendly hotels. Some hotels are opting for LEED (Leadership in Energy and Environmental Design) certification, while others are adopting environmentally friendly programs. Almost all major hotel chains have initiated "green" policies.

Hotel guests can be classified by market segment. The major market segments are corporate individuals, corporate groups, convention and association groups, leisure travelers, long-term stay/relocation guests, airline-related guests, government and military travelers, regional getaway guests, and bleisure travelers. "Guest mix" refers to the variety or mixture of guests who stay at a hotel.

Hotels can be categorized by location: center-city, resort, suburban, highway, and airport are common categories.

Center-city hotels are typically full-service hotels located near their city's government or financial district. Most guests who stay in center-city hotels are in the "corporate individual" or "convention guest" categories.

Resorts are built in destinations that are desirable because of climate, scenery, recreational facilities, or historic interest. Many resorts are patronized for health reasons. While early resorts were usually open only in the summer, most resorts today are open year-round. Most resort business comes from leisure travelers, but resort use by businesses for meetings and incentive programs can be a significant source of revenue. Most resorts are still independent operations. They are expensive to build and operate. However, changing consumer demand has led to a renewed interest in all-inclusive resorts, with Marriott, Wyndham, and Hyatt actively growing their portfolios to include more all-inclusives.

Suburban hotels followed corporations and factories that relocated from downtown to the suburbs because of land costs. Suburban hotels tend to be somewhat smaller than downtown properties and are primarily chain affiliated. Individual business travelers represent their single largest market, although their food and beverage operations are often patronized by the local community.

Highway hotels have evolved from early tourist courts. Large signs, easy access, and ample parking facilities are distinguishing characteristics. Many are franchised. Business travelers are their main source of revenue.

Airport hotels are for the most part affiliated with chains and enjoy some of the highest occupancy rates in the lodging industry. Their biggest operating problem is the need to respond to high demand instantly when weather or other conditions delay flight arrivals and departures.

Hotels can also be categorized by ownership. Most hotels are owned, leased, managed, or franchised by a chain. Nevertheless, many independent hotels have overcome the chains' advantage of economies of scale with other business strategies that allow them to compete effectively. Business philosophies vary from chain to chain. Some hotel chains prefer to own, others to franchise, and others to manage. Many have a mix of the three. In addition, there are some successful management companies that operate and manage chain properties.

Hotels can also be categorized by price. The most important classifications are (1) select-service—economy and budget; (2) mid-price—full-service and select-service; and (3) first-class/luxury.

A significant development in the hotel industry has been the growth of segmentation strategies. To capture more guest markets, companies like Marriott now offer a complete line of properties that range from economy to luxury.

Other types of hotels include boutique/lifestyle hotels, all-suite hotels, conference centers, timeshare properties, condominium hotels, seniors housing, and Airbnb.

Feasibility studies are conducted when new hotels are developed and planned. They help prospective owners obtain financing and help managers prepare operating and marketing plans. Location is a key consideration in all new hotel projects.

Hotel financing covers hard costs, such as the land, building(s), and furniture, fixtures, and equipment; as well as soft costs, such as architectural fees, pre-opening expenses, and financing costs. Financing for new hotels is usually provided in two types of loans—long-term permanent financing loans (mortgage loans) and short-term construction financing loans.

airline-related guests—Airplane crew members; airline passengers needing emergency accommodations are also included in this guest category.

airport hotels—Full-service hotels built near airports.

all-suite hotel—A hotel that features units made up of two connected hotel rooms that sell for approximately the price of one, at lower prices than traditional hotel suites. One room is furnished as a typical hotel guestroom with a bed, the other with a foldout sofa and/or table and chairs.

bleisure—A term that combines the words "business" and "leisure." It refers to the trend of guests blending work travel with leisure travel to save on vacation costs and create a better work–life balance.

boutique hotels—Small hotels, typically 150 to 300 rooms, usually described as "cultural," "historical," and "authentic."

budget hotels—A type of select-service hotel. Budget hotels have low construction and operating costs, allowing them to charge between $45 and $60 per night, a slightly higher rate than economy hotels.

center-city hotels—Full-service hotels located in downtown areas.

condominium hotel—A building or complex with individual rooms that are sold to individual owners. Owners have the option to use units for personal reasons or place them in a rental program managed by a hotel operator.

conference centers—Specialized hotels, usually accessible to major market areas but in less busy locations, that almost exclusively book conferences, executive meetings, and training seminars. Some conference centers provide extensive leisure facilities.

construction financing loan—A short-term loan for use while a hotel is being built, with repayment to be made in three years or less.

convention and association groups—Businesspeople attending a convention or association meeting. The number of guests can run into the thousands.

corporate groups—Small groups of people traveling for business purposes, usually to attend conferences or meetings.

corporate individuals—Individuals traveling for business purposes who are not part of any group.

economy hotels—A type of select-service hotel. Economy hotels have the lowest construction and operating costs, allowing them to charge 25 percent less than budget hotels.

feasibility study—A study commissioned by developers and prepared by consultants to determine the potential success of a proposed hotel on a proposed site.

first-class/luxury hotels—Hotels with high room rates and exceptional service and amenities.

franchise—Refers to (1) the authorization given by one company to another to sell its unique product and service, or (2) the name of the business format or product that is being franchised.

franchisee—The individual or company granted a franchise.

franchisor—The franchise company that owns the trademark, products, and/or business format that is being franchised.

government and military travelers—Guests on a fixed per diem allowance who typically are reimbursed for hotel and other travel expenses.

guest mix—The variety or mixture of guests who stay at a hotel or patronize a restaurant.

hard costs—The land, building, and furniture, fixture, and equipment (FF&E) costs that are basic to hotel and restaurant development.

highway hotels—Hotels built next to a highway. These hotels typically feature large property signs, an entrance where travelers can leave their cars as they check in, and a swimming pool. Parking space is plentiful, and the atmosphere is informal.

hotel chain—A group of affiliated hotels.

independent hotel—A hotel owned by an individual or group of investors not connected with any hotel company.

leisure travelers—Vacationing travelers, often entire families, who typically spend only one night at a hotel unless the hotel is their destination.

lifestyle hotel—While similar to a boutique hotel, a lifestyle hotel generally features contemporary design and décor, provides unique service, and offers high-quality technology.

long-term stay/relocation guests—Individuals or families relocating to an area who require lodging until permanent housing is found.

management company—A company that manages hotels for owners, typically in return for a combination of fees and a share of revenues. A management company may or may not have any of its own funds invested in a hotel that it manages.

mid-price hotels—Hotels that offer facilities and services similar to those at first-class/luxury hotels, but at average rates. They have restaurants and bars, and many have meeting space. Average prices vary by market.

permanent financing loan—A long-term mortgage loan for a hotel, usually up to 25 years. Long-term mortgage loans are obtained from institutions such as insurance companies, pension funds, and banks.

regional getaway guests—Guests who check into a hotel close to home, with or without children, to enjoy a weekend away from daily responsibilities.

resort hotels—Usually located in desirable vacation spots, resort hotels offer fine dining, exceptional service, and many amenities.

segmenting—A method of categorizing hotels by the prices they charge.

select-service hotels—Hotels that do not offer the full range of services customarily associated with hotels. For example, they do not have restaurants or bars. Types of select-service hotels include budget and economy hotels.

seniors housing—Long-term living facilities for senior citizens that can be broken down into four types: independent-living units, congregate communities, assisted-living communities, and continuing-care retirement communities.

soft brands—Also referred to as collections of independent hotels. Established when independent hotels join a larger parent brand or group while preserving their individual identity and unique characteristics. The independent hotels benefit from the established brand's resources, such as reservations systems, distribution channels, loyalty programs, and marketing support.

soft costs—Development costs other than land, building, and furniture, fixture, and equipment (FF&E) costs for a hotel or restaurant project. Soft costs include architectural fees, pre-opening expenses (e.g., for advertising and employee training), and financing.

suburban hotels—Hotels located in suburban areas. Suburban hotels typically belong to a major hotel chain and have 250 to 500 rooms, as well as restaurants, bars, and other amenities found at most downtown hotels.

take-out—The permanent financing secured for a new hotel.

timeshare condominiums—Condominiums for which an owner can purchase a portion of time at the condominium, typically one month to one week, for one-twelfth or one-fiftieth of the condominium's price and share the condominium with other owners. Owners have the right to stay at the condominium during their assigned time or to trade their slot with another owner.

tourist courts—The forerunners of motels, built along highways in the 1920s and 1930s. Typical tourist courts consisted of a simple row of small cabins that often had no private baths.

1. Which hotel was developed as part of a brand extension?
   a. Waldorf Astoria Central Park
   b. The Maybourne Beverly Hills
   c. Hotel del Coronado
   d. Aloft by Starwood

2. Which guest segment describes a traveler who combines work and leisure travel?
   a. Regional getaway guest
   b. Long-term-stay guest
   c. Airline-related guest
   d. Bleisure traveler

3. What is the main difference between a center-city hotel and a resort hotel?
   a. Center-city hotels are developed in metropolitan areas. Resort hotels are developed in desirable vacation spots.
   b. Center-city hotels appeal to budget-conscious travelers. Resort hotels appeal to luxury travelers.
   c. Center-city hotels appeal to leisure travelers. Resort hotels appeal to budget travelers.
   d. Center-city hotels are built close to highways. Resort hotels are built close to airports.

4. Which is a characteristic of airport hotels?
   a. Their demand depends on highway traffic.
   b. They are frequently booked for weddings.
   c. They report some of the highest occupancy rates.
   d. They collect a large amount of revenue from parking fees.

5. A franchisor is defined as
   a. an investment group that manages a hotel.
   b. a contractor who operates a hotel.
   c. a party being granted a franchise.
   d. a party granting a franchise.

6. Which hotel would be categorized as a select-service, economy budget hotel?
   a. Motel 6
   b. The Four Seasons
   c. Hilton Garden Inn
   d. The Standard Hotel

7. Which type of seniors housing would best suit a 74-year-old with no serious health conditions who drives independently?
   a. Assisted-living facility
   b. Congregate community
   c. Independent-living unit
   d. Continuing-care retirement community

8. What type of lodging houses short-term guests and permanent residents?
   a. Airbnb
   b. Timeshare
   c. All-suite hotel
   d. Condominium hotel

9. Which section of a feasibility report includes demographic information?
  a. Market-area characteristics
  b. Site and area evaluation
  c. Competition analysis
  d. Financing costs

10. Which is considered a hard cost in developing a hotel property?
  a. Pre-opening expenses
  b. Architectural fees
  c. Financing costs
  d. The land on which the hotel will be built

11. Historically, what percentage of the cost of a hotel do lenders put up with a permanent financing loan?
  a. 35 to 40 percent
  b. 50 to 55 percent
  c. 65 to 75 percent
  d. 85 to 95 percent

12. What is the purpose of the LEED certification program?
  a. To create more definitive standards for hotel classification
  b. To provide benchmarks for the operation of sustainable buildings
  c. To announce that a hotel incorporates some eco-friendly practices
  d. To announce that a hotel uses green cleaning products

SHORT-ANSWER QUESTIONS

1. How does the hotel industry meet the needs of different kinds of guests?

2. How has technology and the need for sustainability changed the hotel industry?

IS IT WORTH IT?

Brad, a real estate investor, wants to build a soft brand hotel that is a franchise of a major hotel chain. He is looking to open the hotel on Florida's Gulf Coast in a city just south of the Sarasota metropolitan area. The area has had a large population increase since the COVID-19 pandemic and is filled with residents who are retired or looking for a quiet, serene place to live. However, a major disaster and certain lodging trends have impacted the area.

In 2022, a Category 4 hurricane struck the area, eroding beaches, flooding major roads, damaging beachfront homes and hotels, and knocking down trees. Almost six months later, the area had recovered enough for the spring break holiday rush. Tourism began to reach a 60 percent level of business as spring breakers descended on Sarasota.

But a new trend has emerged: because of the popularity of Airbnb rentals with bleisure travelers, many hotels are not at high room occupancy. The local government has tried to crack down on short-term rentals but has not stopped the trend. Many residents own their properties and want to recoup the money paid to their high property taxes by renting out the properties.

Brad is not fully aware of these circumstances and has already decided to build in the area. The decision to proceed with the property build-out is quite risky.

DISCUSSION QUESTIONS

1. Has Brad conducted a full feasibility study?

2. What are the risks associated with the hotel build-out?

3. Should Brad expect a large ROI for this franchise?

J.W. Marriott

J.W. Marriott, Jr. is chairman emeritus of Marriott International, Inc. Mr. Marriott was executive chair and chair of the board before retiring in May of 2022. Mr. Marriott's leadership spanned 66 years, as he guided what was once a family-run root beer stand and restaurant to a global hospitality company that today is comprised of more than 8,500 properties across 31 brands in 138 countries and territories. Mr. Marriott served 40 years as Marriott's chief executive officer before stepping down on March 31, 2012.

Mr. Marriott's passion for the hospitality industry began at an early age. He spent his high school and college years working in a variety of positions in the family's Hot Shoppes restaurant chain. He became a full-time associate in 1956, and soon afterward began overseeing the first Marriott hotel. He became president of the company in 1964 and chief executive officer in 1972. He was elected chair of the board in 1985.

Throughout his career, Mr. Marriott has been known industry-wide for his hands-on management style, which is built on his parents' core value of putting people first. The Marriott corporate culture emphasizes the value that associates bring to the organization.

Mr. Marriott is known as a lodging innovator—shifting the company's business model in the late 1970s from hotel ownership to property management and franchising. His strategic decision allowed the company to accelerate its growth and broaden its leadership position. That transformation culminated in the company's split in 1993 into Marriott International—a hotel management and franchising company headed by Mr. Marriott—and Host Marriott International, a hotel ownership company chaired by his brother, Richard Marriott.

In January 2007, Marriott on the Move, one of the first regular corporate CEO blogs, was launched. Mr. Marriott's award-winning blog extended his global reach and influence that complemented his well-known visits to hundreds of hotels annually before his retirement.

Mr. Marriott serves on the board of trustees of the J. Willard & Alice S. Marriott Foundation. He is a former member of the executive committee of the World Travel & Tourism Council and has served on the board of trustees of the National Geographic Society and as a director of the U.S. Naval Academy Foundation. Previously, Mr. Marriott was chair of the President's Export Council and served on the board of General Motors, Georgetown University, and the Mayo Clinic.

Mr. Marriott grew up in the Washington, D.C., area, where he attended St. Albans School. At the University of Utah, he earned a bachelor's degree in banking and finance, and went on to serve as an officer in the United States Navy. Mr. Marriott is an active member of the Church of Jesus Christ of Latter-day Saints. He is married to the former Donna Garff. They are the parents of four children and have 15 grandchildren, as well as 32 great-grandchildren.

Source: https://news.marriott.com/leadership/j-w-marriott-jr.

WHAT WOULD YOU DO?

A luxury hotel located in a prime location has been facing a decline in guest satisfaction scores over the past year. The hotel is known for its premium amenities, exceptional customer service, and a wide range of dining options. However, the management team has noticed a steady decrease in guest satisfaction scores on review sites like TripAdvisor and Google reviews. The management team is concerned about the negative impact on the hotel's reputation and revenue.

The hotel's management team has identified a few key issues that are affecting the guest experience. First, guests have been complaining about long wait times at check-in and check-out. Second, there have been issues with room cleanliness, and some guests have reported finding stains on linens or towels. Finally, guests have reported a lack of personalized service and attention from the hotel staff. As the general manager, what would you do?

7

HOTEL ORGANIZATION AND MANAGEMENT

Chapter Outline

Learning Objectives

1. Explain how a hotel is organized, distinguish revenue centers from cost centers, and describe the rooms department. (pp. 184–194)

2. Describe a hotel's food and beverage department, and describe the following other hotel revenue centers: golf course and pro shop, health club/spa, and parking department. (pp. 194–203)

3. List hotel cost centers; describe the accounting, human resources, security, information and telecommunications systems, sales and marketing, and property operation and maintenance departments; discuss the utilities cost center; and give examples of what a hotel must do to comply with the Americans with Disabilities Act. (pp. 203–209)

4. Describe hotel control systems, give examples of financial controls used in hotels, summarize the need for (and give examples of) quality controls in hotels, and discuss hotel technology. (pp. 209–219)

accounting department

assets

average daily rate (ADR)

capture rate

catering department

commissions

concession

control system

cost centers

departmental expenses

familiarization (fam) tours

financial controls

food and beverage
department

front office

housekeeping department

human resources
department

key cards

liabilities

meal plan

night audit

nonoperating expenses

occupancy percentage

property management
system (PMS)

property operation
and maintenance
department

purchasing department

quality controls

rentals

reservations department

revenue centers

revenue management

revenue per available room
(RevPAR)

rooms department

room service

sales and marketing
department

security department

undistributed operating
expenses

uniformed service
department

In order to gain a perspective on how hotels are organized, a few hotel characteristics should be noted at the outset:

■ All hotels are in the business of renting rooms.

■ Hotels vary in size, from under 100 rooms to over 5,000.

■ Hotels vary in type. They can be center-city hotels, resorts, highway properties, conference centers, and so on.

■ Hotels vary in the nature and extent of their facilities. Some hotels offer only rooms, while others have coffee shops, gourmet restaurants, swimming pools, golf courses, and other facilities.

■ Hotels vary in the level of service they offer. For example, some offer 24-hour room service, others offer room service from 7 a.m. to 10 p.m. only, and some do not offer room service at all.

Clearly, hotels are not all alike. No matter what category a hotel falls into, however, it must

be organized in order to: (1) coordinate the many specialized tasks and activities necessary to attract and serve guests, and (2) produce a reasonable profit consistent with the amount of money and time invested in the enterprise. Organizing is one of the principal jobs of management. This chapter will introduce the organizational structure of hotels, including functional areas and their responsibilities. Control systems related to financial statements and service quality standards will also be reviewed.

7.1 HOW IS A HOTEL ORGANIZED?

In order to attract and serve guests and make a reasonable profit, hotels are organized into functional areas or departments based on the services the hotel provides. For instance, all hotels have a rooms department to manage guestrooms. If the hotel operates a restaurant or lounge, it is likely to have a food and beverage department as well. Within each department there are specialized functions. The rooms department handles reservations, check-in and check-out activities, housekeeping tasks, and uniformed service activities. At a small hotel, these functions are performed by personnel who report to and take their instructions from the general manager. At a large hotel, rooms personnel report to a rooms department manager. The tasks each employee is responsible for also vary with the size of the hotel. For example, in a small hotel, one person behind the front desk may act as receptionist, cashier, and hotel operator. In a large hotel, different individuals handle these jobs.

Revenue Centers versus Cost Centers

The departments in a hotel can be divided into two main groups. Those that generate operating revenue for the hotel through the sale of services or products to guests are commonly known as **revenue centers** or operated departments. The departments and hotel areas/functions in the other group do not generate revenue directly; instead, they support the proper functioning of the departments that generate operating revenue and are commonly known as **cost centers** or support centers. The expenses of these departments or areas are classified as undistributed operating expenses.[1]

Probably the easiest way to understand revenue and cost centers is to take a look at hotel organization charts. Exhibit 7.1 shows a typical organization chart for a small hotel. As you can see, this hotel has four departments: front office, housekeeping, food and beverage, and building maintenance. The general manager supervises four people, each of whom has the responsibility

and the authority to take care of one of the four principal areas in this hotel. These individuals may or may not supervise other employees, depending on the size of the property. (For example, at a very small property, building maintenance may be handled by just one person.)

Let's examine a much larger hotel that has a much more complex organization. The positions shown in Exhibit 7.2 (or the personnel reporting to these positions) can be placed in the following hotel departments under the revenue center and cost center categories:

Revenue Centers	Cost Centers
Rooms Department	Administrative and General Department
Food and Beverage Department	Information and Telecommunications Systems Department
Other Revenue Centers	Sales and Marketing Department
	Property Operations and Maintenance Department

In order to make hotels more efficient and profitable, there is a trend to combine some departments and eliminate certain middle management positions. At some hotels, the rooms operation and food and beverage operation have been combined into one department, for example. Those areas responsible for generating revenue, such as sales, guestroom reservations, and catering, might be combined into a revenue department.

Exhibit 7.1 Sample Organization Chart—Small Hotel

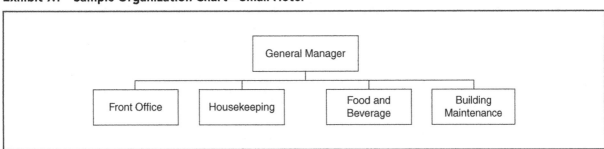

Exhibit 7.2 Executive Committee of a Large Hotel

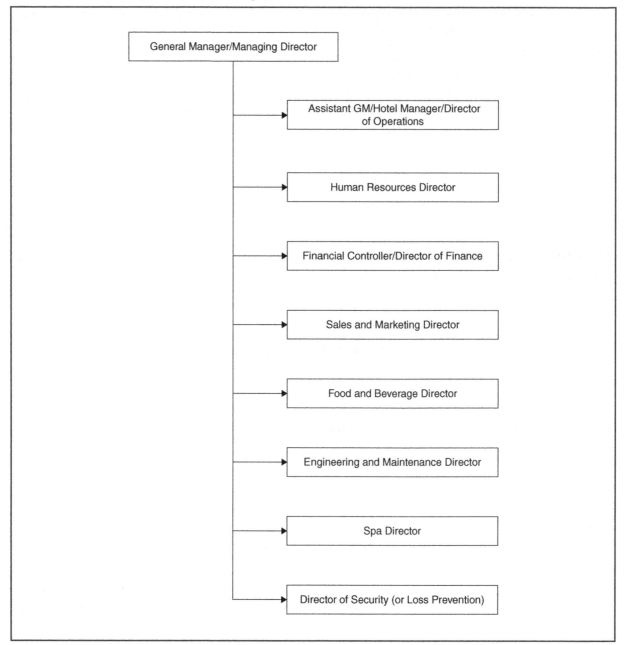

Finally, there might be an administrative department that includes human resources (HR) and accounting.

In some hotel chains, regional management clusters have been formed. Under this system, a single manager (i.e., general manager, controller, or HR director) is in charge of more than one hotel in the region.

At other hotels, a different kind of reorganization is taking place. Based on management concepts that put the customer first, frontline employees are being empowered to solve guest problems and make other decisions— by themselves or in teams. Authority is pushed down to the lowest level in the organization. For some hotels, the sample organization charts shown in this chapter may be more representative of the functions that occur in a hotel rather than the employees who do the job.

Now let's take a closer look at each revenue and cost center.

7.2 REVENUE CENTERS

The two main hotel revenue centers are the rooms department and the food and beverage department. (Casino hotels are an exception to this rule, since their guestrooms are occupied by guests whose primary reason for being at the hotel is to gamble.) Other revenue centers found at some hotels include the golf course and pro shop, health club/spa, and parking department.

Rooms Department

In most hotels, the **rooms department** is the major department and the central reason for the business entity. Most of any hotel's square footage is devoted to guestrooms and areas that support the operation of those rooms. Therefore, the major segment of the building investment and, in most cases, the land cost is related to the rooms department.

For all hotels except casino hotels, guestroom rentals are the single largest source of revenue. Sources of hotel revenue for upper upscale chains, such as Marriott and Hilton, reported by Smith Travel Research (STR) for 2022 are listed below. Note that the percentages do not equal 100 percent because they are based only on the total revenue of hotels that reported each line item:

Rooms	64.1%
Rentals and other income	6.1
Other operated departments	15.3
Food and beverage	22.4[2]

Not only do rooms occupy the most space in a hotel and produce the most revenue, but they also generate the most profit. In a study of U.S. hotels published by CBRE, rooms department income (defined as room revenues or sales less room operating expenses) amounted to about 70 percent of rooms revenue. In other words, for every dollar spent on guestrooms, 70 cents was available for general overhead after deducting the direct rooms department expenses. Per the *Uniform System of Accounts for the Lodging Industry*, the costs to provide housekeeping and complimentary food and beverage are recorded in the rooms department, and rooms department profits comprise 81.9 percent of total departmental profits.[3]

Organization of the Rooms Department. No matter the size or category of hotel, rooms departments are organized and function in a similar manner. Large hotels have more functions and personnel within the department, but this does not change the basic tasks that must be performed.

In a small hotel, the general manager or owner directly oversees the rooms department because of its paramount importance. In a mid-size to large hotel (300 rooms or more), there is likely to be a rooms manager or an executive assistant manager in charge of rooms. In either case, the rooms department is usually organized like the sample organization chart shown in Exhibit 7.3.

As you can see, the rooms department has four functions:

- Front office
- Reservations
- Housekeeping
- Uniformed service

Front office. The **front office** is the command post for processing reservations, registering guests, settling guest accounts (cashiering), and checking out guests. Front desk agents[4] also handle the distribution of guestroom keys as well as mail, messages, or other information for guests.

The most visible part of the front office area is, of course, the front desk. The front desk can be a counter or, in some luxury hotels, an actual desk where a guest can sit down and register. Traditionally, the front desk was placed so that the person behind it had a view of both the front door and the elevator. This was so front desk agents could discourage unwelcome individuals from entering and keep nonpaying guests from departing. Because of modern credit and security procedures, such front desk placement is no

Exhibit 7.3   Sample Organization Chart—Rooms Department

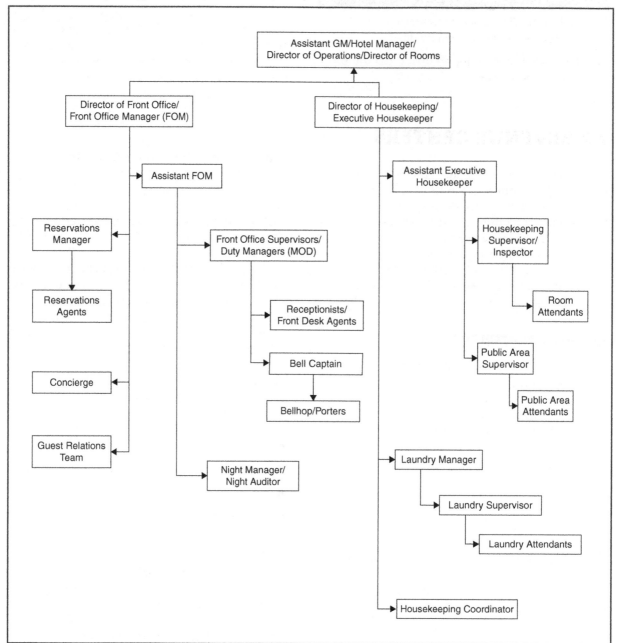

longer necessary. Recent trends in hotel design, especially lifestyle hotels, have emphasized adding experiential social spaces in the lobby, from shared workspaces and bar-centric food and beverage outlets to game rooms. Many of the new designs treated the entire lobby as a food and beverage outlet. This serves as a community gathering spot for travelers and locals, creates a sense of place, and adds an active environment at check-in.

The duties of front desk agents include:

- Greeting guests

- Registering guests

- Establishing a method of payment for the guestroom—credit card, cash, or direct billing

- Assigning guestrooms that are unoccupied and have been cleaned

- Assigning guestroom keys to guests
- Informing guests about their room location and special hotel facilities, and answering questions about the property and the surrounding community
- Calling a bellhop to assist guests with their luggage, if such service is normally provided

In small and mid-size hotels, the front desk agent is also the cashier. Although the front desk station and cashier's station are usually separated in large hotels, employees are often cross-trained to handle both jobs. One important duty of a cashier (or a front desk agent performing cashier duties) is to post charges to guest accounts. This means that the cashier must make sure that all of the expenses a guest incurs, such as restaurant bills that were charged to the guestroom, are added to the bill before it is presented. This task is not necessary in hotels that have a computerized **property management system (PMS)** that interfaces with a point-of-sale (POS) system and automatically posts charges to guest accounts. Once the posting has been accomplished (either manually or electronically), guests can settle their account when they check out. Checking out guests requires tact and diplomacy. Guests often have questions about their charges and, in some cases, may not even be aware that they incurred a charge when using a particular service (e.g., the in-room minibar).

Computerized PMSs have simplified check-in by providing guests the capability to check in using mobile technology through branded mobile applications (apps), such as Hilton Honors or Marriott Bonvoy. At many hotels, it is possible to use apps to make and amend reservations and to use concierge services. A growing use of app technology in hotels is for checking in and checking out. At Marriott, for example, an app allows guests to bypass the normal check-in process and pick up their preprepared key cards at a special mobile check-in desk when they arrive at the hotel. If the guest arrives before the room is available, the hotel can notify the guest when the room is ready via the app. In recent years, mobile key technology check-ins have become commonplace at many hotel brands, such as Choice Hotels, Hilton, Marriott, and Hyatt. Guests are increasingly expecting more integration with their smartphones wherever they travel. Millions of travelers today use their smartphones as a hotel room key. Eliminating disposable plastic key cards improves security and reduces the front desk's workload.

Self-service kiosks in hotel lobbies provide another simplified check-in system. From the lobby kiosk at a citizenM hotel, for example, guests can check in simply by inserting their credit card into the machine to retrieve their reservations information. After the guest selects a room, a room key is dispensed, completing the guest check-in process. Upon checking out, guests

Many hotel lobbies are offering lounge spaces with food and beverage outlets, work areas, and game and activity spaces.

can use the kiosk's terminal to pay their bills and either print a receipt or have it sent to their email on file. Check-out information is then transmitted to the PMS.

One of the most common methods for a guest to review their hotel charges is through the branded app. Many hotels still allow guests to review their bills on the television screens in their guestrooms and then send a signal through the channel selector to acknowledge that their accounts are in order and authorize payment. The bills are then charged to the guests' credit cards. Copies of the guests' hotel bills can be emailed directly to their homes or offices, or picked up in the lobby when the guests depart. Similarly, major hotel brands will allow you to check out of your room via their mobile app.

This system presumes that the guest has used a credit card and a record of that card was taken at registration or during booking. Usually, approval of the card and the guestroom charges are obtained from the credit card company at check-in, not check-out. If a credit card is not used, then the cashier must handle payment by cash or check according to the hotel's policies.

Another important duty performed at the front desk is the **night audit**. The night audit is a review of the guest accounts, also known as accounts receivable, for a single day. The purpose of a night audit is to reconcile the charges or postings to each guest account with the income of each department. For example, the total of room service charges for a day must equal the total of all the room service charges to the guest accounts. Night audits are usually done between 11 p.m. and 6 a.m., when there are few other distracting duties and the hotel's sales outlets are closed. In a small hotel, the night audit is performed by the front desk agent on duty. In a larger property, an auditor from the accounting department usually is assigned this task.

The typical metal guestroom keys and locks have been replaced in many hotels by electronic locking systems that operate with plastic **key cards** or smartphones. An electronic connection between guestroom door locks and a console at the front desk makes it possible to code a key card with each check-in, matching the key card's code with a code programmed into the console for the guest's room. When the guest inserts the key card into a slot in the guestroom doorknob assembly or taps it against the lock, the door is unlocked. The door will stay locked if someone tries to use a key card with a code that does not match the electronic code for the lock. These key cards usually do not have the name of the hotel or the room number on them; so if they are lost, they are of no use to whoever finds them. Some key card systems connect guestroom locks to a central computer so the hotel has a record of everyone who has entered the room (each housekeeping and maintenance employee's key registers its owner's code), along with the time of entry. With smartphone-based locks, guests can use their smartphones as digital keys to access their hotel rooms. Advances in biometric technology currently utilized in airports will soon be integrated into hotel rooms, allowing guests to check in and access their rooms simply with thumbprints or facial recognition. The Department of Homeland Security, American Airlines, and the Walt Disney Company already use biometric technology to streamline their authentication process and prevent fraud.

In addition to their other duties, front desk employees in most cases represent the first and last (and often the only) contact the guest has with hotel personnel. The front desk agent's ability to make guests feel welcome and special has a tremendous impact on the quality of a guest's experience. It's essential, therefore, that the front desk staff be well-trained and that morale be kept high so that interactions with guests and among staff members are always positive.

In order to improve guest relations, more and more hotels are encouraging front office and other employees to take the initiative in resolving disputes themselves rather than referring them to a supervisor. For example, the Ritz-Carlton hotel chain permits all employees to deduct up to $2,000 from a guest's bill if the guest has a legitimate complaint.

Reservations. A **reservations department** is staffed by skilled telemarketing personnel who take reservations over the phone, answer questions about facilities, quote prices and available dates, and sell to callers who are shopping around. The majority of hotel bookings are made online using a central reservations system (CRS) that is either a stand-alone system or part of the PMS. A CRS has a hotel's availability and rates and makes it possible for customers to manage their own reservations by going online to the hotel brand's website or another booking engine. Hotel reservations are received through the following sources:

- Online travel agencies (OTAs), such as Expedia, Orbitz, Travelocity, and Booking.com
- Travel agents
- Independent reservations systems
- Cruise lines and other transportation companies

Many hotels use **revenue management** techniques in the pricing and selling of rooms. For many years, airlines have used sophisticated revenue management pricing systems. These are automated marketing programs that allow the airlines to control the inventory and pricing of airplane seats by forecasting the demand for seats on a given flight or route and then adjusting prices to maximize revenue. Revenue management for hotels means using information, historical and current, to enhance a hotel's ability to carry out a number of common business practices, thereby increasing both its revenues and its customer service capabilities. These practices include:

- Setting the most effective pricing structure for guestrooms
- Limiting the number of reservations accepted for any given night, room type, or length of stay, based on the expected profitability of a reservation
- Reviewing reservations activity to determine whether any inventory control actions should be taken (e.g., lowering rates)
- Negotiating volume discounts with wholesalers and groups
- Providing customers with the right product (the right guestroom type, rate, etc.)
- Obtaining more revenue from current and potential business
- Enabling reservations agents to be effective sales agents rather than mere order takers
- Upselling guests into a more expensive room category

Eric Orkin, an industry consultant, says:

Performance benchmarks in the hotel industry are commonly keyed to room-night or dollar volume. Volume criteria like these make perfect sense when selling a product with a sustained value, but the value of a hotel room varies from day to day and over time. For example, a room on a Saturday during New England fall foliage season is a lot more valuable than the same room on a "mud season" night in the spring. Less obvious, the value of that fall foliage night was high until two days before the date, when bad weather caused a major tour to cancel. Because the hotel was now faced with the prospect of empty rooms, the value of the hotel's rooms dropped.[5]

Revenue management requires the use of complex computer programs to (1) forecast the number of reservations a hotel can expect on a given day (as well as cancellations and no-shows); (2) track the availability of guestrooms; and (3) compute the maximum rates that those rooms can be sold for based on availability, demand, and other factors that fluctuate.

As revenue management systems have become more sophisticated, their scope has expanded. For example, today many hotel companies use revenue management systems to manage their meeting space as well as their guestroom space. By tracking demand for meeting space, the goal of "total hotel revenue management" is to maximize the revenue stream of both room inventories (guestrooms and meeting rooms). There has been a corresponding increase in the status of the revenue manager, now a senior management position reporting to the general manager or the director of sales and marketing.

Some hoteliers feel that revenue management systems sometimes encourage discounting. Others see revenue management as incompatible with good customer service because room rates that frequently change can confuse guests. But, properly used, there is no doubt that revenue management can be an effective reservations tool.

Housekeeping. The **housekeeping department** is another department of the rooms department. Housekeeping is responsible for cleaning the hotel's guestrooms and public areas. In most hotels, this department has the largest staff. In a large hotel, the housekeeping department might consist of an executive housekeeper, an assistant housekeeper, room inspectors, room attendants, a houseperson crew (which cleans the public areas and handles the logistics of moving housekeeping supplies throughout the hotel), a linen room supervisor and attendants, laundry employees, and personnel in charge of employee uniforms (see Exhibit 7.4). Hotels with laundry and valet equipment may use it only for hotel linens and uniforms and send guest clothing to an outside service where it can be handled with specialized equipment.

An executive housekeeper has an enormous amount of responsibility—not only for cleaning and maintenance but also for training staff and controlling large inventories of linens, supplies, and equipment.[6] Housekeeping inspectors supervise room attendants. Room attendants are responsible for cleaning guestrooms according to specified procedures and for maintaining a predetermined level of supplies in the linen closets located on each hotel floor. They are usually assigned a quota of rooms to clean in a given number of hours. Fifteen guestrooms per shift is average, although this figure may vary considerably because of such conditions as geographic location, union contracts, the size of the property, and the wage scale.

When guests check out, it is the room attendants' responsibility to clean the guestrooms so they are available again for rental. This includes such duties as:

- Removing soiled linen and towels and replacing them with fresh ones
- Replacing amenities
- Checking the bed and blankets for damage
- Making the beds
- Emptying trash
- Checking the guestroom for broken appliances, damaged shades or blinds, and leaky faucets
- Checking closets and drawers for items forgotten by guests
- Cleaning the guestroom and bathroom

Some hotels contract with outside cleaning services to clean the hotel's lobbies, restaurants, restrooms, and windows. With the exception of windows, much of this cleaning must be done late at night, and it is difficult for hotels to find supervisors and employees willing to work at those hours. Contract cleaning firms, many of whom handle office buildings and airline terminals as well, are geared to efficiently handle these cleaning tasks during unusual work hours.

Uniformed service. The **uniformed service department**, sometimes referred to as the guest

Exhibit 7.4   Sample Organization Chart—Housekeeping Department

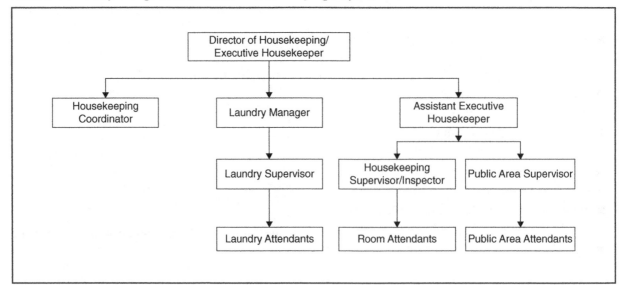

Room attendants are responsible for cleaning guestrooms according to procedures specified by the hotel.

service department, deals with guests' luggage and transportation and provides concierge service. Employees in this department include bellhops (so called because they were originally summoned by a bell), a concierge, and transportation or valet-parking employees. Some large hotels have door attendants who move luggage from cars or taxicabs into the hotel.

Bellhops move guest luggage to and from guestrooms. They also escort guests to their rooms, inspect guestrooms while rooming the guest, and explain the features of the room and the hotel to guests. Bellhops should possess a detailed knowledge of the hotel, including the hours of operation of the hotel's restaurants, lounges, and other facilities. They should also know the local community.

Many hotels have adopted the European system of concierge service. The concierge performs many of the functions that a host might perform for guests in their home. The goal is to give guests personal and attentive service. The concierge is the main source of information about the hotel. They are not only familiar with the hotel's facilities and services but also have a thorough knowledge of the local area. A good concierge knows what's going on in town. They can recommend a romantic candlelit bistro within walking distance or the best steak house in the city. The concierge can make reservations and get theater tickets—or suggest someone who can. They can also recommend secretarial services and copying centers, order limousines, and perform many other services that make guests feel important and well cared for. Some

hotels have a concierge app that guests can use to make requests, even before check-in, and to which hotel staff will respond.

Transportation services include valet parking, either in the hotel's own garage or a nearby facility. If other transportation services are provided, such as an airport shuttle, these are normally handled by the same department. In most large hotels, garages and limousines are handled by outside contractors.

Measuring the Performance of the Rooms Department. The three most commonly used rooms department key performance indicators (KPIs) for measuring department performance are the average daily rate, occupancy percentage, and revenue per available room. These statistics can be calculated daily or for any other time period.

The **average daily rate (ADR)**, also sometimes called average room rate, is simply the amount of rooms revenue divided by the number of rooms occupied for the same period of time. Exhibit 7.5 shows how this is calculated for a single day and a three-day period.

In this example, $155.03 indicates the average amount of revenue for each of the 533 occupied rooms for the three-day period. Most hotels have a number of rate classes targeted at different market segments. There may be different rates for government employees, corporate travelers, and senior citizens, among others. The rates also vary according to room size, location, furnishings, and service. For example, a large corner guestroom on a high

Exhibit 7.5   Average Daily Rate Calculated for Individual Days and a Three-Day Period

Day	Rooms Revenue	÷	Rooms Occupied	=	Average Daily Rate
Monday	$23,800		170		$140.00
Tuesday	$30,000		185		$162.16
Wednesday	$29,000		178		$162.92
Three-Day Figures	$82,800		533		$155.03

floor overlooking a park is more expensive than a smaller room on a lower floor that faces an alley. The price the room is finally sold for will depend on who it is sold to, the location, the day of the week, and possibly the season of the year. Management's goal is to sell the most expensive rooms first. However, guests usually request the lowest-priced rooms. Therefore, the average daily rate is an indicator of the sales ability of those taking reservations, as well as the demand for the various types of guestrooms.

An equally important marketing statistic is the **occupancy percentage**, a measure of how many available rooms in a hotel are occupied by guests over a specific period. It is computed by dividing the number of rooms occupied by the number of rooms available for sale for the same period and multiplying by 100. The number of rooms available for sale may be different from the number of rooms in the hotel. This discrepancy occurs when rooms are being used to house managers and other personnel on a permanent basis, or when rooms are being remodeled. Like the average rate, the occupancy percentage can be calculated for any period of time (see Exhibit 7.6).

Revenue per available room (RevPAR) is a third common statistic that operators use in evaluating the performance of the rooms department. It is computed by dividing room revenue by the number of available rooms for the same period. Alternatively, it can be determined by multiplying the occupancy percentage by the ADR for the same period (see Exhibit 7.7).

These three KPIs are used by managers to assess how the hotel is doing in relation to the budget and the forecast. Another valuable

approach is to measure these KPIs against a defined competitive set. Hotels can receive competitive set data from the firm STR, a global provider of competitive benchmarking information to the hotel industry. (Most chains participate with STR by providing it with their KPI information and in return receive data on each hotel's competitive set.) Comparisons to forecasts and competitive set data can also help management to determine which weeks and months ahead need extra sales efforts. It should be noted that a single KPI cannot be relied on to present an accurate picture of a hotel's financial performance. For example, a hotel might have a 99 percent occupancy percentage and still be failing if the ADR or RevPAR is not high enough to cover all costs and provide a reasonable return on investment.

Food and Beverage Department

Although the rooms department in most hotels generates the greatest amount of revenue, this is not always the case. In a few hotels (most often resorts and convention properties with extensive banquet sales), the **food and beverage department**—responsible for preparing and serving food and beverages within the hotel, including catering and room service—may produce as much revenue as the rooms department, or even more. This is because guests in resorts tend to stay on the premises and may be less price-sensitive because they are on vacation. In convention hotels, the added food sales come from the multitude of restaurants, banquet rooms, and bars typically found in a convention property.

Exhibit 7.6   Occupancy Percentage Calculated for Individual Days and a Three-Day Period

Day	Rooms Occupied	÷	Rooms Available	× 100 =	Occupancy Percentage
Monday	170		200		85.0%
Tuesday	185		200		92.5%
Wednesday	178		200		89.0%
Three-Day Figures	533		600		88.8%

Exhibit 7.7   RevPAR Calculated for Individual Days and a Three-Day Period

Day	Occupancy Percentage	×	Average Daily Rate	=	RevPAR
Monday	85.0%		$140.00		$119.00
Tuesday	92.5%		$162.16		$150.00 (rounded)
Wednesday	89.0%		$162.92		$145.00 (rounded)
Three-Day Figures	88.8%		$155.03		$138.00 (rounded)

Whether the food and beverage operation is large or small, most hotel managers have found that their food and beverage facilities are of paramount importance to the reputation and profitability of the hotel. There is no doubt that in many cases the quality of a hotel's food and beverages powerfully affects a guest's opinion of the hotel and influences their willingness to return. In fact, some hotels are as famous for their restaurants as for their guestrooms. For example, the Fontainebleau Miami Beach Hotel has the StripSteak by Michael Mina restaurant, operated by the famous chef.

Successful hotel operators no longer consider dining facilities merely a convenience for guests. Shifting guest preferences have led to lifestyle food and beverage offerings that mirror current dining trends toward more local and sustainable food offerings. The modern traveler and diner prefers higher quality food and streamlined service over hands-on service styles. A hotel's food and beverage outlets must attract members of the local community, convince hotel guests to dine on the premises, and return a fair profit. The **capture rate**—that is, the percentage of guests who eat meals at the hotel—is measured regularly by many hotels.

Except for limited-service hotels and motels (which achieve that status in large part by staying out of the restaurant business), virtually all lodging facilities offer some level of food and beverage service. Large hotels usually have a wide array of facilities, while small properties may have just one dining room that serves breakfast, lunch, and dinner. Exhibit 7.8 lists the types of food and beverage outlets that may be found in a hotel.[7]

Selecting Food and Beverage Outlets. There are several criteria that managers use to decide what type of food and beverage service should be

Exhibit 7.8   Types of Hotel Food and Beverage Outlets

Foodservice	Beverage Service
Dining Room	Cocktail Lounge
Specialty Restaurant	Public Bar (for guests)
Coffee Shop (mid-price restaurant)	Service Bar (for servers)
Supper Club	Banquets
Snack Bar	Discotheques
Take-Out	Minibars (in guestrooms)
Cafeteria	
Room Service	
Banquets	
Employee Foodservice	

offered in any given hotel. Managers should think about these carefully, both in the initial planning stages of a new hotel and as a hotel matures and the market it appeals to changes.

The first criterion is the type of hotel. Does this property primarily serve transient businesspeople or conventioneers? Is the property a resort? Business clientele are more interested in private dining, while convention hotels need ballrooms for large gatherings. Resorts often do well with specialty restaurants.

Next is the class of hotel. Five-star hotels need five-star restaurants. Moderate-price hotels could not sustain this kind of restaurant quality, nor would their guests expect it.

Competition is another consideration. What kinds of restaurants are already available in the area? If you are surrounded by Italian restaurants, putting one in your hotel would probably not be a good idea. It might be wiser to try something completely different.

Product availability also counts. A fresh-fish restaurant might have a difficult time making it unless it limited itself to the kind of fish that is readily available. The cost of flying in Maine lobster and Dover sole could easily price it out of the market.

Availability of labor is another important consideration. A menu that requires a lot of employees—for example, one that features tableside cooking with dishes like steak Diane and desserts such as crêpe Suzette—might not be practical in a tight labor market.

Quick service dining and table-service dining are also merging in hotels. With labor shortages faced by many lodging operations, food and beverage operators have shifted toward counter-service offerings, but of a higher quality and at a higher price point. Smaller limited-service dining rooms are offering craft cocktails and artisanal appetizers.

Finally, there is the question of demand. Certain kinds of food are more popular in some areas of the country than others. Mexican restaurants are more in demand in the Southwest than the Northeast, for example. Is the type of restaurant in the hotel one that the hotel's guests will want to patronize?

Meal plans. A hotel **meal plan** refers to a package or arrangement offered by hotels that includes meals as part of the guest's stay. There are several meal plans that hotel food and beverage departments offer when you make your room reservations, especially in Asian countries. They include the Full American Plan, the Modified American Plan, the Continental Plan, and the European Plan.

The Full American Plan and the Modified American Plan are usually seen in resort hotels. Under the Full American Plan, the room rate quoted includes all major meals—breakfast, lunch, and dinner. In effect, guests are offered a package price that includes their room and all three meals for as long as they stay. This has great appeal to guests who are concerned with the total cost of their resort vacation and like to budget for it ahead of time. The Modified American Plan provides two meals only—usually breakfast and dinner.

The Continental Plan includes a continental breakfast with the room rate. This plan is also called a Breakfast Plan, and in Bermuda it's known as the Bermuda Plan. With the European Plan, no meals are included in the room rate.

Isolated resorts with few or no restaurants in the surrounding area and no centers of population nearby are more likely to offer an American Plan. These types of resorts were especially popular in the early 1900s, when travelers stayed at resorts for two weeks or more. More commonly found today are breakfast-included options, where guests receive a daily breakfast as part of their stay.

Most guests today do not want to be locked into a meal plan—they prefer the freedom to try other restaurants in the area. As a result, offering a meal plan is not a growing hotel service, since demand for it, on the whole, is decreasing. Hotel managers may wish this were not so. From the hotels' standpoint, there is much better control over purchasing, preparing, and staffing when the number of meals that will be served is known in advance. Moreover, both American plans guarantee food revenue and, to a great degree, beverage revenue as well, since guests often order cocktails before dinner, wine with dinner, or after-dinner drinks.

Organization of the Food and Beverage Department. The food and beverage department of a major hotel can be complex, offering a variety of restaurants and bars, each with its own décor, menu, and style of service. Such a department requires well-trained employees and highly skilled and versatile managers in the kitchen, bar, and service areas.

To get an idea of how a food and beverage department works, we can examine an organization chart of a typical food and beverage operation in a large hotel (see Exhibit 7.9). The person in charge of the food and beverage department reports to the general manager and is known as the food and beverage director. Since this job entails responsibility for a major business entity of the hotel that is staffed by persons with specialized technical skills, the food and beverage director should have a thorough knowledge of general business and management practices. They should also be well versed in the technical aspects of food and beverage preparation and service.

Reporting to the food and beverage manager is the chef, sometimes called the executive chef or head chef, who is in charge of the kitchen staff. Important members of the chef's team are stewards, who make sure all dining rooms, bars, and banquet rooms have sufficient inventories of clean china, glassware, and silverware.

The food and beverage manager oversees multiple food and beverage outlets, ensuring that they run smoothly, profitably, and meet service standards. They must see that waitstaff are well trained and meeting the property's service standards.

In hotels with a lounge, a lounge or bar manager oversees the lounge's operation. They supervise bartenders and beverage servers. The banquet manager and room service manager are in charge of food and beverage areas that will be discussed briefly in the following sections.

Catering. The food and beverage departments of some hotels contain catering departments. (It should be noted that some hotels with catering operations choose to place catering in their sales and marketing department rather than the food and beverage department.) A **catering department's** importance is twofold. Not only is it an image-maker for the hotel, but it also can be the most profitable segment of the food and beverage department. Catering arranges and plans food and beverage functions for (1) conventions and smaller hotel groups, and (2) local banquets booked by the sales department. Catering sales, in some instances, represent as much as 50 percent of a hotel's total food and beverage sales.

Catering is a highly competitive business in most market areas. To succeed, a catering department must have employees with a broad range of abilities and knowledge. Good catering departments excel in sales, menu planning, food

Exhibit 7.9   Sample Organization Chart—Food and Beverage Division

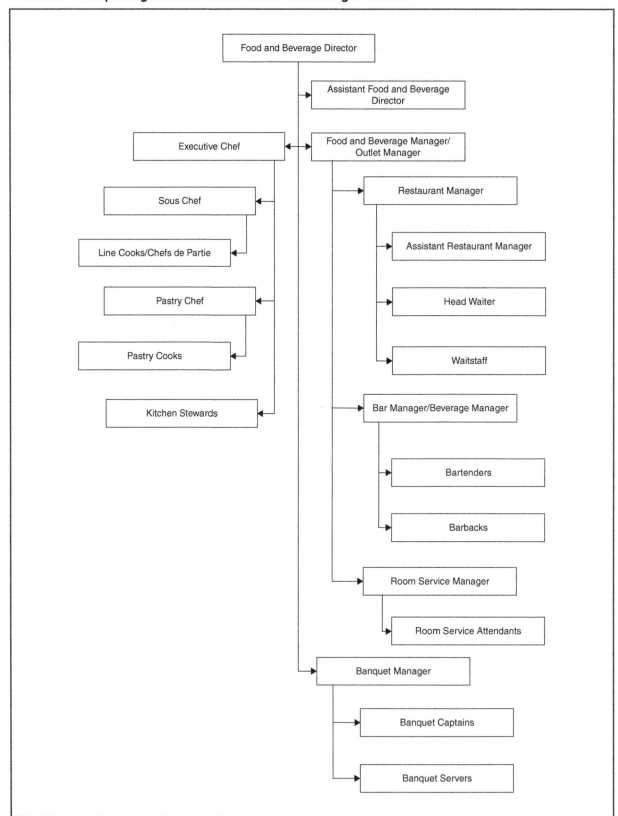

and beverage service (including wines), food production, product knowledge, cost control, artistic talent, and a sense of theater. All of this requires sound technical knowledge as well as skillful use of the hotel's facilities and equipment.

As shown in Exhibit 7.9, the banquet manager reports to the food and beverage director and is in charge of the food preparation and banquet room setups for catering functions. The hotel's catering manager typically reports to the director of sales and marketing and is responsible for selling catered events to clients rather than actually managing the events. Such a division of labor separates the catering area's selling function from the production and service function.

Room service. Most hotels with a food and beverage department provide some type of foodservice to guests in their rooms. **Room service** is a department within a food and beverage department that is responsible for delivering food and beverages to guests in their guestrooms. Employees in the room service department may also be responsible for preparing the food and beverages. Room service is one of the most difficult areas of hotel foodservice to manage and has the greatest potential for losing money.

There are two main difficulties with room service. First, food and beverages are served at great distances from production areas. In resorts where there are cottages for guests, electric carts are often used to transport food. Because of frequent stops along the way, there is a real likelihood of hot items arriving cold and cold items becoming tepid. Second—and, again, because of distance—the productivity of food servers is low; in the same amount of time, restaurant servers can take care of many more guests than room service personnel can. The revenue generated, therefore, is often not sufficient to cover costs. These problems are exacerbated by the fact that the greatest demand for room service is at breakfast, and the most popular type of morning meal is the continental breakfast (juice or fruit, a roll with butter and jam, and a beverage). This meal has a low check average.

To deal with room service costs, many hotels charge higher prices for room service food, as well as an additional charge per order (or per person) for the service. The cost problem can be further alleviated by limiting (1) the number of items on the room service menu, and (2) the hours of service. This does not solve the problem of potentially inferior food quality, however, nor meet the desire on the part of some guests to have a wide variety of food available on the room service menu.

To retain food quality, the food must be delivered to the room as quickly as possible and at the appropriate temperature. This requires proper equipment and a highly efficient room service

A hotel's catering department can account for as much as 50 percent of the hotel's total food and beverage sales.

organization. Many hotels use a doorknob menu that invites guests to order their breakfast the night before, indicating on the menu the items they want and the time they would like to be served. Guests then place the menus on the outside doorknobs of their rooms for collection during the night. This allows the hotel to do a better job because it can plan the number of breakfasts to be served in each time period and organize delivery to the rooms. The use of mobile apps on smartphones even allows guests to place their breakfast order the night before. Some hotels even provide a portable tablet in the room that allows guests to browse their menus and order from the tablet.

Because of the problems associated with delivering a satisfactory room service experience, some hotels have been cutting back on room service, curtailing the number of hours it is available, or doing away with it altogether. The Hyatt Grand Central in New York City cut back its 24-hour room service and now has an 11 p.m. cutoff. Some Hilton Hotels have adopted a more drastic strategy. At the Hilton Hawaiian Village Hotel and at New York's largest hotel, the 2,000-room New York Hilton Midtown, room service has been eliminated and a "grab-n-go" lobby store has opened to serve guests. The growth of food delivery has also replaced the need to include food and beverage outlets in limited-service hotels.

On the other hand, some first-class and luxury hotels view room service as an opportunity. Hoteliers at these properties see room service as an important part of the overall guest experience.

To help guarantee the success of their room service operations, they have redesigned their room service menus to focus on foods that travel well, while still providing a variety of selections. For example, Ritz-Carlton includes pizza, hamburgers, and salads; the Four Seasons serves homestyle dishes, such as chicken pot pie and meat loaf.

Support and control services. Support and control services related to the food and beverage department include the **purchasing department** and the accounting department. Large hotels have a purchasing manager who is responsible for buying all of the products used in the hotel, including food and beverage items. Usually, orders are given to the purchasing department by the chef, the bar manager (or head bartender), or the food and beverage manager. The purchasing department then seeks competitive bids from suppliers, giving them precise specifications for each of the food and beverage items being ordered.

The control aspect of food and beverage is generally under the supervision of the hotel's controller. Reporting to the controller are:

- Receiving clerks, who verify the number and quality of food and beverage items received

- Storeroom clerks, who are responsible for properly storing and issuing items from the food and beverage storeroom

Hotels carefully plan breakfast menus to offer quality items while still meeting customer demand.

- Cashiers in restaurants, coffee shops, and other food and beverage outlets, who handle the settlement of guest checks

Problems in Food and Beverage Operations. Although the food and beverage departments of many hotels show a substantial profit in all of their food and beverage operations, not all food and beverage departments are profitable. Some lose money in all areas, while others lose money in their food operations but make a profit with their beverage operations. Sometimes losses are attributed to bad management alone, but there are a number of other common reasons for losses in food and beverage operations:

- *Long hours of operation.* Hotel restaurants must maintain an adequate level of service even during slow periods in order to satisfy the needs of hotel guests. But the low volume of business during slow times is not always sufficient to cover the cost of operation. Tightly managed employee scheduling can help alleviate this problem.

- *Low check averages.* Low-priced breakfasts and inexpensive snacks served at odd hours are frequently cited as reasons for unprofitability. Clever marketing of more profitable items can help overcome this problem.

- *Too many facilities.* Trying to satisfy a wide variety of hotel guests by having several different types of food and beverage facilities tends to be inefficient from a cost standpoint. However, proper planning, central kitchens, and coordinated menus (so that different recipes use many of the same ingredients) can help solve this problem.

- *High turnover.* Because of the increasing complexity of hotel food and beverage departments, there is a greater need for highly paid personnel. This labor cost cannot be avoided. What can be avoided is a high turnover rate among this group, which increases recruiting and training costs. Good HR management can make a real difference here.

- *Costly entertainment.* Some hotels with several restaurants and bars hire entertainers to entice guests into a night out. Although entertainment is a specialized business, prices charged by entertainers are negotiable. Hotels that use experienced booking agents often have lower entertainment costs and get better entertainers.

- *Insufficient marketing.* In the past, few hotels marketed their food and beverage outlets; some are still guilty of that omission today. But one of the most significant changes in most hotels in recent years is that they are aggressively marketing their restaurants and lounges. Now many hotels compete successfully with freestanding restaurants by employing some of the same techniques that these independents have used so effectively: exciting themes and décor, interesting and dramatic menus, and quality entertainment.

Other Revenue Centers

If there is enough guest demand, a hotel has the potential to sell more than rooms, food, and beverages. Other possible revenue centers that may be found at some hotels include gift shops, newsstands, flower shops, laundry and dry-cleaning services, beauty salons, jewelry stores, and business centers. These revenue centers may be accessible via the lobby or a separate street entrance. Hotel management has the choice of either operating these revenue centers themselves or bringing in others to do it for them.

A **concession** is a hotel facility that might well be operated by the hotel directly, such as a beauty salon or fitness club, but instead is turned over to an independent operator who is responsible for the concession's equipment, personnel, and marketing. The hotel's income from concessions is determined in several ways. It can be a flat fee, a minimum fee plus a percentage of the gross receipts over a specific amount, or simply a percentage of total gross sales.

Rentals are common in many properties. With a rental, the hotel simply rents space to an enterprise such as an office or a store. The rent charged is typically spelled out in a lease, usually a long-term lease, with options to renew and annual rent adjustments specified.

Commissions are fees paid to the hotel by suppliers that are located outside the hotel but provide services for hotel guests. Some examples are car rental agencies, photographers, and dry-cleaning services. They pay a commission to the hotel based on a percentage of their gross sales to guests.

One important aspect of these kinds of arrangements is that unless the company or individual providing the service within the hotel is recognized in its own right (e.g., the Canyon Ranch Spa in the Venetian Hotel in Las Vegas), as far as most guests are concerned, their relationship is not with the vendor but with the hotel. Therefore, the quality and service standards of vendors must conform to the rest of the hotel's operation, or they can negatively affect the guest's perception of the hotel itself. For example, if a gift shop sells tasteless novelties, guests are likely to conclude that the hotel itself has those same tastes and standards. An agreement with a vendor should explicitly spell out standards of cleanliness, personnel dress codes, and other "image" issues, as well as more practical matters such as hours of operation.

To be considered a hotel department in the "other revenue center" category, the department must provide a service that generates revenue and has direct operating expenses, such as payroll. For example, a hotel might operate a health club/spa, a guest laundry, a business center, or a parking facility or service. A golf course or a marina at a resort, if operated by the hotel, would also be grouped in this category. Departments that bring in limited amounts of revenue may be grouped together on the hotel's financial statements as "Minor Operated Departments."

Three revenue centers that deserve special mention because of their importance to the hotels that have them are golf courses and pro shops, health clubs/spas, and parking departments.

Golf Course and Pro Shop. Resorts and other hotels may have a golf course (and accompanying practice facilities) and a pro shop as part of their offerings to guests and others in the surrounding community. Guests may pay to play on the golf course as part of a package that includes their guestroom and other hotel products and services. Other hotel guests, as well as local residents, may pay greens fees to play on the course. Other revenue sources for a hotel that has a golf course include golf lessons; golf course memberships (members may receive preferred tee times and discounts on merchandise in the pro shop); golf equipment rental (clubs, pull carts); golf cart rental; practice range fees; and the proceeds from the sale of clubs, bags, balls, clothing items, and so on in the pro shop.

Health Club/Spa. Today's businessperson may travel with a pair of running shoes and feel that a daily run or workout of some kind is important. Hotels that have recognized this and provided workout facilities and indoor swimming pools have been able to capitalize on this demand and increase their guest base. Other hotels have not kept up with the times and have lost guests who insist on some provision for exercising while they are away from home. Often, guests are not charged for the use of a hotel's basic exercise facilities. However, if a hotel has a health club or spa, guests are usually charged for services such as massages and other body treatments, skin and hair care products and services, manicures, and

Many hotels and resorts now offer health clubs and spas for guests.

so on. Some hotels have recognized the potential to sell access to their health club/spa to office workers and residents near the hotel and have sold health club/spa memberships, thus bringing even more revenue into the hotel.

Parking Department. Hotels in big cities may have a parking department that brings in revenue for the hotel. This revenue is categorized as self-parking revenue, valet parking revenue, and "other revenue" (this includes revenue from such services as gasoline sales and washing the cars of guests). Expenses for this department include labor costs, of course, but also such items as cleaning supplies, complimentary services and gifts to guests, equipment rental, and parking licenses and permits.

Knowledge Check

1. Why are revenue management techniques important for hotels?
2. What are the responsibilities of the food and beverage department and what are some of its challenges?

7.3 COST CENTERS

As mentioned earlier, cost or support centers are hotel departments or areas that do not directly generate revenue. These hotel departments/areas include:

- Administrative and general department
- Information and telecommunications systems department
- Sales and marketing department
- Property operation and maintenance department
- Utilities

Administrative and General Department

This cost center includes the salaries and wages of the hotel's general manager and their office staff as well as the staffs in a broad group of administrative departments (accounting, HR, etc.), plus the related expenses of the hotel's administrative functions.

In full-service and limited-service hotels, total administrative and general costs are approximately 9 percent of total sales.[8] Let's take a look at three of a hotel's key administrative functions: accounting, HR, and security.

Accounting Department. A hotel's **accounting department** is responsible for keeping track of the many business transactions that occur in the hotel. The accounting department does more than simply keep the books—financial management is perhaps a more appropriate description of what the accounting department does. A sample organization chart of an accounting department is shown in Exhibit 7.10.

The responsibilities of the accounting department include:

- Forecasting and budgeting
- Managing what the hotel owns and what money is due from guests
- Controlling cash
- Controlling costs in all areas of the hotel—operating expenses as well as undistributed operating expenses and payroll
- Purchasing, receiving, storing, and issuing operating and capital inventory, such as food and beverages, housekeeping supplies, and furniture
- Keeping records, preparing financial statements and daily operating reports, and interpreting these statements and reports for management

In order to accomplish these diverse functions, the head of accounting—the controller—relies on a staff of auditors, cashiers, and other accounting employees. Not all of the controller's staff works in the hotel's accounting office; accounting functions are performed throughout the hotel. For example, credit staff, front office cashiers, and night auditors work in the front desk area. Cashiers work in the restaurant and bar.

The accounting department bridges and interacts with all of a hotel's revenue and cost departments. In many cases, the controller reports directly to the corporate controller of the parent company (if the hotel is part of a chain or some other corporation). They are responsible for all of

Exhibit 7.10 Sample Organization Chart—Accounting Department

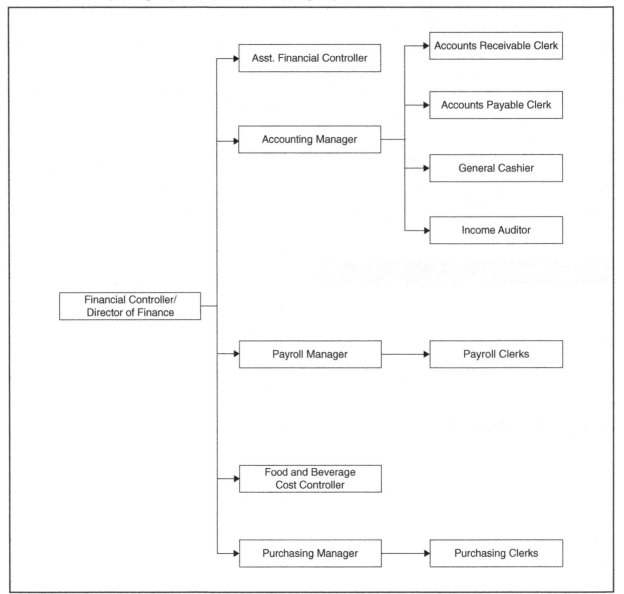

the control functions within the hotel and, in that capacity, also report to the hotel's general manager.

Human Resources Department. Good managers see themselves as developers of people and as guardians of their company's most important asset—its employees. Thus, the old-fashioned personnel department has gone the way of the dinosaur. In the old days, the personnel manager of a company was little more than a clerk. Their job was to accept applications, check references, and keep records of who was hired, fired, and promoted. Today's **human resources department** does much more. Modern HR managers are

concerned with the whole equation of people and productivity—as well as salaries, wages, and benefits. Their job description includes recruiting, hiring, orienting, training, evaluating, motivating, rewarding, disciplining, developing, promoting, and communicating with all the employees of the hotel. Employee satisfaction surveys are used by many hotels to find ways to improve morale.

Security Department. The security of guests, employees, personal property, and the hotel itself is an overriding concern for today's hotel managers. In the past, most security precautions concentrated on the prevention of theft from guests and the hotel. However, today such violent crimes as murder and rape have become a problem for some hotels. Many hotels now worry about terrorism threats. Hotel owners and operators are concerned about their ethical and legal responsibility to protect guests and their property. Not giving security the attention it deserves can be costly. Courts have awarded plaintiffs thousands (in some cases, millions) of dollars as a result of judgments against hotels for not exercising reasonable care in protecting guests.[9]

A hotel security program should be preventive. While ultimate responsibility for security remains with the general manager, most hotels have one or more security officers on staff who are professionally trained in crime prevention and detection.

Traditionally, security has been the responsibility of the front office. The trend today is to give security the status of an independent department reporting directly to the general manager or resident manager, usually called the **security department** but referred to in some hotels as the loss prevention department. In large hotels, the head of the security department may be called the chief of security. This person usually has an extensive background in law enforcement.

Those involved in security should have specialized training in civil and criminal law. They must work closely with local police and fire departments to ensure that all regulations pertaining to hotels are enforced. Applicants for security positions should be trained in self-defense.

A comprehensive security program includes all of the following elements:

- *Security officers.* Security officers make regular rounds of the hotel premises, including guest floors, corridors, public and private function rooms, parking areas, and offices. Their duties involve observing suspicious behavior and taking appropriate action, investigating incidents, and cooperating with local law enforcement officials.

- *Equipment.* Security equipment includes two-way radios; closed-circuit television and motion sensors to monitor entrances, elevators, and corridors; smoke detectors and fire-alarm systems; firefighting equipment,

including extinguishers, hoses, and fire axes; and adequate interior and exterior lighting.

- *Master keys.* Security officers should be able to gain access to guestrooms, storerooms, and offices at all times.

- *Safety procedures.* A well-designed security program includes evacuation plans in case of fire, terrorism, or some other emergency. All employees should be familiar with these plans. Employee training and procedure manuals should include sections on safety.

- *Identification procedures.* Every employee should be issued an identification card that includes their photo. Name tags for employees who are likely to have contact with guests not only project a friendly image for the property but are also useful for security reasons.

Information and Telecommunications Systems Department

The dramatic transformation in how we communicate by phone has prompted a corresponding change in the way telecommunications is reported on a hotel's financial statements. In the not-too-distant past, the hard-wired telephone was the chief method of communication by phone, which meant that telephone service could be a revenue producer for a hotel. Today, most guests travel with their own phones, and a hotel's in-room telephones are used primarily to communicate within the hotel. As a result, hotel telephone service went from a revenue producer for the hotel to an expense, and the Information and Telecommunications Systems line item on hotel financial statements is now classified under Undistributed Operating Expenses.

Costs incurred by this department include the salaries and wages of the information technology (IT) managers and staff (programmers, private branch exchange operators, etc.), and a number of expenses necessary for the operation of the internal telecommunications system. The operating expenses of this department include the computer hardware and software costs of Internet services as well as local and long-distance calls.

Sales and Marketing Department

The mission of a hotel's **sales and marketing department** is to (1) identify prospective guests for the hotel, (2) shape the products and services of the hotel as much as possible to meet the needs of those prospects, and (3) persuade prospects to become guests. This task begins before the first brick is laid.

One way to understand marketing is to look at what it is not. Marketing is not selling. It has been said that the difference between marketing and selling is that selling is getting rid of what you have, while marketing is having what people want. If you have what people want and you tell them about it, sales will come easily—assuming that not many others have it at the same place for the same price at the same time! If you don't have what people want and you are forced to get rid of what you have, then you may have to discount it or promote it heavily; even then, it still might not sell.

Marketing a hotel is not an activity confined to the sales and marketing department; every employee is involved in providing what guests want. It is part of the job of the sales and marketing department to understand the needs and wants of the hotel's guests and advise

management of them so managers can train employees in how to meet those needs and wants.

The sales and marketing department is charged with the responsibility of keeping the rooms in the hotel occupied at the right price and with the right mix of guests. It accomplishes this through many activities, including:

- Contacting groups and individuals

- Using social media

- Advertising in print and on radio, television, and the Internet

- Creating direct-mail and public relations campaigns

- Participating in trade shows

- Visiting travel agents

- Arranging **familiarization (fam) tours** (free or reduced-rate travel packages designed to acquaint travel agents and others with the hotel and stimulate sales)

- Participating in community activities that raise local awareness of the hotel

On average, hotels spend approximately 6 percent of sales on such efforts. This figure is

Exhibit 7.11   Sample Organization Chart—Sales and Marketing Department

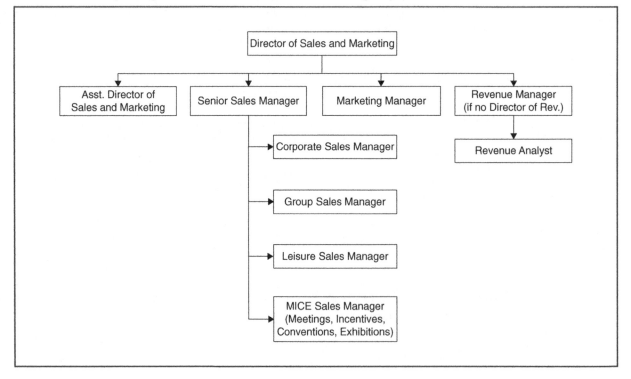

misleading, however, and should be considered cautiously. For example, marketing a new hotel is much more expensive than marketing an established one. The marketing expenses involved in opening a new hotel, such as parties for community leaders and fam tours for travel agents, are often capitalized and charged off over a period of time. The cost of reservations systems is often charged to the rooms department, although it could be argued that such a system is a marketing tool and ought to be treated as a marketing expense.

In most large hotels, the sales and marketing department is headed by a director of sales and marketing (see Exhibit 7.11). Reporting to the director is a senior sales manager, a marketing manager, and a revenue manager. Each of these staff members heads a department that is responsible for a distinct and separate activity within the overall marketing mission.

The sales department is responsible for prospecting for business and making sales calls on individuals and companies. The marketing department attempts to attract guests through advertising and create a positive image of the hotel. Commonly used marketing techniques are news releases about the hotel and its employees or guests and community service activities among managers and employees. Revenue optimization is the responsibility of the revenue manager.

In many ways, the sales and marketing function of a hotel can be considered the very essence of the operation. A frequently quoted remark by management consultant Peter Drucker puts it this way: "There is only one valid definition of business purpose: to create a customer."[10]

Property Operation and Maintenance Department

Taking care of the hotel's physical plant and controlling energy costs are the responsibilities of the hotel engineer and the **property operation and maintenance department**.[11] The physical upkeep of the building, furniture, fixtures, equipment, and plant systems is essential to:

- Slow a hotel's physical deterioration.
- Preserve the original hotel image established by management.
- Keep revenue-producing areas operational.

- Keep the property comfortable for guests and employees.
- Preserve the safety of the property for guests and employees.
- Create savings by keeping repairs and equipment replacements to a minimum.

The property operation and maintenance department is also responsible for heating and air-conditioning systems and the systems that distribute electricity, steam, and water throughout the property.

In order to accomplish the many tasks of the property operation and maintenance department, several types of technicians may be employed: electricians, plumbers, carpenters, painters, refrigeration and air-conditioning engineers, and others. The department is headed by a chief engineer. In small hotels, one all-purpose engineer may perform all engineering functions or subcontract work as needed. In a large hotel, the chief engineer may be called a plant manager. When the size of the hotel warrants, there is also a secretary or administrative assistant to deal with the logistics of handling repair requests and scheduling service. Exhibit 7.12 shows a sample organization chart for the property operation and maintenance department of a convention/resort hotel.

The maintenance and repair work performed by this department's staff is one of two kinds: preventive or as needed. Preventive maintenance is a planned program of ongoing servicing of the building and equipment in order to maintain operations and prolong the life of the facility. Outside contractors may be hired for some jobs either as needed or through a service contract. An important aspect of maintenance work is that in all areas, there should be documentation to track labor and material costs. A master checklist groups the preventive maintenance work to be done on a daily, weekly, and monthly schedule. Detailed equipment checklists outlining tasks to be performed and how long it should take to perform them assist managers in scheduling employees. There are many software programs that can save time by monitoring productivity, costs, and job assignments. Programs such as HotSOS have the capacity to place jobs in a queue that are then sent to the appropriate employee via an electronic device such as a smartphone.

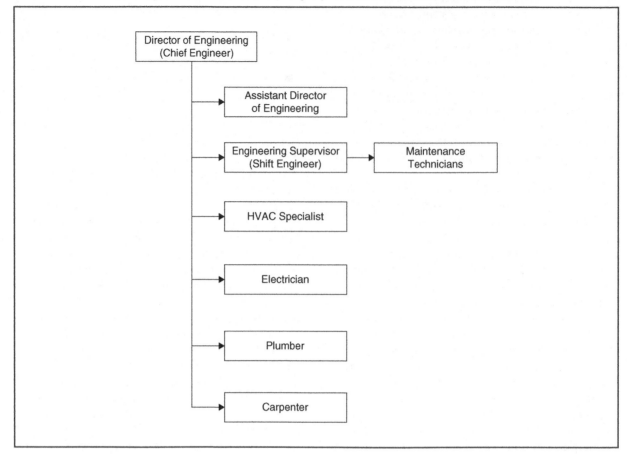

In addition to preventive maintenance, the staff of the property operation and maintenance department performs routine repairs. Repair logs should be used to keep track of the start and finish of each repair assignment. Major projects that require the purchase of building materials may also be undertaken by the property operation and maintenance department. Management usually determines whether extensive repairs, or replacement of equipment not covered by service contracts, is to be done by the hotel's own staff or given to an outside contractor.

In a study of full-service U.S. hotels, PKF Hospitality Group reported that its sample spent 4.5 percent of total sales on maintenance.[12]

Utilities

A hotel's utilities are supervised by the property operation and maintenance department but they are treated as a separate category of expenses in order to better monitor and control the costs. Electricity, oil, water, and steam are some of the major utility expenses. Utility costs average 3.7 percent of hotel revenue.

Knowledge Check

1. What are the responsibilities of the sales and marketing department?

2. How can the property operation and maintenance department help control costs?

7.4 COMPLIANCE WITH THE AMERICANS WITH DISABILITIES ACT

As a result of the Americans with Disabilities Act (ADA), all of the departments of a U.S. hotel must modify existing facilities to some extent and incorporate design features into new construction that make hotel facilities accessible to people with disabilities.[13] People with disabilities, as defined by the ADA, include people who use wheelchairs, other people with mobility impairments, and people with sensory impairments such as blindness and deafness. The ADA covers employees as well as guests.

All hotels are expected to have at least 4 percent of their parking spaces designated as accessible (the figure drops to 2 percent if the parking lot has more than 100 spaces). Parking spaces for people with disabilities must be wide enough for wheelchairs to be unloaded from a van or other vehicle; wheelchair users must be able to easily enter the hotel by means of accessible ramps and doors. Entrances to hotels must have accessible pickup and drop-off points without curbs or other obstructions for a person using a wheelchair or crutches.

Many areas within hotels are affected by the ADA. One section of the registration desk should be low enough for a person using a wheelchair to comfortably see over it. Ramps should be equipped with handrails; stairs require handrails and beveled risers. Restrooms must have accessible stalls that are wide enough for someone to receive assistance from another individual if needed, or to allow someone to enter with a guide dog. Meeting rooms must be equipped with special listening systems for people with hearing impairments. If platforms are used in meeting rooms, they must have accessible ramps. Restaurants must have "accessible paths" at least 36 inches (91.4 centimeters) wide between tables or counters and bars. Merchandise racks in hotel retail shops must be spaced far enough apart for people using wheelchairs to move around and between them.

Guestrooms must be fitted with equipment that can be manipulated by people with severe arthritis, an amputation, or poor control of their hands. Visual fire alarms are required in guestrooms designated for guests with hearing impairments. Numbers on guestroom doors must be tactile so they can be read by touch.

In the first major revision to the ADA, the U.S. Justice Department added guidelines on swimming pool accessibility. Pools that are larger than 300 linear feet of pool wall now require at least two means of access, while smaller pools require just one — which must be either a pool lift or sloped entry.

Many of these changes involve new construction or modifications of existing facilities that are "readily achievable." It is hoped that, in time, all public facilities in the United States, including hotels, restaurants, museums, theaters, shops, and even parks, will make the changes necessary to be fully accessible to people with disabilities. Other countries, notably the United Kingdom and Germany, are making great strides in this area as well.

Knowledge Check

1. What are some things hotels must do to comply with the ADA?
2. What are some issues hotels might face in complying with the ADA?

7.5 CONTROL SYSTEMS

An important part of managing is to measure performance levels and take corrective action if they do not meet the goals of the enterprise. In order to maintain control over all aspects of an organization, managers and owners must first establish goals against which results can be measured. For example, an organization may establish a payroll goal of 30 percent of revenues—that is, the operating plan is to spend 30 percent or less of sales on salaries and other payroll expenses. The plan may also provide that a variance of 2 percent is acceptable, but that anything above that is not. If payroll expenses exceed 32 percent, management must take action.

The ideal **control system** allows managers to quickly recognize and correct deviations from the operating budget (or some other management standard) before they become major problems. One way hotel managers accomplish this is to have accurate forecasting systems. To continue with our payroll example: by being able to forecast with a high degree of accuracy what sales are likely to be in a given period, managers can adjust staffing levels accordingly to meet the payroll goal. For instance, if the dining room manager knows from sales history records that on Monday evenings in February the dining room is likely to serve only 100 meals, then the number of food servers and cooks that will be required is no longer a matter of guesswork but can be carefully planned. Of course, current hotel occupancy and other circumstances must also be taken into account.

In too many cases, corrections are made long after the problem starts. The longer the period between the variation from property goals and the correction, the weaker the control system and the greater the potential for lost revenue and increased costs.

Training plays a key role in control systems. A certain number of errors by front desk personnel and food servers is inevitable—no human system is perfect. But careful training can minimize errors and bring performance levels up to standard.

Many of management's goals can be quantified. The more specific the goal and the easier it is to quantify, the more likely it is that the goal will be met. Guestroom occupancy levels, guest counts in restaurants, and revenue and expense targets are examples of quantifiable goals. Not all goals are easy to measure. For example, an operating plan might have a goal of increasing guest satisfaction or employee morale. However, even there it is possible to be more specific and measure the results accordingly.

Two of the most important types of controls for hotel managers are financial controls and quality controls.

Financial Controls

Among the most useful **financial control** tools are financial statements, operating ratios, and other financial statistics that hotel managers can use to keep track of operations and make sure financial goals are being attained. Investors use them to monitor profitability; lenders view them as measures of financial stability; managers base their planning on them and monitor the success of their planning with them.

In order to understand a hotel financial statement, it is necessary to be familiar with the hotel industry's financial terminology and to understand the manner in which revenues and expenses are grouped by hotel department.

Uniform System of Accounts. In March 1926, the American Hotel & Lodging Association (at that time it was called the American Hotel Association of the United States and Canada) adopted a manual called the *Uniform System of Accounts for Hotels*. The system was formulated by a committee of accountants and hoteliers in New York City. The ninth edition bore a new title to better encompass all segments of the industry: *The Uniform System of Accounts for the Lodging Industry*. It is currently in its 12th edition, in a digital version that is available through a subscription format.

The *Uniform System of Accounts for the Lodging Industry* classifies the different types of hotel revenues and expenses, and groups them in the income statement by department or area. There are two versions of this financial statement: a basic version that is given to external viewers and a much more detailed version (called the summary operating statement) that is shared with and used by the property's managers. This internal version is one of management's major control tools. It shows total sales by product or service category (rooms, food, beverage, etc.) for a stated period of time, the expenses incurred in generating those sales, and the profit earned or the loss incurred as a result of those activities (see Exhibit 7.13).

There are three types of hotel expenses: departmental expenses, undistributed operating expenses, and nonoperating expenses (often called fixed charges or capital costs). **Departmental expenses** are expenses that are charged to specific hotel departments and include a wide range of items, such as rooms department payroll, restaurant laundry, and telephone supplies like message pads and pencils. **Undistributed operating expenses** are costs such as marketing and energy—costs that relate to the entire hotel and not to one specific department. **Nonoperating expenses** are expenses related to the investment, such as insurance on the building and contents, interest on the mortgage loan, and property taxes.

The uniform system also classifies **assets** (something of value that is owned) and **liabilities** (what is owed to creditors). Examples of assets might be the hotel building itself, furniture and equipment, and courtesy vans to transport guests to and from airports. Liabilities include items such as the mortgage loan and food purchases for which payment is due. All of these items are grouped together in a balance sheet (see Exhibit 7.14).

Quality Controls

It is a relatively simple task to standardize the quality and cost of a manufactured product. This is because products, whether they be toasters or skis, are produced in a factory under strictly controlled conditions. Some assembly lines are computerized, and many use robots to perform some functions. Moreover, quality control inspectors not only monitor all operations but can also inspect each finished item before it leaves the plant and a consumer purchases it.

Exhibit 7.13   Summary Operating Statement

	Period Of					
	Current Period			Year-to-Date		
	Actual	Forecast/ Budget	Prior Year	Actual	Forecast/ Budget	Prior Year
Rooms Available:						
Rooms Sold:						
Occupancy:						
ADR:						
Rooms RevPAR:						
Total RevPAR:						

	Period Of											
	Current Period						Year-to-Date					
	Actual		Forecast/ Budget		Prior Year		Actual		Forecast/ Budget		Prior Year	
	$	%[1]	$	%[1]	$	%[1]	$	%[1]	$	%[1]	$	%[1]
Operating Revenue												
Rooms												
Food and Beverage												
Other Operated Departments												
Miscellaneous Income												
Total Operating Revenue												
Departmental Expenses												
Rooms												
Food and Beverage												
Other Operated Departments												
Total Departmental Expenses												
Total Departmental Profit												
Undistributed Operating Expenses												
Administrative and General												
Information and Telecommunications Systems												
Sales and Marketing												
Property Operation and Maintenance												
Utilities												
Total Undistributed Expenses												

(Continued)

Exhibit 7.13   Summary Operating Statement (*Continued*)

	PERIOD OF											
	CURRENT PERIOD						YEAR-to-DATE					
	ACTUAL		FORECAST/ BUDGET		PRIOR YEAR		ACTUAL		FORECAST/ BUDGET		PRIOR YEAR	
	$	%[1]	$	%[1]	$	%[1]	$	%[1]	$	%[1]	$	%[1]
GROSS OPERATING PROFIT												
MANAGEMENT FEES												
INCOME BEFORE NONOPERATING INCOME AND EXPENSES												
NONOPERATING INCOME AND EXPENSES												
Income												
Rent												
Property and Other Taxes												
Insurance												
Other												
TOTAL NONOPERATING INCOME AND EXPENSES												
EARNINGS BEFORE INTEREST, TAXES, DEPRECIATION, AND AMORTIZATION												
INTEREST, DEPRECIATION, AND AMORTIZATION												
Interest												
Depreciation												
Amortization												
TOTAL INTEREST, DEPRECIATION, AND AMORTIZATION												
INCOME before INCOME TAXES												
Income Taxes												
NET INCOME												

Exhibit 7.14 Hotel Balance Sheet

	Assets	Current Year	Prior Year
CURRENT ASSETS			
Cash and Cash Equivalents			
House Banks		$	$
Demand Deposits			
Temporary Cash Investments			
Total Cash			
Restricted Cash			
Short-Term Investments			
Receivables			
Accounts Receivable			
Notes Receivable			
Current Maturities of Noncurrent Receivables			
Other			
Total Receivables			
Less Allowance for Doubtful Accounts			
Net Receivables			
Due To/From Owner, Management Company, or Related Party			
Inventories			
Operating Equipment			
Prepaid Expenses			
Deferred Income Taxes—Current			
Other			
Total Current Assets			
NONCURRENT RECEIVABLES, Net of Current Maturities			
INVESTMENTS			
PROPERTY AND EQUIPMENT			
Land			
Buildings			
Leaseholds and Leasehold Improvements			
Furnishings and Equipment			
Construction in Progress			
Total Property and Equipment			
Less Accumulated Depreciation and Amortization			
Net Property and Equipment			
OTHER ASSETS			
Intangible Assets			
Cash Surrender Value of Life Insurance			
Deferred Charges			
Deferred Income Taxes—Noncurrent			
Operating Equipment			
Restricted Cash			
Pre-Opening Expenses			
Other			
Total Other Assets			
TOTAL ASSETS		$	$
LIABILITIES AND OWNERS' EQUITY			

(Continued)

Exhibit 7.14   Hotel Balance Sheet (*Continued*)

	Current Year	Prior Year
CURRENT LIABILITIES		
Notes Payable		
Banks	$	$
Others		
Total Notes Payable		
Due To/From Owner, Management Company or Related Party		
Accounts Payable		
Accrued Expenses		
Advance Deposits		
Income Taxes Payable		
Deferred Income Taxes—Current		
Current Maturities of Long-Term Debt		
Gift Certificates and Cards		
Other		
Total Current Liabilities		
LONG-TERM DEBT, Net of Current Maturities		
Mortgage Notes, Other Notes, and Similar Liabilities		
Obligations under Capital Leases		
Total Long-Term Debt		
OTHER LONG-TERM LIABILITIES		
DEFERRED INCOME TAXES—Noncurrent		
COMMITMENTS AND CONTINGENCIES		
OWNERS' EQUITY		
TOTAL LIABILITIES AND OWNERS' EQUITY	$	$

Service businesses such as hotels operate under an entirely different set of circumstances. The "product" that a hotel produces—the experience of staying there—is manufactured in the hotel "factory" right in front of the consumer. For example, a guest enters a hotel, goes into the lounge, sits down at a table, and orders a strawberry daiquiri. The product in this case is not simply the daiquiri—it also includes the lounge, the server, and the bartender who mixes the drink. It is this total experience that the guest pays for. If the guest had just wanted a strawberry daiquiri, they could have made one at home or bought a bottled one at the corner liquor store.

Because of the nature of a service business, it is extremely difficult to standardize or even control the service that guests receive. There are too many variables that can interfere with the process—including guests who, for example, may be rude and provoke employees to be rude in return.

Opportunities for guest dissatisfaction abound. Take our guest who ordered the strawberry daiquiri. Possibly the guest had to wait for a table because none were available or the host was out of the room temporarily. Maybe the seating was prompt, but the guest had to wait longer than expected for the order because the ice machine or the drink mixer was broken. Perhaps the bartender was preoccupied with a personal problem instead of concentrating on fixing a perfect strawberry daiquiri. Even if everything else goes well, it can all be spoiled if the guest has to wait too long for the check or if there is a mistake on it. All of these possibilities exist whenever a guest enters the lounge. Any of them can affect the quality of the experience (the product) and thus the guest's perception of the lounge and the hotel. This one transaction is a single example of the many kinds of things that can go wrong in a hotel that is open 24 hours a day, 7 days a week, where guests interact regularly with and receive service from front desk agents, waitstaff, room attendants, bellhops, concierges, valets, maintenance people, and gift shop employees.

Why is guest satisfaction so important? Because dissatisfied guests may not come back and may tell their friends about their unpleasant experiences, which jeopardizes the profit objectives of the organization.

One of the best ways to keep guests satisfied is through product and service consistency. Therefore, product and service are of primary importance. Consistency can only be achieved through **quality controls** such as:

- Setting standards that answer the needs and expectations of guests
- Selecting employees who are capable of achieving those standards and motivated to do so
- Conducting continual training and certification programs for all employees at every level
- Involving employees in structuring job descriptions, setting performance standards, and solving work problems
- Having a feedback system so all managers and employees know that they are achieving what they have set out to do—satisfy the guest
- Rewarding managers and employees for achieving quality goals

Quality programs at hotels go by various names: "quality assurance" and "total quality management" are two examples. Hilton Hotels has the Balanced Scorecard quality program that evaluates financial, operational, and employee performance (as well as customer perceptions) against predetermined objectives and performance measurements. In other words, is the hotel achieving what it wants to achieve from the standpoint of profitability, customer and employee satisfaction, and innovation? Starwood uses Six Sigma, a set of techniques pioneered by Motorola, to improve the quality of the operation by identifying and reducing defects and improving efficiency. Although their names vary, the goal of all such programs is to provide quality service to guests.

Setting Standards. Quality is an overriding concern in the hotel industry, but what does "quality" mean? There is no universal industry agreement on what quality is, nor should there be. Quality has to do with guest expectations versus reality. When guests check into a $40 per night budget hotel, they expect a certain standard of service and no more. If they get what they expect (or a little more), they have enjoyed a quality experience from their point of view. If they get less than what they expected or thought they were paying for, then they will think that they received poor-quality service. The formula is the same for a hotel room that costs $250 per night. A guest who pays that amount has certain expectations. Their perception of quality depends to a large degree on whether those expectations are met or exceeded.

Most hotels strive for quality for their type of product and target market. Quality, then, means that the guest experience—in terms of the cleanliness of the rooms, the taste and presentation of the food, and the physical condition of the hotel—is consistent with what the management has promised and is trying to deliver.

The Ritz-Carlton Hotel Company is known for setting very high standards. According to the chain's management, "Customer satisfaction is a deeply held belief at the Ritz-Carlton and begins with an absolute understanding of the needs and expectations of our customer." The chain achieves this understanding by forming focus groups of Ritz-Carlton current and prospective guests and recording guest preferences that all employees detect and report. This information is used to set guest-service standards.

To achieve quality standards, hotel managers—with the help of individual employees and "quality teams" formed from hotel personnel—must create procedures for hotel staff to follow. For example, when a room attendant has finished cleaning a guestroom, the position of the furniture, the number of towels and other guest amenities, and—most important—the overall cleanliness of the room must be exactly the same every day for every room. How many towels to leave in the bathroom or what constitutes "clean" should not be left to the discretion of the person doing the cleaning. Procedures must be established for each task performed. At the same time, a standard of what is acceptable and what is not must be spelled out for each procedure. It is not reasonable to set standards without specifically detailing the procedures that must be followed in order to achieve those standards.

The following example of a foodservice procedure and standard concerns the task of greeting guests at a table:

Procedure: *After table is seated, greet the guest(s): "Good morning. May I offer you some coffee?" Be pleasant, unhurried. Pour coffee with cup on table, and to right of guest. If tea is served, the teapot is served on a butter plate with a doily, lemon on top of teapot.*

Standard: *Make the guest feel comfortable. Strike a positive note in your "beginning" with the guest.*

Selecting Employees. Ritz-Carlton emphasizes the importance of employee selection in its quality management program. Ritz-Carlton's managers have devised a highly sophisticated predictive instrument, using superior employees as benchmarks, that allows them to determine whether the candidates for a specific position are capable of living up to the chain's service standards.

Training Employees. It is not enough for a hotel to establish standards and procedures and select employees to carry them out. Employees must be shown how to perform the procedures. Employees who have never cleaned a guestroom or waited on a table can't be expected to know what to do simply because they've been given a manual.

To succeed, training must be ongoing and have the full commitment of management. At Ritz-Carlton, all hotels have a director of human resources on staff who is assisted by the hotel's quality leader, who acts as an advisor. Each work area has a departmental trainer who is charged with the training and certification of new employees in that area.

Involving Employees. All successful quality programs use a participative style of management. Judy Z. King, owner and president of Quality Management Services, lists basic beliefs in employee involvement in problem-solving:

1. The person doing the job knows how the job can be done better.

2. Problem-solving and decision-making should be done at the lowest capable level in the organization.

3. People are the greatest untapped resource in the organization.

4. People will meet expectations if they have been enabled to do so and, with encouragement, will exceed them.[14]

Ritz-Carlton employees are expected and empowered to solve problems. On the Ritz-Carlton "Service Values" card that every employee carries, it says, "I own and immediately resolve guest problems." Employees are encouraged to break out of their regular routine and solve guest problems immediately and ensure that they do not recur. Teams of workers from different departments are often put together to resolve conflicts between internal operation problems and external guest expectations.

Evaluating Quality Programs. Management must verify the consistency of product and service quality in order to evaluate the success of its quality efforts. Ritz-Carlton, for example, depends heavily on real-time reports, called "guest incident action forms," that are generated daily by employees. These reports are analyzed and quickly acted on so incidents of guest dissatisfaction will not be repeated.

One of the simplest ways to evaluate the quality of an operation is called "management by walking around." Successful hotel managers have found that taking periodic tours of the hotel and staying alert to what is going on around them are the best ways to ensure that the quality program is working. There is a saying in the U.S. Navy that also applies to the hotel business: "You get what you inspect, not what you expect."

Guest satisfaction surveys are another important evaluation tool. Most chains use an electronic survey emailed to hotel guests within 24 hours of departure. Guests are asked to evaluate the reservations process and the service they received at the hotel by selecting a degree of agreement with a statement about the facilities and the service. Almost all surveys ask whether the guest would stay at the hotel again and the likelihood of recommending the hotel to others. Experience has shown that open-ended questions that ask guests to write a description of their experiences do not work as well as simple rating scales, where guests can indicate their level of satisfaction with various components of the hotel's service and facilities. There should be room on the survey, however, for guests to add comments and identify employees whom they wish to single out either positively or negatively. Today, guests are more likely to share their feedback on various platforms and websites dedicated to travel, such as booking websites, review sites, or social media platforms. Online hotel reviews play a significant role in helping potential guests make informed decisions when choosing accommodations.

Another evaluation method involves hiring outside inspectors, usually referred to as "mystery shoppers." These inspectors, who are not known to hotel employees, make reservations, stay in a guestroom, eat in the dining room, check out, and then prepare elaborate reports on the level of service they received. Some hotels announce inspections in advance and the inspectors are known. While employees often favor this system, the level of management confidence in the results of such inspections tends to be much lower.

Rewarding for Achievement. Today, hotel management executive compensation almost always includes both a salary and a bonus. The bonus can be quite substantial and is a result of hotel owners' desire to motivate their executives to a higher level of performance. Very often bonuses are tied to achieving or surpassing specific goals in the areas of financial performance or guest satisfaction.

Employee recognition programs are also common. These may involve posting photographs of the "employee of the month" in a special frame in the lobby, giving gift certificates or other monetary rewards to high-achieving employees, or setting aside special parking spaces for employees in recognition of their superior job performance.

Hotel Technology

Technology plays a vital role in managing a hotel and providing service to hotel guests.[15] Technology applications have been designed for almost every aspect of hotel operations and control. However, there is no one system that manages all functions, even within individual departments. For example, the rooms department may have one system for guest check-in and check-out, another for voice mail, another for the electronic door locks, and yet another for in-room entertainment. These systems act as one because they are designed to integrate, or interface, with each other.

What follows is a list of some of the most common technology applications that a hotel might have.

Global Distribution System. A global distribution system (GDS) is a computer network that passes inventory and rates for hotels along to travel agents and travel sites. It doesn't maintain the information but passes it from the hotel to the end user (e.g., a travel agent). There are a number of these systems, including Amadeus, Galileo, Sabre, Pegasus, and Worldspan. Twenty percent of a hotel's reservations come through a GDS.

Property Management System. A PMS performs most functions that affect a guest's stay at the hotel. This system shows room availability, handles guest check-in and check-out, maintains a current record of all guest charges, and accepts payment (cash or payment card) when the guest checks out. Other functions of the system include describing the physical characteristics of guestrooms, such as the view, whether there is a balcony, or the type of bed, so the front desk agent has sufficient data to assign a room that will best satisfy the guest.

A number of hotels have kiosks in their lobbies where guests can check in and check out. With the swipe of a payment card or the input of a reservation number, guests can identify themselves; the kiosk has the capability to then assign a room and dispense a key. The guest can check out at the kiosk. They can also use their guestroom television remote and screen or a mobile app to check out before they leave the guestroom. With such a system, guests can view their hotel bills at any time. An interface between the PMS and the kiosk, television, or mobile app is necessary to perform the functions described.

Room reservations may come to a hotel through a CRS, via the Internet, or through a GDS. In all of these cases, an interface with the hotel's PMS is necessary to provide rates and availability to these outlets, to get the reservations to the property, and to have the information available on the PMS when the guest arrives at the hotel.

Another important interface with the PMS is the hotel's revenue management system, which sets the rates in the PMS that are then available to the CRS, Internet outlets, and the GDSs.

Point-of-Sale System. The point-of-sale (POS) system in a hotel's food and beverage outlets must interface with the hotel's PMS in order to verify a hotel guest's name and room number when the guest wants to make a purchase. Once verified, the guest's restaurant or bar charge is accepted and transferred to the guest folio.

Sales and Catering System. Hotels with function rooms that have a considerable number of meetings and catered events would find a sales and catering system helpful. Through an interface with the PMS, the sales staff has access to guestroom availability when negotiating dates with prospective group clients. The system also has the description and availability of all meeting rooms. This facet is especially important in large convention hotels that have a sizeable sales staff selling to different types of clients. Menus for all types of occasions are a feature that allows clients to see what type of food the hotel considers its specialty. An important aspect of a sales and catering system is its ability to prepare contracts for customer signature and prepare banquet event orders for distribution to departments in the hotel involved in putting on the customer's event.

Inventory/Purchasing System. An inventory/purchasing (I/P) system for hotels is similar to I/P systems for restaurants. An I/P system tracks inventories of food and beverages by increasing quantities when items are purchased and decreasing them when they are requisitioned out of storage. The system stores recipe costs and vendor lists, generates reorder reports based on par levels of food or beverage items, and prepares purchase orders.

Accounting System. A hotel's accounting system maintains records of all of a hotel's financial transactions. It is referred to generally as a "back office" system, since it performs out of sight of guests. The system deals with the hotel's general ledger, accounts payable, accounts receivable, and payroll (when payroll is not outsourced to a service company). The general ledger is a record of balance sheet and income statement accounts, and accounts payable is what the hotel owes to its creditors.

Telecommunications System. Today many hotel guests use their mobile phones to communicate with family, friends, and business associates. However, guestroom telephones are still necessary for wake-up calls and other communications between the hotel and guests, and for safety and security reasons. A hotel's call accounting system (CAS) is the software that manages calls made from guestrooms, sending cost information to the hotel's PMS/guest folios. When least-cost routing was adopted by hotels, the CAS searched for the least-expensive carrier to use for the destination of a telephone call. The cost of calls was reduced further with the adoption of Voice over Internet Protocol technology that transmits a call over the Internet rather than a regular telephone line. An important aspect of a hotel's telephone service for guests is voice mail, a system that allows messages to be left for guests during their stay at the hotel.

Electronic Door Lock System. Today it is rare to find a hotel with metal keys for its guestrooms, although there are some small hotels and inns that still use metal keys to help create the ambience of less hectic days. Most hotels use an electronic locking system with plastic key cards that are programmed to open a door during a defined guest stay. In some hotels, the guestroom key card is programmed not only to open the guestroom door, but also to allow hotel entry late at night, or to allow guests access to special facilities such as the hotel's swimming pool, exercise room, or business center. Mobile technology has rapidly modernized the electronic door lock system, and many hotels today offer guests the convenience of using their smartphones in place of plastic key cards. This mobile technology uses Bluetooth or NFC (near field communication) technology in conjunction with a mobile app to turn a guest's mobile phone into their room key. The guest can use their mobile app to unlock their room door by tapping a button on the smartphone, or by simply holding the smartphone close to the door. Just like plastic key cards, the mobile key can also be used to access other hotel facilities, such as the gym or parking garage. When the guest checks out, the PMS automatically alerts the mobile key platform and the digital key is disabled.

The advantages of mobile keys are:

- *An efficient, personalized check-in process.* Guests do not have to wait at the hotel's front desk to get their guestroom assignment and key card upon arrival. Using their mobile app, guests can check in before arrival to the hotel and even select their guestroom and floor. By allowing personalized check-in, hotels can reduce manual administrative load and focus instead on hospitality and welcoming each guest with a smile.

- *Improved security.* Mobile key technology is the safest form of hotel access today. Mobile keys are protected against hacking by the latest encryption technology and transmitted in real time via a secure channel. Guests do not have to worry about misplacing or losing their physical key or key card. Even if a guest misplaces their smartphone, the mobile key is protected first by the password, passcode, or face or fingerprint ID required to access the phone, then by the password, passcode, or face or fingerprint ID required to access the mobile room key app. On top of that, magstripe key cards are easy to duplicate, potentially allowing intruders into guestrooms.

- *Sustainability.* Magstripe key cards are still the cheapest form of guestroom access, but they are prone to demagnetization and are not environmentally friendly: a typical 200-room hotel disposes of approximately 12,000 key cards per year.

Energy Management System. The basic guestroom energy control still found in many hotels is the guest-operated thermostat. More current equipment includes occupancy sensors that adjust guestroom temperature based on guest occupancy. The system is activated by the PMS, which sends a message to the guestroom HVAC equipment when a guest checks in or departs.

Internet Access. Most travelers today expect high-speed wireless Internet access, and most hotels provide this service.

Mobile Technology. Smartphones and tablets are becoming increasingly important in the overall hotel guest experience. Apps have made it convenient to check in or out of a hotel, and they can also assist with many aspects of what happens in between. For example, the Four Seasons Hotels app also includes the ability to make and manage reservations in multiple locations and has a concierge feature that allows guests to arrange luggage pickup; airport transfer; and special requests, such as extra pillows, toiletries, or baby gear. Local recommendations for dining, shopping, and cultural pursuits are additional features. The Mandarin Oriental Hotel Group's app, MO

Hotels, enables the user to see property details using an interactive 3D global view and view local city guidebooks.

Television System. Guests need not be restricted to television stations' programming. Video on demand or pay-per-view options allow guests to select from a wider menu of programs or movies any hour of the day or night and have their selections charged to their guest account. Portable streaming devices, like Amazon's Firestick, allow guests to pack their own movies or shows and watch them in their hotel rooms. Some guestroom television systems provide music and video game options as well as television and movie programming. As mentioned earlier, many hotels allow guests to use the television to review their accounts and check out.

Minibars. The mechanical or stand-alone minibar still found in most hotels requires an attendant to check usage and restock. More current minibars are connected with a PMS interface. Each time an item is removed, it is charged to the guest account. While this system is more expensive, it can reduce labor costs, since an attendant is not required to visit all the rooms—only those that have inventory depleted (this also means one less guest disturbance).

Cloud Computing. With cloud technology, hotel data are stored remotely instead of on computer equipment at an on-site location. The need for excess hardware is reduced, yielding a cost saving for the hotel. With reduced hardware, the demand for electricity is also less, yielding more savings. An added important benefit is that in an emergency, such as a security breach or natural disaster, information would not be lost. Marriott is adopting IBM Cloud technology; IBM will provide enhanced IT operations to Marriott to help the company offer faster digital services to guests staying at Marriott properties across the globe.

Knowledge Check

1. What are two of the most important types of controls for hotel managers and how are they used?

2. How has mobile technology impacted hotel operations?

To efficiently run their hotels, hotel managers organize them into various functional areas and then delegate responsibility and authority. The functional areas are divided into revenue centers and cost (or support) centers. Departments such as rooms and food and beverage are revenue centers; others, like accounting and sales and marketing, are cost centers. The number of such centers depends on the size of the hotel.

In the majority of hotels, the rooms department is the largest and generates the most revenue and profit. It generally consists of four departments: front office, reservations, housekeeping, and uniformed service. Front office duties include checking guests in and out, posting charges to their accounts, and collecting payments. In small hotels, front desk agents may also accept reservations, relay messages to guests, and handle the telephone switchboard.

A hotel's reservations department should be staffed by skilled telemarketing personnel who are able to accept reservations over the phone, answer questions about the hotel and its facilities, and quote guestroom rates and available dates. Since some callers are shopping around, reservationists should be trained to sell the property as well as accept reservations.

The housekeeping department is responsible for cleaning guestrooms and public areas. Often it has the most employees. Besides cleaning, the housekeeping department also takes care of laundry and valet services. Uniformed service employees deal with guest luggage and transportation as well as provide concierge services.

The three most commonly used rooms department key performance indicators (KPIs) for measuring department performance are the average daily rate (ADR), occupancy percentage, and revenue per available room (RevPAR).

The food and beverage department is of paramount importance to a hotel's profitability and reputation. There may be many different types of food and beverage outlets in a hotel. Factors that influence the level of food and beverage service that a hotel offers include the type of hotel, the class of hotel, the competition, product availability, availability of labor, and guest demand. Restaurant managers, beverage managers, and a banquet manager typically report to the food and beverage manager or the food and beverage director. Support and control personnel for the food and beverage department include receiving clerks, storeroom clerks, and cashiers.

The overall profitability of food and beverage operations depends on several factors, including hours of operation, guest check averages, the number and kind of facilities, employee turnover, entertainment costs, and marketing.

Concessions, rentals, and commissions are other sources of hotel revenue. However, managers should make sure that the standards of concessionaires are compatible with those of the hotel. Three revenue centers that play a prominent role at some hotels are golf course and pro shop facilities, health clubs/spas, and parking departments. There are many other revenue centers that may be found at hotels (beauty and barber shops, gift shops, newsstands, etc.).

The administrative and general department, information and telecommunications systems department, sales and marketing department, and property operation and maintenance department are all considered cost centers. The administrative and general department includes the general manager and their staff, and administrative departments such as accounting, human resources, and security. The accounting department is charged with the hotel's financial management. Accounting is headed by a controller who oversees the accounting manager, the payroll manager, the food and beverage cost controller, and the purchasing manager. The human resources department is responsible for recruiting, hiring, orienting, training, evaluating, motivating, rewarding, disciplining, developing, promoting, and communicating with hotel employees. Security of hotel employees and guests is of overriding importance. Hotel security programs are preventive and should be under the direction of a person with law enforcement experience.

The information and telecommunications department went from a revenue producer for hotels to a cost center as guests in greater numbers purchased cell phones or smartphones and used them to make calls when staying at hotels. The sales and marketing department is charged with identifying prospective guests, communicating their needs and wants to hotel management, and persuading prospective guests to stay at the hotel. To accomplish these tasks, the sales and marketing department usually has a director of sales and marketing, a sales manager, a marketing manager, a MICE (meetings, incentives, conventions, exhibits) sales manager, salespeople, and support staff.

The property operation and maintenance department takes care of the hotel's physical plant and utility systems. The department is headed by a chief engineer, assisted by their own staff and outside contractors. Most preventive maintenance duties and repairs are performed by hotel staff.

As a result of the Americans with Disabilities Act (ADA), all of the departments of a U.S. hotel must modify existing facilities to some extent and incorporate design features into new construction that make hotel facilities accessible to people with disabilities. People with disabilities, as defined by the act, include people using wheelchairs, people with mobility impairments, and people with sensory impairments such as blindness and deafness. The ADA covers employees as well as guests.

Hotel managers have two major kinds of controls: financial controls and quality controls. Important financial controls are the hotel's financial statements. These statements are based on those found in the *Uniform System of Accounts for the Lodging Industry.* In this accounting system, hotel expenses are classified as departmental expenses, undistributed operating expenses, and nonoperating expenses. Assets and liabilities are also classified.

Quality controls are essential in order to ensure that standards established by management are adhered to. Hotel managers must establish standards appropriate for their type of hotel, create procedures, and select and train employees carefully if quality guest service is to be achieved. All quality programs require employee involvement. Employees are encouraged to solve problems that interfere with good guest service. To be optimally effective, quality programs should be evaluated to make sure they are truly working, and both managers and employees should be rewarded for achieving quality goals.

Technology plays a vital role in managing a hotel and providing service to hotel guests. Computer applications have been designed for almost every aspect of hotel operations. Two of the most widely used are the property management system (PMS), which performs most functions that affect a guest's stay at the hotel, and an accounting system that records and analyzes the hotel's financial transactions.

accounting department—The hotel department responsible for keeping track of the many business transactions that occur in the hotel and managing the hotel's finances.

assets—Resources available for use by a business (i.e., anything owned by the business that has monetary value).

average daily rate (ADR)—A key rooms department operating ratio: rooms revenue divided by number of rooms sold. Also called average room rate.

capture rate—The percentage of hotel guests who eat meals at the hotel.

catering department—A department within the food and beverage department of a hotel that is responsible for arranging and planning food and beverage functions for (1) conventions and smaller hotel groups, and (2) local banquets booked by the sales department.

commissions—Fees that are paid to the hotel by suppliers that are located outside the hotel but provide services for hotel guests, such as gift shops, car rental agencies, and photographers.

concession—A facility that might well be operated by the hotel directly, such as a beauty salon or fitness club, but is turned over to independent operators. The hotel in turn receives a flat fee, a minimum fee plus a percentage of the gross receipts over a specific amount, or a percentage of total gross sales.

control system—A system of controls that allows managers to quickly recognize and correct deviations from the operating budget, such as financial statements and service quality standards.

cost centers—Departments or areas within a hotel that do not directly generate revenue; they provide support for the hotel's revenue centers. Also known as support centers.

departmental expenses—Expenses that are charged to specific hotel departments; such expenses include a wide range of items, such as rooms department payroll, restaurant laundry, and telephone supplies like message pads and pencils.

familiarization (fam) tours—Free or reduced-rate travel programs designed by hotel personnel to acquaint travel agents and others with the hotel and stimulate sales.

financial controls—Financial statements, operating ratios, and other financial statistics that hotel managers can use to keep track of operations and make sure financial goals are being attained.

food and beverage department—The hotel department responsible for preparing and serving food and beverages within the hotel. Also includes catering and room service.

front office—A hotel's command post for processing reservations, registering guests, settling guest accounts, and checking guests in and out.

housekeeping department—A department of the rooms department responsible for cleaning the hotel's guestrooms and public areas.

human resources department—The hotel department responsible for recruiting, hiring, orienting, training, evaluating, motivating, rewarding, disciplining, developing, promoting, and communicating with hotel employees.

key cards—Plastic cards, resembling credit cards, that are used in place of metal guestroom keys. Key cards require electronic locks.

liabilities—Obligations of a business, largely indebtedness related to the expenses incurred in the process of generating income.

meal plan—A package or arrangement offered by hotels that includes meals as part of the guest's stay.

night audit—An accounting task usually performed between 11 p.m. and 6 a.m. after all a hotel's sales outlets are closed. A night audit (1) verifies that guest charges have been accurately posted to guests' accounts and (2) compares the totals of all accounts with sales reports of operating departments.

nonoperating expenses—Expenses related to the investment in the hotel, such as insurance on the building and contents, interest on the mortgage loan, and property taxes.

occupancy percentage—A measure of how many available rooms in a hotel are occupied by guests over a specific period. It is calculated by dividing the number of rooms occupied by the number of rooms available for a given period.

property management system (PMS)—A computerized system that helps hotel managers and other personnel carry out a number of front-of-the-house and back-of-the-house functions. A PMS can support a variety of applications software that helps managers in their data-gathering and reporting responsibilities.

property operation and maintenance department—The hotel department responsible for taking care of the hotel's physical plant and controlling energy costs.

purchasing department—The hotel department responsible for buying, receiving, storing, and issuing all the products used in the hotel.

quality controls—Standards of operation, quality assurance programs, and other controls that seek to establish and maintain hotel products and services at quality levels established by management.

rentals—Enterprises such as offices or stores that pay rent to a hotel.

reservations department—A department within a hotel's rooms department staffed by skilled telemarketing personnel who take reservations over the phone, answer questions about facilities, quote prices and available dates, and sell to callers who are shopping around.

revenue centers—Departments or areas within a hotel that directly generate revenue through the sale of products or services to guests. Also known as operated departments.

revenue management—A hotel pricing system adapted from airlines that uses a hotel's computer reservations system to track advance bookings and then lower or raise guestroom prices accordingly—on a day-to-day basis—to yield the maximum revenue. Before selling a room in advance, the hotel forecasts the probability of being able to sell the room to other market segments that are willing to pay higher rates.

revenue per available room (RevPAR)—A statistic used by hotel managers to evaluate the performance of the rooms department. It is computed by dividing room revenue by the number of available rooms for the same period. It also can be determined by multiplying the occupancy percentage by the average daily rate for the same period.

rooms department—The largest, and usually most profitable, department in a hotel. It typically consists of four departments: front office, reservations, housekeeping, and uniformed service.

room service—The department within a food and beverage department that is responsible for delivering food and beverages to guests in their guestrooms. May also be responsible for preparing the food and beverages.

sales and marketing department—The hotel department responsible for identifying prospective guests for the hotel, conforming the products and services of the hotel as much as possible to meet the needs of those prospects, and persuading prospects to become guests.

security department—The hotel department responsible for the protection of guests and their property, employees and their property, and the hotel itself.

undistributed operating expenses—Expenses such as marketing and energy—costs that relate to the entire hotel and not to one specific department.

uniformed service department—A hotel department within the rooms department that deals with guests' luggage and transportation and provides concierge services. Also referred to as the guest service department.

1. Which area of a hotel is a revenue center?
   a. Information and telecommunications department
   b. Sales and marketing department
   c. Food and beverage department
   d. Property operations

2. In which hotel would a food and beverage department generate more revenue than a rooms department?
   a. Resort hotel with convention space that has extensive banquet sales
   b. Center-city hotel with three fine dining restaurants
   c. Highway hotel with a complimentary daily breakfast
   d. Condominium hotel with room service options

3. What is the average daily rate if the rooms revenue is $23,800 and there are 170 occupied rooms on a Sunday evening?
   a. $162.94
   b. $162.16
   c. $155.03
   d. $140.00

4. Which is the responsibility of a night auditor?
   a. Arrange excursions and transportation for hotel guests.
   b. Upsell groups into more expensive room categories.
   c. Reconcile charges or postings to guest accounts.
   d. Preassign vacant rooms before check-in.

5. A highway hotel with a full-service restaurant is surrounded by chain restaurants. Few people know about the hotel's restaurant. What problem does the hotel's restaurant have?
   a. High turnover
   b. Low check averages
   c. Costly entertainment
   d. Insufficient marketing

6. Which is not compliant with the Americans with Disabilities Act (ADA)?
   a. Hotel parking lot with 1 percent of its spaces designated as accessible
   b. Swimming pool with 300 linear feet and two ADA access points
   c. Restaurant with a 40-inch-wide path
   d. Lobby restroom with one accessible stall

7. Which department is responsible for keeping revenue-producing areas operational?
   a. Accounting
   b. Human resources
   c. Sales and marketing
   d. Property operation and maintenance

8. What is the simplest way to evaluate the quality of an operation?
   a. Periodic tours of a hotel by management
   b. Guest satisfaction surveys
   c. Industry data polls
   d. Mystery shoppers

9. Which hotel technology passes inventory and rates for hotels to travel sites?
   a. Inventory/purchasing system
   b. Property management system
   c. Global distribution system
   d. Point-of-sale system

10. What is a disadvantage of magstripe key cards?
   a. They are prone to demagnetization.
   b. They cannot access hotel facilities.
   c. They cannot be duplicated.
   d. They are costly.

11. What is the occupancy percentage of a 200-room hotel if 30 rooms are vacant?
   a. 85 percent
   b. 88.8 percent
   c. 89 percent
   d. 92.5 percent

12. How is RevPAR calculated?
   a. Rooms occupied divided by rooms available
   b. Rooms revenue divided by rooms occupied
   c. Average daily rate multiplied by rooms available
   d. Occupancy percentage multiplied by average daily rate

SHORT-ANSWER QUESTIONS

1. How do financial controls contribute to a hotel's success?

2. What are the challenges of delivering consistent quality control at a hotel?

ROOM RATES, REVIEWS, AND REFUNDS

In early February 2020, Marcia books a trip to Switzerland for the end of March of that year. All the hotels she books are refundable except one. The most generous cancellation policy of that hotel is a partially refundable rate with a nonrefundable deposit. She calls the hotel to get more information about its policy. Since the nonrefundable rate is about 20 to 25 percent lower than the partially refundable rate, Marcia decides to go for the nonrefundable rate. She also decides to upgrade to a room with a more scenic view, which a reservations agent at the hotel enthusiastically describes to her. Marcia knows that staying there could be a once-in-a-lifetime opportunity—it is a popular hotel with rave reviews and a prime location in the Swiss Alps.

Then the COVID-19 pandemic starts to affect Europe. There are a growing number of cases in Switzerland. Marcia decides to cancel her trip. Marcia used miles to book her airline ticket and the airline graciously waives the mileage redeposit fee. After canceling the refundable hotels she booked, she contacts the booking site she used to see what she can do about the nonrefundable charge at the Swiss Alps hotel. The booking site contacts the property to see whether it is willing to issue a refund, but it sticks to its cancellation policy.

Marcia then calls customer service for her credit card company to see whether she has any recourse. But because Switzerland is not officially on the list of places under a travel advisory, the credit card company refuses to dispute the charge. Marcia decides to contact the hotel directly and negotiates credit for a future stay. She will have to pay any difference in rates, and the next booking will also be nonrefundable, but it is better than nothing.

DISCUSSION QUESTIONS

1. How might the cancellation policy of the Swiss Alps hotel affect its future bookings?

2. Which revenue centers or cost centers have likely made the Swiss Alps hotel successful?

Seth McDaniels

Seth McDaniels, general manager of the Wyndham Grand Clearwater Beach in Florida, is known for his exceptional leadership and accomplishments in the hospitality industry. McDaniels has held key positions that have allowed him to make a significant impact in various areas of hotel management and operations.

As vice president for openings and experience at Davidson Hospitality Group, he was responsible for overseeing new build openings, acquisitions, and dispositions across the company. During his tenure, he achieved unprecedented growth, converting and opening over 35 hotels, marking the largest expansion in Davidson's history.

Prior to joining Davidson, McDaniels held key positions at Hyatt and its parent organization, Two Roads Hospitality. In those positions, he demonstrated his expertise in pre-opening activities, budget development, and implementing operational standards for lifestyle brands. He successfully managed the transition, opening, and disposition of 25 properties during his four-year tenure.

McDaniels's leadership abilities were evident during his time as the general manager at The Epiphany, where he repositioned the property to launch the prestigious Nobu Hotel in Palo Alto, California. Overseeing all operational departments, he led the property to be recognized as the top hotel in overall service and ADR within the Two Roads portfolio.

Throughout his career, McDaniels has held various leadership positions with Kimpton Hotels & Restaurants, including managing The Goodland in Santa Barbara, California, and EPIC Hotel in Miami, Florida. These experiences further showcased his versatility and success in managing different properties.

McDaniels earned a bachelor of science degree in hospitality management from Florida International University's Chaplin School of Hospitality & Tourism Management. His education, combined with his extensive hands-on experience, has solidified his reputation as a respected and accomplished professional in the industry.

A 150-room hotel in a major city has been experiencing declining occupancy rates and revenue over the past year. The hotel is part of a well-known chain and has a reputation for high-quality service. But in recent months, customer complaints have increased, and staff morale is low. The hotel management team needs to identify the root causes of these issues and come up with a plan to improve the situation. What would you do as the general manager?

8

CLUB MANAGEMENT

Chapter Outline

Learning Objectives

1. Summarize background information about clubs; list and describe types of private clubs; and describe country, golf, city/athletic, and yacht clubs. (pp. 232–239)

2. Compare equity clubs with corporate or developer clubs; outline club organization and the duties and personal attributes of and advancement opportunities for a club manager; list and describe typical revenue sources for clubs; and discuss club expenses, control, and technology. (pp. 239–249)

KEY TERMS

administrative skills

assessment

athletic club

beach club

city/athletic club

city club

club manager

common interest realty association (CIRA)

conceptual skills

corporate club

country club

dining club

equity club

fraternal clubs

golf club

golf committee

initiation fee

membership dues

military club

social club

sports activities fees

technical skills

university club

visitors' fees

yacht club

In this chapter, we will discuss the organization and management of private clubs. The chapter describes the different kinds of clubs and their membership composition. It also explains how clubs are owned, organized, and managed. We then examine the unique aspects of clubs, including their sources of revenue, and profile several prominent clubs and their memberships.

8.1 BACKGROUND ON CLUBS

Private clubs are gathering places for club members only. They bring together people of like interests. Those interests could be recreational, social, fraternal, or professional.

Private clubs are not an invention of modern society. Wealthy citizens of ancient Greece and Rome formed clubs. Clubs have been an integral part of the social fabric of upper-class English society for centuries. As the English colonized the world, they established clubs; English social clubs and the golf club of St Andrews in Scotland are the forerunners of city clubs and country clubs in the United States. Some U.S. city clubs, such as the Somerset Club in Boston, the Detroit Club, and the Wilmington Club in Delaware, date back to the mid-nineteenth century. Perhaps the oldest country club in the United States—founded in 1882—is The Country Club, located in Brookline, Massachusetts.

In many parts of the world, the club you belong to is an indication of your position in society. Comedian Groucho Marx sent a telegram to the Friars Club, to which he belonged: "Please accept my resignation. I don't want to belong to any club that will accept me as a member." Marx was commenting on the fact that many people join clubs to enhance their own social status. While some clubs continue to be vestiges of the class system, by and large the exclusionary aspect of private clubs in the United States has changed due to equal rights legislation and society's increased social consciousness.

Perhaps one of the most notable clubs in the world is the Mar-a-Lago Club on Palm Beach Island in Florida. It is currently the only private club in the world to attain the prestigious 6-Star Diamond Award from the American Academy of Hospitality Sciences. Its amenities include an oceanfront swimming pool and beach club, a spa, six tennis courts, a full-size croquet court, a chip and putt golf course, a fitness center, and European indoor and terrace dining.

Today, there are about 4,000 private clubs in the United States, providing diverse opportunities in management. Private club management is closely related to hotel and foodservice management. Often the manager of a club is called the chief operating officer. Many of a club manager's responsibilities in the areas of guest relations, human resources management, marketing, control, and maintenance are similar to those of a hotel manager. Most clubs have dining facilities; some have multiple dining rooms and lounges as well as extensive private meeting rooms for catered events. In addition to these facilities, many city clubs have gymnasiums, racquetball courts, and guestrooms for overnight guests. Country clubs may have dining rooms, meeting rooms, one or more golf courses, a tennis club, a beach club, and even a skeet- and trap-shooting club. Such country clubs are like resort hotels, except that they are not open to the public.

Clubs managed by the same company, as well as independent city and country clubs, have various types of reciprocal agreements so their members can use the facilities of similar clubs when traveling. For example, the members of the historic Fort Orange Club in Albany, New York, may dine at the University Club of San Francisco, stay at London's Sloane Club, and play golf at the Dataw Island Club in South Carolina. Typically, members secure an introductory guest card or letter of introduction to the club that they wish to visit before leaving on their trip, although simply presenting their current membership card to their own club will often get them into an affiliated club.

There are some similarities in the organization of clubs and hotels. A basic difference between clubs and hotels is that the club's "guest" is a dues-paying member with a financial and emotional attachment to the club; whereas hotels are open to the public, and the relationship between the guest and the hotel is less personal.

Knowledge Check

1. How does membership in a club affect social status?

2. What is a fundamental difference between clubs and hotels?

Exhibit 8.1   Breakdown of Club Types

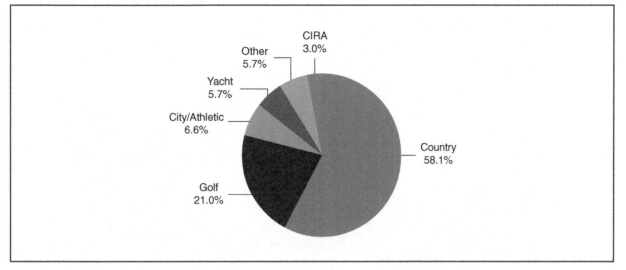

Source: Club Management Association of America, *2022 Finance and Operations Report,* https://www.cmaa.org/media/2zdnrdhg/2022cmaafinanceandoperationsreportexecuti vesummary.pdf.

8.2 TYPES OF CLUBS

The Club Management Association of America (CMAA) classifies clubs into four basic types:

1. Country
2. Golf
3. City/Athletic
4. Yacht

There are some private clubs that do not easily fit into these classifications. We will discuss these clubs under a fifth classification called "other clubs." See Exhibit 8.1 for a breakdown of private club types according to the CMAA.

Due to the growth of planned communities, condominiums, cooperatives, and homeowner associations in the twentieth century, **common interest realty associations (CIRAs)** were formed to govern and manage common-interest communities. CIRAs are commonly known as homeowners associations (HOAs), condominium associations, cooperative associations, or planned-community associations. CIRAs are responsible for overseeing shared areas, amenities, and services within the community, and they enforce rules and regulations to maintain the community's standards and protect property values. They provide a variety of benefits, such as shared amenities, property maintenance, community events, and a sense of belonging for residents.

Country Clubs

The largest type of private club is the country club. **Country clubs** are primarily recreational and social facilities for individuals and families who live nearby. These clubs often have separate children's facilities and do a large catering business since it is common for members to hold bar and bat mitzvahs, weddings, and other social events at them. Country clubs offer a host of amenities—likely racquet sports— tennis, pickleball, platform tennis, etc., and aquatics (pool, etc.) in addition to golf.

Since country clubs need a great deal of land (one 18-hole golf course typically requires a minimum of 110 acres), they are usually located in suburban or rural areas. Exceptions sometimes occur when a city develops to the extent that the urban sprawl comes up to or surrounds the club. The Hillcrest Country Club in Los Angeles is a case in point. When it opened in 1920, the locale was suburban Los Angeles; now it is surrounded by Beverly Hills and Century City. Other once-suburban country clubs include the Chevy Chase Country Club in metropolitan Washington, D.C.,

Country clubs need a great deal of land.

and the Everglades Country Club on fashionable Worth Avenue in Palm Beach, Florida.

In some cases, new country clubs are financed by prospective members, who are asked to invest in the club by buying shares of stock. A new club can cost $50 million to build. It is not unusual for members who wish to join to be asked to buy as much as $150,000 worth of stock, as well as pay membership dues of at least $1,000 per month.

In addition to a clubhouse with one or more dining rooms and function rooms, most country clubs have at least one golf course and one swimming pool. In the 1970s, the popularity of tennis grew so much that tennis courts became almost a mandatory part of a country club's recreational facilities. In a study conducted by the CMAA, 80 percent of the country clubs reporting had outdoor tennis courts and 10 percent had indoor courts. Other facilities mentioned in the study were steam rooms, fitness and exercise rooms, paddle tennis, and racquetball. Clubs that provide experiences for the entire family are growing in popularity.[1]

A number of country clubs are known for their beautiful facilities and exclusivity. One is the Onwentsia Club in Lake Forest, Illinois. The golf course of the Mid-Ocean Club in Bermuda, founded in 1921, has been played by former British prime minister Winston Churchill, presidents Dwight Eisenhower and George H.W. Bush, and baseball legend Babe Ruth; the *World Atlas of Golf* calls its par-4 fifth hole "one of the world's unforgettable holes."[2] Other clubs are famous for their outstanding golf courses and the tournaments held there. Examples include California's Pebble Beach Country Club in Pebble Beach and the Royal St. George's Golf Club in Sandwich, England.

Golf Clubs

A **golf club** refers to a private establishment or facility where golf is played. The primary difference between golf clubs and country clubs is golf clubs focus on one amenity—golf. Golf clubs typically feature an 18-hole course, but some may have more or fewer holes. In addition to golf courses, these clubs often offer various services to enhance the members' experiences, such as a clubhouse and practice facilities. The clubhouse serves as the central gathering place for members. It may house a pro shop, locker rooms, dining areas, lounges, and administrative offices. Many golf clubs have practice areas, such as driving ranges, putting greens, chipping areas, and practice bunkers, where members can work on their golf skills. Golf clubs often have restaurants, bars, and banquet facilities for members to enjoy meals, socialize, and host events.

Membership in a golf club is typically exclusive and requires an application process and payment of annual dues. Each club may have different membership categories, such as full golf members, social members, and junior members.

Golf clubs are known for providing a luxurious and recreational environment for golf enthusiasts where they can enjoy their favorite sport, connect with fellow members, and relax in a serene setting. An example of a golf club is the Augusta National Golf Club, one of the most prestigious and iconic golf clubs in the world. Located in Augusta, Georgia, it is renowned for hosting the Masters Tournament, one of the four major championships in professional golf. Augusta National is synonymous with the Masters Tournament, which is held annually in early April. The tournament is one of the most anticipated events in golf, attracting top professional players from around the world and captivating golf enthusiasts. The club's membership has historically been limited to a select group of prominent individuals. One of the unique traditions at Augusta National is the awarding of the Green Jacket to the winner of the Masters Tournament. The winner gets to keep the jacket for one year and then returns it to the club.

City/Athletic Clubs

The CMAA classifies city and athletic clubs as one category. A **city/athletic club** is an urban recreational and social facility. These clubs vary in size, type, facilities, and membership. Some city/athletic clubs own their own real estate; others lease space in office buildings or hotels. What they have in common is that foodservice is generally offered, and a manager is hired to oversee the entire operation. For clarity, we will discuss city and athletic clubs separately.

Athletic. Athletic clubs, also known as sports clubs or fitness clubs, are facilities that provide a range of athletic- and fitness-related amenities and services designed to promote physical activity, health, and well-being. They cater to individuals who are interested in sports, fitness, and recreational activities. Athletic clubs are as varied as the club industry itself. The New York Athletic Club, founded in 1868, occupies an entire building in midtown Manhattan, with extensive health and sports facilities, 200 guestrooms, a dining room with a sweeping view of Central Park, its Tap Room

and Cocktail Lounge, and extensive meeting and banquet rooms. (Travers Island, the club's 30-acre "summer home" on Long Island Sound, has a clubhouse; an Olympic-size saltwater pool; and facilities for tennis, rowing, and yachting.)

Equinox is a luxury fitness club with locations in various cities in the United States and internationally. It offers a premium experience, attracting individuals seeking high-quality fitness facilities and personalized attention with state-of-the-art fitness equipment, group exercise classes, spa services, and high-end amenities. Equinox positions itself as a lifestyle brand, aiming to provide a comprehensive approach to health and well-being for its members.

The YMCA, or Young Men's Christian Association, has a long and storied history. It was founded in London by George Williams in 1844 as a Christian movement to promote the spiritual and physical well-being of young men during the early stages of the Industrial Revolution. Over time, the YMCA expanded its focus and began serving a broader community, including women and children. Today, the YMCA is a diverse organization with programs for people of all ages and backgrounds, promoting health, fitness, education, and social responsibility.

City. City clubs can refer to various types of private clubs located in urban areas, such as social clubs, dining clubs, or university clubs. City clubs bring together individuals who share common interests, hobbies, or social activities. These clubs provide a platform for members to engage in recreational, cultural, or social pursuits, fostering a sense of community and camaraderie among like-minded individuals. The difference between social clubs, dining clubs, and university clubs are their primary purposes.

Social. Social clubs are clubs where members go to meet each other to enjoy leisurely activities. These clubs were modeled after men's social clubs in London, such as Boodle's, St. James, and White's, where people from similar backgrounds could meet at the end of the day for cocktails and general companionship or entertainment unrelated to business. Indeed, in some social clubs, it was considered bad manners to talk about business.

The oldest social club in the United States is said to be the Fish House in Philadelphia, founded in 1732. To ensure that the Fish House would always be socially oriented rather than business oriented, it was formed as a men's cooking club, with each member taking turns preparing meals for the membership.[3] Social clubs in Manhattan include the Union League Club, founded in 1863; the Knickerbocker Club, named in honor of a character created by writer Washington Irving; and the Links Club, which was originally established "to promote and conserve throughout the United States the best interests and true spirit of the game of golf." Links Club members include business leaders and politicians from all over the country. The most well-known social club on the West Coast, San Francisco's Bohemian Club, was founded in 1872. It occupies a handsome red-brick Georgian clubhouse on the side of Nob Hill and features a 750-seat theater where members perform amateur theatricals. The club also owns a 280-acre estate in the Sierra Nevada where members gather every summer for a two-week "encampment," during which there are poetry readings, musical productions, and concerts presented by the club's own 70-piece orchestra.[4]

In recent years, social clubs have had to reinvent themselves to reflect changes in the societal attitudes of their members. The Westmoreland Club in Wilkes-Barre, Pennsylvania, is one example. Founded in 1873, it is impressive enough that the club has survived through all of the national and regional economic downturns over the years. Adding to the club's remarkable history is its recent transformation from a special occasion destination into a more regularly frequented place to meet and dine with friends and business associates. How was this accomplished? Dining was made less formal by the introduction of a casual restaurant and an Internet café with the services and ambience of a Starbucks. A concierge service was established to assist members with their entertainment, travel, and business needs. Recognizing the increasing interest in sustainability, the club grows fresh ingredients for its restaurants in an area outside the club. More than 50 social events are spread throughout the year and have achieved enviable status. The Westmoreland Club's ability to adapt to changing times by offering facilities, services, and events that meet twenty-first-century needs have made it once again "indispensable to its members."[5]

Another example of a social club is the Carlyle & Co., Rosewood Hong Kong Hotel's new private membership club. Unlike other social clubs that choose members based on wealth, social status, and profession, Carlyle & Co. selects members with similar personalities, passions, interests, and stories. Its aim is to bring together a rich culture of unique individuals, each adding a new dimension to the club's membership. Members have access to a 25,000-square-foot social sanctuary above Rosewood Hong Kong that features a well-appointed music room designed to hold performances from world-class musicians, a wine cellar, and a chef's table designed for intimate fine dining experiences. There is also a fitness studio, pool, gym, game room, dedicated tailor, and an on-site barber.

A less formal social club dedicated to creativity, exclusivity, and community is Soho House. It has over 110,000 members across 27 locations in 12 countries. It was featured in the television show *Sex and the City*. Soho House is probably the most talked about and least "private" private club in the world. What started out in London on top of a restaurant as a media- and arts-focused alternative to European aristocracy has now become a go-to place for those who want to embrace celebrity culture and share their most public "private" moments on social media. This has been called "high public exclusivity," meaning *"don't talk to me, but just watch me and be jealous. Telling someone to meet you at Soho House for lunch is a not-so-subtle humble brag — you may want to get lunch but what you really want is for them to know you are a member, a sort of status voyeurism."*[6] Soho House's acquisition of Cecconi's, one of London's best-loved Italian restaurants, helped its expansion across Europe and into the United States. Soho House has also launched Soho Works, an exclusive coworking space, and Soho Home, where members can buy furniture and interior items found in Soho House.

Dining. Dining clubs, also known as supper clubs or gastronomic clubs, are private social establishments centered around communal dining experiences. These clubs typically focus on providing their members with unique culinary experiences, often featuring gourmet meals prepared by professional chefs or talented home cooks. The concept of dining clubs has a long history, and they continue to be popular in various forms around the world. Dining clubs vary in their structure, purpose, and exclusivity. Some are formal, invitation-only establishments, while

8

CLUB MANAGEMENT

erings of like-minded

club is the
ciety (IWFS).
al organization
appreciation and
onomy, and cultural
don in 1933 by
IWFS has grown
of chapters and
nizes events,
ctivities that
ns and wines of
nal wine tastings
casual gatherings
events often
rts in the fields of
gh its events and
a platform for
nowledge, form
create memories
s of the table.

are private clubs
ividuals otherwise
, university
s nature are quite
sity Club in Seattle
rsity. You only have
be eligible to

join. Other university clubs are for graduates of specific schools and exist in cities where there may be a large concentration of alumni who either live there or visit often. In New York City, for example, Harvard, Princeton, Yale, Cornell, and the University of Pennsylvania each have their own clubs with restaurants, health clubs, guestrooms, and regular activities such as lectures and concerts. The Harvard, Yale, and Princeton clubs are owned by their members; the Cornell and Pennsylvania clubs are university owned. The largest of these clubs is the Yale Club. Guestrooms, dining facilities, meeting and banquet rooms, an indoor swimming pool, and a gymnasium are provided for Yale (and Dartmouth) alumni. The club stands on the exact spot where one of Yale's most celebrated sons, Nathan Hale, uttered the famous phrase, "I regret that I have but one life to give for my country," before being hanged as a spy by the British during the American Revolution.

Yacht. Yacht clubs cater to individuals who share a passion for boating, yachting, and maritime activities. These clubs provide a social and recreational hub for yacht owners and sailing enthusiasts, offering a range of amenities and services related to boating, water sports, and nautical activities. They are located near large bodies of water, and their main purpose is to

f yacht clubs is to provide marinas and other facilities for boat owners.

provide marinas and other boating facilities for boat owners. While many of these clubs have tennis courts, swimming pools, and elaborate clubhouses with dining rooms and lounges, others provide only the bare necessities of dock space, fuel, and boating supplies. Some provide sailing programs to introduce young enthusiasts to the world of boating and sailing through educational and recreational activities. Yacht clubs may host regattas and races for members and as part of regional or national competitions. One famous yacht club is the Grosse Pointe Yacht Club in Grosse Pointe Shores, Michigan, founded in 1923 by a group that included automaker Edsel Ford. The club's facilities include an enormous ballroom, a domed main dining room overlooking the harbor, and slips for 300 boats.

Other Clubs

There are other types of private clubs that engage professional managers to operate their facilities and manage their social and recreational programs, such as beach clubs, fraternal clubs, and military clubs. While these clubs are not as common as country clubs, golf clubs, city/athletic clubs, or yacht clubs, they are managed by professionals who play a crucial role in creating positive experiences for club members and ensuring that clubs remain financially viable.

Beach. A **beach club** is a type of private or commercial establishment located along a beachfront that provides various amenities and services for its members or guests. Beach clubs are popular in coastal destinations and tropical resorts, offering a range of recreational activities and relaxation opportunities. The primary feature of a beach club is its direct access to a beach or shoreline. Members and guests can enjoy the beach and access to the ocean for swimming, sunbathing, and water sports. Beach clubs provide an ideal setting for individuals and families to relax, enjoy recreational activities, and immerse themselves in the natural beauty of coastal regions. They offer a luxurious and convenient escape for those seeking a beachside retreat. One example is Nikki Beach Club, a luxury beach club brand with locations in various international destinations, including Miami Beach, Saint-Tropez, Ibiza, and Dubai.

Fraternal. Fraternal clubs are social organizations or associations that bring together individuals who share common interests, values, or affiliations. These clubs are often founded on principles of brotherhood, friendship, and mutual support. Fraternal clubs typically have a strong sense of community and aim to foster belonging and camaraderie among their members. Fraternal organizations sometimes own or rent entire buildings or floors within a building. Some offer food and beverage service, overnight accommodations, and rooms for meetings and recreation. Fraternal clubs also require professional managers.

The Elks Club and Rotary International are examples of fraternal clubs. Elks Clubs actively contribute to the betterment of their communities through charitable endeavors. The Elks Club's commitment to service, tradition, and fellowship has made it a significant and enduring presence in American society since its founding in 1868. Rotary International started as Rotary Club in 1905 to bring together professionals from different vocations to foster friendships, exchange ideas, and serve communities. The name "rotary" was chosen because the club initially rotated its meetings among members' offices. The Rotary Club's early meetings were characterized by a focus on ethics, service, and camaraderie. Today, Rotary International is one of the largest and most influential service organizations in the world, with over 1.2 million members in more than 35,000 clubs across nearly every country in the world. Rotary's dedication to service, community engagement, and international collaboration has made a significant and lasting impact on lives and communities around the globe.

Military. Military clubs are social organizations or associations that bring together current and former members of the military, as well as their families and supporters. These clubs provide a sense of community and camaraderie for individuals who have served or are currently serving in the armed forces. Military clubs often focus on fostering friendships, providing support, and engaging in activities that honor and recognize the sacrifices and service of military personnel. Examples of military clubs are the American Legion and Veterans of Foreign Wars.

8.3 CLUB OWNERSHIP

Private clubs are usually owned in one of two ways. A club can be owned by some of its members; such clubs are called equity clubs. Those members who fund the purchase or development of an equity club are known as founder members. Or a club can be owned by a company that sells memberships. These for-profit clubs are known as corporate or developer clubs, or—less frequently—as proprietary clubs.

Equity Clubs

Equity clubs are generally nonprofit since they are typically formed simply for the enjoyment of their members. Members are either (1) founder members or (2) those who pay a one-time initiation fee and annual dues. If an equity club has an excess of revenues over expenses, the profits are not given back to the founder members but instead are invested in improving the club's facilities and services. The nonprofit statute of the tax law exempts equity clubs from federal and state income taxes, although they may be required to pay taxes on unrelated income (e.g., nonmember functions) as well as federal and state payroll taxes.

Nontransfer of profits to members is only one part of what gives an equity club its nonprofit status. To receive a tax exemption, an equity club must be formed solely for pleasure and recreation, and must not discriminate on the basis of sex, race, or religion against anyone who wishes to become a member. Discrimination is often practiced on other grounds, however. Sometimes clubs charge high initiation fees or require members to buy expensive bonds or membership shares. And it is perfectly within the rights of a club to turn down applicants because they are not qualified by reason of accomplishment, professional occupation, or—as in the case of the Bohemian Club—artistic talent.

Corporate or Developer Clubs

As mentioned earlier, **corporate clubs** or developer clubs operate for profit and are owned by individuals or corporations. Those who wish to become members purchase a membership, not a share in the club. Members may or may not be involved in running the club. Sometimes developers sell or turn over the club to its members when all memberships are sold. The cost of the clubhouse is paid for by initiation fees or real estate sales.

Corporate or developer clubs proliferated with the real estate boom in office buildings, condominiums, and single-housing developments. Just as having dining clubs in office buildings helped developers rent office space, a country club at the center of a condominium or housing development was a good marketing tactic that not only helped to sell or lease properties but also raised their prices by offering an added value to buyers.

The major company in the business of club management is ClubCorp. This Dallas-based company owns or operates more than 200 country clubs, city clubs, sports clubs, and resorts in the United States and Mexico. It was in 1984, with the purchase of the Pinehurst Resort and Country Club in North Carolina, that ClubCorp broadened its business by going into resort hotel management. In view of the similarities between country clubs and resorts, this was not a surprising move. Later, ClubCorp added daily fee golf courses to its management. In 2013 it became a publicly traded company on the New York Stock Exchange.

8.4 CLUB ORGANIZATION

How a club is organized depends to a large extent on whether the club is nonprofit or for-profit. In a nonprofit equity club, the members elect a board of directors (sometimes called a board of governors) to oversee the budget and set policy affecting membership and club use. The board is the governing body, and the club manager reports to the board and implements its policies and decisions (see Exhibit 8.2). In a for-profit corporate or developer club, the club manager reports to and receives instructions on club policies, procedures, and standards from the club's owners (see Exhibit 8.3). A corporate or developer club may have a board of directors made up of club members if the owners wish to give the members some sense of authority, but generally this board merely advises the owners and does not make policy. Exhibits 8.4 and 8.5 show the organization of a city club and a small country club.

The number of members on an equity club's board usually ranges from 12 to 25, although sometimes it is even higher. Board officers typically include a chairperson (usually last year's president), president, vice president, and treasurer.

Committees are extremely important to club morale and operation because they allow more members to participate in club leadership. In addition to special committees that are appointed for specific social or sporting events, clubs generally have five standing committees: a house committee, a membership committee, a finance and budget committee, an entertainment committee, and an athletic committee.[7]

The Club Manager

Club managers are hired professionals responsible for guiding all of the elements of a private club's operation. They were not considered necessary until the early 1920s. Up to that time, most private clubs were managed by their members through the club's standing committees and board of governors. Generally, the clubhouse was run by a steward, and the sports facilities were overseen by a sports professional. Today, club management is a profession requiring special training and expertise.

The duties of a **club manager** can vary considerably, depending on the kind of club they work for and the way it is organized. Some clubs have a general manager in the club manager position; others have a clubhouse manager. The difference is that a general manager has responsibility for all the employees of the club, while a clubhouse manager may only be responsible for employees working in the clubhouse. For example, a country club may have a clubhouse manager in charge of clubhouse operations and personnel, while the club's sports facilities are operated by athletic professionals. Areas of competency needed by club managers are listed in the following sections. In corporate or developer clubs, the trend is to have one general manager in charge of everything because members are too busy to take an interest in all of the details involved in running a club.

According to CMAA, club managers must possess these competencies, grouped into three skill areas (conceptual, administrative, and technical).

Conceptual. Conceptual skills refer to the ability of an individual to think critically, analyze complex situations, and grasp the bigger picture. For a club manager, these skills are important for effective governance and strong leadership qualities. They are also needed for educating the board on best practices, conducting performance reviews, strategic planning, active listening, conflict resolution, negotiation, time management, ethical conduct, innovation, diversity, coaching, delegation, inspiration, philanthropy, and representing the club's brand.

Exhibit 8.2   Sample Organization Chart for an Equity Club

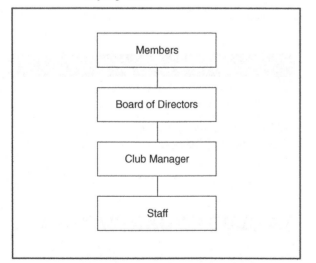

In an equity club, the members own the club and elect a board of directors (who are also members of the club) to oversee the budget and set club policies. The club manager reports to the board or a member of the board.

Exhibit 8.3   Sample Organization Chart for a Corporate or Developer Club

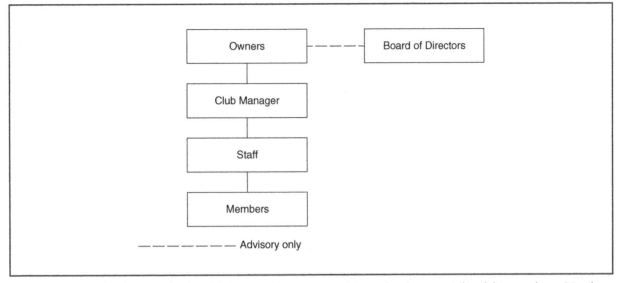

In a corporate or developer club, the club is owned by a corporation or developer, not the club's members. Members may or may not be involved in running the club. For example, the club's owners may form a board of directors, made up of club members, to advise them on club matters. The club manager reports to the corporation or developer, not the club's members.

Exhibit 8.4   City Club Organization

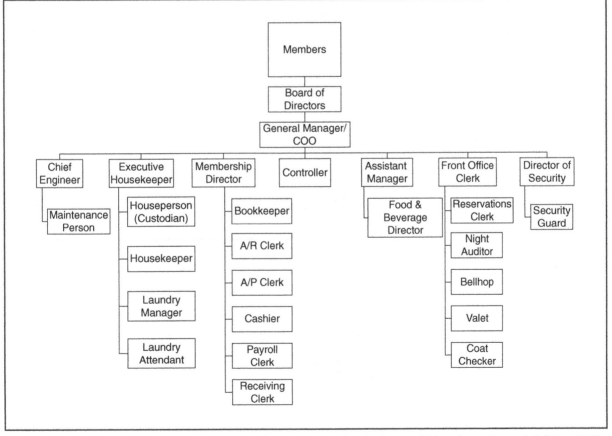

Source: Club Managers Association of America, *Job Descriptions for the Private Club Industry*, Seventh Edition, 2012.

Exhibit 8.5 Small Country Club Organization

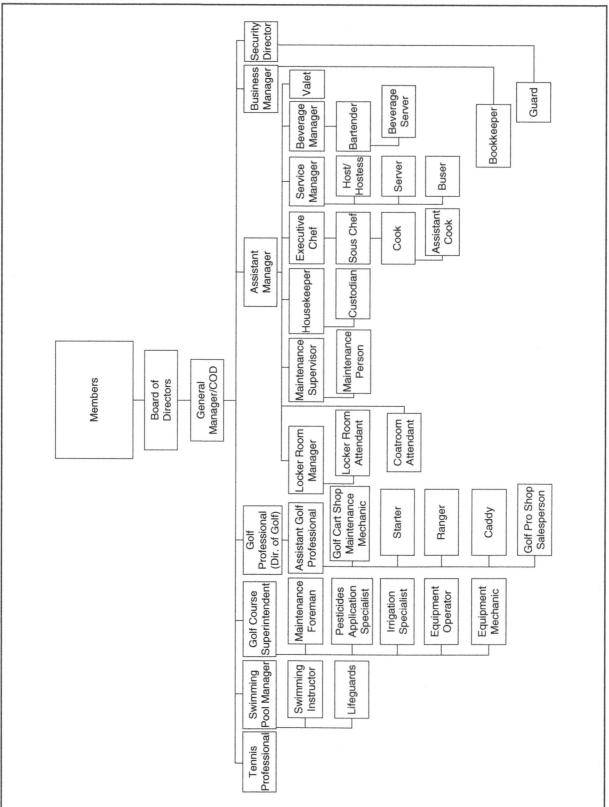

Source: Club Managers Association of America, *Job Descriptions for the Private Club Industry,* Seventh Edition, 2012.

Administrative. Administrative skills refer to a set of competencies that involve effectively managing and organizing tasks, resources, and processes within an organization. Club managers must possess a wide range of skills to effectively oversee club operations. They need to be well versed in understanding financial standards, conducting annual audits, managing budgets, and analyzing data for decision-making. Additionally, club managers must ensure compliance with legal requirements, safety regulations, tax laws, and privacy policies. They also play a vital role in managing professional resources: handling employee policies, recruitment, orientation, and performance reviews; and developing strategies for employee growth and succession planning. Managers also oversee member services, marketing initiatives, and media presence, as well as conduct market research to retain current members and attract new ones.

Technical. Technical skills refer to a specific set of abilities and knowledge required to perform tasks related to a particular field or profession. Technical skills in club management involve computer proficiency, including knowledge of operating systems and relevant software applications. Data analysis skills involve interpreting data using statistical tools and programming languages like Python or R. Other technical skills required in club management include facilities management, food and beverage expertise, golf and sports management, information technology (IT) management, and integrated technology planning. These technical skills are crucial for efficient and effective operations within a club environment.[8]

In one respect, a club manager's job is more complex than the job of a hotel or restaurant manager. The jobs are similar in that all these managers must manage physical facilities, employees, and services in order to meet economic objectives. Each must hire, train, fire, and set standards of service. Where the jobs differ—and what makes a club manager's job more complex—is that club managers must share planning and budgeting responsibilities with an on-site board of directors, and club members have a more direct say in whether a manager keeps their job than hotel or restaurant guests do. In an equity club, a club manager must find a way to keep two groups relatively happy: (1) a board whose members may have diverse points of view because they were elected by different

factions within the club's membership that do not agree, and (2) a variety of members with differing desires and needs. To do this, a club manager must be a master politician.

Advancement in the club management field may require more mobility than in the hotel field. According to surveys done by CMAA, fewer than 20 percent of all CMAA-member club managers were employed as an assistant manager or department head at the same club they now manage.[9] An assistant manager or department head who wishes to advance usually must move to a different club. Club managers who wish to advance to a larger and more prestigious club obviously have to change jobs, which usually requires moving. But many club managers develop such a satisfying relationship with club members and officers that they never consider moving on. A study by GGA Partners in collaboration with CMAA reported that the average tenure of club managers is 7.3 years. On average, club managers are 51 years old and 80 percent of them are male.[10]

Knowledge Check

1. How is a club manager's role more complex than a hotel or restaurant manager's role?

2. How are clubs organized differently from hotels?

8.5 CLUB OPERATIONS

Clubs are similar to other hospitality businesses in that they generate revenue and incur expenses. Differences between clubs and other hospitality businesses can be found in the clubs' sources of revenue.

Revenue

Since a club is a private enterprise used primarily by members, the bulk of its revenue is derived from its members. Typical sources of club revenue are:

■ Membership dues

■ Initiation fees

- Assessments
- Sports activities fees
- Food and beverage sales
- Other sources of revenue (e.g., rooms revenue)

Membership dues, initiation fees, assessments, and sports activities fees help set clubs apart from hotels and restaurants, since hotels and restaurants do not earn revenue from these sources. Exhibit 8.6 shows the sources of club revenue.

Membership Dues. Membership dues are the cost to a member for the exclusivity of the club. Unlike an operation open to the public, a private club has a limited number of patrons and hence a limited source of revenue. Membership dues subsidize all of the club's operating costs and fixed charges. Dues vary based on the type of club (city or country), the number of members, and the extent of the club's facilities and services. Because country clubs are generally more expensive to operate than city clubs, they usually have higher dues. The income per member derived from dues alone averages $5,140 for country clubs, compared to only $2,065 for city clubs.[11]

It is common for a club to charge several levels of dues based on different types of membership. This makes it possible for more people to join and thus increases the membership base, which decreases costs for each member.

A good example of how a city club offers different types of memberships is the Cornell Club of New York. The Cornell Club occupies a 15-floor building with guestrooms, dining rooms, a lounge, a health club, and private meeting rooms. Here are the types of memberships (each with a different dues structure) available:

- *Resident*—a member who resides or works within New York City
- *Suburban*—a member who resides within 50 miles of New York City but not within the city itself and does not work in New York City
- *Nonresident*—a member who resides more than 50 miles from New York City

Each of these memberships has six different levels of dues, based on the number of years the member has been out of college. It is presumed, of course, that the members who have been graduates for the greatest number of years can afford the highest dues.

Exhibit 8.6   Sources of Club Revenue

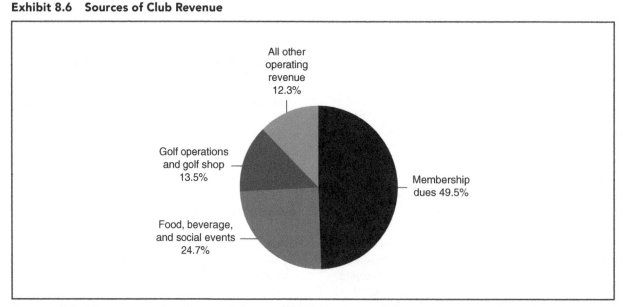

Source: Club Management Association of America, *2022 Finance and Operations Report*, https://www.cmaa.org/media/2zdnrdhg/2022cmaafinanceandoperationsreportexecutivesummary.pdf.

In addition to these memberships, the Cornell Club offers special memberships for people who are not Cornell graduates but are associated with the university (e.g., full-time faculty and staff). These special memberships are also categorized as resident, suburban, or nonresident. There is even a Cornell couple membership and a spouse membership.

Country clubs usually have a larger number of membership categories than city clubs. Some people are just interested in a social membership at a country club—they wish to eat there and socialize with friends at the swimming pool but are not interested in playing golf or tennis. Other members want to make full use of the club's recreational facilities and purchase a regular or active membership. Some clubs offer single or family memberships. A few country clubs have a nonresident category. Many have a lifetime membership option for those willing to make a large one-time payment for lifetime privileges.

An example of a club that offers its members a wide variety of memberships is the Grosse Pointe Yacht Club (GPYC). This club offers a choice of active, social, legacy, and nonresident memberships. An active member can vote and enjoys all privileges (dining, tennis, pool, bowling, paddle tennis, and boating). A social membership excludes voting and boating. A legacy member is defined as a child of a GPYC member and is similar to a social member, who has no voting or boating privileges. A nonresident member is a member who does not have their principal residence or place of business within 75 miles of the club and has access to all amenities and facilities. Within each of these categories, there are three levels of membership dues defined by age, beginning with 21- to 25-year-olds. There is even a special membership for clergy.

Initiation Fees. Most clubs charge new members an **initiation fee**, which in most cases is nonrefundable. Clubs vary in how they handle initiation fees. Some consider them contributions to capital and show them as additions to founder members' equity (for equity clubs) or owners' equity (for corporate or developer clubs). Others add them to reserve funds for specific capital improvement projects, such as refurbishing the clubhouse. Initiation fees typically range from $500

to $10,000, although a few clubs charge $100,000 or more.

Assessments. One-time or periodic **assessments** are sometimes imposed on members instead of increasing dues. Some assessments cover operational shortfalls. Others are used to raise capital for improvements to the club. Assessments are unpopular with members since they are unanticipated expenses. Therefore, instead of assessments, many clubs prefer to impose minimum spending requirements, usually on food and beverages. If a member does not spend a specified amount on food and beverages either on a monthly, quarterly, or annual basis, a bill is sent for the difference.

Sports Activities Fees. City clubs do not record revenue from sports activities because they typically do not charge members extra for using the club's recreational facilities. On the other hand, **sports activities fees** (including golf) account for 14.6 percent of total country club revenues.[12] In country clubs where golf and tennis are significant activities, a golf professional and a tennis professional are responsible for programs in these sports. Fees are charged for playing tennis or golf and rental fees are charged for golf carts.

A golf course is an expensive facility, each year costing more than $45,000 per hole to maintain depending on whether it is a private, semiprivate, or municipal course (see Exhibit 8.7). Labor constitutes the largest expense category, at 56.74 percent. As a rule, revenue derived directly from golf operations covers only about half of golf costs. Membership dues or profits from other departments are necessary to make up the difference.

Sometimes other recreational facilities exist, such as a swimming pool, a health spa, or volleyball or squash courts. Members at most country clubs pay fees to use these facilities except for swimming pools; swimming is usually free. If a club offers a lot of sports options, an athletic director might well be added to the staff to supervise all of the club's recreational facilities and programs.

Clubs with athletic facilities have committees for specific sports. Country clubs with a golf course have a **golf committee** that reports to the club's board and advises it on policies, such as

Exhibit 8.7   Golf Course Expenses

Average Cost per Hole	All Country Clubs in the Study
Salary and Wages	$31,581
Payroll Taxes and Employee Benefits	6,268
Course Supplies and Contracts	13,887
Other Expenses	8,003
Total Golf Department	$59,738

Source: *Clubs in Town & Country*, North American Edition, 2015 (Fairfax, VA: PBMares, LLP, 2015), p. 11.

appropriate course use and hours of operation. The committee works with the club's management in planning tournaments and preparing the golf course budget.

Food and Beverage Sales. After dues income, sales of food and beverages are the major source of revenue in both city clubs and country clubs. Like hotels and resorts, clubs often have more than one dining facility. City clubs with a single dining room tend to keep it formal and add a more informal tap room or grill. Country clubs usually operate snack bars at the pool or golf course, an informal dining room for lunch, and a formal dining room.

A club's dining facilities must compete with restaurants in the surrounding area in terms of food quality and value. Wine tastings, dinners featuring steak or lobster, and special dinners prepared by visiting chefs are among the promotional techniques used to draw members. Club chefs are often promoted heavily.

In general, club members hold their club to higher standards of food quality and service than they do of public restaurants. For this reason, foodservice often becomes the main focus of the club, requiring the greatest part of the club manager's efforts.

Other Sources of Revenue. In addition to membership dues, initiation fees, assessments, sports activities fees, and food and beverage sales, there are other sources of revenue for clubs.

Most clubs charge **visitors' fees** for nonmembers who are guests of members and use rooms, buy food and beverages, or use recreational facilities. Often there are service charges on food and beverage sales, which may be distributed to employees or, as in most cases, used to offset the club's labor costs. Country clubs may offer their facilities for weddings, corporate events, parties, and other special occasions. They charge rental fees for use of event spaces, which provides an additional source of revenue. City clubs with overnight accommodations generate revenue from guestroom sales and may offer laundry and valet services for a fee. Country clubs have pro shops, operated by the club or a concessionaire, that sell sports equipment, apparel, and in some cases a broad range of gift items.

Expenses

Payroll and related costs are the single largest expense in operating a club, representing 59 percent of club expenses in city clubs and 56 percent in country clubs (see Exhibit 8.8). The largest segment of payroll expenditure is in the food and beverage operation. The second-largest expense for both city clubs and country clubs is "other operating expenses," at 20 percent and 18 percent, respectively. The third-largest expense for both city and country clubs is "food and beverage" (at 15 percent for city clubs and 18 percent for country clubs).

After membership dues, sales of food and beverages are the major source of revenue in both city and country clubs.

Exhibit 8.8   Sources of Club Expenses

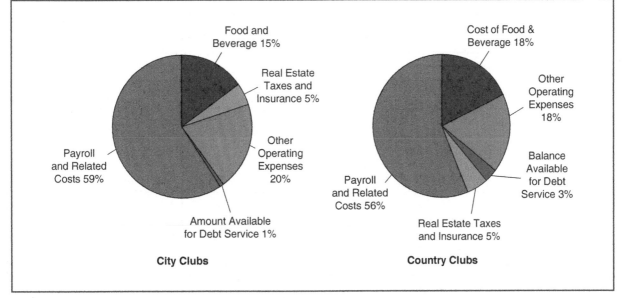

City Clubs

Food and Beverage 15%
Real Estate Taxes and Insurance 5%
Other Operating Expenses 20%
Amount Available for Debt Service 1%
Payroll and Related Costs 59%

Country Clubs

Cost of Food & Beverage 18%
Other Operating Expenses 18%
Balance Available for Debt Service 3%
Real Estate Taxes and Insurance 5%
Payroll and Related Costs 56%

Source: *Clubs in Town & Country*, North American Edition, 2015 (Fairfax, VA: PBMares, LLP, 2015), pp. 9, 19.

Control

Like hotels and restaurants, clubs have a uniform accounting system; the *Uniform System of Financial Reporting for Clubs* is in its seventh revised edition.[13] In addition to a classification of accounts, the system provides for a reporting method that separates revenues and expenses into departments, much like a hotel does. This allows a club's managers, board of directors, members, and—if it is a corporate or developer club—owners to easily review operating results by department. The primary difference between hotels and clubs is identification of a separate revenue for membership dues.

In 2018, *Accounting Standards Codification Topic 606: Revenue from Contracts with Customers* (ASC 606) changed the reporting of initiation fees, one-time payments made by new club members when they join a club. Depending on the nature of the contract and the specific services offered by the club, the initiation fee can be amortized over the life of the membership. If the initiation fee is part of a broader contract, the club needs to determine the standalone selling price of the initiation services. Clubs should also consider whether the initiation fee is refundable or nonrefundable. The treatment of revenue recognition may differ based on this distinction. As accounting rules can be complex, it is best to seek guidance from accounting professionals or auditing firms.

Technology

Clubs have tended to be slow in adopting technology, mostly due to budgetary constraints.

However, most clubs have websites that are used by their members to find club information and make reservations. The following is a list of how members use their club's website, starting with the most frequent search:

- Club calendar
- Member statement
- Member roster
- Tee times
- Event registration
- Online payment
- Dining reservations[14]

Few clubs have a dedicated IT staff, which means that support and maintenance of the technology is a challenge, as is keeping up with the latest technology changes. Most clubs do have a wide range of software (see Exhibit 8.9) that can be used in managing the clubhouse and recreation activities. Wireless paging, cell

Exhibit 8.9   Software Most Used by Private Clubs

Irrigation Software	87.9%
Payroll Software	79.9%
Point of Sale	78.3%
Accounting/Back Office Software	78.0%
Time Management Software	73.0%
Security Cameras	65.9%
Tee Times/Tennis Court Reservations Software	62.0%
Catering/Sales Software	61.4%
Human Resources Software	56.8%
Energy Management Systems	53.7%
Spa Management Software	46.9%
Dining/Event Reservations Software	45.2%
Mobile Applications	44.0%

phone paging, and tablets are used by some country clubs to communicate to members such information as changes in tee times or adjustments to tennis lesson schedules.

8.6 OUTLOOK

Over the past 30 years, golf and country clubs have faced diminishing membership due to aging members. However, the COVID-19 pandemic was beneficial in many ways for clubs. Why? The nature of private clubs and their exclusivity made members feel safe; there was an abundance of outdoor spaces and programming available at country clubs. The ability to work from home meant that members were spending more time at their clubs, and those with active memberships were able to use clubs as staycation locations when travel was restricted.

In addition, many club managers were able to cut their expenses by reducing their hours and offering less subsidized programming, strategies that will likely stay in place permanently. In a study conducted by Gold Life Navigators and Club Benchmarking in 2021, 44 percent of all clubs surveyed reported having membership waitlists. The percentage of clubs with waitlists increases as the cost to join goes up.[15]

Successful club managers have leveraged their amenities and continued to innovate their offerings by staying a step ahead of their members' wants. These changes include having smaller, more nimble boards; incorporating technology like golf simulators; attracting millennials; reinventing dining and social spaces; and focusing more on fitness and wellness.[16]

Private clubs date back to ancient Greece and Rome, but the true forerunners of American private clubs (which now number more than 4,000) are the social and golf clubs of England and Scotland. While there are many similarities to managing clubs and hotels, there are some differences as well. The most distinct differences between managing clubs and hotels lies in their business models and target markets. A club typically operates with a membership model, where individuals must be dues-paying members to access the club's facilities and services. Club revenue largely comes from membership fees, and the focus is on creating a community and social environment for members. On the other hand, hotels cater to the general public and generate revenue from room bookings, dining services, event spaces, and other guest-related amenities. The nature of private clubs means club management must focus on providing services and amenities that cater to the specific interests and preferences of its members. In contrast, hotel management seeks to attract a diverse range of guests and must cater to the needs of various types of travelers.

There are four basic types of clubs—country, golf, city/athletic, and yacht.

The largest type of private club is the country club. Country clubs are primarily recreational and social facilities for individuals and families who live nearby. Since country clubs need a great deal of land for their golf course(s) and other facilities, they are usually located in suburban or rural areas.

A golf club is a private establishment or facility where golf is played. The primary difference between golf clubs and country clubs is that golf clubs focus on one amenity—golf. In addition to golf courses, these clubs often offer various services to enhance the members' experiences, such as a clubhouse and practice facilities.

A city/athletic club is an urban recreational and social facility. These clubs vary in size, type, facilities, and membership. Some city/athletic clubs own their own real estate; others lease space in office buildings or hotels. Athletic clubs, also known as sports clubs or fitness clubs, are facilities that provide a range of athletic- and fitness-related amenities and services designed to promote physical activity, health, and well-being. City clubs can refer to various types of private clubs located in urban areas, such as social clubs, dining clubs, or university clubs.

Other kinds of clubs include beach clubs, fraternal clubs, and military clubs.

Most private clubs are equity clubs or corporate (or developer) clubs. Equity clubs are owned by a group of founder members and are generally nonprofit, since they are formed for the enjoyment of their members rather than for money-making purposes. Corporate or developer clubs are for-profit clubs owned by individuals or companies that sell memberships in the clubs.

A club's organization depends on whether it is an equity or a corporate or developer club. The club manager is the hired professional responsible for guiding all of the elements of a club's operation.

The bulk of club revenues is derived from club members. These revenues fall into the following classifications: membership dues, initiation fees, assessments, sports activities fees, food and beverage sales, and other sources of revenue.

Membership dues are the cost to a member for the exclusivity of the club. It is common for city and country clubs to have several different types of memberships. A city club might have different membership dues for resident, suburban, and nonresident members, reflecting the location of the member's residence in relation to the location of the club. Country clubs tend to use a different type of dues structure, based on use of recreational facilities, a member's age, and other factors. In addition to dues, clubs generally charge initiation fees and, in some cases, special assessments.

Next to dues, food and beverage sales are the major source of club revenue. Other sources of revenue include guestroom sales (for city clubs), visitors' fees, and service charges on food and beverage sales. A club's payroll and related costs are its largest expense.

Like hotels and restaurants, clubs have their own uniform system of financial reporting that helps club managers control and manage operations.

administrative skills—A set of competencies that involve effectively managing and organizing tasks, resources, and processes within an organization.

assessment—A one-time or periodic charge imposed on private club members to cover operational shortfalls or raise capital for improvements to the club.

athletic club—Also known as a sports club or fitness club, this facility provides a range of athletic- and fitness-related amenities and services designed to promote physical activity, health, and well-being, catering to individuals who are interested in sports, fitness, and recreational activities.

beach club—A type of private or commercial establishment located along a beachfront that provides various amenities and services for its members or guests.

city/athletic club—An urban recreational and social club that varies in size, type, facilities, and membership.

city club—A term for various types of private clubs, such as social clubs, dining clubs, or university clubs, located in urban areas. City clubs bring together individuals who share common interests, hobbies, or social activities. These clubs provide a platform for members to engage in recreational, cultural, or social pursuits, fostering a sense of community and camaraderie among like-minded individuals.

club manager—The hired professional responsible for guiding all the elements of a private club's operation. Often referred to as the club's general manager or chief operating officer.

common interest realty association (CIRA)—Commonly known as a homeowners association (HOA), condominium association, cooperative association, or planned-community association. CIRAs are responsible for overseeing shared areas, amenities, and services within the community, and they enforce rules and regulations to maintain the community's standards and protect property values.

conceptual skills—The ability of an individual to think critically, analyze complex situations, and grasp the bigger picture.

corporate club—A for-profit private club owned by an individual or a company that sells memberships in the club. Also called a developer or proprietary club.

country club—Primarily a recreational and social facility for individuals and families who live nearby the club. Country clubs often have separate children's facilities and do a large catering business while offering a host of amenities—likely racquet sports (tennis, pickleball, platform tennis, etc.) and aquatics (pool, etc.), in addition to golf.

dining club—Also known as a supper club or gastronomic club, this is a private social establishment centered around communal dining experiences. A dining club typically focuses on providing its members with unique and exclusive culinary experiences, often featuring gourmet meals prepared by professional chefs or talented home cooks.

equity club—A nonprofit private club whose members buy shares in the club and, after expenses have been paid, invest any revenues left over in improvements to the club's facilities and services.

fraternal clubs—Social organizations or associations that bring together individuals who share common interests, values, or affiliations. These clubs are often founded on principles of brotherhood, friendship, and mutual support among their members.

golf club—A private establishment or facility where the sport of golf is played, typically featuring an 18-hole golf course, although some may have more or fewer holes.

golf committee—A private country club committee composed of club members who establish golf course policy, review golf course budgets and operations, and oversee the care of the golf course(s).

initiation fee—A typically nonrefundable charge that new members must pay to join a private club.

membership dues—The cost to a private club member for the exclusivity provided by the club's limited membership. Membership dues subsidize all of the club's operating costs and fixed charges.

military club—A social organization or association that brings together current and former members of the military, as well as their families and supporters.

social club—A club where members go to meet each other and enjoy leisurely activities.

sports activities fees—Fees that country clubs charge members and visitors for using the club's recreational facilities.

technical skills—A specific set of abilities and knowledge required to perform tasks related to a particular field or profession.

university club—A private club for university graduates or individuals otherwise affiliated with a university.

visitors' fees—Charges to nonmembers of a private club who are guests of members and use rooms, buy food or beverages, or use recreational facilities.

yacht club—A type of social club that caters to individuals who share a passion for boating, yachting, and maritime activities.

1. Which describes the key difference between clubs and hotels?
   a. Clubs bring together people of like interests. Hotels may or may not bring together people of like interests.
   b. A general manager is at the top of a club's organization. Members are at the top of a hotel's organization.
   c. Clubs are an invention of modern society. Hotels are historical institutions.
   d. Like hotels, clubs are open to the public.

2. Which club belongs in the "city/athletic club" category?
   a. The New York Athletic Club
   b. The Elks
   c. Grosse Point Yacht Club
   d. Pebble Beach Country Club

3. Which kind of club operates as a nonprofit club?
   a. Social
   b. Equity
   c. Corporate
   d. University

4. If an equity club has a net profit, how is the profit dispersed?
   a. It is invested in club facilities and services.
   b. It is returned to club members.
   c. It is used to pay taxes.
   d. It is donated to charity.

5. Which company is in the business of club management?
   a. Marriott International
   b. Starwood, Inc.
   c. IHG Group
   d. ClubCorp

6. Which technical skill is important for club managers?
   a. Technical writing
   b. IT management
   c. Engineering
   d. Coding

7. Which revenue stream is usually nonrefundable?
   a. Sports activities fees
   b. Membership dues
   c. Assessments
   d. Initiation fees

8. Which rate would apply to a member who lives more than 50 miles away from the Cornell Club of New York?
   a. International rate
   b. Nonresident rate
   c. Suburban rate
   d. Resident rate

9. What are the largest costs associated with club operations?
   a. Food and beverage costs
   b. Payroll and labor costs
   c. Maintenance costs
   d. Legal costs

10. What are two basic ways private clubs can be owned?
    a. Company owned or university owned
    b. Member owned or company owned
    c. Member owned or hotel owned
    d. Member owned or equity owned

11. From where is the bulk of club revenue derived?
    a. Membership dues and fees
    b. Guestroom sales
    c. Visitors' fees
    d. Rental fees

12. Why is support for technology a challenge for clubs?
    a. Club managers are mostly resistant to new technology.
    b. Club members are unaware of new technology.
    c. Few clubs have a dedicated IT staff.
    d. There is high turnover for IT staff.

SHORT-ANSWER QUESTIONS

1. What are opportunities and challenges associated with a career in club management?

2. What recent changes have clubs made to attract new members?

DRESS CODE COMMUNICATION

The Beehive Country Club is one of the most prestigious private country clubs in the country. It opened in 1924, and its double 18-hole Blue Course has hosted five major golf championships. It was a biennial stop on the professional golf association tour for many years. Also, the country club is home to the largest clubhouse in the country. The club has an indoor duckpin bowling alley, a tennis club, a grand ballroom, an indoor pool, a lap pool with diving boards, a children's pool and main pool, a fitness center, and a grand foyer. Food and beverage outlets include seven restaurants, three bars, and many beverage carts. The club has 21 overnight guest accommodations and has hosted several famous weddings. It also has a spa, massage services, an indoor hot tub, and men's and women's locker rooms.

Beehive's Blue Course membership is highly sought after, but it has a hefty price tag—a $120,000 initiation fee. To be a member of the course is to gain access to some of the most beautiful, high-end courses in the world. Membership packages include access to championship courses, private lessons, and exclusive events. Members also enjoy a variety of amenities, including a restaurant and pro shop. Membership is limited to just 300 people.

Recently, club management has changed the long-held club dress code for sports-related activities. This has caused frustration among the longtime members who are paying expensive dues. Members must now wear all-white clothing on the golf course or at the tennis club. The previous dress code was that members wear predominately white clothing (70 percent visibility). Frustrated members are petitioning to vote out club management over the dress code, monetary loss from canceled memberships, and a recent 30 percent increase in membership dues. The club is also dealing with declining membership due to aging members. The growing tension between management and the members must be alleviated.

DISCUSSION QUESTIONS

1. Is the change in the dress code unreasonable for members?

2. What is at risk for club managers if they do not change their policies?

3. What challenges with membership does club management face?

Brett Morris

Brett Morris, the general manager and COO at The Club at Admirals Cove in Jupiter, Florida, is a highly respected figure in the club industry. With an impressive track record spanning over 30 years, Morris has become known for his exceptional leadership and numerous achievements.

A visionary leader committed to excellence, his remarkable accomplishments have left an indelible mark on the industry. In recognition of his outstanding contributions, Morris was named the 2022 CMAA Club Executive of the Year and received the prestigious 2016 James H. Brewer Award for Excellence in Club Management. These accolades serve as testament to his ability to guide clubs toward unparalleled success and create extraordinary experiences for their members.

In addition to his professional achievements, Morris is dedicated to giving back to the industry. He is highly sought after as a speaker and mentor, and his wisdom and expertise are valued by aspiring professionals. As a director and recipient of the FLCMAA Jay DiPietro Award for Most Valuable Member in 2019, Morris has demonstrated his commitment to serving the industry. Furthermore, his role as a faculty member for the esteemed Business Management Institute allows him to share his profound insights on various topics, including food and beverage trends, crisis management, and club culture.

His passion for the industry goes beyond traditional leadership roles. His dedication and experience continue to inspire professionals in the industry.

You were recently hired to be the general manager of a private club. The average age of members joining a private club today is about 42 years old. The millennial generation comprises the largest demographic since the baby boomers. For the next 10 years, this is the generation that club managers will be trying to attract. This generation typically has two children. The current offerings at clubs are geared toward members who are 55 or older. However, you cannot change your amenities to attract only one demographic, since you will risk alienating your older members. What strategy will you adopt to attract the millennial generation?

AN INTRODUCTION TO THE MEETINGS AND EVENTS INDUSTRY

Chapter Outline

Learning Objectives

KEY TERMS

association

certified meeting professional (CMP)

conference centers

consumer show

convention

convention and visitors bureau (CVB)

convention services manager (CSM)

destination wedding

event

Events Industry Council (EIC)

exhibition

exposition

force majeure

general service contractor (GSC)

incentive trips

management meetings

meeting

product launches

professional and technical meetings

sales meetings

social events

special events

stockholders meetings

supplier

third-party meeting planners

trade show

training seminars

In this chapter, we will develop an understanding of the various terminologies used in the meetings and events industry. Then we will review the abundance of opportunities available in the meetings and events industry, identify where meetings and events are held, and review the planning process for successful meeting or event execution.

9.1 OVERVIEW OF THE MEETINGS AND EVENTS INDUSTRY

The meetings and events industry has completely transformed over the last 30 years with the introduction and advancement of new technology. The role of the meeting and event professional, what is expected from meetings and events, the logistics and design process, and the importance of meetings and events to an organization's overall strategy have changed. These areas continually evolve as the fundamental purpose of meetings and events changes.

The terms *meeting* and *event* are defined differently, and although a meeting is technically classified as an event, the industry is often referred to as the "meetings and events industry." In some countries, this is further expanded into meetings, expositions, events, and conventions (MEEC); whereas in other countries, the industry is referred to as the meetings, incentives, conventions, and exhibitions (MICE) industry. These areas can be pictured in a massive Venn diagram, with areas having both common and unique attributes.

While there are many organizations and definitions surrounding this field, the meetings and events industry often looks to the **Events Industry Council** (formerly the Convention Industry Council), or EIC, to create industry standards and definitions. The EIC is an umbrella organization for all meeting and event organizations. The EIC also curates the industry's glossary of terms and provides certifications for the meetings and events industry. The EIC is the global voice of the business events industry on advocacy, research, professional recognition, and standards. It has over 30 member organizations representing over 103,500 individuals and 19,500 firms and properties involved in the events industry. The EIC has four signature programs: Sustainability and Social Impact, Accepted Practices Exchange (APEX), Knowledge, and Leadership.[1]

The broadest term that encompasses every area of the industry is *event*. The EIC defines an **event** as "an organized occasion such as a meeting, convention, exhibition, special meeting, gala dinner, etc. An event is often composed of

A meeting is just one type of event—and meeting types vary as well.

several different yet related functions."[2] Specific categories of events would include meetings, trade shows, and conventions. The EIC defines a **meeting** as "an event where the primary activity of the participants is to attend educational and/or business sessions, participate in discussions [and] social functions, or attend other organized events. There is no exhibit component."[3] To make this part easier to comprehend, think of a meeting as a group of people listening to content, discussing among themselves, or doing activities. Technically, you could consider every single class you attend as a meeting!

A trade show is different and is an often-overlooked area by students if you are not in a major convention city such as Chicago, Orlando, or Las Vegas. A **trade show**, or an exhibition, is a series of "booths" where companies can set up their products or advertise services that they are

Trade shows are exhibition events to promote products and services within a particular industry.

Exhibit 9.1   Meetings and Events Industry

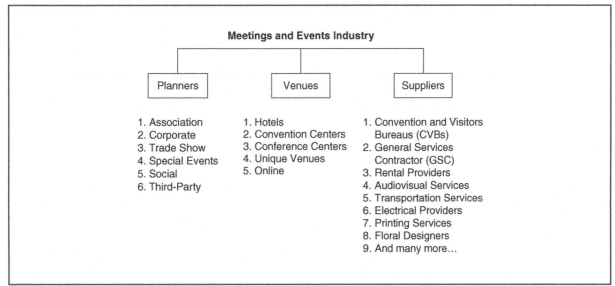

Meetings and Events Industry

Planners	Venues	Suppliers
1. Association	1. Hotels	1. Convention and Visitors Bureaus (CVBs)
2. Corporate	2. Convention Centers	2. General Services Contractor (GSC)
3. Trade Show	3. Conference Centers	3. Rental Providers
4. Special Events	4. Unique Venues	4. Audiovisual Services
5. Social	5. Online	5. Transportation Services
6. Third-Party		6. Electrical Providers
		7. Printing Services
		8. Floral Designers
		9. And many more…

trying to sell to the attendees. Trade shows can be simple, small rows of pipe and drape booths or elaborate, custom-built structures. In Europe, trade show booths are all hard-wall systems—never pipe and drape.

As an attendee at a trade show, you walk around and talk with exhibitors, trying to find out what products and services would best fit your organization. Trade shows are typically held for members of a common industry and are not open to the public. There is a trade show for almost every industry. For example, the International Pizza Expo has taken place for over 35 years and is held every spring in Las Vegas. The expo brings together hundreds of vendors who sell everything from dough, cheese, meats, and sauce to ovens, freezers, and packaging. There are also marketing and food safety vendors.

Although trade shows can be stand-alone events, they often have an educational component in a separate space at the venue. An event with a meeting and trade show component is called a **convention** (meeting + trade show = convention).

9.2 OPPORTUNITIES IN THE MEETINGS AND EVENTS INDUSTRY

The meetings and events industry has something for everyone. Whether you love some calculated risk and enjoy traveling to new venues or are risk averse and want to coordinate at one site only, there is a career path for you. To dive into those, we will look at the various types of meetings and events. Each section will describe the types and their associated career paths.

Association Meetings and Events

Associations are groups of people that band together for a specific purpose. You can think of them as a professional version of a club where everyone is interested in the same area and comes together to advance knowledge, socialize with like-minded professionals, and advocate for their industry. There can be an association for anything—from the American Management Association to the Dairy Farmers of America Association to the Professional Elvis Impersonators Association. There are over 30 associations within the meetings and

events industry alone, including the Corporate Event Marketing Association, Event Service Professionals Association, International Association of Exhibitions and Events, the International Live Events Association, and the Professional Convention Management Association.[4]

The association area of the industry is often overlooked by meetings and events students because they assume expertise in the association's purpose is a requirement. No matter what association you work for, your main duties involve planning and hosting its meetings and events. Over half of the associations registered in the United States have a trade show component as well, so event professionals in this area may also manage sales and logistics for trade show vendors.

Prior to the COVID-19 pandemic, associations largely held one major national or international convention per year as well as several smaller trainings and board and continuing education meetings. During and after the pandemic, many associations switched to hosting up to four regional conventions. This shift has been seen as an advantage from a planning perspective because it allows planners access to more locations. There are few sites that can host 50,000 people in one area, but many can host 10,000 participants; and more options means more negotiating power when it comes to costs. From an attendee perspective, regional locations are often easier to access, take less time away from family and work, and provide more direct regional networking opportunities.

It is important to recognize that attendance at association meetings is voluntary. Marketing is essential to recruit attendees, and planners should pay special attention to city choice, site location, and any additional social programs that are being offered to draw more attendance.

Before the pandemic, locations for annual events were often confirmed three to five years in advance for larger meetings; smaller meetings could be secured between five to eight months in advance. Post-pandemic, the contract window has shortened for groups that have multiple options. If an association can choose among many cities, they may contract 18 months to 3 years in advance for larger meetings and 6 months or less for smaller meetings. This allows the planner to evaluate situational factors, such as discriminatory state laws that could affect image or attendance, environmental and weather conditions, health concerns, and unexpected developments, and choose the city that best suits their meeting.

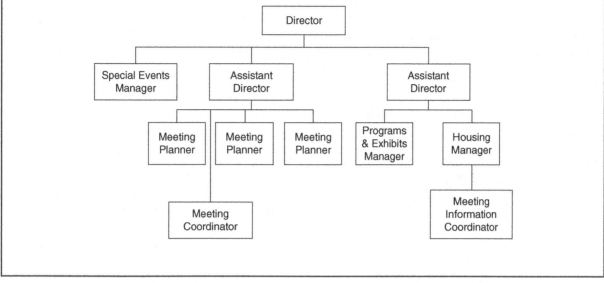

Associations vary greatly in size. Some may be completely volunteer based, some may have only one or two paid positions, and some may have a staff of more than 50 professionals. Depending on the size of the association, the career opportunities may be specific to events or broader to include marketing as well.

Smaller associations with no paid staff or executive director may pay an association management company (AMC) to manage their association. These companies are separate businesses typically made up of project and finance managers; accountants; and marketing, sales, and event professionals. Associations can hire an AMC on a fee-for-service basis to take care of specific aspects of their affairs, from planning a meeting to full management of financials, tax reporting, marketing and sales, and events. Nearly 1 in 5 associations outsource trade show services and nearly 1 in 10 outsource event strategy and management at large. Examples of AMCs include IMN Solutions, Paragon Events, and Talley Management Group; for those who enjoy planning events for a variety of associations at the same time, AMCs are a viable career path.

Mid-size to large associations may hire their own in-house event professional (see Exhibit 9.2). This is often considered a great starter job in the meetings and events industry because it requires less experience than other areas of the industry. In-house association planners spend a lot of time focused on a handful of events each year, overseeing the events from start to finish and getting to know all their aspects.

Corporate Meetings and Events

Corporate meetings and events are hosted by corporations. Depending on the size of the corporation, meetings and events can be its own department or placed within marketing, communications, or public relations. The size of the events department also varies, from 1 person to 20 or more depending on the size and purpose of the company. Large corporations like Coca-Cola, McDonald's, and Meta all have event management departments.

Corporate meetings and events professionals typically plan many more events per year, from 20 to over 100, and are in a faster, more innovative environment. Events can range widely, from traditional meetings to special events. A list of events and their definitions is below.

Management meetings. Management meetings include everything from financial reviews to strategic planning sessions. Management meetings make up the largest category in the corporate meetings market. There is an average of 45 attendees at management meetings, which can include specific department managers or the organization's executive management at large.

Training seminars. **Training seminars** rank second in number of meetings held. They provide training for employees at all levels.

Sales meetings. National and regional **sales meetings** are essential for teaching sales techniques, introducing new products, building morale, and motivating sales personnel. National sales meetings average 3.6 days with 104 attendees; regional sales meetings average 42 attendees and last an average of 2.5 days.

Product launches. New products are showcased to employees at **product launches**. These meetings are also used to motivate dealers or distributors who are not employees (e.g., introducing new car models to dealers). Product launches last one to two days on average.

Professional and technical meetings. **Professional and technical meetings** are used to provide information or teach new techniques to employees in technical and professional fields. Accountants need to learn about new tax laws and rulings every year, for example.

Incentive trips. Often a combination of meetings and recreation, **incentive trips** are rewards to customers, retailers, distributors, or employees. Spouses are often invited to attend these trips.

Stockholders meetings. These are gatherings where the owners of a company, the shareholders or stockholders, come together to discuss and make important decisions about the company's affairs. **Stockholders meetings** are annual events that usually last a day, with an average attendance of 95 owners of company stock.

Other corporate meetings. Other corporate meetings include press conferences, public forums, and other gatherings that a corporation might sponsor.

Because of the fast-paced environment and wide range of events, most corporate event planner jobs require three to five years of previous experience. Although there are no typical career paths in this industry, planners may start in associations for a few years and then transition to corporate events. Corporations tend to include certifications such as the **certified meeting professional (CMP)** in their minimum qualifications for jobs. The CMP certification was launched in 1985 to enhance the knowledge and performance of meeting professionals, promote the status and credibility of the meeting profession, and advance uniform standards of practice. Today, the CMP credential is recognized globally as the badge of excellence in the events industry. The qualifications for certification are based on professional experience, education, and a rigorous exam.

Corporate meetings and events come in a variety of shapes and sizes.

Corporate meetings and events can be hosted internally for staff and externally for customers. Internal events require a much smaller lead time since they typically have mandatory attendance and do not last as long. However, external, customer-facing events are similar to association events in that marketing is essential for attendance. Corporate events tend to have larger budgets and therefore interactions with higher-scale customers. Some corporations may even pay for the travel and lodging of customers to create a captive audience at an event. The corporation gives the customers a memorable experience while also pitching their new products or services. One example would be a product launch. If Apple is releasing a new product, it may host a product launch and invite its top retail buyers to attend to create excitement and make it more likely that they will stock the product. A corporate event sponsor could also invite influencers to generate more positive word-of-mouth advertising. A product launch also allows an organization to explain all the features of the new item.

Trade Shows

Trade shows is an umbrella term often used to describe many different areas of this part of the industry. You will most often hear *trade shows* and *exhibitions* used interchangeably and *consumer shows* and *public shows* used interchangeably. The main difference between these two categories is that the former is business to business (B2B), whereas the latter is business to consumer (B2C). Expositions is a term used almost exclusively in North America and includes all these categories. Below are trade show definitions you may hear.

Trade show. A trade show is an exhibition of products and/or services held for members of a common or related industry. A trade show is not open to the general public.

Exhibition. An **exhibition** is an event at which products, services, or promotional materials are displayed to attendees visiting exhibits on the show floor. An exhibition is primarily focused on B2B relationships.

Exposition. A term primarily used in North America, **exposition** is another name for a large exhibit, trade show, or public show.

Consumer show. A **consumer show** is often B2C, typically open to the public, and usually requires an entrance fee. If you have heard of a Holiday Expo, a Women's Expo, or an RV show, these are all considered consumer shows. Consumer shows differ from trade shows in that trade shows are typically B2B and not open to the public.

The slight differences and large overlaps between these terms can make it difficult to keep them straight. For the purposes of this chapter, the main focus is on B2B shows, and they are referred to broadly as "trade shows."

Trade shows require a lot of space for vendors to set up and display their products. Therefore, they typically take place in convention centers, exhibit halls, or in hotel exhibit space. Trade shows can be included in an association's annual convention and can be a significant source of revenue for the sponsoring association.

Most trade shows can be subdivided into four categories: industrial, wholesale/retail, professional or scientific, and public or consumer. Industrial shows are events used by manufacturers to exhibit their products to other manufacturers. At an industrial show, buyers are typically purchasing materials and inventory that they will remanufacture into a processed product or resell as is or in some adapted form.

Wholesale and retail trade shows are collections of exhibits specific to one or more closely associated trades. In most instances, the buyers represent businesses that are shopping for services and products to use in their business. The World Travel Mart, held annually in London, is an example of a wholesale and retail trade show. At this show, several hundred hotels, airlines, cruise lines, tour operators, and tourism boards from major countries staff booths and attempt to persuade travel agents to recommend their offerings. One of the largest wholesale and retail trade shows in the United States is held every May in Chicago by the National Restaurant Association. This show attracts almost 2,000 exhibitors and is attended by more than 42,000 delegates from all over the world.

Professional or scientific exhibitions are usually associated with meetings of professional groups, educators, scientists, and other people who could be considered end users.

Public or consumer shows are the only wholesale and retail trade shows open to the public. Newspapers and other media sponsor shows for their advertisers. At these shows, the public can browse among exhibits, view videos, and attend presentations. Other popular consumer shows include antique shows, art shows, and various shows that appeal to collectors.

Special Events

The **special events** sector of the industry broadly consists of private events, public events, fairs and festivals, sporting events, and concerts. Special events can occur on their own, but can also represent an aspect of a larger, more formal business event. An example is a convention where attendees are in meeting rooms all day, and the event planner stages a gala dinner with Cirque de Soleil performers. In this case, they are considered special events because they are outside the normal business program.

Special events are normally entertainment or hospitality based. A private event is aimed at a specific audience of invited guests. These can include brand events (award ceremonies, openings, premieres), charity fundraisers, and other nonprofit events. Public events, on the other hand, are open to the public and usually held in public spaces. These can include community celebrations, government events, parades, and demonstrations. Sometimes public events can overlap with other categories, such as a bike race that is a sporting event open to the public. It's important to distinguish the purpose of the event and not just its format.

While some public events are included in fairs and festivals, not all fairs and festivals are open to the public. Fairs and festivals are categorized first by the land on which they are set. Are they on public land or privately owned land? Then they are categorized by the hosting organization: is it a for-profit company or a nonprofit group? Examples of commercial festivals include Burning Man, the South Beach Wine & Food Festival®, and Coachella. There are specific companies that produce "brand-owned" festivals, creating brand-marketing events using a festival format to appeal to consumers in a more experiential format. Ben & Jerry's One World, One Heart Festival, and the Virgin Group's V Festival are examples of these.

Sporting events include local, state, regional, national, and international competitions. In the United States, these are events like the U.S. Open, the Kentucky Derby, and the Super Bowl. Internationally, these include the Wimbledon Tennis Championships, the Tour de France, and the World Cup. On state and local levels, such events can include bike rides, marathons, equestrian shows, boat races, rodeos, and school sports teams.

Finally, there are special events that involve music: individual concerts, band tours, and multi-act festivals. For sporting and music events, there are many career opportunities from both the venue side and the performing side. From a venue side, many of the positions stated previously for hotels can be found at arenas and concert venues. From the performing side, many sports teams and music groups hire logistics managers to coordinate travel, food and beverage, and lodging. Some may travel with the group, and some may work remotely.

Social Events

Several times throughout our lives, we reach milestones that we wish to celebrate, including births, baptisms, bar and bat mitzvahs, birthdays, engagements, weddings, anniversaries, and retirements. Many planners specialize in arranging these **social events** and enjoy knowing that one successful event can lead to long-term relationships with clients that can span generations. The types of venues that hold social events include hotels (especially those with extensive meeting space), private clubs (country, yacht, and city clubs), wineries, resorts, and small event centers. If you are a meeting planner preparing for a wedding, your clients may have their ceremony in a church and then hold their reception at a country club, hotel, or resort. Other clients may wish to plan a **destination wedding**, a wedding held at an exotic or remote location. The nature of social event planning can vary greatly depending on where you live. For example, Los Angeles may support high-end luxury weddings where planners can design million-dollar events, but other cities may not have that kind of demand or ability to charge as much.

Third-Party Meeting and Event Planning

Third-party meeting planners, or independent meeting planners, are not associated with a company and provide their services as an independent contractor. Many of these planners started at companies to learn about the industry and then decided to work for themselves. Third-party meeting planners can work in any area of the industry and choose the jobs they want to

Planning one successful social event can lead to connections for countless future celebrations.

accept. Some may only do on-site coordination, some may do all planning, and others may serve in sales and marketing support roles. While these independent professionals are known as meeting planners in North America, in other parts of the world they are called professional conference or congress organizers.

Knowledge Check

1. Why is a career in planning association meetings often overlooked?
2. What types of meetings do corporations typically hold?

9.3 WHERE MEETINGS ARE HELD

Meetings and events can be held anywhere, but their venues tend to fall under certain categories. These include hotels, convention centers, unique venues, and online.

Hotels

Many meeting and event management programs in universities started under hospitality or hotel and restaurant programs. Meetings and events were traditionally held in hotels because the sleeping rooms were located there, providing easy access for the attendees. As demand grew for meetings and events, so did the food and beverage departments and audiovisual departments in hotels. Hotel event spaces often include carpet, tables and chairs, lighting, access to electrical outlets, stages, and additional services they charge fees to use.

According to Kalibri Labs HQ, the U.S. meetings industry generates approximately $300 billion annually, with about $30 billion in hotel rooms revenue attributed to meetings and events.[5] When you consider ancillary spending, such as food and beverage, equipment rental, audiovisual services, and ground transportation, the industry contributes another $110 billion in revenue. In fact, in some markets, hotels receive such a direct impact from meetings and events business that they expanded from having a few meeting spaces to having an on-site convention center.

Convention and Conference Centers

Convention centers are also frequently used for meetings and events. Whereas hotels provide many services included in their room rates,

When the size is right, hotels are convenient for meetings and conferences.

convention centers charge for individual services. Meeting professionals will pay to bring in their own carpet, pay for tables and chairs, and pay to plug into outlets.

Convention centers provide a lot more space and flexibility, which is appealing for trade and consumer shows. Recognizing that trade shows are increasingly tied to education meetings, convention centers built or redesigned since 2010 include some carpeted spaces to create a warmer environment for keynotes and breakout rooms.

Conference centers are a smaller version of convention centers and hotels. They are often designed to host small meetings and can contain lodging. They are typically all-inclusive and higher end. Some are owned by corporations, such as American Express, IBM, and JP Morgan Chase Bank. Many universities have also built conference centers, such as Florida International University on its Biscayne Bay campus.

Unique Venues

Examples of unique venues include wineries, amusement parks, castles, cruise ships, trains, museums, and parks. Some of these businesses rely on meetings and events to be profitable (e.g., wineries). For others, meetings and events are just a portion of their business (meetings on cruise lines account for 1 percent to 15 percent of the industry's overall business). Unique venues can often be included in a meeting as a location for a special reception, opening night, VIP or sponsor outing, or something similar.

As hotels and convention centers have increased their prices and attendees look for more one-of-a-kind experiences, meeting planners have increased their use of unique venues. For example, the Professional Convention Management Association closed down the Gas Lamp district in San Diego for one of its receptions. At a Meeting Professionals International event, the Indianapolis Motor Speedway was shut down so attendees could ride on the track with trained drivers.

Any of these venues offer a wide variety of meeting and event careers, ranging from event concierge to event coordinator. Sales teams are also involved in venue events and typically responsible for bringing meetings and events to their property. Some may build a relationship with a client for years before a contract comes to fruition. These sales positions are often divided into different markets (social vs. business) or by the number of days until the event (events less than one year away or more than one year away). Once the sale is secured, the client is turned over to a **convention services manager (CSM)** who sees to it that everything the venue promised to the group is delivered. They become the on-site event coordinator who represents the venue. In smaller venues, the sales manager and CSM may be the same person.

Wineries are just one example of unique event venues.

Banquet captains and managers are also key in these positions since they work with event coordinators to help execute the events on-site.

These are good positions for people who love to see a new event every day, like to know what they have in-house and on hand at every moment, and enjoy fixing problems. They might not enjoy the nitty-gritty details of planning an event for over a year, but they love the energy in an event room and seeing events set up and torn down every day.

Online Meetings

Before the COVID-19 pandemic, online meetings might have been held for smaller internal meetings or for dispersed teams through Zoom or other video conferencing apps. The pandemic sped up the acceptance and quality of online meetings. Although online events will never replace face-to-face gatherings, they can be used strategically to increase touch points with attendees, decrease costs, and show live meetings (which can be more engaging than passive webinars).

Companies that once held four meetings each year might now choose to do winter and summer sessions online and meet in person in the spring and fall. A meeting professional knows how to incorporate online events strategically. Many new career positions were developed during the pandemic to provide digital concierges, online event coordinators, and virtual production teams. This is an area that will continue to expand as the metaverse becomes widespread and artificial intelligence increases its impact on the industry.

> **Knowledge Check**
>
> **1.** How do unique venues enhance the experience of meeting attendees?
>
> **2.** How has the increased adoption of online meetings changed the industry?

9.4 SUPPLIERS

If you are not a planner, then you are a supplier. A **supplier** is any company that provides facilities, products, or services that a meeting planner needs. Let's explore supplier careers as we walk through how an event planner might plan an event.

An event planner will probably hear of a destination through one of many tourism organizations. Countries, states, and counties often have their own tourism organizations— all of these provide viable career paths. Some tourism departments are well funded and spend significant amounts on advertising and promoting their destinations. Tourism departments can maintain overseas offices with salespersons who call on travel agencies and tour operators to persuade them to promote their destination. In some destinations, the government's tourism department stages or helps fund events such as festivals, golf or tennis tournaments, regattas, and even dog shows. Typically, these departments employ nationals of their country to attend trade shows and create and coordinate events designed to entice travelers to visit their countries. Career opportunities consist of positions in sales, marketing, and administration. Their job is heavily involved in marketing and advertising the attractions that distinguish their destination from others. Once an event planner hears of a destination, they may decide to reach out.

Most event planners will first come into direct contact with a location through the city's **convention and visitors bureau (CVB)** such as Visit Orlando or the Greater Miami Convention and Visitors Bureau. These are nonprofit organizations whose job is to bring business (specifically, room nights) to their destination. They are able to provide many services free of charge to event planners, such as sending out requests for proposals, providing event swag for the city, and making connections. Associations often will contact a CVB and ask for the names of hotels in the area that meet certain criteria for their meetings. For example, an association meeting planner might ask for a list of downtown hotels with 100 rooms available March 5 to 8 that have 10,000 feet of exhibit space. The CVB will then reach out to appropriate venues and tell them about this inquiry so those interested can contact the meeting planner directly.

These bureaus almost never book hotel rooms for meeting planners, but in some cities they serve as the marketing and sales arm for the city's convention center. They also place advertising on behalf of their destinations, produce brochures and films, research potential markets, and provide maps and other materials to visitors who request them. These can also be referred to as destination marketing organizations. Job duties are often separated into industries from a sales perspective, so there might be one sales coordinator position specific to sporting events, one specific to associations, and one specific to special events and bus tours.

Once the event planner has received proposals, they would then select and work with the contracted venue. If they have a trade show component, they may choose to work with a **general service contractor (GSC)**. GSCs were previously known as decorators. This term is still used by some meetings and event professionals. GSCs work as a true partner in the planning process, providing additional support and coordination. Once a vendor has paid for their booth space, a GSC will coordinate with them about floor plans, furniture, decorations, electricity, food and beverage, floral, and shipping and handling. Most GSCs now have their own graphics, marketing, and printing departments that are fee-for-service beyond trade show services. There are many career paths available with GSCs, from logistics and graphics to event strategy and design. Popular GSCs include Freeman, Global Exhibitions Company, and Shepherd.

If the trade show is a large show or there is a special event where a concert or outside stage is needed, the event planner may also need to secure electrical. Can you imagine if 100 or more vendors were trying to plug into a single outlet on the hotel wall? There are special companies that do electrical for the event industry. One example is Edlen Electrical. While some career paths at these companies are specific to electrical, there are sales positions and on-site coordinator positions as well.

After securing the trade show vendor and any necessary electrical, the event planner will need to coordinate the rest of the logistics. This could include additional rentals, printing, or floral that the GSC does not handle. If the event is providing transportation to and from the airport or any offsite venue, then transportation needs to be coordinated. This is an excellent career path for those who love logistics and coordinating times, locations, and personalized services. VIP transports, bus tours, limos, and more would all be coordinated through a transportation services company.

Outside of the venue and food and beverage, one of the largest costs is audiovisual. This includes all televisions, screens, projectors, Wi-Fi, speakers, microphones, computers, clickers, and any other technology. Most hotels have an exclusive service provider, which means that the event planner would have to use them or pay large fees to bring in an external vendor. Convention centers may have an exclusive provider or a list of preferred providers to choose from. Unique venues may or may not let you bring in your own audiovisual. This is a large cost that needs to be considered when selecting a location.

9.5 THE MEETING AND EVENT PLANNING PROCESS

In 2009, a worldwide collective of event and tourism organizations gathered to develop a list of meeting and business event competency standards (MBECS). They wanted to set expectations for what meeting and event planners should know to be successful in this field. The book of competencies they created has become the basis for many meeting and event management programs in higher education. In 2012, the U.S. Bureau of Labor Statistics officially separated the meetings and events industry as a stand-alone career path outside of hospitality and tourism. This has led to an increase in universities offering this program of study. There are entire degrees in meeting and event planning that consist of many classes.

This section will give a brief overview of some of the MBECS in a general format. If meeting and event planning is something that you would like to pursue, then you should explore these areas in much more depth. The MBECS are public and free to download.[6]

Objectives

To plan a successful meeting or event, a meeting planner must know the objectives of the meeting. This is the first step and often overlooked from an organizational standpoint. If all stakeholders are not on the same page regarding what constitutes a successful event, the executive suite will often default to profit—which is not always the appropriate objective. Knowing the objectives of the meeting will give the event planner a better idea of how much time to schedule for the meeting and what type of format or agenda is best. There are three general meeting objectives—business, educational, or social—and any of the three can be combined.

An appropriate meeting site depends on the meeting's objectives. For example, a two-day meeting of quick service franchisees from all over the United States might best be held in a centrally located, large hotel connected to a major airport so attendees can get to the meeting site and return

Objectives, scheduling, and format are a few of the many factors that planners need to know for successful events.

home quickly and economically. On the other hand, a meeting meant to motivate salespeople to exceed their quotas in the year ahead and reward them for their past year's performance is frequently held at a resort in a warm climate (Hawaii and Florida are popular destinations).

Scheduling and Format

The next issue to address is the amount of time needed to achieve the meeting's objectives. The dates of the meeting are also important. A toy show must occur early enough in the year for retailers to place their orders in time for Christmas. Boat shows are typically held in the spring, just before the boating season begins. Television executives gather every January to show off new programs to advertisers and stations so the fall season programming can be finalized. Meeting planners should be careful to pick a time that does not conflict with another meeting that might require the presence of or attract the same delegates. Planners should also avoid religious and national holidays.

Once the length of the meeting and the dates have been established, it is time to make decisions about the meeting's format. The format is the overall schedule of events: What is going to happen during the meeting and in what order? When will the meeting start and end? What will be the times and length of meals? Coffee breaks? Social events? How many general sessions, roundtable discussions, and workshops will there be? If there is a trade show, when will it open and close? How many exhibitors will be involved and how much time will they need to accomplish their objectives? If there are tours, when will they occur and how long will they take? In today's fast-paced and technology-enhanced world, it is critically important for meeting planners to consider the level of engagement by the attendees. Instead of trying to fight for attendees' attention with their smart devices, consider incorporating technology that will enhance their engagement at the meetings.

Choosing a Location and Facility

Some meeting locations are predetermined. Many corporations hold their meetings at their own headquarters, for example. Other organizations change the meeting site from year to year to ease travel costs for delegates from different geographic areas. Location is also affected by the nature of the organization. One would not expect a religious group to meet in Las Vegas or Atlantic City, where many of the leisure activities available are not compatible with the group's values. The transportation logistics involved are also a consideration. How accessible is the meeting site to airports? In Europe, where trains are used extensively for intercity travel, accessibility to the train station can be a major consideration.

Once the location has been chosen, a facility must be selected. Will it be a resort, center-city hotel, conference center, or cruise ship? Outside of availability, a facility's size and cost are two of the major considerations here. In terms of size, a facility must have enough guestrooms, meeting rooms, and exhibit space. There is a popular expression in the meetings and events industry: "Dates, rates, and space—choose two." If the group is set on a specific date with a certain amount of space, the rates will be much higher. If the group wants all the space for a lower rate, then it has to be flexible with the dates. If the group wants specific dates at a specific rate, then it has to be flexible with the space available.

Factors to consider when choosing a facility include the following:

- Are the guestroom accommodations adequate? Are there a sufficient number of suites for VIPs and hospitality functions?

- Is Wi-Fi available in the guestrooms? Can it be complimentary per the contract, or is it a charge for the attendees? Is Wi-Fi available in the lobby and other public areas?

- Can the meeting rooms be set up in a variety of styles? Theater, schoolroom, and hollow square are some of the basic styles (see Exhibit 9.3).

- What types of amenities and recreational facilities are offered? This can be very important for meetings where relaxation is an objective. Some groups insist on resorts with golf courses, tennis courts, and spas; others want hotels located in or near scenic attractions.

- Are the meeting rooms adequately soundproofed? Meetings and activities in adjoining rooms should not intrude on each other.

- Does the resort, hotel, or cruise ship offer adequate audiovisual facilities? Is there a good sound system, especially for large rooms? What about the lighting? State-of-the-art

Seating possibilities and décor are among the decisions to make when choosing a facility.

Exhibit 9.3   Sample Meeting Room Setups

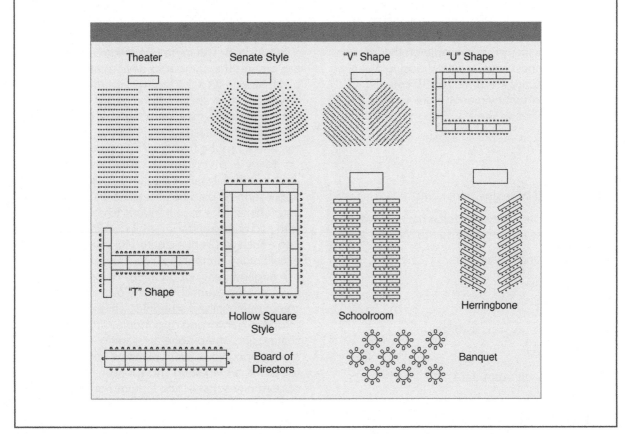

Source: Adapted from *The Convention Liaison Council Manual*, 4th ed.

lighting facilities include track lighting and theatrical lighting equipment. What kind of projection equipment is available?

- How far are the meeting rooms from the guestrooms? Can the meeting rooms be reached without climbing stairs? Are there a sufficient number of conveniently located elevators or escalators? These access issues have taken on added importance since the Americans with Disabilities Act was passed.

- Are you able to bring in your own suppliers, or do you have to use the facility's exclusive or preferred vendors?

Of course, an association or corporation's budget is a determining factor in where the meeting will be held. Some industry groups can afford to meet at upscale hotels; others have more modest budgets. The price of many items is a matter of negotiation between the venue and the meeting's sponsor. Questions for negotiation include whether there will be a charge for meeting room space, what the functions will cost, whether the venue is willing to pay for any of the functions (such as a manager's reception), what the guestrooms will cost, and how many guestrooms will be provided on a complimentary basis.

There are many lists available on the Internet of what is a "must have" when choosing a venue. Here is a standard list of the top 10 criteria deemed important by meeting planners in selecting a meeting site:

1. Location
2. Parking
3. Food and beverage minimums
4. Contract flexibility and force majeure, which became very important during the pandemic
5. Services and amenities
6. Layout
7. Insurance
8. Ambience and accessibility
9. Acoustics
10. Flexibility on event date

Force majeure is a legal term that refers to unforeseeable and unavoidable circumstances or events that prevent a party from fulfilling its contractual obligations. These events are typically beyond the control of the parties involved and are considered external, extraordinary, and often of a disruptive nature. Force majeure events can include natural disasters (e.g., earthquakes, floods, hurricanes), acts of terrorism, government actions or regulations, labor strikes, war, and other events that make it impractical or impossible for a party to perform its contractual duties.

Event Technology

Technology has changed how we prepare and execute an event and how we evaluate it after it concludes. Before a meeting or event, an event website is created to provide information about the event, create buzz, and help people register. The website should be mobile friendly so people can access and navigate it easily with a smartphone or tablet. Social media is another way to create interest and market an event. Social networks such as Instagram, Facebook, LinkedIn, and X can be used to connect potential attendees to an event and provide information and updates.

During the event, the facility should have enough bandwidth—the amount of information that can travel through a communications line—for all attendees. The more bandwidth a facility has, the greater the number of devices attendees can use to connect to the facility's Internet to send emails, post on social media, or surf the web. Many attendees may bring three or more devices (e.g., tablets, smartphones, laptops) that they wish to connect to the facility's Wi-Fi network.

Many event organizers will create mobile apps specifically tailored to their event. These applications should be accessible via smartphones and tablets, allowing attendees to connect with each other and with exhibitors. A mobile app—such as Cvent—created for the event is an excellent investment that provides attendees with rich engagement opportunities before, during, and after the event. The app allows attendees to create personalized schedules while encouraging attendee networking opportunities through contact sharing and one-on-one messaging. In addition, a mobile app allows event planners the opportunity to sell more marketing and sponsorship opportunities that will be featured on the app; communicate directly with attendees through push notifications and instant updates; and track, measure, and analyze attendee engagement in real time while providing data and analytics.

After an event, meeting planners will often distribute online evaluations and surveys to attendees to gauge the success of and overall satisfaction with an event. This surveying method saves paper and the cost of mailing surveys. Planners will also pose questions and monitor feedback on social media regarding the success of an event.

During the Event

In order to perform these tasks successfully, meeting planners must be superb negotiators and diplomats. The organizations they work for and the people who attend the meetings expect them to choose the best sites and arrange for the best accommodations and transportation at the lowest prices. They want their food and beverage service and their social events to be superior—and they expect all of this to happen without any mishaps or delays. Meeting planning is a difficult job, requiring a high degree of specialized knowledge.

During the meeting, the planner is usually busy and under a great deal of pressure to keep things moving smoothly and resolve problems that come up. Meeting planners often arrive at a site a day or two in advance to ensure that all the elements they have negotiated and contracted are in place. Are the hotels prepared to receive the delegates? Is transportation in place? Are the meeting rooms arranged as they should be? Have the arrangements for guest speakers been confirmed? Are there any problems with setting up the trade show? Cell phones and short-wave radio communications are often required to keep the planner in touch with staff in different parts of the venue—and with other venues in the city in the case of a larger convention.

Even when things are going well, unanticipated events can threaten a convention's success. Speakers can fail to show up; weather can disrupt transportation arrangements; and fires, strikes, or demonstrations can occur. Good meeting planners devise contingency plans to handle all of these situations.

After a meeting is over, the planner must still deal with a number of crucial tasks. Equipment and exhibit booths must be packed and shipped. Invoices from hotels, restaurants, and other facilities must be checked and settled. Equally important, the meeting must be evaluated from the point of view of the attendees, the sponsor, and the exhibitors. This information provides feedback for future meeting planning.

Knowledge Check

1. What are some factors a meeting planner must consider when choosing a facility?

2. How important is communication during an event?

Event planners work through the events to ensure that everything runs smoothly.

9.6 MEETINGS AND EVENTS INDUSTRY CAREERS

Event planning has become a popular career track in a number of universities due to the growing demand for professional management. Individuals; companies; and charitable, social, and trade organizations rely on trained and experienced people to create and execute their events. The diversity of events that a professional event planner might be called on to create and execute is one aspect of this career that is appealing to many. Although some independent event planners specialize in certain kinds of events (e.g., weddings), others accept the challenge of any type of event—personal, cultural, leisure, or organizational. Weddings and anniversaries are personal events, while an art fair is an example of a cultural event. Leisure events include concerts and organized recreational activities. Events produced for businesses or charitable groups are classified as organizational. All types of events, no matter the category, require organizational skills and technical knowledge on the part of the event planner.

Companies that have many events throughout the year might have their own in-house event planners, or they might call on an event planning company or independent event planner. University graduates have numerous opportunities for careers in event planning. They can join an organization's event department or a company specializing in producing special events, or become an independent planner.

Event planners coordinate every aspect of the event. In some cases, they may select the city or hotel, or some other venue (e.g., a park, convention center, or historic building). Bryant Park in New York City was the venue for New York Fashion Week for many years. The Baltimore Aquarium and the Smithsonian Institution in Washington, D.C., rent certain areas to event and meeting planners for dinners and receptions. The center of downtown is used for the three-day Wine & Food Classic in Aspen, Colorado. Since event planners must deal with other contractors, such as caterers, audiovisual companies, decorators, florists, and transportation services, they must have knowledge of those functions. Creativity is an important trait for an event planner.

Many clients expect the planner to recommend a unique location or create a one-of-a-kind event.

Over the last decade, the career paths for business event planners have split into two main areas (not including social events). Meeting planners historically have handled logistics only; now they are expected to oversee design, evaluation, and reporting. Therefore, the meetings and events industry has been trying to change the job title from meeting planner to "business event strategist" or "business event professional" and encourage the position to be included in more strategic conversations at higher levels in an organization.

It is still a completely viable career path to become a meeting and event planner who coordinates logistics (secures event space, coordinates catering, and selects audiovisual). This has become a lower-paid career path, and the duties can often be divided up and spread among administrative assistants and office managers. Another viable career path is the event designer, who often looks at an organization's overall marketing plan, decides on strategic touch points, and designs event experiences that provide tangible value to the organization. These positions are often higher up in the company and have larger salaries.

People who plan, organize, and coordinate meetings, conventions, and trade shows may have various job titles. Only in the largest associations are such people engaged full time in meeting planning and given titles such as "meeting planner," "meeting coordinator," or "exhibits manager." Many meeting and event professionals have job titles that relate to other activities they perform, such as sales, marketing, or administration. For example, the marketing manager of a company may also be its convention manager or meeting planner. This can make it difficult for those trying to find a career in the industry to use the appropriate search terms to find the positions online. Many different titles should be searched to find available opportunities.

Knowledge Check

1. What are some career paths in the meetings and events industry?

2. What could be advantages of working as an independent event planner?

A meeting is a group of two or more people who gather together for a specific purpose. A meeting can consist of a few people in a conference room or 100,000 delegates at a major convention center using a dozen or more hotels in a large city. Many specialized services, facilities, and technologies may be used.

Meetings are held by associations, corporations, and governments. There are also trade shows that may be a part of or independent from a meeting or convention. Four kinds of trade shows are industrial, wholesale/retail, professional or scientific, and public or consumer.

Planners can specialize in special events (e.g., fairs and festivals, sporting events, and concerts), social events (e.g., births, bar and bat mitzvahs, and weddings). Planners can become independent contractors, working in any area of the industry.

Almost any kind of facility can be used to hold a meeting. Meetings have been held at amusement parks, football stadiums, and castles. Hotels, conference centers, universities, and cruise ships also serve as popular meeting venues. Online meetings are becoming more popular because of new technology and the general acceptance of online meetings during and after the COVID-19 pandemic.

Suppliers are companies that provide facilities, products, and services that a meeting planner needs. In choosing a location, planners may first some into contact with a city's convention and visitors bureau. Planners may also work with a general services contractor, who coordinates things like floor plans, furniture, decorations, and electricity.

One of the first questions a meeting planner needs to address is the objective (or objectives) of the meeting. Some meeting locations will obviously be more appropriate than others once objectives have been set. The next question is the amount of time needed to achieve the stated objectives. The dates of the meeting are also important. Once the length of the meeting and the dates have been established, it is time to make some decisions about the format—the meeting's overall schedule of events. What is going to happen during the meeting and in what order?

Some meeting locations are predetermined. Many corporations hold their meetings at their own headquarters, for example. Other organizations move their meetings around to ease the travel costs for delegates from different geographic areas. Once the location has been established, a facility must be chosen. Size and cost are two of the major considerations here. Others include guestrooms, meeting rooms, amenities and recreational facilities, soundproofing, technology, adequate access, and budget.

During the actual meeting, the planner is usually very busy and under a great deal of pressure to keep things moving smoothly and resolve problems that come up. After a meeting is over, there are still a number of crucial tasks left for the meeting planner. Evaluation for future planning purposes is one of the most important of these.

Meeting planners may hold a variety of job titles within an organization. People who are actively engaged in meeting planning can be found in associations, corporations, and governments. Meeting planners historically have handled logistics only; now they are expected to oversee design, evaluation, and reporting. This has split the career path for planners into two main areas: a business and event strategist who is included in higher-level strategic conversations or a planner who coordinates logistics.

KEY TERMS

association—A group of people banded together for a specific purpose.

certified meeting professional (CMP)—A CMP certification enhances the knowledge and performance of meeting professionals, promotes the status and credibility of the meeting profession, and advances uniform standards of practice. The qualifications for certification are based on professional experience, education, and a rigorous exam.

conference centers—Smaller versions of convention centers and hotels. They are often designed to host small meetings and can contain lodging.

consumer show—Also known as a public show. It differs from a trade show in that trade shows are typically business to business and not open to the public. A consumer show is often business to consumer, typically open to the public, and usually requires an entrance fee. A Holiday Expo, a Women's Expo, and RV shows are considered consumer shows.

convention—An event that has a meeting and a trade show component.

convention and visitors bureau (CVB)—A nonprofit service organization that promotes a destination and sometimes provides services for meetings and conventions.

convention services manager (CSM)—A member of hotel or resort staff who is responsible for all aspects of a convention.

destination wedding—A wedding held at an exotic or remote location.

event—An organized occasion such as a meeting, convention, exhibition, special meeting, gala dinner, and so on. An event is often composed of several different yet related functions.

Events Industry Council (EIC)—Formerly known as the Convention Industry Council, the EIC is an umbrella organization for all meeting and event organizations, and its mission is to create industry standards and definitions.

exhibition—An event at which product, services, or promotional materials are displayed to attendees visiting exhibits on the show floor. These are primarily focused on business-to-business relationships.

exposition—A term primarily used in North America, this is another term for a large exhibit, trade show, or public show.

force majeure—Unforeseeable circumstances that prevent someone from fulfilling a contract.

general service contractor (GSC)—An organization that provides event management and exhibitors with a wide range of services, sometimes including but not limited to distributing the exhibitor manual, installation and dismantling, creating and hanging signs and banners, laying carpet, material handling, and providing booth/stand furniture.

incentive trips—Often a combination of meetings and recreation, incentive trips are rewards to customers, retailers, distributors, or employees. Spouses are often invited to attend.

management meetings—These gatherings include everything from financial reviews to strategic planning sessions. Management meetings make up the largest category in the corporate meetings market.

meeting—An event where the primary activity of the participants is to attend educational and/or business sessions, participate in discussions and social functions, or attend other organized events. There is no trade show component.

product launches—Events at which new products are showcased to employees. These meetings are also used to motivate dealers or distributors who are not employees (e.g., introducing new car models to dealers). Product introductions last one to two days on average.

professional and technical meetings—Gatherings used to provide information or teach new techniques to employees who work in technical and professional fields. Accountants need to learn about new tax laws and rulings every year, for example.

sales meetings—Sales meetings are essential for teaching sales techniques, introducing new products, building morale, and motivating sales personnel. National sales meetings average 3.6 days with 104 attendees. Regional sales meetings average 42 attendees and last an average of 2.5 days.

social events—Events whose purpose is not business focused and often celebrate such milestones as births, baptisms, bar and bat mitzvahs, birthdays, engagements, weddings, anniversaries, and retirements.

special events—A category consisting of private events, public events, fairs and festivals, sporting events, and concerts.

stockholders meetings—Annual events where owners of company stock meet. They usually last a day, with an average attendance of 95 stockholders or shareholders.

supplier—Any company that provides facilities, products, or services that the meeting planner needs.

third-party meeting planners—Also known as independent meeting planners. These planners are not associated with a company and serve as independent contractors. Third-party meeting planners can work in any area of the industry and can choose what jobs they want to accept. In other parts of the world, they are called professional conference or congress organizers.

trade show—An exhibition of products and/or services held for members of a common or related industry. Not open to the general public.

training seminars—Training seminars, which rank second in number of meetings held, provide training for employees at all levels.

1. Which describes meetings and events?
   a. An event comprises several different functions. A meeting is a type of event.
   b. A meeting comprises several different functions. An event is a type of meeting.
   c. An event requires planning. A meeting does not require planning.
   d. An event is a small gathering. A meeting is a large gathering.

2. Trade shows are usually not open to
   a. the general public.
   b. business vendors.
   c. company executives.
   d. industry professionals.

3. Which event is considered a consumer show?
   a. Fundraising gala and auction
   b. Automobile expo
   c. Pediatric conference
   d. College fair

4. Which makes up the largest category in the corporate meetings market?
   a. Training seminars
   b. Stockholders meetings
   c. National sales meetings
   d. Management meetings

5. Which event is considered a special event?
   a. The National Restaurant Association Show
   b. Food and Wine Classic in Aspen
   c. Bitcoin conference
   d. World Travel Mart

6. What is essential in planning an association meeting?
   a. Securing a convention center
   b. Marketing to recruit attendees
   c. Hiring a third-party meeting planner
   d. Advertising to the public in newspapers

7. Which meeting location has the most expansive reach?
   a. Convention centers
   b. Unique venues
   c. Online
   d. Hotels

8. Which term refers to unforeseeable circumstances that prevent contract fulfillment?
   a. Confidentiality breach
   b. Force majeure
   c. Negligence
   d. Vis major

9. Which aspect are meeting planners now expected to handle?
   a. Design
   b. Logistics
   c. Communication
   d. Facility selection

10. Once an event planner has selected a city for an event, they will most likely reach out to a(n)
   a. convention and visitors bureau.
   b. general services contractor.
   c. food and beverage vendor.
   d. audiovisual vendor.

11. General service contractors were previously known as
   a. logistic coordinators.
   b. IT technicians.
   c. decorators.
   d. exhibitors.

12. What is another term for a meeting planner?
   a. Conferences services specialist
   b. Hospitality event specialist
   c. Business event professional
   d. Business professional

SHORT-ANSWER QUESTIONS

1. How does the meetings and events industry support the hotel industry?

2. How has the COVID-19 pandemic affected the meetings and events industry?

CASE STUDY

ALL FOR NOTHING

It's the spring of 2018. A major restaurant week is underway in Southern California, and events are planned throughout the area. With warm weather and great promotional efforts, the week is turning out to be a success. There's also an impressive lineup of celebrities and world-renowned chefs scheduled to attend several events.

It is the second-to-last day of the restaurant week, and food lovers have purchased $100 tickets for a meet and greet with a famous Italian chef, plus cocktails, appetizers, live music, and swimming pool access. For the venue, event planners and marketers have selected a casual seafood restaurant that can accommodate 150 guests. It has an outdoor bar, space for live entertainment, and a 3-foot pool. The planners go over final logistics with each other before the event, but they do not confirm the expected head count with the event marketers. The event marketers have sold over 200 tickets for the event.

It is the day of the event. Ticketed guests who arrive early are admitted early. Guests who arrive later cannot find parking. An hour into the event, the celebrity chef arrives but does not mingle with ticketed guests. He makes one appearance to greet guests over a microphone while live music is playing. In addition, the event runs out of food and cocktails, forcing ticketed guests to purchase food from the restaurant. Highly annoyed, guests start leaving the venue. Some have only stayed 15 minutes at the venue.

The guests complain that they paid $100 for nothing.

DISCUSSION QUESTIONS

1. What were some problems with this event?

2. What mistakes did the event planners and event marketers make?

3. How could the event planners and event marketers have better communicated with each other?

Lee Brian Schrager

Lee Brian Schrager is a renowned event planner, media relations expert, and the creator of the Food Network South Beach Wine & Food Festival presented by Capital One (SOBEWFF®) and the New York City Wine & Food Festival presented by Capital One (NYCWFF). He is chief communications officer and senior vice president of corporate social responsibility at Southern Glazer's Wine & Spirits, the world's leading distributor of beverage alcohol. In this role, he oversees the company's internal and external communications function, as well as its corporate giving and volunteering programs.

Schrager studied at the Culinary Institute of America and Florida International University's Chaplin School of Hospitality & Tourism Management. He actively contributes to *Ocean Drive* magazine and serves on the board of Trustees for the Pérez Art Museum Miami. Schrager is also a member of the Culinary Council for God's Love We Deliver in New York City and serves as a judge for the annual Forbes 30 Under 30 list and American Airlines' annual *Celebrated Living* Platinum List Awards.

Celebrating its tenth year in 2011, the SOBEWFF® was marked by Schrager's first book release, the *Food Network South Beach Wine & Food Festival Cookbook*. He has since published two more cookbooks: *Fried & True* in May 2014 and *America's Best Breakfasts* in April 2016.

A core aspect of Schrager's business philosophy is giving back to the community. Both SOBEWFF® and NYCWFF are charitable organizations, collectively raising over $50 million for various charitable causes.

WHAT WOULD YOU DO?

You are an event manager responsible for organizing a charity fundraiser gala for a well-known nonprofit organization. The event is scheduled to take place at a luxurious hotel ballroom, and the guest list includes several high-profile donors and celebrities.

During the planning process, you discover that the hotel's owner is a major donor to a competing charity. You also find out that the owner has been accused of making inappropriate remarks to female staff members in the past.

As an event manager, you are responsible for ensuring that the event is successful and meets the expectations of both the nonprofit organization and its donors. However, you also have a responsibility to uphold ethical standards and maintain the reputation of the nonprofit organization.

How would you handle this situation?

10

FLOATING RESORTS: THE CRUISE LINE BUSINESS

Chapter Outline

Learning Objectives

1. Summarize the beginnings of the cruise industry, describe the birth of modern cruising, and describe the cruise industry of today. (pp. 288–292)

2. Explain how a cruise ship is organized and managed. (pp. 293–304)

KEY TERMS

captain

chief housekeeper

chief officer

cruise director

environmental officer

flags of convenience

food and beverage manager

galley

hotel director

lido deck

physician

purser

shore excursions

sitting

ton

turnaround day

The *Icon of the Seas*, a Royal Caribbean International ship, is the largest and most expensive cruise ship built to date. Costing an estimated $1.35 billion, it has 2,805 staterooms that can accommodate 7,600 passengers who can sleep, dine, and be entertained on 20 decks and eight themed "neighborhoods" located throughout the vessel. The *Icon of the Seas* ship features 40 new and returning dining, bar, and nightlife options across its decks, along with a conference center, medical center, pharmacy, outdoor movie screen, casino royale, and music hall. This magnificent ship symbolizes just how far the modern cruise line industry has come in the last few decades.

The cruise industry has experienced impressive growth since 1970, when it was estimated that just 500,000 people took a cruise each year. By 2019 more than 29 million people reported having taken a vacation on a cruise ship somewhere in the world that year.[1] Growth in demand has required expanded fleets, and more than 50 new cruise ships have been launched since 2010.[2] Half of all new cruise ships built in 2022 and beyond will be powered by liquified natural gas.[3] This dramatic growth bodes well for hospitality program graduates who want to consider a career in the cruise industry. The passenger services aboard these ships are managed by hotel managers (many of whom come from fine hotels and hospitality schools), who supervise food and beverage managers, executive chefs, maître d's, and chief housekeepers, among others. These managers are recruited worldwide and are offered salaries competitive with land-based resorts. Even on land there are many hospitality-related positions now available in the cruise industry. Carnival Cruise Lines, the world's largest cruise company, employs about 100,000 people in hotel and foodservice operations, sales and marketing, entertainment and casino management, itinerary planning, finance, human resources, information systems, marine operations, and new construction.

Yet, cruise lines are still in their infancy. North America, at 51 percent, has the largest share of all cruise passengers, followed by Europe at 21 percent. The rest of the world makes up 22 percent of the market—and when you consider that the rest of the world makes up about 83 percent of the world's population, the potential for growth is tremendous.[4] Only 20 percent of American adults have ever taken a cruise. It is, however, the fastest growing segment of the hospitality industry, and it appears to generate the highest rates of customer satisfaction. Cruise Lines International Association reports that there were 1.1 million full-time equivalent cruise industry employees in 2019, generating over $50 billion in wages and salaries. The industry contributed over $154 billion to the global economy in 2019. Despite the economic devastation suffered by the cruise industry from the COVID-19 pandemic, with an estimated $77 billion loss in global economic activity, the industry continues to exhibit resiliency and optimism—74 percent of cruisers reported that they are likely to cruise again in the next few years, and two out of three are willing to cruise within a year.[5]

This chapter will explore the evolution of the cruise industry from steamship transportation to floating vacation resorts, cruise line management, and career opportunities for those who are interested in this exciting and dynamic industry.

10.1 EARLY CRUISES

If you define a cruise as going to a number of ports for the purpose of sightseeing and ending up back where you started, then perhaps the first person to take a cruise and write about it was the English novelist William Makepeace Thackeray. In 1844, the Peninsular and Oriental Steam Navigation Company, popularly known as the P&O, invited Thackeray to travel on board its ships to Greece, the Holy Land, and Egypt. His book *Notes of a Journey from Cornhill to Grand Cairo* told of the trip. Thackeray reported getting seasick; complained about the prices, bugs, and lack of pretty women in Athens; and objected to the beggars he encountered while climbing the pyramids in Egypt. Even so, he said he had a good time and recommended that others consider taking the journey.

The first U.S.-origin cruise was probably the 1867 voyage of the paddle-wheel steamer *Quaker City*, with an itinerary similar to Thackeray's except that it started from New York. Among the passengers was the American writer Mark Twain, who chronicled his adventures in *The Innocents Abroad*. Twain, too, became a cruising enthusiast. He described how every evening after dinner, guests would promenade the deck, sing hymns, say prayers, listen to organ

Passenger cruising emerged in the nineteenth century. Paddle-wheel steamers carried cargo, mail, and passengers along U.S. rivers.

music in the grand saloon, read, and write in their journals. Sometimes dances were held on the upper deck, accompanied by music that Twain did not particularly enjoy. "However," he wrote, "the dancing was infinitely worse than the music." When the ship rode to starboard, "the whole platoon of dancers came charging down to starboard with it and brought up in mass at the rail; and when it rolled down to port, they went floundering down to port with the same unanimity of sentiment. The Virginia reel, as performed on board the *Quaker City*, had more genuine reel about it than any reel I ever saw before."[6]

Transportation and Immigration

From the time of the *Quaker City* to the late 1950s, far more people crossed the Atlantic from necessity rather than for pleasure. This was the peak period of immigration to the United States, and travel conditions for most passengers were miserable. Even for those traveling first class, the trip was often uncomfortable because voyages were long and there were no ports to stop at. Shipbuilders tried their best to make people forget that they were at sea. The English architect

Arthur Davis, who designed some of the great Cunard liners, put it this way:

The people who use these ships are not pirates, they do not dance hornpipes; they are mostly seasick American ladies, and the one thing they want to forget when they are on the vessel is that they are on a ship at all. If we could get ships to look inside like ships, and get people to enjoy the sea, it would be a very good thing; but all we can do as things are is to give them gigantic floating hotels.[7]

The other objective, of course, was to make the ships go as fast as possible so that the voyages would last only a few days instead of two weeks. On the whole, this strategy worked, and passengers began to regard steamships as both luxurious and unsinkable.

This complacency was shattered when on her maiden voyage, one of the most luxurious ships afloat, the White Star liner *Titanic*, struck an iceberg and sank in the North Atlantic in the early morning hours of April 15, 1912. This 46,329-ton liner (less than one-third the size of today's largest ships) carried 2,228 passengers and crew. In 2 hours and 40 minutes, 1,523 perished—most of them second- and third-class passengers trapped because *Titanic's* 20 lifeboats could carry only about half of those on board. At first, because most passengers were convinced that the ship would not sink, they did not rush to fill the boats. Confusion and a lack of preparedness compounded the problem; 40 percent of the available lifeboat seats stayed empty as the boats were lowered. Boat number one, with a capacity of 40, was launched with only five passengers and seven crew.

The sinking of *Titanic* was one of the saddest nights in maritime history. Stories of courage and cowardice survive to this day. For example, Isidor Straus, co-owner of Macy's department store, and his wife, Ida, were returning home from a vacation on the French Riviera. Mrs. Straus refused to board a lifeboat without her husband. "I will not be separated from my husband," she said. "As we have lived, so shall we die. Together." Historians tend to blame Captain Edward Smith (who went down with his ship) and White Star's managing director, Bruce Ismay (who was on board but managed to escape) because allegedly they were eager to run on schedule and arrive at the announced time, when the press would be waiting. Even though they were advised that there were icebergs in the area (another ship, the *Californian*, just 20 miles away, had stopped for the night because of the same warnings), the ship did not slow down.

After the *Titanic* disaster, ships crossing the North Atlantic were moved to a more southerly route, more lifeboats were added, 24-hour wireless watches at sea were required, and other safety measures were implemented.

New Passengers and New Directions

By the 1920s, the transatlantic passenger business was booming again—until the United States curtailed its open-door immigration policy. Since the passenger lines earned most of their revenue from this source, a new kind of passenger had to be found. World War I had created an interest in Europe among Americans, and immigrants' accommodations were turned into "tourist class" cabins that soon filled with teachers, students, and sightseers who wanted to visit London, Paris, Rome, or some of the Belgian and French battlegrounds they had read about. There was another incentive as well. Prohibition had dried up America in 1920. Those who enjoyed a martini or Scotch and soda could get as many as they wanted on an ocean voyage!

Spending a week at sea soon became the fashionable thing to do. The press ran frequent articles about the lavish and expensive first-class lifestyles displayed on board, where people dined, danced, and partied all night with exciting, interesting, and often rich companions. Going to Europe on a transatlantic liner was the best of all travel experiences.

With the arrival of the Great Depression in 1929, many who had previously enjoyed European vacations could no longer afford the expense. In response, steamship lines started to offer cheaper alternatives, including short, inexpensive vacation/party cruises to Nova Scotia, the Bahamas, and Bermuda. The ships used for these cruises had been designed for transatlantic traffic and were not really suited for cruising, especially in warm waters. They were not air-conditioned, and their lack of outdoor deck space and swimming pools was not the atmosphere of a resort at all. As the cruising market grew, however, new and more luxurious ships were deployed, and with them came more expensive and longer itineraries. Ships became more open and more resort-like. Posters showed passengers dressed in leisure clothes around an outdoor pool instead of dressed in business suits strolling an enclosed deck.

Up to World War II, the major steamship lines were owned by European interests. When the war started, almost all of those vessels were converted into troop ships or stayed in port. This situation continued until 1945, when the rebuilding of Europe once again spurred a growing demand for ocean liners. For the first time, the United States recognized that it might need its own troop ships and subsidized the building and operation of new vessels. The *United States*, launched in 1951, was designed to be the fastest ship of its size afloat. On its very first transatlantic crossing, it set a new world record of 3 days, 10 hours, and 40 minutes, beating *Queen Mary's* record by a full 10 hours.

The postwar boom marked the last days of the great steamship liners. Besides the *United States* and *Queen Mary*, there were the *Queen Elizabeth*, the French Line's *France*, Holland America's *Rotterdam*, and a host of sleek Italian liners built for warm-water cruising in the Mediterranean. These ships crossed the Atlantic, cruised to exotic ports, and circled the globe.

The cruise world started to come apart in 1958, when Pan American World Airways offered its first nonstop, transatlantic crossing on a Boeing 707 jet. Ocean-going passenger ships were effectively out of business as a means of transportation. Some ships were mothballed, such as the *United States*. Others were scrapped. The *Queen Mary* became a landlocked hotel in Long Beach, California. The *France* was converted to a cruise ship and continued to sail as the *Norway* until 2006, when it was retired from service and scrapped.

Knowledge Check

1. What safety measures were implemented for ships after the *Titanic* disaster?

2. What contributed to the decline of cruising in the 1950s?

10.2 THE BIRTH OF MODERN CRUISING

There were no modern cruise lines until the early 1960s, when Miami entrepreneur Leslie Frazer chartered two ships, the *Bilu* and *Nili*, and marketed them exclusively for cruises.

In 1966, Ted Arison, a young Israeli from Tel Aviv who had started and lost two air cargo businesses, joined with Norwegian Knut Kloster to bring the *Sunward*, the first new vessel built especially for cruising, into the market. They formed a cruise line called Norwegian Caribbean Line (now called Norwegian Cruise Line) to market the vessel. By 1971, the NCL fleet had added three more ships, the *Starward*, *Skyward*, and *Southward*. NCL helped transform South Florida's cruise industry from a regionally marketed collection of old transatlantic liners to a nationally marketed business featuring brand-new vessels designed specifically for Caribbean cruising.

At the same time, a former Miami Beach hotelier named Ed Stephan had dreams of starting his own cruise line. After producing some designs and plans, he traveled to Norway and enlisted the help of prominent shipping executives. Thus, another industry giant, Royal Caribbean Cruise Lines (RCCL; now Royal Caribbean International), was born. RCCL quickly launched a modern fleet based on Stephan's innovative designs of ships with a sleek, yacht-like profile and an observation lounge located in the ship's funnel, high above the superstructure, which was inspired by Seattle's Space Needle. By 1972, the RCCL fleet consisted of the *Song of Norway*, *Nordic Prince*, and *Sun Viking*.

By the early 1970s, the U.S. cruise business was no longer limited to Florida. A Seattle businessman, Stanley McDonald, founded Princess Cruise Lines on the West Coast, offering cruises to the Mexican Riviera. It was an instant hit, and by 1972 Princess had four vessels. At the same time, a former bush pilot, Chuck West, was building a seasonal cruise business along Alaska's Inside Passage. West's cruise line was part of his overall tour operation, which he called Westours.

In 1977, Princess scored a coup that would forever change the image of cruising. Most people had no idea what taking a cruise was like. A television production company, Aaron Spelling Productions, decided to use a luxury cruise ship as the location for a major TV series. Princess made two of their vessels, the *Island Princess* and the *Pacific Princess*, available for the filming. The series was called *The Love Boat*, and in nine years of production, it featured stories of people who fell in love, solved personal problems, or just had a great adventure while on a cruise. There is little doubt that the program popularized the idea that a cruise was not a vacation just for the rich and famous.

Carnival Is Born

In 1971, the partnership between Ted Arison and Knut Kloster broke up. Arison decided to leave NCL and start his own business. With the help of a friend, Meshulam Riklis, Arison bought a laid-up ocean liner, the *Empress of Canada*, renamed it the *Mardi Gras*, and founded Carnival Cruise Lines.

What is now the world's largest cruise company did not have a very auspicious beginning. When the *Mardi Gras* entered service on March 7, 1972, it ran aground at the tip of Miami Beach shortly after leaving the dock. It sat there for a full 24 hours while tourists along the shoreline gazed in amazement before it was refloated. It did not help that Carnival's only ship was an old one competing in a sea of new vessels. Carnival's vice president of sales and marketing at that time, Bob Dickinson, mulled over the problem of how to get more people to take a Carnival cruise. He concluded that people were not really looking for a specific ship or port when they went on a cruise vacation; what they really wanted was to have fun. Dickinson's solution was to provide more activities and entertainment onboard ship than Carnival's competitors and call his ship "The Fun Ship." This was a total reversal of cruise marketing. Up to that time, cruise promotion had been destination-driven. Dickinson decided to make the ship itself the destination. Because it was an old ship, the company was forced to offer very low prices, which attracted a younger crowd. Until then, cruises had been viewed as suitable only for wealthy, older people. This was a whole new market. The younger age and informality of the passengers added to the "fun" on the ship, and Carnival was able to deliver on its promise. By 1975, the line was profitable and started adding more ships to its fleet. Dickinson's strategy, which changed consumers' perception of cruising from a rather stodgy pastime for the rich to a fun and affordable vacation for the masses, was probably the defining event in the development of the modern cruise industry.

The Cruise Industry Today

Cruise lines are divided into four market segments by the Cruise Lines International Association. The largest category by far is the contemporary/value segment, which is dominated by the popular-priced, mass-market lines. These lines tend to get a lot of their business from first-time cruisers. Carnival, Norwegian, and Royal Caribbean are all part of this segment. The premium cruise lines charge more and carry fewer passengers per **ton** of space. (In the shipping business, the tonnage of a ship usually refers to the ship's volume, not weight; thus, a ton is a unit for measuring the total cubic capacity of a

cruise ship.) Celebrity, Holland America, and Princess are in this category. The luxury segment is the top of the line. Seabourn, Crystal, Cunard, and Silversea are all examples of luxury cruise lines. The final segment is called "specialty" lines, which concentrate on niche destinations and various riverboat cruises; Windjammer Barefoot Cruises and Windstar are two companies in this category.

There are three giant players in the industry: the largest is Carnival, with nine brands; next is Royal Caribbean, which also operates Celebrity Cruises and Azamara Club Cruises, and owns Pullmantur (based in Spain) and CDF Croisières de France; the third largest is NCL, which also owns Oceania and Regent Seven Seas Cruises. The Caribbean, Bahamas, and Bermuda remain the top cruise destinations, followed by Asia and China.

The average cruise passenger is 47 years old, cruises an average of seven days, and spends an average of $385 in a port city before embarking on a cruise. Passengers also spend an average of $750 in port cities over the course of a typical seven-day cruise. Millennials are the most enthusiastic cruisers of the future. Looking ahead, the cruise industry continues to focus on destination stewardship by collaborating with local communities.[8]

Knowledge Check

1. What revived the cruise industry in the 1960s?

2. What was the inspiration for Carnival Cruise Lines?

A modern cruise ship.

10.3 CRUISE SHIP ORGANIZATION

As has been said, cruise ships today are floating vacation resorts. In terms of organization, they are very similar to hotels in some ways. While each cruise line has its own unique organization for its ships, all cruise ships generally follow a similar pattern. Exhibit 10.1 shows a sample cruise ship organization chart. At the top is the captain, who has responsibility for the engine, deck, and hotel departments. Within each of those departments, there is an individual in charge, usually a chief officer or director. The engine department is led by the chief engineer; the deck department is led by the first officer; and the hotel department is led by the hotel director, who is responsible for food and beverage, housekeeping, pursers, casinos, concessions, and entertainment. Entertainment is led by the cruise director.

Because this chapter concentrates on the hospitality aspects of a cruise, we will focus on hotel directors and those who report to them (after briefly discussing the captain's position).

Captain

Although a cruise ship can be compared to a hotel, it is in fact a vessel at sea and is therefore first and foremost operating under maritime laws. It is under the command of the **captain**, who is responsible for the ship's operation and the safety of all aboard. It is the captain's job to see that all company policies and rules are followed, as well as national and international laws. The captain has legal authority to enforce these laws, an

Exhibit 10.1 Sample Cruise Ship Organization Chart

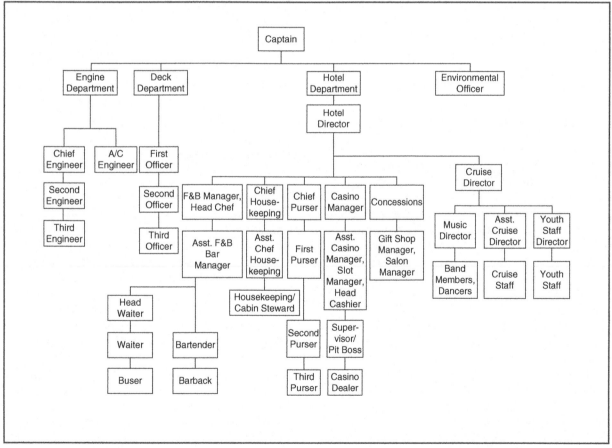

Source: "Cruise Ship Ranks and Hierarchy," CruiseShipJobs.com, https://cruiseshipjobs.com/career-advice/cruise-ship-ranks/.

authority granted by the country in which the ship is registered.

Vessels also must comply with the laws of the ports they sail from and to. For example, personnel from the U.S. Coast Guard and the U.S. Centers for Disease Control and Prevention regularly inspect all ships sailing to and from U.S. ports for compliance with U.S. safety and sanitation laws.

As just mentioned, directly reporting to the captain are the **chief officer** (called the staff captain on some lines), who is second in command and also the captain's deputy; the chief engineer, who is in charge of the ship's physical plant; the hotel director, who is in charge of hotel, guest services, housekeeping, and food and beverage; and the **environmental officer**, who is responsible for compliance with international and local environmental regulations. These people (and some members of their staffs) are officers and wear uniforms with appropriate stripes indicating their rank and department. To some extent, a cruise ship is a paramilitary organization. Rank, regulations, and discipline are taken very seriously. All officers have duties they must perform; otherwise, they are subject to discipline. Unlike hotel or restaurant employees on land, a cruise ship's officers and crew members cannot walk off the job or refuse to obey commands.

Hotel Director

Among the senior officers reporting to the captain, the **hotel director** has the largest staff (see Exhibit 10.2). The hotel director and the people working for them are directly responsible for creating the vacation experience that the cruise line offers. Today, many cruise ship hotel directors are recruited from land-based resorts. For example, both Carnival and Royal Caribbean recruit at schools of hospitality management for entry-level positions in their hotel divisions.

This job has some similarities to a general manager's job in a land-based hotel, but also many differences. One major difference is that there is no sales or marketing staff to supervise; another is that passengers do not have to check in (i.e., arrange for their length of stay and pay for their accommodations) onboard the ship: these functions are performed on shore. Besides being ultimately responsible for food and beverage services and housekeeping services, the hotel director may be responsible for medical care, entertainment, and shore excursions. In addition, there are casino operations, the beauty salon, the health spa, gift shops, photography services, and more to oversee. On some cruise lines, many of these services are concessions. For instance, cruise ship beauty salon and health spa services typically are provided by Steiner-Transocean, a London-based company. The large lines run their own food and beverage operations, but some of the smaller ones use outside caterers, known as ship's chandlers, to provide both the food and the personnel. In these cases, the hotel director is responsible only for housekeeping duties and planning social activities for passengers.

Just as the scope of their duties varies from cruise line to cruise line, some hotel directors are given more autonomy than others. There are vessels where virtually every decision is made on shore in advance or is relayed to the hotel director via email or satellite telephone when the ship is at sea.

Hotel directors on cruise ships typically spend four months at sea, followed by two months off. Many have families who occasionally join them on short cruises. Salaries are competitive with land-based jobs. Indeed, considering that for much of the year their housing, medical care, and food are supplied free of charge, hotel directors on cruise ships often fare better economically than their land-based counterparts.

Other Officers

Under the hotel director on most cruise ships are a purser, food and beverage manager, chief housekeeper, cruise director, and human resources manager. These positions will be explored in the following sections. On large, resort-style cruise ships such as Holland America's Vista Class, there are additional personnel reporting to the hotel director, including a controller, shore excursions manager, onboard marketing manager, and guest relations manager. The onboard marketing manager is responsible for all of the ship's concessions, including the casino. Note in Exhibit 10.2 that instead of a single food and beverage manager, the position's responsibilities have been divided into two positions, a culinary operations manager and a beverage manager. In a circumstance like this, all kitchen and dining room staff report to the culinary operations manager.

Exhibit 10.2   Hotel Department, Large Cruise Ship

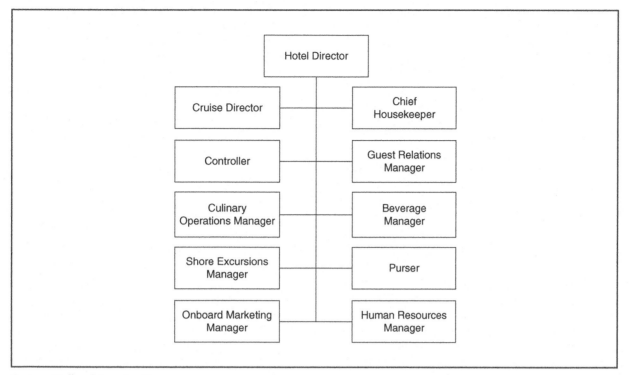

Source: Holland America Line.

Purser. One of the most important departments in the hotel division is the purser's office. The **purser** is the ship's banker, information officer, human resources director (except on larger ships), and complaint handler. The purser is also second in command of the hotel division and is in charge of the division whenever the hotel director is off the ship. The purser's office runs the ship's front office, including the management of guest accounts or folios, and clears the ship at foreign ports. In some ways, it is similar to the front office department of a hotel. What was traditionally called the "purser's desk" is now typically called guest services, guest relations, passenger services, or reception desk.

On some ships, the purser is responsible for revenue accounting; on other ships, however, that is an accounting function managed by a controller. The purser (and the controller, if the ship is large enough to justify such a position) reports to the hotel manager. Whether a purser or a controller performs the function, the system of revenue control is the same. All sales at outlets onboard the ship, such as dining rooms, bars, and shops, are captured on a point-of-sale system that interfaces with the ship's property management system and are recorded on the guests' folios.

Most cruise ships use a credit system to handle guest accounts. Checks and/or cash are not accepted for transactions onboard. After passengers board, they are asked to come to the purser's office and register their credit card (if they have not already done so before boarding the ship). All charges incurred on board are then billed to that card. If they do not have a credit card, they are asked for a cash deposit. When the deposit is used up, credit is cut off until another cash deposit is made. Ships do not accept checks because there is no feasible method for clearing them while at sea or in a foreign port. Technology makes it possible for the ships to issue an all-purpose, magnetic-coded card to each passenger that serves as identification, door key, and charge card. On some cruise lines, these cards also show the bearer's lifeboat assembly station, dining time, and table assignment, as well as serve as a security device to track who has gone ashore and returned. The advent of wearable technology, such as the Ocean Medallion being implemented by Carnival, allows cruisers to unlock their staterooms, swipe and pay, and even order food and drinks without the need to carry a magnetic-coded card.

The purser holds most of the money on the ship and acts as a central bank for the ship's cash needs at the front desk and for payroll and the casino. Passengers can convert their traveler's checks in the purser's office to get cash for duty-free shopping or for playing games of chance in the ship's casino. The purser provides currency exchange and makes change. The amount of cash a large ship carries can be substantial; more than $500,000 is not unusual.

The purser's staff also handles passenger problems like lost luggage and broken plumbing, as well as cabin upgrades (when they are available). The job is considered attractive. Living conditions are good, and pursers are allowed to mingle with passengers in specified public areas when they are off duty.

Food and Beverage Manager. Research shows that one of the most important components of every cruise, from the passenger's point of view, is the food. It is the thing people are most likely to remember and talk about. Over the years, cruises have built a reputation for serving very good food and a lot of it. It goes back to the early days of steamship travel when César Ritz designed a Ritz-Carlton restaurant for the Hamburg-Amerika Line. While food is included in the price of every cruise, beverages are not (except on the most luxurious of ships), and they are the largest single source of onboard revenue for all of the major lines. These two factors make the job of the **food and beverage manager** the linchpin of every successful cruise. In addition to feeding the passengers, the food and beverage department is also responsible for feeding the ship's crew members—a challenging task because they are onboard for months at a time, represent many different cultures and nationalities, have nowhere else to go, and must be satisfied if they are to satisfy guests.

Reporting to the food and beverage manager typically are the assistant food and beverage manager, executive chef, maître d' (dining room manager), bar manager, and provision master or storekeeper (see Exhibit 10.3).

Food and beverage managers who come from a hotel background describe their job as being very different on a cruise ship. Diderik Van Regemorter, a 15-year Marriott veteran who became a hotel manager with Holland America, makes these observations:

There is a tremendous difference between food and beverage services in a hotel and onboard a ship. The ship is a very closed environment. You live with the people you work with, so it's extremely important to develop good interpersonal skills. Also, the number of stripes you carry on your shoulders is very important. It makes a big difference in the amount of attention you get from others.

My responsibilities are also different. While I do all of the ordering as far as items and quantity, I don't get involved with the financial details. In a hotel, I had to control wages, overtime, and other costs, as well as generate income. I do have a consumption budget, but I don't worry about food costs. I don't even know what it costs to feed a passenger.

Serving tables on a cruise ship is very different from a hotel as well. The group being served stays the same for a whole week. This enables the waiter to develop a relationship with the guests and learn their preferences. After the first night, experienced servers remember whether guests like coffee, tea, or espresso, regular or decaffeinated, with or without sugar and cream. In a hotel, waiters have other concerns, such as handling cash and the number of people they have to serve at one time.

Another difference is the way we do our cooking. The majority of our galley crew are trained cooks. The levels and positions are different. We still use the traditional French culinary setup. We use a lot more labor, which in part accounts for the high quality of our food. We do everything from scratch. We bake our own bread daily. We make our stock from bones. We buy a whole hindquarter and cut it down. Nothing goes to waste. We don't have leftovers. We have a limited storage capacity and no trucks come by to take away what we don't use. We know exactly how many people are coming and what they will order. That's because even though we have a lot of choices, we serve the same menu on every cruise.

Our passengers expect quite a bit when it comes to food. They don't expect the same things they would have at home or even in an ordinary restaurant. I like to compare the food we serve daily to what you might order when you go to

Exhibit 10.3   Food and Beverage Department, Large Cruise Ship

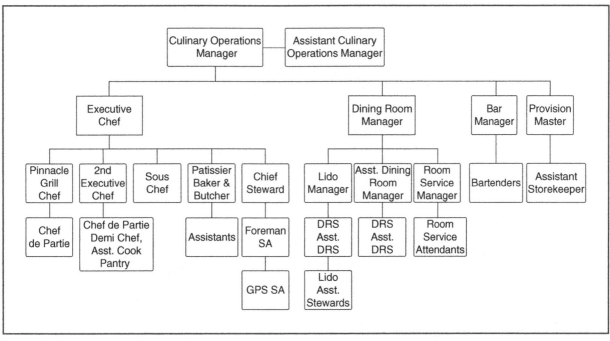

Source: Holland America Line.

that extraordinary restaurant for a special occasion. That's why lunch is four or five courses, and dinner six or seven. If you feel like eating lobster or rack of lamb, price is no consideration because you've already paid for it.

On land it's not possible to give 800 people a quality dining experience in an hour and forty minutes. But I have 107 people in our galley and they don't have to worry about what people are going to order or when to prepare it. All they have to worry about is taking orders from 108 waiters and cooking them individually. Having a ship that's consistently full removes a lot of uncertainty and allows us to produce really fine food and serve it in style.[9]

Several points that Van Regemorter makes are important to note. Safety, sanitation, and health are the most important considerations on any ship. This means that the **galley**, the shipboard equivalent of a kitchen, must be a highly disciplined operation. Everything must be done according to regulation; there can be no exception. There are many instances where one small error has caused hundreds to get sick.

As Van Regemorter points out, one of the ways this discipline is achieved, which is very different from in a hotel or restaurant on land, is that everyone is taking orders from a person who has not just economic power over them but legal power. Not obeying orders from an officer on a ship is a form of mutiny. In reality, everyone strives very hard to get along because it is not practical to quit in the middle of the ocean thousands of miles away from home! Food and beverage managers need even better people skills—including tact and diplomacy—than land-based food and beverage managers because they must work long hours with their employees every single day for months at a time.

Another important difference that should be noted, which was also alluded to by Van Regemorter, is that the food and beverage department on a ship has less direct involvement with food costs than a land-based resort. The cruise industry calculates its costs very carefully, but this is done by managers in cruise line offices on shore. Computer perpetual inventory systems provide a very detailed analysis of the food and beverage items consumed aboard ship, together with a daily food cost expressed in dollars per passenger day. Management expects the ship's food staff to be only generally aware of these daily costs but to respond to them, if necessary, so that both guest satisfaction and corporate financial targets are maintained.

RCL's *Symphony of the Seas* feeds around 6,600 passengers and 2,200 crew on a typical seven-day itinerary. This requires about 60,000 eggs; 9,700 pounds of chicken; 20,000 pounds of potatoes; and 700 pounds of ice cream. In addition, 450 cases of champagne are brought onboard at the start of each cruise. This kind of consumption and the resulting cost savings through bulk purchasing are only possible because cruise lines standardize menus on their ships whenever possible. To facilitate this, cruise lines typically build several ships of the same size and class, which allows them to have similar galleys and passenger counts. Predictable demographics and ship itineraries make accurate forecasting possible. Royal Caribbean knows that when its ships put escargot on the French evening menu, which occurs on the fifth night out, 22 percent of the 1,800 passengers on each ship will most likely order it. Standardization is everything.

Because of its limited shelf life and storage temperature constraints, provisioning fresh produce is a major activity for cruise ships. At each port, the logistics of provisioning must be conducted like clockwork. The ship's inventory

From fine dining to breakfast buffets, cruise ships offer an array of culinary experiences.

compliance officer, the food and beverage manager, the provision master, and the chef and storekeepers all play a role to ensure that the supplies and produce they receive meet the cruise operator's standards. Just as important as provisioning is waste management. All major cruise lines go to great lengths to highlight their waste mitigation efforts. Carnival Corporation installed nearly 600 food waste biodigesters across its fleet as part of its overall commitment to environmental compliance. These biodigesters use a natural aerobic digestion process to efficiently break down food waste by utilizing a mix of beneficial microorganisms, enabling the systems to process anything that can be consumed by humans.

Serving is another very different matter on a cruise ship. The problem is time. Except for the smaller luxury ships, no cruise vessel today has enough main dining room seats to handle more than half of its passengers at the same time. While two dinner **sittings**—a sitting is the time allotted for serving one complete meal to a group of diners—was the former standard (and still is on some ships), today's lifestyles demand a more flexible approach to dinner. For example, Carnival offers four sittings in its main dining room; Norwegian Cruise Line lets passengers dine anytime during an extended time period between 5:30 p.m. and 10 p.m. Almost all cruise lines are including daytime dining options.

On the dinner menu of every cruise line, there is always a choice of four or five appetizers, a couple of soups and different salads, four or five entrées, and several desserts. (It is, in fact, this abundant choice that helps create the feeling of fine dining as opposed to banquet service.) Many people order wine as well. Because the dining experience is such an important part of a cruise vacation, passengers must not feel that they are being rushed or receiving banquet-style service. On the contrary, most cruise passengers expect their server to know them by name, be aware of their preferences, discuss each menu item with them, and exchange a menu item for another if it does not meet their expectations. Since the server's compensation comes almost entirely from tips, it is important that they meet or exceed passenger expectations. The average food server's base salary is less than $100 monthly plus room, board, and medical services. But their tips (on the major lines, passengers tip an average of $3 to $4 per person, per day, in the dining room and to

cabin stewards) make it possible to bring home compensation of $24,000 per year—tax-free in most cases and with virtually no expenses.

The cruise lines use many strategies to turn the tables in their dining rooms without making passengers feel rushed. For instance, there are typically two live shows each evening in the ship's main auditorium. There are more live shows in the alternate auditorium and sometimes a midnight performance as well. Passengers who want a good seat for a show—or a movie—leave the dining room promptly after dinner. Movie theaters showing first-run productions are a staple of some ships. Holland America's movie theaters on its newest ships (e.g., the *Amsterdam*) are especially luxurious and match most theaters that you are likely to find on land.

To respond to the demand of passengers who do not want to eat at specified times, many ships offer specialty restaurants in addition to their main dining rooms. For example, Crystal Cruises offers two or more alternative dining venues on its ships. On Carnival cruises, passengers can pay a nominal charge, from $15 per person, to dine in one of their specialty restaurants. Reservations are still required, but there is more flexibility. The ships of some other cruise companies have opened up their lido deck dining area for informal dining at night, in addition to its normal operating times during the day. (The **lido deck** is the deck on which the ship's main swimming pool is located.) Some ships have 24-hour pizzerias. The dining concept embraced by most major lines is that passengers should be able to eat when they want, where they want, and with whom they want rather than at fixed times and fixed tables.

Just as the passengers need to be fed at all hours, so do the officers and crew. Dining facilities are usually open for them many hours of the day, with cooks on duty.

Finally, students should understand that as important as the food is to the passengers, beverages are even more important to the cruise lines. Beverages are the single largest source of onboard revenue on major mass-market cruise lines. As a rule, ships generate more bottom-line profit selling drinks than they do in their casinos or shops. For this reason, drinks are served in almost every part of the ship at any time when an area is likely to be in use. Moreover, drinks often must be served promptly because passengers are on some kind of schedule, wanting cocktails before dinner or a drink before a show starts, for example.

The lido deck is the deck on which the ship's main swimming pool is located.

This level of service requires a substantial commitment of well-trained personnel who can mix and serve a large number of drinks fairly rapidly. This staff must be well supervised.

Chief Housekeeper. The **chief housekeeper** (also called the chief steward) runs a department that is very similar to the housekeeping department of any hotel (see Exhibit 10.4). The chief housekeeper's staff is responsible for the cleaning and general maintenance of all cabins and interior areas on the ship. The staff controls a large inventory of bed and bath linens, soaps and other bathroom amenities for passengers, and cleaning supplies and chemicals. (A perpetual inventory is used to track most of these operating supplies.) The department staff is also responsible for passenger laundry and dry cleaning, as well as cleaning all cabin linens, table linens, towels, and the crew's uniforms. The housekeeping department's cabin stewards are also responsible for cabin foodservice, and for loading and unloading luggage and delivering it to passengers' cabins.

The most important difference between housekeeping on shore versus at sea is that guests in hotels rarely interact on a regular basis with the persons who clean their rooms; on ships, they always do. Cabins on a ship are serviced twice a day—generally while passengers are having breakfast and again while they are at dinner. In addition, cabin stewards are on duty a good part of the morning and evening (70 hours per week is

normal for this position) and assist passengers with other matters such as lifeboat drills, wheelchairs, and pressing clothes for the captain's party for those passengers who request it. Like the ship's food servers, cabin stewards depend largely on tips for their compensation, so they learn their guests' names and generally find as many ways as they can to be helpful. Good cabin stewards can be crucial to a guest's total cruise experience.

The busiest day for the housekeeping department is **turnaround day**. This is the day a ship finishes a cruise and starts another one. A typical 70,000-ton vessel may have 600 or more cabins, with an average of two people in each cabin. Each cabin may have two to three pieces of luggage. That's 2,400 to 3,600 pieces of luggage to be unloaded and loaded in a single day! Moreover, departing passengers are usually off the ship between 9 and 10 a.m., and new passengers begin to arrive by noon. The ship often sails by 5 p.m. That means that all of the ship's cabins must be completely cleaned, the linens changed, and all major lounges and other public spaces vacuumed and polished—all in three or four hours.

Cruise Director. The **cruise director** and their staff are among the most visible crew members on board from the passengers' point of view (see Exhibit 10.5). Members of this department are the entertainers, musicians, and children's counselors, and they direct all of the entertainment activities.

An important part of the cruise staff's job is to sell and coordinate the shore excursions.

Exhibit 10.4   Housekeeping Department, Large Cruise Ship

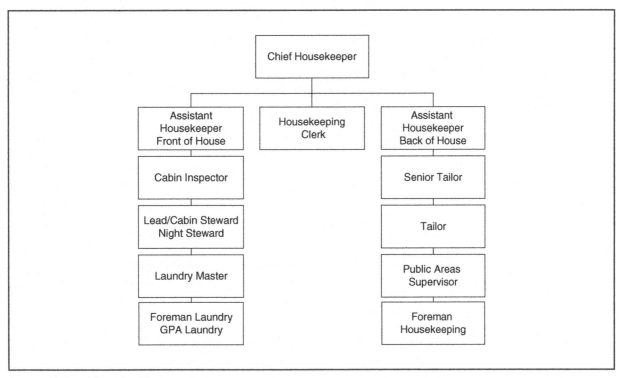

Source: Holland America Line.

Exhibit 10.5   Cruise Director's Staff, Large Cruise Ship

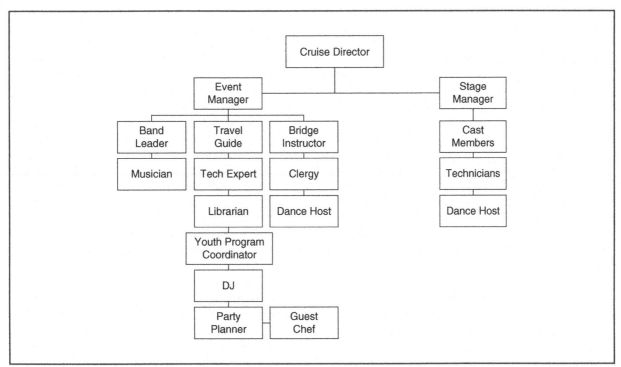

Source: Holland America Line.

Shore excursions are specially arranged trips, tours, and activities that occur off the ship and a significant part of onboard revenue for any cruise line. In Alaska, passengers can go whitewater rafting, walk on or fly over glaciers, and attend salmon bakes. In the Caribbean, there are snorkeling expeditions, beaches, tours of old sugar plantations, Mayan ruins, rainforests and volcanoes, and opportunities to play golf, visit nightclubs, shop, and more. In Europe, there are tours to the Acropolis in Athens, gondola rides in Venice, and visits to Pompeii in Naples. Typically, these tours are contracted from local tour operators. They are sold in advance on the ship so that when it arrives in port, a sufficient number of tour buses and guides are available for each activity. It is important that tours run as scheduled since ships spend a limited amount of time in port. This can be a logistical problem when you are handling five or six different tours for more than 1,000 passengers.

Before a ship arrives in port, a member of the cruise staff usually gives a destination-and-shopping talk in one of the ship's auditoriums. All of the large cruise lines recommend certain onshore shops whose merchandise they know to be fairly priced and reliable. These shops pay a promotional fee to the cruise line, in return for which their location and merchandise are promoted by the line. Often the cruise line guarantees that if there is any problem with a purchase and the shop will not make an adjustment, the line itself will.

Another important duty of the cruise staff is to prepare the daily activity calendar. The ship publishes a daily schedule for all passengers; it is distributed to their cabins the night before. If the ship is going to be in port, the schedule shows its arrival and departure times, tour departure times, when and where the ship's meals will be served, what onboard activities will be available, library hours, the times movies will be shown, and other information of interest to passengers. When the ship has a day at sea, the cruise staff usually is very busy running a myriad of activities. There are aerobic classes; bingo games; tennis tournaments; dance lessons; carved-ice and cooking demonstrations; talks on such topics as personal finance, popular health, or the history and politics of the region where the ship is sailing; art auctions; bridge lessons; and more. All of these activities must be scheduled, promoted, and run by the cruise department.

Finally, the cruise director is responsible for monitoring the quality of the live shows and other entertainment offered nightly to passengers. The revues and other acts are cast, rehearsed, and produced by people outside the cruise department; in most instances they are the work of independent producers and agents. Carnival Cruise Lines is an exception; it produces and stages all of its own entertainment. Royal Caribbean produces some of its own entertainment and subcontracts the rest. In some cases, the cruise director or a member of the cruise staff acts as master of ceremonies. The cruise director is also responsible for providing feedback to the home office concerning audience reaction. Obviously, the demographics of the passengers, which vary by season and itinerary, affect the suitability of the entertainment.

Human Resources Manager. The human resources function of recruiting and hiring staff is done by land-based, not shipboard, human resources (HR) personnel. Background checks, medical exams, and visa requests must be done before a crew member is hired and placed with a ship. Land-based HR staff must arrange for getting the newly hired crew members to their ship assignments, which could be thousands of miles from the ship line's home base. Once the crew is aboard, the ship's human resources manager is responsible for ongoing training and crew welfare. Recreation and educational programs are necessary to occupy crew members during their free time. Members of the crew are allowed to charge purchases they make onboard ship and, accordingly, folios must be established for them. This is another responsibility of the ship's HR department.

Physician. In the hotel business, when guests get sick, a doctor is called in; if guests need further medical attention, they are rushed to a hospital. Since this is not possible on a ship at sea, all cruise ships carry a **physician** and at least one nurse.

The nature of the business makes this a critical position on any ship. Despite the fact that the age of the average cruise passenger is dropping, cruise ships get a good number of older passengers and passengers with disabilities. *Symphony of the Seas* has 46 cabins that accommodate passengers with disabilities, *Carnival Destiny* has 25 cabins, and Holland America's *Rotterdam VI* has 23. All modern cruise ships are completely accessible, which also makes them attractive for older passengers or those with arthritis or other mobility issues. Considering that cruise ships are not yet subject to the Americans with Disabilities Act because they sail under **flags of convenience**, they appear to be way ahead of the hotel industry in this matter. The reasons for this are simple: 61 million Americans (27.2 percent) reported having some kind of disability in 2021 and accommodating them is a sound marketing strategy. Moreover, it's the right thing to do. Princess has created the Love Boat Access Program, which includes a brochure highlighting accessible features on each ship, many of which were suggested by passengers. These features include wheelchair gangways, Braille elevator buttons, phone amplifiers, and visual smoke detectors. Princess also developed tenders (launches that run between the ship and shore) that are designed to board wheelchairs, as well as gangway crawlers that carry people in wheelchairs and others who find ascending steep stairways difficult. Most ships accommodate service animals for guests with visual impairments.

To assist the physician, modern cruise ships are equipped with state-of-the-art medical centers. Physicians onboard ships have emergency room training, and their equipment includes cardiac defibrillators, x-ray machines, operating tables, hospital beds, and enough prescription drugs to stock a small pharmacy. Consequently, the lead nurse is responsible for a perpetual inventory system to control the drugs. The object of onboard medical care is to treat minor injuries and stabilize major medical conditions until patients can be evacuated. The most common injuries among elderly passengers are falls, caused by their limited mobility and balance issues on a moving vessel. Other common ailments among passengers and crew members are motion sickness and hangovers, urinary tract infections, ear infections, and allergies. Operators do not like to talk about it, but ships have morgues as well.

Princess's former fleet medical officer, Dr. Allister Smith, points out that, statistically speaking, only 3 percent of passengers may become critically ill, and his medical staff treats more crew members than passengers. Smith says practicing medicine at sea is not the same as onshore:

> Time, which is one of the main tools doctors use, is taken away from you at sea. If a patient has certain symptoms ashore, you can wait and see what happens. But with a passenger, if the ship is in port and the patient perhaps seriously ill, a decision must be made on the spot to put him ashore.

Flags of Convenience

The laws under which a cruise ship operates depend on where it is registered. The choice of country depends on many factors, including the financing of the vessel, the cost of operation, or the route the vessel sails. The flag-of-convenience tradition dates back to the early days of naval warfare, when merchant ships—to avoid being attacked—carried the flag of a neutral nation, thus protecting their passengers and cargo from the ravages of war.

Staffing considerations play an important part in the decision about which country's flag a cruise ship will sail under. Many countries, including the United States, Norway, and Britain, have strict regulations concerning unionized labor that tend to create a high labor cost for cruise lines. Countries such as Panama, Liberia, Bermuda, and the Bahamas do not have such laws, so many cruise ships are registered there.

Unions are not the only issue. Some countries require that a large proportion of the crew serving on a cruise ship flying their flag must be citizens. For example, the United States requires that all cruise ships registered as U.S. ships must employ only officers licensed in the United States, and three-quarters of the unlicensed crew must be U.S. citizens. Cruise lines do not like to operate with these types of labor restrictions because they wish to recruit from various countries to find the best people for the job. The British, Italians, Greeks, Dutch, and Norwegians are known for their nautical skills and rigorous training, for example. Similarly, French, German, and Austrian foodservice personnel are in high demand. Major cruise lines recruit from all of these groups; therefore, their ships have a truly international crew that would be impossible to achieve if they flew the flags of countries with restrictive labor laws.

Environment, Health, Safety, and Security

All of the major cruise lines have policies and procedures to protect the environment and to ensure the health, safety, and security of passengers and crew. The cruise industry has been focusing on its commitment to a cleaner, more sustainable future by investing in ships with new technologies and cleaner fuels, such as liquified natural gas, in order to reduce carbon emissions. Fourteen ports worldwide currently offer cruise ships the ability to plug in and turn off their engines. Advanced water treatment systems are built into 99 percent of all new ships on order, bringing global capacity served by these systems to 78.5 percent.[10] Carnival, for example, has a maritime policy and compliance group that deals with these issues, develops standards, and shares best practices with all of their brands. International, national, and local regulations set many of the standards to protect the environment in matters related to the discharge of black water (sewage) and gray water (shower and sink water), disposal of garbage, air emissions, and oily discharge.

Cruise ships carrying thousands of passengers and crew must be concerned about spreading sickness. Today, hand-sanitizer dispensers are placed at the beginning of buffet lines on most cruise ships. Reminders are posted throughout a ship advising crew and passengers to wash their hands often, especially after using the lavatory. In order to minimize slips and falls, warning notices are placed throughout ships, calling attention to steps and wet decks. On all Carnival ships, U.S. standards are followed for food handling, storage, and preparation, and the maintenance of kitchen equipment. Fire prevention and the capability to extinguish any fire that might occur is a major concern for all cruise lines. Accordingly, smoking policies are strictly enforced and fire extinguishing equipment checked on a regular basis.

The cruise lines are responsible for passenger and crew security while they are onboard, but security issues may also arise when passengers are at a port-of-call. Procedures are set to deal with any threats that may arise at a port or at sea. All Carnival brands, for example, have an emergency response system in place to deal with a variety of safety and security issues.

Knowledge Check

1. What are the main responsibilities of a cruise ship captain? What are the main responsibilities of a cruise ship's hotel director?

2. What are the food and beverage manager's responsibilities? What are the chief housekeeper's responsibilities?

CHAPTER SUMMARY

The cruise industry has experienced impressive growth since 1970, when it was estimated that just 500,000 people took a cruise each year; today, that number has increased to almost 30 million. The passenger services aboard cruise ships are managed by hotel directors, pursers, food and beverage managers, chief housekeepers, cruise directors, and human resources managers, many of whom come from fine hotels and hospitality schools. Only 20 percent of Americans have ever taken a cruise.

The first person to take a cruise and write about it was the English novelist William Makepeace Thackeray on the P&O to Greece, the Holy Land, and Egypt. The first U.S.-origin cruise was probably the 1867 voyage of the paddle wheel steamer *Quaker City*, with an itinerary similar to Thackeray's cruise, except that it started from New York. Among the passengers was the American writer Mark Twain, who chronicled his adventures in *The Innocents Abroad*.

From the time of the *Quaker City* to the late 1950s, far more people crossed the Atlantic from necessity than for pleasure. This was the period of massive immigration to the United States, and travel conditions for most passengers crossing the Atlantic were miserable. Even for those traveling first class, the trip was often uncomfortable because voyages were long and there were no ports to stop at.

Up to World War II, the major steamship lines were owned by European interests. When the war started, almost all of the vessels were converted into troop ships or stayed in port. This situation continued until 1945, when the rebuilding of Europe spurred a growing demand for ocean liners. For the first time, the United States recognized that it might need its own troop ships and subsidized the building and operation of new vessels. The *United States*, launched in 1951, was designed to be the fastest ship of its size afloat.

The postwar boom marked the last days of the great steamship liners. Besides the *United States* and *Queen Mary*, there were the *Queen Elizabeth*, the French Line's *France*, Holland America's *Rotterdam*, and a host of sleek Italian liners built for warm-water cruising in the Mediterranean.

The cruise world started to come apart in 1958, when Pan American World Airways offered its first nonstop, transatlantic crossing on a Boeing 707 jet. Ocean-going passenger ships were effectively out of business as a means of transportation.

Modern cruising was born in the 1960s and 1970s with the formation of Norwegian Caribbean Line, Royal Caribbean Cruise Lines, Princess Cruise Lines, and Carnival Cruise Lines. Carnival's strategy of focusing on the cruise ships themselves as the center of the cruise vacation experience changed consumers' perception of cruising from a stodgy pastime for the rich to a fun vacation for the masses. This marketing innovation was probably the defining event in the development of the modern cruise industry.

Cruise lines are divided into four market segments by the Cruise Lines International Association: contemporary/value, premium, luxury, and specialty. The average cruise passenger is 47 years old, cruises an average of seven days, and spends an average of $750 in port cities over the course of the cruise.

Today's cruise ships are floating vacation resorts. In some ways, they are very similar to hotels in how they are organized. At the top is the captain, who is responsible for the ship's operation and the safety of all those onboard. Four people typically report directly to the captain: the chief officer, the chief engineer, the hotel director, and the environmental officer. The hotel director is in charge of the ship's hotel division and oversees a purser, food and beverage manager, chief housekeeper, cruise director, human resources manager, physician, and sometimes the heads of other smaller departments and concessions. Besides being ultimately responsible for food and beverage services and cabin services, the hotel director may also be responsible for entertainment and shore excursions.

The purser is the ship's banker, information officer, human resources director (on small cruise ships), and complaint handler. The purser is second in command of the hotel division.

The food and beverage manager oversees the assistant food and beverage manager, executive chef, maître d', bar manager, and provision master. Because of safety and sanitation requirements—as well as passenger expectations—food and beverage operations on cruise ships are highly disciplined operations. Beverages are the single largest source of onboard revenue on every major cruise ship.

The chief housekeeper is responsible for the cleaning and general maintenance of all cabins and interior areas of the ship. The housekeeping department also takes care of passenger laundry and dry cleaning, as well as cleaning all cabin linens, table linens, towels, and the crew's uniforms. The busiest day for the housekeeping department is turnaround day, when the ship finishes a cruise and starts another.

The cruise director's staff directs all guest activities and includes entertainers, musicians, and children's counselors. They also sell and coordinate shore excursions and prepare the daily activity calendar.

The human resources manager is responsible for the crew's welfare and ongoing training. This manager is responsible for the recreation and educational programs necessary to occupy crew members during their free time.

Modern cruise lines pay a great deal of attention to medical care. All ships carry at least one physician and a nurse. The physician typically has a state-of-the-art medical center onboard with which to treat patients. Devotion to accessibility makes cruise ships attractive vacations for older people and people with disabilities.

captain—The person on a cruise ship who is responsible for its operation and the safety of all those onboard. The captain sees that all company policies and rules, as well as national and international laws, are followed.

chief housekeeper—The person on a cruise ship who is responsible for the cleaning and general maintenance of all cabins and interior areas on the ship. The chief housekeeper is also responsible for passenger laundry and dry cleaning, as well as cleaning cabin linen and table linen, towels, and the crew's uniforms. Also called the chief steward.

chief officer—The captain's second in command and deputy. Also called the staff captain on some cruise lines.

cruise director—Oversees a staff responsible for managing a ship's entertainers, children's counselors, and guest activities, including selling and coordinating shore excursions.

environmental officer—Responsible for compliance with international and local environmental regulations.

flags of convenience—Refers to the practice of registering ships in a country other than that of ownership or the country where the ship's operators and crew are based. This practice allows shipowners to take advantage of certain benefits and lower costs associated with the chosen flag state's maritime regulations and tax laws.

food and beverage manager—The person on a cruise ship who is responsible for providing quality food and beverage service to passengers and crew members; they typically report to the hotel manager.

galley—The shipboard equivalent of a kitchen.

hotel director—The person on a cruise ship who runs the hotel division. Besides being ultimately responsible for food and beverage services and housekeeping services, the hotel manager may oversee medical care, entertainment, shore excursions, casino operations, the beauty salon, the health spa, gift shops, photography services, and more—in short, everything that helps create the vacation experience that the cruise line offers.

lido deck—The deck that contains a cruise ship's main swimming pool. It is usually a center for many onboard activities.

physician—The person on a cruise ship who is responsible for the medical care of passengers and crew members; they typically have a state-of-the-art medical facility in which to work and one or more nurses to assist in the care of patients.

purser—The second in command within the hotel department and a cruise ship's banker, information officer, human resources director, and complaint handler.

shore excursions—Specially arranged trips, tours, and activities that occur off the ship. They are a significant part of onboard revenue for any cruise line.

sitting—The time allotted for serving one complete meal to a group of diners.

ton—A unit for measuring the total cubic capacity of a cruise ship.

turnaround day—The day when a cruise ship finishes one cruise and starts another.

REVIEW QUESTIONS

1. What attracted passengers to cruising in the 1920s?
   a. Interest in Europe and escape from Prohibition
   b. Mass interest in fun, affordable vacations
   c. Interest in river cruising
   d. Interest in the Bahamas

2. What is now the world's largest cruise line?
   a. Royal Caribbean International
   b. Norwegian Cruise Line
   c. Carnival Cruise Line
   d. Disney Cruise Line

3. What is the average age of cruise passengers?
   a. 39
   b. 47
   c. 53
   d. 62

4. What are the main responsibilities of a cruise ship's captain?
   a. The operation of the ship's front office
   b. The operation of the ship's physical plant
   c. The operation of the ship and the safety of passengers
   d. Compliance with international and environmental regulations

5. What is one way the duties of a cruise hotel director are different from those of a general manager at a land-based hotel?
   a. A cruise hotel director does not oversee food and beverage.
   b. A cruise hotel director does not oversee a marketing staff.
   c. A cruise hotel director does not oversee guest relations.
   d. A cruise hotel director does not oversee housekeeping.

6. What U.S. government organizations inspect cruise ships sailing to and from U.S. ports?
   a. Citizenship and Immigration Services and Environmental Protection Agency
   b. Food and Drug Administration and Department of Agriculture
   c. Coast Guard and Centers for Disease Control and Prevention
   d. Department of Homeland Security and Border Patrol

7. What are the responsibilities of a cruise ship's purser?
   a. Prepares the daily activity calendar and oversees entertainment
   b. Acts as the central bank of the ship and handles complaints
   c. Recruits and hires staff
   d. Feeds guests and staff

8. Which position is responsible for compliance with international and local environmental regulations?
   a. Environmental officer
   b. Cruise director
   c. Chief officer
   d. Captain

9. What area of a cruise ship is the galley?
   a. Captain's office
   b. Main dining room
   c. Main kitchen
   d. Main deck

10. Which employee is most visible on a cruise ship?
    a. Captain
    b. Purser
    c. Cruise director
    d. Executive chef

11. Why have cruise lines made ships more physically accessible?
    a. They want to appeal to older guests and guests with disabilities.
    b. They must comply with the Americans with Disabilities Act.
    c. They must comply with international laws.
    d. They have received too many complaints.

12. To whom does a cruise director report?
    a. Captain
    b. Chief officer
    c. Hotel director
    d. Chief engineer

SHORT-ANSWER QUESTIONS

1. Why is cruise food and beverage service so important, and how is it different from hotel food and beverage service?

2. What has the cruise industry done to become more sustainable?

CASE STUDY

ENHANCEMENT OF THE SEAS

Breezeway Cruises is a pioneer of small-ship, ultra-luxury cruising. It continues to be a leader in this unique style of travel. Its intimate, all-suite ships, which carry between 458 and 600 guests each, sail to the world's most desirable destinations at peak seasons. On board, guests are served by an award-winning crew, handpicked and extensively trained to deliver Breezeway's signature style of thoughtful and personalized hospitality. Breezeway's ships attract accomplished people who enjoy traveling well and sharing fun and adventure with other interesting people. Many of them have found the Breezeway cruise experience to be their preferred method of travel and return regularly to sail with the cruise line.

A problem facing Breezeway is that the company has done the bare minimum to comply with environmental regulations (and has at times violated them). This is important, since cruise ships can leave a large ecological footprint. Additionally, it has not adequately prepared for a new strain of flu that has been affecting some cruise lines this season.

DISCUSSION QUESTIONS

1. What have been some key success factors for Breezeway?

2. What are some potential problems Breezeway could face?

3. How could Breezeway improve its environmental and safety practices?

Arnold Donald

Arnold Donald is the former vice-chair of Carnival Corporation & PLC, the world's largest cruise company, which comprises nine renowned cruise brands: Carnival Cruise Line, Holland America, Princess, Seabourn, AIDA, Costa, Cunard, P&O UK, and P&O Australia.

In addition to his role at Carnival, Donald holds positions on the boards of Bank of America Corporation; Salesforce, Inc.; MP Materials; and Foster Farms. He has also been appointed chair of the World Travel and Tourism Council, a distinguished organization that represents the global travel and tourism industry, while advocating for the positive economic impact of travel and tourism worldwide.

Donald's impressive career includes over two decades at Monsanto Company, where he served as corporate senior vice president and held the positions of president in both the consumer and nutrition sector and the agricultural sector. Following his time at Monsanto, he assumed the role of chairperson at Merisant, a company known for its leading global sweetener brands, Equal and Canderel.

Before his tenure as CEO at Carnival began in 2013, Donald held prominent leadership positions as president and CEO of the Executive Leadership Council, a professional network and leadership forum for African American executives of Fortune 500 companies, as well as president and CEO of the Juvenile Diabetes Research Foundation International.

A native of New Orleans, Donald holds a Bachelor of Arts degree from Carleton College, a Bachelor of Science degree in mechanical engineering from Washington University in St. Louis, and a master's degree in business administration from the University of Chicago Graduate School of Business.

Currently, Donald actively serves on the boards of several nonprofits, including Tulane University, Carleton College, and Washington University. He has previously served on boards of the Greater New Orleans Foundation; St. Louis-based BJC Healthcare; and Crown Holdings, Inc.

WHAT WOULD YOU DO?

There are many job opportunities on board a cruise ship, from hotel director to purser to cruise director. However, the hours are long (wait staff often work up to 70 hours per week), there are no days off, you are on call 24/7, the food is not the same for guests and crew members, and you are committing to a six-month contract at sea. You are also likely to share a cabin unless you are fortunate to hold an officer position. Yet, working on cruise ships has its benefits. What are some of the most desired perks, and what kind of skills do you need?

11

GAMING AND
CASINO HOTELS

Chapter Outline

Learning Objectives

1. Summarize the history of gaming around the world and in the United States, describe casino hotels, and explain differences between the organization and management of casino hotels and other types of hotels. (pp. 316–324)

2. Describe casino operations, including casino games, terminology, employees, customers, marketing, and controls and regulation. (pp. 324–330)

KEY TERMS

cashier's cage

credit slip

croupier

drop box

fill slip

floor people

grind players

high-end players

hold percentage

junkets

markers

pit

pit boss

slots drop

slots hold

slot machines

table drop

table games

table win

This chapter is about gambling, or *gaming*, which is what it has come to be called in the industry; the two words are interchangeable. For the most part, the focus will be on gaming within hotels, although freestanding casinos, riverboat gambling, offshore gaming junkets, and Internet gambling are proliferating. The chapter will start with a brief history of gaming and then look at casino hotels—including the games that are played there, who plays them, and who conducts them. It concludes with a discussion of how casinos with hotels and other non-gaming amenities are marketed, controlled, and regulated.

11.1 THE STORY OF GAMING

No one knows when gambling first started. The first recorded accounts date back to early Chinese dynasties in 2300 BC. Some of the earliest pieces of gaming evidence come from ancient Egypt; dice have been found by archeologists in pyramid excavations. It appears that gamblers back then faced the same problems that they do today. People who couldn't pay their gambling losses were punished and made to work off their debts. Ancient Greeks considered gambling immoral, but it occurred anyway; historians relate that Greek soldiers played dice before the offensive against Troy. Both the Old and New Testaments mention gambling. Indeed, Roman centurions gambled for Christ's robes at his crucifixion. While there were laws barring gambling during the early period of the Roman Empire, gambling was later embraced and became a popular diversion for Roman citizens. Romans enthusiastically bet on gladiators, lions against Christians, chariot races, and other sports held in venues like the Colosseum.

After the Crusades (circa AD 1100–1300), gambling spread throughout Europe. In fact, games that evolved into dice games, roulette, and blackjack had their roots in medieval times. Craps, for instance, began as a game called "hazard" that English knights played. By the seventeenth century, forms of roulette and blackjack were popular in Europe.

The elegant casinos of Baden-Baden, Germany, and Monaco in Monte Carlo were built in the mid-nineteenth century and became favorites of European royalty and the aristocracy. Gambling was legalized in Britain in the 1960s to assist churches in collecting funds. Today, there are 9,362 gambling properties in 161 countries, including the United States, China (Macau), South Africa, France, Colombia, and 18 Caribbean countries. In recent years, online gambling has grown to over 4,000 sites.[1] Casinos are owned by a variety of entities, including individuals, corporations, tribes, and governments. The ownership structure of a casino varies depending on the location, regulations, and type of casino.

Gaming in the United States

Following the discovery of the New World, Spanish and Portuguese sailors brought dice and cards with them on the first expeditions; in leisure moments, they raced their horses, wagering on the results. Native Americans shaped their own dice from fruit pits and joined in the games.

Early American colonists developed a taste for gambling as well. It was one way, for example, to finance the Revolutionary War. They justified their popular lotteries by using the money raised to fund other worthy causes, such as municipal projects and colleges and universities. Columbia, Dartmouth, Harvard, and Yale were all partially funded by lotteries. Card games, too, were widely played.

By the early nineteenth century, some places in the United States had established reputations as favorite gambling destinations. The most prominent of these was New Orleans, conveniently situated on the Mississippi River and a major port. By 1810 the city was said to have as many gambling halls as the four largest American cities put together. But gambling attracted criminals as well as average citizens. Riverboats were known to be home to card sharps and professional gamblers, and there were many instances of travelers being cheated out of all their money.

Prior to 1861 and the start of the Civil War, there was a move to prohibit gambling in most states. In the latter part of the nineteenth century, lotteries were outlawed by the federal government. However, other forms of gambling continued to survive in a few places, including on riverboats on the Ohio and Mississippi rivers and in the states that were on those rivers.

Gaming in Nevada and New Jersey. By the early twentieth century, gambling had become illegal in most states. Even Nevada, which had allowed it since 1868, outlawed it in all forms in

1910. But in 1931, during the Great Depression, Nevada's legislature decided to revive gaming as a means to economic recovery. Almost all forms of gambling were again permitted.

The first Nevada casinos were mostly converted stores, but by 1935 clubs began to appear, first in Reno and later in Las Vegas. In 1946, the Flamingo Hotel and Casino opened—the first elegant casino hotel that included entertainment. Opening night featured a bevy of Hollywood movie stars as performers and guests. They would return regularly, giving Las Vegas a reputation as a glamorous vacation spot. With the opening of The Mirage Hotel & Casino Resort in 1989, the era of the mega-destination resort began. The Mirage cost $630 million and was the most expensive casino hotel to be built anywhere in the world up to that time. Other mega-hotels would follow, and today Las Vegas is the home of 25 of the 50 largest hotels in the world, each of them a casino hotel located on the Las Vegas Strip. The largest is the Venetian Resort, which comprises the Venetian and the Palazzo Towers; with 7,092 rooms; 2.2 million square feet of meeting and exhibit space; more than 40 restaurants; and more than 60 retail shops. These two properties were formerly owned by Las Vegas Sands Corporation, which sold them in 2021 to focus its attention internationally.

Caesars Entertainment is one of the largest casino companies in the world, with 65 casinos in the United States and casino interests on four continents.[2] In addition to operating casino hotels in Las Vegas under the Harrah's name, the company runs Caesars Palace, Paris Las Vegas, Rio, and Bally's. In 2020, Caesars Entertainment merged with Eldorado Resorts, Inc., creating the largest casino and gaming company in the United States.[3] The MGM Mirage Company has the largest number of casino hotels in Las Vegas, including four of the world's largest hotels: the MGM Grand, the Mandalay Bay, ARIA Resort & Casino, and the Bellagio. Exhibit 11.1 shows the leading casino companies worldwide by revenue.

In 1976, legalized casino gambling was allowed in depressed Atlantic City, New Jersey, mainly for many of the same economic reasons that had appealed to Nevada. The first casino hotel in Atlantic City was created by Resorts International (which had already developed Paradise Island in the Bahamas).

A more recent addition to the gaming industry in the United States is the Racino, a pari-mutuel racetrack with a casino. This concept started in West Virginia in 1990 and has now spread to 15 states. Initially, only slot machines were allowed, but table games have been gradually added in some states.

Today, gambling in one form or another is permitted almost everywhere in the United States. Hawaii and Utah are the only two states that prohibit all forms of gambling.

Riverboat and Offshore Gambling. By 1997, six states had legalized riverboat gambling, giving it a firm foothold. Laws concerning these gambling operations, however, vary considerably. For example, in Iowa the boats are required to leave the shore and take gamblers on cruises. In Illinois, cruises last for approximately two hours. In Mississippi, the boats are not allowed to leave the dock and guests can gamble as long as they wish. Some major hospitality companies have taken an interest in riverboat gambling operations.

In coastal states such as Florida, Georgia, and Texas, offshore gambling is gaining in popularity. Large tour boats and even a few small, obsolete

Exhibit 11.1 Leading Casino Companies Worldwide

Casino	Leading Casino Companies Worldwide Revenue/Billions
MGM Resorts International	$12.55
Caesars Entertainment, Inc.	10.59
Flutter Entertainment	7.66
PENN Entertainment, Inc.	6.4
Entain	5.0

Source: James Hall, "Leading Casino Companies by Revenue 2022," Casino Tops Online, https://www.casinotopsonline.com/casino-news/leading-casino-companies-by-revenue-2022.

The Paris Las Vegas features a 50-story replica of the Eiffel Tower.

cruise ships offer gambling "cruises to nowhere." These boats sail three miles offshore before they open their casinos, and they usually stay out three or four hours.

Indian Gambling. With the passing of the Indian Gaming Regulatory Act (IGRA) in 1988, Congress made it legal for Native Americans to open casinos on their property in states where gambling is allowed. The purpose of the act was to promote tribal economic development, protect Indian gaming from organized crime, and establish an appropriate regulatory body. Today Connecticut, Minnesota, Florida, and many other states have major casino operations on reservations. In fact, the third-largest casino in the world—Foxwoods Resort Casino—is located on a Native American reservation in Ledyard, Connecticut; it is run by the Mashantucket Pequot Tribal Nation. Besides three hotels, there is a casino with more than 7,000 slot and video poker machines; 380 gaming tables; and a 3,800-seat bingo hall.

Gaming around the World

Several countries have legalized and regulated gambling to varying extents. Some of the notable gambling countries are discussed next.

Macau, China. Macau is the only place in China where gambling is legal, and it draws visitors not only from that country but also from around the world. Gambling revenue in Macau is six times greater than in Las Vegas. However, since the COVID-19 pandemic, Macau's gambling revenue has dropped below that of Las Vegas. Legal gambling was introduced to Macau as a monopoly in 1850 by the Portuguese government in hopes of generating revenue. In 1999, Macau was transferred to the People's Republic of China as a Special Administrative Region, and in 2001 gambling was deregulated. Initially, three companies won concessions: SJM Holdings (which has roots in Macau), U.S.-based Wynn Resorts, and a joint venture between Galaxy Entertainment (Hong Kong) and Las Vegas Sands (United States). Wynn Resorts subsequently sold a sub-concession to a Hong Kong and Australian group, while SJM Holdings made a similar deal with MGM Resorts. At the end of 2021, there were 42 casinos in Macao. SJM has 23 casinos, followed by Galaxy with six casinos, Venetian with five, Melco Crown (previously known as Melco PBL) with four, and Wynn and MGM with two each.[4] Macau has five of the world's biggest casinos, the Venetian Macau, the City of Dreams Resort, Wynn Macau, Pointe 16 Macau, and the Sands Macau. It has surpassed Las Vegas as the largest international casino gambling destination.

Monte Carlo, Monaco. Gaming in Monte Carlo is an integral part of the city's allure and reputation as a glamorous and luxurious destination. It is renowned for its iconic Casino de Monte-Carlo, designed by architect Charles Garnier, which opened its doors in 1863 and has become a symbol of elegance and opulence. The Casino de Monte-Carlo offers a variety of traditional casino games, including roulette, blackjack, poker, baccarat, and slot machines. It is known for its lavish interiors, stunning architecture, and high-stakes gambling experiences, attracting both high rollers and tourists from around the globe.

Gaming in Monte Carlo is not just about the casinos; the entire city exudes luxury and sophistication, creating a unique and unforgettable gambling experience for visitors. The elegant surroundings, beautiful landscapes, and upscale amenities make Monte Carlo a magnet for those seeking a glamorous gaming adventure in one of the world's most exclusive destinations.

Other countries that have legalized gaming are the United Kingdom, Australia, Singapore, Canada, South Africa, New Zealand, Spain, Germany, France, Russia, the Netherlands, South Korea, Japan, the Philippines, and Cambodia. It's important to note that gaming laws and regulations can vary significantly from one country to another. Some countries have strict regulations and only allow certain forms of gaming, while others have more liberal gaming laws. Additionally, some countries have restrictions based on age or specific regions.

Knowledge Check

1. How did gaming in the United States evolve?

2. What was the significance of gambling becoming legalized in Las Vegas?

11.2 CASINO HOTELS

The best way to understand casino hotels is to think of them not as hotels with casinos attached, but as casinos with guestrooms, restaurants, shopping arcades, and even theme parks. Many of the casino hotels in Las Vegas are more like casino resorts,

luxurious destinations that combine world-class casino gaming with upscale accommodations, dining, entertainment, and amenities.

At the heart of a Las Vegas casino resort is its expansive gaming floor, offering a wide array of table games such as blackjack, roulette, craps, poker, and baccarat. Slot machines, video poker, and other electronic gaming options add to the diverse gaming experience. High-stakes areas, known as high-limit rooms, cater to players seeking exclusive and premium gaming experiences.

Beyond the casino floor, the resort offers opulent hotel accommodations with luxurious suites and guestrooms, featuring modern amenities and stunning views of the famous Las Vegas Strip or surrounding desert landscapes. Many casino resorts boast elaborate pools and spa facilities, creating a relaxing oasis for guests to unwind and rejuvenate.

Dining options at a Las Vegas casino resort are a highlight in themselves, with a variety of choices ranging from celebrity chef restaurants to international cuisine, gourmet buffets, and casual dining experiences. Lavish shows, concerts, and live entertainment are a hallmark of Las Vegas resorts, with world-class performers taking the stage to entertain guests.

Additionally, Las Vegas casino resorts often feature shopping promenades, nightclubs, bars, and lounges, providing guests with a vibrant and immersive experience. Some resorts even have outdoor attractions such as water features, gardens, or theme park-like rides.

Las Vegas casino resorts are known for their grand architecture, dazzling lights, and captivating themes that transport visitors to different worlds. At New York-New York Las Vegas Hotel & Casino, guests can stroll through an indoor replica of Central Park, ride the Manhattan Express roller coaster, shop along Park Avenue, and visit a huge replica of the Statue of Liberty. At the Venetian, guests can take a gondola ride on a re-creation of the Grand Canal.

The $1 billion MGM Grand Las Vegas (including The Signature at MGM Grand) is, for the moment, the world's third-largest hotel complex. Besides 29 restaurants; 6,852 guestrooms (including 751 suites); 29 private villas; and a casino the size of four football fields (with 3,000 slot machines); the hotel boasts two wedding chapels for couples who want to get married during their stay.

At New York-New York Las Vegas Hotel & Casino, guests can shop along Park Avenue, ride a roller coaster, and visit a 150-foot-tall replica of the Statue of Liberty.

The Palazzo, developed by the Las Vegas Sands company at a cost of $1.8 billion, is the largest building in terms of floor space in the Western Hemisphere. It opened in December 2007 as an extension of the Venetian Casino Resort and is the largest LEED-certified building in the United States.

In December 2008, Steve Wynn opened the Encore Hotel, a $2.3 billion casino resort with 2,034 guestrooms. It is connected to the Wynn by a shopping arcade and was originally conceived as an expansion of that hotel but developed its own identity as a resort. The hotel features five restaurants and seven bars; a 74,000-square-foot casino; a nightclub; and 27,000 square feet of retail space. One of the restaurants, a 152-seat steak house, is named Sinatra after the departed crooner Frank Sinatra and has on display Grammy and Oscar statuettes on loan from the Sinatra estate.

One of the most ambitious projects developed in Las Vegas is the MGM Mirage's City Center. Located on the Strip between the Monte Carlo and the Bellagio, it is a 77-acre hotel, residential, and entertainment complex that cost $8.5 billion. Three hotels with a total of 6,000 hotel rooms share the site with 2,400 condominiums. The Vdara, the Mandarin Oriental, and the ARIA hotels opened in December 2009. ARIA is the first hotel on the Las Vegas Strip to generate its own electricity. The SLS Las Vegas opened in 2014 with 1,620 rooms and suites; it was the redevelopment of the legendary Sahara Hotel. By Las Vegas standards, it was done at the relatively modest sum of $415 million.

On June 24, 2021, the Las Vegas strip was reinvigorated following a dismal economic year caused by the COVID-19 pandemic. Resorts World Las Vegas opened with much fanfare, including fireworks and a traditional lion dance meant to herald in luck and prosperity at the Asian-themed property. The project was built by Malaysia-based Genting Group for $4.3 billion and features 66-story, ruby-red towers with over 3,500 rooms from three Hilton brands. It includes a 5,000-seat theater; over 40 food and beverage venues integrated with online food delivery provider Grubhub (which allows guests to order food for pickup or delivery to rooms or the pool complex); 70,000 square feet of boutiques; a nightclub and a day club; 1,400 slot machines; 117 table games; and a 30-table poker room. The resort features technology enhancements such as contactless check-in and room unlocking with smartphones, a fully integrated Resorts World app that allows guests to pay for gaming from a smartphone, and Las Vegas's first cash-free casino. Casino guests load their digital wallets or enroll in Play+, which connects to a bank, credit, debit, or PayPal account.[5]

In Macau, the City of Dreams opened in 2009 at a cost of $2.1 billion with 1,400 rooms and a 420,000-square-foot casino. The resort's impressive water show, House of Dancing Water, was created by longtime Cirque du Soleil director

Franco Dragone. The show features 80 performers from around the world and takes place in a special round theater with a pool that holds 3.7 million gallons of water.

One of the most dazzling and expensive casino hotels is the Marina Bay Sands in Singapore, developed at a cost of $5.7 billion. This 2,561-room hotel has a 2.9-acre terrace on the 57th floor that includes a 150-meter infinity pool, restaurants, nightclubs, gardens, and a public observatory on the cantilever with 360-degree views of Singapore.

Revenue

Before the advent of the mega-casino resorts (also known as integrated resorts), the casino was the major source of revenue at Las Vegas hotels. Gambling accounted for about 58 percent of total hotel revenue. The win percentage of the various gambling games on the Las Vegas Strip breaks down as follows:

Baccarat	14.70%
Blackjack	14.18
Craps	15.95
Roulette	20.14
Ultimate Texas Hold'em	23.24
Three-Card Poker	31.91
Slot Machines	8.14[6]

In 1989, the Mirage Hotel & Casino Resort set a new standard for casino hotel development by making the hotel itself an attraction through architecture, design, and entertainment. Meanwhile, at Caesars Palace, Wolfgang Puck opened his highly respected Spago restaurant and started a trend of upscale celebrity chef restaurants, establishing Las Vegas as a culinary capital. Today, casino hotels have a more diversified revenue stream than in the past. As hotel developers made rooms and suites more luxurious, higher room rates were charged. Shopping arcades are an integral part of every mega-resort, and shopping has become a major part of the vacation experience in Las Vegas. The Forum Shops of Caesars Palace was the first shopping arcade destination. In its more than 800,000 square feet of space, there are 160 mostly upscale boutiques and specialty food shops. Brand names such as Burberry, Dior, Louis Vuitton, and Gucci are located there. It is the highest-grossing mall in the United States. The Wynn Las Vegas has an art gallery with 15 priceless paintings, including a Rembrandt, a Picasso, and a Vermeer. Las Vegas has become a center of dining, entertainment, and luxury shopping, resulting in a more varied economic base. Yet another new revenue stream emerged in 1999 when the opening of the Venetian Hotel led to the rapid expansion of the city's meetings business. The new emphasis on meetings has helped drive hotel food and beverage revenue during the mid-week period, when rooms were traditionally sold at discounted prices. While gambling still accounts for most of a casino hotel/ resort's revenue at 35.5 percent, guestrooms now account for 27.8 percent of revenue, food and beverage accounts for 23.6 percent, and "other" accounts for 13.1 percent.[7]

Organization and Management

The most striking difference between a casino hotel and other types of hotels is in the organization and management of the facility. This point cannot be overemphasized because it changes completely the way casino hotels are operated compared to traditional hotels. In casino hotels, the hotel operation is subordinate to the gambling operation. The vice president of hotel operations is not in complete control of the hotel; they report to a higher resident authority who usually holds the title of casino hotel president. There is also a vice president of casino operations, who is as important as the hotel manager when it comes to making decisions about almost everything. That's not all. Other vice presidents also make a lot of decisions that in a typical hotel or resort are handled as part of hotel operations. In Exhibit 11.2, note that there are a total of nine vice presidents reporting to the president. In addition to the vice presidents of hotel operations and casino operations, there is a vice president of administration (who handles human resources), a vice president of marketing, a vice president of finance, and a vice president of security. Why have these departments been separated from the hotel operation? Because decisions

Exhibit 11.2 Sample Casino Hotel Organization Chart

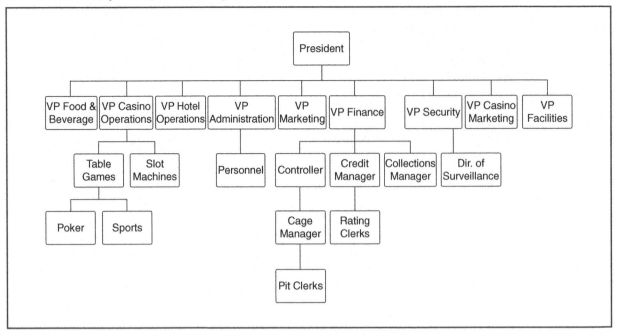

made in these departments affect not just hotel operations but casino operations as well.

For example, controls, credit, and the management of cash are not matters for either the hotel manager or the casino manager to determine independently because decisions about them affect both the hotel operation and the casino operation. Therefore, there is a separate finance department. Marketing, too, is unique. Gamblers are one audience, resort and convention guests another—hence two different marketing departments. But they're all at the same property at the same time.

The bottom line is that the vice president of hotel operations in many large Las Vegas and Atlantic City casino hotels is not in charge of the entire hotel; rather, they are only in charge of the rooms department and hotel services such as the spa, transportation, and pool (see Exhibit 11.3).

The Importance of Food and Beverage.
While food and beverage operations are extremely important to any resort operation, they play an additional role in casino hotels. They make gaming convenient by "fueling" the players. It isn't necessary to wander far or leave the premises in order to get any kind of dining experience—from a pastrami sandwich to Chateaubriand.

In some casino hotels, the food and beverage department is operated as a separate division under its own vice president. At the Mirage, this division, which has 14 food outlets, is the largest of all in terms of number of employees. The MGM Grand has nine chef-driven restaurants—all of them imaginatively decorated—as well as a variety of other outlets, including a 24-hour café and a New York-style deli. The amount of food consumed daily at the hotel during a peak business period is mind-boggling: 10,000 eggs; 2,650 pounds (1,193 kilograms) of beef; 640 pounds (288 kilograms) of chicken; and 270 pounds (122 kilograms) of shrimp, for example. An in-house bakery, which produces 99 percent of MGM Grand's baked goods, prepares 9,000 rolls; 3,000 pastries; 200 cakes; and 150 pies each day. As many as 80,000 cocktails are poured on a busy day.[8]

However, contrary to many people's perceptions about the buffets in Las Vegas, it is not the food-waste capital. Yalmaz Siddigui, vice president of corporate sustainability at MGM Resorts International from 2016 to 2022, who oversaw the company's 30 hotel and gaming offerings around the world, referred to Las Vegas as "one of the cities with the best programs in terms of managing food waste in a couple ways—donating it to people in need, sending it to farms so it becomes feed for animals, sending oil to become biofuel."[9] In fact, MGM Resorts has been named on the U.S. Environmental Protection Agency's list of Food Loss and Waste 2030 Champions, which recognizes companies

Exhibit 11.3   Sample Organization Chart for Hotel Operations within a Casino Hotel

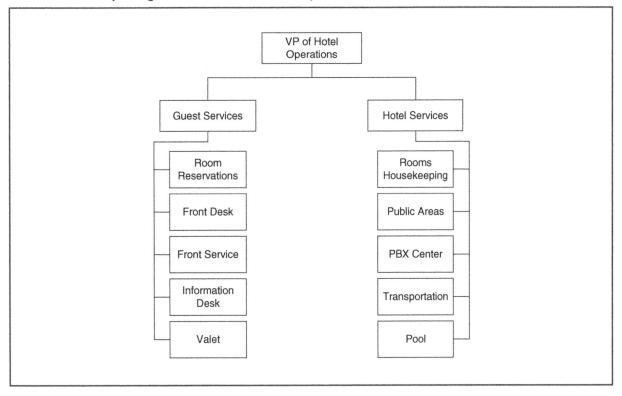

committed to reducing their food loss and waste by 50 percent over the next decade.

One successful marketing tool for casino-hotel food and beverage departments has been the use of brand-name restaurants. At the Bellagio, there is Michael Mina, Spago, and Le Cirque. At the Mandalay Bay Hotel, there is Rivea by Chef Alain Ducasse and Lupo by Wolfgang Puck.

Service Demands. Service operations in casino hotels are unique as well. Both entertainment and food are important components of the gambling experience. They provide opportunities for winners to celebrate and losers to console themselves. Because of all the services they provide, casino hotels are even more labor-intensive than other kinds of hotels. Elaborate and extensive entertainment and multiple dining facilities with all-night service mean that the number of employees per hotel room may be three or four times higher than in conventional hotels and resorts.

Despite the complexity of operating casino hotels, they are tremendously attractive cash cows to knowledgeable operators who have experience running them. Although not all casino hotels have been financially successful, those that are successful generate profits far in excess of other hotels.

One typical source of tension that may arise among casino managers, hotel managers, and food and beverage managers is how much money the casino division will be charged for the complimentary rooms and food and beverages given to guests to encourage them to come to the hotel and gamble. Another source of tension between the casino division and the rooms division involves guestroom inventory. Research has shown that most people take gambling trips—especially to Las Vegas and Atlantic City—on impulse, planning them no more than 48 hours in advance. This means that a casino hotel must keep a certain number of guestrooms available at all times for this last-minute traffic. On the other hand, popular resort hotels with casinos tend to fill their guestrooms five or six weeks in advance, especially around holidays. Enough rooms must be held open so that the hotel is not forced to turn away gamblers—its most profitable source of revenue—due to lack of rooms. However, if too many rooms are held, the hotel is stuck with empty guestrooms that could have been sold. As you can see, casino hotel managers must perform a fine balancing act to plan correctly.

Casino Operations

Since the hotel operations within casino hotels are very similar to hotel operations within all types of hotels and resorts, this section concentrates on what makes casino hotels unique: their casino operations. The section will describe casino games and look at casino terminology, employees, customers, marketing, and controls and regulation.

Casino Games. There are basically two types of casino games: (1) those classified as **table games** and (2) slot machines. The most common table games include baccarat, blackjack, craps, and roulette. Table games are played on a table and typically involve one or more dealers, or croupiers, facilitating the play.

Table games. *Baccarat* was named after an Italian word meaning "zero." It went from Italy to France in the fifteenth century, where it was known as *chemin de fer*. The object of the game is to come as close as possible to the number 9, which is known as a "natural." (Scoring an 8 is the second-best hand and is also known as a natural.) It is played with eight complete decks of cards. The cards are shuffled by the croupier (dealer), cut, and placed in a special box referred to as the "shoe." The shoe is passed to a player who becomes the banker. The first and third cards dealt from the shoe constitute the player's hand; the second and fourth cards are the banker's hand. Face cards and 10 count as 0, aces count as 1, and all other cards count at face value. The hand with the highest point total closest to 9 wins.

Blackjack is played at a table that can seat six or seven players across from a dealer. Here the object is to get closer to 21 than the dealer. (All players play against the dealer, not against each other.) Players who go over 21 automatically lose. The shoe can contain between one and eight decks. The dealer gives each player two cards face up; the dealer gets one card face up and one card face down. Kings, queens, jacks, and 10s each count as 10. Aces count as 1 or 11, as the player or dealer wishes. All other cards count at their face value. Additional cards may be distributed to each player, if the player desires, and the dealer may or

may not take additional cards, depending on the initial hand dealt. The game continues until all the players stand pat with their hands; each player's total is then compared with the dealer's total to see who wins.

Craps is considered by many players to be the most exciting game in any casino. Because there are so many betting variations, craps can be a complicated game. It is played on an oval table covered with green felt. The table is marked with all of the possible bets that can be made. A pair of dice is thrown by one of the players designated as the "shooter." Other players bet with or against the shooter by putting their chips on sections of the table that are marked *pass* line, *don't pass* line, *come* field, etc. In the most basic bet, players who bet on the pass line win if the shooter rolls a 7 or 11; they lose if the shooter rolls "craps," which is 2, 3, or 12. Of course, there are many other ways to win and lose, and the action moves very fast—which is why the game is often perceived as difficult.

Roulette is the simplest table game of them all. In American roulette, the table consists of a revolving wheel in which there is a ball and slots numbered from 1 to 36; in addition, there are two symbols, 0 and 00 (in most other countries, there is only one zero). On the table, there is a diagrammed area with each number and symbol marked. Players place their chips on a number or symbol, and the dealer spins the roulette ball in the opposite direction of the spinning wheel. When the ball falls into a slot on the roulette wheel, the dealer places a marker on the winning number on the table layout and pays the winning bet(s), if any.

Ultimate Texas Hold'em is a variation of the classic poker game Texas Hold'em. Instead of competing against other players, players compete only against the dealer. To start the game, the player must make equal bets into the ante and blind circles. There is also an option to make a bet on Trips, which pays if the final five-card hand equals three-of-a-kind or better. The player may raise prior to the flop or at the conclusion of each round of action; however, the earlier the raise is made, the higher the value of the bet.

Three-card poker has gained popularity in Las Vegas casinos because it is easy to learn. The objective of the game is to make the best poker hand possible using only three cards. Players compete against the dealer and can also win based on how good their cards are. Once the cards are dealt, a player determines whether they are

Manual dexterity is an important skill for dealers.

Roulette is the simplest of the casino table games.

going to place a play wager or fold. If the dealer has a hand of jack-high or worse, then the play wager is returned to the player. If it is queen-high or better, then the play wager is paid out at 1 to 1 if the player's hand is better than the dealer's.

Of the table games, blackjack is the most popular in the United States, followed by craps and roulette. People who gamble regularly know that a player has a good chance of winning in blackjack, where the house odds (depending on the player's skill level) can be less than 2 percent. With craps, the house advantage is only 1.4 percent. In American roulette, the house advantage is 5.26 percent.

In European casinos, where roulette is the most popular game, gaming is generally considered more of an entertainment than a way of winning money. The odds are a little better for players of French roulette, however, because the wheel has only one 0. With French roulette, the house advantage is only 2.63 percent.

Slot machines. Much of the gaming in American casinos involves **slot machines**, also known as fruit machines, pokies, or one-armed bandits. Slot machines are designed to offer games of chance where players bet money on the outcome of a spin or series of spins. Slots are by far the most profitable games from a casino's point of view. The percentage of money the casino keeps is usually high, and slots are the least labor-intensive of all games, requiring no dealers or other attendants except for employees who maintain the machines, make change, and empty and refill the hoppers. There are also a high number of bets made every hour on a slot machine, and the more bets, the more the casino makes.

The amount of money slot machines pay out is controlled in every jurisdiction. For example, in Atlantic City, slot machines must pay back 83 percent, or 83 cents out of every dollar bet; the house keeps 17 cents. Nevada does not regulate the payback, but the state's Gaming Control Board, as a policy, does not approve any game that pays back less than 75 percent. In order to attract business in competitive markets, casinos may pay back more, hoping to make their profit on the increased betting volume. Some casinos in Nevada have been known to pay back 99 percent in winnings.

Casino Terminology. Before going any further, some key terms used in casino management should be introduced:

- *Markers.* **Markers** are printed or written forms that look like bank checks; they are used to extend credit to a player. They are IOUs that players can give to dealers to buy chips, instead of using cash. Markers have no cash value; they simply record the amount of credit that the casino is willing to extend to a player.

Typically, the casino agrees not to cash these markers for 30 or 45 days, giving the player time to deposit enough money in their bank account to cover them.

- *Cashier's cage.* The **cashier's cage**, generally referred to simply as "the cage," is where chips and cash are stored, where checks are cashed, where credit cards are accepted, and where markers are approved. It is the control center for the flow of chips to and from tables.

- *Pit.* A group of tables within a casino that defines a management section is called a **pit**. A pit can be made up of tables featuring the same game or tables featuring a combination of games. For example, there may be four craps tables and four roulette tables in one pit, or simply eight craps tables. The manager of a pit is called the **pit boss**.

- *Fill and credit slips.* Each gaming table has an inventory of chips. At the end of each shift, the inventory at every table is restored to the original amount. If the inventory is depleted, a **fill slip** is completed and additional chips are issued from the cage. If there is an excess of chips, a **credit slip** is completed and the extra chips are returned to the cage.

In modern casinos, these pieces of paper have been replaced by a computer network so requests can be transmitted electronically from the pit. If there is no computer system, security guards are utilized to carry credit and fill slips back and forth to the cage.

Much of the gaming in American casinos involves slot machines.

- *Drop box.* Each gaming table is equipped with a box that locks in place beneath the table. Cash and markers received from players are deposited through a slot into this **drop box**. At the end of a shift, boxes are removed from the tables and brought to a count room. At specific times, they are opened and the contents counted carefully under strict supervision. When the box is removed from a gaming table, the slot is automatically locked and can be reopened only by keys that are under the control of the casino's accounting team.

- *Table drop.* The **table drop** is the amount of money and markers in a gaming table's drop box that players have exchanged for chips at that table. It may or may not represent the amount placed on bets at that table, since players often carry chips from one table or game to another, or cash them in. The table drop, however, is a good measure of the gaming activity within a casino.

- *Slots drop/hold.* The **slots drop** is the amount of money played through a slot machine; the **slots hold** represents the amount of money that a slot machine does not pay back to players as wins.

- *Table win.* The **table win** is the amount of a bet at a table minus the amount that is paid back to the players. It is calculated as follows:

Opening chip inventory

+	Fill slips
−	Credit slips
−	Closing chip inventory
TOTAL =	Total chips won or transferred from the table

Once the total chips won or transferred from the table are determined, a second calculation is required to arrive at the table win:

Table drop

−	Total chips won or transferred from the table
TOTAL =	Table win

- *Hold percentage.* The **hold percentage** is a calculation to determine the percentage of chips purchased at a table by customers that is won back by the casino. It is calculated as follows:

$$\text{Win} \div \text{Drop} = \text{Hold}$$

For example, if the table win is $1,000 and the table drop is $4,000, then the hold is 25 percent. In other words, the casino won (kept) 25 percent of the chips purchased at that table.

Anti-Theft Technology. Many casino robbery movies have been made, and the most popular is probably the *Ocean's Eleven* series. However, casinos have implemented cutting-edge technologies that are very good at stopping theft. Even before you enter the premises, license plate readers have compared your license plate against a list of known gambling addicts or criminals. Once you enter the door, biometric face recognition is employed, and you are compared against the images of suspected criminals in the casino's database. At the baccarat table, a system known as Angel Eye reads the invisible barcodes printed on each card to keep track of the cards being dealt and compares the dealer's hands against its result to prevent card switching. Radio-frequency identification (RFID) embedded in chips ensures that counterfeit chips are not cashed out at the cage and tracks the chips loaned out to players and their statistics. A robust software combines RFID chips data with an overhead video camera that continuously analyzes all kinds of statistics on the table and identifies when a player is counting cards or collaborating with the dealer. Lastly, Non-Obvious Relationship Awareness (NORA) software is used when the pit boss suspects collusion between players or player and dealer to identify relationships that may not be obvious.

Casino Employees. Casinos are staffed by **croupiers**, or dealers, whose job it is to conduct the table games, collect bets, and pay the winning bets of players. Casino managers expect dealers to be friendly and fast. Manual dexterity and math skills are also important. Like all casino employees, dealers are carefully screened for honesty. They are also under constant electronic and personal surveillance. The average salary is $32,000 to $58,000, including benefits. Dealers can also earn large sums in tips that may account for 50 to 80 percent of their salary. Some players not only tip dealers generously, but they also place a bet for the dealer at the same time that they place one for themselves (for good luck).

Floor people are casino employees who supervise dealers. They are trained to enforce good dealing procedures, resolve disputes, and watch for cheaters. Today's cheaters are often extremely sophisticated; some use computers and other electronic devices. A floor person usually supervises two to four tables and reports to a pit boss.

A pit boss manages a larger group of tables and pays special attention to tables with high action. A big part of a pit boss's job is to make sure that gamblers placing large bets are happy. Often pit bosses act as hosts for these gamblers.

The person in charge of the casino at any given time is the shift manager. Shift managers work six to eight hours at a time. Under the shift manager is the games manager, who is responsible for all of the table games.

All of these employees have high-pressure jobs because they are responsible for so much cash. In a large casino, it is not unusual for betting activity to reach $1 million an hour. Many casinos win $1 million for their owners in a single day.

Students interested in a career in gaming usually get specialized training and experience, which is available at gaming institutes. These are private schools that teach the skills needed to fill jobs such as croupier and casino manager. The majority of hospitality students, however, are drawn to a casino's hotel operations and food and beverage operations, which are extensive in the gaming industry. Career tracks in the rooms, food and beverage, and sales and marketing divisions—all leading to general management positions—are possible at casino hotels.

Casino Customers. Casinos often divide their customers into two broad groups: grind players and high-end players. Both are vital to the long-term health of a gaming establishment.

Grind players generally enter a casino with a budget. They have decided to play $25, $200, or some other relatively modest amount. When their budgeted amount is gone or when they have won enough to make them feel lucky, they happily leave. Gaming for them is a form of entertainment, and their losses are viewed as the price of that entertainment.

High-end players (often called "high rollers" or "high-stakes players") are a different breed of gambler. Gaming for them represents a chance to experience a meaningful risk, a big thrill, for which they are prepared to put down a large amount of money. It is difficult to estimate how much a high-end player will bet because it depends on a casino's particular market. A player with $5,000 to spend during a weekend of gambling would typically be considered a high roller. Some high-end players bet much more than that, however—sometimes as much as $500,000 on a single bet!

High-end players play regularly and expect to suffer big losses at times. They minimize their losses by negotiating with the casinos where they play regularly. Rebates, gifts, free guestrooms, and free food are four common ways casinos help ease the sting of losing. Often the value of these rebates and complimentary items can reach as high as 25 to 50 percent of what the player lost. Rebates are most common in baccarat, where typically the highest sums are wagered; rebates are negotiated in advance.

Casino managers have been known to present Rolex watches to high-end players and their spouses when they arrive at the hotel. These players may leave with a Lexus or BMW if their losses (the casino's winnings) are significant enough.

On the Las Vegas strip, the highest rollers of all are called "whales." One of these was Kerry Packer, an Australian media tycoon. During one July weekend at the Bellagio in Las Vegas, Packer reportedly lost $20 million, a loss so huge that it sent ripples through casino stocks on Wall Street and spurred heated debate back in Australia. "This is not someone else's money, this is mine and I'm entitled to spend it any way I choose," Packer said. "I understand that it's a lot of money and I understand how it comes as a shock to some. But the truth of the matter is that I like to have a bet now and then." Packer was also reputed to be one of the biggest winners in Las Vegas history; in 1995, he reportedly won more than $20 million at the MGM Grand. Packer liked baccarat and blackjack, and he played hard and fast, betting up to $250,000 a hand and playing several hands at a time. He gambled for short stints, a few hours at a time, making him even more threatening to a casino's bottom line; if he got ahead, he was likely to head out the door before the house could recover.[10]

Some high-end players have "personal representatives" who approach the casino's managers to negotiate terms before the players arrive. This representative asks questions like the following:

- What kind of action are you expecting? (How much money do you expect my client to play?)
- How many hours a day do you expect my client to play?
- What percentage of my client's gambling losses will you cover through complimentary items?
- How long will you hold my client's markers?
- Will you give my client a discount if they pay off the markers immediately?
- Will you offer a suite and food and beverages for some of my client's friends and relatives who don't gamble but would like to stay at your hotel?

A personal representative usually receives a commission of 10 percent of the money the casino wins from the client. Casino hotels view high-end players differently, as their profit margins are substantially higher. Many casinos consider you a whale if you gamble over the $1 million bankroll mark and your bets are usually more than $25,000 per hand. They will ensure that you have the best experience while you are there and often provide luxury amenities such as free suites, unlimited food and beverages, top-notch entertainment, and even private air and ground transportation.

Casino Marketing. There are three separate markets that casinos generally target. The *high end*, as has been discussed, is made up of those people who are willing to gamble $5,000 or more on every visit to a casino. Since they are, for the most part, experienced gamblers who play regularly and make credit arrangements in advance, they are well known to casino operators. This kind of gambler is recruited through agents and friends. Marketing to them consists mainly of offering rebates; complimentary lodging, food, and entertainment; and often gifts as well.

The *middle-range* customer can be described as the person who spends between $3,000 and $5,000 per gambling trip. Many casinos

call this segment their core market. The key to marketing to these customers is first to identify and track them—a task that has become much easier because of computer technology. Modern casinos use an automated rating system that tracks frequency of play, amount of time played, the particular games played, and the size of the average bet to assign a theoretical value or a certain number of points to players. With this information, a direct-mail campaign can be created offering everything from junkets to room discounts and special events for those who qualify. What is offered is calculated very carefully, based on how much a player is expected to (or agrees to) play. Some casino hotels comp up to 40 percent on table games and 30 percent on slot machines of the total amount the player gambles, whether the player wins, loses, or breaks even. This sum is applied against the room and food and beverage charges that the player incurs at the hotel.

Casino junkets are sometimes advertised or organized by brokers. **Junkets** are partially or completely paid trips to a casino, organized by a casino or gaming representative. Guests generally agree, in advance, to play a certain amount of money over a certain period of time—usually four hours a day. Casino personnel monitor the action carefully. These junkets often lure first-time visitors who may then be invited back based on their observed performance.

Once a casino has identified one of these valuable middle-range players, it may send them a regular newsletter, along with invitations to play in special tournaments, join the casino's VIP club, and attend parties or events organized around special holidays.

Low-end players are very important for the health of any casino. Because their game of choice is often slot machines, they help create a busy ambience and can be very profitable since the house odds on slots are significantly better than with other games. Bus tours, which are particularly popular in Atlantic City because of its proximity to New York City and Philadelphia, are the major marketing tool for this market. These tours operate on regular schedules. Players on a tour are usually refunded the amount of the bus fare in the form of vouchers good for free meals, show tickets, and rolls of quarters or tokens for playing the slots.

Typically, low-end players on bus tours spend about six hours in town. To keep players in a particular casino—so they don't wander off to visit a competitor down the street—casinos may offer free cocktails and hold frequent drawings for automobiles and cash.

Future marketing trends. As gaming continues to grow, gamblers have become more sophisticated. Casinos that cater to the grind market have been forced to offer complimentary items to grind players who've learned that part of the game is to recover some of their losses. Many casinos in Las Vegas have formed slot clubs. These clubs cost nothing to join. Members are issued electronic cards, which they enter into slot machines before starting to play. The cards record the volume of play, and players are awarded points based on how much they bet. These points can be exchanged for food, beverages, guestrooms, or gifts.

Casino Controls and Regulation. Because of the high volume of cash and credit transactions at casinos, controls within them must be stringent. There are many opportunities for customer and employee dishonesty. Because a casino's gambling operations do not earn money by selling services or products such as overnight accommodations or food, there is no way of measuring what has been "sold." Nor is it practical to record every single gambling transaction. So how does a casino make certain it keeps all of the cash it earns?

Casinos use three kinds of controls:

■ *Accounting controls* include sophisticated formulas to calculate expected profitability by the game, by the table, and by the shift. As previously mentioned, there are numerous credit and cash control procedures that are carefully followed as well.

■ *Equipment controls* involve equipment such as electronic surveillance cameras, safes, lock boxes, RFID chips, and so on.

■ *Human controls* are found at every staff level, from pit bosses to security guards. There are on-site inspectors (electronic as well as human) monitoring every part of the casino and every transaction.

Casinos are carefully regulated by the governments that sanction them. This is necessary to ensure that the government collects its share of the proceeds, as well as to discourage organized criminal activities. Legislation usually dictates the casino's size, types of games permitted, investigation and licensing of employees, hours and days of operation, marketing activities, and type and size of public space.

While regulations differ from state to state, the Nevada model of gaming control is widely copied. Nevada has two regulatory/oversight bodies that deal with gaming and report directly to the governor: the Gaming Commission and the Gaming Control Board. The Gaming Commission is charged with enacting necessary gaming regulations, issuing licenses, and handling disciplinary matters. The Gaming Control Board investigates applicants, enforces regulations, and audits the books and control systems of casinos.

Knowledge Check

1. How are casino hotels organized and managed differently from other types of hotels?

2. What two broad groups of customers are vital to the long-term health of a gaming establishment? What are their characteristics?

The first recorded account of gambling dates back to early China. Today, casinos exist in many countries. Casinos are owned by a variety of entities, including individuals, corporations, tribes, and governments.

Gambling was accepted early on in regions of the United States, and riverboats became popular venues. But by the early twentieth century, gambling had become illegal in most of the country. In 1931, it was revived in Nevada, and in 1976 it became legal in New Jersey. Today, gambling exists in most states in one form or another—if not throughout the state, it can be found on Indian reservations, on riverboats, and offshore.

The best way to understand casino hotels is to think of them not as hotels with casinos attached, but as casinos with guestrooms, restaurants, shopping arcades, and even theme parks. In casino hotels, the hotel operation is subordinate to the gambling operation. As a result, many activities that come under the hotel manager's jurisdiction in non-casino hotels, such as food and beverage service and marketing, are separated from the hotel manager's duties in casino hotels. This may cause some tension between the hotel manager and the casino manager of a casino hotel.

There are basically two types of casino games: table games and slot machines. The most common table games include baccarat, blackjack, craps, and roulette. Of the table games, blackjack is the most popular in the United States, followed by craps and roulette. Slots are the most profitable games for a casino because of the percentage of money the casino gets to keep and the low labor requirements.

Casino employees include croupiers (dealers), floor people, pit bosses, and shift managers. From an operational point of view, casinos often divide their customers into two broad groups: grind players and high-end players. While these are the two kinds of customers playing, from a marketing point of view, there are three markets that casinos generally target with promotional activities: high-end, middle-range, and low-end. Different strategies are used to attract each market.

There are three kinds of controls that casinos use: accounting controls, equipment controls, and human controls. Casinos are carefully overseen by the governments that sanction them. While regulations differ from state to state, the Nevada model of gaming control is widely copied.

KEY TERMS

cashier's cage—Generally referred to simply as "the cage," this is the area within a casino where chips and cash are stored, checks are cashed, credit cards are accepted, and markers are approved. It is the control center for the flow of chips to and from gaming tables.

credit slip—A form that states the amount of excess chips at each gaming table at the end of a shift. Extra chips are returned to the cage along with the credit slips.

croupier—An attendant or dealer at a gaming table who conducts the game, collects bets, and pays the winning bets of players.

drop box—A locked box beneath each gaming table into which the cash and markers received from players are deposited. At the end of a shift, boxes are removed from the tables and brought to a count room, where they are opened and the contents counted under strict supervision.

fill slip—A form that states the amount of chips short at each gaming table at the end of a shift.

floor people—Casino employees who supervise dealers. They are trained to enforce good dealing procedures, resolve disputes, and watch for cheaters.

grind players—Gamblers who budget a modest amount for gaming and usually leave the casino when that amount is spent. They view gaming as entertainment and their losses as the price of that entertainment.

high-end players—Gamblers who gamble regularly, are prepared to gamble a large amount of money, and expect to suffer big losses at times. Often called "high rollers" or "high-stakes players," high-end players may bet as much as $500,000 on a single bet.

hold percentage—A calculation to determine the percentage of chips purchased at a gaming table by customers that is won back by the casino. It is calculated as follows: Win ÷ Drop = Hold.

junkets—Partially or completely paid trips to a casino, organized by a casino or gaming representative. Guests generally agree, in advance, to play a certain amount of money over a certain period of time—usually four hours per day.

markers—Printed or written IOUs that extend credit to a player; players can use them rather than cash to buy chips from dealers. Typically, the casino agrees not to cash markers for 30 or 45 days, giving players time to deposit enough money in their bank account to cover their markers.

pit—A group of gaming tables within a casino that defines a management section. A pit can be made up of tables featuring the same game or tables featuring a combination of games. For example, there may be four craps tables and four roulette tables in one pit or simply eight craps tables.

pit boss—The manager who oversees a group of gaming tables, called a pit, within a casino.

slots drop—The amount of money played through a slot machine.

slots hold—The amount of money that a slot machine does not pay back as wins.

slot machines—Also known as fruit machines, pokies, or one-armed bandits. Slot machines are designed to offer games of chance where players bet money on the outcome of a spin or series of spins.

table drop—The amount of money and markers in a gaming table's drop box that players have exchanged for chips at that table. The table drop is a good measure of gaming activity within a casino.

table games—A category of casino games that are played on a table and typically involve one or more dealers, or croupiers, facilitating the play.

table win—The amount of a bet at a gaming table minus the amount that is paid back to the players.

1. Which city was the most prominent for gambling in the United States in the early nineteenth century?
   a. Biloxi
   b. Las Vegas
   c. Atlantic City
   d. New Orleans

2. Which game was popularized and played by English knights?
   a. Craps
   b. Poker
   c. Roulette
   d. Blackjack

3. Which accounts for most of a casino hotel's revenue?
   a. Food and beverage
   b. Conventions
   c. Gambling
   d. Rooms

4. Which position is at the top of a casino hotel's organization?
   a. Vice president of casino operations
   b. Vice president of hotel operation
   c. Casino hotel president
   d. General manager

5. Which is the simplest table game?
   a. Blackjack
   b. Baccarat
   c. Roulette
   d. Craps

6. Who supervises dealers in a casino?
   a. Pit bosses
   b. Croupiers
   c. Floor people
   d. Collections managers

7. Why are slots the most profitable games for casinos?
   a. Slots are the most exciting games.
   b. Only one dealer is required for every slot machine.
   c. The percentage of money that casinos keep from slot machines is high.
   d. Slot machines occupy a significant amount of floor space.

8. Which describes a high-end player?
   a. Player with $5,000 to spend during a weekend of gambling
   b. Player with $2,000 to spend during a weekend of gambling
   c. Player with $1,000 to spend during a weekend of gambling
   d. Player who goes beyond their budget

9. What does a player obtain to extend their credit?
   a. Chip exchange
   b. Credit slip
   c. Fill slip
   d. Marker

10. What is the major marketing tool for low-end players?
   a. Bus tours
   b. Newsletters
   c. Casino junkets
   d. Direct-mail campaigns

11. What is the biggest threat to casino controls and regulations?
   a. Customer and employee dishonesty
   b. Violence against employees
   c. Technology failure
   d. Strict legislation

12. What are the two basic types of casino games?
   a. Card games and slot machines
   b. Table games and slot machines
   c. Poker and slot machines
   d. Roulette and card games

SHORT-ANSWER QUESTIONS

1. How has gambling contributed to the travel and tourism industry in the United States?

2. Why are casino jobs high-pressure?

VIP

A frequent guest of a casino resort in Arizona makes a last-minute decision to travel there for a weekend stay. The guest enjoys gambling as a leisure activity and is a well-respected gambler in the casino. When the guest arrives, they are usually met by a casino host and treated as a VIP because of their level of betting at the blackjack tables. The guest is worth approximately $600,000 in casino earnings per year for the hotel.

Due to their last-minute arrangements, however, the guest doesn't notify a casino host that they are on their way. Upon arrival, the guest notices that the front desk check-in area is extremely busy. The hotel is installing self-check-in kiosks to speed up the check-in process, but they are not operational yet. In addition, big groups in town for a conference are waiting to check in.

The VIP guest waits in line for 20 minutes. When they try to check in, they are told that the hotel is at 100 percent occupancy. The front desk representative acts impatiently when the guest states that they are a frequent customer. In a fit of frustration, the guest leaves the hotel. They figure that all casinos have similar odds at the blackjack table and another property might show them more respect.

DISCUSSION QUESTIONS

1. What kind of casino customer is the guest?

2. What could the front desk representative have done differently to appease the guest? What could the hotel do differently to avoid this situation in the future?

Cynthia Kiser Murphey

Cynthia Kiser Murphey is an exceptional leader and the general manager of Palms Casino Resort, the first casino resort owned by a Native American tribe in Las Vegas.

In her role as general manager, Murphey is responsible for overseeing the gaming, hospitality, and food and beverage operations of the 766-room casino resort and Palms Place condominiums.

Murphey's passion for the hospitality industry was ignited at a young age, driving her to pursue studies in hotel management in the vibrant city of Las Vegas—the Entertainment Capital of the World. After graduating from the University of Nevada, Las Vegas (UNLV), she embarked on her career in gaming and hospitality in the city. She held various leadership positions at MGM Resorts International, including the role of senior vice president of human resources. Following this, she served as president and chief operating officer of New York-New York Las Vegas Hotel & Casino for 12 years. In this influential role, she oversaw the operations and refurbishments of the 2,000-room property located on the iconic Las Vegas Strip.

As one of the pioneering female presidents on the Strip, Murphey spearheaded initiatives that transformed the resort into a vibrant and sought-after indoor and outdoor entertainment destination.

During her tenure at MGM, Murphey played a vital role in the successful launch of three mega-resorts, including the world's largest hotel. Her leadership extended to community relations, where she was instrumental in shaping public opinion on gaming in Michigan and Massachusetts, ultimately contributing to regulatory approvals in both regions.

Murphey holds a bachelor's degree in hotel and restaurant management as well as a master's degree in hotel administration from UNLV. She actively participates in various charitable and professional organizations, earning notable recognition as one of the "People to Watch" by *Global Gaming Business* magazine. Additionally, she has been honored with a lifetime achievement award from *Las Vegas Magazine*. She takes immense pride in her more than 20 years of service as a trustee to the UNITE HERE National Fund, an organization dedicated to providing outstanding health benefits to employees in the hospitality industry.

Murphey's dedication to developing individuals, supporting communities, and delivering exceptional guest experiences has been central to her distinguished career.

It's a Friday night, and the bustling casino floor is alive with the sound of slot machines, the clatter of chips, and the chatter of excited patrons. Sarah, a seasoned gambler, has been a regular at this casino for several years. She's a high roller, meaning she frequently wagers large sums of money and has a reputation for being a loyal customer.

As Sarah makes her way through the casino floor, she's greeted by several staff members who know her by name. The pit boss approaches her and offers her a free meal at the casino's upscale restaurant. He tells Sarah that this is their way of thanking her for her patronage. Sarah accepts the offer and heads to the restaurant, where she enjoys a delicious meal with her friends.

After dinner, Sarah heads back to the gaming floor and starts playing at one of her favorite slot machines. A few minutes into her game, a casino host approaches her and introduces himself. He tells her that he's there to make sure she's comfortable and to assist her with anything she needs. Sarah appreciates the gesture and tells the host that she's doing fine.

As Sarah continues playing, the casino host periodically checks in with her, offering her drinks and snacks. He also informs her that she has earned some complimentary slot play as a reward for her loyalty. Sarah is thrilled and continues playing, knowing that the more she wagers, the more perks she'll receive.

At the end of the night, Sarah decides to cash out her winnings and head home. Before she leaves, the casino host approaches her once more and thanks her for her business. He hands her a complimentary hotel room voucher and tells her it's their way of showing appreciation. Sarah smiles and thanks him, feeling valued and appreciated as a loyal customer.

As Sarah leaves the casino, she reflects on the night and how much she enjoyed being a part of the comping program. Why do casinos offer comps to customers like Sarah?

12

THE MANAGEMENT OF HOSPITALITY ENTERPRISES

Chapter Outline

Learning Objectives

1. Describe management and summarize the contributions to management theory made by Frederick Taylor, Henri Fayol, and Peter Drucker. (pp. 340–342)

2. Identify and describe four basic leadership strategies used by managers. (pp. 342–345)

3. Identify and discuss current labor trends and legislation affecting the hospitality industry. (pp. 345–347)

4. Describe elements of a good human resources program. (pp. 347–357)

5. Distinguish marketing from selling, identify and explain the Four P's of Marketing, and describe how a marketing plan is developed. (pp. 358–362)

6. Explain the role and importance of public relations and publicity. (pp. 362–363)

KEY TERMS

advertising

classical school

competitive pricing

consumer-based pricing

cost-plus pricing

crowdsourcing

distribution channels

diversity training

elasticity of demand

empowerment

Four P's of Marketing

full-time-equivalent (FTE) employee

integrated marketing communications

job breakdown

job description

job list

loss-leaders

marketing

marketing mix

networking

performance review

productivity standards

publicity

public relations (PR)

What does it mean to be a manager in today's hospitality industry? This chapter will examine some traditional management ideas rooted in the manufacturing economy of the early twentieth century. Then it will move forward in time to explore the thinking of contemporary management theorists about a more diverse twenty-first-century economy focused on service. It should become clear that management involves much more than just being the boss—communication, leadership, and emotional awareness all play their part. You will also learn about the importance of managing human resources within the hospitality industry. No other industry provides so much contact between employees and customers and so many opportunities to either reinforce a positive experience or create a negative one. Lastly, you will learn how hospitality companies market and sell their products and services, both online and offline. The Four P's of Marketing—product, place, price, and promotion—will be covered, along with how hotels and restaurants go about developing a marketing plan.

12.1 A MANAGER'S JOB

In a hospitality business, "management" can look very different from day to day. One day you may be reviewing your company's goals and setting department benchmarks to meet them or preparing an employee's performance evaluation. The next day you may be mediating a dispute between team members, counseling a troubled associate, or trying to calm an angry guest. The day-to-day functions of a manager can vary depending on the size of their establishment, their specific segment of the hospitality industry, and the individual responsibilities of their role.

As these examples illustrate, management is not something you undertake with a textbook open in front of you. Management is more like the extended, semistructured improvisation of a skilled soccer team or a jazz quartet. Every day will bring fresh challenges but not necessarily the hoped-for rewards. The work itself must reward you; pats on the back or thanks from associates and customers are gratifying when they occur but can never be counted on.

It's often simple to single out the managers in a contemporary hotel, restaurant, or club. In addition to their titles, they may have nice offices—or at least a desk somewhere. At high levels, their jobs might come with perks such as company cars, country club memberships, and expense accounts. This would seem absurd to early management theorists, who would have scoffed at the idea that a manager does anything but command, control, punish, and reward their workers—certainly no hobnobbing at the country club.

This outlook had its highest expression in the **classical school** of management, founded by Frederick W. Taylor (1856–1915). The classical school of management sees workers as rational people interested primarily in making money. This management approach addresses an employee's economic and physical needs, but not their social needs or need for job satisfaction. An American industrial engineer who managed the Midvale Steel Company in Philadelphia, Taylor revolutionized manufacturing by coming up with scientific principles of production. According to these principles, there was one best way to do every job, and that one best way could be revealed by undertaking a job analysis. Workers should therefore be trained to do their jobs using only the "best way" devised by management and paid according to how rapidly and how well they performed. Taylor suggested using a "differential rate system of piece work," under which one of two rates would be paid for a job: "a high price per piece, in case the work is finished in the shortest possible time and in perfect condition, and a low price, if it takes a longer time to do a job, or if there are any imperfections in the work."[1]

While Taylorism was primarily focused on worker productivity, other models were concerned with defining the duties and functions of managers. Henri Fayol, a French mining engineer and the manager of a large coal mining enterprise, came up with five management functions early in the last century. They were originally translated into English as follows:

1. Planning
2. Organizing
3. Commanding
4. Coordinating
5. Controlling

Fayol has proven pretty durable, and you'll likely find some version of his management functions in many textbooks. In some cases, however, the terminology has been modified to reflect changing times and approaches. For example, Fayol meant "controlling" in the way we understand quality management now: you get feedback on the process of interest, evaluate the feedback, and modify the process as needed. In addition, "leading" often now replaces the earlier command and coordination functions, while "planning" is often updated to "forecasting."

Peter Drucker, the great (and somewhat more contemporary) management theorist, believed that a manager has two broad goals. The first is "creation of a true whole that is larger than the sum of its parts, a productive entity that turns out more than the sum of the resources put into it."[2] This is one of the few assertions in management theory that is as suitable for today's service-dominated economy as it was for the manufacturing age.

Drucker compared a manager to a conductor of an orchestra who is able to pull together the music played by each musician into a beautiful symphony. (That particular metaphor has been around for a while!) Drucker pointed out that unlike conductors, who have a composer's score in front of them and only have to interpret it, managers must also write their own score. In effect, then, managers are composers as well as conductors.

The second broad goal of a manager, as identified by Drucker, is to "harmonize in every decision and action the requirements of [the] immediate and long-range future."[3] This vision of the future, taken in concert with the first goal, is what separates managers from supervisors. Supervisors only implement established policies. Although they may act like orchestra conductors at times—that is, lead and direct their employees—it is not their job to compose the music; that has already been done by higher-level managers. Nor do supervisors worry about the long range; they take care of what's going on today.

On a more fundamental level, Drucker concluded that several basic tasks were common to all managers:[4]

- Setting objectives

- Organizing

- Motivating and communicating

- Measuring performance

- Developing people

Let's take a look at each of these management tasks in turn.

Setting Objectives

A manager sets objectives. Unlike a worker or supervisor, a manager must decide what goals and objectives their department or organization should strive to achieve. The manager then decides what work must be done to reach those objectives and, finally, directs and communicates with their employees to get the work done. Multiple studies demonstrate that goals must be properly set—not too easy, not too difficult. If a team expends little or no effort meeting an objective, it probably wasn't worth accomplishing in the first place. If a goal is too difficult or unreasonable, frustration sets in. The savvy manager knows the "sweet spot" for a goal: difficult enough to motivate and get the team focused and working, but not so hard that everybody throws their hands up in disgust and walks away.

Organizing

A manager organizes. A manager must analyze the work for which their department is responsible, divide that work into various jobs, and assign the jobs to employees, some of whom may need additional training in order to handle them. All of the classic management texts emphasize that managers must know how to delegate. According to author Wess Roberts, even Attila the Hun, the notorious fifth-century leader who forged 70,000 barbarians into a well-disciplined army, understood this concept.

Motivating and Communicating

Above all, managers must be communicators. A skilled manager knows how to turn groups of individuals into high-functioning, tightly focused, task-oriented teams. In order for a manager to be a good communicator, good people skills are mandatory; managers must communicate with employees (and other stakeholders) and understand that people have different communication capacities and styles. Managers must also know how to deal with conflict—mostly to resolve it, but sometimes to deliberately create it in order to reveal underlying issues affecting performance.

Perhaps the most important (and most difficult) obligation a manager has is to monitor and control perceptions of organizational equity (fairness). This is an important element of motivating workers. Reflect on your own work experiences. At every job, you probably had a pretty solid idea of your worth, of the job rewards you deserved. (Rewards in this sense might mean money or promotion, but also might mean praise, more challenging work, or anything else you value.) Inevitably, you compare your standing to that of your fellow workers you judge to be peers. What if one or more of your peers are not working as hard as you are, but they are getting the same rewards? The perceived unfairness leads to job dissatisfaction, which may lead to diminished performance—and perhaps even turnover if you decide to quit. For managers to effectively motivate their employees, they must make wise and fair decisions regarding rewards and accurately assess employees' work performance. Only then can rewards be distributed fairly.

Measuring Performance

Managers decide what factors are important to the success of their organizations and then establish standards against which to measure individual or group performance. Obviously, to be most effective the criteria must be fairly and equitably applied across all groups and people.

Developing People

Managers develop people, including themselves, by creating an atmosphere that values ongoing learning. Along with offsite seminars and educational programs, on-the-job training is one of the main tools that managers use to develop their employees. Development doesn't always imply formal, extended training. Small "bites" of constructive feedback from attentive managers can be just as effective.

Successful managers recognize that the people who work for them are their most important resource. They also know that setting an example is the surest and best way to develop people. It's by following a good leader that people learn how to become leaders themselves.

"What a manager does can be analyzed systematically," Peter Drucker maintained. "What a manager has to be able to do has to be learned (though perhaps not always taught). But [there is] one quality [that] cannot be learned, one qualification that the manager cannot acquire but must bring with him. It is not genius; it is character."[5] J. Willard Marriott, founder of the hotel chain bearing his name, believed the same. In a letter to his son when Bill Jr. took over the reins of the company, the elder Marriott wrote, "A leader should have character, be an example in all things. This is his greatest influence."[6]

Knowledge Check

1. Why is it important for managers to be good motivators and communicators?

2. What is the benefit of developing people?

12.2 THE IMPORTANCE OF LEADERSHIP

Let's start this section with a simple definition of leadership: "Leadership is a process whereby an individual influences a group of individuals to achieve a common goal."[7]

Taken from Peter G. Northouse's excellent book *Leadership: Theory and Practice*, this is the most succinct definition that succeeds in capturing all the essential components of leadership. Leading will always involve influence (which comes in many flavors) and process. That means that fulfilling a common goal is a matter of exchange between leader and followers, and not a one-way monologue. Leadership is a group creation.

Any discussion of influence requires a discussion of power. Why do followers work toward a common goal outlined by the leader? Because their performance has implications for them.

Scholars have identified several bases for power, any or all of which you might have encountered on the job. See if these sound familiar:

1. *Referent power*—You like and identify with the leader.

2. *Expert power*—The leader knows more than you.

3. *Legitimate power*—A rank or title is involved; think of a judge or a military office.

4. *Reward power*—Think of a supervisor empowered to give rewards (desirable shifts, bonuses) to those who work hard.

5. *Coercive power*—Too often mistaken for true leadership, coercive power is the power to punish.

Of course, any given supervisor or manager may exert a blend of these types of power. To further complicate matters, in the real world, the person whom workers turn to for leadership may not necessarily be their supervisor—for example, it may be just a coworker who knows what's going on and how to get things done.

The late Warren Bennis—an industrial psychologist and advisor to four American presidents—concluded that managers who succeed do so by *leading*. Bennis believed that managing and leading are both important to organizations, but they are profoundly different:

> *To manage means to bring about, to accomplish, to have charge of, responsibility for, to conduct. Leading is influencing, guiding in direction, course, action, opinion. The distinction is crucial.* Managers are people who do things right and leaders are people who do the right thing. *The difference may be summarized as activities of vision and judgment*—effectiveness—*versus activities of mastering routines*—efficiency.[8]

Bennis concluded that business leaders employed four basic leadership strategies: attention through vision, meaning through communication, trust through positioning, and self-development.

Strategy I: Attention through Vision

Leaders create focus. Ray Kroc of McDonald's told Bennis, "Perhaps [the ability to lead] is a combination of your background, your instincts, and your dreams." Leaders envision their organization's future and share that convincingly with all stakeholders. Before the first load of concrete was poured, Walt Disney knew what Disneyland would look like, how people would feel after spending a day there, and how he would get them to feel that way. Kemmons Wilson dreamed of a network of roadside inns no more than 100 miles apart that would have special facilities for children. His dreams became Holiday Inn.

Strategy II: Meaning through Communication

But dreams alone are not enough. Successful leaders drive others to share those dreams and help turn them into reality. Communication is the key. As Bennis put it:

> *How do you capture imaginations? How do you get people aligned behind the organization's overarching goals? How do you get an audience to recognize and accept an idea? Workers have to recognize and get behind something of established identity. The management of meaning, the mastery of communication, is inseparable from effective leadership.*[9]

Effective leadership requires effective communication. Some leaders write inspiring memos. Others hold meetings complete with models, drawings, and charts to get their ideas across. Many use analogies, comparing what they want things to be like to something that everyone already understands. Bennis pointed out that such communication has little to do with facts—rather, it concentrates on direction. The idea is to get everyone in the organization to share the same ideas and dreams so that they will all hear the same music and play the same tune—based not on having a songbook in front of them, but because they just know instinctively what the tune should sound like.

Strategy III: Trust through Positioning

Leaders not only have a vision and can communicate that vision in a way that gets everyone behind it; they also know how to steer a steady course in the direction they've chosen. People who work for effective leaders trust their reliability. They know that their leaders will do what they have said they will do, whatever it takes. Ritz-Carlton's managers expect their employees to satisfy guests—whatever it takes—and every employee knows that they mean it.

Effective leaders hold on to their principles, ideas, and visions and are not deterred by obstacles, no matter how insurmountable they seem. The people who work for them know this and trust them to carry out their vision. In this respect, such leaders are no different from the legendary generals in military history, whose soldiers knew that they would fight until they achieved victory and thus were willing to fight alongside them.

Strategy IV: Self-Development

Bennis believed that effective leaders are out on the front line leading the charge most of the time. "Our top executives spent roughly 90 percent of their time with others," he reported, "and virtually the same percentage of their time concerned with the messiness of people problems."[10] He calls this "the creative deployment of self." Leaders know what they are good at, and they are constantly using their personal strengths to achieve their goals. At the same time, they understand their weaknesses and compensate for them. If they believe they can't compensate for their weaknesses (e.g., by surrounding themselves with a staff competent in the areas in which they do not excel), they typically do not take the job. "It's the capacity to develop and improve their skills that distinguishes leaders from followers," Bennis observed.[11] Leaders generally do this without being prodded. They have a strong feeling of self-worth—they know who they are and what they can do—and they act based on that confidence in themselves and their own abilities.

In addition, leaders value and respect others. They understand that you can't get others to follow you willingly unless it feels good to them. Leaders seldom criticize others. A former NFL head coach told Bennis that he

> never criticizes his players until after they're convinced of his unconditional confidence. After that's achieved, he might say (if he does spot something that can help a player), "Look, what you're doing is 99 percent terrific, but there is that 1 percent factor that could make a difference. Let's work on that."[12]

Leaders are not afraid to make mistakes. They believe that making mistakes may be the best way to learn—not only about themselves but about their employees. Right-thinking leaders empower their employees to solve problems; if they make a mistake, they're expected to learn from it and get better at their jobs. It makes their jobs more rewarding because they are given a chance to act like a leader—to climb on the tightrope and walk it and take responsibility for their own actions. Sure, there are risks, but there are also rewards. Companies that encourage their employees to take risks, to fail, and to be rewarded when they succeed develop a strong group of well-trained leaders who also know how to follow.

In the best companies, all employees are encouraged to become leaders by owning customers' problems and solving them. By being given the resources and authority to make decisions independently, they have **empowerment**: they are authorized to solve customers' problems without needing to seek prior approval from their supervisors. This requires great trust on the part of their leaders. It also requires a well-trained group of people that *can* be trusted. As Bennis pointed out, leaders who trust themselves understand instinctively that it is necessary to trust others.

In the best companies, employees are encouraged to own customers' problems and solve them.

As invigorating as empowerment is for your workers, nothing erodes morale more than *false* empowerment. Have you ever worked a job where you had responsibility for, say, guests' satisfaction but received none of the support necessary to make it possible? Or worse, you were undercut

Opportunities to make a good impression on guests abound in the hospitality industry.

at every turn? True leaders eradicate this morale killer from their organizations. They make sure that empowerment is real and their people are supported through thick and thin.

12.3 LABOR TRENDS

By any measure, one of the most serious challenges the hospitality industry faces is the shortage of qualified workers. Many industry leaders feel that the shortage of qualified labor makes it difficult to expand their brands and provide excellent service. High turnover of staff also negatively impacts the industry's ability to provide consistent service and control labor costs. Demographic changes provide a clue to some of the causes of the industry's labor challenges.

Changing Demographics

Most observers agree that there are several key demographic trends that will have a significant impact on the American workforce and consequently on all U.S. businesses in the coming years.

Population Growth. In the 1950s, the U.S. population was growing at a rate of as high as 2 percent annually. Starting in the twenty-first century, many millennials postponed marriage and childbearing, and stricter immigration restrictions led to population growth dropping to 0.46 percent in 2018–2019. During the first full year of the COVID-19 pandemic, 2020–2021, annual growth fell to a historic low of 0.16 percent as a result of the substantial rise in deaths and declines in births and immigration. As the U.S. birth rate continues to decrease and the number of deaths rise (due to an aging population), immigration will play an ever more important role in shaping the American workforce.

The Aging Work Force. Labor trends continue to show that the U.S. workforce is aging.

The median age of the U.S. labor force was 35.4 years in 1986, according to the U.S. Bureau of Labor Statistics; projections expect that by 2030, the labor force will grow by 96.5 percent among people ages 75 and older.[13] The ongoing increase in older workers is due to a number of reasons, including the following:

- Many individuals are living longer and healthier lives.

- Today's higher-educated workforce tends to stay in the workforce longer.

- Defined contribution plans give incentives to older workers to continue contributing to their retirement plans by remaining employed and delaying retirement.

- The eligible age for collecting full retirement Social Security benefits began to increase as of 2000.

- The cost of health insurance continues to rise.

The good news for hospitality managers is that an older labor force is usually more experienced and productive. However, the bad news is that there are fewer younger workers available in today's labor force to start in entry-level positions and work their way up.

Generation Y or Millennials. Individuals born between 1978 and 1995 and identified by advertisers and others as "Generation Y" or "millennials" have entered the workforce with different attitudes about work than those who preceded them. Millennials are technologically savvy, exhibit a high degree of independence, and seek flexibility in their work–life balance. They have high expectations of their employers and do not hesitate to challenge the status quo. Seeking to advance on their terms, they are ready to move to the next employment opportunity as soon as it arises. Their expectations differ greatly from their older counterparts in the workforce, who tend to be more traditional, prefer the status quo, and remain loyal to their current employer. This may be especially challenging for managers in the hospitality industry, who are expected to lead an increasingly diverse workforce with very different expectations.

The Increase in Women Workers. Because of the rising cost of living and the increase in the number of single-parent households, the number of women joining the U.S. workforce has grown steadily since the middle of the twentieth century. In 1955, only 35 percent of women worked outside the home, but today more than half of all women are in the workforce. In 2022, the labor force participation rate—the percentage of the population working or looking for work—for all mothers with children under age 18 was 72.9 percent.

The Shifting Population. There has been a large influx of immigrants from the Caribbean, Central and South America, and Asia who have settled in the southern and western United States. The 10 fastest-growing states are in the West and South. This means that there is a labor shortage in some areas of the country, but not in all.

Transitions in Education. As industries continue to require more knowledge from their workers, degrees of some sort—either from a university, junior college, or technical school—will be important for job attainment and workers' earnings. Between 2020 and 2021, the mean nominal earnings of workers ages 18 and older rose about $6,900 for people whose highest credential was a bachelor's degree. In 2022, more U.S. immigrants (15.2 percent) held advanced degrees, such as master's degrees, than U.S. natives (14 percent). Also in 2022, 39 percent of women ages 25 and older completed a bachelor's degree or more as their highest level of educational attainment, compared to 36.2 percent of men in the same age range. However, undergraduate college enrollment dropped 8 percent from 2019 to 2022—the steepest decline

on record. The decline has been attributed to disruptions from the COVID-19 pandemic, students considering alternatives to higher education, and concerns about student debt.

The Diversity of the Workforce. In 1960, only 10 percent of Americans belonged to a minority group. Today, 25 percent of all Americans are nonwhite. By the year 2050, Blacks, Hispanics, Asians, and Native Americans will represent more than 50 percent of the U.S. population, and non-Hispanic whites will become the new minority. Clearly, as more and more managers and employees from diverse races and cultures are brought together in the workplace, there is an increasing need for diversity training and a better understanding on the part of managers of how to manage a diverse workforce.

High Turnover

High turnover rates are another labor problem that hospitality managers must cope with. According to the American Hotel & Lodging Association, employee turnover in the hotel industry is between 60 percent to more than 300 percent annually. One hotel operator reports that most departing employees are room attendants, food servers, and bussers, and nearly half of them leave during the first two weeks of employment. One result of this high turnover rate is that many hotel and restaurant employees are not well trained or experienced enough to provide the quality of service customers expect.

The number of women employed in the hospitality industry continues to grow.

It is difficult to pin down all the reasons for the industry's high turnover rates, but there are a few that may be universal. One reason is improperly managing expectations during the hiring process, resulting in hospitality workers getting disillusioned after learning that they need to work on holidays or weekends, have limited opportunities for advancement, and don't receive enough training and supervision. Many receive inadequate training, make mistakes, get discouraged, and quit. While on-the-job training may be the cheapest form of training, it is also the most traumatic for employees.

Knowledge Check

1. How have changing demographics affected the American workforce?

2. What are some reasons for high turnover in the hospitality industry?

12.4 LEGISLATION

It is important for hospitality managers to understand legislation that has an impact on the way they manage their businesses. In 1938, Congress passed the Fair Labor Standards Act, which established laws concerning wages and overtime. Employees of service industries were exempt until 1967, and it was not until 1979 that all of the provisions were in force. The law addressed such issues as the employment of minors and equal pay for men and women who perform the same kind of work.

A number of other federal and local laws have influenced human resources practices. The Civil Rights Act of 1964 bans discrimination on the basis of race, gender, religion, or national origin. One result of this law was the formation of the Equal Employment Opportunity Commission (EEOC), which oversees the enforcement and administration of this law. In recent years, the EEOC has expanded its horizons to cover sexual harassment cases.

The Occupational Safety and Health Act of 1970 spells out what constitutes safe working conditions. In addition, it requires employers to make sure that workers have necessary safety equipment while on the job and that equipment, such as meat slicers and ladders, conforms to safety standards. The Occupational Safety and

Health Administration (OSHA) was established to oversee worker safety.

The Americans with Disabilities Act (ADA) of 1990 and the changes made by the ADA Amendments Act of 2008 are designed to protect the civil rights of people who have physical or mental disabilities. Employers may not deny jobs to people with disabilities who are capable of performing the jobs and must provide reasonable access to the workplace for them (e.g., accessible parking spaces and ramps for wheelchairs).

The Family and Medical Leave Act of 1993 provides that employees must be given up to 12 weeks off per year without pay if they need it for the birth or adoption of a child, or because of an illness of the employee or a family member. Effective January 2009, the regulations were revised to add military family leave entitlements for eligible family members.

The Illegal Immigration Reform and Immigrant Responsibility Act of 1996 establishes penalties for employers who knowingly hire undocumented workers. It also prohibits employment discrimination on the basis of national origin or citizenship.

Knowledge Check

1. What does the Family and Medical Leave Act ensure for families?

2. What did the Fair Labor Standards Act establish?

12.5 HUMAN RESOURCES PROGRAMS

A sound human resources (HR) program typically contains the following elements:

- It truly cares about employees.
- It defines the job.
- It establishes productivity standards.
- It recruits the most suitable job candidates.
- It selects the best applicants.
- It implements continual training and career development programs.
- It motivates employees so they want to stay with the company.

- It offers competitive employee benefit options.
- It evaluates employees.

We'll take a look at each of these elements in the following sections.

Caring about Employees

There is a growing recognition among managers in service industries that you can't expect employees to treat customers any better than they themselves are treated. The Ritz-Carlton Hotel Company refers to its employees in its mission statement as "internal customers" and believes that in order for its employees to offer quality service to guests, Ritz-Carlton must first offer it to employees. The company promotes a corporate culture that encourages employees to stop their day-to-day routine to help fellow employees. This helps eliminate internal competition and builds stronger employee teams.

At McDonald's, teenage employees are told that "working part time is an excellent way for you to learn about the real world. But it's more important for you to make education Priority #1. At McDonald's, our commitment is to help students explore the best of both worlds."[14] This communicates to employees McDonald's belief in the importance of education.

Both of these companies recognize that when they talk about being in the "people business," they mean the people who work for them as well as the people who buy from them. Companies with successful HR programs recognize that people are the most valuable resource they have and ensure that every step within their program takes into account the basic worth of individuals and their sensitivities and vulnerabilities. These companies say, in effect, "We are employers who care about the people who work for us."

Defining the Job

Before the right person can be hired to perform a particular job, managers must understand exactly what the job involves so an applicant's skills and the requirements of the job can be matched accurately.

The task of analyzing a job is somewhat more complicated in the hospitality industry than elsewhere. The job of a spot welder, for example, is essentially the same whether the welding takes place on top of a skyscraper or in a machine shop. But a food server's job can vary tremendously depending on the time of day, the operation's physical layout and design, whether they are working at a local diner or a fine dining restaurant, the operation's equipment, and the guests' expectations. Even merchandising techniques can affect a food server's job: in most restaurants, guests order off a printed menu; in others, servers are expected to show a blackboard to diners or memorize the daily specials.

Since the same job can differ from property to property, independent hotels and restaurants must perform their own job analyses in order to understand how jobs are done at their particular properties. Hotels and restaurants that belong to chains do not typically perform their own job analyses; this task is done at corporate headquarters. For example, Days Inn's franchise division commissioned the School of Industrial and Systems Engineering at the Georgia Institute of Technology to prepare an analysis of Days Inn's room-cleaning procedures. The Georgia Tech analysts concluded that all major tasks in room cleaning fall into "natural groupings," or job blocks, and recommended that Days Inn adopt the room-cleaning sequence shown in Exhibit 12.1.

This is only part of the job analysis of a typical room attendant position. The complete description might also cover the room attendant's responsibility for stocking the in-room cart with sheets, pillowcases, towels, glasses, soap, toilet paper, stationery, and other items, as well as more detail on how beds should be made, toilets cleaned, and so on.

Once a job has been analyzed, a number of documents can be prepared to help employees understand and learn the job, including job lists, job breakdowns, and job descriptions.

As the name implies, a **job list** is simply a list of the tasks that must be performed by the individual holding that particular job (see Exhibit 12.2). Job lists are useful as training tools and can serve as reminders for new employees.

Job lists are the foundations for **job breakdowns**—specific, step-by-step procedures for accomplishing a task (see Exhibit 12.3). The first column in Exhibit 12.3 shows a task (7) from the job list shown in Exhibit 12.2. The second column breaks down the task by identifying the steps that an employee must take to accomplish the task. These steps are written as performance standards. The third column, "Additional

Exhibit 12.1 Sample Guestroom Cleaning Sequence

Preliminary

The room attendant enters the room, turns on the light, and opens the curtains. They place the in-room cart at the side of the vanity. They then make a forward sweep through the room, picking up room trash. They deposit the trash in the main cart outside the door and return to the room.

↓

Block 1

From the vanity, the room attendant makes a second sweep through the room, gathering all dirty terry, placing terry on the used bed, and wrapping the dirty linen around it. If two beds are used, then they place the ball on the second bed, wrapping the dirty linen from that bed around it. Note that the procedure eliminates stuffing linen and terry into a pillowcase. This is a time-consuming procedure. The room attendant takes the ball and places it in the main cart outside the door.

↓

Block 2

From the main cart, they take all necessary clean linen, reenter the room, and make the bed(s).

↓

Block 3

From the beds, they go directly to the vanity and perform all necessary work, including terry restocking. They do not need to move away from the vanity due to the convenience of the in-room cart.

↓

Block 4

They move the in-room cart next to the bathroom. Here, they perform all bathroom cleaning tasks.

↓

Block 5

They make a circuit of the room to dust. Returning to the in-room cart, they move it next to the desk, clean the desk mirror, replace the trash can bag, and restock necessary stationery supplies. Then, moving the in-room cart toward the door, they take the in-room cart outside the room.

↓

Block 6

Removing the vacuum (or other carpet-cleaning tool) from the main cart, they vacuum the room.

Information," explains why each step of the task is performed and may also include such information as desired attitudes when performing the step, safety tips, or pointers on how to reach the performance standard. In the other columns, managers can record information for quarterly performance evaluations. As you can see, a job breakdown can be as useful in evaluating employees as in training them.

Once a job list and a job breakdown have been developed for a particular job, a **job**

description can be written that outlines (1) the title that goes with the job, (2) the person to whom the employee reports, (3) the work to be performed (in general terms), (4) the education or skills the employee must have, and (5) the physical requirements of the job. A job description can be useful in a number of ways. It can be used as a recruiting tool to show prospective employees the nature of the work to be performed; it is an excellent training tool; supervisors can use it to monitor work in progress; and it can be

Exhibit 12.2   Sample Job List for a Housekeeping Room Attendant

	Date: XX/XX/XX
JOB LIST	

Position: Housekeeping Room Attendant

Tasks: Employees must be able to:

1. PARK in designated area.
2. WEAR proper uniform.
3. PUNCH in.
4. PICK up clipboard and keys.
5. MEET with supervisor.
6. OBTAIN supplies.
7. PLAN your work.
8. ENTER the room.
9. CHECK guest's linen refreshment preference.
10. PREPARE the room.
11. MAKE the beds.
12. GATHER cleaning supplies.
13. CLEAN the bathroom.
14. DUST the room.
15. CHECK/REPLACE paper supplies and amenities.
16. CLEAN windows.
17. INSPECT your work.
18. VACUUM the room.
19. LOCK the door and mark your report.
20. TAKE breaks at designated times.
21. RETURN and restock cart.
22. RETURN to housekeeping with clipboard and keys.
23. PUNCH out.

Exhibit 12.3   Sample Job Breakdown for a Housekeeping Room Attendant

POSITION: Housekeeping Room Attendant, morning shift

NAME:

SUPERVISOR:

JOB LIST	PERFORMANCE STANDARDS	ADDITIONAL INFORMATION	1st QTR Yes/No	2nd QTR Yes/No	3rd QTR Yes/No	4th QTR Yes/No
7. PLAN YOUR WORK.	A. STUDY your assignment sheet.	Early service requests, rush rooms, check-outs, VIPs, and no-service requests will be noted on your chart.				
	B. CLEAN check-outs first, whenever possible.	Cleaning check-outs first gives the front desk rooms to sell.				
	C. CLEAN early service requests as noted on your report.					
	D. CLEAN VIP rooms before lunch, whenever possible.	A VIP is our most important guest.				
	E. LOCK your cart room door and proceed to your section.					
	F. HONOR "do not disturb" signs.	We must honor the privacy of guests. Many guests like to sleep in. Never knock on a door that has a "do not disturb" sign.				
	G. CHECK rooms marked c/o and then check the rooms that are circled on your report. These are rooms due to check out.	Rooms marked c/o have already checked out at the front desk. Check-out time is noon.				
	H. PLAN your work around early service requests.	If you have early service requests, be sure to clean these rooms at the proper time.				

used as the basis for employee evaluation. Job descriptions can also ease employee anxiety because they specify in writing the person to whom the employee reports and the responsibilities of the employee.

Establishing Productivity Standards

A good HR program has **productivity standards**. Productivity standards tell managers how long it should take employees to complete tasks using the best methods management has devised and how much work can be performed in a given time period. Productivity standards are often based on a manager's personal experience, the business's historical records, and industry standards.

In order to know whether productivity standards are being met, employee productivity must be measured. Productivity can be measured in dollars or units produced or served.

When productivity is expressed in dollars, it can be calculated by two different methods. The first consists of dividing sales by payroll costs:

$$\frac{\$10,000,000\,(sales)}{\$2,500,000\,(payroll)} = \$4$$

In this example, every $1 of payroll expended produced $4 of sales.

The second method of calculating productivity using dollars consists of dividing sales by the number of **full-time-equivalent (FTE) employees**, which is a measure used by organizations to represent the total number of worked hours of an employee, expressed as a full-time employee's workload. It is a way to quantify the total hours worked by all employees, taking into account both full-time and part-time employees and converting them into an equivalent number of full-time employees. For example, four part-time employees who each work 10 hours a week would, for statistical purposes, be recorded as one FTE employee:

$$\frac{\$10,000,000\,(sales)}{280\,(FTE\ employees)} = \$35,714\,(rounded)$$

In this example, $35,714 was generated for every FTE employee.

These are very basic examples of measuring productivity. More complex systems are often used to determine productivity by department. For example, what is the catering sales revenue generated from each inbound call, from a salesperson, or from a referral? Does understaffing a restaurant dining room increase the available earning capacity of each server but at the same time reduce the overall food and beverage sales because customers are frustrated with the wait times?

Productivity standards are not only essential for payroll control—they are also important in job analysis and as measures of expectation when recruiting, training, or evaluating an employee.

Managers should never assume that high productivity equals guest satisfaction and business success. While managers of service businesses must watch their productivity measures carefully in order to achieve their economic goals, they must also remember that success in business has qualitative as well as quantitative dimensions. In other words, successful businesses base their productivity standards in part on guest expectations, not on profitability or efficiency objectives alone. For example, the Bob Evans restaurant chain bases many of its productivity standards on its guests' expectations and carefully measures how well it meets those expectations. Guests should not have to wait for a table for more than 15 minutes; after guests are seated, an employee should come by with water and a greeting within 60 seconds; food should arrive at the table no longer than 10 minutes after guests order it; and a vacated table must be readied for new guests within 5 minutes.

Recruiting Suitable Candidates

Once the various jobs have been defined and productivity standards established, recruiting workers becomes the top priority for managers. A major goal of recruiting is to find the best workers available who find the job attractive and are willing to work for the wages offered by the business. This task is complicated by the fact that, in the hospitality industry, work skills alone are not a sufficient measure of a person's suitability for a job. Personality must also be taken into consideration if the position involves interaction with guests.

Internal and External Sources of Employees. All sources of new employees fall into one of two categories: internal or external. Of these, internal sources are the least costly and often the most reliable. One internal source consists of recruits recommended by current employees. Since employees have a good understanding of the nature of the work involved, and since they tend to be careful about whom they recommend, employees often bring in recruits who do very well. In tight labor markets, employees may be paid a referral fee if the new recruit stays for a certain length of time (typically 90 days). Postings on the company intranet, internal bulletin boards, and company newsletters are ways of getting the news of job openings to employees.

Often, employees will suggest friends and relatives for positions. Some businesses have rules prohibiting family members from working together. These rules are typically a result of previous negative experiences or of fears that if one member of a family leaves the company, other members may leave as well. There are also legitimate concerns about a conflict of interest (e.g., if an employee oversees a relative). However, there are many examples of family members working for the same employer at the same time quite successfully, so a complete ban on such hires is unwise.

Another internal source of applicants for a vacant job is the current staff. Promoting from within establishes the operation as a good place to work—one in which opportunities are available for those who want them, are suitable for promotion, and work hard. In fact, a strong internal promotion policy is in itself a valuable recruiting tool, and many companies spell out internal career ladders as part of their recruitment program. For example, many of the Domino's Pizza franchisees were once store managers—owning your own store is part of the career track that is offered as a recruitment incentive. More than 50 percent of Marriott's managers have been promoted from within. Nine out of 10 salaried employees at table-service restaurants started out as hourly workers. Loews Hotels has career monitoring days for line-level employees.

There are also some potential problems associated with internal promotion. An employee applicant who loses a position to another employee (or to an outside applicant) might turn their disappointment into negative actions, such as not performing up to standards or complaining

In the hospitality industry, work skills alone are not a sufficient measure of a person's suitability for the job. Personality must also be taken into consideration, especially if the position involves interaction with guests. It's easier to teach job skills than to teach someone to have a pleasing personality and a warm smile; that's why some HR managers "hire the smile" when recruiting for many positions.

on the job (which could affect the morale of others). In general, employers who use internal promotion effectively also have strong employee counseling programs.

External sources for employees can be informally tapped. Managers and supervisory staff are often able to locate new personnel through their social and professional contacts. In many cases, this involves recruiting from competitive operations. Companies find that being heavily involved in local community affairs makes them more approachable and that a larger number of people apply for job openings than would otherwise.

Classified advertising and direct mail are examples of formal external recruiting methods. Classified advertising can be placed in local daily newspapers, in industry journals, and even on radio stations. Sending email and direct mail to schools, colleges, and seniors' groups are also good ways to reach job candidates. This approach is likely to be especially successful in markets where there are new hotels and restaurants opening, plus it can help to promote the new business. An advantage of **advertising**—a communication strategy used by businesses and organizations to promote their products, services, or ideas to a target audience— and direct mail is that they generally produce a large number of applicants. After all, everyone looking for a job is likely to apply for what sounds like an attractive position. A disadvantage of the direct mail recruiting method is that many applicants are not qualified and must be screened out by the HR department. This can be time-consuming and expensive.

One of the most successful recruiting tools is the Internet. While sites like Indeed post the largest number of job openings, there are some recruiting sites devoted just to the hospitality industry, such as Hcareers. Hospitality companies often have employment sections on their websites where a candidate can apply or submit a résumé online.

Other formal external sources that are often used to recruit employees are state government employment offices and private employment agencies. People who are out of work and wish to receive unemployment compensation are usually required to register with state employment offices, so these offices usually have sizable lists of candidates. Many of these individuals may not be qualified for hospitality jobs, however, and must be screened carefully. There are some private employment agencies that charge a fee

for placing an individual with a company; the fee is paid by either the employee or the employer. These agencies are mostly used to find supervisory and management personnel.

The city school systems in New York City and Miami–Dade County have their own "Academies of Tourism." These academies help high school students gain an awareness and understanding of the hospitality and tourism industry. All the students work in an internship their senior year; some continue their education in culinary schools or hospitality programs in college, while others go directly into the workforce. In many communities, students in hospitality, tourism, or culinary programs offered by junior colleges and four-year institutions are eager to gain work experience while in school.

The National Restaurant Association has identified several sometimes-overlooked population groups that can answer the needs of the restaurant industry and other hospitality organizations. These groups include minorities, workers with disabilities, older adults, and workers with limited skills. The National Restaurant Association points out that some individuals within these groups might need help in improving their English-speaking skills. Special job trainers or equipment might be needed for workers with disabilities. New career ladders might be needed for older workers.

A good deal of recruiting is done by companies at colleges that teach hospitality management. A hotel or restaurant chain may offer graduates an opportunity to enter a management training program that, upon completion, qualifies them for a supervisory position at one of its properties. Or graduates may receive direct placement offers. With these, graduates are put directly into supervisory or management positions and are given on-the-job training. Often, direct placement recruiting is done by independent hotels/restaurants and private clubs that do not offer full-scale management training programs.

Some hotels and foodservice companies employ the services of executive recruiters. Companies usually engage these recruitment firms to find people for senior management positions. Executive recruiters receive substantial fees for their services.

Another recruitment technique is networking. With **networking**, either online or via other methods of communication, current employees contact or are contacted by friends, classmates, and former associates about a job opening. Most observers agree that the majority of management positions are filled via networking rather than through advertising.

Of course, many graduates from hospitality programs—and supervisors and managers already employed in the industry—find their own positions by directly contacting the companies they would like to work for.

Selecting the Best Applicants

Selecting the right employees has long been considered one of the keys to operating a successful hospitality business. As mentioned earlier, personality must be considered as well as skills. In 1917, the great hotelier Ellsworth Statler told his hotel managers to "hire only good-natured people." That is still a good idea today.

Selecting an applicant to fill a position involves five steps:

1. Receiving and processing applications

2. Interviewing applicants

3. Evaluating applicants

4. Checking references

5. Hiring the selected person

These steps should not be taken lightly. Top-notch companies go about hiring people carefully for even the lowest-paid positions. Selectivity is the watchword. At the Walt Disney World Resort, no candidate for a salaried or managerial-level position is hired on the basis of one interview; at least two are required.

Implementing Continual Training and Career Development Programs

Training is one of the most crucial parts of an HR program, but it is more often talked about than practiced. When an operation gets busy, training is often overlooked or temporarily suspended due to lack of time or lack of trainers.

Training is enormously demanding. It should be an ongoing process for all current employees; for new employees, the training process or program has to be started all over again at square one. Training is also expensive—employees who

are learning are not fully productive. For these reasons, there is a great temptation to take shortcuts in training procedures. Managers often rationalize their negligence by telling themselves that current employees don't need to be trained, or on-the-job training is good enough for new hires. Yet, without training at all levels within the organization, there can be no consistency of product and service. Training is the process that teaches trainees the knowledge and skills they need to operate within the standards set by management. Training also attempts to develop within employees a positive attitude toward guest service.

Poor training contributes to high turnover and substandard job performance. Employees should feel comfortable in their jobs and be able to do them well so they do not become discouraged and quit. To train their employees well, many companies use techniques like the video-assisted testing described earlier for new job applicants. At Domino's, McDonald's, and Wendy's, training programs introduce new items and emphasize product consistency and control standards. The Cheesecake Factory has a comprehensive six- to eight-week training program for store managers and kitchen managers.

For new hires, training should begin on the first day with a welcoming orientation at which the employees are introduced to basic elements of the company's culture, important company policies and practices, and their new colleagues. This type of orientation session can help create a positive first impression of the company. The Cheesecake Factory's online learning management system, Cheesecake U, hosts training programs and courses for company-wide staff.

Training must be continuous and ongoing. A company with an active training program expresses a commitment to its employees. A training program should define who will be trained (ideally, all categories and levels of employees), who will be responsible for training (corporate staff, on-site managers, supervisory personnel), and the training aids and techniques that will be used.

Regular, ongoing training on basic job tasks is necessary at all levels of an organization. Unless continuing positive reinforcement is provided, employees tend to forget some of what they learned. In addition to ongoing training in employees' regular duties, it is often necessary to hold extra training sessions on topics such as sanitation and fire safety.

Training helps give employees confidence.

While most training focuses on knowledge and skills, equally important are other issues that directly affect employees' job satisfaction and attitudes. Many of these issues fall under the broad heading of diversity. **Diversity training** programs seek to make all workers feel comfortable in the work atmosphere—no matter their race, culture, gender, or age. Diversity programs are not the same as affirmative action programs. Affirmative action programs were created as a result of government mandates to eliminate discrimination based on gender and race. By their very nature, they have accelerated more diversity among workers, which has led to a greater need for diversity training.

Motivating and Retaining Employees

Finding ways to motivate and retain workers is perhaps a manager's most difficult challenge. The importance of having employees who are motivated is clear. The present shortage of workers demands that individual workers increase their productivity. How can managers increase

productivity? According to a National Science Foundation report that reviewed 300 studies of productivity, pay, and job satisfaction,

Increased productivity depends on two propositions. First comes motivation: arousing and maintaining the will to work effectively—having workers who are productive not because they are coerced, but because they are committed. Second is reward. Of all the factors that help to create highly motivated and highly satisfied workers, the principal one … appears to be that effective performance be recognized and rewarded in whatever terms are meaningful to the individual—financial, psychological, or both.[15]

The message is clear. Motivation is a matter of commitment. A manager can only motivate employees to do their best at what the manager wants them to do if it is something the employees want to do as well. Bill McLean, former CEO of a major bank, puts it this way: "You need not read further concerning motivation unless you genuinely understand that to get employees to perform minimum duties, one only needs to drive them. To gain their top performance, one must inspire them to drive themselves."[16]

Employee Benefit Options

Including employee benefits as part of a compensation program has become even more important in the competitive environment in which hospitality organizations operate today. Benefits such as paid time off, vacation time, personal days, and paid holidays are critical in an industry that typically operates 24 hours a day, 365 days a year. Work–life balance has become an important concept in an increasingly stressful society. Additionally, offering benefit options such as health insurance (medical, dental, vision), company-matched 401(k) retirement plans, and employee assistance programs contribute to a company's ability to attract and retain talented staff. Of course, there are expenses associated with these programs, but in order to compete, most hospitality organizations find that these are necessary expenses.

Because of the increasing cost of health insurance, employers try to make plans more affordable by offering a variety of medical and dental plans with different options (high or low deductibles, varying office-visit co-pays, etc.) and sharing the expense for these benefits with their employees (i.e., asking employees to pay a portion of the cost). Due to the employer's purchasing power with the health insurance companies, the cost is less to employees than if they searched for insurance on their own.

Other employee benefits usually found in the hospitality industry include offering complimentary meals or meals offered at a minimal charge, free dry cleaning of uniforms, free parking, discounted or complimentary travel/room nights, and tuition reimbursement programs.

Evaluating Employees

Although we are discussing evaluation last, it should be clear by this time that evaluation occurs in almost every part of an HR program, from selection and hiring to training and motivating. Companies that do a good job of

developing, motivating, and retaining employees recognize that where there are problems, they are often the result of a flawed system rather than a flawed person. For example, if a server frequently has trouble delivering room service breakfast orders on time, you can't blame them for this problem if the only service elevator is always tied up by housekeepers eager to get their guestrooms cleaned.

Employee **performance reviews** are typically held every 3, 6, or 12 months. New employees are usually reviewed more frequently than experienced ones. The purpose of performance reviews is not to confront employees with their shortcomings. The performance review is a natural step that follows selection, training, and motivating. It lets employees know how well they have learned to do what the company expects of them, and it lets managers know how well they are doing in hiring the right people and training them. Performance reviews are also coaching tools that managers can use to improve employee performance.

Good performance reviews are specific and objective. Before meeting with an employee, some managers fill out a review form on which they can rate the employee's knowledge, skills, and personal attributes—often on some kind of numerical basis. During the review, the manager shares these ratings with the employee and gives them a chance to comment on them. Some companies have the employee fill out the same form before the review meeting so the manager and the employee can compare ratings. The manager can recommend follow-up training, coaching, and counseling if those seem called for. Some companies have the manager and the employee draw up a joint goal-setting agreement in which the two agree on (1) what will be done on both sides to improve the employee's performance in their current job, and (2) what the manager and employee will do to prepare the employee for a more rewarding position.

Knowledge Check
1. Why is it important for businesses to analyze jobs?
2. What are some internal and external sources of employees?

12.6 MARKETING HOSPITALITY

In recent years, there has been a dramatic change in how businesses are marketed. Television, newspapers, and magazines are losing ground to digital platforms. In the pre-Internet days, companies disseminated their marketing messages in several ways: they used a sales staff, print or broadcast advertising, promotions, and perhaps a contracted public relations expert to help them get newspapers and magazines to take notice of the business. These traditional methods are still used, but to a lesser degree each year. Today, the Internet has become the primary means of communicating with hotel, restaurant, airline, and other hospitality and travel customers. Generation Z and millennial travelers are making travel decisions based on social media images.

In some businesses, television continues to command the largest segment of the advertising budget, but today one rarely sees a television commercial for hotels. Jumeirah Hotels & Resorts, in a shift from traditional print and broadcast advertising, spends over 50 percent of its marketing budget on digital marketing. The Wyndham Hotels & Resorts and Accor are at similar levels of spending. There are some independent hotels where digital marketing is as high as 95 percent of the marketing budget.[17]

The fundamentals of marketing are the same with or without the Internet. Having a grasp of basic marketing concepts can help hospitality managers and others create and execute their companies' digital as well as non-digital marketing strategies.

The purpose of a business is to get and keep customers—without customers there is no business. Professor Theodore Levitt of the Harvard Business School points out that

> customers are constantly presented with lots of options to help them solve their problems. They don't buy things, they buy solutions to problems. ... No business can function effectively without a clear view of how to get customers, what its prospective customers want and need, what options its competitors give them, and without explicit strategies and programs focused on what goes on in the marketplace.[18]

That is what marketing is: the effort to determine and meet the needs and wants of current and potential customers.

There is an important distinction between selling and marketing that many students fail to recognize. This is due to confusing terminology that is commonly used in business. Often, people whose jobs are in sales are called "marketing representatives." The title suggests that the words "sales" and "marketing" are interchangeable; they are not. **Marketing** is a much broader term that includes sales and a great deal more. It is a system of interrelated activities formulated to help managers plan, price, promote, and make available services or products to customers and potential customers in a particular target market. The primary goal of marketing is to create awareness, generate interest, and ultimately drive sales or adoption of the offerings. Marketing lays the foundation for sales by creating awareness and generating interest, while sales activities are focused on converting leads into paying customers. The difference between the two has often been stated this way: *selling is getting rid of what you have; marketing is having what people want.*

Some marketers look at it this way: marketing is the art of *buying from* customers, which is exactly the opposite of *selling to* customers. In other words, customers have money in their pockets that you, the salesperson, want to "buy." How can you buy the customer's money? By paying for it with a product or service. This marketing approach to selling can help you sell in two ways. First, your focus is on the customers rather than on your products. Instead of focusing on the attributes of your products, you focus on persuading customers to "sell" you their money, which usually leads you to study your customers and their needs and wants. Second, you have a different attitude toward customers—you value them more and approach them more carefully because you realize you are trying to convince them to give up something of value.

The Four P's of Marketing

The list of activities that can be included in the efforts to get and keep customers is quite extensive. For a restaurant, the things that influence whether customers eat there include the location, décor, menu, quality and presentation of food, type of service, and prices. All of these are marketing decisions first and foremost. To make these decisions, a restaurant's managers must determine (1) what their current and potential customers need or want, (2) how to provide it, and (3) how to persuade current and potential customers to patronize the restaurant. These activities break down into four basic responsibilities that are popularly called the "**Four P's of Marketing**": product, place, price, and promotion.

How businesses allocate their resources among product, place, price, and promotional efforts varies widely, because it depends on the objectives of each business. In a sense, the Four P's are like the ingredients in a recipe for success, and the relative proportion of resources allocated to each effort and the way these four marketing efforts are combined is often referred to as the **marketing mix**. The focus of the marketing mix is the target customers and the employees who serve them.

Product: What Do You Sell? The term "product" as used in the hospitality field can have several meanings. Obviously, a product can be a guestroom or a meal that a hotel or restaurant provides to guests. A hospitality product can also be an intangible service, such as a food server serving a meal or a bellhop carrying a guest's luggage. Product can also refer to a hotel or restaurant's concept. For example, a Fairfield Inn is an economy product designed specifically to appeal to business travelers. In this case, "product" refers to all the things that make the experience of staying at a Fairfield Inn what it is— its philosophy, facilities, amenities, level of service, and the tangible products it sells to guests.

A hotel or restaurant's concept—the type of establishment it is or will be—should be first and foremost a marketing decision that is based on providing a better solution to a customer's problem, which might be anything from finding a place for a quick bite to eat to searching for a site to hold a wedding reception for 300 people. To come up with a successful concept for a hospitality business requires a clear understanding of what people are looking for and what competitors already offer them. Only a business that understands what consumers' needs are—and can satisfy those needs—has a hope of succeeding.

Today, hospitality products—either the physical facility or the services provided—may not be developed by the company's owners and creative team alone. For example, the concept of **crowdsourcing** invites customers to offer their suggestions for improving a company's products. Marriott's campaign "Travel Brilliantly" focused on millennials by welcoming these guests to share their suggestions for enhancing their hotel experiences. Two of their suggestions were adopted by Marriott: "easier access to healthier foods and pop-up shops stocked with bona fide local gifts" and "regional touches that let a hotel really reflect its location."[19]

Place: Where Do You Sell It? "Place" also has several meanings in hospitality marketing. To begin with, it clearly refers to the physical location of the business, which, as has been shown previously, can be crucial to its success. This physical meaning of "place" can have a profound effect on marketing methods. For instance, the fact that a large number of Holiday Inns are located all over the United States means that people are reminded of the Holiday Inn name wherever they go. When they are in a strange town, the Holiday Inn is a familiar place. Moreover, because Holiday Inn is everywhere, its corporate management can advertise on national television or in national magazines, which would be too costly and inefficient for many of its competitors.

Place is also the sites where the reservations for the hotel are made, referred to today as **distribution channels**. This can occur on the hotel's own website or the website of the chain to which the hotel belongs (in the case of chain properties). It can also take place via telephone at the hotel or at the hotel's central reservations office, at a travel agency (by phone or in person), or on the Internet with an online travel agency (OTA) such as Expedia.

Price: What Do You Sell It For? Too often, hotels and restaurants set their prices on a cost-plus pricing method. **cost-plus pricing** is determining a price by taking the total cost of providing a product or service and adding to it (1) a percentage to cover overhead or fixed expenses and (2) a predetermined gross profit margin. It is assumed that food costs, for example, should be 30 percent of the menu item's total cost to a guest. But this model ignores how guests feel about what they are getting and what they are willing to pay for it. The basic flaw with cost-plus pricing is that guests don't care what your costs are. Moreover, it doesn't take into account a notion that almost all retailers understand: some items are

The term *product* as used in the hospitality industry can have several meanings. A hospitality product can be tangible—such as a bottle of fine wine—but it can also be an intangible service, such as a sommelier's suggestion for just the right wine for a special occasion.

loss-leaders, items that are not profitable but which attract customers to stores, where they may buy other items that are profitable. Typically, bars and lounges that offer a free or nominally priced buffet during happy hour are purposely sacrificing the low profit margin on their food in order to gain higher profits from beverage sales.

Cost-plus or product-driven pricing is used by many businesses to set prices, but consumers ultimately decide whether they will pay for what is being offered. If they won't pay the price set by management, the price must be adjusted or the product or service must be dropped. Therefore, **consumer-based pricing** is a much more realistic method of setting prices. With consumer-based pricing, companies first determine what customers want, what they are willing to pay for it, and then figure out a way to deliver that product or service at the desirable price.

Hotels and restaurants that use consumer-based pricing try to give customers what they expect (or more than they expect) for the price being charged. Businesses that set prices with the customer in mind also recognize that consumers may perceive a larger difference between $9.95

and $10 than there actually is, and so try to keep their prices at the lower figure. There is another psychological factor at work in pricing—the assumption that quality costs money and you must pay more to get better quality. Restaurants that have a real quality advantage over competitors in terms of product or service also have a definite pricing advantage. Even if it costs them less than it costs their competitors to produce a meal, they can charge more and their sales will actually increase since many people believe that extra quality is worth more money.

There are many other methods of pricing besides cost-plus and consumer-based pricing. One is **competitive pricing**. With competitive pricing, hotels base room rates on what their competitors charge. This strategy can work only as long as consumers see all of the competing hotels as being equal. If there is a perceivable difference (e.g., one hotel is brand new while the others are much older), then competitive pricing will favor the hotel that appears to offer the most, the newest, or the nicest facilities.

There is a phenomenon known as **elasticity of demand**—the response by customers to changes in price. Elasticity of demand is important to understand, because if demand for a product or service is elastic, then managers can raise or lower consumer demand through various strategies, including raising or lowering prices. If demand for a product or service is low at one price, then lowering that price may increase the demand. For example, in many cities, rates for hotel rooms are high during the week because business travelers will pay high prices for the rooms. Those same guestrooms may go unoccupied on weekends, however, when demand from business travelers drops off significantly. The rooms may be sold if the prices for them are lowered enough so they appeal to a different guest group—families or singles wanting a weekend getaway package, for example.

If demand is inelastic, then demand will vary little if at all, no matter what type of price adjustments are made. This is the experience of resorts in areas such as Bermuda (in the winter when it is too cold) and Palm Springs, California (in the summer when it is too hot), where lowered room rates and special promotional advertising have not been entirely successful in raising room occupancies to an acceptable level during the off-season. Many people do not want to go to Bermuda or Palm Springs during the off-season, no matter how attractive the price.

Students interested in pricing should recognize that for the purposes of this book, we have simplified this subject considerably. For example, today most hotels use revenue management computer programs to set their prices. Revenue management programs seek to optimize the revenue a hotel receives in any given period by adjusting the rates that are offered to different market segments based on the projected supply of rooms and the demand for them. Revenue management is a system originally developed by the airlines to allocate the number of seats on each flight that would be available for each of the different fares that airlines offer. These numbers change constantly as reservations come in and forecasts are adjusted accordingly.

With the aid of revenue management systems, airlines, hotels, and car rental places have been able to adjust prices based on demand. The result is that the price of an airline seat or a hotel room or a rental car could go up or down from one hour to the next, a state of affairs that is accepted by the hotel, airline, and car rental market but not by restaurant customers. Variable restaurant pricing

from one hour to the next or even over longer periods would be certain to cause customer resistance. In addition, until digital equipment becomes standard, the cost of constantly reprinting menus would make such a course prohibitively expensive.

Promotion: How Do You Spread the Word? The fourth "P" in marketing stands for "promotion." It is placed last because promotional decisions ideally should be made after product, place, and price decisions have been made. Promotion consists of all the ways an enterprise tries to persuade people to buy its products and services, including use of online technologies through website advertising, email promotions, and social networks. All promotional activities fall into one of six categories:

- Personal selling
- Advertising
- Public relations and sponsorship marketing
- Sales promotion
- Direct marketing communications
- Point-of-purchase communications

Traditionally, companies have looked at these functions separately. There is a school of thinking, however, that says that these tasks are various forms of *marketing communications* and that to be effectively managed, they should be integrated. **Integrated marketing communications** is one model that many firms use in organizing their marketing activities. All activities, whether they involve personal sales calls, advertising programs, or tent cards for the dining room, are coordinated. This ensures that the organization sends out messages to its employees, customers, the press, and others that are consistent and directed at achieving the overall mission of the organization.

However, while these various forms of marketing communications should be integrated, each has unique strengths and weaknesses. Personal selling is used as the primary way to attract corporate and group business. Advertising both offline and online is often targeted at leisure travelers (who cannot be reached by direct sales), or designed to build an image for a brand name such as Hilton or Marriott. Public relations often has a much wider audience and attempts to influence individuals and groups not reached by traditional personal selling or advertising—employees, community opinion leaders, financial institutions, unions, and others. Sales promotion is used to quickly boost sales.

To succeed, a hotel or restaurant must know how to use promotional activities and how to organize and combine them so they work together to produce a synergistic effect—one where the whole is greater than the sum of its parts. The principal tool used to accomplish this is the hotel or restaurant's marketing plan.

A marketing plan is a blueprint for organizing, in the most efficient way possible, a business's marketing strategies and activities. New marketing plans are usually created on a regular basis. Many businesses create one every year, others may create marketing plans every two, three, or five years. Good plans are always reviewed and often revised on a quarterly basis to take current conditions into account. A good marketing plan encompasses a feasibility study of the current situation, often called SWOT analysis (SWOT stands for strengths, weaknesses, opportunities, and threats); establishes clear and concise marketing objectives that are specific and measurable; develops strategies that help the organization achieve its marketing objectives via tactics or action plans; implements controls that will allow the organization to monitor the progress of the marketing plan; and establishes a budget prior to launching the marketing plan.

Knowledge Check

1. Why is consumer-based pricing a realistic method of price setting?
2. What is the benefit of using a revenue management program?

12.7 PUBLIC RELATIONS

A hospitality company does not function in a vacuum but rather as part of a society that consists of the people who work for it, the people and companies who do business with it, the public at large, and the government that regulates and taxes it. These groups are known as a company's "publics." In order for a company to effectively deal with these publics, a relationship of trust must exist. Employees will not cooperate with or put forth their best efforts for a company that they do not trust or that they feel is taking advantage of them. The public will not buy services or products from a company that, in their estimation, is not responsible or trustworthy: if they can't trust the company or its owners, how can they trust the products or services it sells? And the government, as the protector of the society it governs, is especially vigilant in dealing with a company that it regards as not operating in the public interest. Given these circumstances, every hotel, restaurant, travel agency, tour company, and other hospitality business should give some thought to the relationships it has with all of the various publics it interacts with. The techniques that a company uses to improve these relationships are known as **public relations**, or **PR**.

The goal of public relations is usually to improve the climate or atmosphere in which a company operates. Here are some results a company might expect from a successful public relations campaign:

- Its products and services are better known.
- Its relationship with employees has improved.
- Its public reputation has improved.

In developing and implementing public relations plans, companies often use a simple five-step process:

1. *Research or fact-finding.* The purpose of research or fact-finding is to identify the attitudes of the company's various publics, who the key opinion leaders are, and what must happen to change bad perceptions or reinforce good ones.

2. *Planning.* A public relations strategy is devised that will produce the desired outcome(s).

3. *Action.* Action steps are taken to implement the strategy.

4. *Communication.* The company's actions are communicated to the interested publics.

5. *Measurement or evaluation.* The results of the public relations campaign are studied to see whether the desired outcomes have been achieved or whether more action is needed.

For example, a chain restaurant that receives pressure from the public to use more sustainable packaging may hire an environmental consultant to evaluate packaging alternatives and solutions. Then, the chain may put some of these solutions into practice (e.g., using recycled paper products or limiting plastic straw use). To communicate the changes, the chain may write about them in its annual report.

12.8 PUBLICITY

Public relations and publicity are often confused with each other, but they are not the same thing. Richard Weiner defines **publicity** as "a public relations technique in which information from an outside source—usually a public relations practitioner—is used by the media. A message is developed and distributed, without specific payment to the media, through selected outlets (magazines, TV, and so on) to further particular interests of the clients."[20]

Publicity is sometimes called "free advertising," but this is a misnomer. Advertising is paid for and advertisers control the message in their ads. Publicity is not paid for by the advertiser, and the media—not the advertiser—control the message because they are writing or broadcasting stories that they consider newsworthy, which also just happen to mention a company or be about a company. Since publicity is not paid for by an advertiser, it has more credibility with consumers than an ad. Unfortunately, from a company's standpoint, publicity can be unfavorable as well as favorable. A newspaper article about a restaurant's unlawful discrimination in hiring or a TV story about a cruise ship fire are examples of bad publicity.

New hotels and restaurants usually work hard to publicize their grand openings and often receive a good deal of attention and publicity. Press kits are the most common publicity materials prepared by a property. These kits generally consist of a series of fact sheets about the property; some news releases about the building, the architects, the general manager, and other key property personnel; and several glossy photos.

However, grand openings occur only once, and businesses need publicity throughout their lives. News outlets receive thousands of press releases every week and generally discard most of them. Therefore, it is often necessary to stage special events or create new products or services to focus the media's attention and give them something newsworthy to write about.

Hotels and restaurants often try to stimulate publicity by inviting travel editors and writers to visit. Sometimes these invitations are arranged by publicists who organize all-expenses-paid press tours. However, while freelancers often accept invitations to go on these tours, many of the top news organizations and travel magazines will not publish anything that a journalist writes while enjoying a free trip because they believe the journalist is likely to be biased. Their editors and writers usually pay for everything when they visit a hotel or restaurant and report on both the positives and the negatives they encounter.

However, a hotel or restaurant need not wait for media representatives to tell their story. The Internet provides multiple ways to reach millions of existing and prospective customers with company information that other media outlets may or may not choose to pick up.

CHAPTER SUMMARY

By now, it should be clear that managing people who serve people is a distinct slice of the larger management world. The management of hospitality enterprises is complex. It involves developing leadership skills, managing human resources, and allocating resources properly to ensure your business will succeed and thrive. Having a sound marketing plan is one of the most important aspects of a successful business, but you must also be competent with technical knowledge and in your role as a hospitality manager and leader.

A manager's job is similar to that of a conductor of an orchestra in that they must take all of the individual parts of a company and harmonize them into a whole. The manager must also compose the music that the orchestra is going to play.

The classical school of management was founded by Frederick Taylor, who focused his attention on improving worker productivity. Taylor believed that there was a best way to perform every job and workers should therefore be paid according to how rapidly and how well they performed. Although some hailed Taylor's methods, many considered his approach to be too rigid.

Other theorists tried instead to define the duties and functions of managers. Henri Fayol concluded that there were five management functions. As originally translated into English, they were planning, organizing, commanding, coordinating, and controlling. Since "commanding" and "controlling" seem rather harsh to today's ears, these terms are now often modified.

More recently, Peter Drucker concluded that a manager has two broad goals. The first is "creation of a true whole that is larger than the sum of its parts." The second is to "harmonize in every decision and action the requirements of [the] immediate and long-range future." According to Drucker, managers have five basic tasks to perform: setting objectives, organizing, motivating and communicating, measuring performance, and developing people.

Almost everyone agrees that managers need to be leaders. Leadership requires four basic strategies: attention through vision, meaning through communication, trust through positioning, and self-development. Successful managers know what they want their businesses to accomplish, clearly communicate that vision to their employees, are good at overcoming obstacles, and are out front leading the charge most of

the time. They aren't afraid to make mistakes and strive to improve themselves and their skills. Leaders also empower their employees to solve problems and become leaders themselves.

It is critical that hospitality managers be prepared for the real challenges they will face in managing others. It is difficult to attract and retain the right talent within an industry where high turnover is almost a certainty. Managers must be prepared to lead others successfully in order to minimize the circumstances that cause turnover. With ever-increasing legislation that influences how a manager can deal with specific situations that arise in day-to-day operations, it is imperative that managers understand the implications of the various laws concerning workers and the workplace, including the Civil Rights Act, the Americans with Disabilities Act (ADA) and the ADA Amendments Act of 2008, and the Family Medical Leave Act, to name just a few.

As part of their strategy to deal successfully with employee issues, many hospitality companies have developed HR programs. An HR program typically involves a corporate philosophy that values employees. It also includes job analyses; productivity standards; and employee recruitment, selection, training, motivation, benefits, and evaluation programs.

Jobs should be analyzed to establish the best way to perform them. Once jobs are understood, job lists, job breakdowns, and job descriptions can be prepared. These are helpful in recruiting, training, and evaluating employees.

Productivity can be expressed in dollars or in units produced or served. But productivity standards cannot be based on numbers alone—they must take into account quality goals and guest expectations as well.

Effective recruiting demands an understanding of the local labor market. The goal of recruiting is to find the best workers available who find the vacant jobs attractive and are willing to work for the wages the business can pay. Recruiters can use internal sources (current employees and people recommended by them) and external sources (those recruited through advertising, community involvement, and employment agencies). Sometimes-overlooked groups that can help answer the hospitality industry's labor needs include minorities, workers with disabilities, older adults, and workers with limited skills. There are many job programs in place to help hospitality businesses find and train potential employees in these groups.

Selecting a job applicant to fill a vacancy involves five steps: receiving and processing applications, interviewing applicants, evaluating applicants, checking references, and hiring the selected person.

Training is one of the most crucial parts of a human resources program. Unfortunately, training is often neglected. Basic steps in the training process are establishing a training policy, defining training needs, planning the training, preparing the employees for training, conducting the training, and evaluating the training. Ongoing coaching by managers is a valuable follow-through on all types of training. Today, many companies supplement traditional training methods with online courses.

A manager who wants motivated workers must gain their commitment to the company and its goals. Offering a competitive benefit package is also important in an increasingly competitive environment for talented staff.

Evaluating employees is the final step in a human resources program. Employees need to know how they are doing; regularly scheduled performance reviews help accomplish this. Companies that do a good job of retaining, developing, and motivating employees recognize that where there are problems, they are often the result of a flawed system rather than a flawed person.

The purpose of a business is to get and keep customers. For that to happen, you must have an understanding of marketing concepts. There is a real difference between selling and marketing. Selling is getting rid of what you have; marketing is having what customers want. The marketing concept can be defined as the effort to determine and meet the needs and wants of current and potential customers.

The Four P's of Marketing are product, place, price, and promotion. The term *product* as used in the hospitality field can have several meanings. Obviously, a product can be a guestroom or a meal that a hotel or restaurant provides to guests. A hospitality product can also be an intangible service, such as a bellhop carrying a guest's luggage.

"Place" refers to the physical location of a property. It also refers to distribution channels—the places where a sale of a guestroom or a restaurant reservation is made, which can be over the Internet, via the telephone, or at a travel agency.

There are three methods of pricing commonly used in the hospitality industry: cost-plus pricing, consumer-based pricing, and competitive pricing. There are other, more complicated approaches to pricing as well. Some hotels, for example, employ revenue management techniques to optimize the revenue they receive in any given period by adjusting the guestroom rates that are offered to different market segments based on the projected supply of rooms and the demand for them.

Promotion decisions are made after the first three marketing P's are established. Promotion consists of all the ways a business tries to persuade consumers to buy its products and services. All promotional activities fall into one of six categories: personal selling, advertising, public relations and sponsorship marketing, sales promotion, direct marketing communications, and point-of-purchase communications.

To properly allocate marketing resources, a company should begin with a marketing plan. A good marketing plan consists of several parts: situation analysis, objectives, strategies, tactics (or action plans), controls, and budgets.

Every hotel, restaurant, travel agency, tour company, and other hospitality enterprise should give some thought to its public relationships—that is, the relations it has with all of the various "publics" (clients, employees, government agencies, etc.) it interacts with. The techniques that a company uses to improve these relationships are known as "PR," or public relations. In developing and implementing public relations plans, companies often use a simple five-step process: research or fact-finding, planning, action, communication, and measurement or evaluation.

Publicity is a public relations technique in which information from an outside source—usually a public relations practitioner—is used by the media. Hotels and restaurants often receive a lot of publicity at their grand openings. The need for publicity continues throughout the life of a business.

advertising—A communication strategy used by businesses and organizations to promote their products, services, or ideas to a target audience.

classical school—A school of management thought in which workers are seen as rational people interested primarily in making money. This management approach addresses an employee's economic and physical needs, but not their social needs or need for job satisfaction.

competitive pricing—Basing prices on what competitors charge.

consumer-based pricing—Pricing based on what consumers are willing to pay.

cost-plus pricing—Determining a price by taking the total cost of providing a product or service and adding to it (1) a percentage to cover overhead or fixed expenses, and (2) a predetermined gross profit margin.

crowdsourcing—Obtaining ideas or content by asking for contributions from groups of people, generally via the Internet.

distribution channels—Intermediaries through which a service or product passes.

diversity training—Training that seeks to make all workers feel comfortable in their workplace, no matter their race, culture, gender, or age.

elasticity of demand—A measure of customer responsiveness to changes in price.

empowerment—Being authorized to solve customers' problems without needing to seek prior approval from supervisors.

Four P's of Marketing—The four basic marketing responsibilities: product, place, price, and promotion.

full-time-equivalent (FTE) employee—A measure used by organizations to represent the total number of worked hours of an employee, expressed as a full-time employee's workload. It is a way to quantify the total hours worked by all employees, taking into account both full-time and part-time employees and converting them into an equivalent number of full-time employees. For example, four part-time employees who each work 10 hours per week would, for statistical purposes, be recorded as one FTE employee.

integrated marketing communications—A marketing model in which all marketing activities are coordinated, ensuring that all corporate marketing messages are consistent and directed at achieving the organization's overall mission.

job breakdown—The specific, step-by-step procedures for accomplishing each task of a particular job.

job description—A recruiting and training tool that outlines for a particular job (1) the title that goes with the job, (2) the person to whom the employee reports, (3) the work to be performed (in general terms), (4) the education or skills the employee must have, and (5) the physical requirements of the job.

job list—A list of the tasks that must be performed by the individual holding a particular job.

loss-leaders—Items sold at or below cost in order to attract customers to a business, where they may buy other items that are profitable.

marketing—A system of interrelated activities formulated to help managers plan, price, promote, and make available services or products to customers and potential customers in a particular target market. The primary goal of marketing is to create awareness, generate interest, and ultimately drive sales or adoption of the offerings.

marketing mix—The variety of marketing activities in which a business engages.

networking—A process whereby current employees contact, or are contacted by, friends, classmates, and former associates about a job opening. This can happen online or via other methods of communication.

performance review—A meeting between a manager and an employee to (1) let the employee know how well they have learned to meet company standards, and (2) let the manager know how well they are doing in hiring and training employees. Typically held every 3, 6, or 12 months, depending on the employee's performance and experience.

productivity standards—Measurements that tell managers how long it should take an employee to complete tasks using the best methods management has devised and how many tasks an employee can perform in a given time period. This measurement differs according to the task the employee is performing.

publicity—Mention in the media about an organization's people, products, or services.

public relations (PR)—A systematic effort by a business to communicate favorable information about itself to various internal and external publics in order to create a positive impression.

1. According to Peter Drucker, what is the first broad goal of a manager?
   a. Harmonize in every decision and action the requirements of the immediate and long-range future.
   b. Create a true whole that is larger than the sum of its parts.
   c. Set objectives and organize.
   d. Motivate employees.

2. Which management task involves dividing work into jobs?
   a. Organizing
   b. Setting objectives
   c. Measuring performance
   d. Motivating and communicating

3. Which leadership strategy involves envisioning and sharing a business's future?
   a. Trust through positioning
   b. Meaning through communication
   c. Attention through vision
   d. Self-development

4. Which is a reason for the growing number of older workers in the U.S. labor force?
   a. High turnover in the labor force
   b. The rising costs of health insurance
   c. The need for a two-income household
   d. The need for a high degree of independence

5. Which act prohibits employment discrimination based on national origin?
   a. Fair Labor Standards Act
   b. Americans with Disabilities Act
   c. Occupational Safety and Health Act
   d. Illegal Immigration Reform and Immigrant Responsibility Act

6. Which tells managers how long it should take to complete tasks using methods that management has devised?
   a. Job list
   b. Job breakdown
   c. Job description
   d. Productivity standards

7. Which is an internal source of employees?
   a. Direct mail
   b. Classified advertising
   c. Government employment offices
   d. Current employee recommendations

8. Which of the Four P's of Marketing includes crowdsourcing?
   a. Price
   b. Place
   c. Product
   d. Promotion

9. Which describes a public relations effort?
    a. A restaurant advertises its grand opening.
    b. A hotel invites a travel writer to stay at one of its locations.
    c. A restaurant chain joins an environmental task force.
    d. A restaurant invites a food writer to a monthly event.

10. Which term describes the response by customers to changes in price?
    a. Cost-plus pricing
    b. Competitive pricing
    c. Elasticity of demand
    d. Consumer-based pricing

11. What is the last step in developing a public relations plan?
    a. Action
    b. Planning
    c. Research or fact-finding
    d. Measurement or evaluation

12. Which leadership strategy is associated with making mistakes and developing solutions?
    a. Trust through positioning
    b. Meaning through communication
    c. Attention through vision
    d. Self-development

SHORT-ANSWER QUESTIONS

1. How important are managers to the success of an organization?

2. Why is ongoing training, including diversity training, important for employees?

TRAINING AND TURNOVER

An independent beachfront hotel has been open for about 11 months. Its main restaurant has grown in popularity with locals and guests, but the restaurant staff has experienced high turnover. Jill, the head waiter, has been with the restaurant for three months. The job description for her position had been minimal, but she had worked as a head waiter before and was excited about working at the new location. Jill quickly realized that the job required more managerial tasks than she was used to. She also had very little initial training with the restaurant's point-of-sale system and had to quickly learn it on the job.

Jill has asked for more training from the restaurant's manager, but the manager always seems too busy to have an in-depth conversation about her concerns. Jill has noticed that other employees have had similar concerns over lack of training and confusion about duties. She likes her customers and coworkers, but she is not sure how much her manager is interested in developing the restaurant team.

DISCUSSION QUESTIONS

1. What are some human resources issues that the restaurant is experiencing?

2. What can the hotel do to better retain and develop its restaurant employees?

3. What leadership strategies and tasks could the manager improve?

Alba Castillo Baylin

Alba Castillo Baylin is vice president of stakeholder and community management at the Coca-Cola Company's North America operating unit. In this role, she leads stakeholder partnerships, philanthropy strategy, community marketing and engagement, nonprofit board placement, employee volunteerism, and disaster relief.

Previously, Baylin held the position of vice president of customer marketing for the company's North America Foodservice customers. Before that, she served as Coca-Cola's group director of Hispanic marketing, leading the company's largest ever Hispanic-focused marketing program for the 2014 FIFA World Cup. This program won multiple awards for digital and social media.

Joining Coca-Cola in 1999 after 10 years in the hospitality industry, Baylin took on roles of increasing responsibility in worldwide public affairs and communications, strategic partnership marketing, and customer and commercial leadership. For six years, she was assigned to the company's Latin America group, first as director of revenue growth management and later as group director of shopper marketing.

Baylin has been recognized by *Ser Padres* magazine as one of 25 Latina Executive Moms Making a Difference. In 2019, she was inducted into Delta Sigma Pi as the national honorary member of the year. The following year, Florida International University's (FIU) Chaplin School of Hospitality & Tourism Management named her Distinguished Alumnus of 2020. She is a strong advocate for community service and serves on the boards of the Georgia State University (GSU) Foundation, the Woodruff Art Center's Alliance Theatre, Junior Achievement of Georgia, Leadership Atlanta, and UnidosUS.

Born in Bucaramanga, Colombia, Baylin holds a Bachelor of Science degree from FIU and an MBA from the Robinson College of Business at GSU. She is married to Marc Baylin and is a proud mom to her 12-year-old daughter, Sofia.

WHAT WOULD YOU DO?

You have recently started your first job as an assistant manager of a fast-casual restaurant. It is a brand-new store filled with employees of all ages, and you are the youngest member of the management team. You feel like you need to make a name for yourself and at the same time let your employees know that they can count on you. During the first three months, everything goes fine. Then one holiday weekend, you experience an abnormal number of callouts: employees phoning in to say they can't come in because they are sick. You have no recourse but to work the entire weekend with a skeleton crew, leaving you exhausted. On Monday morning, you hear through the grapevine that many of the employees who called out were actually spending their holiday weekend together on a yacht! Two months later, this happens again. How do you address this with your employees?

13

FRANCHISING IS BIG BUSINESS

Chapter Outline

Learning Objectives

1. Explain what a franchise is, describe types of franchises, summarize the history of franchising, and explain how franchising works. (pp. 376–383)

2. State common reasons individuals give for wanting to buy a franchise, outline the advantages and disadvantages of owning a franchise, list advantages and disadvantages for franchisors, and summarize other franchising issues. (pp. 383–388)

business format franchise

encroachment

Franchise Disclosure Document (FDD)

franchising

initial franchise fee

product or trade-name franchise

promotional assistance

royalty fee

KEY TERMS

This chapter covers franchising in the hospitality industry. U.S. franchises generate around $670 billion in revenue for the U.S. economy each year, with about one-third of this coming from quick service restaurants. While franchising is prevalent in various industries, including quick service, retail, hotels, automotive, and many others, there are specific laws and regulations that protect both the franchisor and franchisee's interests and ensure fair business practices within the franchise relationship. We will review the history of franchising, the reasons for its popularity, the advantages and disadvantages of owning a franchise, and how franchising works.

13.1 WHAT IS A FRANCHISE?

In its simplest form, the word *franchise* refers to the authorization given by a company to another company or an individual to sell its unique products and services. Franchising is a marketing or distribution system: the franchisor grants an individual or company the right to conduct business according to the franchisor's guidelines, for a specified time and in a specified place, for a fee.

A franchisee may be a single-unit owner or have a multiunit franchise. As the term suggests, a single-unit owner has the right to open and operate one franchise unit. It does not exclude that individual from buying additional single units. If that occurs, the franchisee is a multiple, single-unit owner. A multiunit franchisee is given the right to open and operate more than one unit in a defined area.

Let's review the following terms, which will be used throughout the chapter:

- **Franchise**—In addition to the meaning mentioned earlier, "franchise" can also refer to the name of the business format or product that is being franchised. The Marriott Corporation grants Residence Inn franchises as well as Courtyard by Marriott franchises and others.

- **Franchisor**—The franchise company that owns the trademark, products, and/or business format that is being franchised.

- **Franchisee**—The individual or company granted the right to do business under the franchisor's name. A person who buys a Dairy Queen franchise is a franchisee.

- **Franchising**—The major trade association in franchising, the International Franchise Association, defines **franchising** as "a continuing relationship in which the franchisor provides a licensed privilege to do business, plus assistance in organizing, training, merchandising, and management in return for a consideration from the franchisee."

Franchise rights vary. Most franchisors grant franchisees the right to use the franchise name and its distinctive trademark, logo, architecture, and interior design. Some franchisors also sell their method of operation or designate territories in which the franchisee may operate. In some cases, the franchisor may grant the franchisee the right to sell the franchisor's product(s); for example, franchisees of Baskin-Robbins ice cream stores have the right to sell Baskin-Robbins ice cream.

Hotel and restaurant franchising is big business. It has been the dominant method for worldwide restaurant expansion for decades. McDonald's, the largest chain in number of units, has over 40,000 stores in 119 countries, of which 93 percent are franchised.[1] For many of the hotel chains, franchising is becoming the preferred expansion strategy. Wyndham Hotels & Resorts, the leader in hotel franchising, is basically a franchising company. Its 24 brands located in 60 countries total more than 9,100 hotels, all of which are franchised.[2] Oyo Hotels & Homes is another franchised model, but the exact number of hotels it partners with can fluctuate due to factors such as new partnerships, expansions, or changes in business strategies. It's worth noting that Oyo is known for its asset-light model, partnering with independent hotels and providing them with brand affiliation and technology support. See Exhibits 13.1 and 13.2 for the chains with the most franchised hotels and quick service restaurants.

Types of Franchises

There are two types of franchises: the product or trade-name franchise and the business format franchise.

The **product or trade-name franchise** is a supplier–dealer arrangement whereby the dealer (franchisee) sells a product line provided by the supplier (franchisor) and, to some degree, takes on the identity of the supplier. This is the type of franchise that exists in the automobile, gasoline service station, and soft drink industries.

Exhibit 13.1   Top 10 Franchised Hotel Chains in the World

	Chain	Hotels
1.	Jin Jiang International	10,000+
2.	Wyndham Hotel Group	9,300
3.	Huazhu World Group	8,176
4.	Marriott International	7,887
5.	Choice Hotels International	7,100
6.	Hilton	6,200
7.	IHG (InterContinental Hotels Group)	5,700
8.	Accor Group	5,100
9.	BTH Hotels	4,895
10.	OYO[a]	20,000+

Note: 2022 data. [a]OYO leases and franchises hotels, homes, and living spaces. Its inventory can fluctuate from 20,000 to 10,000 in a month.

Exhibit 13.2   Top 10 Franchised Quick Service Restaurant Chains in the United States

	Chain	2021 Units	2021 Sales (in billions)
1.	McDonald's	13,438	$45.96
2.	Starbucks	15,450	24.3
3.	Chick-fil-A	2,732	16.7
4.	Taco Bell	7,002	12.6
5.	Wendy's	5,938	11.11
6.	Dunkin'	9,244	10.42
7.	Burger King	7,105	10.03
8.	Subway	21,147	9.35
9.	Domino's	6,560	8.64
10.	Chipotle	2,966	7.55

Source: Samanda Dorger, "Supersized: 30 Biggest Fast-Food Chains in the U.S.," TheStreet, August 16, 2022, https://www.thestreet.com/personal-finance/30-biggest-fast-food-chains-in-the-us#gid=ci02a857df700025f2&pid=15-mcdonalds-yaoinlove--shutterstock.

The majority of total franchise sales in the United States are from product or trade-name franchising.

Business format franchises, which include quick service restaurants and lodging chains, are characterized by an ongoing business relationship between franchisor and franchisee that includes not only the product, service, and trademark but also the entire business concept itself.

The majority of the growth in franchising has been in the business format franchise category. Besides foodservice operations and hotels, this category includes nonfood retailers, personal and business services, real estate services, and other service businesses. Restaurants make up the majority of business format franchises.

Knowledge Check

1. How do franchise rights vary?
2. What is the main difference between the two types of franchises?

13.2 THE HISTORY OF FRANCHISING

Franchising is not a new concept. A precursor of modern franchising occurred in Roman times, when private citizens bid for the right to operate tax-collecting "franchises" for the government. These "franchisees," called "publicans," kept a percentage of the taxes they collected for themselves. It was a lucrative business—especially for the unscrupulous—and publicans were generally detested, as the biblical phrase "publicans and sinners" reminds us.[3] This form of franchising existed in the Middle Ages as well, when royalty and church officials rewarded important citizens with the right to collect revenues in return for "various services or considerations."[4]

Product or Trade-Name Franchising

All of the early franchises were product or trade-name franchises that allowed individuals or companies willing to put up their own capital to sell and, in some cases, make the franchisor's product. The only restrictions on franchisees were on what they sold and the territory where they sold it.

In 1851, I.M. Singer & Company used franchising to develop a network of sewing machine dealers throughout the United States. Under the Singer concept, a dealer was allowed to open a Singer Sewing Machine store in return for an agreement to sell only Singer machines and supplies. Since people did not know how to use these new sewing machines, the dealers also provided service in the form of sewing lessons. This was the beginning of modern franchising systems.

Because the Singer company had a unique product that was in demand, and one that dealers could not obtain unless they agreed to open a Singer Sewing Machine store, the company did very well. However, franchising did not catch on in a big way until the production of automobiles and soft drinks in the early 1900s.

Just as in the case of Singer sewing machines, automobiles were new and complicated mechanical devices requiring service and repair. No one was willing to buy a horseless carriage unless there was someone nearby who could fix it if it broke down. Automobile manufacturers, most notably General Motors at first, came up with a solution similar to the Singer company's: they established dealerships to sell and service their cars. Because dealers were located in the communities where the cars were sold, they were trusted neighbors who could be relied on to back up the promises made by the automobile manufacturers. Not surprisingly, the petroleum companies that grew along with the automobile dealers adopted the same form of distribution. Even today, gas stations are, for the most part, individually owned small businesses that have the right to use a company's trade name and sell its products.

The first Coca-Cola franchise was granted in 1899. Franchising was necessary because Coca-Cola was packaged in a unique glass bottle that consumers paid a deposit for and returned to the company. Handling the bottles required local bottling companies that could pick them up, wash them, and reuse them. Moreover, it was expensive to ship bottled drinks all over the country from the company's headquarters in Atlanta, Georgia. In order to expand, Coca-Cola gave franchisees the right to build Coca-Cola bottling plants in return for purchasing Coca-Cola's bottles and syrup. Coca-Cola also agreed to train its bottlers in production techniques and marketing. Soon Coca-Cola bottling plants were established all over the United States.

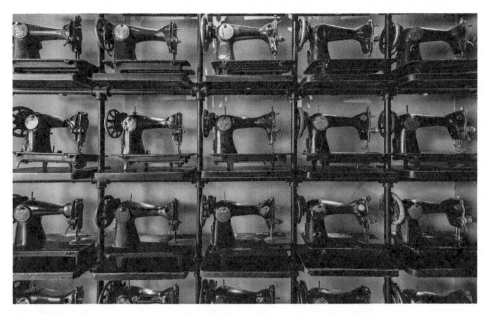

The Singer company sold sewing machines like these in the 1900s.

Each Singer or General Motors franchise involved a relationship between the manufacturer (franchisor) and the retailer (franchisee) who sold the manufactured product(s) directly to the public. Note that in both cases, the retailer performed a service (product servicing and repair) for the franchisor in addition to selling the product. This was one reason why franchising was the most efficient form of distribution for these products. In the case of Coca-Cola, the relationship was between the manufacturer (franchisor) and a wholesaler (franchisee). Coca-Cola's wholesalers did not sell directly to the public, but delivered Coca-Cola to retail soda fountains and grocery stores. Again, however, the franchisee (wholesaler) performed a service for the franchisor: in this case, bottling the product. These new products—sewing machines, cars, and soft drinks—required the seller to provide services as well as the product itself, making franchising necessary and practical.

Business Format Franchising

The first person to pioneer the idea of the business format franchise in the hospitality industry was Howard Dearing Johnson, founder of the Howard Johnson Company. Johnson started his chain in 1925 with a drugstore that he successfully converted into an ice cream parlor. By 1928, he had two thriving ice cream parlors and decided to open a third that would serve food as well. This was his first restaurant. A friend offered Johnson some land so Johnson could build a second restaurant. Johnson had no more capital to invest, however, and convinced his friend to build the restaurant. Johnson would provide him with a franchise to sell Howard Johnson ice cream as well as assist in the design and supervision of the restaurant.

The friend's restaurant was an instant success, and Johnson realized that he had found a way to expand his business without investing any money of his own. Johnson decided to continue with the strategy of encouraging others to build Howard Johnson restaurants, which would sell Howard Johnson ice cream and other products that he would supply. He continued to assist in the design and management of these new restaurants so he could help make them successful. Johnson did not ask for a royalty on sales for these extra services; his sole profit came from the sale of Howard Johnson products. By the end of 1936, there were 61 Howard Johnson's restaurants, most of which were franchises; by 1939, there were 107 restaurants operating in a half dozen states.[5] In 1954, Johnson entered the lodging business by franchising his first motor lodge in Savannah, Georgia. By 1969, there were 391 lodges, 90 percent of which were franchises. After 11 more years of continued growth, Howard B. Johnson, son of the founder, sold Howard Johnson's to Imperial Group Ltd., a British corporation. Imperial sold the company to Marriott in 1985. Marriott kept a few of the bigger hotels and quickly sold the rest of the lodging properties to Prime Motor Inns; Marriott then sold the freestanding Howard Johnson's restaurants to various buyers over the next few years. The "Howard Johnson" hotel name is now owned by Wyndham Hotel Group.

In spite of Johnson's success, franchising did not catch on with the rest of the hospitality industry until the early 1950s. Lodging's most notable early franchising success was Holiday Inn. Kemmons Wilson and a partner owned three successful Holiday Inn motor hotels in the early 1950s and wanted to expand nationwide. They decided to finance their expansion by selling Holiday Inn franchises to franchisees who would build their Holiday Inns according to a set format and contribute some money from each guestroom for advertising.

The beginning of the franchise giant McDonald's was a drive-in, self-service restaurant in San Bernardino, California, built in 1948 by two brothers, Maurice and Richard McDonald. In 1954, Ray Kroc, a milkshake-machine salesman, called on the McDonald brothers to deliver eight of his Multimixer machines. What he found was an efficient octagonal assembly-line operation turning out beverages, french fries, and 15-cent hamburgers. As Kroc tells it, "When I saw it working that day in 1954, I felt like some latter-day Newton, who'd just had an Idaho potato caromed off his skull."[6] Kroc understood what made the restaurant a success. In his book, *Grinding It Out: The Making of McDonald's*, he explained what went through his mind:

> I've often been asked why I didn't simply copy the McDonald brothers' plan. They showed me the whole thing and it would have been an easy matter, seemingly, to pattern a restaurant after theirs. Truthfully the idea never crossed my mind. I saw it through the eyes of a salesman. Here was a complete package. I could get out and talk up a storm about it. ... Besides, the brothers did have some equipment that couldn't be readily copied. They had a specially fabricated aluminum griddle for one thing, and the setup of all the rest of the equipment was in a very precise step-saving pattern. Then there was the name. I had a strong intuitive sense that the name McDonald's was exactly right. I couldn't have taken the name. But for the rest of

> it, I guess the real answer is that I was so naive or honest that it never occurred to me that I could take their idea and copy it and not pay them a red cent.[7]

The McDonald brothers, who drove Cadillacs and lived together in a luxurious home, were not interested in expanding. They were happy with what they had achieved and did not want to work any harder. In exchange for $2 million, they granted Kroc an exclusive 10-year franchise. He agreed to put up buildings exactly like the one their architect had drawn up, complete with the golden arches. The McDonald brothers inserted contractual clauses that obligated Kroc to follow their plans down to the last detail—even to signs and menus. And there was a clause that prohibited Kroc from doing anything differently without a registered letter of permission from the two brothers. It was agreed that Kroc could charge franchisees 1.9 percent of their gross sales and that he would give 0.5 percent of that to the McDonalds. Kroc was also allowed to charge a franchise fee of $950 to cover the expenses he incurred in finding a suitable location for each franchise and a contractor who would build to the McDonalds' specifications.

Kroc brought in Harry Sonneborn to assist him, and the two planned the future of their new enterprise. They realized that for their franchise to succeed, they had to do more than simply sell prospective franchisees a name and a menu. Besides, a hamburger—ready-made according to the franchisor's specifications—could not be sold to a franchisee like Howard Johnson's ice cream; franchisees would have to cook their own hamburgers. Kroc wrote:

> We agreed that we wanted McDonald's to be more than just a name used by many different people. We wanted to build a restaurant system that would be known for food of consistently high quality and uniform methods of preparation. Our aim, of course, was to ensure repeat business based on the system's reputation rather than on the quality of a single store or operator. This would require a continuing program of educating and assisting operators and a constant review of their performance. It would also require a full-time program of research and development. I knew in my bones that the

key to uniformity would be in our ability to provide techniques of preparation that operators would accept because they were superior to methods they could dream up for themselves.[8]

Here Kroc expresses the heart of the concept of modern franchising: a franchise company's reputation depends on the quality and consistency of all of its franchises, and quality and consistency are maintained by ongoing training and development. In 1961, Kroc bought out the McDonald brothers for an additional $2.7 million. As mentioned earlier, today there are about 40,000 McDonald's units in 119 countries.

Knowledge Check

1. How did I.M. Singer & Company contribute to franchising?

2. How did Howard Johnson contribute to business format franchising?

13.3 HOW FRANCHISING WORKS

In order to obtain a license from a franchisor, a franchisee must pay a fee for the privilege of using the franchisor's name, identity, business systems, operating procedures, marketing techniques, and (in the case of hotels) reservations system. The typical franchise fee arrangement has two parts: (1) an initial franchise fee, payable upon signing the franchise agreement, and (2) ongoing fees.

Initial franchise fees vary. They are calculated by assigning a monetary value to the following:

- The franchisor's goodwill
- The value of the new franchise unit's trading area or territory
- The average cost of recruiting a franchisee
- The cost of training a franchisee
- The cost of signs, ads, plans, and other aids

The goodwill of a business—the reputation or prestige it enjoys among customers—is an intangible asset that is easier to estimate for an established franchisor, such as McDonald's, than for a new franchisor. Although intangible, goodwill can be calculated by relating it to the franchisor's profits (profits being one measure of the amount of goodwill a franchisor enjoys). For example, if a franchisor's franchises average $150,000 in profits per year, the value of the goodwill for a new franchise might be two-and-a-half times that, or $375,000. A percentage of the goodwill charge—anywhere from 4 percent to 12 percent—could be part of the initial franchise fee. Franchisors differ in how they calculate goodwill and how they charge it to their franchisees.

Some territories are more valuable than others, due to their demographic makeup and the propensity of their residents to eat out. Therefore, a new franchise's location would be considered in setting the initial franchise fee.

The value of recruiting, training, and aids such as signs and advertising is easier for the franchisor to calculate since it can refer to actual costs.

Fees

As just indicated, franchise fees consist of an initial franchise fee and various other ongoing fees, one of which, a royalty fee, is always charged to franchisors.

Initial Fee. Restaurant franchisors generally charge a flat franchise fee for one unit; some franchisors charge a reduced rate for additional units. On the other hand, hotel franchisors base their **initial franchise fee** on the number of guestrooms the franchisee builds, with a minimum fee plus an amount per room over a defined minimum number of rooms. For example, a minimum fee for a hotel with 100 rooms would be $50,000, but a hotel with 150 rooms would be $50,000 plus $300 per room over 100 rooms, or $65,000 ($50,000 + $15,000). Some hotel companies quote an amount per room with a total minimum. Here are some examples of initial franchise fees:

Franchisor	Initial Franchise Fee
Subway	$10,000–$15,000 (depending on country)
Papa John's	$25,000

Franchisor	Initial Franchise Fee
McDonald's	$45,000
Hilton Hotels & Resorts	$75,000, plus $400 for each additional guestroom or suite over 250
Red Roof Inn	$30,000

Royalty Fee. Ongoing franchise fees vary; one of them is a royalty fee. All franchisors charge a **royalty fee**, a fee usually calculated on a percentage of the franchisee's sales. As with initial franchise fees, royalty fees are related to the value of the franchise. Examples of typical royalty fees are as follows:

Franchisor	Percent of Gross Revenues
Subway	8.0%
KFC	5.0%
Hilton	5.0%
McDonald's	12.5%

Other Fees. Fees for advertising and marketing, training, and pre-opening support are charged by both restaurant and hotel franchisors. One of the major benefits of a hotel franchise is the franchisor's reservations system. The fee for that service is either a percentage of room revenue or a dollar amount per available room per month.

Initial Investment

Although most restaurant franchises are still considered small businesses, the initial investment required to establish a successful franchise can be substantial due (among other factors) to the cost of real estate, construction, and property taxes. For example, the total investment to acquire a new McDonald's ranges from almost $1 million to $2.1 million. The land is owned by McDonald's, and the rent is based on a percentage of monthly sales. Some hotel franchises cost even more. For example, a Homewood Suites by Hilton franchise can cost from $9.9 million to $20 million. Because of the high cost of franchises, franchisors want

to be sure that their franchisees will have enough capital to operate their units until they start making a profit. For this reason, some franchisors require their franchisees to have a minimum personal net worth. This amount varies from franchisor to franchisor. One franchisor, Pizza Hut, requires a $700,000 net worth and $350,000 in liquid assets to open a franchise in the United States.

Franchise Regulations

Franchising is regulated in the United States by the Federal Trade Commission and a number of states. In those states with special regulations, a franchisor must register with the proper state authority before offering a franchise for sale within the state. State and local restrictions take precedence if they are more demanding than federal requirements.

All franchisors must comply with Federal Trade Commission Rule 436.1, which requires that a prospective franchisee be given a prospectus—the **Franchise Disclosure Document (FDD)**, formerly known as the Uniform Franchise Offering Circular, or UFOC. This prospectus is a disclosure document that informs the franchisee about certain vital aspects of the franchisor and the franchise agreement before the agreement is signed. This disclosure statement must be in the hands of the prospective franchisee 14 days prior to signing the franchise agreement so the franchisee can have ample time to study it and understand the risks involved. The FDD covers everything from the franchisor's history and financial condition to the detailed terms of the sales agreement. Franchisees should study the FDD carefully before buying a franchise. There are 23 categories of information that must be provided by the franchisor to the prospective franchisee at least 14 days prior to the execution of the franchise agreement; this information is found in the FDD.[9] These categories include:

1. The Franchisor and any Parents, Predecessors, and Affiliates

2. Business Experience

3. Litigation

4. Bankruptcy

5. Initial Fees

6. Other Fees

7. Estimated Initial Investment

8. Restrictions on Sources of Products and Services

9. Franchisee's Obligations

10. Financing

11. Franchisor's Assistance, Advertising, Computer Systems, and Training

12. Territory

13. Trademarks

14. Patents, Copyrights, and Proprietary Information

15. Obligation to Participate in the Actual Operation of the Franchise Business

16. Restrictions on What the Franchisee May Sell

17. Renewal, Termination, Transfer, and Dispute Resolution

18. Public Figures

19. Financial Performance Representations

20. Outlets and Franchisee Information

21. Financial Statements

22. Contracts

23. Receipts

International Adaptation

Although franchising is all about standardization, there are times when a franchisor needs to adapt to local cultures and laws of specific countries. For instance, McDonald's strategies for international markets focus on segmentation and experimentation and product testing. Appetites of Japanese also differ from appetites of Americans. Thus, the serving size of burgers, fries, and drinks is smaller in Japan. In China, McDonald's uses meat from chicken thighs in its chicken burgers because of a local preference for dark meat. In Muslim countries, pork has been replaced with fish, and rice is often offered as well. Switzerland is the only country that offers McRaclette, a beef sandwich made with raclette cheese, a unique raclette sauce, onions, and gherkin pickles.

Similarly, hotel chains have different products in different countries. In the United States, the Holiday Inn franchise is a mid-scale, no-frills hotel designed to serve business and leisure travelers who want reliability and convenience. But in China, you can easily find Holiday Inns that are five-star, with full-service restaurants and amenities. Many of them are upper upscale hotels with luxurious lobbies and teahouses.

Knowledge Check

1. Why is it important for a prospective franchisee to consider the initial investment costs of owning a franchise?

2. What is a Franchise Disclosure Document?

13.4 OWNING A FRANCHISE

Franchising has not only been a boon to companies seeking to expand quickly; it is also one of the ways individuals can realize the dream of having their own business. Ray Kroc considered it the quickest way to capture the American dream and was proud of the fact that people credited him with making many of his associates millionaires. Subway is one of the largest and most widespread quick service chains globally, and its franchisees are mostly family-run businesses owned by immigrants.

Success doesn't happen for every franchisor, however. Starting a business is risky, and success depends heavily on the franchisor. Obviously, the franchise company also plays a role. Experienced franchise companies with successful track records are more likely to provide the kind of advice and support that translates into profitability.

Franchising gives an individual entrepreneur a chance to compete in the marketplace against giant companies. It provides some insurance for success because when franchisees buy a franchise, they buy (1) a format and formula, and (2) the experience of the franchisor, who is expected to teach them what they need to know to succeed.

The Development Group, a consulting firm that sells franchises for its clients, asked prospective franchisees why they wanted a franchise. Their answers were revealing:

■ Self-management was the most important reason given: 73 percent of applicants saw owning a franchise as a way to be their own boss.

Franchising gives an individual entrepreneur a chance to compete in the marketplace.

- Financial independence was a close second: 69 percent of applicants thought owning a franchise was a better way to ensure financial security than depending on a paycheck from someone else.

- Career advancement ranked third (53 percent of applicants). If you own your own franchise, you don't have to wait for someone else to promote you. You can move as fast as you are able.

- New skills/training was cited by 49 percent as their main reason for buying a franchise. Many people, for example, would like to own their own hotel or restaurant but simply don't know how. Good franchise companies provide training and assistance.

- A franchise was seen by 32 percent as a long-term investment that would appreciate in value.

Advantages

There are many advantages to owning a franchise in addition to those just cited, including:

- Site-selection assistance
- Credit
- Construction expertise
- Fixtures and equipment assistance
- Training
- Promotional assistance
- Economies of scale
- Ongoing support

Site-Selection Assistance. The first advantage for franchisees is that their franchisor will help them select a good site for their business. Almost all successful franchisors know exactly what kinds of sites work best for their franchises. In many cases, the franchisor selects the site, buys or leases the land, puts up the building, and then leases it to the franchisee. In other instances, the franchisees do all of this for themselves. But even then, franchisors almost always approve sites based on their experience concerning the amount and kind of population needed in an area, traffic patterns, and other considerations.

Choice Hotels International, which franchises Comfort Inn, Quality, Clarion, and Econo Lodge, among others, offers prospective franchisees help with not only site selection but also site acquisition and site and market assessment. Some restaurant franchisors do the same, though the process varies. For example, the Subway sandwich chain requires franchisees to find their own locations but assists in evaluating the site selected by the franchisee. McDonald's picks locations for its franchisees based on sophisticated surveys and demographic studies.

Credit. Some franchisors may help provide financing to qualified applicants. This help can be in the form of offering loans or guarantees, locating potential lenders, or preparing a loan package or business plan that can be shown to a bank or other potential lender. Some franchisors have been known to accompany franchisees in their visit to the lender. Many people have been able to get into the franchise business by using all kinds of creative financing plans and more than one source of capital. These include lines of credit, Small Business Administration loans, employee stock options (ESOPs), credit unions, insurance policies, venture capital, and trade credit (from suppliers). Some franchisors even have lease programs that allow prospective franchisees to lease units with an option to buy them.

Construction Expertise. Most franchisors supply franchisees with architectural and floor plans for the franchise building. Choice International has plans available for three different styles of two-story, 100-unit Sleep Inns and furnishes all interior and exterior designs and site plans, including landscaping. McDonald's and Burger King have a large variety of interior designs to choose from, depending on the market and the amount the franchisee is able to invest.

Some franchisors also help the franchisee employ the builder and supervise the construction. Since most franchisees do not have experience in this area, the assistance of a construction professional can mean considerable savings. Choice International provides preliminary and code-modified working drawings, elevations, and floor plans, as well as all structural, mechanical, plumbing, and electrical drawings necessary to complete the hotel. When the hotel is finished, a Choice International representative conducts a final site inspection to make sure that everything was done properly.

Fixtures and Equipment Assistance. Franchisors help franchisees select, purchase, and install fixtures and equipment. The Subway chain provides store design and equipment ordering guidance. Sheraton issues a product catalog as well as a guestroom design catalog with different interior design schemes that fit the Sheraton image.

Training. Classroom and on-the-job training is a major part of most franchise programs. As noted earlier, 49 percent of all franchisees list training as their main reason for buying a franchise. Many franchisors have extensive training programs because it is in their best interest to see that franchisees meet franchise standards.

Subway offers an intensive two-week training program that includes basic business operations, management techniques, and hiring skills. The program is conducted in a classroom and at one of the Subway restaurants. There are also follow-up programs for management. The KFC program is four days of 8 to 10 training hours per day. The franchisee or the manager and one other key person must attend the training. McDonald's has a two-week training program at Hamburger University in Chicago that follows on-the-job training at an operating store; every seven years, franchisees are invited back for an additional one-week course. McDonald's also has Hamburger Universities in places such as Hong Kong, London, Tokyo, Sydney, Hamburg, China, Singapore, and Dubai. Most of the hotel franchisors have training at their headquarters or conducted at individual hotels by field representatives.

Promotional Assistance. Promotional assistance—that is, help with advertising, sales, and public relations—is one of the main strengths a franchisor can offer a franchisee. Most franchisors charge franchisees a marketing or advertising fee that is used to purchase television time, radio spots, and newspaper ads; support promotional efforts on social media; and produce other promotions such as coupons, sweepstakes, or contests. Burger King charges each franchisee an advertising royalty of 4 percent of monthly sales. This money is used for advertisements and commercials. The company also helps franchisees with cooperative advertising plans, offers ongoing sales incentives, and sponsors periodic awards for superior sales and quality. Wendy's charges 2 percent of gross sales for national advertising and another 2 percent for local advertising efforts.

Advertising and sales efforts in the lodging industry can be complicated. For Hilton Hotel's Garden Inns, a monthly program fee of 4.3 percent of gross rooms revenue is charged.

A franchisor's regional representatives give franchisees ongoing support.

The program fee covers advertising, promotion, publicity, public relations, market research, hotel directories, and developing and maintaining the reservations system. Additional charges are levied for marketing programs not covered under the program fee, including Hilton Honors Worldwide (Hilton's guest frequency and reward program).

Economies of Scale. Because they are part of a franchise chain, franchisees receive the advantages of economies of scale in purchasing supplies, equipment, and advertising.

Ongoing Support. The franchisor remains available to the franchisee on an ongoing basis after the franchise unit becomes operational. Franchisors have regional representatives and district managers who regularly meet with franchisees. Franchisors help franchisees with merchandising and day-to-day problems. As members of a franchise organization, franchisees have access to many types of specialists that they would otherwise have to hire.

Disadvantages

Despite all the advantages of franchising, there are problems that have caused some franchisees to regret their decision to purchase a franchise. Disadvantages include:

- Restrictions
- Unwanted products or procedures
- Unwanted advertising
- Unprotected territories
- Cancellation
- Inadequate training

Restrictions. A major disadvantage of franchising is that most franchise contracts restrict franchisees a great deal. A franchisor's success depends on having consistent quality throughout the system. When people check in at a Holiday Inn anywhere in the United States, they expect to find the same kind of room, similarly priced and furnished, with the same kind of amenities. A Big Mac or a Whopper is expected to taste exactly the same whether it is purchased in Los Angeles or London. This means that franchisors must strictly enforce their standards. Operators of Holiday Inns *must* furnish and maintain guestrooms in a certain way; Holiday Inn kitchens *must* adhere to certain standards, and staffing *must* be at required levels. A McDonald's franchisee *must* prepare hamburgers and other products to company standards, and a Dunkin' franchisee *must* make new donuts every four hours. All of these franchisors run regular and unannounced inspections, and franchisees who fail to adhere to standards run the risk of having their franchise canceled. This is not an idle threat. Every year, some franchisees have their contracts canceled for failure to follow company guidelines.

These restrictions mean that some franchisees cannot be as creative as they'd like to be. They can't come up with their own advertising campaigns or introduce new menu items. Restaurant chains are especially strict about their menus. Franchisees cannot add or subtract anything from menus or change recipes in any way without permission, and permission is seldom granted; though on very rare occasions, a franchisee will get an idea approved. McDonald's likes to point out that several of its menu items evolved from the ideas of its operators. Ray Kroc credited franchisee Lou Groen with inventing Filet-O-Fish to help him in his battle against the Big Boy chain in the Catholic parishes of Cincinnati; Jim Delligatti in Pittsburgh came up with the idea for the Big Mac; Herb Peterson in Santa Barbara created the Egg McMuffin; and Harold Rosen in Enfield, Connecticut, came up with the Shamrock Shake, a special green milkshake served around St. Patrick's Day.[10]

Unwanted Products or Procedures. When new products or procedures are introduced, franchisees must embrace them whether they want to or not. Originally, many McDonald's operators did not want to open for breakfast—it meant dramatically increased labor costs and a whole new shift. They doubted that they would sell enough breakfasts to make it pay. But when the company decided to advertise the new breakfast hours on television, every franchisee needed to open at 6 a.m.

Unwanted Advertising. A franchisor's advertising program can be another cause of franchisee dissatisfaction. When Burger King decided to launch a television campaign featuring "Herb the Nerd," many franchisees did not like it. They felt it actually drove away customers. Nevertheless, they were forced to accept it and pay for it until the company itself decided the campaign was not effective and canceled it. In some cases,

franchisees feel the franchisor's national campaign does not help them, although it may benefit franchisees elsewhere.

Unprotected Territories. Another area of dispute between franchisors and franchisees involves territories. Many franchisors do not grant specific territories. This means they allow a new franchisee to establish a new unit as close as a mile or two away from an existing unit if business in the area warrants it. This is called **encroachment**. There have been a number of lawsuits brought against franchisors by franchise operators over this issue.

Legislation to protect franchisees' rights, and the formation of a number of franchise owners groups, are restricting the power of franchisors to control their operators' destinies. In many cases, these groups now have a voice in determining company policies on encroachment into their territories, as well as input on new product introductions and advertising campaigns.

Cancellation. Franchisees are not always guaranteed that they will be able to renew their franchise after the initial 20-year period (the usual length of a franchise contract). If a franchisee has not been adhering to the standards set by the company, for example, the franchisor may decide not to renew the franchise. The franchisor may also decide not to renew for reasons outside the franchisee's control. Theoretically, a franchisee might spend a lifetime building a business and then be unable to pass it on to their children because the franchise contract expired and was not renewed.

Inadequate Training. Not all franchisors provide high-quality training programs to their franchisees. Sometimes a franchisor's salespersons misrepresent the training that franchisees will receive.

Advantages and Disadvantages for Franchisors

Franchising has advantages and disadvantages for the franchisor as well. On the advantages side, little to no capital is required for expansion because the franchisees provide the funding. Franchisors can expand their companies quickly, while transferring the investment risk to the franchisees. Because a franchise unit is owned by a local individual or company, the franchisor gains an involved and motivated on-site manager who is a member of the community. This means the franchisee is likely to be accepted by the local community, and the franchise is in the hands of someone who knows local authorities and ordinances.

The downside is that the franchisor gives up the profits generated by its franchise units, settling for royalties instead. Also, the franchisor surrenders a certain amount of control to the franchisees. In company-owned units, it is easier to make changes in operating procedures and marketing approaches and get feedback from unit managers.

Knowledge Check

1. What are some reasons franchisees purchase a franchise?
2. From a franchisee's point of view, what are some advantages and disadvantages of owning a franchise?

13.5 FRANCHISING ISSUES

Franchising will continue to be a major force in the expansion of the hospitality industry. There are problems, however, that strain franchisor–franchisee relations. The most common areas of disagreement include encroachment, financial violations such as unpaid royalty charges, and contract violations.

Some segments of the hotel and restaurant business have reached a mature stage of growth. New concepts are more difficult to come by, and franchise chains and individual franchisees are competing for market share with each other. Franchisors, however, have not been taking these signs of a mature market lying down. Instead, they have reached out to penetrate new markets. The strategy of a number of restaurant chains is to establish outlets in nontraditional locations such as supermarkets, convenience stores, airports, schools and colleges, ballparks, and hospitals.

In the lodging industry, too, franchising is in transition. Hotel chains have introduced new brands under their trade name or a new name. As a result of this branding strategy, some franchisees have accused hotel franchisors of encroachment. Franchisors have countered with impact studies and defined geographic areas for each franchisee to allay fears about encroachment.

Knowledge Check

1. What are the most common areas of disagreement in franchisor–franchisee relations?
2. How have franchisors penetrated new markets?

CHAPTER SUMMARY

Franchising is a marketing or distribution system. In its simplest form, the term *franchise* refers to the authorization given by one company to another to sell its unique products or services.

There are two types of franchises: the product or trade-name franchise and the business format franchise. The product or trade-name franchise is a supplier–dealer arrangement whereby the dealer (franchisee) sells a product line provided by the supplier (franchisor) and to some degree takes on the identity of the supplier. Business format franchises are ongoing business relationships between franchisors and franchisees in which franchisors sell their product(s), service(s), trademark, and the business concept itself to franchisees in return for royalties and other franchise fees.

Franchising is not a new concept. In 1851, I.M. Singer & Company used franchising to develop networks of sewing machine dealers all over the United States. The first person in the hospitality industry to pioneer the idea of the business format franchise was Howard Johnson, founder of the Howard Johnson Company.

The evolution of franchising was driven by the desire of some companies to expand their business, coupled with the desire of entrepreneurs like McDonald's founder Ray Kroc to take a successful idea and build on it, rather than risk starting from scratch. Franchising also provided companies with an alternative method of financing growth other than through company-owned units.

The typical franchise fee arrangement has two parts: (1) an initial franchise fee, payable upon signing the agreement, and (2) ongoing fees, which consist of royalties (based on monthly gross sales) and advertising and marketing fees. In addition to these fees, there is an initial investment required to purchase or lease the physical facility, equipment, and supplies necessary to operate the franchise. Before selling a franchise, franchisors are required by the Federal Trade Commission to submit a Franchise Disclosure Document (FDD) to the prospective franchisee.

Franchising is one way for individuals to run their own businesses. When people buy a franchise, they buy (1) a format and formula, and (2) the experience of the franchisor, who will teach them what they need to know to succeed. One study showed that prospective franchisees had the following reasons for wanting their own franchise: self-management, financial independence, career advancement, new skills/training, and long-term investment.

There are many other advantages to owning a franchise. Franchisors help franchisees with site selection, credit, construction, fixtures and equipment, training, pre-opening and opening activities, promotional assistance, economies of scale, and ongoing support.

Franchising is not for everyone. Many franchisees do not like the restrictions imposed on them by their franchise agreement. Franchisors have tough standards and usually do not hesitate to cancel the franchises of operators who will not adhere to those standards. Franchisees must also go along with—and help pay for—the franchisor's advertising and marketing program, whether they agree with it or not. Sometimes there are disputes over territories.

Franchising has disadvantages for the franchisor as well. While little or no capital is required to expand (because funding is provided by the franchisee), the franchisor gives up the profits generated by the franchise units, settling for royalties instead. Also, the franchisor surrenders a certain amount of control to the franchisees.

There is no doubt that franchising will continue to be a major force in the expansion of the hospitality industry. But there are many upheavals taking place due to the expansion strategies of franchisors.

KEY TERMS

business format franchise—An ongoing business relationship between a franchisor and a franchisee in which the franchisor sells its products, services, trademark, and business concept to the franchisee in return for royalties and other franchise fees.

encroachment—Placing a branded hotel or restaurant in the vicinity of other hotels or restaurants with the same or a related brand.

Franchise Disclosure Document (FDD)—A prospectus that outlines certain vital aspects of a franchisor and its franchise agreement. By law, the FDD must be given to a potential franchisee before the franchisee signs the franchise agreement. (Formerly known as the Uniform Franchise Offering Circular, or UFOC.)

franchising—A continuing relationship in which the franchisor provides a licensed privilege to do business, plus assistance in organizing, training, merchandising, and managing, in return for a financial consideration from the franchisee.

initial franchise fee—While restaurant franchisors generally charge a flat franchise fee for one unit, hotel franchisors base their initial franchise fee on the number of guestrooms the franchisee builds, with a minimum fee plus an amount per room over a defined minimum number of rooms.

product or trade-name franchise—A supplier–dealer arrangement whereby the dealer (franchisee) sells a product line provided by the supplier (franchisor) and to some degree takes on the identity of the supplier.

promotional assistance—Help with advertising, sales, and public relations. It is one of the main strengths a franchisor can offer a franchisee.

royalty fee—A fee calculated on a percentage of a franchisee's sales.

1. What is the definition of a franchisor?
    a. The individual or company granted the right to conduct business
    b. The owner of the trademark, product, or business format
    c. An individual who gives a franchise ongoing support
    d. The name of the business format or product

2. Who pioneered the idea of the business format franchise in the hospitality industry?
    a. I.M. Singer
    b. Coca-Cola
    c. Ray Kroc
    d. Howard Dearing Johnson

3. What is the definition of a franchisee?
    a. The individual or company granted the right to conduct business
    b. The owner of the trademark, product, or business format
    c. An individual who gives a franchise ongoing support
    d. The name of the business format or product

4. What is the initial franchise fee for a hotel usually based on?
    a. Number of units built
    b. Number of hotels built
    c. Number of guestrooms built
    d. Number of projected guests

5. Which is calculated in an initial franchise fee?
    a. Franchisor's goodwill
    b. Construction costs
    c. Training costs
    d. Royalties

6. Which government agency regulates franchising?
    a. Better Business Bureau
    b. U.S. Department of Labor
    c. Federal Trade Commission
    d. U.S. Small Business Administration

7. What is the Franchise Disclosure Document?
    a. Prospectus that outlines vital aspects of a franchisor and its franchise agreements
    b. Estimate of how much a franchise will make in its first year
    c. Legal agreement to open a franchise
    d. License from a franchisor

8. What is the most important reason franchisees want a franchise?
    a. Financial independence
    b. Career advancement
    c. Self-management
    d. New skills and training

9. What is a major disadvantage of franchise ownership?
   a. Credit
   b. Restrictions
   c. Economies of scale
   d. Gaining royalties instead of profits

10. Which example describes encroachment?
   a. A new burger restaurant opens within a mile of another restaurant within the same brand.
   b. A coffee shop in an airport serves specialty drinks not offered at its other locations.
   c. A donut shop has different operational hours from another location 10 miles away.
   d. A casual restaurant in a suburban location has different menu prices from a location in a major metropolitan area.

11. Which is a disadvantage for a franchisor?
   a. Surrender of control
   b. Unwanted advertising
   c. Unwanted procedures
   d. Lack of capital

12. What is key to succeeding in international markets?
   a. Acquiring enough capital
   b. Providing adequate training
   c. Having construction expertise
   d. Adapting to local cultures and laws

SHORT-ANSWER QUESTIONS

1. How has franchising changed the hospitality industry?

2. Why do franchisors hold franchisees to such strict standards?

LESS IS MORE

Since 2016, Georgia-based Cool Grill has been a trusted Southeastern food franchise committed to maintaining the highest standards in serving fresh, high-quality food. There are no freezers or microwaves at Cool Grill's locations because fresh products are delivered and prepared by hand daily. Priding itself on maintaining the highest industry standards, Cool Grill refuses to let its commitment to high-quality food suffer because of its rapid growth.

The director of compliance joined the Cool Grill team in 2018. Before joining Cool Grill, she had spent 30 years in restaurant brand development and organic farms management, so she was no stranger to food safety issues associated with fresh food.

Because consumers are becoming more health-conscious, many restaurants have also adopted Cool Grill's emphasis on fresh ingredients. However, Cool Grill recognizes that just because a restaurant promises fresh food, it doesn't necessarily mean the food is safe. Food must be handled appropriately to be considered "fresh." The director of compliance and her team recognize these complexities in the food regulatory landscape. They are also keenly aware of the investment Cool Grill has made in consumer confidence and its brand image.

The entire company has made a significant effort to ensure that Cool Grill's food is both fresh and safe. It requires employees to conduct regular inspections to maintain compliance with regulations and industry best practices. However, Cool Grill is facing problems with availability of organic ingredients in some of its franchise locations. This has resulted in closure of half of its locations and threatens its expansion plans into the Northeast.

DISCUSSION QUESTIONS

1. What is unique about Cool Grill's product?

2. What are some successful things about Cool Grill and its operational team?

3. How could Cool Grill's franchise model be reevaluated to improve the company's outlook?

Kemmons Wilson

Kemmons Wilson (1913–2003) was an American entrepreneur and philanthropist best known as the founder of Holiday Inn, one of the world's largest hotel chains. His visionary approach to the hospitality industry revolutionized the concept of affordable, standardized accommodations and laid the foundation for modern hotel chains.

Growing up during the Great Depression, he learned the value of hard work and perseverance at an early age. Wilson started his first business venture at the age of 17, selling popcorn to moviegoers in his hometown.

In 1951, Wilson embarked on a family vacation that would ultimately shape his future. Frustrated by the inconsistent quality and high prices of the existing lodging options, he decided to create his own motel chain with a focus on affordable rates, cleanliness, and standardized amenities. This led to the founding of Holiday Inn in 1952, with its first location in Memphis, Tennessee.

Wilson's commitment to quality and innovation propelled Holiday Inn to unprecedented success. He introduced numerous industry innovations, including centralized reservations, air conditioning in every room, in-room telephones, and swimming pools. Wilson's emphasis on consistent quality across Holiday Inn locations set a new standard for the hospitality industry.

Under Wilson's leadership, Holiday Inn grew rapidly, expanding throughout the United States and internationally. By the 1960s, it became one of the largest hotel chains in the world. The success of Holiday Inn made Wilson a prominent figure in the business world and a respected entrepreneur.

Today, Holiday Inn stands as a testament to Wilson's vision and remains an iconic brand in the global hospitality landscape. His contributions to the industry and his philanthropic efforts have had a lasting impact, making Kemmons Wilson a revered figure in both business and community circles.

As an entrepreneur, you have always succeeded in your business ventures, even while you were in college. After graduation, you launch your first fast-casual Mediterranean grab-n-go concept. Located within three blocks of a college campus, your first-year sales revenue exceeds your projections by 200 percent! You use your profits to open a second location downtown, which is also a huge success. By now, you are confident that you have found the perfect formula for a business venture that is scalable. However, you do not have enough capital to open a third location, even though your customers are asking you to expand. What should you do?

14

HOW MANAGEMENT COMPANIES MANAGE HOTELS

Chapter Outline

Learning Objectives

1.   Identify unique management characteristics of the hotel business, explain why hotel management companies came into existence, and summarize the history of management companies. (pp. 398–400)

2.   Describe a hotel management contract. (pp. 400–406)

KEY TERMS

approval provision

asset manager

basic fees

fee structure provision

gross operating profit

incentive fee

management contract

operating expenses provision

operating term provision

operator investment provision

operator-reimbursable expenses

post-opening management fees

pre-opening management fees

real estate investment trust (REIT)

reporting requirements provision

technical assistance fees

termination provision

This chapter covers hotel management companies and their methods of operation. First, it explains the beginnings of management companies and continues by describing their history and evolution. It then focuses on management contracts between hotel owners and management companies, identifying and explaining major contract provisions and the reasons for them. Finally, the chapter describes the opportunities and risks for hotel owners and management companies when they enter into management contracts.

14.1 WHY MANAGEMENT COMPANIES EXIST

The growth and prosperity of hotel management companies, and the unique and changing nature of their relationships with hotel owners, underscore the fact that hotels are a special kind of real estate. They are very different from office buildings and shopping malls, for example.

To begin with, unlike most other businesses, hotels operate 24 hours a day. Moreover, unlike 24-hour operations such as all-night gas stations or drugstores, hotels must provide a multitude of readily available specialized services. At full-service properties, guests expect that food and beverage service will be provided—in some cases, 24 hours a day. Rooms must be cleaned daily. Full-service hotels may also offer laundry and valet services, meeting and convention rooms and services, fitness clubs, tennis courts and golf courses, airport limousines, concierge services, business centers, Wi-Fi and secretarial services. The number and range of facilities and services that a lodging property offers depend on the property's biggest guest group, positioning, and market segmentation.

In fact, a hotel is a miniature, self-sustaining society. Managers of large hotels often compare what they do to running a small city. Many large hotels have their own energy-generating facilities, security forces, and shopkeepers. Guests sleep, eat, work, play, and sometimes even live in hotels. The hotel is the guests' headquarters—their office and home, the center of their daily business and social life. Because a hotel can be so many things, managing it can be complex and extremely demanding. Managers and their staffs must be prepared to cope with a variety of activities and emergencies while maintaining and controlling the hotel's physical plant.

Managing a hotel requires special expertise. Buying a franchise is one way that inexperienced hotel owners can try to acquire that expertise. When they buy a franchise like Holiday Inn, they buy an established image, a tested and successful operating system, employee training programs, marketing and advertising programs, and reservations systems.

Many hotel companies previously believed that while a franchise agreement provides systems, programs, and training, it does not provide the experienced managers and employees necessary to consistently operate a hotel in accordance with brand standards of quality. For this reason, branded hotel management companies, such as Hilton and Marriott, often chose to manage new properties themselves rather than sell franchises. They understood that they could not write down everything they knew in training manuals, and that mastery of the science of running a hotel could not be easily acquired in a short training course. (This management preference still generally holds for luxury and strategic flagship properties and in international markets.)

As the industry evolved, hotel ownership became increasingly institutionalized, with owners having more than one hotel. Professional hotel managers, many having previously worked with branded hotel management companies, began to manage hotels on behalf of these owners under a franchise agreement. Thus, the independent hotel management company was born. The emergence of extremely competent independent management companies that could maintain brand equity made the franchise model increasingly palatable, if not preferred, among branded hotel companies and hotel investors alike.

Knowledge Check

1. What was the impetus of the independent hotel management company?

2. Why is it important to have managers with expertise in running a branded hotel or franchise?

14.2 THE EVOLUTION OF MANAGEMENT COMPANIES

For hundreds of years, hotels were started, owned, and operated by hoteliers, just as restaurants were started by chefs. These hoteliers were usually small entrepreneurs who knew how to manage a single hotel.

But as the lodging industry grew rapidly in the last half of the twentieth century and evolved into the new millennium, a new breed of owners appeared. These new owners were increasingly institutional investors who regarded the buildings and land they occupied as attractive investments, or they were property owners who felt that a hotel would be the best use for their real estate. While many of these new owners were comparatively sophisticated and experienced real estate investors, many knew little about running the day-to-day operations of the hotels they owned. Fortunately, there was a burgeoning number of options available to them for running their hotels. Many hired professional hotel managers and operated their hotels as independent properties. In order to generate business and name recognition, they sometimes tied in with a referral service such as Best Western or a marketing group like Preferred Hotels & Resorts.

With the growing preference for boutique and lifestyle hotels, as well as Internet-enabled distribution systems, many started opting for new affiliation arrangements, such as soft brands, which afforded the benefits of powerful centralized systems and loyalty programs while allowing individual properties to retain a unique and authentic personality. Of course, the option to affiliate with branded management companies like Hyatt and Accor remained attractive, especially as many of these companies developed a variety of new brands for an ever-expanding array of property types (extended stay, select service, lifestyle, etc.) across a wide spectrum of price points and geographies. Branded hotel management companies were more than receptive to the idea because it meshed perfectly with their evolving business models, which hinged on growing their fees and earnings base without the financial risk of hotel development and ownership.

From the standpoint of these new owners—who were real estate investors, not hoteliers—the most logical way to employ a hotel company was a lease, an instrument that they were very familiar with. Under this arrangement, a hotel owner or developer—which might be an individual, a company, or even a government—would simply rent out a structure to a hotel company either as a fully developed and furnished turnkey operation or, more likely, as an unfurnished building that had to be outfitted by the hotel company. For instance, the government of Bermuda constructed the town of Saint George's first hotel, expecting the hotel would bring tourists to that part of the island. The building was then leased to the Holiday Inn Corporation. Subsequently the hotel has been leased to several other operators.

Under early lease arrangements, the hotel company was responsible for hiring and managing the entire staff of the hotel, collecting all the revenues from sales, and paying all operating costs. It also paid rent to the owners for the use of the facility. In return, the company received a share of the hotel's **gross operating profit**, calculated by deducting operating costs from total revenue. Obviously, the hotel's fixed charges—such as depreciation, interest on borrowed capital, and real estate taxes—were paid by the owner of the building. For a few leased hotels, the rental agreement was based on a percentage of total sales. Sometimes the rent was based on a combination of a percentage of sales as well as a share of the gross operating profit.

Another typical arrangement was the two-thirds/one-third lease. Here, two-thirds of the gross operating profit went to the owner and one-third went to the hotel company. This kind of arrangement was the basis of the contract made in 1954 between Hilton Hotels and the Puerto Rican government, the lessee and lessor, respectively, of the Caribe Hilton Hotel in San Juan. Hilton used the same formula to expand to Turkey, Mexico, and Cuba. It was in Cuba, after Fidel Castro's takeover and the disruption of operations because of the revolution, that Hilton recognized the potential for losses due to circumstances beyond its control. According to Charles A. Bell, executive vice president of Hilton International in its formative years, "That is why Hilton converted their profit-sharing lease agreement into management contracts under which the owners took the risk of operating losses, as well as debt service, and had the ongoing responsibility of supplying working capital."[1] Today, leasing is not at all preferred by branded or independent hotel management companies, precisely for this reason.

While Hilton was growing by leasing new properties and creating new types of leases, the InterContinental Hotels Group, now IHG, was pioneering the management contract. In the early 1950s, IHG signed its first management contracts with the respective owners of the Tequendama in Bogotá, Colombia, and the Tamanaco in Caracas, Venezuela, while the hotels were still under construction. Instead of paying rent and keeping the hotels' profits, IHG did not pay rent and received from each owner a management fee (which originally was based on a fixed fee per room) and an "incentive fee." The incentive fee was a percentage of the hotel's gross operating profit, plus reimbursement of IHG's overhead—specific expenses incurred by IHG in managing the property.

Incentive fees are now a regular part of management contracts, but in the 1950s this concept was a real innovation. The term **incentive fee** describes that portion of the management fee that is based on a percentage of a negotiated level of profitability. For example, one basis is a percentage of operating cash flow after debt service (CFADS), usually some percentage of adjusted gross operating income (AGOP) and, often, after a preferred owner return (usually calculated as percentage of total cost). It is called an incentive fee because it is designed to motivate the hotel company to produce maximum profit for the owners so the hotel company can collect the maximum incentive fee. As it gained more experience with this concept, IHG switched from a fixed fee per room to a percentage of gross revenue plus a percentage of gross operating profit with no reimbursement of company overhead. At first, IHG made a small investment in each of the hotels it managed so it could be a director on the boards of the companies that owned the hotels. Later, in Europe and Asia, IHG invested as much as one-third of the project cost.

One of the pioneers of independent management companies in the United States was Robert M. James, former president of Regal-AIRCOA (now Richfield Hospitality, Inc.). When James started his company in 1971, few U.S. hotels were operating under management contracts. In 1970, there were fewer than 10 management companies operating 22 properties.

Since contracting with a hotel owner to manage the hotel for them was virtually a new field, there was little information or experience to guide the first U.S. management companies.

To help remedy this situation, James started the International Council of Hotel and Motel Management Companies—a committee of the American Hotel & Lodging Association—which enabled management company representatives to meet with one another and learn more about management contracts.

It did not take long for the strategy of separating hotel ownership from hotel management to gain traction, and over the next four decades the number of independent management companies mushroomed. Exhibit 14.1 lists today's top 20 independent management companies.

> **Knowledge Check**
>
> 1. What are the benefits of a soft brand affiliation?
>
> 2. How do incentive fees benefit hotel companies?

14.3 MANAGEMENT CONTRACTS

A hotel **management contract** is a written agreement between the owner of a hotel and a hotel management company whereby the management company assumes the responsibility of operating the hotel and receives a fee for its service. The operator (management company) can be a brand operator with a familiar name and market image, such as Hyatt or Marriott. It can also be an independent management company. Independent management companies operate franchise hotels as well as independent hotels. For example, Aimbridge Hospitality manages properties under various franchises such as Marriott, Hilton, and Sheraton, as well as independent hotels and resorts such as the Charles Hotel in Cambridge, Massachusetts, and the Roosevelt Hotel in New York City.

Under the earliest management contracts, the operator was simply regarded as a company hired to perform a service, much as an architectural firm might be hired to draw the plans for a hotel. The management company got paid for performing those services but took no financial risk and therefore was not entitled to any profits. However, as noted previously, that basic concept

Exhibit 14.1   Top 20 Independent Management Companies

	Company	Number of Hotels
1.	Aimbridge Hospitality	1,500
2.	Hotel Equities	252
3.	HHM Hotels	235
4.	Pyramid Global Hospitality	220
5.	Highgate	176
6.	Concord Hospitality Enterprises	145
7.	GF Hotels & Resorts	130
8.	TPG Hotels	130
9.	Davidson Hospitality Group	129
10.	Crestline Hotels & Resorts	123
11.	Nationwide Hotel Management Company	122
12.	Remington Hotels	121
13.	Crescent Hotels & Resorts	115
14.	McKibbon Hospitality	109
15.	Real Hospitality Group	109
16.	Kinseth Hospitality Companies	100
17.	Atrium Hospitality	83
18.	HEI Hotels & Resorts	82
19.	Dimension Development	80
20.	Driftwood Hospitality Management	74

Source: Josiah Mackenzie, "Guide to Hotel Management Companies for 2023," Hotel Operations, 2023, https://hoteloperations.com/hotel-management-companies/#The_10_biggest_hotel_management_companies_for_2023.

has evolved over time. Other changes to the basic concept are as follows:

■ At one time, most financing of lodging facilities in the United States was done by insurance companies and lending institutions. They invested for the long term, hoping to realize both profits and appreciation on the value of the property. Today, the situation has evolved to include a greater variety of equity and debt participants. Current investors include private equity funds (e.g., Blackstone,

Starwood, Cerberus, and Apollo), **real estate investment trusts (REITs)**, and high-net-worth individuals. (A REIT is like a mutual fund; it allows individuals to combine their resources to invest in income-producing sovereign wealth funds and properties or lend funds to developers and builders.)

■ Most major hotel brands follow an "asset-light" strategy, having sold most of their owned properties to equity investors while retaining long-term management contracts. In Europe and the Pacific Rim, financial institutions still play an important role in financing hotels, while in some countries governments provide needed funds.

■ The relationship between owners and operators has dramatically shifted. There has been a significant change in management contracts due to increased competition among operators (both the branded chains and the independent management companies) and the more active role of increasingly professional institutional owners in managing their investments.[2] The relative bargaining strengths and negotiating abilities of the owner and the operator affect how the risks are shared.

■ Environmental concerns have slowed hotel development in ecologically sensitive areas in the United States and abroad. Today, it is recognized that hotels and resorts might damage such areas, so it is harder to get approval to build. Often, the cost of meeting environmental requirements can substantially increase the capital required to develop a new property.

■ With the economic downturn at the end of the first decade of the twenty-first century, hotel development was stalled, resulting in few new management contracts available and a shift in bargaining power to the hotel owners. Even as the economic environment changed and worldwide hotel development resumed, owners remained emboldened to negotiate more favorable contractual provisions.

With each economic downturn or "black swan" event, like the COVID-19 pandemic, the relationship between hotel management companies and the hotel owners continues to shift. Generally, these challenging moments reveal operating inefficiencies, many of which can be remedied with better use of evolving technologies. Owners increasingly demand that operators focus only on value-added tasks, while branded and independent management companies continue to gain scale through consolidation. Such trends are resulting in generally improving margins for all types of hotel properties.

Because of these reasons, hotel owners have become even less willing to take all of the financial risk. The stakes have gotten too high.

Contract Provisions

The provisions of a management contract are important not only to the owner and the operator but also to the lenders who finance the project. Lenders want assurance that the hotel owner and the management company operating the hotel have a reasonable opportunity to make a profit. They also want to be sure that differences between the owner and the management company have been resolved in advance; otherwise, the viability of the project may be jeopardized.

Contract provisions detail the exact terms that the parties have agreed on. Although the basic provisions of all management contracts are similar, there can be significant differences from contract to contract. These differences include the amounts invested by the owner and the management company; the nature and amount of control exercised by each party; fee structures, including the incentive arrangement; and contract termination provisions.

In the following sections, we discuss some of the major terms and provisions often addressed in hotel management contracts.[3]

Operating Term. The **operating term provision** defines the length of the initial term of the contract and its renewal options. The management company (hereafter referred to as the "operator") usually prefers a long initial period, while the owner usually prefers a shorter one. James Eyster and Jan de Roos, in their study of management contracts, explain that while a long-term contract offers stability for the operator, owner, and lender, it is a disadvantage to the owner if the owner wants to remove the operator before the contract comes up for renewal.[4] Operators generally favor long-term contracts because such contracts give them more time to recover a return on their investment in training and implementing brand standards. They also favor long-term contracts because of the importance of stable long-term fees to their valuations as "asset light" management companies. Owners, on the other hand, "prefer to have shorter terms or exit terms to minimize the risk of being tied to an agreement that they may eventually determine is not maximizing the value of their asset."[5] The lenders' concern is that the term of the contract and the term of the loan coincide, making it probable that the hotel will be run by only one operator throughout the loan's payback period. Such a stable situation makes it more likely that there will be an uninterrupted flow of revenues and profits to cover debt payments.

The length of the contract is often a serious negotiating point. An HVS study reports that initial contract terms for the chain brands are typically 10 to 30 years, while for independent management companies the initial contract term is usually 3 to 10 years. In some cases, contract terms with independent management companies and luxury and upper upscale hotel owners are longer.[6] Shorter and more easily terminated independent management company contracts are a couple of the reasons driving the increasing popularity of independent management companies.

Fee Structure. The **fee structure provision** outlines the fees the owner must pay to the operator for managing the property. This is one of the most important contract provisions because it affects both the owner's and operator's profits. The fee structure is negotiable and will vary from contract to contract depending on the bargaining power of the parties. Eyster and de Roos categorize the payments owners make to operators into four areas.

Technical assistance fees cover the time and expertise of the operator as a consultant in the design of the facilities. Architectural and interior design are the services most commonly rendered, although help with restaurant layout, equipment selection, and security concerns such as lighting and locking systems are often involved as well.

Pre-opening management fees are similar to technical assistance fees in that they cover work done by the operator before the hotel opens. Pre-opening management activities include planning, staffing, training, marketing, budgeting, and other activities that the operator must perform before the property is ready to receive guests. These activities are very important, especially for hotel owners with no previous experience, since they may well influence the hotel's long-term success.

Post-opening management fees are fees paid by a hotel owner to a management company for managing the property. They are almost always based on some kind of formula. It is typically a basic fee plus an incentive. **Basic fees**, also known simply as "management fees," are the fees paid to the operator for managing the property. In the case of a chain operator such as Hilton or Marriott, the fee also covers the use of the established brand name. As has been noted, an independent management company does not bring a recognizable name to the negotiating table. If the owner wants a franchised name like Hampton Inn or Embassy Suites or wants the property to be part of a referral reservations system like that of Best Western, they must deal directly with the franchisor or reservations system. That cost is distinct and separate from the management fee. This is the main justification for a chain operator's higher management fee; a chain operator gives the owner's hotel an established name. The important thing in determining an equitable management fee is to relate the fee to the services received and to define the level of profit upon which the incentive fee is based. The average basic fee in the Americas ranges from 2.9 to 3.7 percent of gross revenue. The incentive fee is a negotiated figure and there are a number of ways to calculate it. There are other methods that allow the owner to receive a designated percentage return on the total project cost or the owner's invested equity before the operator's incentive fee. While specific terms vary with each deal and are usually considered proprietary information, today's management contracts typically reflect base fees of 2 percent to 4 percent of total hotel revenue, coupled with an incentive fee of certain negotiated percent of AGOP, before or after an owner/investor's return, a stated reserve for replacement, and the asset management fee.[7]

Operator-reimbursable expenses are incurred when a management company's corporate office provides centralized reservations systems, bulk purchasing services, national advertising campaigns, and accounting services. Travel costs of corporate staff who supervise the hotel are also considered operator-reimbursable expenses. Each managed property reimburses the operator for its share of these costs.

Reporting Requirements. The **reporting requirements provision** defines the types of reports that will be provided by the operator to the owner and outlines how frequently they will be provided. These reports include budgets, financial statements, variance reports between budget and actual performance, market plans, audited statements, and—in some cases—weekly and daily activity reports.

Approvals. Since the management contract is an agreement between the hotel's owner and operator, decisions about the hotel's development or operation generally require input from both parties, or at least an approval from one party of the other's decision. The agreement should have an **approval provision** that defines in what areas approvals are necessary. Most contracts require the owner's approval of the hotel's general manager, controller, and director of sales. Today's lenders are no longer entirely passive; they may involve themselves in such areas as the hotel's asset positioning in the marketplace, the annual operating and capital budget, and executive positions in the hotel. In many cases, owners are concerned about restaurant concepts and marketing and pricing strategies as well.

Contract provisions relating to owner input have given owners and lenders, or their representatives (**asset managers**), more of a voice in operational decisions. According to James Eyster, involvement has increased considerably in operational decisions, the hotel's operating policies, the budgeting process, and personnel selection.

Although the operating companies continue to set standards, owners—through on-site representatives or representation on policymaking committees—take part in the decision-making process. In the past, the operator was responsible for developing and following the operating budget. Today, in most cases, owners provide input and have the right to approve the budget. Also, owner control over capital replacement or improvement budgets has increased significantly. Line staff members are sometimes employees of the owner under the relationship established by some management contracts, with the executive staff employed by the operator. Owners now have a greater say in the selection of the general manager and other key department heads.[8]

Even when communication between the owner and the operator is good, they may not always agree, so the contract should contain provisions for settling disputes. A number of management contracts contain an arbitration provision, specifying that the arbitration come from a qualified person or firm.[9]

Performance. Performance clauses that allow the owner to terminate the management company have become a more common addition to management contracts. According to Stephen Rushmore, performance clauses usually contain the following: "the criteria standard; an implementation period; ability for operator to cure; and exceptions to termination."[10] The criteria standard is generally a dual benchmark of revenue and achievement of a certain percentage of the approved operating budget. A common revenue test is revenue per available room (RevPAR) compared to that achieved by a competitive set of hotels. The percent of budget ranges significantly, but it is usually between 75 percent and 90 percent.

The implementation period is the time that the management company has to achieve the standards mentioned above. It could be anywhere from one to three years, depending on the market conditions. Also, it may vary between a new hotel, which requires a period of time to develop business, and an existing hotel, where the new management company must merely put in place its marketing and operating systems rather than develop business from scratch.

If expected levels of profitability are not met, some contracts require that the management company give or lend the owner "sufficient funds to make up the difference between the stipulated level of net income defined in the standards and the actual level."[11]

Circumstances beyond the control of the management company, such as natural disasters or terrorist attacks, alter the market environment and are legitimate reasons for not achieving the negotiated performance standards. Hence the management agreement must be specific as to the exceptions that are acceptable.

Termination. All management contracts contain a **termination provision** that outlines the conditions and terms under which either party (the hotel or the client) can end the contractual agreement before its original expiration date. Conditions that can end a contractual agreement include the following:

- Nonperformance of a contract provision by the other party (sometimes with a one-time right to "cure"—that is, make things right), which usually goes into effect two to three years after the opening of the hotel or the beginning of the contract. Nonperformance benchmarks could be based on a minimum average daily rate (ADR) index or a RevPAR index compared to a competitive set of properties if the owner's return is less than expected or there is a negative cash flow.
- One of the parties filing for bankruptcy.
- One of the parties causing licenses to be suspended or revoked.[12]

Some contracts include other reasons for termination. These relate to the damage or loss of the property or the sale of the property. Sometimes there is a "termination without cause" provision. If a contract is terminated without cause, the owner must pay a penalty fee to the operator to compensate for the loss of profits anticipated by the operator.

Operator Investment. Operators or management companies are primarily in the business of managing. On the other hand, owners prefer a good-faith investment on the part of the operator. Today, more operators are investing in the properties they manage, usually in the form of loans or equity. When an operator loans money to an owner, the management contract specifies the amount in the **operator investment provision**; how the loan will be used (as initial working capital, for example, or to cover negative cash flows); the term of the loan; and the interest rate. When the investment is an equity contribution, it may be in the form of cash, free technical services, waived pre-opening management fees, or even conversion of incentive fees.[13]

Operating Expenses. In addition to the normal costs of operating a hotel, an operator will incur expenses in its home office or on the premises of the property itself. Expenses such as centralized advertising, reservations systems, and computer and accounting services are typical of the costs that an operator sometimes charges to the hotel's owner. The operator should clearly state the operating expenses it will pass on to the owner in the **operating expenses provision**—this helps avoid challenges by the owner later on.

Other Provisions. Other provisions of most management contracts include those that:

- Restrict the operator from competing in the same market area by operating another property within the area (unless approved by the owner).
- Specify the methods of transferring ownership or management interests to others by either party through a sale or a lease.
- Stipulate exclusive rights to work with each other on future hotels.
- Define the rights of each party in case the property is damaged or condemned.
- Provide indemnification for the adverse performance of the other party.
- Lay out a plan for a cash reserve for the replacement of furniture, fixtures, and equipment.

Advantages and Disadvantages

Management contracts have advantages and disadvantages for each of the parties involved. One of the primary disadvantages for owners is that while a management contract relieves them of day-to-day operating responsibilities, they still have to carry all or most of the financial burden. Although operators have increasingly provided loans and equity investments in recent years, owners are still primarily responsible for funding their properties. They must make up for losses or insufficient revenues to cover operating costs. In addition, management fees reduce owner profits.

Owners do, however, benefit from management contracts. The primary advantage is that they buy the services of an established hotel operator with a proven track record and a good reputation. Although a management fee must be paid, the potential for profit is increased. An experienced operator can offer marketing expertise and systems of cost control that would otherwise not be available to the owner.

At first, it may appear that operators have few serious disadvantages in a management contract arrangement. One of the greatest advantages, from an operator's point of view, is that it can control a large number of properties with a relatively limited investment. The operator's financial risk is much lower than that of the owner.

Nevertheless, there are disadvantages to a management contract for operators as well. An operator's reputation is on the line every day at every hotel it manages. The operator must look to the owner for funding when there is a shortfall in revenues. If the owner refuses to supply it or does not have it, the resulting substandard services and facilities will reflect on the operator. In addition, the operator's real opportunity for profit lies in the incentive fee. An operator dealing with a difficult or poorly financed owner will probably never realize the anticipated profits.

A further disadvantage is that, unless the operator has provided equity, the owner may make decisions regarding the property's development or sale without the operator's input. The owner can also dismiss the operator or not renew the contract at the end of its term, possibly damaging the operator's reputation and taking away its opportunity to realize profits from the work it has done. A hotel is rarely an overnight success; it usually takes years to realize an operating profit, and only those who are in it for the long haul are likely to reap the rewards.

On the whole, management contracts are carefully crafted so that all parties are well protected. But even with the best intentions, sometimes there are serious disagreements between owners and operators. An example of what can happen surfaced publicly when Broadreach Capital Partners, owners of the Four Seasons Aviara Resort in Carlsbad, California, attempted to oust the hotel company and replace Four Seasons with Dolce Hotels and Resorts. Broadreach had signed a 30-year contract with Four Seasons in 1995 that included three 20-year options, so that the potential term of the contract had a 90-year span. However, a clash surfaced when the owners and the operator could not agree on the 2009 operating budget. Although the contract contained a provision for settling disputes, both parties brought the disagreement to court. The owners claimed that Four Seasons was not operating in a cost-effective manner, and they wanted the hotel company out immediately. In fact, representatives of the owners arrived at the property late at night to change the locks of management offices, according to a Four Season's assertion. On the other hand, Four Seasons argued that Broadreach burdened the hotel with onerous debt and requested that the court stop the owners from seizing the hotel and require them to abide by the dispute-settlement provision in the management contract—namely, arbitration. The court agreed and ordered the parties to arbitrate. They did so, and the arbitration panel ruled that Broadreach had to pay Four Seasons in order to sever the contract.

According to Eyster and de Roos, dispute settlement provisions are relatively new to management contracts. They appear now rather frequently. According to their research, "Most owners and operators interviewed recommend that the arbitration clause state clearly whether all contract provisions should be subject to arbitration or whether arbitration should be limited to specific disputes."[14] In the case of the Broadreach and Four Seasons dispute, the management agreement had a broad arbitration clause. If an "owner wants to reserve its right to litigate certain aspects of the relationship with the manager in court, then it should customize the provision appropriately" by either explicitly excluding or stating potential areas of dispute.[15]

While this kind of incident is highly unusual, serious disagreements do happen occasionally, and it illustrates the necessity of both parties understanding what they get and what they give up in a management contract.

Knowledge Check

1. Why are contract provisions important?

2. From a hotel owner's point of view, what are advantages and disadvantages of management contracts?

Hotels are a special kind of real estate. They are small, self-sufficient communities, and they need people with hotel expertise to operate them. In the last half of the twentieth century, inexperienced hotel owners such as investors and real estate developers began to acquire hotel properties. These owners realized that the best way to gain hotel management expertise was to bring in experienced hotel operators by (1) leasing the hotel to them or (2) signing a management contract with them that allowed them to run the hotel.

With the first leasing agreements, the operator paid rent for the building but kept whatever profits were made. With the first management contracts, operators did not pay rent and did not keep all of the hotel's profits—they received a basic fee to cover their overhead costs plus a share of the profits or an incentive fee.

A management contract is a written agreement between an owner of a hotel and a hotel management company (operator) in which the owner employs the operator as an agent to assume full responsibility for managing the property. The operator can be a hotel chain with an established brand name or an independent management company.

There are several reasons why management contracts are still evolving. Most new hotel owners are interested in optionality, including the possibility of shorter-term ownership. Hotel development has slowed because the tax structure and business climate have changed, and environmental concerns have become more important. Most reasons have to do with the increased sophistication of professional hotel ownership and trends concerning the size and focus of hotel management companies themselves. Evolving technologies and the consumer demand preferences of millennials and Generation Z travelers are prompting the development of all sorts of new blended hotel/branded residential products, which in turn are spawning new brands, operating models, and financing structures—all of which will eventually have to be accommodated in new contract terms.

The most important provisions in a management contract are those dealing with the operating term, the fee structure, reporting requirements, approvals, performance, termination of the contract, operator investment, and operating expenses.

From an owner's point of view, the advantage of hiring a management company is that it relieves them of the burden of running the hotel and provides the hotel with experienced management personnel and operating systems. The disadvantages are that the owner is still responsible for paying the bills, even though the management company operates the hotel, and management fees reduce the owner's profits.

Hotel management companies benefit from management contracts because the companies can grow without putting up large amounts of capital, keeping their financial risk low. However, difficult or under-financed owners can damage an operator's reputation and deprive it of profits that it has earned. The owner can also dismiss the operator who built the business, even if the hotel is showing a profit.

KEY TERMS

approval provision—The provision of a hotel management contract specifying which operator decisions require management approval. The mechanism for settling owner–operator disputes is sometimes included in this provision.

asset manager—The owner's representative monitoring the operation of the hotel.

basic fees—Fees paid by a hotel owner to a management company for managing the property. In the case of a chain management company, the fees also cover the use of the established brand name. Also called "management fees."

fee structure provision—A provision in a contract between a hotel owner and a hotel management company that outlines the fees the owner must pay to the management company for managing the property.

gross operating profit—Profit calculated by deducting operating costs from total revenue.

incentive fee—That portion of the management fee (paid by hotel owners to hotel management companies) that is based on a percentage of income before fixed charges (also known as gross operating profit) or on a percentage of cash flow after debt service.

management contract—A written agreement between the owner of a hotel and a hotel management company whereby the management company assumes the responsibility of operating the hotel and receives a fee for its service.

operating expenses provision—The provision in a hotel management contract that outlines the expenses the management company will pass on to the hotel's owner.

operating term provision—The provision of a hotel management contract that defines the length of the initial contract and its renewal options.

operator investment provision—The provision of a hotel management contract outlining the details of the operator's investment in the property.

operator-reimbursable expenses—Expenses a hotel management company's corporate office incurs in providing services (e.g., bulk purchasing services and national advertising campaigns) to its managed properties. Each managed property reimburses the management company for its share of these costs.

post-opening management fees—Fees paid by a hotel owner to a management company for managing the property; they are almost always based on some kind of formula that incorporates a basic fee plus an incentive.

pre-opening management fees—Fees paid by a hotel owner to a management company for work done before the opening of the hotel, including planning, staffing, training, marketing, budgeting, and other activities that the management company must perform before the property is ready to receive guests.

real estate investment trust (REIT)—An investment instrument, somewhat like a mutual fund, that allows individuals to combine their resources to invest in income-producing properties or lend funds to developers or builders.

reporting requirements provision—The provision of a hotel management contract that stipulates the types of reports the management company must provide to the owner and how often they must be submitted.

technical assistance fees—Fees paid by a hotel owner to a management company covering the time and expertise of the company as a consultant in the design and plan of the facilities.

termination provision—A clause that outlines the conditions and terms under which either party (the hotel or the client) can end the contractual agreement before its original expiration date.

1. Why did branded hotel management companies initially not sell franchises?
   a. There was too much financial risk.
   b. They did not think it would be profitable.
   c. They did not want to lose control of quality.
   d. Mastery of running a hotel could not be learned in a short time.

2. Which describes an incentive fee?
   a. Operating expenses that are padded on to an owner
   b. Fee to cover the use of an established brand name
   c. Fee paid by a hotel owner to a management company
   d. Portion of a management fee based on a percentage of income before fixed charges

3. Which defines the length of an initial contract?
   a. Fee structure provision
   b. Operating term provision
   c. Operating expense provision
   d. Operator investment provision

4. What is the benefit of a real estate investment trust?
   a. Funds in the trust are not affected by income losses.
   b. Individuals are not subjected to withdrawal penalties.
   c. Profits generated from a contract are paid back to the trust.
   d. Individuals can combine resources to invest in income-producing properties.

5. Which cost is considered an operator-reimbursable expense?
   a. Food and beverage expenses
   b. National advertising campaigns
   c. Third-party concierge services
   d. Housekeeping expenses

6. What is the average basic fee in the Americas?
   a. 2.5 to 3.2 percent of gross revenue
   b. 2.9 to 3.7 percent of gross revenue
   c. 3.3 to 4.2 percent of gross revenue
   d. 3.5 to 4.4 percent of gross revenue

7. A contract includes damage to property as a reason to dissolve a management contract. Which provision includes this?
   a. Operating expense provision
   b. Operating term provision
   c. Termination provision
   d. Approval provision

8. What is a disadvantage of management contracts for operators?
   a. Decisions about development or sale can be made without their input.
   b. They must oversee the day-to-day operating responsibilities.
   c. They must make up for insufficient revenues.
   d. Fees reduce their profits.

9. Which condition would not allow either party of a management contract to terminate their agreement?
   a. Suspension of licenses
   b. Filing for bankruptcy
   c. Change in overtime labor laws
   d. Nonperformance of a contract provision

10. Which could be a conflict of interest in hotel operations?
   a. A hotel operator receives a bonus payment from a hotel owner.
   b. A hotel owner hires a hotel operator to manage five motels off a highway exit.
   c. A hotel owner has managing contracts with three different types of hotels.
   d. A hotel operator manages multiple hotel properties under different owners in the same location.

11. What is one reason why management contracts are still evolving?
   a. Owners no longer want to lease hotels.
   b. Owners are taking on more financial risks.
   c. Contracts no longer have termination provisions.
   d. New hotel owners are interested in short-term ownership.

12. Which hotel brand pioneered the first management contract?
   a. IHG
   b. Starwood
   c. Hilton Hotels
   d. Marriott International

SHORT-ANSWER QUESTIONS

1. What are some of the industry-wide changes responsible for the evolution of management contracts?

2. What are the differences between a lease and a management contract?

CONTRACT CONUNDRUMS

The owner of a large hotel resort attempted to physically oust its management company from the property in fall of 2018. Employees of the management company reported that security guards hired by the owner threatened to fire them and attempted to change door locks, all while guests were staying in the hotel. Employees contacted local authorities, who prevented the ousting and stated that eviction would require a court order. The drama resulted in a lawsuit filed by the management company against the owner of the hotel.

Tension between the management company and the hotel owner began the previous winter when the owner attempted to terminate their contract. The owner claimed that the management company, ABC Hotels, had not maximized the profits of the newly renovated property (a $240 million renovation had been completed two years prior). ABC Hotels had been contracted to manage the hotel through 2040.

Eventually, a court ruled in favor of the hotel owner, citing that hotel owners have the right to terminate management contracts at will.

DISCUSSION QUESTIONS

1. Under what conditions was the owner attempting to terminate the management contract?

2. Was it ethical for the owner to evict the hotel employees in the way that it did?

3. What could the owner have put in the management contract to define expectations more clearly for the management company?

Jonathan M. Tisch

Jonathan M. Tisch is co-chairman of the board of Loews Corporation and executive chairman of its subsidiary Loews Hotels & Company. Prior to assuming the role of executive chairman, Tisch was chairman and CEO of Loews Hotels and has been an officer of the company since 1986.

Tisch has led Loews's expansion and emergence as a prominent and respected hotel company with a widely praised culture that embraces the power of partnerships—with team members, guests, communities, and owners. He was voted "Hotelier of the World" by *Hotels* magazine.

Recognized nationally as a statesman for the multibillion-dollar travel and tourism industry, Tisch is chairman emeritus of the U.S. Travel Association and previously served as chairman of the Travel Business Roundtable and the American Hotel & Lodging Association. Tisch also served for nearly six years as chairman of NYC & Company, New York City's official tourism agency, and was chairman of New York Rising, which was established to bring back visitors and revive the economy after 9/11. *Crain's New York Business* named him one of the "Top 10 Most Influential Business Leaders" and inducted him into its Hall of Fame.

Tisch is the author of three bestselling books: *The Power of We: Succeeding Through Partnerships*; *Chocolates on the Pillow Aren't Enough: Reinventing the Customer Experience*; and *Citizen You: Doing Your Part to Change the World*. He hosted the Emmy-nominated television series *Beyond the Boardroom*.

Tisch is a champion of corporate responsibility and active citizenship. More than 25 years ago, he initiated the Loews Hotels Good Neighbor Policy, a recipient of the U.S. President's Volunteer Service Award. He is currently vice chair emeritus of the board of trustees of his alma mater, Tufts University, and is the naming benefactor of the Jonathan M. Tisch College of Civic Life at Tufts.

In 2017, he was honored by the New York University School of Professional Studies with the naming of the Jonathan M. Tisch Center of Hospitality, of which he has been a driving force for years.

Imagine that you are the CEO of a hotel management company that oversees several hotels in different regions. One of your hotels in a developing country is facing a labor dispute. Workers are protesting low wages, poor working conditions, and lack of benefits. The workers have formed a union and are demanding collective bargaining rights, but the hotel management is resisting their demands and threatening to replace them with nonunion workers.

As the CEO, you must make a decision that balances the financial interests of the hotel with the ethical considerations of social responsibility and labor rights. What are some solutions that you may consider?

ETHICS IN HOSPITALITY MANAGEMENT

Chapter Outline

15.1 **What Is Ethics?**

15.2 **Social Responsibility and Business Ethics**

15.3 **Ethical Issues in Hospitality**

15.4 **Must There Be a Code of Ethics?**

Learning Objectives

1. Define ethics, distinguish social responsibility from business ethics, describe six kinds of moral reasoning, and compare the ethical standards of business and poker. (pp. 416–419)

2. Explore whether honesty is always the best policy, give examples of different viewpoints concerning morality, contrast deontology with utilitarianism, and explain the concept of ethical relativism. (pp. 419–422)

3. Describe ethical issues in the hospitality industry, explain the need for a code of ethics for hospitality businesses, define the term "stakeholder," and identify three questions individuals should ask themselves when making a decision. (pp. 422–434)

KEY TERMS

categorical imperative
code of ethics
deontology
ethical relativism
ethics
social responsibility
stakeholder
utilitarianism

In this chapter, ethics in the hospitality industry is defined and discussed. The chapter distinguishes ethics from social responsibility and explores how values are arrived at. Concepts such as whether it is ever right to lie are examined. Ethical issues in hospitality, such as discrimination, environmental issues, advertising claims, and truth-in-menu laws, are discussed. Finally, an ethical litmus test is offered.

15.1 WHAT IS ETHICS?

There is a children's story about a group of blind men from "Indostan" who, by touching an elephant, attempt to describe to each other what it is like. The first man, falling against the elephant's side, says that the elephant is like a wall. The second, feeling the elephant's tusk, tells the others that the elephant is like a spear. The third, with the animal's trunk in hand, says that the elephant is like a rope. The fourth is certain an elephant is like a tree, having touched a leg; the fifth blind man feels the elephant's ear and concludes that elephants are like fans. The sixth, seizing its tail, pronounces that an elephant is like a snake:

So these men of Indostan

Disputed loud and long

Each in his own opinion

Exceedingly stiff and strong;

Though each was partly in the right

And all were in the wrong![1]

Trying to describe ethics is similar to the blind men describing the elephant. Depending on how we approach the question and our own system of values, we can come up with very different answers.

Ethics is a set of moral principles and values that we use to answer questions of right and wrong, good or bad, just or unjust. Ethics can also be defined as the study of the general nature of morals and of the moral choices made by individuals in their relationships with others.

There is evidence that many people have forgotten the true meaning of ethics. Today, we tend to think of ethics in pragmatic terms—our choices are based on what seems reasonable or logical to us according to our own personal value system. This is called "ethical relativism" because it casts ethics as being relative to what the situation is or how we feel about it.

In truth, ethics is something different. The very concept of ethics suggests that there is a real distinction between good and bad, right and wrong, and that it is our obligation to do our best to distinguish between these and try to do what is right. Although we all have different personal values and morals, we should recognize that there are some universal principles that virtually all religions, cultures, and societies agree on. These principles form the basis of ethical behavior. The foundation of all of these principles is the belief

Social responsibility and ethics should be a part of the hospitality business plan.

that other people's rights are as important as our own, and that it is our duty not to harm others if we can avoid it. In fact, it is our duty to help others whenever possible. This idea is at the heart of the value system of most societies, tribes, and organizations. Without it, we would not be able to live and work together.

Knowledge Check

1. What is the true meaning of ethics?
2. Why is ethics important in decision-making?

15.2 SOCIAL RESPONSIBILITY AND BUSINESS ETHICS

It is important to distinguish between social responsibility and business ethics. The concept of **social responsibility** suggests that "at any one time in any society there is a set of generally accepted relationships, obligations, and duties between the major institutions and the people. Philosophers and political theorists have called this set of common understandings 'the social contract.'"[2] This contract differs among societies and may change over time. For example, today we expect that businesses will take care (1) not to pollute the air we breathe or the water we drink, (2) not to damage the ozone layer, (3) to offer fair wages and employee benefits, (4) to provide a satisfactory product or service at a reasonable price, and (5) to in some way participate in making the community in which they operate a better place. These are not ethical considerations—they are part of a "deal" that says that we as consumers expect companies to act in this manner because they are a part of the society we all share.

Because hospitality companies serve as key players in the global tourism industry, they have a social responsibility to ensure that their operations align with sustainable practices and contribute to the well-being of the communities in which they operate. This responsibility includes minimizing their environmental impact, treating their employees fairly and ethically, and supporting local businesses and economies.

Furthermore, hospitality companies should prioritize the safety and satisfaction of their guests, providing a welcoming and inclusive environment that respects diversity and promotes responsible travel behavior. By fulfilling their social responsibility, hospitality companies not only enhance their reputation and profitability but also play a vital role in creating a more sustainable and equitable world. For example, Starbucks is committed to advancing racial and social equity in our society. It established representation goals, to be met by 2025, which include achieving at least 30 percent Black, Indigenous, and People of Color (BIPOC) representation at all corporate levels and at least 40 percent representation in all retail and manufacturing roles. The goals also include achieving representation of women at 55 percent in all retail roles, 50 percent in corporate roles, and 30 percent in manufacturing roles.

Hilton is another company with an outstanding social conscience. In selecting Hilton as one of the "100 Best Companies to Work For," *Fortune* magazine noted that 97 percent of Hilton employees say it is a great place to work, compared to 57 percent of employees who work at a typical U.S.-based company. McDonald's joined the United Nations Race to Zero campaign and charted a course for net zero emissions by 2050. It has achieved an almost 3 percent reduction in absolute greenhouse gas emissions from its restaurants and offices since 2015.

Ethical behavior is a whole different matter. In the twenty-first century, the United States has seen unethical behavior by corporate executives far in excess of anything witnessed before. For example, a scandal hit Facebook in March 2018 when *The Guardian* and *The New York Times* reported that a firm called Global Science Research had harvested data from millions of Facebook users in 2013—without their explicit consent. This led to Cambridge Analytica using those data to create highly targeted ads to encourage users to vote for Donald Trump and Brexit. Another example of unethical and illegal conduct involved Apple's Batterygate scandal. Apple was accused of hampering the performance of select iPhone models to improve battery life. Other examples include the Ponzi scheme[3] masterminded by Bernard Madoff, an investment advisor and stockbroker, who defrauded thousands of his clients of a reported $21 billion—the largest financial investor fraud in history committed by a single person. In 2016, it was revealed that Wells Fargo employees had opened millions of accounts without customers' consent in an effort to reach the bank's aggressive goals, a sign of systemic cultural failure. In another spectacular failure of business ethics, Dennis Kozlowski, the former CEO of Tyco, and two other executives were charged with looting their company of $600 million and using the money to fund lavish lifestyles that included expensive Manhattan condos, vacation homes, ski chalets, and fine art collections. Investigators charged that Kozlowski once spent $1 million in company funds on a birthday party thrown on the island of Sardinia for his wife, a party that featured gladiators, chariots, horses, lions, and an ice sculpture of Michelangelo's David with vodka gushing out of it for partygoers.

How We Arrive at Our Values

Author Hunter Lewis says that there are six ways in which we arrive at our values—our personal beliefs about what is "good" and "just." The six kinds of moral reasoning are as follows:

1. *Authority.* Beliefs can be derived from an authority. Here we take someone else's word, such as that of the Bible or the church.

2. *Deductive logic.* Deductive logic is another basis for our beliefs. Here is a simple example of deductive logic: If all chocolate is fattening, and if this dessert is chocolate, then this dessert must be fattening.

3. *Sense experience.* Often, we arrive at beliefs through sense experience. In these cases, we gain direct knowledge through our five senses. We decide that something is true because we heard it; can see it with our own eyes; or can touch it, taste it, or smell it.

4. *Emotion.* Emotion can dictate our beliefs. We may "feel" that something is true. Sometimes our emotions concerning others influence our ideas about them. For example, if we love someone, we tend to idealize them. Violent criminals might have parents who say, "He's a nice boy" or "But she's really a good girl."

5. *Intuition.* Intuition is another way to arrive at knowledge. Here, we use our unconscious or intuitive mind to process information and discover the solution to a problem. Sometimes we refer to our intuition as "a gut feeling."

6. *Science.* Science is the basis of some beliefs. When we use the scientific method, we use our senses to collect facts, our intuition to develop a hypothesis, our logic to experiment, and our senses again to complete the test. Physicians use this process to arrive at their beliefs about the causes of disease and what cures to prescribe.[4]

Although we may use all six techniques of moral reasoning at one time or another, Lewis believes that each of us has a dominant or primary technique. To discover your dominant technique, Lewis suggests that you ask yourself whom you would confide in if you had a serious personal issue on your mind and wanted advice.

If your answer is a priest, a minister, a rabbi, or another religious leader, your primary mode is to use authority as the basis for your beliefs. If you ask a professor of philosophy to help you, then you are looking for someone who can think through your problem in a highly structured or logical way. If your confidant is a professor of history and literature who is also a good friend, then you are relying on their own personal sense experience plus the experience of Western culture as contained in its history and literature. Suppose you turn to a family member or close friend. Here, your dominant reasoning style can be characterized as emotional. Clearly, you are looking for empathy from a member of your peer group. Some people would seek an answer from a Buddhist or guru of immense calm and unspoken wisdom. They would be hoping to use meditation and other tools to unlock their powers of intuition. If you don't recognize yourself in any of these groups, perhaps you would consult a psychologist who could offer an appraisal based on social science methods and principles.[5]

The point is that we are all likely to have a different set of values or ethics, depending on which moral reasoning technique is our dominant one. To many of us, some actions are wrong because the Bible or the Torah or the Koran says so. To others, actions are wrong only if our friends and family would condemn them. Some believe that anything is OK "so long as it isn't against the law" or even "so long as you don't get caught." Nearly everyone agrees that it is a good idea to tell the truth, and that stealing from others is wrong.

Is Business Like Poker?

There is a school of thought that recognizes that honesty is the best policy and it is never right to lie or steal, but holds that the rules of business are different and that behavior that is unacceptable elsewhere is legitimate in the business world.

Business writer Alfred Carr attracted a good deal of attention by comparing business to a poker game:

> No one expects poker to be played on the ethical principles preached in churches. In poker it is right and proper to bluff a friend out of the rewards of being dealt a good hand. Poker's own brand of ethics is different from the ethical ideals of civilized human relationships. The game calls for distrust of the other fellow. It ignores the claim of friendship. Cunning, deception and concealment of one's strength and intentions, not kindness and open-heartedness, are vital in poker. No one thinks any worse of poker on that account. And no one should think any the worse of the game of business because its standards of right and wrong differ from the prevailing traditions of morality in our society.[6]

While Carr's argument might seem to make sense at first glance, Robert Solomon and Kristine Hanson—authors of *It's Good Business*, a book about business ethics—point out that it shows a misunderstanding of both poker and business:

> Bluffing isn't lying, which is as forbidden in playing poker as it is in business. Most business is conducted in conversation where truth and mutual trust are essential. … A poker game involves only its players; business is essential to the well-being of the entire society. The rules of poker protect the game and its players; the rules of business protect everyone else, too. Carr's suggestion ignores that core of ethics that does not vary from community to community—which we call "morality." Morality consists of those basic rules which are not merely a matter of a single game or practice, but provide the preconditions of every game, every practice. Carr may be trivially correct when he says the rules of poker are different from the rules of other games and practices, but he is quite wrong when he suggests that this constitutes a divergence from morality.[7]

Solomon and Hanson point out that the ultimate goals of business are to promote a good life for every individual and wealth for the nation as a whole. The goal of poker is to redistribute the wealth among a small group of players. Both involve risk-taking, strategy, and the need to make calculated decisions based on available information. But because the goals are different and much more is at stake in the business world, the rules of poker and business should and must be different.

Is Honesty Always the Best Policy?

According to some moral philosophers, honesty is the only acceptable policy. They argue that all lying, whether "little white lies" or vicious falsehoods, injures both the liar and the person lied to, and may injure society as well. When someone lies to Congress about the extent of U.S. military involvement in an area or the cost of a weapon or social welfare program, the result is that our elected officials do not have the information they need to protect our interests, which is what we elected them to do.

The principle involved here is described by Sissela Bok, author of *Lying: Moral Choice in Public and Private Life*, who writes, "All our choices depend on our estimates of what is the case; these estimates must in turn often rely on information from others. Lies distort this information and therefore our situation as we perceive it, as well as our choices."[8] When we lie to others, Bok argues, we take away their right to make their own choices and instead manipulate them by giving them false information on which to base their decisions. In a real sense, we are taking away their freedom. Unless we have a very strong reason for doing so, lies cannot and should not be tolerated.

Liars like to believe that their reasons for lying are sound. Most liars do not believe that anyone should lie to them but justify their own behavior on the grounds that they are protecting someone else's feelings or confidences, or that their lie is necessary to protect their business or employees. Each person must decide for themselves what is a good reason to lie. Clearly, if a robber walks into your business asking for all your money, and you say all you have is in the cash register, when in fact there is a considerable amount stored in the back room, then this is a matter of self-preservation and lying is justified. What about telling an employee whom you are letting go that you do not have enough work, when your real reason is that the person is incompetent? In this case, it might be easier to lie; but one could argue that it is kinder in the long run to be honest with the employee so they can look for more suitable work. Each situation must be looked at individually, with our bias always on the side of telling the truth.

In general, honesty is considered the best policy in most situations. Being truthful and transparent in your interactions with others can help build trust, strengthen relationships, and create a foundation of integrity that is beneficial in both personal and professional contexts.

Ultimately, you should base your decision to be honest on thoughtful consideration of the potential consequences and the values and principles that are most important to you. While honesty is generally valued as an important virtue, there may be times when it is necessary to weigh other factors and make a more nuanced decision.

The Search for a Common Moral Ground

Despite the fact that everyone may use a different set of values to determine what is ethical, many philosophers and educators who have spent their lives thinking about ethics have concluded that there are some universal moral imperatives or obligations that form the basis of civilized behavior and are necessary for any society to function. Michael Josephson is an attorney and founder of the Joseph and Edna Josephson Institute for the Advancement of Ethics, a nonprofit institute that has been at the forefront of defining ethical behavior for businesses. In an interview with Bill Moyers on the Public Broadcasting System, Josephson said:

> History, theology, philosophy will show that every enlightened civilization has had

a sense of right and wrong and a need to try to distinguish them. Now we may disagree over time as to what is right and what is wrong—but there has never been a disagreement in any philosophy about the importance of knowing the difference. The things that are right are the things that help people and society. They are things like compassion, honesty, fairness, accountability. They are absolute universal ethical values.[9]

Josephson points out that the Golden Rule—"Do unto others as you would have them do unto you"—had been incorporated into Greek and Chinese culture thousands of years before Jesus articulated his version.[10]

Josephson believes that most people have a built-in sense of what is right and wrong. The proof, he says, is that we feel guilt and shame when we do the wrong thing. Despite that knowledge, we often ignore our ideals about what constitutes proper behavior. There are a number of reasons for this. We have become a rights-oriented society. Sometimes we feel we have a right to certain things, but we have forgotten that with those rights come certain responsibilities. Too often, says Josephson, we measure our lives by what we get, what we acquire, and who we know. "It's the need to win, to be clever, and to be successful in other people's eyes that sometimes causes people to sacrifice the fundamental ideals," he says.

Former U.S. diplomat Max Kampelman puts it this way: "There is a hole in our moral ozone layer. There is a vast difference between the right to do something, which is important, and doing something right, which is equally important."[11]

Sometimes businesspeople feel that the only way to be competitive and win is to be completely selfish—put their own interests above those of everyone else. Josephson tells the story of a lawyer who goes on a camping trip with a friend. They both are hiking with backpacks when suddenly they see a cougar about 20 yards away. The lawyer takes off his backpack, and the friend says, "What are you going to do?" The lawyer says, "I'm going to run for it." The friend says, "But you can't outrun a cougar." And the lawyer says, "I don't have to outrun the cougar. I just have to outrun you."[12]

Some justify the philosophy of putting your own interests ahead of everyone else's by saying that life is like having your hand in a bucket of water—when you remove it, the water settles down within moments and no one knew you ever lived; therefore, you should try to get everything you can for yourself, because it will make no difference to anyone else in the long run. There is another way of looking at the world and your place in it: you can make a permanent and positive impact on society by doing what you can to make positive differences in the lives of others. You can bring some of them happiness and joy, and help alleviate the pain and suffering of others.

Sometimes people argue that when you are dealing with unethical people, you have to be unethical too, or you will be stepped on. Josephson says, "There is usually a choice of ethical and unethical behaviors. We tell people, unless you have three alternatives to every major problem, you haven't thought hard enough. As soon as you have three, you can find one that's ethical."[13]

Eventually, most of us come to believe in the philosophy of helping people rather than taking advantage of them or using them for our own benefit. Sadly, for many of us, this occurs late in life when we have learned that accomplishing a particular task or career goal did not bring us the satisfaction we had hoped for. As Josephson observes, "We know that nobody on a deathbed says, 'I wish I had spent more time at the office.' People's values begin to change when they reflect upon how futile most of the flurry of activity was. And the fact is that a good conscience is the best pillow. Living a good life is the most important thing for us."[14]

Deontology versus Utilitarianism. There are two major traditions that dominate current thinking in moral philosophy: deontology and utilitarianism.[15]

Deontology holds that basic or universal ideals should direct our thinking. Deontology is based on the beliefs of Immanuel Kant, an eighteenth-century German philosopher. Kant thought that the human mind could not possibly comprehend or arrive at the truth about God or the universe through pure logic or thought. He said that the only judgments we were capable of making were those based on evidence that we could see or prove the existence of. Kant believed in the existence of God, but said we have to take this on faith, since we cannot prove it by pure logic. Once we admit there is a God, then it is possible to make logical and reasonable

assumptions about what is expected of us and how we are required to act. In short, there is a scientifically arrived-at ideal that is necessary for humans to adhere to and for which adequate evidence exists, once we admit there is a God. Deontology proposes that ethical behavior is simply a matter of doing God's will. Since most of us believe that God is good, then goodwill or loving other human beings as God loves us is the universal principle on which all moral behavior must be based.

Along with the concept of goodwill is a concept of duty to keep our promises, which is known as Kant's **categorical imperative**—an absolute and universally binding moral law. Kant believed in always telling the truth because if we cannot believe what others tell us, then agreements and even conversations between people are not possible. Would you loan money to someone if you knew that they had no intention of repaying it, even though they promised to do so? Deontology, in effect, says that the only way to measure whether an action is ethical is to ask whether we would be willing to live in a world where *everyone* routinely did the same thing. If our actions would be acceptable to us as a universal law, then they are correct and ethical.

Conversely, **utilitarianism** does not seek universal principles that can be applied to all situations, but instead says that ethical behavior consists of acting in such a way as to achieve the greatest good for the greatest number. One determines this by "performing a social cost/benefit analysis and acting on it."[16] Authors Donald Robin and Eric Reidenbach show that this philosophy is grounded in the ideas of Adam Smith, who said that "capitalistic systems, by providing the greatest material good for the greatest number, are considered ethical from a perspective of economic philosophy."[17] They point out, however, that there are some major criticisms of utilitarianism that should be considered. One is that an action might do a small amount of good for a large number of people while at the same time severely injuring a small group. For example, is it always ethical to build a mega-resort on a pristine beach in an underdeveloped country? Such a complex benefits tourism but is often a disaster for the local community. A mega-resort introduces pollution, large numbers of visitors, and noise to the area, and may lead to the destruction of the local culture. Moreover, utilitarianism suggests that each action should be judged on its own merits. When we do this, there is a lack of consistency that opens the door to generalizations and excuses. We cannot say that anything is either moral or immoral, ethical or unethical, if "it all depends." For example, can an accountant embezzling company funds be excused because they believe the company is "ripping people off, so why shouldn't I?" Generally, we reject that kind of rationalization because it is entirely subjective.

Ethical Relativism. Ethical relativism suggests that there are no universal ethical principles at all; each issue must be considered in its situational or cultural context. For example, it might be unethical to bribe a government official in the United States to obtain a building permit or zoning variance, but quite acceptable in some other countries where bribes are a routine part of doing business. (Students should note that while one can debate whether bribing government officials is ethical or not, it is most definitely against U.S. law for any American corporation or citizen to do so.) This kind of reasoning is also known as "situational ethics." It is a convenient ethical code for those who are not sure what their ethical values are or how they are arrived at; however, like utilitarianism, it provides little guidance for those who believe in a clear and consistent code of ethics.

Knowledge Check

1. What is the difference between social responsibility and business ethics?
2. What is the difference between deontology and utilitarianism?

15.3 ETHICAL ISSUES IN HOSPITALITY

The hospitality industry faces several ethical issues that can impact the well-being of employees, guests, and the wider community. Some of the most common ethical issues in hospitality include:

- *Labor practices.* Ensuring fair wages, reasonable working hours, and a safe work environment for hospitality employees is crucial. Ethical issues may arise if workers are underpaid, subjected to long hours without proper compensation, or face unsafe conditions.

- *Diversity and inclusion.* Promoting diversity and inclusion in the workplace is an ethical responsibility for hospitality businesses. Discrimination based on race, gender, ethnicity, or other factors should be actively prevented.

- *Environmental impact.* The hospitality industry has a significant environmental footprint. Ethical concerns arise regarding waste management, energy consumption, and sustainable practices to reduce the impact on the environment.

- *Responsible tourism.* Hospitality businesses often operate in destinations that rely heavily on tourism. Encouraging responsible tourism practices, respecting local cultures, and preserving natural resources are ethical imperatives.

- *Fair pricing and transparency.* Ethical issues may emerge when hotels or travel agencies engage in deceptive pricing practices or hidden fees, leading to misleading customers.

- *Privacy and data protection.* Protecting guest privacy and data is critical. Ethical concerns arise when hospitality establishments mishandle or misuse guest information.

- *Human trafficking and child labor.* The hospitality industry can be vulnerable to human trafficking and child labor. Establishments need to implement strict policies to prevent and combat them.

- *Food safety and quality.* Ethical responsibility includes ensuring that food served to guests meets proper safety and quality standards.

- *Marketing and advertising.* Hospitality businesses should adhere to ethical marketing practices, avoiding misleading advertisements or false claims.

- *Intellectual property rights.* Respect for intellectual property rights, such as copyrights and trademarks, is essential in hospitality, particularly when using images or designs.

- *Community engagement.* Ethical engagement with the local community involves supporting local businesses, contributing to community development, and giving back to the regions where the establishments operate.

Overall, addressing these ethical issues in hospitality requires a commitment to ethical leadership, responsible business practices, and ongoing engagement with stakeholders to ensure that the industry operates in a way that is sustainable, fair, and socially responsible.

Here are a few examples of decisions that a hotel general manager or someone in a similar position at a club or restaurant might make in the ordinary course of business:

New Menu
You have just approved a new menu that retains many of your favorite high-calorie, high-cholesterol, high-sodium foods. There are no nutritious alternatives on the menu. You reason that hotel guests liked what was on the old menu and they will keep coming back.

Bumped Reservation
You have just been approached by an influential guest regarding a birthday party he would like to hold at the hotel two months from now. Unfortunately, just yesterday the hotel's meeting room was booked for that date. The guest asks you to bump the person who reserved the room. He suggests you tell that person the sales manager made a mistake in booking the room when it had previously been reserved. You agree to do so.

Cashier's Integrity
You decide to test a cashier's integrity. The cashier has been with the company 10 years and has a flawless record. You slip a $50 bill in the register receipts. At the end of the day, the cashier shows a $5 overage. Upon questioning, the cashier admits to pocketing the $45 difference.

Free Wine
You recently purchased 20 cases of wine for the hotel from a new beverage supplier. Without your advance knowledge, the supplier delivered one free case of wine to your residence.

You decide to keep the free case for your personal use, since it did not influence the purchase of the 20 cases for the hotel.[18]

In a *Lodging* magazine poll, 400 lodging managers were asked whether they agreed with the ethics of the manager's decision in each of these hypothetical scenarios. The results of that poll are shown in Exhibit 15.1.

The "new menu" scenario considers how much responsibility each of us must take for the welfare of others. We may not consider ourselves our brother's keeper, but it can be argued that as hospitality professionals, it is our duty to include low-calorie, nutritious meals on the menu so we can meet the needs of guests who must, for health reasons, be careful about what they eat.

We were told by one knowledgeable hotelier that meeting room reservations get "bumped" all the time. That may be so, but if we are going to respect the rights of others, the fair decision is to allow the person who made the reservation first to keep it. Moreover, it is wrong to lie and say the other reservation was made earlier when it was not. On the other hand, if we are ethical relativists, we might argue that we could lose a substantial amount of business if we do not go along with this influential guest. This could also result in laying off employees or facing other consequences that might hurt others.

The case of the cashier's integrity also bears on the rights of others. Is it fair to put a loyal employee to a test of this nature without warning them in advance, especially when there is no evidence that anything is wrong? Would we like to be treated this way?

The free wine scenario poses the question of what constitutes honesty. The wine may have been delivered after the hotel's wine was ordered, but it still represents an unauthorized payment to the manager for "services rendered." The manager could return the free case and ask the supplier to show their appreciation for the order by giving the hotel an appropriate discount on its next wine purchase. Or the manager might give the extra case of wine to the hotel so the hotel could profit from its sale. One test of whether it is ethical to keep this wine for personal use would be for the manager to ask how they would feel if other managers at the

Exhibit 15.1   Ethics Poll of Lodging Managers

The New Menu, Bumped Reservation, Cashier's Integrity, and Free Wine scenarios (described in the text) were presented to lodging managers by *Lodging* magazine. When rating the manager's decision or actions in each of the scenarios, the polled managers were asked whether they (a) strongly agreed, (b) moderately agreed, (c) were unsure, (d) moderately disagreed, or (e) strongly disagreed. Here are the results:

New Menu	
a. Strongly agree	6.1%
b. Moderately agree	15.5%
c. Unsure	8.9%
d. Moderately disagree	24.9%
e. Strongly disagree	44.6%

Comment: The responses suggest a fairly high level of health consciousness among hotel managers.

Bumped Reservation	
a. Strongly agree	1.3%
b. Moderately agree	5.1%
c. Unsure	4.6%
d. Moderately disagree	13.7%
e. Strongly disagree	75.3%

Comment: Clearly, managers believe that guest favoritism leads to guest dissatisfaction.

Cashier's Integrity	
a. Strongly agree	36.5%
b. Moderately agree	25.6%
c. Unsure	9.4%
d. Moderately disagree	11.7%
e. Strongly disagree	16.8%

Comment: A minority of managers evidently believed that the test put too much pressure on the employee; however, 62.1% agreed with the manager's test.

Free Wine	
a. Strongly agree	7.4%
b. Moderately agree	16.5%
c. Unsure	10.6%
d. Moderately disagree	17.5%
e. Strongly disagree	48.0%

Comment: 65.5% of respondents apparently felt that acceptance of the wine could influence future beverage purchases by the hotel.

Source: Adapted from Raymond S. Schmidgall, "Hotel Scruples," *Lodging*, January 1991, 38–40.

hotel found out about it. Along with many other hospitality companies, Hilton Hotels Corporation has a strict policy that prohibits its managers and other company personnel from accepting gifts from people with whom they do business; there is even a sample "gift response" letter in the company's *Code of Conduct* booklet for managers.

The Yale Center for Emotional Intelligence, in partnership with the Faas Foundation, conducted a comprehensive nationwide survey involving over 14,500 employees from various industries. The goal was to gain insight into the work experiences of Americans. The sample represented a diverse range of industries and demographics that reflect the U.S. economy's distribution.

The survey aimed to understand the frequency of unethical pressure experienced by workers and the level of fear they had in speaking up at work. Additionally, it explored employees' emotional experiences in the workplace and their perception of their supervisors' emotional intelligence.

The findings were concerning. The majority of workers reported rarely or never experiencing pressure to act unethically. However, 11 percent acknowledged facing such pressure occasionally, and an alarming 12 percent experienced it frequently to almost always. In total, 23 percent of respondents, or nearly one in four individuals, felt compelled to engage in actions that they knew were wrong.[19]

Linda K. Enghagen surveyed 113 four-year colleges and universities on ethical issues in hospitality and tourism. While 35 issues were raised, the 10 that received the most mentions were:

- Managing an ethical environment
- Relations with customers and employees
- Honesty
- Employee privacy rights
- Alcohol/drug testing
- Environmental issues
- Relations with foreign governments
- Codes of ethics and self-governance
- Employee abuse of alcohol/drugs
- Conflicts of interest[20]

These issues reflect the academic perspective. Industry leaders have cited many other ethical problems that concern them. These include:

- Travel agent commissions
- Overbooking
- Human trafficking
- Employment discrimination by age, gender, or race
- Kickbacks
- Concealing income from the Internal Revenue Service
- Revenue management
- Advertising claims
- Raiding of the competition's staff
- Truth-in-menu laws
- Meeting the needs of customers and employees with disabilities
- Adequate safety and security measures

Let's take a closer look at some of these industry issues.

Environmental Issues

The hospitality and tourism industry is known to have significant impacts on the environment. Some of the main environmental concerns in the hospitality and tourism industry are:

- *Carbon emissions.* The hospitality and tourism industry is a significant contributor to carbon emissions, which contribute to climate change. Air travel, transportation, and energy use in hotels and resorts are the main sources of carbon emissions.

- *Energy consumption.* The industry uses a lot of energy for heating, cooling, lighting, and other purposes. Energy consumption contributes to carbon emissions and also leads to the depletion of nonrenewable resources.

- *Water consumption.* The industry uses a lot of water for various purposes, including landscaping, cleaning, and laundry. Water consumption can lead to water scarcity and environmental degradation, particularly in regions with limited water resources.

- *Waste generation.* The industry generates a significant amount of waste, including food waste, packaging, and other materials. Improper waste disposal can lead to pollution, littering, and damage to natural habitats.

- *Destruction of natural habitats.* Tourism development can lead to the destruction of natural habitats, particularly in areas with sensitive ecosystems, such as coastal areas and forests. Development can also lead to soil erosion, deforestation, and loss of biodiversity.

Preserving and protecting the resources of tourist destinations has become a topic of major importance. Every time a hotel or an attraction is added to an area already crowded with visitors, there is a legitimate concern about its long-term impact on the environment. Many destinations have already taken major steps to preserve their natural resources. In Bermuda, the number of hotel rooms has been restricted to 10,000 for many years, and cruise ship visits are restricted. In Egypt, officials have reduced the visiting hours at the pyramids at Giza and limited the number of tourists who can visit at one time.

Much of the concern revolves around hotel and restaurant development, which is inevitable at popular tourist destinations. If visitors are allowed to visit a site, they need to be accommodated while they are there. This dilemma is faced not only by developing nations but also by highly developed industrialized countries where overbuilding has already caused major damage.

Starbucks has made a commitment to cut its carbon, water, and waste footprints by half by 2030. Each year, the company issues a Global Environmental and Social Impact Report outlining its progress toward this commitment and goals it has achieved. For example, one goal was "50 percent reduction in waste sent to landfill from stores (including packaging that leaves stores)." The company reported that "in FY22, 28 percent of operational waste was diverted from landfill, a 2-percentage point increase over FY19." This was achieved by reducing single-use plastics and packaging waste by implementing innovative programs, such as Starbucks Borrow a Cup Program, 100 percent reusable operating models, financial incentives and promotions, new customer experience upgrades, and an emphasis on personal cups and its "For Here Ware."[21]

One hotel company that takes its environmental responsibilities seriously is IHG, which has created an online sustainability system for use in all of its properties. The system, known as "Green Engage," allows IHG to design, build, and run more sustainable hotels. The advanced online system allows a hotel to measure the

Sorting bins are a small eco-friendly tool at some modern hotels.

impact on the environment from the day-to-day running of the hotel. Furthermore, hotels are given guidelines to manage, assess, and report their energy and water usage, waste consumption, and effect on their community.[22]

Many hotels urge guests to save water (the water used by the hotels' laundries) by reusing towels rather than asking for fresh ones every morning. Modern cruise ships burn waste in onboard incinerators or compact and store it until it can be properly disposed of on land.

Fairmont Hotels & Resorts has a chain-wide Fairmont Green Partnership program. At each Fairmont hotel, a "green team" (made up of staff volunteers) oversees existing environmental initiatives and looks for new areas where environmentally friendly practices and policies can be introduced. Fairmont's director of environmental affairs believes that environmental responsibility is also good business. For example, Fairmont's five properties in British Columbia saved enough energy through environmentally friendly practices to power one hotel for an entire year.[23] Fairmont Hotels was selected as one of Canada's "Top 100 Employers" for its "earth-friendly" programs, based on the company's success at integrating environmental values as part of the company culture.

In addition to the hotel companies just mentioned, most of the other major hotel organizations have sustainability programs.

Marriott International, Wyndham Worldwide, Hyatt Hotels Corp., and Hilton Worldwide have corporate environmental officers and property sustainability teams that train and measure sustainability program effectiveness.[24]

There are many environmentally conscious restaurants around the world that have led the way in sustainable practices. Here are a few examples:

- *Noma, Copenhagen, Denmark.* This Michelin-starred restaurant is known for its commitment to sustainable and locally sourced ingredients. The restaurant has its own urban farm, where it grows herbs, vegetables, and flowers. The restaurant also uses renewable energy sources and practices waste reduction and recycling.

- *Blue Hill at Stone Barns, New York.* This farm-to-table restaurant is located on an 80-acre farm and uses ingredients sourced from the farm and other local producers. The restaurant also uses sustainable practices such as composting, rainwater harvesting, and solar power.

- *Silo, Brighton, United Kingdom.* Silo is a zero-waste restaurant that uses local, organic, and seasonal ingredients. The restaurant uses reusable containers, composts food waste, and recycles all other materials. Silo also produces its own flour and brews its own beer.

Some restaurants compost food waste as part of their sustainability plan.

- *Attarine, Jakarta, Indonesia.* Attarine was a sustainable restaurant that used local and seasonal ingredients and practiced responsible sourcing. The restaurant also used energy-efficient appliances, composted food waste, and used recycled materials for furniture and décor.

- *Brae, Birregurra, Australia.* Brae is a farm-to-table restaurant that sources its ingredients from its own organic farm and other local producers. The restaurant uses renewable energy sources, composts food waste, and uses recycled materials for building and décor.

These restaurants demonstrate that sustainable and environmentally sensitive practices can be integrated into the restaurant industry without compromising on quality or taste. By adopting sustainable practices, restaurants can contribute to a more sustainable future.

Discrimination

Even though it is unlawful, and companies may have their own policies forbidding it, discrimination of one sort or another can still occur in the workplace. Some managers may have value systems that lead them to discriminate in certain instances, perhaps unconsciously. Because there are so many subtle forms of discrimination—based on age, race, religion, gender, sexual orientation, nationality, or physical attributes—discrimination may be one of the most common violations of ethics found in the hospitality industry, and one of the most difficult to recognize. In many cases, it is neither malicious nor intentional. That does not excuse it, however, and managers must know where they are likely to find it and how to eliminate it.

Discrimination in the hospitality industry is a significant issue that affects many employees and customers. Discrimination can take many forms, including the following:

- *Racial discrimination.* Discrimination based on race, ethnicity, or national origin is prohibited in many jurisdictions. This includes treating individuals unfairly because of their skin color, ancestry, or cultural background.

- *Gender discrimination.* Gender discrimination is treating individuals unequally due to their gender or sex. This can include differential treatment based on being male, female, or nonbinary.

- *Age discrimination.* This is discrimination against individuals due to their age (this could be discrimination against older adults or younger people). This may include discriminatory hiring practices, pay inequity, or harassment based on age.

- *Sexual orientation discrimination.* This is discrimination against individuals based on their sexual orientation, such as being lesbian, gay, bisexual, or heterosexual.

- *Religious discrimination.* This discrimination occurs when people are unfairly treated based on their religious beliefs or practices. This can involve prejudice or bias against particular religions or discrimination against individuals who do not adhere to any religion.

- *Disability discrimination.* Disability discrimination is treating people unfairly due to their physical or mental disabilities, whether visible or invisible. This can involve denying access to services or opportunities.

- *Marital status.* Some laws prohibit discrimination based on a person's marital status (whether they are single, married, divorced, or widowed).

- *Pregnancy.* Discrimination against pregnant women or individuals based on pregnancy status is often prohibited.

- *Nationality or immigration status.* Discriminating against individuals based on their nationality or immigration status is prohibited in many jurisdictions.

Almost all discrimination involves fear of one sort or another. We live in uncertain times; huge political and social upheavals have taken place. These changes are bound to make us uneasy. Many of us are afraid of losing our jobs. Others are afraid of losing power or prestige, or simply not "belonging" anymore. One way these fears manifest themselves is through discrimination. Discrimination allows us to express those fears and rationalize them by giving them faces and names. Unfortunately, many opportunists have made a career out of exploiting our concerns and thus have muddied the waters even more. Their ideas fuel our fears, and sometimes these fears express themselves in the workplace.

One of the most serious and blatant forms of discrimination still practiced in many parts of the world is racial. Many people believe that affirmative action programs are necessary to give minority groups and others opportunities that have been denied to them in the past. The hospitality industry faces the same challenges as the rest of society.

Many hospitality companies recognize the problem of racial discrimination and are doing something about it. Hilton Worldwide, for example, has implemented both an Ownership Diversity outreach program to encourage minority and female entrepreneurs to become owners of its properties, and an award-winning Supplier Diversity program that has led to the development of supplier relationships with more than 4,600 women- and minority-owned businesses.[25]

Gender discrimination is another form of discrimination that must be addressed. For years, most male chefs believed that women had no place in professional kitchens, but that belief is slowly fading. Sometimes this is based on fallacies such as "it's a man's world" or "those large pots are too heavy for a woman to lift." But discrimination is not confined to the kitchen. Female general managers of hotels are still relatively scarce when one considers that more than half of most hotels' employees are women. There are also questions of salaries and promotions. Male managers often assume that since a married woman has a husband to help support her, she is in less need of a raise. Sometimes a female manager is not offered a promotion that involves a transfer to another city because it is wrongly assumed that her husband's job dictates where the family will live. Women have been denied sales positions because it was felt that men were better suited for traveling and going out drinking with clients. In other words, a female manager is just not "one of the boys." Discrimination on this basis is clearly unethical, as well as unlawful in the United States.

No discussion of discrimination is complete without mentioning age discrimination, a global problem. Companies under economic pressure to cut costs often look first to older workers, who often enjoy high earnings (due in part to their years of service). In the long run, they may cost the company more if they stay employed until retirement and become entitled to a pension.

Many companies favor younger applicants when reviewing job applications.

Discrimination in the hospitality industry can have serious consequences, including legal action, negative publicity, and damage to reputation. To address discrimination in the industry, it is important to promote diversity and inclusion and provide training and education around issues of discrimination and bias. Additionally, policies and procedures should be put in place to ensure that discrimination is not tolerated in any form and that individuals who experience discrimination have a safe and supportive environment in which to report it. By promoting diversity and inclusivity, the hospitality industry can create a more welcoming environment for all employees and customers.

Sexual Harassment

Another ethical problem in the workplace is sexual harassment. Men as well as women can be victims of sexual harassment by superiors. Sexual harassment by employers includes asking their employees for dates, making sexual jokes or comments, touching employees inappropriately, or suggesting that sex will result in a promotion. The pressure to not complain when one's job and economic well-being are on the line is sometimes overwhelming. Companies cannot and should not allow anyone to believe for a moment that such behavior will go unnoticed or be excused.

The U.S. Equal Employment Opportunity Commission has developed guidelines designed to prevent discrimination on the basis of sex. The guidelines detail the following three examples of misconduct that constitute sexual harassment:

- When submission to such conduct is made a term or condition of an individual's employment, either explicitly or implicitly;

- When submission to or rejection of such conduct by an individual is used as a basis of employment decisions; and

- When such conduct has the purpose or effect of unreasonably interfering with an individual's work performance or creating an intimidating, hostile, or offensive work environment.[26]

The third guideline, which cites a "hostile" work environment, should be of particular interest to managers, since it is a more subtle violation of

The U.S. Equal Employment Opportunity Commission guidelines are designed to prevent discrimination on the basis of sex, including sexual harassment. Companies must be attentive to any such behaviors.

the law and may not manifest itself in such obvious circumstances as employment or promotions. In 1986, the U.S. Supreme Court handed down a landmark decision, *Meritor Savings Bank* v. *Vinson*, that acknowledged the existence of a "hostile work environment" as a basis for a claim of sexual harassment.[27] The courts have, in a series of subsequent decisions, clarified the types of conduct that might support a claim of a hostile work environment. These include "treating women with less respect than men or being abusive to women but not men, and published images or remarks or spoken comments portraying women or men in a sexually demeaning manner."[28]

While the precise definition of sexual harassment remains a controversial subject, that does not mean that managers should feel powerless to act to prevent it. Managers need to be extremely sensitive to the feelings as well as the behavior of their staff members. If employees feel that they are being sexually harassed, they have a right to be protected from such behavior.

Advertising Claims

The purpose of advertising is to sell products and services. Most people understand this and therefore are skeptical about advertising claims. However, some advertising claims may be misleading or exaggerated, which can harm consumers and undermine trust in the industry. Here are some examples of advertising claims in hospitality and tourism:

- *Luxury.* Many hotels and resorts claim to offer a "luxury" experience, but the term is not well-defined and can be subjective. Some properties may use the term to suggest high-end amenities and personalized service, while others may simply use it as a marketing ploy to charge higher rates.

- *Authenticity.* Tourist destinations may promote their "authentic" culture or heritage, but this claim can be difficult to verify and may overlook the complex history and diversity of the region. Some destinations may even create a false sense of authenticity by staging cultural events or limiting visitors' interactions with local residents.

- *Sustainability.* Increasingly, hotels and tour operators are promoting their environmental and social sustainability practices, but some claims may be greenwashing or exaggerating their impact. For example, a hotel may claim to be "carbon neutral" but still rely heavily on nonrenewable energy sources.

A realistic image of a Hawaiian beach on a beautiful day.

■ *Price.* Many hotels and airlines use price-based advertising claims to attract customers, such as "lowest rates guaranteed" or "discounted fares." However, these claims may not always be accurate, and consumers may be required to meet certain conditions or book well in advance to secure the advertised price.

Exaggeration in brochures and other travel advertising is "motivated by the fact that so much of the industry is so price-driven that the line between telling people a reasonable truth and beefing it up to be competitive is crossed all the time," says Sven-Olof Lindblad, president of Special Expeditions, a specialty cruise line. Travel advertising shouldn't give people "an impression that something is going to be something that it absolutely is not," such as "a picture of a beach in Honolulu with not a footprint on it, and two people walking alone into the sunset. Give me a break. That's out of the question."[29]

There is a difference between puffery and outright deception. Resorts advertising that they are "on the beach" should be on the beach and not across the street from it. Some resorts advertise that they offer golf, but neglect to mention that the course they use is 20 miles away and starting times are difficult to come by. If a rate is advertised, it should be one that is readily available.

In an unusual dispute that garnered a good deal of negative publicity for all concerned, Killington Ski Resorts of Vermont hired an engineering firm to measure its ski terrain and the terrain of nine other New England resorts. It then launched an advertising campaign charging its competitors with exaggerating their number of trails, the depth of their snow, snow conditions, and acreage of skiable terrain. The resort placed large advertisements in national newspapers that said, "You can't ski on hype. This time of year, the hype on the trails is usually thicker than the snow." The ad then illustrated how much terrain Killington had that could be skied and compared it with other resorts in the area.[30] In a related case, Sunday River Ski Resort in Maine filed a complaint charging Sugarloaf/USA with misleading advertising. In its advertising, Sugarloaf claimed that it was only 35 miles farther from Portland, Maine, than Sunday River. Sunday River said Sugarloaf was at least 42.6 miles farther. Sugarloaf changed its ads to say it was 39 miles farther.[31]

Unlike a television or a sweater, which can be returned if it is not satisfactory, a vacation is not returnable and represents an investment in time that cannot be replaced. Hoteliers have a moral duty to disclose all of the relevant details of their properties so consumers can make a fair judgment as to whether their expectations are going to be met.

Overall, advertising claims in hospitality and tourism can be powerful tools for attracting customers, but they must be accurate, transparent, and verifiable to avoid misleading or harming consumers. It's important for travelers to do their own research, read reviews, and compare options before making a booking decision.

Truth-in-Menu Laws

Many states have enacted truth-in-menu laws. In some states, fines can be as high as $500 for misrepresenting a menu item. But beyond legal obligations, there is a moral obligation to present what is being sold fairly and honestly. People have a right to know what they are eating and a right to enough information to make a fair evaluation about whether they are getting their money's worth. If a menu offers a 12-ounce sirloin steak, then it ought to be 12 ounces every time it is served. Honest restaurateurs are proud of the fact that their gulf shrimp really comes from the Gulf of Mexico, and their prime beef really is prime and not a lower grade. These may seem like minor points, but consumers have indicated that they are important to them.

Truth-in-menu laws are regulations that require restaurants and food establishments to accurately describe the dishes they offer on their menus. The purpose of these laws is to prevent misleading or deceptive descriptions that could harm consumers and undermine trust in the food industry. Here are some key features of truth-in-menu laws:

- *Accurate descriptions.* Truth-in-menu laws require that menus accurately describe the dishes they offer, including the ingredients, preparation methods, and portion sizes. This information must be consistent with what is actually served to the customer.

- *Language restrictions.* Some truth-in-menu laws may prohibit the use of certain terms or phrases that could mislead consumers. For example, a restaurant may not be able to describe a dish as "organic" unless it meets specific certification standards.

- *Disclosure requirements.* Some truth-in-menu laws may require restaurants to disclose certain information about the dishes they offer, such as allergen information, nutritional content, or the source of the ingredients.

- *Enforcement.* Truth-in-menu laws are typically enforced by government agencies or industry organizations. Violations can result in fines, legal action, or loss of licenses.

- *Variations.* The specifics of truth-in-menu laws may vary by jurisdiction and may apply differently to different types of food establishments. For example, laws may differ for quick service restaurants, table-service restaurants, and food trucks.

Overall, truth-in-menu laws are intended to protect consumers and promote transparency in the food industry. They help ensure that customers can make informed decisions about what they eat and encourage restaurants to provide high-quality and honest descriptions of their dishes.

Knowledge Check

1. What are some typical ethical dilemmas hospitality managers face?

2. What are some ways local, state, and federal governments have responded to ethical issues in the hospitality industry?

15.4 MUST THERE BE A CODE OF ETHICS?

Hospitality businesses that do not already have a code of ethics should develop one that employees can live by and make decisions with while at work. A **code of ethics** is s a set of principles, guidelines, and standards that govern the behavior and conduct of individuals or professionals within a particular organization, industry, or community. It outlines the moral and ethical responsibilities of individuals and provides a framework for making ethical decisions and handling various situations with integrity and responsibility. Without such a code, how can a manager know what the company considers ethical or unethical? If every manager makes decisions based on their own ethical code, then a corporation may have no ethics at all or a lot of different ethical codes, depending on who is calling the shots. "Thirty years ago, all [business] values and ethics were primarily informal," says Michael G. Daigneault, president of the Ethics Resource Center. "It was assumed you were a good person and would do the right thing. ... Today organizations are realizing they are the transmitters of values. Many institutions have created codes of ethics, put ethics officers in place, and are offering ethics training. The pendulum has now swung over to formal ethics."[32]

A company's ethics should reflect the company's mission and must be communicated to those who are responsible for carrying out that mission. Hospitality is a "people business"; ethics deals with our relationships with other people. For this reason, a code of ethics is almost mandatory for hospitality businesses whose managers want to achieve a unified direction and a satisfactory level of control over the conduct of business.

There is ample evidence to suggest that without a code of ethics, some managers will make unethical decisions. According to a survey done by *Personnel Journal* magazine, middle managers—especially those 40 to 45 years old—are the most likely executives to do something unethical.[33] Some of these managers have a desire to "make it before it's too late," and strive to advance by shortcuts. In addition, they may have developed the attitude that "the company owes me" and therefore may be prone to cheating on expense accounts or making purchasing deals that benefit them.[34]

In the survey by Yale Center for Emotional Intelligence, workers were asked what kinds of unethical behavior they witnessed. Twenty-nine percent of the workers said they encountered experiences that could be described as rule violations, followed by lying (27 percent) and an unhealthy work environment (also 27 percent). Workers also mentioned sacrificing safety (9 percent), discrimination (3 percent), stealing (3 percent), and bullying (2 percent) as examples of unethical behavior in the workplace.[35]

Other managers don't cheat or lie on purpose; they just make decisions without thinking about all of the ethical implications or potential pitfalls. Archie B. Carroll, professor emeritus at the University of Georgia, divides businesspeople into three categories—moral, immoral, and amoral—and says the vast majority fall into the third category. These people do not aggressively cheat; they just do not think about ethics, and then stumble into unethical territory without realizing it. That's why a written ethics policy is so important. Ask most businesspeople

about their basic responsibilities and they'll list two: making money and obeying the law, says Carroll. In fact, there's a third: "They have a responsibility to be ethical. Which essentially means to be fair and just and to avoid harm in the marketing and sales of their product." Responsibility to ethics, he says, is no less fundamental than profitability and legality.[36]

One hotel company that has a strict and explicit code of ethics is Marriott International. Marriott's managers are expected to strictly comply with all of the company's Business Conduct Guide. The policies are quite lengthy and include the following:

Protecting Confidential Information

Everyone is responsible for protecting the confidentiality of Marriott's proprietary information, except when disclosure is authorized or legally mandated.

This duty applies to all associates. It applies during both working and nonworking hours and extends beyond your employment with Marriott.

Do not share Marriott's confidential information with: 1) associates who are not authorized to receive it or do not have a business need for the information; or 2) persons outside Marriott, unless there is a legitimate and authorized business purpose for the disclosure, or unless disclosure is required by law.

Confidential Information Includes:

- *Information that derives value from not being known to the public*

- *Undisclosed or commercially sensitive information that might be of use to Marriott's competitors*

- *Information that might harm Marriott, our shareholders, our customers, or our associates, if disclosed.*[37]

While there is no single universal ethics code for all hotels, many hotel chains and industry organizations have their own code of ethics and conduct that their properties are expected to follow. These codes are designed to outline the ethical standards and values that hotels should uphold in their operations and interactions with guests, employees, and the community. Typical ethical principles and areas covered in a hotel code of ethics are as follows:

- *Integrity and honesty.* Hotels are expected to demonstrate integrity, honesty, and transparency in all their dealings with guests, employees, suppliers, and the public.

- *Fair treatment.* Hotels should treat all guests and employees fairly and without discrimination, regardless of race, gender, nationality, religion, or any other characteristic.

- *Guest privacy and data security.* Ensuring the privacy and security of guest data and personal information is a crucial ethical consideration in the hospitality industry.

- *Employee well-being.* Hotels should prioritize the well-being and safety of their employees, offering fair wages, a safe work environment, and opportunities for professional growth.

- *Sustainability and environmental responsibility.* Ethical hotels promote sustainability practices to minimize their environmental impact and contribute positively to their local communities.

- *Customer service excellence.* Hotels should prioritize exceptional customer service and strive to meet or exceed guests' expectations.

- *Responsible marketing and advertising.* Ethical hotels should engage in honest and transparent marketing and advertising practices, avoiding misleading or deceptive claims.

- *Community engagement.* Hotels are encouraged to actively engage with the local community, support local initiatives, and act as responsible corporate citizens.

Some Ethical Litmus Tests

Even with laws and company policies and rules, ethical behavior is an intensely personal matter that every manager and employee must wrestle with. There are no easy guidelines that apply equally well in all circumstances. Ethical philosophers often talk about the moral duty of taking into account the interests of all stakeholders in arriving at a decision. A **stakeholder** is anyone who is affected by the outcome of a given decision. These could be your employees or your boss, the owners of the company you work for, the families of your employees, or the community in which the business operates. Sometimes managers or employees who are forced to implement unethical policies become whistleblowers and let other stakeholders know what is happening rather than be a silent part of an unethical action or plan.

In their book *The Power of Ethical Management*, Ken Blanchard and Norman Vincent Peale list three simple questions that they believe managers should ask themselves when making a decision:

1. *Is it legal?* Will I be violating either civil law or company policy?

2. *Is it balanced?* Is it fair to all concerned in the short term as well as the long term? Does it promote win-win relationships?

3. *How will it make me feel about myself?* Will it make me proud? Would I feel good if my decision were published in the newspaper? Would I feel good if my family knew about it?[38]

Knowledge Check

1. Why is it important that a business have a code of ethics?

2. What three questions should managers ask themselves when making a decision?

Ethics is a set of moral principles and values that we use to answer questions of right and wrong. It focuses on moral choices and relationships with others. Although we all have different personal values and morals, there are some universal principles that virtually all religions, cultures, and societies agree on. The basis of all of these principles is that other people's rights are as important as our own, and that it is our duty not to do anything to harm others.

Social responsibility is not the same as ethics, although the concepts are related. Companies have an unwritten social contract with society covering their rights and obligations. Ethics consists of "doing the right thing" in areas that may be entirely unrelated to that social contract, such as dealing with employees and customers.

There are six ways in which we arrive at our values about what is "good" and "just": authority, deductive logic, sense experience, emotion, intuition, and science. One of these ways is usually dominant within an individual and tends to influence the way they arrive at personal values. Although everyone is likely to have different values, most agree that it is a good idea to tell the truth whenever possible, and that stealing from others is wrong.

Some have argued that business is like poker and thus principles of ethical behavior do not apply in business. However, a careful examination shows that because businesses have different goals and there is much more at stake, the rules of business and poker must and should be different.

Honesty is always the best policy. When we lie, we manipulate other people and impair their ability to make choices based on true information. People should think carefully before telling a lie and have some very good reasons for violating this cardinal rule of ethics.

The most basic ethical rule is the Golden Rule: Do unto others as you would have them do unto you.

There are two major traditions that dominate current thinking in moral philosophy: deontology and utilitarianism. Deontology holds that basic or universal ideals should direct our thinking. These include keeping one's promises and always telling the truth. Utilitarianism says that there are no basic or universal ideals; ethical behavior consists of doing the greatest good for the greatest number. This philosophy is based on the ideas behind capitalism.

Many people who cannot choose between these two traditions prefer ethical relativism, also known as situational ethics. However, by definition, situational ethics is ambiguous and thus cannot be incorporated into any management system.

Hospitality managers are faced with a variety of ethical decisions daily. What should be done to preserve and protect the environment has become an ethical question of major importance in the hospitality industry. Many destinations have already taken major steps to preserve their natural resources, and hotel and restaurant companies are implementing recycling programs.

One of the most serious ethical issues facing the industry is discrimination not only in hiring and promotion but also in treatment of guests. Discrimination can be based on race, ethnicity, gender, or other characteristics.

Another ethical problem that must be addressed in the workplace is sexual harassment. Companies cannot and should not allow anyone to believe that sexual harassment will go unnoticed or will be excused.

Advertising claims should not misrepresent the truth or create unrealistic expectations. Menus should honestly describe what is being sold.

Many hotel companies have adopted their own code of ethics outlining the ethical standards and values that hotels should uphold in their operations and interactions with guests, employees, and the community. A good litmus test of an ethical decision is to ask these questions: (1) Is it legal? (2) Is it balanced? and (3) How will it make me feel about myself?

KEY TERMS

categorical imperative—A moral obligation or command that is unconditionally and universally binding.

code of ethics—A set of principles, guidelines, and standards that govern the behavior and conduct of individuals or professionals within a particular organization, industry, or community. It outlines the moral and ethical responsibilities of individuals and provides a framework for making ethical decisions and handling various situations with integrity and responsibility.

deontology—A system of ethics that assumes God exists and holds that basic or universal ideals should direct our thinking.

ethical relativism—The philosophical view that ethical choices should be based on what seems reasonable or logical according to one's own value system. Also known as situational ethics.

ethics—(1) A set of moral principles and values that individuals use to answer questions of right and wrong; (2) the study of the general nature of morals and of the specific moral choices to be made by individuals in their relationships with others.

social responsibility—A set of generally accepted relationships, obligations, and duties between the major institutions and the people.

stakeholder—Anyone who is affected by the outcome of a given decision.

utilitarianism—A system of ethics based on the greatest good for the greatest number of people.

1. Ethics is considered
   a. a set of principles and values used to determine right and wrong.
   b. personal choices used to navigate our professional careers.
   c. self-reflection about our choices.
   d. personal values we inherit.

2. What philosophical tradition is based on the beliefs of Immanuel Kant?
   a. Ethical relativism
   b. Utilitarianism
   c. Deontology
   d. Narcissism

3. What kind of moral reasoning involves following a "gut feeling" to arrive at knowledge?
   a. Science
   b. Intuition
   c. Authority
   d. Deductive logic

4. Which statement is an example of deductive logic?
   a. If six employees in the same department quit, then leadership is failing.
   b. The new president of a college loves students; therefore, she will make a great leader.
   c. An employee sees a black cat on the way to work and then has a bad day. Black cats are bad luck.
   d. If all chocolate is fattening, and if this dessert is chocolate, then this dessert must be fattening.

5. Which is an example of following truth-in-menu laws?
   a. Selling a cheaper cut of steak than what is advertised on a menu
   b. Calling a restaurant "farm to table" and sourcing all ingredients from local farms
   c. Labeling a dish "organic" when its ingredients have not been certified as organic
   d. Withholding nutritional information about a drink that is advertised as sugar-free

6. Which is an example of a misleading advertising claim?
   a. Providing a virtual tour of a beach resort on a website
   b. Honoring a first responders discount at a donut shop
   c. Booking a hotel stay, including resort fees, on a third-party website
   d. Selling excursions on a discount site and then not honoring the discount

7. A female front desk attendant is paid less than a male counterpart who has the same level of experience and expertise. What type of discrimination is this?
   a. Sexual orientation discrimination
   b. Gender discrimination
   c. Racial discrimination
   d. Age discrimination

8. Which is an example of a sustainable environmental practice in action?
   a. A restaurant sources ingredients from local farms only.
   b. A restaurant manager talks about switching to metal straws.
   c. A hotel claims to be carbon-neutral but still relies heavily on nonrenewable energy sources.
   d. A cruise line advertises its water sustainability program but has not yet put the program in place.

9. Which is an ethical concern around food safety?
  a. Water consumption
  b. Cultural sensitivity
  c. Hygiene standards
  d. Data breaches

10. Which is an ethical question managers should ask themselves when making a decision?
  a. Is it legal?
  b. Should I avoid the issue?
  c. How will this affect shareholders?
  d. Does it align with our public relations campaign?

11. What organization has developed guidelines designed to prevent sexual discrimination?
  a. U.S. Department of Labor
  b. U.S. Department of Commerce
  c. U.S. Department of Agriculture
  d. U.S. Equal Employment Opportunity Commission

12. Which is an example of situational ethics?
  a. An employee is fired for stealing.
  b. A restaurant does not honor an expired coupon.
  c. Plagiarism is considered unethical in one culture but not in another.
  d. A hotel property decides to implement a composting program, but its sister property does not.

SHORT-ANSWER QUESTIONS

1. How can an organization benefit from having a code of ethics?

2. What would you do if your boss asked you to do something that you believe is unethical?

FAIR WARNING

A suburban highway hotel adds an 18 percent charge to gift shop purchases when they are charged to a guestroom. Gift shop employees have been instructed to encourage shoppers to charge their purchases to guestrooms. For example, when they check out a guest, they are trained to ask, "For your convenience, would you like me to charge this to your room?"

The policy is noted only on the guest's final bill at check-out. Most guests don't notice the charge and just pay their bill. Front desk agents have been instructed to remove the additional fee if a guest complains. The hotel brings in several hundred dollars per week from the policy.

At check-out time, a guest notices the additional charge on her bill. She asks the front desk agent what the additional charge is for. The front desk agent politely explains the policy, showing her the small print on her bill.

The guest becomes irritated and demands that the charges be removed immediately. She also says she's going to post a negative review about the hotel on social media. She then insists on seeing the general manager and tells him that in addition to social media posts, she's going to submit her story to a local news station.

DISCUSSION QUESTIONS

1. What ethical issues are involved with the hotel policy?

2. What ethical issues are involved for the hotel employees?

3. What do you think the general manager should do?

Rachel Humphrey

Rachel Humphrey is the founder of the Women in Hospitality Leadership Alliance and is a board member, principal, and interview host for DEI Advisors. Before retiring in August 2021, Humphrey served as the executive vice president and chief operating officer of the Asian American Hotel Owners Association (AAHOA), the nation's largest and most influential hotel owners association, and as a member of its executive leadership team. Humphrey joined AAHOA in 2015 after more than 20 years as a trial lawyer. She was responsible for AAHOA's day-to-day operations in addition to managing its franchise relations and overseeing the association's education initiatives. Humphrey led AAHOA as its interim president and CEO for most of 2019, during which she served on the AAHOA board of directors. She has been recognized as one of the most "Influential Women in Hospitality," one of the "Top 50 Women in Travel," one of the "100 Most Powerful People in USA Hospitality," and one of the "100 Most Inspirational People in Hospitality." Humphrey has also received numerous awards and recognitions for her leadership and service to the hospitality industry. She is dedicated to advancing women in leadership in the hospitality industry. In addition to the Alliance and DEI Advisors, Humphrey serves on the boards of Women in Travel Thrive and the Kennesaw State University Coles College of Business. She is also a frequent speaker at industry conferences and serves on numerous advisory boards within the hospitality industry.

Imagine that you are a hotel manager in a popular tourist destination. Your hotel has a policy of overbooking rooms to ensure maximum occupancy, which has been a successful business strategy in the past. However, on one particular day, several guests arrive to check in and find that their rooms are not available due to overbooking. One of the guests is a family with young children who have been traveling all day and are visibly upset.

As a manager, you must make a decision that balances the hotel's financial interests with the ethical considerations of customer service and respect for the guests' needs. What are some ethical considerations that you might take into account to resolve this dilemma?

APPENDIX A

KEY HOTEL MANAGEMENT POSITIONS

Hotel Executive Committee (Reports to the General Manager/Managing Director)

Title	Description
General Manager (GM)/ Managing Director	Oversees operations, strategy, and profitability.
Assistant GM/Hotel Manager/Director of Operations	Assists the GM in decision-making, oversees daily operations, and steps in during the GM's absence.
Director of Human Resources	Oversees the human resources functions of the hotel, sets policies, and aligns HR strategies with hotel objectives. Leads staff recruitment, training, payroll, and employee welfare.
Financial Controller/ Director of Finance	Manages finances, budgets, and financial reporting.
Director of Sales and Marketing	Oversees promotion strategies, guest attraction, and partnership management.
Director of Food and Beverage	Oversees all food and beverage operations of the hotel, from restaurants to catering. Ensures profitability and maintains quality standards. Responsible for all dining, catering, and bar operations.
Director of Engineering	Responsible for entire hotel's maintenance and engineering department, ensuring that the hotel remains in top operational order. Sets departmental objectives, budgets, and oversees larger renovation projects. Directs the upkeep, maintenance, and repair strategies of the resort's facilities and equipment.
Spa Director	Oversees the entire spa's operations, from treatments to sales and staffing. Responsible for budgeting, setting targets, and ensuring profitability.
Director of Loss Prevention	Oversees the security and safety of the hotel, including asset protection, guest safety, staff safety, and emergency response planning.

Accounting Department (Reports to Financial Controller/Director of Finance)

Title	Description	Advancement Opportunity
Financial Controller/ Director of Finance	Manages finances, budgets, and financial reporting.	
Assistant Financial Controller	Supports the financial controller in the execution of financial strategies and operations.	Financial Controller
Accounting Manager	Manages day-to-day accounting operations, ensuring accuracy and compliance with financial regulations.	Assistant Financial Controller
Payroll Manager	Manages staff payroll, ensuring timely and accurate payment, tax deductions, and other payroll-related tasks.	
Food and Beverage Cost Controller	Specializes in controlling costs within the food and beverage department, monitoring waste, and ensuring efficient purchasing.	
Purchasing Manager	Manages the procurement of goods and services for the hotel, ensuring cost-effective purchasing and timely deliveries.	

Food and Beverage Department (Reports to Director of Food and Beverage)

Title	Description	Advancement Opportunity
Director of Food and Beverage	Oversees all food and beverage operations of the hotel, from restaurants to catering. Ensures profitability and maintains quality standards. Responsible for all dining, catering, and bar operations.	
Assistant Director of Food and Beverage	Supports the food and beverage director and may oversee specific outlets or projects.	Director of Food and Beverage
Executive Chef	Heads the kitchen, sets the menu, and ensures food quality and presentation standards.	Director of Food and Beverage
Sous Chef	The second-in-command in the kitchen, often managing day-to-day operations and supporting the executive chef.	Executive Chef
Food and Beverage Manager/Outlet Manager	Manages multiple food and beverage outlets, ensuring that they meet service standards and run smoothly and profitably.	Director of Food and Beverage

(Continued)

Food and Beverage Department (Reports to Director of Food and Beverage) (*Continued*)

Title	Description	Advancement Opportunity
Restaurant Manager	Manages daily operations of the restaurant, from staffing to guest satisfaction.	Food and Beverage Manager
Bar Manager/ Beverage Manager	Oversees the operations of the bar, from drink preparation to inventory control.	Food and Beverage Manager
Banquet Manager	Oversees the operations of banquet events, from weddings to conferences.	Food and Beverage Manager

Rooms Division (Reports to Assistant General Manager/Hotel Manager/Director of Operations/ Director of Rooms)

Title	Description	Advancement Opportunity
Assistant GM/Hotel Manager/Director of Operations/Director of Rooms	Assists the GM in decision-making, oversees daily operations, and steps in during the GM's absence.	
Director of Front Office/ Front Office Manager (FOM)	Manages front desk operations, reservations, and guest services.	Assistant GM
Assistant Front Office Manager	Assists FOM and often manages specific functions like reservations or night operations	Director of Front Office/ FOM
Night Manager/Night Auditor	Manages front office operations overnight.	Assistant Front Office Manager
Front Office Supervisors/ Manager on Duty (MOD)	Responsible for managing front office operations during their shifts.	Assistant Front Office Manager
Reservations Manager	Oversees room bookings and maintains balance of room reservations, whether group or individual.	Assistant Front Office Manager
Director of Housekeeping/ Executive Housekeeper	Ensures overall cleanliness and presentation of rooms and public areas.	Assistant GM
Assistant Executive Housekeeper	Directly assists the executive housekeeper, often managing daily operations and coordinating with floor supervisors.	Executive Housekeeper
Laundry Manager	Manages all laundry operations, ensuring clean linen and uniforms and their timely delivery.	Executive Housekeeper

Engineering Department (Reports to Director of Engineering/Chief Engineer)

Title	Description	Advancement Opportunity
Director of Engineering/ Chief Engineer	Responsible for the entire hotel's maintenance and engineering department, ensuring that the hotel remains in top operational order. Sets departmental objectives and budgets. Oversees larger renovation projects. Directs upkeep, maintenance, and repair strategies for the hotel's facilities and equipment.	
Assistant Director of Engineering	Assists the chief engineer and takes charge in their absence. May manage specific projects or tasks within the department.	Director of Engineering

Human Resources Department (Reports to Director of Human Resources)

Title	Description	Advancement Opportunity
Director of Human Resources	Oversees the human resources (HR) functions of the hotel, setting policies and aligning HR strategies with hotel objectives. Leads staff recruitment, training, payroll, and employee welfare.	
Assistant Director of Human Resources	Assists the director and often manages specific HR functions or projects.	Director of Human Resources

Loss Prevention Department (Reports to Director of Loss Prevention)

Title	Description	Advancement Opportunity
Director of Loss Prevention	Responsible for the security and safety of the hotel, including asset protection, guest safety, staff safety, and emergency response planning.	
Assistant Director of Loss Prevention	Assists the director in daily operations, handles specific projects, and oversees certain areas of the property.	Director of Loss Prevention

Sales and Marketing Department (Reports to Director of Sales and Marketing)

Title	Description	Advancement Opportunity
Director of Sales and Marketing	Oversees promotion strategies, guest attraction, and partnership management.	
Assistant Director of Sales and Marketing	Assists the director and might be responsible for specific segments or strategies.	Director of Sales and Marketing
Senior Sales Manager	Directly supervises sales executives and coordinates sales strategies for different market segments.	Assistant Director of Sales and Marketing
Marketing Manager	Oversees the marketing strategies, campaigns, and brand positioning of the hotel.	Assistant Director of Sales and Marketing
Revenue Manager	Focuses on pricing strategies, analyzing market demand, and ensuring revenue growth.	Assistant Director of Sales and Marketing

Spa Department (Reports to Spa Director)

Title	Description	Advancement Opportunity
Spa Director or Manager	Oversees the spa's operations, from treatments to sales and staffing. Responsible for budgeting, setting targets, and ensuring profitability.	
Assistant Spa Manager	Assists the director in daily operations, handles specific projects, and oversees spa retail and operations.	Spa Director or Manager

APPENDIX B

KEY FOOD SERVICE MANAGEMENT POSITIONS

Restaurant Positions

Title	Description	Advancement Opportunity
Banquet Manager	Coordinates exceptional events for guests. Ensures smooth event execution and maintains high standards of customer satisfaction at events held in an operation's banquet facility. Excellent leadership skills, attention to detail, and ability to multitask are crucial in creating unforgettable experiences for clients and guests.	Catering Manager
Beverage Manager	Oversees all aspects of the beverage program within a restaurant. This role involves managing the bar operations, creating and maintaining beverage menus, supervising staff, managing inventory, and ensuring excellent customer service. Plays a vital role in driving revenue, maintaining high-quality standards, and enhancing the overall guest experience.	Food and Beverage Director
Catering Manager	Oversees all aspects of an operation's catering commitments, including planning, organizing, and executing catering events. Exceptional leadership skills, attention to detail, and passion for delivering outstanding customer experiences are key to success in this role. Candidates who thrive in a fast-paced environment, possess excellent organizational abilities, and have a genuine love for food and hospitality are ideal.	Food and Beverage Director
Controller	Manages and oversees the financial operations of a restaurant, implementing and maintaining robust financial controls, analyzing financial data, preparing accurate financial reports, and providing strategic insights to enhance profitability and operational efficiency.	General Manager
Dining Room Manager	Primarily responsible for ensuring the smooth and efficient operation of the dining area in a restaurant, overseeing the dining room staff, maintaining a high level of customer service, and ensuring an exceptional dining experience for guests. The role involves managing daily operations, coordinating with other departments, and implementing strategies to enhance the overall dining room experience.	Assistant General Manager

(Continued)

Title	Description	Advancement Opportunity
Executive Chef	Creates and implements innovative menus, oversees kitchen operations, and ensures the highest quality of food and customer satisfaction. Exceptional culinary expertise, leadership skills, and creative flair are instrumental to support the restaurant's success and reputation.	Food and Beverage Director
Food and Beverage Director	Oversees and manages all aspects of the food and beverage operations within a restaurant. Works closely with the restaurant management team to ensure the highest level of guest satisfaction, operational efficiency, and profitability.	General Manager
General Manager— Full Service	Oversees all aspects of the restaurant's operations. Primary function is to ensure exceptional customer service, maintain high-quality standards, and drive profitability. The GM leads a team of employees, implements operational strategies, manages financial aspects, and fosters a positive, inclusive work environment. Strong leadership skills, industry knowledge, and business acumen contribute to this role's success.	
General Manager— Quick Service	Oversees and manages all aspects of the restaurant's operations. The primary function is to ensure excellent customer service, maximize profitability, and maintain a positive work environment. The GM leads a team of employees, implements company policies and procedures, and upholds quality and safety standards.	
Kitchen Manager	Oversees all kitchen operations, ensuring the efficient and smooth functioning of the culinary department in a restaurant. Primary focus is to maintain high-quality standards, manage a team of kitchen staff, and collaborate with other departments to deliver exceptional culinary experiences to customers.	Food and Beverage Director
Public Relations/ Marketing Manager	Develops and executes comprehensive public relations and marketing strategies to enhance an operation's image, drive customer engagement, and support the growth of the business.	

Restaurant Positions

Title	Description	Advancement Opportunity
Service Manager/ Dining Room Manager	Ensures the smooth and efficient operation of the restaurant's front-of-house service, overseeing the service staff, managing customer interactions, and working closely with other managers to maintain exceptional service standards. Responsibilities include staff supervision, training, customer satisfaction, and operational efficiency.	Assistant General Manager
Shift Manager	Supervises and coordinates the activities of the restaurant staff during a specific shift. The primary objective is to ensure efficient operations, exceptional customer service, and a positive dining experience for all patrons. The position requires strong leadership, organizational skills, and the ability to handle various responsibilities simultaneously.	Service Manager/Dining Room Manager
Sommelier/Wine Steward	Curates an exceptional wine list. Recommends suitable pairings and educates guests on the nuances of wine appreciation. The position calls for close collaboration with the operation's culinary team to ensure harmonious combinations of food and wine and the ability to act as a brand ambassador by delivering a personalized and memorable wine experience to guests.	

Corporate Positions

Title	Description
Brand Management Specialist	Develops and executes comprehensive brand strategies that resonate with the restaurant brand's target audiences and reinforce the company's values and positioning. Ability to work closely with cross-functional teams, including marketing, operations, and culinary, to ensure consistency and alignment in all brand-related initiatives is critical to the success of this position. Expertise in brand management and a passion for storytelling contributes to enhancing the brand image, driving customer engagement, and fostering brand loyalty.
Chief Executive Officer (CEO)	A restaurant company CEO shapes the company's strategic direction, driving growth and fostering a culture of excellence. They are ultimately responsible for the overall performance and growth of the company. Exceptional leadership skills, industry expertise, and strategic mindset are critical in driving the mission and ensuring a company's long-term success.

(Continued)

Corporate Positions (*Continued*)

Title	Description
Chief Financial Officer (CFO)	The CFO plays a crucial role in shaping a brand's financial strategy, optimizing operational efficiency, and maximizing profitability across all restaurant locations.
Chief Operating Officer (COO)	The COO ensures the seamless execution of the business strategy, driving operational excellence. Responsibilities include developing and implementing strategies that align with the company's vision, values, and long-term goals. A deep understanding of the restaurant industry, exceptional leadership skills, and a proven track record of successfully managing complex operations in a fast-paced environment contribute to the success of this position.
Chief Diversity, Equity, and Inclusion Officer	A chief diversity, equity, and inclusion officer is responsible for developing and implementing a comprehensive strategy that advances a culture where all are welcome, feel they belong, and know they can contribute. Collaborates with leaders across the company to weave inclusive culture principles into company processes, policies, and practices. Cultivates an environment where every employee feels valued and respected and has an equal opportunity to contribute and thrive.
Equipment Specifier	Researches, selects, and procures the equipment needed for a brand's restaurants. The main objective is to identify, evaluate, and recommend the most suitable tools, appliances, and machinery for the restaurants' operations. This position requires expertise and attention to detail to streamline processes, enhance productivity, and improve overall efficiency.
Facilities Designer	Designs, plans, and oversees the construction and renovation projects for restaurant facilities. This role requires a blend of artistic vision, technical expertise, and project management skills to ensure the successful execution of facility projects.
Franchise Liaison	A restaurant's franchise liaison is the crucial link between a restaurant company and its franchisees. The liaison ensures effective communication, collaboration, and support. They are responsible for building strong relationships, overseeing franchise operations, and driving the growth and success of the franchise network.
Human Resources Specialist	A human resources specialist is responsible for supporting employees and management by implementing and overseeing all HR programs, benefits packages, hiring, and related initiatives. They contribute to the overall success of the company by ensuring a positive, inclusive, and engaging work environment; promoting employee satisfaction; and fostering a culture of growth and excellence.
Marketing Executive	Develops and implements comprehensive marketing strategies that align with the company's objectives and brand vision. Duties include leading a team of marketing professionals and collaborating closely with cross-functional departments to drive revenue growth, enhance customer loyalty, and expand the brand's market presence. Innovative, creative thinking, a strategic mindset, and a deep understanding of the restaurant industry are crucial to the success of this position.

Corporate Positions

Title	Description
Menu Research and Development Specialist	Develops and enhances the brand's menu offerings to ensure that they align with a culinary vision and meet the evolving tastes and preferences of customers. This role works closely with the executive chef, culinary team, and management to create innovative and exciting menu items that showcase the brand's commitment to quality, flavor, and presentation.
Real Estate/Location Specialist	A real estate/location specialist plays a critical role in the company's expansion strategy by identifying and securing prime real estate locations for restaurant outlets. A keen understanding of market trends, excellent negotiation skills, and the ability to forge strong relationships with landlords and brokers are key to the success of this position.
Sustainability Specialist	Identifies opportunities to reduce environmental impact, improve resource efficiency, and promote social responsibility across all aspects of operations.

Source: "Restaurant Industry Job Descriptions," National Restaurant Association, https://restaurant.org/education-and-resources/learning-center/workforce-engagement/restaurant-industry-job-descriptions/.

APPENDIX C

SAMPLE RÉSUMÉ

FULL NAME

City, State | Phone Number | Email Address

EXPERIENCE

Job Title   **Start Date–End Date (or Present)**

Most Recent Employer, City and State

- List responsibilities.
- Describe accomplishments.
- Use strong action verbs.
- Include specific numbers and details.

Front Desk Manager   **July 2021–December 2022**

Bellinger Inn and Suites, Rolling Hills, WI

- Supervised a front desk team of 5–6 representatives.
- Processed and audited daily reservations reports.
- Coordinated operations with housekeeping and maintenance departments.
- Increased average online customer service score to 91% from 88%.

Front Desk Representative   **March 2019–June 2021**

Pine Creek Hotel and Resort, Mokane Plains, WI

- Managed reservations for 65 hotel rooms.
- Addressed all online inquiries and answered phone calls.
- Processed guest arrivals and departures using a property management system.

Education

School or Institution   **Month and Year Awarded**
Expected or awarded degree or certification

Midwest State University   **December 2021**
Bachelor of Arts in Hospitality and Tourism Management

American Hotel & Lodging Educational Institute   **May 2020**
Hospitality Manager Certificate

Professional Skills

- Leadership
- Communication
- Customer service
- Languages: Spanish and English

GLOSSARY

accounting department—The hotel department responsible for keeping track of the many business transactions that occur in the hotel and managing the hotel's finances.

administrative skills—A set of competencies that involve effectively managing and organizing tasks, resources, and processes within an organization.

advertising—A communication strategy used by businesses and organizations to promote their products, services, or ideas to a target audience.

airline-related guests—Airplane crew members; airline passengers needing emergency accommodations are also included in this guest category.

airport hotels—Full-service hotels built near airports.

all-suite hotel—A hotel that features units made up of two connected hotel rooms that sell for approximately the price of one, at lower prices than traditional hotel suites. One room is furnished as a typical hotel guestroom with a bed, the other with a foldout sofa and/or table and chairs.

ambience—The décor, lighting, furnishings, and other factors that create a feeling about or an identity for a restaurant.

approval provision—The provision of a hotel management contract specifying which operator decisions require management approval. The mechanism for settling owner–operator disputes is sometimes included in this provision.

areas of dominant influence (ADI)—A term used in the television industry to describe areas covered by the signals of major television stations as measured by Arbitron, a national TV rating service.

assessment—A one-time or periodic charge imposed on private club members to cover operational shortfalls or raise capital for improvements to the club.

asset manager—The owner's representative monitoring the operation of the hotel.

assets—Resources available for use by a business (i.e., anything owned by the business that has monetary value).

association—A group of people banded together for a specific purpose.

athletic club—Also known as a sports club or fitness club, this facility provides a range of athletic- and fitness-related amenities and services designed to promote physical activity, health, and well-being, catering to individuals who are interested in sports, fitness, and recreational activities.

average daily rate (ADR)—A key rooms department operating ratio: rooms revenue divided by number of rooms sold. Also called average room rate.

balance sheet—A financial statement that provides a snapshot of a restaurant's financial position at a specific point in time. It presents a summary of a restaurant's assets, liabilities, and shareholders' equity and shows the balance between these three components.

banquet or catering manager—A hotel manager responsible for arranging and planning food and beverage functions for (1) conventions and smaller hotel groups, and (2) local banquets booked by the sales department.

bars and taverns—Locations where drinks, especially alcoholic drinks, are served, sometimes with limited food options. It can be a local neighborhood corner bar or a sports bar with many televisions and many types of snack foods.

bar's par—The amount of each type of beverage established for behind-the-bar storage, based on expected consumption.

basic fees—Fees paid by a hotel owner to a management company for managing the property. In the case of a chain management company, the fees also cover the use of the established brand name. Also called "management fees."

beach club—A type of private or commercial establishment located along a beachfront that provides various amenities and services for its members or guests.

bleisure—A term that combines the words "business" and "leisure." It refers to the trend of guests blending work travel with leisure travel to save on vacation costs and create a better work–life balance.

blind receiving—A receiving system in which the supplier gives the receiving clerk a list of items being delivered but not the quantities or weights, thereby forcing the clerk to count or weigh the incoming products and record the results. These results are later compared with the supplier's invoice.

boutique hotels—Small hotels, typically 150 to 300 rooms, usually described as "cultural," "historical," and "authentic."

budget hotels—A type of select-service hotel. Budget hotels have low construction and operating costs, allowing them to charge between $45 and $60 per night, a slightly higher rate than economy hotels.

budgeting—The forecasting of revenues, expenses, and profits.

business format franchise—An ongoing business relationship between a franchisor and a franchisee in which the franchisor sells its products, services, trademark, and business concept to the franchisee in return for royalties and other franchise fees.

capacity-constrained businesses—Businesses that produce products or services that cannot be inventoried or stored for future use. Success depends on their ability to efficiently match production capacity to consumer demand at any given moment.

capital investment budget—A financial plan that outlines the projected spending on long-term assets or capital projects over a specified period. Also known as a capital expenditure budget or capital budget.

captain—The person on a cruise ship who is responsible for its operation and the safety of all those onboard. The captain sees that all company policies and rules, as well as national and international laws, are followed.

capture rate—The percentage of hotel guests who eat meals at the hotel.

career path/career ladder—A series of positions an individual may take on the way to their ultimate career goal. Some companies lay out sample career paths or ladders for their employees.

career portfolio—A job search tool that expands on a job applicant's résumé by giving additional information about the applicant's talents, communications skills, creativity, leadership qualities, social responsibility, critical thinking, and teamwork.

cash flow statement—A financial statement that tracks the inflow and outflow of cash from a restaurant over a specific period. It provides insights into the sources and uses of cash, allowing owners and stakeholders to understand how cash is being generated and utilized within the business.

cashier's cage—Generally referred to simply as "the cage," this is the area within a casino where chips and cash are stored, checks are cashed, credit cards are accepted, and markers are approved. It is the control center for the flow of chips to and from gaming tables.

casual dining restaurant—A restaurant distinguishable by a combination of décor, informal atmosphere, and eclectic menu that draws from ethnic and traditional offerings.

categorical imperative—A moral obligation or command that is unconditionally and universally binding.

catering—The business of providing food, beverages, and other related services for special events, gatherings, or occasions. It involves preparing, delivering, and serving meals at a specific location chosen by the client, such as a venue, office, or private residence.

catering department—A department within the food and beverage department of a hotel that is responsible for arranging and planning food and beverage functions for (1) conventions and smaller hotel groups, and (2) local banquets booked by the sales department.

center-city hotels—Full-service hotels located in downtown areas.

certified meeting professional (CMP)—A CMP certification enhances the knowledge and performance of meeting professionals, promotes the status and credibility of the meeting profession, and advances uniform standards of practice. The qualifications for certification are based on professional experience, education, and a rigorous exam.

chased-demand strategy—A management strategy in which capacity can, to a limited extent, be varied to suit the level of demand.

chief housekeeper—The person on a cruise ship who is responsible for the cleaning and general maintenance of all cabins and interior areas on the ship. The chief housekeeper is also responsible for passenger laundry and dry cleaning, as well as cleaning cabin linen and table linen, towels, and the crew's uniforms. Also called the chief steward.

chief officer—The captain's second-in-command and deputy. Also called the staff captain on some cruise lines.

city/athletic club—An urban recreational and social club that varies in size, type, facilities, and membership.

city club—A term for various types of private clubs, such as social clubs, dining clubs, or university clubs, located in urban areas. City clubs bring together individuals who share common interests, hobbies, or social activities. These clubs provide a platform for members to engage in recreational, cultural, or social pursuits, fostering a sense of community and camaraderie among like-minded individuals.

classical school—A school of management thought in which workers are seen as rational people interested primarily in making money. This management approach addresses an employee's economic and physical needs, but not their social needs or need for job satisfaction.

club manager—The hired professional responsible for guiding all the elements of a private club's operation. Often referred to as the club's general manager or chief operating officer.

code of ethics—A set of principles, guidelines, and standards that govern the behavior and conduct of individuals or professionals within a particular organization, industry, or community. It outlines the moral and ethical responsibilities of individuals and provides a framework for making ethical decisions and handling various situations with integrity and responsibility.

commissions—Fees that are paid to the hotel by suppliers that are located outside the hotel but provide services for hotel guests, such as gift shops, car rental agencies, and photographers.

common interest realty association (CIRA)—Commonly known as a homeowners association (HOA), condominium association, cooperative association, or planned-community association. CIRAs are responsible for overseeing shared areas, amenities, and services within the community, and they enforce rules and regulations to maintain the community's standards and protect property values.

competitive pricing—Basing prices on what competitors charge.

conceptual skills—The ability of an individual to think critically, analyze complex situations, and grasp the bigger picture.

concession—A facility that might well be operated by the hotel directly, such as a beauty salon or fitness club, but is turned over to independent operators. The hotel in turn receives a flat fee, a minimum fee plus a percentage of the gross receipts over a specific amount, or a percentage of total gross sales.

condominium hotel—A building or complex with individual rooms that are sold to individual owners. Owners have the option to use units for personal reasons or place them in a rental program managed by a hotel operator.

conference centers—Smaller versions of convention centers and hotels. They are often designed to host small meetings and can contain lodging.

construction financing loan—A short-term loan for use while a hotel is being built, with repayment to be made in three years or less.

consumer-based pricing—Pricing based on what consumers are willing to pay.

consumer show—Also known as a public show. It differs from a trade show in that trade shows are typically business to business and not open to the public. A consumer show is often business to consumer, typically open to the public, and usually requires an entrance fee. A Holiday Expo, a Women's Expo, and RV shows are considered consumer shows.

contribution margin—A food or beverage item's selling price minus the cost of the ingredients used to prepare the item.

controller—Manages the accounting department and all of its functions, including management of credit, payroll, guest accounts, and cashiering activities.

control system—A system of controls that allows managers to quickly recognize and correct deviations from the operating budget, such as financial statements and service quality standards.

convention—An event that has a meeting and a trade show component.

convention and association groups—Businesspeople attending a convention or association meeting. The number of guests can run into the thousands.

convention and visitors bureau (CVB)—A nonprofit service organization that promotes a destination and sometimes provides services for meetings and conventions.

convention services manager (CSM)—A member of convention center, hotel, or resort staff who is responsible for all aspects of a convention.

corporate club—A for-profit private club owned by an individual or a company that sells memberships in the club. Also called a developer or proprietary club.

corporate groups—Small groups of people traveling for business purposes, usually to attend conferences or meetings.

corporate individuals—Individuals traveling for business purposes who are not part of any group.

cost centers—Departments or areas within a hotel that do not directly generate revenue; they provide support for the hotel's revenue centers. Also known as support centers.

cost of food sold—The cost of the food sold to a guest. It is calculated based on beginning inventories, closing inventories, and food purchases for the period between the two inventories, minus complimentary meals.

cost-plus pricing—Determining a price by taking the total cost of providing a product or service and adding to it (1) a percentage to cover overhead or fixed expenses, and (2) a predetermined gross profit margin.

country club—Primarily a recreational and social facility for individuals and families who live nearby the club. Country clubs often have separate children's facilities and do a large catering business while offering a host of amenities—likely racquet sports (tennis, pickleball, platform tennis, etc.) and aquatics (pool, etc.), in addition to golf.

credit slip—A form that states the amount of excess chips at each gaming table at the end of a shift. Extra chips are returned to the cage along with the credit slips.

croupier—An attendant or dealer at a gaming table who conducts the game, collects bets, and pays the winning bets of players.

crowdsourcing—Obtaining ideas or content by asking for contributions from groups of people, generally via the Internet.

cruise director—Oversees a staff responsible for managing a cruise ship's entertainers, children's counselors, and guest activities, including selling and coordinating shore excursions.

cyclical menu—A menu that changes every day for a certain number of days, then repeats the cycle. A few cycle menus change regularly but without any set pattern. Also known as a cycle menu.

demographic information—Statistical information (such as age and income) about a population, used especially to identify markets.

deontology—A system of ethics that assumes God exists and holds that basic or universal ideals should direct our thinking.

departmental expenses—Expenses that are charged to specific hotel departments; such expenses include a wide range of items, such as rooms department payroll, restaurant laundry, and telephone supplies like message pads and pencils.

destination wedding—A wedding held at an exotic or remote location.

dining club—Also known as a supper club or gastronomic club, this is a private social establishment centered around communal dining experiences. A dining club typically focuses on providing its members with unique and exclusive culinary experiences, often featuring gourmet meals prepared by professional chefs or talented home cooks.

direct purchase—Food sent directly from the receiving area to the kitchen or dining room rather than to a storage area.

distribution channels—Intermediaries through which a service or product passes.

diversity training—Training that seeks to make all workers feel comfortable in their workplace, no matter their race, culture, gender, or age.

dogs—Unpopular menu items with a low contribution margin.

drop box—A locked box beneath gaming tables into which cash and markers received from players are deposited. At the end of a shift, boxes are removed from the tables and brought to a count room, where they are opened and the contents counted under strict supervision.

economy hotels—A type of select-service hotel. Economy hotels have the lowest construction and operating costs, allowing them to charge 25 percent less than budget hotels.

ecotourism—Responsible travel to natural areas that conserves the environment and improves the well-being of local people.

elasticity of demand—A measure of customer responsiveness to changes in price.

empowerment—Being authorized to solve customers' problems without needing to seek prior approval from supervisors.

encroachment—Placing a branded hotel or restaurant in the vicinity of other hotels or restaurants with the same or a related brand.

environmental officer—An officer on a cruise ship responsible for compliance with international and local environmental regulations.

equity club—A nonprofit private club whose members buy shares in the club and, after expenses have been paid, invest any revenues left over in improvements to the club's facilities and services.

Escoffier, Georges Auguste—A French chef (1847–1935) who is considered the father of modern cookery. His two main contributions were (1) the simplification of classical cuisine and the classical menu, and (2) the reorganization of the kitchen.

ethical relativism—The philosophical view that ethical choices should be based on what seems reasonable or logical according to one's own value system. Also known as situational ethics.

ethics—(1) A set of moral principles and values that individuals use to answer questions of right and wrong; (2) the study of the general nature of morals and of the specific moral choices to be made by individuals in their relationships with others.

ethnic restaurant—A restaurant featuring a particular cuisine, such as Chinese, Italian, or Mexican.

event—An organized occasion such as a meeting, convention, exhibition, special meeting, gala dinner, and so on. An event is often composed of several different yet related functions.

Events Industry Council (EIC)—Formerly known as the Convention Industry Council, the EIC is an umbrella organization for all meeting and event organizations, and its mission is to create industry standards and definitions.

exhibition—An event at which product, services, or promotional materials are displayed to attendees visiting exhibits on the show floor. These are primarily focused on business-to-business relationships.

exposition—A term primarily used in North America, this is another term for a large exhibit, trade show, or public show.

familiarization (fam) tours—Free or reduced-rate travel programs designed by hotel personnel to acquaint travel agents and others with the hotel and stimulate sales.

family dining restaurant—A restaurant that caters to families—with an emphasis on satisfying the needs of children—and serves breakfast, lunch, and dinner, while offering traditional menu items.

fast-casual restaurant—A restaurant that combines elements of quick service and casual dining. These establishments offer higher-quality food and a more upscale dining experience compared to traditional quick service chains, while still maintaining speed and affordability.

feasibility study—A study commissioned by developers and prepared by consultants that seeks to determine the potential success of a proposed business on a proposed site.

fee structure provision—A provision in a contract between a hotel owner and a hotel management company that outlines the fees the owner must pay to the management company for managing the property.

fill slip—A form that states the amount of chips short at each gaming table at the end of a shift.

financial controls—Financial statements, operating ratios, and other financial statistics that hotel managers can use to keep track of operations and make sure financial goals are being attained. For restaurants, tools that managers use to measure the worth of a restaurant and its level of sales, costs, and profitability.

fine dining restaurant—A restaurant that features luxury dining and an exciting menu (not necessarily French or haute cuisine, however), and employs well-trained, creative chefs and skilled food servers. Fine dining restaurants are generally small and independently operated, with more employees per guest than other types of restaurants.

first-class/luxury hotels—Hotels with high room rates and exceptional service and amenities.

first-in, first-out (FIFO)—An inventory method used to rotate and issue stored food, so items that have been in storage the longest are used first.

fixed menu—A menu with a set list of items that is used for several months or longer before it is changed. Also known as a static menu.

flags of convenience—Refers to the practice of registering ships in a country other than that of ownership or the country where the ship's operators and crew are based. This practice allows shipowners to take advantage of certain benefits and lower costs associated with the chosen flag state's maritime regulations and tax laws.

floor people—Casino employees who supervise dealers. They are trained to enforce good dealing procedures, resolve disputes, and watch for cheaters.

food and beverage department—The hotel department responsible for preparing and serving food and beverages within the hotel. Also includes catering and room service.

food and beverage manager—Directs the production and service of food and beverages. On a cruise ship, they typically report to the hotel manager.

food cost—The cost of food used in the production of a menu item.

food cost percentage—A financial metric used in the restaurant industry to measure the proportion of a restaurant's revenue that is spent on the cost of ingredients and food items used in menu preparation. It is calculated by dividing the total cost of food by selling price.

food hall—A type of marketplace or large indoor space that features a diverse collection of food vendors, stalls, and eateries in a communal setting. It is a modern take on traditional markets and offers a wide range of culinary options in a single location.

force majeure—Unforeseeable circumstances that prevent someone from fulfilling a contract.

Four P's of Marketing—The four basic marketing responsibilities: product, place, price, and promotion.

franchise—Refers to (1) the authorization given by one company to another to sell its unique product and service, or (2) the name of the business format or product that is being franchised.

Franchise Disclosure Document (FDD)—A prospectus that outlines certain vital aspects of a franchisor and its franchise agreement. By law, the FDD must be given to a potential franchisee before the franchisee signs the franchise agreement. (Formerly known as the Uniform Franchise Offering Circular, or UFOC.)

franchisee—The individual or company granted a franchise.

franchising—A continuing relationship in which the franchisor provides a licensed privilege to do business, plus assistance in organizing, training, merchandising, and managing, in return for a financial consideration from the franchisee.

franchisor—The franchise company that owns the trademark, products, and/or business format that is being franchised.

fraternal clubs—Social organizations or associations that bring together individuals who share common interests, values, or affiliations. These clubs are often founded on principles of brotherhood, friendship, and mutual support among their members.

front office—A hotel's command post for processing reservations, registering guests, settling guest accounts, and checking guests in and out.

front office manager—Responsible for all hotel front desk operations, including managing front desk employees.

full-service restaurant—A restaurant that provides table service; a diverse menu with appetizers, entrées, desserts, and beverages; and a staff of servers to assist customers throughout their meal. Full-service restaurants often have additional amenities such as reservations, private dining, and catering services.

full-time-equivalent (FTE) employee—A measure used by organizations to represent the total number of worked hours of an employee, expressed as a full-time employee's workload. It is a way to quantify the total hours worked by all employees, taking into account both full-time and part-time employees and converting them into an equivalent number of full-time employees. For example, four part-time employees who each work 10 hours per week would, for statistical purposes, be recorded as one FTE employee.

fusion cuisine—A style of cooking in which chefs take ingredients or techniques from more than one cuisine and create new dishes with the results.

galley—The shipboard equivalent of a kitchen.

general manager—The chief operating officer of a hotel or restaurant.

general service contractor (GSC)—An organization that provides event management and exhibitors with a wide range of services, sometimes including but not limited to distributing the exhibitor manual, installation and dismantling, creating and hanging signs and banners, laying carpet, material handling, and providing booth/stand furniture.

golf club—A private establishment or facility where the sport of golf is played, typically featuring an 18-hole golf course, although some may have more or fewer holes.

golf committee—A private country club committee composed of club members who establish golf course policy, review golf course budgets and operations, and oversee the care of the golf course(s).

government and military travelers—Guests on a fixed per diem allowance who typically are reimbursed for hotel and other travel expenses.

grind players—Gamblers who budget a modest amount for gaming and usually leave the casino when that amount is spent. They view gaming as entertainment and their losses as the price of that entertainment.

gross operating profit—Profit calculated by deducting operating costs from total revenue.

gross profit—Selling price minus the cost of food.

guest mix—The variety or mixture of guests who stay at a hotel or patronize a restaurant.

hard costs—The land, building, and furniture, fixture, and equipment (FF&E) costs that are basic to hotel and restaurant development.

high-end players—Gamblers who gamble regularly, are prepared to gamble a large amount of money, and expect to suffer big losses at times. Often called "high rollers" or "high-stakes players," high-end players may bet as much as $500,000 on a single bet.

highway hotels—Hotels built next to a highway. These hotels typically feature large property signs, an entrance where travelers can leave their cars as they check in, and a swimming pool. Parking space is plentiful, and the atmosphere is informal.

hold percentage—A calculation to determine the percentage of chips purchased at a gaming table by customers that is won back by the casino. It is calculated as follows: Win ÷ Drop = Hold.

hospitality—The act of being welcoming, friendly, and generous toward guests or visitors. It involves making people feel comfortable, providing them with what they need, and creating a positive and enjoyable experience for them.

hospitality industry—The hospitality industry encompasses businesses that provide accommodations, dining, and various services designed to offer a welcoming and enjoyable experience for travelers, tourists, and guests.

hotel chain—A group of affiliated hotels.

hotel director—The person on a cruise ship who runs the hotel division. Besides being ultimately responsible for food and beverage services and housekeeping services, the hotel manager may oversee medical care, entertainment, shore excursions, casino operations, the beauty salon, the health spa, gift shops, photography services, and more—in short, everything that helps create the vacation experience that the cruise line offers.

hotel manager—A person in charge of daily hotel operations. Areas of responsibility include the front office, reservations, and housekeeping, as well as such sources of revenue as gift shops and recreational facilities. May be responsible for the food and beverage department as well.

housekeeping department—A department of the rooms department responsible for cleaning the hotel's guestrooms and public areas.

housekeeping manager—Responsible for coordinating the housekeeping staff and making sure they have all the supplies and equipment needed to do the job. This includes hiring, firing, training, scheduling, and budgeting.

human resources department—The hotel department responsible for recruiting, hiring, orienting, training, evaluating, motivating, rewarding, disciplining, developing, promoting, and communicating with hotel employees.

human resources (HR) manager—Responsible for overseeing the management and administration of the HR function within an organization. They play a critical role in attracting, developing, and retaining a qualified workforce while ensuring compliance with employment laws and regulations. They are also in charge of employee relations, which includes counseling employees, developing and administering programs to maintain and improve employee morale, monitoring the work environment, and so on.

incentive fee—That portion of the management fee (paid by hotel owners to hotel management companies) that is based on a percentage of income before fixed charges (also known as gross operating profit) or on a percentage of cash flow after debt service.

incentive trips—Often a combination of meetings and recreation, incentive trips are rewards to customers, retailers, distributors, or employees. Spouses are often invited to attend.

income statement—Also known as a profit and loss (P&L) statement, it summarizes the revenues, expenses, and resulting net income or loss of a restaurant over a specific period. It provides a detailed breakdown of a restaurant's financial performance, specifically its ability to generate profits.

independent hotel—A hotel owned by an individual or group of investors not connected with any hotel company.

information technology (IT) manager—Oversees a hotel's computerized management information systems. May write simple computer programs and instruction manuals for employees.

initial franchise fee—While restaurant franchisors generally charge a flat franchise fee for one unit, hotel franchisors base their initial franchise fee on the number of guestrooms the franchisee builds, with a minimum fee plus an amount per room over a defined minimum number of rooms.

initiation fee—A typically nonrefundable charge that new members must pay to join a private club.

intangible products—The primary products of hospitality-oriented organizations. Intangible products, such as comfort, enjoyment, and pleasant experiences, relate to guests' emotional well-being and expectations. They present very different management and marketing challenges than do tangible products, such as automobiles or boxes of cereal.

integrated marketing communications—A marketing model in which all marketing activities are coordinated, ensuring that all corporate marketing messages are consistent and directed at achieving the organization's overall mission.

job breakdown—The specific, step-by-step procedures for accomplishing each task of a particular job.

job description—A recruiting and training tool that outlines for a particular job (1) the title that goes with the job, (2) the person to whom the employee reports, (3) the work to be performed (in general terms), (4) the education or skills the employee must have, and (5) the physical requirements of the job.

job list—A list of the tasks that must be performed by the individual holding a particular job.

junkets—Partially or completely paid trips to a casino, organized by a casino or gaming representative. Guests generally agree, in advance, to play a certain amount of money over a certain period of time—usually four hours per day.

key cards—Plastic cards, resembling credit cards, that are used in place of metal guestroom keys. Key cards require electronic locks.

leisure travelers—Vacationing travelers, often entire families, who typically spend only one night at a hotel unless the hotel is their destination.

level-capacity strategy—A management strategy in which the same amount of capacity is offered, no matter how high the consumer demand.

liabilities—Obligations of a business, largely indebtedness related to the expenses incurred in the process of generating income.

lido deck—The deck that contains a cruise ship's main swimming pool. It is usually a center for many onboard activities.

lifestyle hotel—While similar to a boutique hotel, a lifestyle hotel generally features contemporary design and décor, provides unique service, and offers high-quality technology.

limited-service restaurant—Also known as quick service or fast-casual restaurants, they provide fast and efficient food service with minimal table service. These restaurants are designed to offer quick meals to customers who are looking for convenience, speed, and affordability.

long-term stay/relocation guests—Individuals or families relocating to an area who require lodging until permanent housing is found.

loss-leaders—Items sold at or below cost in order to attract customers to a business, where they may buy other items that are profitable.

management company—A company that manages hotels for owners, typically in return for a combination of fees and a share of revenues. A management company may or may not have any of its own funds invested in a hotel that it manages.

management contract—A written agreement between the owner of a hotel and a hotel management company whereby the management company assumes the responsibility of operating the hotel and receives a fee for its service.

management meetings—These gatherings include everything from financial reviews to strategic planning sessions. Management meetings make up the largest category in the corporate meetings market.

markers—Printed or written IOUs that extend credit to a player; players can use them rather than cash to buy chips from dealers. Typically, the casino agrees not to cash markers for 30 or 45 days, giving players time to deposit enough money in their bank account to cover their markers.

marketing—A system of interrelated activities formulated to help managers plan, price, promote, and make available services or products to customers and potential customers in a particular target market. The primary goal of marketing is to create awareness, generate interest, and ultimately drive sales or adoption of the offerings.

marketing manager—Develops and implements a marketing plan and budget.

marketing mix—The variety of marketing activities in which a business engages.

meal plan—A package or arrangement offered by hotels that includes meals as part of the guest's stay.

meeting—An event where the primary activity of the participants is to attend educational and/or business sessions, participate in discussions and social functions, or attend other organized events. There is no trade show component.

membership dues—The cost to a private club member for the exclusivity provided by the club's limited membership. Membership dues subsidize all of the club's operating costs and fixed charges.

mid-price hotels—Hotels that offer facilities and services similar to those at first-class/luxury hotels, but at average rates. They have restaurants and bars, and many have meeting space. Average prices vary by market.

military club—A social organization or association that brings together current and former members of the military, as well as their families and supporters.

moments of truth—Critical interactions or touch points between a customer and a company that significantly influence the customer's perception of the brand.

multiplier effect—The hidden or indirect benefits of travel and tourism to a community, measured by adding up all the expenditures of travelers in the community and then multiplying that figure by a factor (known as the multiplier) to arrive at the amount of income that stays in the community and is generated by these expenditures.

networking—A process whereby current employees contact, or are contacted by, friends, classmates, and former associates about a job opening. This can happen online or via other methods of communication.

night audit—An accounting task usually performed between 11 p.m. and 6 a.m. after all a hotel's sales outlets are closed. A night audit (1) verifies that guest charges have been accurately posted to guests' accounts and (2) compares the totals of all accounts with sales reports of operating departments.

nonoperating expenses—Expenses related to the investment in the hotel, such as insurance on the building and contents, interest on the mortgage loan, and property taxes.

occupancy percentage—A measure of how many available rooms in a hotel are occupied by guests over a specific period. It is calculated by dividing the number of rooms occupied by the number of rooms available for a given period.

operating budget—A financial plan that outlines the anticipated income and expenses of an organization or business over a specific period, typically a fiscal year.

operating expenses provision—The provision in a hotel management contract that outlines the expenses the management company will pass on to the hotel's owner.

operating term provision—The provision of a hotel management contract that defines the length of the initial contract and its renewal options.

operator investment provision—The provision of a hotel management contract outlining the details of the operator's investment in the property.

operator-reimbursable expenses—Expenses a hotel management company's corporate office incurs in providing services (e.g., bulk purchasing services and national advertising campaigns) to its managed properties. Each managed property reimburses the management company for its share of these costs.

performance review—A meeting between a manager and an employee to (1) let the employee know how well they have learned to meet company standards, and (2) let the manager know how well they are doing in hiring and training employees. Typically held every 3, 6, or 12 months, depending on the employee's performance and experience.

permanent financing loan—A long-term mortgage loan for a hotel, usually up to 25 years. Long-term mortgage loans are obtained from institutions such as insurance companies, pension funds, and banks.

perpetual inventory system—A system for tracking inventory by keeping a running balance of inventory quantities—that is, recording all additions to and subtractions from stock.

physician—The person on a cruise ship who is responsible for the medical care of passengers and crew members; they typically have a state-of-the-art medical facility in which to work and one or more nurses to assist in the care of patients.

pit—A group of gaming tables within a casino that defines a management section. A pit can be made up of tables featuring the same game or tables featuring a combination of games. For example, there may be four craps tables and four roulette tables in one pit or simply eight craps tables.

pit boss—The manager who oversees a group of gaming tables, called a pit, within a casino.

plowhorses—Popular menu items with a low contribution margin.

post-opening management fees—Fees paid by a hotel owner to a management company for managing the property; they are almost always based on some kind of formula that incorporates a basic fee plus an incentive.

pre-opening management fees—Fees paid by a hotel owner to a management company for work done before the opening of the hotel, including planning, staffing, training, marketing, budgeting, and other activities that the management company must perform before the property is ready to receive guests.

price and sights group—The group of travelers interested in doing the most things for the least amount of money while on vacation.

prime costs—The cost of food sold plus payroll costs (including employee benefits). These are a restaurant's highest costs.

primes—Menu items with a low food cost and a high contribution margin.

productivity standards—Measurements that tell managers how long it should take an employee to complete tasks using the best methods management has devised and how many tasks an employee can perform in a given time period. This measurement differs according to the task the employee is performing.

product launches—Events at which new products are showcased to employees. These meetings are also used to motivate dealers or distributors who are not employees (e.g., introducing new car models to dealers). Product introductions last one to two days on average.

product or trade-name franchise—A supplier–dealer arrangement whereby the dealer (franchisee) sells a product line provided by the supplier (franchisor) and to some degree takes on the identity of the supplier.

professional and technical meetings—Gatherings used to provide information or teach new techniques to employees who work in technical and professional fields. Accountants need to learn about new tax laws and rulings every year, for example.

promotional assistance—Help with advertising, sales, and public relations. It is one of the main strengths a franchisor can offer a franchisee.

property management system (PMS)—A computerized system that helps hotel managers and other personnel carry out a number of front-of-the-house and back-of-the-house functions. A PMS can support a variety of applications software that helps managers in their data-gathering and reporting responsibilities.

property operation and maintenance department—The hotel department responsible for taking care of the hotel's physical plant and controlling energy costs.

psychographic research—Research that attempts to classify people's behavior in terms of their lifestyles and values.

publicity—Mention in the media about an organization's people, products, or services.

public relations (PR)—A systematic effort by a business to communicate favorable information about itself to various internal and external publics in order to create a positive impression.

purchase specification—A detailed description—for ordering purposes—of the quality, size, weight, and other characteristics desired for a particular item.

purchasing department—The hotel department responsible for buying, receiving, storing, and issuing all the products used in the hotel.

purser—The second in command within the hotel department and a cruise ship's banker, information officer, human resources director, and complaint handler.

puzzles—Unpopular menu items with a high contribution margin.

quality controls—Standards of operation, quality assurance programs, and other controls that seek to establish and maintain hotel products and services at quality levels established by management.

quality group—The group of travelers for whom the quality of their vacation is of paramount importance. They want, and are willing to pay for, first-class accommodations and service.

quick service restaurant (QSR)—A restaurant that offers a narrow selection of food, provides limited service, and focuses on speed of preparation and delivery.

real estate investment trust (REIT)—An investment instrument, somewhat like a mutual fund, that allows individuals to combine their resources to invest in income-producing properties or lend funds to developers or builders.

regional getaway guests—Guests who check in to a hotel close to home, with or without children, to enjoy a weekend away from daily responsibilities.

rentals—Enterprises such as offices or stores that pay rent to a hotel.

reporting requirements provision—The provision of a hotel management contract that stipulates the types of reports the management company must provide to the owner and how often they must be submitted.

requisition form—A written order used by employees that identifies the type, amount, and value of items needed from storage.

reservations department—A department within a hotel's rooms department staffed by skilled telemarketing personnel who take reservations over the phone, answer questions about facilities, quote prices and available dates, and sell to callers who are shopping around.

resort hotels—Usually located in desirable vacation spots, resort hotels offer fine dining, exceptional service, and many amenities.

restaurant manager—Oversees the operations of a restaurant, ensuring its efficient functioning and overall success. They are responsible for managing various aspects of the restaurant, including staff supervision, customer service, financial performance, and administrative tasks.

résumé—A concise document that provides a summary of an individual's education, work experience, skills, and qualifications.

revenue centers—Departments or areas within a hotel that directly generate revenue through the sale of products or services to guests. Also known as operated departments.

revenue management—A hotel pricing system adapted from airlines that uses a hotel's computer reservations system to track advance bookings and then lower or raise guestroom prices accordingly—on a day-to-day basis—to yield the maximum revenue. Before selling a room in advance, the hotel forecasts the probability of being able to sell the room to other market segments that are willing to pay higher rates.

revenue manager—Recommends room rate strategies based on demand and market conditions.

revenue per available room (RevPAR)—A statistic used by hotel managers to evaluate the performance of the rooms department. It is computed by dividing room revenue by the number of available rooms for the same period. It also can be determined by multiplying the occupancy percentage by the average daily rate for the same period.

rooms department—The largest, and usually most profitable, department in a hotel. It typically consists of four departments: front office, reservations, housekeeping, and uniformed service.

room service—The department within a food and beverage department that is responsible for delivering food and beverages to guests in their guestrooms. May also be responsible for preparing the food and beverages.

royalty fee—A fee calculated on a percentage of a franchisee's sales.

sales and marketing department—The hotel department responsible for identifying prospective guests for the hotel, conforming the products and services of the hotel as much as possible to meet the needs of those prospects, and persuading prospects to become guests.

sales manager—Conducts sales programs and makes sales calls on prospects for group and individual business. Reports to the marketing manager.

sales meetings—Sales meetings are essential for teaching sales techniques, introducing new products, building morale, and motivating sales personnel.

security department—The hotel department responsible for the protection of guests and their property, employees and their property, and the hotel itself.

segmenting—A method of categorizing hotels by the prices they charge.

select-service hotels—Hotels that do not offer the full range of services customarily associated with hotels. For example, they do not have restaurants or bars. Types of select-service hotels include budget and economy hotels.

seniors housing—Long-term living facilities for older adults that can be broken down into four types: independent-living units, congregate communities, assisted-living communities, and continuing-care retirement communities.

service—The act of providing assistance, help, or support to someone or fulfilling a particular need or request.

shore excursions—Specially arranged trips, tours, and activities that occur off the ship. They are a significant part of onboard revenue for any cruise line.

sitting—The time allotted for serving one complete meal to a group of diners.

slot machines—Also known as fruit machines, pokies, or one-armed bandits. Slot machines are designed to offer games of chance where players bet money on the outcome of a spin or series of spins.

slots drop—The amount of money played through a slot machine.

slots hold—The amount of money that a slot machine does not pay back as wins.

social club—A club where members go to meet each other and enjoy leisurely activities.

social events—Events whose purpose is not business focused and often celebrate such milestones as births, baptisms, bar and bat mitzvahs, birthdays, engagements, weddings, anniversaries, and retirements.

social responsibility—A set of generally accepted relationships, obligations, and duties between the major institutions and the people.

soft brands—Also referred to as collections of independent hotels. Established when independent hotels join a larger parent brand or group while preserving their individual identity and unique characteristics. The independent hotels benefit from the established brand's resources, such as reservations systems, distribution channels, loyalty programs, and marketing support.

soft costs—Development costs other than land, building, and furniture, fixture, and equipment (FF&E) costs for a hotel or restaurant project. Soft costs include architectural fees, pre-opening expenses (e.g., for advertising and employee training), and financing.

special events—A category consisting of private events, public events, fairs and festivals, sporting events, and concerts.

specialty menu—A menu that differs from the typical breakfast, lunch, or dinner menu. Specialty menus are usually designed for holidays and other special events or for specific guest groups. Examples include children's, beverage, dessert, and banquet menus.

sports activities fees—Fees that country clubs charge members and visitors for using the club's recreational facilities.

stakeholder—Anyone who is affected by the outcome of a given decision.

standard recipe—A formula for producing a food or beverage item specifying ingredients, the required quantity of each ingredient, preparation procedures, portion size and portioning equipment, garnish, and any other information necessary to prepare the item.

stars—Popular menu items with high contribution margins.

stockholders meetings—Annual events where owners of company stock meet. They usually last a day, with an average attendance of 95 stockholders or shareholders.

strategic planning—The process of setting goals, defining strategies, and making decisions to guide an organization toward its desired outcomes. It involves systematically analyzing an organization's internal and external environment, assessing its strengths and weaknesses, identifying opportunities and threats, and developing a comprehensive plan of action.

suburban hotels—Hotels located in suburban areas. Suburban hotels typically belong to a major hotel chain and have 250 to 500 rooms, as well as restaurants, bars, and other amenities found at most downtown hotels.

sun and surf group—The group of travelers seeking a vacation spot where there is good weather, guaranteed sunshine, and a beautiful beach.

supplier—Any company that provides facilities, products, or services that the meeting planner needs.

sustainable tourism development—Tourism that has a low impact on a locale's environment and culture and conserves the ecosystem while generating income and employment.

SWOT—An acronym for Strengths, Weaknesses, Opportunities, and Threats. A SWOT analysis helps companies assess how well they are serving their current markets, which is an important step in the strategic planning process.

table drop—The amount of money and markers in a gaming table's drop box that players have exchanged for chips at that table. The table drop is a good measure of gaming activity within a casino.

table games—A category of casino games that are played on a table and typically involve one or more dealers, or croupiers, facilitating the play.

table-service restaurant—A restaurant where customers or guests are seated at tables and served by wait staff.

table win—The amount of a bet at a gaming table minus the amount that is paid back to the players.

take-out—The permanent financing secured for a new hotel.

technical assistance fees—Fees paid by a hotel owner to a management company covering the time and expertise of the company as a consultant in the design and plan of the facilities.

technical skills—A specific set of abilities and knowledge required to perform tasks related to a particular field or profession.

termination provision—A clause that outlines the conditions and terms under which either party (the hotel or the client) can end the contractual agreement before its original expiration date.

third-party meeting planners—Also known as independent meeting planners. These planners are not associated with a company and serve as independent contractors. Third-party meeting planners can work in any area of the industry and can choose what jobs they want to accept. In other parts of the world, they are called professional conference or congress organizers.

timeshare condominiums—Condominiums for which an owner can purchase a portion of time at the condominium, typically one month to one week, for one-twelfth or one-fiftieth of the condominium's price and share the condominium with other owners. Owners have the right to stay at the condominium during their assigned time or to trade their slot with another owner.

ton—A unit for measuring the total cubic capacity of a cruise ship.

tourist courts—The forerunners of motels, built along highways in the 1920s and 1930s. Typical tourist courts consisted of a simple row of small cabins that often had no private baths.

trade show—An exhibition of products and/or services held for members of a common or related industry. Not open to the general public.

training seminars—Training seminars, which rank second in number of meetings held, provide training for employees at all levels.

travel and tourism industry—A collection of organizations and establishments that derives all or a significant portion of its income from providing goods and services to travelers.

turnaround day—The day when a cruise ship finishes one cruise and starts another.

undistributed operating expenses—Expenses such as marketing and energy—costs that relate to the entire hotel and not to one specific department.

uniformed service department—A hotel department within the rooms department that deals with guests' luggage and transportation and provides concierge services. Also referred to as the guest service department.

university club—A private club for university graduates or individuals otherwise affiliated with a university.

utilitarianism—A system of ethics based on the greatest good for the greatest number of people.

visitors' fees—Charges to nonmembers of a private club who are guests of members and use rooms, buy food or beverages, or use recreational facilities.

yacht club—A type of social club that caters to individuals who share a passion for boating, yachting, and maritime activities.

ENDNOTES

CHAPTER 1

1. Danny Myer, *Setting the Table: The Transforming Power of Hospitality in Business* (New York, NY: Harper, 2006), 65.

2. Christopher H. Lovelock, *Services Marketing*, 2nd ed. (Englewood Cliffs, NJ: Prentice-Hall, 1991), 7. The author gratefully acknowledges the concepts formulated by Dr. Lovelock upon which much of the subsequent discussion is based.

3. Ibid., 9

4. "Our Values," Shake Shack, https://shakeshack.com/stand-for-something-good#/.

5. Timothy W. Firnstahl, "My Employees Are My Service Guarantee," *Harvard Business Review*, July–August 1989, 29.

6. Kathleen Cullen and Caryl Helsel, "Defining Revenue Management," HSMAI Foundation Special Report, 2006.

7. James L. Heskett, *Managing in the Service Economy* (Boston: Harvard Business School Press, 1986), 5–25.

8. Ibid., 96–97.

9. Firnstahl, 30.

10. Jan Carlzon, *Moments of Truth* (Cambridge, Mass.: Ballinger, 1987), 21–29.

11. Josh D'Amaro, "A Place Where Everyone Is Welcome," *Disney Parks Blog*, April 13, 2021, https://disneyparks.disney.go.com/blog/2021/04/a-place-where-everyone-is-welcome/.

CHAPTER 2

1. United Nations, "Growing at a Slower Pace, World Population Is Expected to Reach 9.7 Billion in 2050 and Could Peak at Nearly 11 Billion Around 2100," June 17, 2019, https://www.un.org/development/desa/en/news/population/world-population-prospects-2019.html.

2. Alison Fox, "This Is What Paid Vacation Looks Like Outside of the U.S.," *Travel and Leisure*, November 23, 2019, https://www.travelandleisure.com/trip-ideas/yoga-wellness/guaranteed-paid-vacation-time-outside-the-us.

3. "Impact Assessment of the COVID-19 Outbreak on International Tourism," UNWTO (website), https://www.unwto.org/impact-assessment-of-the-covid-19-outbreak-on-international-tourism.

4. Somerset R. Waters, *Travel Industry World Yearbook: The Big Picture—1998* (Rye, NY: Child and Waters, 1998).

5. Andrew Vladimir, *The Complete Travel Marketing Handbook* (Chicago: NTC Business Books, 1988), 5.

6. "Impact Assessment of the COVID-19 Outbreak."

7. Daniel Goleman, "Head Trips," *American Health*, April 1988, 58.

8. Ibid.

9. MMGY Travel Intelligence LLC, *2022 Portrait of American Travelers*.

10. Pierre L. van den Berghe, "Cultural Impact of Tourism," *VNR's Encyclopedia of Hospitality and Tourism* (New York: Van Nostrand Reinhold, 1993), 627.

11. "Sustainable Development," UNWTO (website), https://www.unwto.org/sustainable-development.

12. "What Is Ecotourism?," International Ecotourism Society (website), https://ecotourism.org/what-is-ecotourism/.

13. Arenas del Mar Beachfront & Rainforest Resort, https://www.arenasdelmar.com.

CHAPTER 3

1. Jordan Hollander, "75+ Hospitality Statistics You Should Know," *Hotel Tech Report*, May 17, 2023, https://hoteltechreport.com/news/hospitality-statistics.

2. American Hotel & Lodging Association, *AHLA's State of the Hotel Industry 2021*, January 21, 2021, https://www.ahla.com/sites/default/files/2021_state_of_the_industry_0.pdf.

3. National Restaurant Association, *2023 State of the Restaurant Industry*, March 2023.

4. National Restaurant Association, *Restaurant Employee Demographics* (Data Brief), March 2022, https://restaurant.org/getmedia/21a36a65-d5d4-41d0-af5c-737ab545d65a/nra-data-brief-restaurant-employee-demographics-march-2022.pdf.

5. Tim McDonald, "Humanics: A Way to 'Robot-Proof' Your Career?," BBC, January 27, 2019, https://www.bbc.com/worklife/article/20190127-humanics-a-way-to-robot-proof-your-career.

6. Eric Amel et al., "Independent Restaurants ... Economic Activity That Is at Risk ... Due to the COVID-19 Pandemic," getbento.com, https://media-cdn.getbento.com/accounts/cf190ba55959ba5052ae23ba6d98e6de/media/EmH1JsVMRNylmKAeF2FJ_Report.pdf.

7. Joshua Kurlantzick, "Growing Your Business Your Way," *Entrepreneur*, November 1, 2003, https://www.entrepreneur.com/article/65008.

8. Dahlia Snaiderman, "What Is the Average Restaurant Revenue for a New Restaurant?," *Toast*, https://pos.toasttab.com/blog/on-the-line/average-restaurant-revenue.

9. U.S. Small Business Administration, "10 Steps to Start Your Business," May 3, 2023, https://www.sba.gov/content/follow-these-steps-starting-business.

10. Vincent Onyemah, Martha Rivera Pesquera, and Abdul Ali, "What Entrepreneurs Get Wrong," *Harvard Business Review*, May 2013 (91:5), 74–79.

CHAPTER 4

1. National Restaurant Association, https://restaurant.org.

2. Eric Amel et al., "Independent Restaurants ... Economic Activity That Is at Risk ... Due to the COVID-19 Pandemic," getbento.com, https://media-cdn.getbento.com/accounts/cf190ba55959ba5052ae23ba6d98e6de/media/EmH1JsVMRNylmKAeF2FJ_Report.pdf.

3. Sky Ariella, "45+ Must-Know US Restaurant Industry Statistics [2023]: How Many Restaurants Are in the U.S.," July 3, 2023, *Zippia Inc.*, https://www.zippia.com/advice/restaurant-industry-statistics/.

4. National Restaurant Association, *Restaurant Employee Demographics* (Data Brief), March 2022, https://restaurant.org/getmedia/21a36a65-d5d4-41d0-af5c-737ab545d65a/nra-data-brief-restaurant-employee-demographics-march-2022.pdf.

5. Business Wire, "Fast Casual Restaurants Market in the US to Grow by $150.10 Billion in 2020 ...," November 3, 2020, https://www.businesswire.com/news/home/20201103005389/en/Fast-Casual-

Restaurants-Market-in-the-US-to-Grow-by-150.10-Billion-in-2020-Chipotle-Mexican-Grill-Inc.-Firehouse-Restaurant-Group-Inc.-Godfathers-Pizza-Inc.-and-YUM%21-Brands-Inc.-Emerge-as-Key-Contributors-to-Growth-Technavio.

6. National Restaurant Association, *2022 State of the Restaurant Industry*, February 2022.

7. Michael Roman, "Catering From a Chef's Point of View," *Roman's Opinion*, November 29, 2012, https://romansopinion.blogspot.com/2012/11/catering-from-chefs-point-of-view.html.

8. National Restaurant Association, https://restaurant.org.

9. Mary Scoviak-Lerner, "Great Hotel Restaurants," *Hotels*, August 2000.

10. Emma Liem Beckett, "Ghost Kitchens Could Be a $1T Global Market by 2030, Says Euromonitor," *Restaurant Dive*, July 10, 2020, https://www.restaurantdive.com/news/ghost-kitchens-global-market-euromonitor/581374/.

11. Alicia Kelso, "How the Pandemic Accelerated the US Ghost Kitchen Market '5 Years in 3 Months'," *Restaurant Dive*, October 5, 2020, https://www.restaurantdive.com/news/how-the-pandemic-accelerated-the-us-ghost-kitchen-market-5-years-in-3-mont/585604/.

12. Caroline Price. "What Is the Restaurant Failure Rate?," *Toast*, https://pos.toasttab.com/blog/on-the-line/restaurant-failure-rate.

13. Jeremy Repanich, "More Than 70,000 Restaurants Closed Because of the Pandemic, a New Report Estimates," *Robb Report*, June 27, 2022, https://robbreport.com/lifestyle/news/how-many-restaurants-closed-pandemic-1234694652/.

14. *Wall Street Journal*, August 14, 2000.

15. Ron Zemke and Dick Schaaf, *The Service Edge* (New York: New American Library), 297.

16. Deborah Silver, "Site Seeing," *Restaurants & Institutions*, January 15, 2000.

17. Available annually at https://www.bls.gov/cex/.

CHAPTER 5

1. Karl Albrecht and Ron Zemke, *Service America* (Homewood, IL: Dow Jones-Irwin, 1985), 49.

2. National Restaurant Association, *2022 State of the Restaurant Industry*, February 2022.

3. Ibid.

4. Ilaria Urbinati, "Ken Fulk on Maximalism & the Art of Entertaining," *Leo*, December 8, 2021, para. 1, https://www.leoedit.com/lifestyle/ken-fulk-on-creating-a-space-for-entertaining/.

5. Erika Adams, "Chef Thomas Keller on Creating Destination Restaurants," *Skift Table*, September 27, 2018, para. 14, https://table.skift.com/2018/09/27/chef-thomas-keller-on-creating-a-sense-of-place-in-restaurants/.

6. *Nation's Restaurant News*, April 11, 2005, and *Nation's Restaurant News*, August 15, 2005.

7. National Restaurant Association, *2022 State of the Restaurant Industry*, February 2022.

8. Ibid.

9. National Restaurant Association, *2020 Restaurant Industry Forecast*.

10. Michael L. Kasavana and Donald I. Smith, *Menu Engineering* (Okemos, MI: Hospitality Publications, 1982).

11. Mohamed E. Bayou and Lee B. Bennett, "Profitability Analysis for Table-Service Restaurants," *Cornell Quarterly*, April 1992, 50

12. Ibid.

13. Ibid., 55.

14. Stephen G. Miller, "The Simplified Menu-Cost Spreadsheet," *Cornell Quarterly*, June 1992, 85.

15. Lendal H. Kotschevar, *Management by Menu*, 2nd ed. (Chicago: National Institute for the Foodservice Industry/William C. Brown, 1987), 261.

CHAPTER 6

1. "Mission and Vision," U.S. Green Building Council, https://www.usgbc.org/about/mission-vision.

2. "In the LEED," *Lodging*, February 2009, 34.

3. Information provided by STR, September 2015.

4. Albert J. Gomes, *Hospitality in Transition* (Houston, TX: Pannell Kerr Forster, 1985), 32–34. Although the hotel industry has been through many changes since Gomes's book was published, the industry's guest markets can still be categorized as described in the following sections.

5. "Business Travelers: Hotel Location Matters Most," *USA Today*, April 27, 2014.

6. MBO Partners, *State of Independence in America 2020 Report*, https://www.mbopartners.com/state-of-independence/soi-2020/.

7. Donald E. Lundberg, *The Hotel and Restaurant Business*, 5th ed. (New York: Van Nostrand Reinhold, 1989), 185.

8. Club Med, https://www.clubmed.co.nz/l/your-happy-place.

9. "Conference Centers," *The Convention Liaison Council Manual*, 6th ed. (Washington, D.C.: Convention Liaison Council, 1994), 17.

10. Penn, Schoen & Berland Associates, *AIF Vacation Timeshare Owners Report*, https://www.arda.org/.

11. Steve Rushmore, "What Is a Condo-Hotel?," *Hotels*, November 2004.

12. Binu, "People Who Use Airbnb Don't Want to Go Back to Hotels," *Vafion* (blog), www.vafion.com/blog/more-people-who-use-airbnb-dont-want-to-go-back-to-hotels-says-goldmansachs-survey/.

CHAPTER 7

1. For more details, see the *Uniform System of Accounts for the Lodging Industry*, 12th revised ed. (New York: Hotel Association of New York City, 2023). The *USALI* is discussed in greater detail later in the chapter, in the section on financial controls.

2. STR, *2023 Global Hotel Profitability Review (2022 Data)*, 2023.

3. Robert Mandelbaum, "Trends in Rooms Department Costs: A Study in Fixed and Variable Expenses," *Lodging*, December 21, 2021, https://lodgingmagazine.com/trends-in-rooms-department-costs-a-study-in-fixed-and-variable-expenses/.

4. Titles for front desk employees vary within the industry. Hotels may refer to their front desk employees as front desk agents, front desk representatives, front desk clerks, guest service representatives, front office agents, or something similar.

5. Eric B. Orkin, Yield Management Conference, March 26–27, 1992, Dallas, Texas.

6. The housekeeping department, from an executive housekeeper's perspective, is the subject of Aleta A. Nitschke and William D. Frye's *Managing Housekeeping Operations*, revised 3rd ed. (Lansing, MI: American Hotel & Lodging Educational Institute, 2008).

7. For students desiring a good introductory text to food and beverage operations, see Jack D. Ninemeier, *Management of Food and Beverage Operations*, 6th ed. (Lansing, MI: American Hotel & Lodging Educational Institute, 2016).

8. PKF Hospitality Research, *Trends in the Hotel Industry, USA Edition, 2015*.

9. Legal ramifications of hotel security are covered in Jack P. Jefferies and Banks Brown, *Understanding Hospitality Law*, 5th ed. (Lansing, MI: American Hotel & Lodging Educational Institute, 2010). The security responsibilities of hotel managers and hotel security programs are the subject of David M. Stipanuk and Raymond C. Ellis, Jr.'s *Security and Loss Prevention Management*, 3rd ed. (Lansing, MI: American Hotel & Lodging Educational Institute, 2013).

10. Peter E. Drucker, *Management: Tasks, Responsibilities, Practices* (New York: Harper & Row, 1974), 61.

11. For more information on the responsibilities of the hotel engineer and the hotel's property operation and maintenance department, see David M. Stipanuk, *Hospitality Facilities Management and Design*, 4th ed. (Lansing, MI: American Hotel & Lodging Educational Institute, 2015).

12. PKF Hospitality Research, *Trends in the Hotel Industry, USA Edition, 2009*.

13. Much of the following information appeared in John P.S. Salmen, "The ADA and You," *Lodging*, November 1991, 97–107.

14. Judy Z. King, Sixth Annual AH&LA National Conference for Quality, San Francisco, July 7–9, 1993.

15. For this section on hotel technology, the author relied on *An Introduction to Hotel Systems*, 2nd ed. (Lansing, MI: American Hotel & Lodging Educational Institute, 2006), and information provided by technology consultant Jules Sieburgh.

CHAPTER 8

1. National Club Association, *Club Industry Trends and Economic Outlook*, 2009.

2. Bermuda Department of Tourism.

3. Stephen Birmingham, *America's Secret Aristocracy* (New York: Berkley Books, 1990), 209.

4. Ibid., 213.

5. National Club Association and McMahon Group, *Club Trends*, 2, no. 1 (Winter 2015).

6. David Litwak, "The Rise of Soho House Part I: Highly Public Exclusivity and The New Aristocrats," *Café Society*, June 30, 2021, https://cafesociety.maxwellsocial.com/p/the-rise-of-soho-house-part-i-highly.

7. Ted E. White and Larry C. Gerstner, *Club Operations and Management*, 2nd ed. (New York: Van Nostrand Reinhold, 1991).

8. "Competency Areas," Club Management Association of America, https://www.cmaa.org/learn/competency-areas/#:~:text=Personal%20strategic%20plan%3B%20self%2Dimprovement,motivation%3B%20collaborative%3B%20philanthropic%3B%20empathetic.

9. Ibid., 32.

10. GGA Partners, *A Club Leader's Perspective: Emerging Trends & Challenges*, 2021.

11. Kevin F. Reilly, *Clubs in Town & Country*, North American Edition, 2015 (Fairfax, Virginia: PBMares, LLP, 2009), 4, 13.

12. Ibid., 6.

13. The *Uniform System of Financial Reporting for Clubs*, Seventh Revised Edition, was published in 2013 by the Club Managers Association of America and Hospitality Financial and Technology Professionals (HFTP), the international society for financial and technology professionals in the hospitality industry.

14. Tanya Venegas, Jessica Howton, and Jackie Abrams, "Club Technology Resource Needs: What Clubs Want to Know," NCA-HFTP Technology Task Force, 2011, https://www.hftp.org/i/downloads/Resources_IT_Best_Practice_Club_Tech_resource.pdf.

15. Scott Kauffman, "Private Club Waitlists Are at an All-Time High," *Golf Inc.*, December 2, 2021, https://golfincmagazine.com/content/private-club-waitlists-are-all-time-high/.

16. Frank Vain, "What's Next for Private Clubs?" (CMAA Golden State Chapter Webinar, July 21, 2022), https://mcmahongroup.com/whats-next-for-private-clubs-cmaa-golden-state-chapter-webinar/.

CHAPTER 9

1. "About Us," Events Industry Council, https://eventscouncil.org.

2. Events Industry Council Industry Glossary, s.v. "Event," https://insights.eventscouncil.org/Industry-glossary/Glossary-Details/PID/405/mcat/403/EDNSearch/E.

3. Events Industry Council Industry Glossary, s.v. "Meeting," https://insights.eventscouncil.org/Industry-glossary/Glossary-Details/PID/405/mcat/403/EDNSearch/M.

4. A full list of Events Industry Council members can be found here: https://eventscouncil.org/EIC-Members/Association-Members.

5. Kalibri Labs, *U.S. Groups & Meetings: The Economics and Complexity of Intermediation*, 2018, https://22486350.fs1.hubspotusercontent-na1.net/hubfs/22486350/US%20Groups%20%26%20Meetings.pdf.

6. Meeting Professionals International, *Meeting and Business Event Competency Standards Curriculum Guide, (MBECS)*, 2012, https://www.mpi.org/docs/default-source/Research-and-Reports/MBECS-Guide-APP-2-Standards.pdf.

CHAPTER 10

1. Cruise Lines International Association, *The Economic Contribution of the International Cruise Industry Globally in 2019*, 2020, chrome-extension://efaidnbmnnnibpcajpcglclefindmkaj/https://europe.cruising.org/wp-content/uploads/2021/08/Global-Cruise-Impact-Analysis-2020-V1.0-1.pdf.

2. Cruise Lines International Association, *2022 State of the Cruise Industry Outlook*, https://cruising.org/-/media/clia-media/research/2022/clia-state-of-the-cruise-industry-2022_updated.ashx.

3. Ibid.

4. Ibid.

5. Cruise Lines International Association, *2021 State of the Cruise Industry Outlook*, https://cruising.org/-/media/research-updates/research/2021-state-of-the-cruise-industry_optimized.ashx.

6. Much of the information cited in this chapter was originally researched and developed by Bob Dickinson and Andy Vladimir for *Selling the Sea: An Inside Look at the Cruise Industry* (New York: Wiley, 1997).

7. John Maxtone-Graham, *The Only Way to Cross* (New York: Macmillan, 1972), 112–113.

8. Cruise Lines International Association, *2022 State of the Cruise Industry Outlook*.

9. Dickinson and Vladimir, 88–92.

10. Cruise Lines International Association, *2021 State of the Cruise Industry Outlook*.

CHAPTER 11

1. Worldwide Casinos, Horse Tracks and Other Gaming," Casino City, https://www.casinocity.com/casinos.

2. "Caesars Properties," Caesars Entertainment, https://investor.caesars.com/caesars-properties.

3. Resorts World Las Vegas, https://www.rwlasvegas.com.

4. Chi Chuen Chan, William Wai Lim Li, and Eugene Chung Ip Leung, "The History and Development of Casino Gaming in Macau," in *Problem Gambling in Hong Kong and Macao*, (Springer, 2016).

5. "Take Cashless for a Spin with Play+," Resorts World Las Vegas, https://www.rwlasvegas.com/gaming/playplus/.

6. Center for Gaming Research, *Nevada Gaming Win 2022*, https://gaming.library.unlv.edu/reports/2022 NevadaGamingWin_oar.pdf.

7. Nevada Gaming Control Board, *Annual Nevada Gaming Abstract*, 2012–2021, https://gaming.nv.gov/index.aspx?page=144.

8. Deborah Silver, "Lion's Share," *Restaurants & Institutions*, May 1, 2000.

9. DeMarco Williams, "How MGM Resorts Has Become the Face of Eco-Friendly Elegance," *Forbes*, February 28, 2020.

10. Rebecca Trounson, "Big Spender Not Sweating Fat Vegas Loss," *Miami Herald*, October 2, 2000.

CHAPTER 12

1. Frederick W. Taylor, "A Piece Rate System," *Scientific Management: A Collection of the More Significant Articles Describing the Taylor System of Management*, edited by Clarence Bertrand Thompson (Cambridge, MA: Harvard University Press, 1914), 637.

2. Peter F. Drucker, *Management: Tasks, Responsibilities, Practices* (New York: Harper & Row, 1974), 398.

3. Ibid., 399.

4. Ibid., 400–401.

5. Ibid., 402.

6. Robert O'Brien, *Marriott: The J. Willard Marriott Story* (Salt Lake City: Deseret, 1987), 265.

7. G. Northouse, *Leadership: Theory and Practice*, 7th ed. (Thousand Oaks, CA: Sage Publications, 2015), 6.

8. Warren Bennis and Burt Nanus, *LEADERS: The Strategies for Taking Charge* (New York: Harper & Row, Perennial Library Edition, 1986), 21. All anecdotes in this section are from Bennis and Nanus.

9. Ibid., 33.

10. Ibid., 56.

11. Ibid., 60.

12. Ibid., 64.

13. U.S. Bureau of Labor Statistics, "Projections Overview and Highlights, 2020–30," in *Monthly Labor Review*, October 2021, https://www.bls.gov/opub/mlr/2021/article/projections-overview-and-highlights-2020-30.htm.

14. From a letter by Edward H. Rensi, president, McDonald's U.S.A., printed as an introduction to *Ingredients for Success: Food for Thought on Finding Your First Job,* produced in conjunction with the American School Counselor Association.

15. Ron Zemke and Dick Schaaf, *The Service Edge: 101 Companies That Profit from Customer Care* (New York: New American Library, 1989), 72.

16. J. W. McLean, *So You Want to Be the Boss? A CEO's Lessons in Leadership* (Englewood Cliffs, NJ: Prentice-Hall, 1990), 44.

17. "The Digital Marketer," *Hotels Magazine*, January/February 2015, 24–25, https://library.hotelsmag.com/publication/?m=18711&i=242800&p=28&ver=html5.

18. Theodore Levitt, *The Marketing Imagination* (New York: Macmillan, 1983), xii–xiii.

19. "Marriott Discovers Crowdsourcing Is the Key to Welcoming Millennials," MGD, MGD Solutions, https://www.mdgsolutions.com/learn-about-multi-location-marketing/marriott-discovers-crowdsourcing-is-the-key-to-welcoming-millennials/.

20. Richard Weiner, *Webster's New World Dictionary of Media and Communications* (New York: Simon & Schuster, 1990), 381.

CHAPTER 13

1. "McDonald's: Number of Restaurants Globally (2005–2021)," GlobalData, https://www.globaldata.com/data-insights/foodservice/mcdonalds-number-of-restaurants-globally/.

2. "Franchise Opportunities," Wyndham Hotels & Resorts, https://development.wyndhamhotels.com.

3. N. G. L. Hammond and H. H. Scullard, eds., *The Oxford Classical Dictionary* (Oxford, England: Clarendon Press, 1979), 613, 898–899.

4. Charles L. Vaughn, *Franchising* (Lexington, MA: Lexington Books, 1974), 11.

5. Hammond and Scullard, 15–17.

6. Ray Kroc and Robert Anderson, *Grinding It Out: The Making of McDonald's* (New York: Berkeley Books, 1978), 71.

7. Ibid., 72–73.

8. Ibid., 86.

9. U.S. Federal Trade Commission Legal Library, "Franchise Rule: 16 CFR Parts 436 and 437," https://www.ftc.gov/legal-library/browse/rules/franchise-rule.

10. Kroc and Anderson, 173–174.

CHAPTER 14

1. Charles A. Bell, "Agreements with Chain-Hotel Companies," *Cornell Quarterly*, February 1993, 28.

2. James J. Eyster, "Hotel Management Contracts in the U.S.," *Cornell Quarterly*, June 1997, 14.

3. These provisions and some of the comments about them are adapted from Stephen Rushmore, "Make Sure Management Contracts Contain These Terms," *Lodging Hospitality*, April 1988. The author also wishes to acknowledge his debt to Professor James J. Eyster. Many of the observations and comments relating to these provisions are based on Eyster and de Roos's *The Negotiation and Administration of Hotel and Restaurant Management Contracts*.

4. James J. Eyster and Jan A. de Roos, *The Negotiation and Administration of Hotel Management Contracts*, 4th ed. (Pearson, 2009).

5. Hans Detlefsen and Matt Glodz, "Hotel Management Contracts: Historical Trends," HVS, January 2013.

6. Ibid.

7. Telephone interview with Jay Litt, principal, LittKM Group, an ownership and asset management company.

8. Eyster, "Hotel Management Contracts in the U.S.," 15.

9. Ibid., 33.

10. Stephen Rushmore, "Performance Clauses Essential in Contract," *Hotels*, November 2002, 36.

11. Ibid.

12. Eyster, *Negotiation and Administration*.

13. Eyster, "Hotel Management Contracts in the U.S.," 22.

14. Eyster and de Roos.

15. Cecelia L. Fanelli and Jonathan D. Twombly, "Four Seasons Aviara Case: Using an Arbitration Clause," *Hotels*, June 3, 2009.

CHAPTER 15

1. John Godfrey Saxe, *The Blind Men and the Elephant* (New York: McGraw-Hill, 1963).

2. George A. Steiner, "Social Policies for Business," *California Management Review*, Winter 1972, 17–24, cited by Donald P. Robin and Eric Reidenbach in "Social Responsibility, Ethics, and Marketing Strategy: Closing the Gap Between Concept and Application," *Journal of Marketing*, January 1987, 45.

3. A Ponzi scheme is an investment scam in which individuals are enticed by a fraudster or fraudsters to make "investments" in a financial venture that promises an unusually consistent and/or unreasonably high rate of return. Money from later investors is used to pay earlier investors, giving the illusion of profitability and encouraging both current and new "investors" to contribute more money to the scheme. The scheme does little or no legitimate business; it just recycles money from its investors and depends on a constant stream of new investors to fund the payouts to earlier investors and line the pockets of the fraudster(s). Ultimately, a Ponzi scheme will collapse when there are no more new investors to supply new money for the older investors, or when an economic downturn leads a large number of investors to demand their money back. The fraudster(s) will face multiple criminal charges when caught. This method of financial fraud is named after U.S. swindler Charles Ponzi, who ran an investment scheme in 1919–20, but the method predates him.

4. Adapted from Hunter Lewis, *A Question of Values* (New York: Harper & Row, 1990), 10–11.

5. Ibid., 16–17.

6. Alfred Carr, "Is Business Bluffing Ethical?," *Harvard Business Review*, January/February 1968, cited by Robert C. Solomon and Kristine R. Hanson in *It's Good Business* (New York: Atheneum, 1985), 91.

7. Solomon and Hanson, 90–93.

8. Sissela Bok, *Lying: Moral Choice in Public and Private Life* (New York: Random House, 1979), 20.

9. Bill Moyers, "Ethical Dilemmas," *New Age Journal*, July/August 1989, 45.

10. Ibid. The phrase Josephson refers to appears in the New Testament: "Therefore all things whatsoever ye would that men should do to you, do ye even so to them: for this is the law and the prophets" (Matthew 7:12, King James Version).

11. Ambassador Max Kampelman, speaking at Florida International University's graduation ceremony, May 3, 1993, Miami, Florida.

12. Moyers, 97.

13. Ibid.

14. Ibid.

15. Robin and Reidenbach, 46.

16. Ibid.

17. Ibid., 47.

18. Adapted from Raymond S. Schmidgall, "Hotel Scruples," *Lodging*, January 1991, 38–40.

19. Zorana Ivcevic, Jochen I. Menges, and Anna Miller, "How Common Is Unethical Behavior in U.S. Organizations?," *Harvard Business Review*, https://hbr.org/2020/03/how-common-is-unethical-behavior-in-u-s-organizations.

20. Linda K. Enghagen, "Ethics in Hospitality/Tourism Education: A Survey," supplied by the author. Professor Enghagen has been most helpful in the formulation of some of the ideas presented here.

21. Starbucks, *Starbucks Fiscal 2022 Global Environmental & Social Impact Report*, 2023, https://stories.starbucks.com/uploads/2023/06/Starbucks-2022-Global-Environmental-and-Social-Impact-Report.pdf.

22. "IHG Green Engage Hotels," IHG Hotels & Resorts, https://www.ihg.com/content/us/en/support/green-engage-hotels.

23. Jeff Hale, "We'll Leave the Lights On for You? Not Any More," *The (Toronto) Globe and Mail*, April 20, 2007, B8.

24. Nancy Loman Scanlon, "Sustainability," *Hotel Business*, February 7–20, 2010.

25. Hilton Supply Management, *Supplier Diversity 2022 Annual Report*, https://www.mysupplymanagement.com/media/tnnlywfr/2022supplierdiversityannualreport.pdf.

26. Arthur J. Hamilton and Peter A. Veglahn, "Sexual Harassment: The Hostile Work Environment," *Cornell Quarterly*, April 1992, 88.

27. Ibid.

28. Ibid., 90.

29. Gary Langer, "Business Ethics," *travel COUNSELOR*, June 1996, 19.

30. Marj Charlier, "Resort Ads Caught Snowing the Ski Set," *Wall Street Journal*, December 22, 1992, B-1.

31. Ibid.

32. Cheryl-Anne Sturken, "What's Your Ethics IQ?" *Meetings & Conventions*, August 1997, 50.

33. Study by *Personnel Journal*, November 1987, cited in "Survey: Middle Managers Most Likely to Be Unethical," *Marketing News*, November 6, 1987, 6.

34. Ibid.

35. Ivcevic, Menges, and Miller.

36. Langer, 19.

37. Marriott International's entire Business Conduct Guide can be found on the company's website: https://www.marriott.com/Multimedia/PDF/CorporateResponsibility/Marriott_Business_Conduct_Guide_English.pdf.

38. Ken Blanchard and Norman Vincent Peale, *The Power of Ethical Management* (New York: Morrow, 1988), 27.

INDEX

Page entries indicating figures are in italics.

suburban, 154–155
sustainability, 146
technology, 145–146
trends, 144–145
utilities, 208. *see also* food
and beverage department;
gaming and casino hotels;
guests and guestrooms;
housekeeping department;
reservations department;
rooms department;
uniformed service
department
Housekeeping department, 59, 72,
191–192, *192*, 222
Howard Johnson, 379–381
Human literacy, 55
Human resources department, 59,
72, 204, 222
Human resources (HR) managers,
59, 72, 302, 307
Human trafficking, 422
Humphrey, Rachel, 440

I

Icon of the Seas (ship), 288
Illegal Immigration Reform and
Immigrant Responsibility Act of
1996, 347
Incentive fee, 400, 408
Incentive trips, 264, 278
Inclusion, 19. *see also* disabilities;
mobility
Income statement, 121, *122*, 135
Independent hotels, 156,
158–159, 175
Independent restaurants, 60–61
Independent-living units, 165
Indian Gaming Regulatory Act
(IGRA), 318
Indigenous people. *see* BIPOC (Black,
Indigenous, and People of Color)
Industry recruiters, 69
Information and
telecommunications systems
department, 205
Information technology (IT)
managers, 59, 72
Initial franchise fee, 381, 390
Initiation fees, 245, 251
Instagram, 69, 274

Intangible products, 7, 22
Integrated marketing
communications, 361, 366
Intellectual property rights, 422
InterContinental Hotels Group, 400
Internet of Things (IoT), 30
Inventory, 130, 132, 135
Ismay, Bruce, 290
It's Good Business (Solomon and
Hanson), 419

J

Job
analysis, 348
breakdown, 348–349, 366
description, 349, *351*, 366
list, 348, *350*, 366
restructuring, 16
skills inventory, 55
Joseph and Edna Josephson
Institute for the Advancement of
Ethics, 420
Josephson, Michael, 420
Junkets, 329, 332

K

Kant, Immanuel, 421
Key cards, 222
Key performance indicators (KPIs),
193–194
King, Judy Z., 216
Komodo, 76, 83
Kozlowski, Dennis, 418
Kroc, Ray, 111, 380–381
Kuk, Alex, 138

L

Labor, 345–347
Labor practices, 422
Leadership, 11, 341–345
Leadership: Theory and Practice
(Northouse), 342–343
LEED certification program, 146
Legal holidays, 30
Leisure time, 30
Leisure travelers, 148, 175
Level-capacity strategy, 12, 22

Lewis, Hunter, 418
Liabilities, 210, *214*, 222
Lido deck, 299, 307
Lifestyle hotel, 162, 175
Limited-service restaurants,
53, 80, 101
LinkedIn, 69–70, 274
Lockdowns. *see* COVID-19
pandemic
Lodging, 52–53, 57–60, 120–121.
see also hotels
Long-term stay/relocation guests,
149, 175
Loss-leaders, 360, 366
Love Boat Access Program, 303
Lovelock, Christopher H., 7, 9
Low-end players, 329–330
Luxury hotels, 57, 161, 174
Luxury restaurants, 82–83
*Lying: Moral Choice in Public and
Private Life* (Bok), 419

M

Madoff, Bernard, 417–418
Managed foodservice companies,
62–63
Management company, 156, 175
Management contract, 400, 408
Management meetings,
263–264, 278
Management training
programs, 354
Managers
asset, 404, 408
banquet or catering, 58, 72,
199, 269
casino, 323, 327, 328
classical school of
management, 340
club, 240–243
controllers, 58–59, 72, 200–201,
203, 295
convention services managers
(CSMs), 268, 278
encouraging employees to act
like, 17–18
executive housekeepers, 192
food and beverage, 58, 72,
296–300, 307
foodservice, 64–65
front office, 59, 72

Operating term provision, 402–403, 408
Operational controls, 119–130
Operator investment provision, 405, 408
Operator-reimbursable expenses, 403, 408
Orkin, Eric, 191
Outback Steakhouse, 82, 97

P

Packer, Kerry, 328
Panera Bread, 86
Payroll control, 16
People of color. *see* BIPOC (Black, Indigenous, and People of Color)
People's Express, 17
Performance reviews, 357, 366
Permanent financing loans, 171, 175
Perpetual inventory systems, 130, 133, 297
Pit, 326, 332
Pit boss, 326, 332
Place, 359
Planned-community associations, 233
Population, 30, *31*, 345
Post-opening management fees, 403, 408
Pregnancy discrimination, 428
Pre-opening management fees, 403, 408
Price, 13, 37, 43, 82–83, 359–360
Privacy and data protection, 422
PRIZM, 98
Product, 359
Product launches, 264, 278
Product or trade-name franchise, 376, 378–379, 390
Productivity standards, 352, 367
Professional and technical meetings, 264, 278
Profit and loss (P&L) statement. *see* income statement
Profitability analysis, *125*
Promotion, 361

Promotional assistance, 385–386, 390
Property management system (PMS), 189–190, 223
Property operation and maintenance department, 207–208, *208*, 223
Psychographic research, 37, 43
Public relations (PR), 362–363
Publicity, 363, 367
Purchase specification, 127
Purchasing department, 125–127, *126*, 200, 223
Purser, 295, 307

Q

Quaker City (ship), 288–289
Quality controls, 210–217, 223
Quality group, 37, 43
Quantum of the Seas (ship), 88
Queen Mary (ship), 290–291
Quick service restaurants (QSR), 86–87, 101

R

Racism and racial discrimination, 109, 428, 429
Radio-frequency identification (RFID), 327
Real estate investment trust (REIT), 402, 408
Receiving, 127
Recipes, 113, *114*
Recreation, 32, 36
Recreation and sports venues, 64
Recruiting and hiring, 18–19
Regional getaway guests, 150, 175
Registration, 145, 189–190
Religious discrimination, 428
Rentals, 201, 223
Reporting requirements provision, 404, 408
Reservations department, 190–191, 223, 423
Resort conference centers, 163
Resort hotels, 57, 175

Resorts World Las Vegas, 320
Responsible tourism, 422
Restaurants
    accounting systems, 120–121
    affordability, 97
    ambience, 111–112, 135
    atmosphere, 83
    balance sheet, 121, 135
    bar's par, 130, 135
    blind receiving, 127, 135
    budgeting, 121–123, 135
    capital investment budget, 98
    cash flow statement, 121, 135
    casual dining, 83–85, 101
    chain, 61–62
    chatbots, 99
    concept, 95–96
    contribution margin, 135
    controlling costs, 130–131
    corrections foodservice, 90
    cuisine, 82, 101
    customer payment, 129
    direct purchase, 128, 135
    education market, 89
    environmentally conscious, 427–428
    failure, 94
    family dining, 85–86, 101
    fast-casual, 61, 86, 101
    feasibility studies, 97–98
    financial controls, 120–121, 135, 210, 222
    fine dining, 60–61, 80, 101
    food costs, 123, *123*, 129–130, 135
    food service, 128–129
    food storage, 128
    forecasting, 125
    full-service, 81–82, 101
    ghost kitchens, 93
    gross profit, 124, 135
    guests, 110–111
    healthcare market, 89–90
    high-priced, 83
    hotel, 64
    income statement, 121, *122*, 135
    independent, 60–61
    inventory/purchasing (I/P) systems, 120, 220
    limited-service, 53, 80, 101